INTRODUCTION TO C++ PROGRAMMING:

BRIEF EDITION

D. S. MALIK

COURSE TECHNOLOGY
CENGAGE Learning

Australia • Brazil • Japan • Korea • Mexico • Singapore • Spain • United Kingdom • United States

COURSE TECHNOLOGY
CENGAGE Learning

Introduction to C++ Programming: Brief Edition
by D. S. Malik

Acquisitions Editor: Amy Jollymore
Senior Product Manager: Alyssa Pratt
Editorial Assistant: Patrick Frank
Marketing Manager: Bryant Chrzan
Content Project Manager: Matt Hutchinson
Art Director: Marissa Falco
Copyeditor: Chris Clark
Proofreader: Foxxe Editorial Services
Indexer: Liz Cunningham
Compositor: Integra

For product information and technology assistance, contact us at
Cengage Learning Customer & Sales Support, 1-800-354-9706
For permission to use material from this text or product, submit all requests online at **cengage.com/permissions**

Further permissions questions can be emailed to
permissionrequest@cengage.com

ISBN-13: 978-1-4239-0246-1

ISBN-10: 1-4239-0246-7

Course Technology
25 Thomson Place
Boston, MA 02210
USA

Cengage Learning is a leading provider of customized learning solutions with office locations around the globe, including Singapore, the United Kingdom, Australia, Mexico, Brazil, and Japan. Locate your local office at:
international.cengage.com/region

Cengage Learning products are represented in Canada by Nelson Education, Ltd.

For your course and learning solutions, visit
course.cengage.com

Course Technology, a part of Cengage Learning, reserves the right to revise this publication and make changes from time to time in its content without notice.

PowerPoint is a registered trademark of the Microsoft Corporation; Pentium is a registered trademark of Intel Corporation; IBM is a registered trademark of International Business Machines Corporation.

The programs in this book are for instructional purposes only. They have been tested with care, but are not guaranteed for any particular intent beyond educational purposes. The author and the publisher do not offer any warranties or representations, nor do they accept any liabilities with respect to the programs.

Purchase any of our products at your local college store or at our preferred online store **www.ichapters.com**

Printed in Canada
1 2 3 4 5 6 7 13 12 11 10 09 08

TO

Sadhana Malik

BRIEF CONTENTS

TABLE OF CONTENTS

8 | NAMESPACES, THE class string, AND USER-DEFINED SIMPLE DATA TYPES   475

9 | POINTERS   517

PREFACE

Welcome to *Introduction to C++ Programming*. Designed for a first Computer Science C++ course (CS1), this text provides a breath of fresh air for you and your students. The CS1 course is the foundation of the Computer Science curriculum. Hence, our primary goal is to educate, motivate, and excite your programming students, regardless of their levels and prospective career directions. Motivation breeds excitement for learning. Motivation and excitement are critical factors that lead to the success for the programming student.

Warning: This text can be expected to create a serious reduction in the demand for programming help during your office hours. Other side effects include significantly diminished student dependency on others while learning to program.

Our primary focus in writing this text is on student learning. Therefore, in addition to clear explanations, we address the key issues that otherwise impede student learning. For example, a common question that arises naturally during an early programming assignment is: "How many variables and what kinds are needed in this program?" We illustrate this important and crucial step by helping students learn why variables are needed and how data in a variable is manipulated. Next, students learn that the analysis of the problem will spill the number and types of the variables. Once students grasp this key concept, control structures, (selection and loops) become easier to learn. The second major impediment in learning programming is parameter passing. We pay special attention to this topic. First, students learn how to use predefined functions and how actual and formal parameters relate. Next, students learn about user-defined functions. They see visual diagrams that help them learn how functions are called and how formal parameters affect actual parameters. Once students have a clear understanding of these two key concepts, they readily assimilate advanced topics.

The topics are introduced at a pace that is conducive to learning. The writing style is friendly, engaging, and straightforward. It parallels the learning style of the contemporary CS1 student. Before introducing a key concept, the student learns why the concept is needed and then sees examples illustrating the concept. Special attention is paid to topics that are essential in mastering the C++ programming language and in acquiring a foundation for further study of computer science.

Other important topics include debugging techniques and techniques for avoiding programming bugs. When a beginner compiles his or her first program and sees that the number of errors exceeds the length of this first program, he or she becomes frustrated by the plethora of errors, only some of which can be interpreted. To ease this frustration and help students learn to produce correct programs, debugging and bug avoidance techniques are presented systematically throughout the text.

Traditionally, a C++ programming neophyte needed either a working knowledge of another programming language or at least a programming mentality. This book assumes no prior programming experience and no special mindset. However, a background in mathematics including college algebra is assumed.

Approach

The programming language C++, which evolved from C, is no longer considered an industry-only language. Numerous colleges and universities use C++ for their first programming language course. C++ is a combination of structured programming and object-oriented programming, and this book addresses both types. Furthermore, in July 1998, ANSI/ISO Standard C++ was officially approved. This book focuses on ANSI/ISO Standard C++.

Chapter 0 briefly reviews the history of computers and programming languages. The reader can skim quickly and become generally familiar with the hardware and software components of the computer. This chapter gives an example of a C++ program and describes how a C++ program is processed. The two basic problem-solving techniques, structured programming and object-oriented design, are presented.

Because input/output is fundamental to any programming language, it is introduced early, and is covered in appropriate detail in Chapter 2. After completing Chapters 1 and 2, students are familiar with the basics of C++ and are ready to write programs that are complicated enough to do some computations.

Chapters 3 and 4 introduce control structures to alter the sequential flow of execution. Chapter 5 studies user-defined functions. Since parameter passing is a fundamental concept in any programming language, several examples including visual diagrams help readers understand this concept. It is recommended that readers with no prior programming background spend extra time on Chapter 5.

Chapter 6 discusses arrays in detail. Chapter 7 begins the study of Object-Oriented Programming (OOP) and introduces classes. The first half of this chapter shows how classes are defined and used in a program. The second half of the chapter introduces abstract data types (ADTs). This chapter shows how classes in C++ are a natural way to implement ADTs.

Chapter 8 discusses the namespace mechanism of ANSI/ISO Standard C++, the string type, and the user-defined simple data type (enumeration type), The earlier versions of C did not include the enumeration type. This book is organized such that readers can skip the section on enumeration types during the first reading without experiencing any discontinuity, and then later go through this section.

Chapter 9 studies pointers in detail. Chapter 10 describes various searching and sorting algorithms as well as an introduction to the **vector** class.

Chapter 11 presents recursion. Several examples illustrate how recursive functions execute.

Appendix A lists the reserved words in C++. Appendix B shows the precedence and associativity of the C++ operators. Appendix C lists the ASCII (American Standard Code for

Information Interchange) and EBCDIC (Extended Binary Coded Decimal Interchange Code) character sets. Appendix D has two objectives. First, we discuss how to convert a number from decimal to binary and binary to decimal. We then discuss additional input/output functions. Appendix E provides the answers to odd numbered exercises in the book.

How to Use This Book

This book can be used in two ways. One approach is to study all chapters in sequence. However, Chapters 6 and 7 can be studied in any order. If you decide to study Chapter 7 before Chapter 6, then study the discussion of arrays and classes in Chapter 7 after studying Chapter 6. Chapter 9 on pointers can be studied before Chapter 7. In fact after studying first seven chapters, remaining chapters can be studied in any order.

1. Study chapters in the sequence.
2. Study first seven chapters in sequence and then study the remaining chapters in any order.
3. Study first five chapters in sequence and then study Chapter 7 followed by Chapter 6. The remaining chapters can be studied in any order.

FEATURES OF THE BOOK

This statement stores **35** in **a** and **67** in **b**. The reading stops at the **.** (the decimal point). Because the next variable **c** is of type `int`, the computer tries to read **.** into **c**, which is an error. The input stream then enters a state called the **fail state**.

What actually happens when the input stream enters the fail state? Once an input stream enters a fail state, all further I/O statements using that stream are ignored. Unfortunately, the program quietly continues to execute with whatever values are stored in variables, and produces incorrect results. The program in Example 2-9 illustrates an input failure. This program on your system may produce different results.

EXAMPLE 2-9

```cpp
//************************************************************
// Author: D.S. Malik
//
// Input Failure program
// This program illustrates input failure.
//************************************************************

#include <iostream>                                   //Line 1

using namespace std;                                  //Line 2

int main()                                            //Line 3
{                                                     //Line 4
    int a = 10;                                       //Line 5
    int b = 20;                                       //Line 6
    int c = 30;                                       //Line 7
    int d = 40;                                       //Line 8

    cout << "Line 9: Enter four integers: ";          //Line 9
    cin >> a >> b >> c >> d;                           //Line 10
    cout << endl;                                     //Line 11

    cout << "Line 12: The numbers you entered are:"
         << endl;                                     //Line 12
    cout << "Line 13: a = " << a << ", b = " << b
         << ", c = " << c << ", d = " << d << endl;   //Line 13

    return 0;                                         //Line 14
}                                                     //Line 15
```

Sample Runs: In these sample runs, the user input is shaded.

```
Sample Run 1

Line 9: Enter four integers: 34 K 67 28

Line 12: The numbers you entered are:
Line 13: a = 34, b = 20, c = 30, d = 40
```

Four-color interior design shows accurate C++ code and related comments.

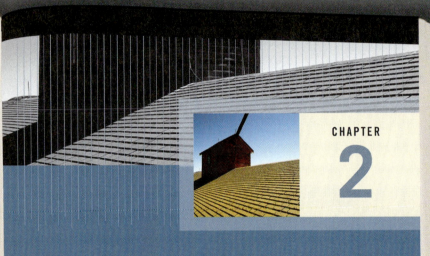

CHAPTER

2

INPUT/OUTPUT

IN THIS CHAPTER, YOU WILL:

- Discover how to input data into memory using input statements
- Explore how to read data from the standard input device
- Learn how to debug a program using `cout` statements
- Learn how to debug a program by understanding error messages
- Explore how to use the input stream functions `get`, `ignore`, and `clear`
- Become familiar with input failure
- Learn how to perform input and output operations with the `string` data type
- Learn how to format output using the manipulators `fixed`, `showpoint`, `setprecision`, `setw`, `left`, and `right`
- Become familiar with file input and output

Learning Objectives offer an outline of the C++ programming concepts discussed in detail in the chapter.

Input (Read) Statement

In the previous chapter, you learned how to put data into variables using the assignment statement. In this section, you learn how to put data into variables from the standard input device using C++'s input (or read) statements.

NOTE   In most cases, the standard input device is the keyboard.

When the program gets the data from the keyboard, the user is said to be interacting with the program.

Putting data into variables from the standard input device is accomplished through the use of **cin** and the operator **>>**. The syntax of **cin** together with **>>** is:

```
cin >> variable >> variable ...;
```

This is called an **input (read)** statement. In C++, **>>** is called the **stream extraction operator**.

NOTE   Recall that in a syntax, the shading indicates the part of the definition that is optional.

EXAMPLE 2-1

Suppose that **miles** is a variable of the data type **double**. Further suppose that the input is **73.65**. Consider the following statement:

```
cin >> miles;
```

This statement causes the computer to get the input, which is **73.65**, from the standard input device, and store it in the variable **miles**. That is, after this statement executes, the value of the variable **miles** is **73.65**.

To use **cin** in a program, the program must include the header file **iostream**. Like the identifier **cout**, the identifier **cin** is also declared in the header file **iostream**, but within the **namespace std**. Therefore, after including this header file and the statement, **using namespace std;**, we can refer to **cin** without using the prefix **std::**.

Example 2-2 further explains how to input numeric data into a program.

Notes highlight important facts about the concepts introduced in the chapter.

In C++, `switch`, `case`, `break`, and `default` are reserved words. In a `switch` structure, first the **expression** is evaluated. The value of the **expression** is then used to perform the actions specified in the statements that follow the reserved word `case`. Recall that, in a syntax, shading indicates an optional part of the definition.

Although it need not be, the **expression** is usually an identifier. Whether it is an identifier or an expression, the value can be only integral, such as `int` or `char`. The **expression** is sometimes called the **selector**. Its value determines which statement is selected for execution. A particular `case` value should appear only once. One or more statements may follow a `case` label, so you do not need to use braces to turn multiple statements into a single compound statement. The `break` statement may or may not appear after each statement. Figure 3-4 shows the flow of execution of the `switch` statement.

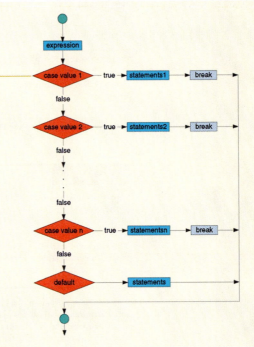

FIGURE 3-4 `switch` statement

More than 140 visual diagrams, both extensive and exhaustive, illustrate and explain otherwise difficult concepts.

EXAMPLE 3-3

Expression	Value	Explanation
`(14 >= 5) && ('A' < 'B')`	true	Because `(14 >= 5)` is true, `('A' < 'B')` is true, and true `&&` true is true, the expression evaluates to true.
`(24 >= 35) && ('A' < 'B')`	false	Because `(24 >= 35)` is false, `('A' < 'B')` is true, and false `&&` true is false, the expression evaluates to false.

3

Table 3-8 defines the operator `||` (or). From this table, it follows that **Expression1 || Expression2** is true if and only if at least one of the expressions, **Expression1** or **Expression2**, is true; otherwise, **Expression1 || Expression2** evaluates to false.

TABLE 3-8 The `||` (Or) Operator

Expression1	Expression2	Expression1 || Expression2
true (nonzero)	true (nonzero)	true (1)
true (nonzero)	false (0)	true (1)
false (0)	true (nonzero)	true (1)
false (0)	false (0)	false (0)

EXAMPLE 3-4

Expression	Value	Explanation
`(14 >= 5) || ('A' > 'B')`	true	Because `(14 >= 5)` is true, `('A' > 'B')` is false, and true `||` false is true, the expression evaluates to true.
`(24 >= 35) || ('A' > 'B')`	false	Because `(24 >= 35)` is false, `('A' > 'B')` is false, and false `||` false is false, the expression evaluates to false.
`('A' <= 'a') || (7 != 7)`	true	Because `('A' <= 'a')` is true, `(7 != 7)` is false, and true `||` false is true, the expression evaluates to true.

Numbered *Examples* illustrate the key concepts together with the relevant code. The programming code in these examples is numbered for easy reference, and is followed by a Sample Run. Careful explanations describe what each program statement does. The rationale behind each program statement is discussed in detail.

PROGRAMMING EXAMPLE: Classify Numbers

This program reads a given set of integers and then prints the number of odd and even integers. It also outputs the number of zeros.

The program reads 20 integers, but you can easily modify it to read any set of numbers. In fact, you can modify the program so that it first prompts the user to specify how many integers are to be read.

Input 20 integers—positive, negative, or zeros.

Output The number of zeros, even numbers, and odd numbers.

PROBLEM ANALYSIS AND ALGORITHM DESIGN

After reading a number, you need to check whether it is even or odd. Suppose the value is stored in **number**. Divide **number** by 2 and check the remainder. If the remainder is 0, **number** is even. Increment the even count and then check whether **number** is 0. If it is, increment the zero count. If the remainder is not 0, increment the odd count.

The program uses a `switch` statement to decide whether **number** is odd or even. Suppose that **number** is odd. Dividing by 2 gives the remainder 1 if **number** is positive and the remainder -1 if it is negative. If **number** is even, dividing by 2 gives the remainder 0 whether **number** is positive or negative. You can use the mod operator, %, to find the remainder. For example,

6 % 2 = 0; -4 % 2 = 0; -7 % 2 = -1; 15 % 2 = 1.

Repeat the preceding process of analyzing a number for each number in the list.

This discussion translates into the following algorithm:

1. For each number in the list, do the following:
   a. Get the number.
   b. Analyze the number.
   c. Increment the appropriate count.
2. Print the results.

Variables Because you want to count the number of zeros, even numbers, and odd numbers, you need three variables of the type `int`—say, **zeros**, **evens**, and **odds**—to track the counts. You also need a variable—say, **number**—to read and store the number to be analyzed, and another variable—say, **counter**—to count the numbers analyzed. Therefore, you need the following variables in the program:

```
int counter;    //loop control variable
int number;     //variable to store the number read
int zeros;      //variable to store the zero count
int evens;      //variable to store the even count
int odds;       //variable to store the odd count
```

5

```
MTH    ****************************************
       ^^^^^^^^^^^^^^^^^^^^^^^^^^^^^^^^^^^^^^^^^

PHY    ****************************************
       ^^^^^^^^^^^^^^^^^^^^^^^^^^^^^^^^^^^^^^^^^

Group 1 -- ***
Group 2 -- ^^^
Avg for group 1: 82.04
Avg for group 2: 82.01
```

The complete program listing is available at the Web site accompanying this book.

QUICK REVIEW

1. Functions are like miniature programs and are called modules.
2. Functions enable you to divide a program into manageable tasks.
3. The C++ system provides the standard (predefined) functions.
4. To use a standard function, you must:
    i. Know the name of the header file that contains the function's specification
    ii. Include that header file in the program
    iii. Know the name and type of the function, and know the number and types of the parameters (arguments)
5. There are two types of user-defined functions: value-returning functions and void functions.
6. Variables defined in a function heading are called formal parameters.
7. Expressions, variables, or constant values used in a function call are called actual parameters.
8. In a function call, the number of actual parameters and their types must match with the formal parameters in the order given.
9. To call a function, use its name together with the actual parameter list.
10. A value-returning function returns a value. Therefore, a value-returning function is used (called) in either an expression or an output statement, or as a parameter in a function call.
11. The general syntax of a user-defined function is:

```
functionType  functionName(formal parameter list)
{
    statements
}
```

5

Quick Review offers a summary of the concepts covered in the chapter, reinforcing learning. After reading the chapter, students can review the highlights of the chapter and then test themselves using the ensuing exercises.

33. In row processing, a two-dimensional array is processed one row at a time.

34. In column processing, a two-dimensional array is processed one column at a time.

35. When declaring a two-dimensional array as a formal parameter, you can omit the size of the first dimension but not the second.

36. When a two-dimensional array is passed as an actual parameter, the number of columns of the actual and formal arrays must match.

37. C++ stores two-dimensional arrays in a row order form in computer memory.

EXERCISES

1. Mark the following statements as true or false.

   a. A `double` type is an example of a simple data type.

   b. A one-dimensional array is an example of a structured data type.

   c. Arrays can be passed as parameters to a function either by value or by reference.

   d. A function can return a value of type array.

   e. The size of an array is determined at compile time.

   f. The only aggregate operations allowable on `int` arrays are the increment and decrement operations.

   g. Given the declaration

   ```
   int list[10];
   ```

   the statement

   ```
   list[5] = list[3] + list[2];
   ```

   updates the content of the fifth component of the array `list`.

   h. If an array index goes out of bounds, the program always terminates in an error.

   i. In C++, some aggregate operations are allowed for strings.

   j. The declaration

   ```
   char name[16] = "John K. Miller";
   ```

   declares `name` to be an array of 15 characters because the string `"John K. Miller"` has only 14 characters.

   k. The declaration

   ```
   char str = "Sunny Day";
   ```

   declares `str` to be a string of an unspecified length.

   l. As parameters, two-dimensional arrays are passed either by value or by reference.

```
myObject1.printX();
cout << endl;
myObject1.printCount();
cout << endl;
myObject2.printCount();
cout << endl;
```

10. Draw the UML class diagram of the `class` `thermometer` given in Example 7-2.

PROGRAMMING EXERCISES

1. Write a program that converts a number entered in Roman numerals to decimal. Your program should consist of a `class`, say `romanType`. An object of type `romanType` should do the following:

   a. Store the number as a Roman numeral.

   b. Convert and store the number into decimal form.

   c. Print the number as a Roman numeral or decimal number as requested by the user. (Write two separate functions, one to print the number as a Roman numeral and the other to print the number as a decimal number.)

   The decimal values of the Roman numerals are:

M	1000
D	500
C	100
L	50
X	10
V	5
I	1

   Remember, a larger numeral preceding a smaller numeral means addition, so `LX` is `60`. A smaller numeral preceding a larger numeral means subtraction, so `XL` is `40`. Any place in a decimal number, such as the 1s place, the 10s place, and so on, requires from zero to four Roman numerals.

   d. Test your program using the following Roman numerals: `MCXIV`, `CCCLIX`, and `MDCLXVI`.

2. Write the definition of the `class` `dayType` that implements the day of the week in a program. The `class` `dayType` should store the day, such as `Sun` for Sunday. The program should be able to perform the following operations on an object of type `dayType`:

   a. Set the day.

   b. Print the day.

   c. Return the day.

   d. Return the next day.

7

SUPPLEMENTAL RESOURCES

The following supplemental materials are available when this book is used in a classroom setting. All of the teaching tools available with this book are provided to the instructor on a single CD-ROM.

Electronic Instructor's Manual

The Instructor's Manual that accompanies this textbook includes:

- Additional instructional material to assist in class preparation, including suggestions for lecture topics.
- Solutions to all the end-of-chapter materials, including the Programming Exercises.

ExamView®

This textbook is accompanied by ExamView, a powerful testing software package that allows instructors to create and administer printed, computer (LAN-based), and Internet exams. ExamView includes hundreds of questions that correspond to the topics covered in this text, enabling students to generate detailed study guides that include page references for further review. These computer-based and Internet testing components allow students to take exams at their computers, and save the instructor time because each exam is graded automatically.

PowerPoint Presentations

This book comes with Microsoft PowerPoint slides for each chapter. These are included as a teaching aid either to make available to students on the network for chapter review, or to be used during classroom presentations. Instructors can modify slides or add their own slides to tailor their presentations.

Distance Learning

Course Technology is proud to offer online courses in WebCT and Blackboard. For more information on how to bring distance learning to your course, contact your local Cengage Learning sales representative.

Source Code

The source code is available at **www.course.com**, and also is available on the Instructor Resources CD-ROM. If an input file is needed to run a program, it is included with the source code.

Solution files

The solution files for all programming exercises are available at **www.course.com** and are available on the Instructor Resources CD-ROM. If an input file is needed to run a programming exercise, it is included with the solution file.

ACKNOWLEDGMENTS

There are many people that I must thank who, one way or another, contributed to the success of this book. I am thankful to Professors S.C. Cheng, Randall Crist, and John N. Mordeson for constantly supporting this project. I would like to thank my wife Sadhana and my daughter Shelly. They cheered me up whenever I was overwhelmed during the writing of this book. I am thankful to my parents for their blessings.

I owe a great deal to the following reviewers who patiently read each page of every chapter of the current version and made critical comments to improve on the book: Phillip Barry, University of Minnesota; Raffi Khatchadourian, Ohio State University; and Amar Raheja, California State University Pomona. Additionally, I express thanks to the reviewers of the proposal package: Joan Harnett, Manhattan College; Jeanna Matthews: Clarkson University; and Brian Noble, University of Michigan. The reviewers will recognize that their criticisms have not been overlooked, adding meaningfully to the quality of the finished book. Next, I express thanks to Amy Jollymore, acquisition editor, for recognizing the importance and uniqueness of this project. All this would not have been possible without the careful planning of Product Manager Alyssa Pratt. I extend my sincere thanks to Alyssa. I also thank Tintu Thomas of Integra Software Services for assisting us in keeping the project on schedule and the QA department of Course Technology for carefully testing the code.

I welcome any comments concerning the text. Comments may be forwarded to the following e-mail addresses: `malik@creighton.edu`.

D.S. Malik

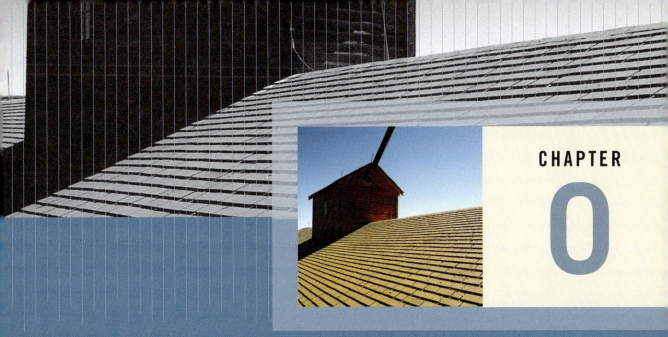

AN OVERVIEW OF COMPUTERS AND PROGRAMMING LANGUAGES

IN THIS CHAPTER, YOU WILL:

- Learn about different types of computers
- Explore the hardware and software components of a computer system
- Learn about the language of a computer
- Learn about the evolution of programming languages
- Examine high-level programming languages
- Discover what a compiler is and what it does
- Explore how a C++ program is processed
- Learn what an algorithm is and explore problem-solving techniques
- Become aware of structured design and object-oriented design programming methodologies

Introduction

Terms such as "the Internet," which were unfamiliar just a few years ago, are now common. Elementary school students regularly "surf" the Internet and use computers to design their classroom projects. Many people use the Internet to look up information and to communicate with others. These Internet activities are all made possible by the availability of different software, also known as computer programs. Software is developed by using programming languages. The programming language C++ is especially well suited for developing software to accomplish specific tasks. Our main objective is to teach you how to write programs in the C++ programming language. Before you begin programming, it is useful if you understand some of the basic terminology and different components of a computer. We begin with an overview of the history of computers.

A Brief Overview of the History of Computers

The first device known to perform calculations was the abacus. The abacus was invented in Asia, but was used in ancient Babylon, China, and throughout Europe until the late Middle Ages. The abacus uses a system of sliding beads in a rack for addition and subtraction. In 1642, the French philosopher and mathematician Blaise Pascal invented the calculating device called the Pascaline. It had eight movable dials on wheels that could calculate sums up to eight figures long. Both the abacus and the Pascaline could perform only addition and subtraction operations. Later in the seventeenth century, Gottfried von Leibniz invented a device that could be used to add, subtract, multiply, and divide.

In 1819, Joseph Jacquard, a French weaver, discovered that the weaving instructions for his looms could be stored on cards with holes punched in them. While the cards moved through the loom in sequence, needles passed through the holes and picked up threads of the correct color and texture. A weaver could rearrange the cards and change the pattern being woven. In essence, the cards programmed a loom to produce patterns in cloth. At first glance, the weaving industry might seem to have little in common with the computer industry. However, the idea of storing information by punching holes on a card turned out to be of great importance in the later development of computers.

In the early and mid-1800s, Charles Babbage, an English mathematician and physical scientist, designed two calculating machines—the difference engine and the analytical engine. The difference engine could perform complex operations such as squaring numbers automatically. Babbage built a prototype of the difference engine, but the actual device was never produced. The analytical engine's design included an input device, data storage, a control unit that allowed processing instructions in any sequence, and output devices. However, the designs remained in the blueprint stage. Most of Babbage's work is known through the writings of his colleague Ada Augusta, Countess of Lovelace. Augusta is considered the first computer programmer.

At the end of the nineteenth century, U.S. Census officials needed help to accurately tabulate the census data. Herman Hollerith invented a calculating machine that ran on

0

electricity and used punched cards to store data. Hollerith's machine was immensely successful. Hollerith founded the Tabulating Machine Company, which later became the computer and technology corporation known as IBM.

The first computer-like machine was the Mark I. In 1944, it was built jointly by IBM and Harvard University, under the leadership of Howard Aiken. Punched cards were used to feed data into the machine. The Mark I was 52 feet long, weighed 50 tons, and had 750,000 parts. In 1946, the ENIAC (Electronic Numerical Integrator and Computer) was built at the University of Pennsylvania. It contained 18,000 vacuum tubes and weighed some 30 tons.

The computers that we know today use the design rules given by John von Neumann in the late 1940s. His design included components such as arithmetic logic unit, control unit, memory, and input/output devices. These components are described in the next section. Von Neumann computer design makes it possible to store the programming instructions and the data in the same memory space. In 1951, the UNIVAC (Universal Automatic Computer) was built and sold to the U.S. Census Bureau.

In 1956, the invention of transistors resulted in smaller, faster, more reliable, and more energy-efficient computers. This era also saw the emergence of the software development industry with the introduction of FORTRAN and COBOL, two early programming languages. In the next major technological advancement, tiny integrated circuits, or chips, replaced transistors. Chips are smaller and cost less than transistors, and a single chip can contain thousands of circuits. They give computers tremendous processing speed.

In 1970, the microprocessor, an entire central processing unit (CPU) on a single chip, was invented. In 1977, Stephen Wozniak and Steven Jobs designed and built the first Apple computer in Jobs's garage. In 1981, IBM introduced its personal computer (PC). In the 1980s, clones of the IBM PC made the personal computer even more affordable. By the mid-1990s, people from many walks of life were able to afford them. Computers continue to become faster and less expensive as technology advances.

Modern-day computers are powerful, reliable, and easy to use. They can accept spoken-word instructions and imitate human reasoning through artificial intelligence. Expert systems assist doctors in making diagnoses. Mobile computing applications are growing significantly. Using handheld devices, delivery drivers can access global positioning system (GPS) satellites to verify customer locations for pickups and deliveries. Cell phones permit you to check your e-mail, make airline reservations, see how stocks are performing, and access your bank accounts.

Although there are several categories of computers, such as mainframe, midsize, and micro, all computers share some basic elements.

Elements of a Computer System

A computer is an electronic device capable of performing instructions. The basic instructions that a computer performs are input (get data), output (display result), storage, and arithmetic and logical operations. Programs are executable collections of instructions.

In today's market, personal computers are sold with descriptions such as Pentium 4 Processor 2.80 GHz, 512MB RAM, 100GB HD, VX750 17″ Silver Flat CRT Color Monitor; preloaded software such as operating systems, games, and encyclopedias; and application software such as word processors and money management programs. These descriptions represent two categories: hardware and software. Items such as "Pentium 4 Processor 2.80 GHz, 512MB RAM, 100GB HD, VX750 17″ Silver Flat CRT Color Monitor" fall into the hardware category; items such as "operating systems, games, encyclopedias, and application software" fall into the software category. Let's look at the hardware first.

Hardware

Major hardware components include the central processing unit (CPU); main memory (MM), also called random access memory (RAM); input/output devices; and secondary storage. Some examples of input devices are the keyboard, mouse, and secondary storage. Examples of output devices are the screen, printer, and secondary storage. Let's look at each of these components in more detail.

CENTRAL PROCESSING UNIT

The **central processing unit (CPU)** is the brain of the computer and the single most expensive piece of hardware in a personal computer. The main components of the CPU are the control unit (CU), arithmetic logic unit (ALU), and registers. Figure 0-1 shows how certain components of the CPU fit together.

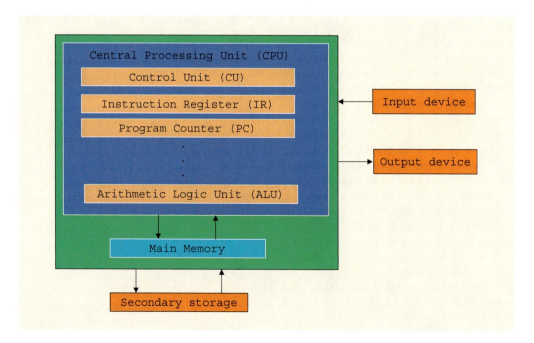

FIGURE 0-1   Hardware components of a computer

0

- The **control unit (CU)** has three main functions: fetch and decode the instructions, control the flow of information (instructions or data) in and out of main memory, and control the operation of the CPU's internal components.
- The **arithmetic logic unit (ALU)** carries out all arithmetic and logical (decision-making) operations.
- The CPU contains various registers. Some of these registers are for special purposes. For example, the **instruction register (IR)** holds the instruction currently being executed. The **program counter (PC)** points to the next instruction to be executed. All registers provide temporary storage. (For example, intermediate results of a calculation may be stored in temporary storage.)

MAIN MEMORY

The **main memory** is directly connected to the CPU. All programs must be loaded into main memory before they can be executed. Similarly, all data must be brought into main memory before a program can manipulate it. When the computer is turned off, everything in main memory is lost for good.

The main memory is an ordered sequence of cells, called **memory cells**. Each cell has a unique location in main memory, called the **address** of the cell. These addresses help you access the information stored in the cell. Figure 0-2 shows main memory with some data.

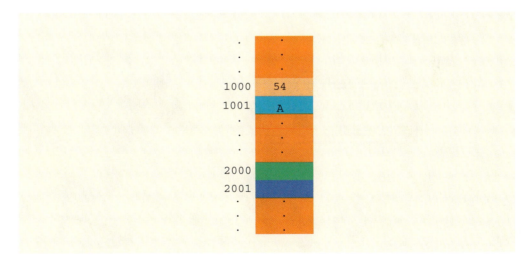

FIGURE 0-2 Main memory with storage cells and some data

Today's computers come with main memory consisting of millions to billions of cells. Although Figure 0-2 shows data stored in cells, the content of a cell can be either a programming instruction or data. Moreover, this figure shows the data as numbers and letters. However, as explained later in this chapter, main memory stores everything as sequences of 0s and 1s. The memory addresses also are expressed as sequences of 0s and 1s.

SECONDARY STORAGE

Because programs and data must be stored in main memory before processing, and because everything in main memory is lost when the computer is turned off, information stored in main memory must be transferred to some other device for longer-term storage. A device that stores longer-term information (unless the device becomes unusable or you change the information by rewriting it) is called **secondary storage**. To be able to transfer information from main memory to secondary storage, these components must be connected directly to each other. Examples of secondary storage are hard disks, 3.5-inch disks, flash memory, Zip disks, and CD-ROMs.

INPUT/OUTPUT DEVICES

For a computer to perform a useful task, it must be able to execute programs, process data, and display the results of calculations. The devices that feed data and programs into computers are called **input devices**. The keyboard, mouse, and secondary storage are examples of input devices. The devices that the computer uses to display or store results are called **output devices**. A monitor, printer, and secondary storage are examples of output devices. Figure 0-3 shows some input and output devices.

Input devices   Output devices

FIGURE 0-3 Some input and output devices

0

Software

Software consists of programs written to perform specific tasks. For example, word processors are programs that you use to write letters, papers, and even books. Similarly, an operating system is a program that monitors the overall activities of a computer and provides services. Some of these services include memory management, input/output activities, and storage management. Some other examples of programs are spreadsheets and games. All software is written in programming languages.

The Language of a Computer

A computer is an electronic device. Electrical signals move along channels inside the computer. There are two types of electrical signals: analog and digital. **Analog signals** are continuous waveforms used to represent things such as sound. Audio tapes, for example, store data in analog signals. **Digital signals** represent information with a sequence of 0s and 1s. A 0 represents a low voltage, and a 1 represents a high voltage. Digital signals are more reliable carriers of information than analog signals and can be copied from one device to another with exact precision. You might have noticed that when you make a copy of an audio tape, the sound quality of the copy is not as good as the sound quality on the original tape. On the other hand, when you copy a CD, the copy is as good as the original. Computers use digital signals.

Because digital signals are processed inside a computer, the language of a computer, called **machine language**, is a sequence of 0s and 1s. The digit 0 or 1 is called a **binary digit**, or **bit.** Sometimes a sequence of 0s and 1s is referred to as a **binary code** or a **binary number**.

Bit: A binary digit 0 or 1.

A sequence of eight bits is called a **byte**. Moreover, 2^{10} bytes (1024 bytes) is called a **kilobyte (KB)**. Table 0-1 summarizes the terms used to describe various numbers of bytes.

TABLE 0-1 Binary Units

Unit	Symbol	Bits/Bytes
Byte		8 bits
Kilobyte	KB	2^{10} bytes = 1024 bytes
Megabyte	MB	1024 KB = 2^{10} KB = 2^{20} bytes = 1,048,576 bytes
Gigabyte	GB	1024 MB = 2^{10}MB = 2^{30} bytes = 1,073,741,824 bytes
Terabyte	TB	1024 GB = 2^{10} GB = 2^{40} bytes = 1,099,511,627,776 bytes
Petabyte	PB	1024 TB = 2^{10} TB = 2^{50} bytes = 1,125,899,906,842,624 bytes
Exabyte	EB	1024 PB = 2^{10} PB = 2^{60} bytes = 1,152,921,504,606,846,976 bytes
Zettabyte	ZB	1024 EB = 2^{10} EB = 2^{70} bytes = 1,180,591,620,717,411,303,424 bytes

Every letter, number, or special symbol (such as * or {) on your keyboard is encoded as a sequence of bits, each having a unique representation. The most commonly used encoding scheme on personal computers is the *seven-bit* **American Standard Code for Information Interchange (ASCII)**. The ASCII data set consists of 128 characters numbered 0 through 127. That is, in the ASCII data set, the index (also called position) of the first character is 0, the index of the second character is 1, and so on. In this scheme, A is encoded as the binary number 1000001. In fact, A is the 66th character in the ASCII character code, but its index is 65 because the index of the first character is 0. Furthermore, the binary number 1000001 is the binary representation of 65. The character 3 is encoded as 0110011. Note that in the ASCII character set, the index of the character 3 is 51, so the character 3 is the 52nd character in the ASCII set. It also follows that 0110011 is the binary representation of 51. For a complete list of the printable ASCII character set, refer to Appendix C.

NOTE The number system that we use in our daily life is called the **decimal system** or **base 10**. Because everything inside a computer is represented as a sequence of 0s and 1s, that is, binary numbers, the number system that a computer uses is called **binary** or **base 2**. We indicated in the preceding paragraph that the number 1000001 is the binary representation of 65. Appendix D describes how to convert a number from base 10 to base 2 and vice versa.

0

Inside the computer, every character is represented as a sequence of *eight* bits, that is, as a byte. Now the eight-bit binary representation of 65 is 01000001. Note that we added 0 to the left of the seven-bit representation of 65 to convert it to an eight-bit representation. Similarly, the eight-bit binary representation of 51 is 00110011.

ASCII is a seven-bit code. Therefore, to represent each ASCII character inside the computer, you must convert the seven-bit binary representation of an ASCII character to an eight-bit binary representation. This is accomplished by adding 0 to the left of the seven-bit ASCII encoding of a character. Hence, inside the computer, the character A is represented as 01000001, and the character 3 is represented as 00110011.

There are other encoding schemes, such as EBCDIC (used by IBM) and Unicode, which is a more recent development. EBCDIC consists of 256 characters; Unicode consists of 65,536 characters. To store a character belonging to Unicode, you need two bytes.

The Evolution of Programming Languages

The most basic language of a computer, the machine language, provides program instructions in bits. Even though most computers perform the same kinds of operations, the designers of the computers might have chosen different sets of binary codes to perform the operations. Therefore, the machine language of one machine is not necessarily the same as the machine language of another machine. The only consistency among computers is that in any modern computer, all data is stored and manipulated as binary codes.

Early computers were programmed in machine language. To see how instructions are written in machine language, suppose you want to use the equation

wages = rate · hours

to calculate weekly wages. Further suppose that the binary code 100100 stands for load, 100110 stands for multiplication, and 100010 stands for store. In machine language, you might need the following sequence of instructions to calculate weekly wages:

```
100100 010001
100110 010010
100010 010011
```

To represent the weekly wages equation in machine language, the programmer had to remember the machine language codes for various operations. Also, to manipulate data, the programmer had to remember the locations of the data in the main memory. This need to remember specific codes made programming not only very difficult, but also error-prone.

Assembly languages were developed to make the programmer's job easier. In assembly language, an instruction is an easy-to-remember form called a **mnemonic**. For example,

Table 0-2 shows some examples of instructions in assembly language and their corresponding machine language code.

TABLE 0-2 Examples of Instructions in Assembly Language and Machine Language

Assembly Language	Machine Language
LOAD	100100
STOR	100010
MULT	100110
ADD	100101
SUB	100011

Using assembly language instructions, you can write the equation to calculate the weekly wages as follows:

```
LOAD rate
MULT hours
STOR wages
```

As you can see, it is much easier to write instructions in assembly language. However, a computer cannot execute assembly language instructions directly. The instructions first have to be translated into machine language. A program called an **assembler** translates the assembly language instructions into machine language.

Assembler: A program that translates a program written in assembly language into an equivalent program in machine language.

Moving from machine language to assembly language made programming easier, but a programmer was still forced to think in terms of individual machine instructions. The next step toward making programming easier was to devise **high-level languages** that were closer to natural languages, such as English, French, German, and Spanish. Basic, FORTRAN, COBOL, Pascal, C, C++, C#, and Java are all high-level languages. You will learn the high-level language C++ in this book.

In C++, you write the weekly wages equation as follows:

```
wages = rate * hours;
```

The instruction written in C++ is much easier to understand and is self-explanatory to a novice user who is familiar with basic arithmetic. As in the case of assembly language, however, the computer cannot directly execute instructions written in a high-level language. To run on a computer, these C++ instructions first need to be translated into machine language. A program called a **compiler** translates instructions written in high-level languages into machine code.

Compiler: A program that translates instructions written in a high-level language into the equivalent machine language.

Processing a C++ Program

The following is an example of a C++ program:

```
#include <iostream>

using namespace std;

int main()
{
    cout << "Welcome to C++ Programming." << endl;

    return 0;
}
```

At this point, you need not be too concerned with the details of this program. However, if you run (execute) this program, it will display the following line on the screen:

```
Welcome to C++ Programming.
```

Recall that a computer can understand only machine language. Therefore, to run this program successfully, the code first must be translated into the machine language. In this section, we review the steps required to execute programs written in C++.

To process a program written in C++, you carry out the following steps, as illustrated in Figure 0-4.

1. You use a text editor to create a C++ program following the rules, or *syntax,* of the high-level language. This program is called the **source code** or **source program**. The program must be saved in a text file that has the extension `.cpp`. For example, if you saved the preceding program in the file named `firstCPPProgram`, then its complete name is `firstCPPProgram.cpp`.

   Source program: A program written in a high-level language.

2. The C++ program given in the preceding section contains the statement `#include <iostream>`. In a C++ program, statements that begin with the symbol # are called preprocessor directives. These statements are processed by a program called a **preprocessor**.

3. After processing preprocessor directives, the next step is to verify that the program obeys the rules of the programming language—that is, the program is syntactically correct—and translate the program into the equivalent machine language. The *compiler* checks the source program

for syntax errors and, if no error is found, translates the program into the equivalent machine language. The equivalent machine language program is called an **object program**.

Object program: The machine language version of the high-level language program.

4. The programs that you write in a high-level language are typically developed using an **integrated development environment (IDE)**. The IDE contains many programs that are useful in creating your program. For example, IDE contains the necessary code (program) to display the results of the program and several mathematical functions to make the programmer's job somewhat easier. Therefore, if certain code is already available, you can use this code rather than writing your own code. Once the program is developed and successfully compiled, you must still bring the code for the resources used from the IDE into your program to produce a final program that the computer can execute. This prewritten code (program) resides in a place called the **library**. A program called a **linker** combines the object program with the programs from libraries.

Linker: A program that combines the object program with other programs in the library, and is used in the program to create the executable code.

5. You must next load the executable program into main memory for execution. A program called a **loader** accomplishes this task.

Loader: A program that loads an executable program into main memory.

6. The final step is to execute the program.

Figure 0-4 shows how a typical C++ program is processed.

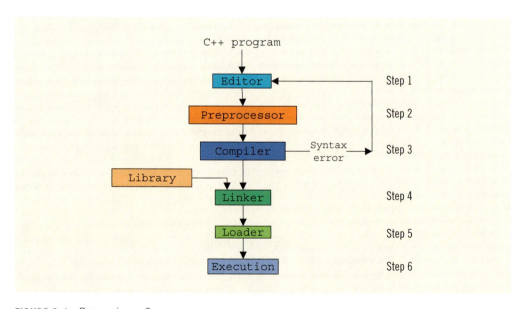

FIGURE 0-4 Processing a C++ program

0

As a programmer, you need to be concerned only with Step 1. That is, you must learn, understand, and master the rules of the programming language to create source programs.

As noted earlier, programs are developed using an IDE. Well-known IDEs used to create programs in the high-level language C++ include Visual C++ 2005 Express and Visual Studio .Net (from Microsoft), C++ Builder (from Borland), and CodeWarrior (from Metrowerks). These IDEs contain a text editor to create the source program, a compiler to check the source program for syntax errors, a program to link the object code with the IDE resources, and a program to execute the program.

These IDEs are quite user friendly. When you compile your program, the compiler not only identifies the syntax errors, but also typically suggests how to correct them. Moreover, with just a simple command, the object code is linked with the resources used from the IDE. The command that does the linking on Visual C++ 2005 Express and Visual Studio .Net is **Build** or **Rebuild**; on C++ Builder, it is **Build** or **Make**; and on CodeWarrior, it is **Make**. (For further clarification regarding the use of these commands, check the documentation of these IDEs.) If the program is not yet compiled, each of these commands first compiles the program and then links and produces the executable code.

Programming with the Problem Analysis–Coding–Execution Cycle

Programming is a process of problem solving. Different people use different techniques to solve problems. Some techniques are nicely outlined and easy to follow. They not only solve the problem, but also give insight into how the solution was reached. These problem-solving techniques can be easily modified if the domain of the problem changes.

To be a good problem solver and a good programmer, you must follow good problem-solving techniques. One common problem-solving technique includes analyzing a problem, outlining the problem requirements, and designing steps, called an **algorithm**, to solve the problem.

Algorithm: A step-by-step problem-solving process in which a solution is arrived at in a finite amount of time.

In a programming environment, the problem-solving process requires the following three steps:

1. Analyze the problem, outline the problem and its solution requirements, and design an algorithm to solve the problem.
2. Verify that the algorithm works and implement the algorithm in a programming language, such as C++.
3. Maintain the program by using and modifying it if the problem domain changes.

Figure 0-5 summarizes this three-step programming process.

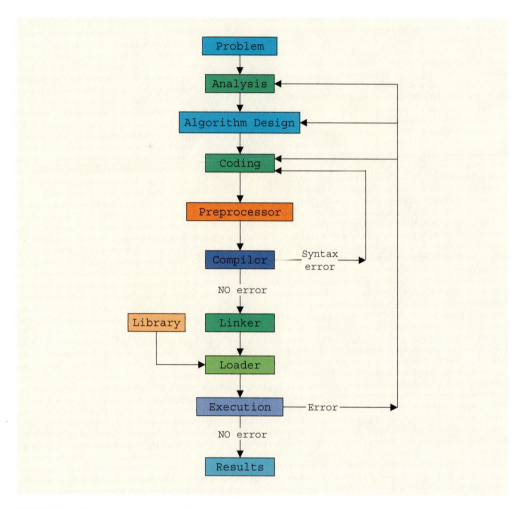

FIGURE 0-5 Problem analysis–coding–execution cycle

To develop a program to solve a problem, you start by analyzing the problem. You then design the algorithm; write the program instructions in a high-level language, or code the program; and enter the program into a computer system.

Analyzing the problem is the first and most important step. This step requires that you do the following:

1. Thoroughly understand the problem.
2. Understand the problem requirements. Requirements can include whether the program requires interaction with the user, whether it

0

manipulates data, whether it produces output, and what the output looks like. If the program manipulates data, the programmer must know what the data is and how it is represented. That is, you need to look at sample data. If the program produces output, you should know how the results should be generated and formatted.

3. If the problem is complex, divide the problem into subproblems and repeat Steps 1 and 2. That is, for complex problems, you need to analyze each subproblem and understand each subproblem's requirements.

After you carefully analyze the problem, the next step is to design an algorithm to solve the problem. If you broke the problem into subproblems, you need to design an algorithm for each subproblem. Once you design an algorithm, you need to check it for correctness. You can sometimes test an algorithm's correctness by using sample data. At other times, you might need to perform some mathematical analysis to test the algorithm's correctness.

Note that the algorithm design may itself be an iterative process. Problems discovered in the algorithm design feed back into an understanding of problem analysis. Once you have designed the algorithm and verified its correctness, the next step is to convert it into an equivalent programming code. You then use a text editor to enter the programming code or the program into a computer. Next, you must make sure that the program follows the language's syntax. To verify the correctness of the syntax, you run the code through a compiler. If the compiler generates error messages, you must identify the errors in the code, remove them, and then run the code through the compiler again. When all the syntax errors are removed, the compiler generates the equivalent machine code, the linker links the machine code with the system's resources, and the loader places the program into main memory so that it can be executed.

The final step is to execute the program. The compiler guarantees only that the program follows the language's syntax. It does not guarantee that the program will run correctly. During execution the program might terminate abnormally due to logical errors, such as division by zero. Even if the program terminates normally, it might still generate erroneous results. Under these circumstances, you may have to reexamine the code, the algorithm, or even the problem analysis.

Your overall programming experience will be successful if you spend enough time to complete the problem analysis before attempting to write the programming instructions. Usually, you do this work on paper using a pen or pencil. Taking this careful approach to programming has several advantages. It is much easier to discover errors in a program that is well analyzed and well designed. Furthermore, a thoroughly analyzed and carefully designed program is much easier to follow and modify. Even the most experienced programmers spend considerable time analyzing a problem and designing an algorithm.

Throughout this book, you will not only learn the rules of writing programs in C++, but you will also learn problem-solving techniques. The Programming Examples, in each chapter, help you learn techniques to analyze and solve the problems and also help you understand the concepts discussed in the chapter. To gain the full benefit of this book, we recommend that you work through the Programming Examples at the end of each chapter.

Next, we provide examples of various problem-analysis and algorithm-design techniques.

EXAMPLE 0-1

In this example, we design an algorithm to find the perimeter and area of a rectangle.

To find the perimeter and area of a rectangle, you need to know the rectangle's length and width. The perimeter and area of the rectangle are then given by the following formulas:

```
perimeter = 2 × (length + width)
area = length × width
```

The algorithm to find the perimeter and area of the rectangle is:

1. Get the length of the rectangle.
2. Get the width of the rectangle.
3. Find the perimeter using the following equation:

   ```
   perimeter = 2 × (length + width)
   ```

4. Find the area using the following equation:

   ```
   area = length × width
   ```

EXAMPLE 0-2

In this example, we design an algorithm that calculates the sales tax and the price of an item sold in a particular state.

The sales tax is calculated as follows: The state's portion of the sales tax is 4% and the city's portion of the sales tax is 1.5%. If the item is a luxury item, such as a car costing over $50,000, then there is a 10% luxury tax.

To calculate the price of the item, we need to calculate the state's portion of the sales tax, the city's portion of the sales tax, and, if it is a luxury item, the luxury tax. Suppose `salePrice` denotes the selling price of the item, `stateSalesTax` denotes the state's sales tax, `citySalesTax` denotes the city's sales tax, `luxuryTax` denotes the luxury tax, `salesTax` denotes the total sales tax, and `amountDue` denotes the final price of the item.

To calculate the sales tax, we must know the selling price of the item and whether the item is a luxury item.

0

The `stateSalesTax` and `citySalesTax` can be calculated using the following formulas:

```
stateSalesTax = salePrice × 0.04
citySalesTax = salePrice × 0.015
```

Next, you can determine `luxuryTax` as follows:

```
if (item is a luxury item)
   luxuryTax = salePrice × 0.1
otherwise
   luxuryTax = 0
```

Next, you can determine `salesTax` as follows:

```
salesTax = stateSalesTax + citySalesTax + luxuryTax
```

Finally, you can calculate `amountDue` as follows:

```
amountDue = salePrice + salesTax
```

The algorithm to determine `salesTax` and `amountDue` is, therefore:

1. Get the selling price of the item.
2. Determine whether the item is a luxury item.
3. Find the state's portion of the sales tax using the formula:

    ```
    stateSalesTax = salePrice × 0.04
    ```

4. Find the city's portion of the sales tax using the formula:

    ```
    citySalesTax = salePrice × 0.015
    ```

5. Find the luxury tax using the following formulas:

    ```
    if (item is a luxury item)
        luxuryTax = salePrice × 0.1
    otherwise
        luxuryTax = 0
    ```

6. Find `salesTax` using the formula:

    ```
    salesTax = stateSalesTax + citySalesTax + luxuryTax
    ```

7. Find `amountDue` using the formula:

    ```
    amountDue = salePrice + salesTax
    ```

EXAMPLE 0-3

In this example, we design an algorithm to play a number-guessing game.

The objective is to randomly generate an integer greater than or equal to 0 and less than 100. Then prompt the player (user) to guess the number. If the player guesses the number correctly, output an appropriate message. Otherwise, check whether the guessed number is less than the random number. If the guessed number is less than the random number generated, output the message: "Your guess is lower than the number. Guess again!" Otherwise, output the message: "Your guess is higher than the number. Guess again!" Then prompt the player to enter another number. The player is prompted to guess the random number until the player enters the correct number.

The first step is to generate a random number as described earlier. C++ provides the means to do so, which is discussed in Chapter 4. Suppose `num` stands for the random number, and `guess` stands for the number guessed by the player.

After the player enters the `guess`, we compare the `guess` with the random number as follows:

```
if (guess is equal to num)
    Print "You guessed the correct number."
otherwise
    if guess is less than num
        Print "Your guess is lower than the number. Guess again!"
otherwise
        Print "Your guess is higher than the number. Guess again!"
```

We can now design an algorithm as follows:

1. Generate a random number and call it `num`.

2. Repeat the following steps until the player has guessed the correct number.
    a. Prompt the player to enter `guess`.
    b.

```
    if (guess is equal to num)
            Print "You guessed the correct number."
    otherwise
        if guess is less than num
            Print "Your guess is lower than the number. Guess again!"
    otherwise
            Print "Your guess is higher than the number. Guess again!"
```

In Chapter 4, we write a program that uses this algorithm to write a C++ program to play the guessing the number game.

The type of coding used in Examples 0-1 to 0-3 is called **pseudocode**, which is an outline of a program that could be translated into actual code. Pseudocode is not written in a particular language, nor does it have syntax rules; it is mainly a technique to show programming steps quickly and easily.

Programming Methodologies

0

Two popular approaches to programming design are the structured approach and the object-oriented approach, both of which are outlined in the following sections.

Structured Programming

Dividing a problem into smaller subproblems is called **structured design**. Each subproblem is then analyzed and a solution is obtained to solve the subproblem. The solutions to all the subproblems are then combined to solve the overall problem. This process of implementing a structured design is called **structured programming**. The structured design approach is also known as **top-down design**, **bottom-up design**, **stepwise refinement**, and **modular design**.

Object-Oriented Programming

Object-oriented design (OOD) is a widely used programming methodology. In OOD, the first step in the problem-solving process is to identify the components called objects, which form the basis of the solution, and to determine how these objects interact. For example, suppose you want to write a program that automates the video rental process for a local video store. The two main objects in this problem are the video and the customer.

After identifying the objects, the next step is to specify for each object the relevant data and possible operations to be performed on that data. For example, for a video object, the data might include:

- Movie name
- Starring actors
- Producer
- Production company
- Number of copies in stock

Some of the operations on a video object might include:

- Checking the name of the movie
- Reducing the number of copies in stock by one after a copy is rented
- Incrementing the number of copies in stock by one after a customer returns a particular video.

The preceding information illustrates that each object consists of data and operations on that data. An object combines data and operations on the data into a single unit. In OOD, the final program is a collection of interacting objects. A programming language that implements OOD is called an **object-oriented programming (OOP)** language. You will learn about the many advantages of OOD in later chapters.

Because an object consists of data and operations on that data, before you can design and use objects, you need to learn how to represent data in computer memory, how to manipulate data, and how to implement operations. In Chapters 1 and 2, you will learn the basic data types of C++ and discover how to represent and manipulate data in computer memory. Chapter 2 discusses how to input data into a C++ program and output the results generated by a C++ program.

To implement operations, you write algorithms and implement them in a programming language. Because a data element in a complex program usually has many operations, to separate operations from each other and to use them effectively, in a convenient manner, you use functions to implement algorithms. You will learn the details of functions in Chapter 5. Certain algorithms require that a program make decisions, a process called selection. Other algorithms might require certain statements to be repeated until certain conditions are met, a process called repetition. Still other algorithms might require both selection and repetition. You will learn about selection and repetition mechanisms, called control structures, in Chapters 3 and 4. Also, in Chapter 6, using arrays, you will learn how to manipulate data when data items are of the same type, such as items in a list of sales figures.

Finally, to work with objects, you need to know how to combine data and operations on that data into a single unit. In C++, the mechanism that allows you to combine data and operations on that data into a single unit is called a class. You will learn how classes work, how to work with classes, and how to create classes in Chapter 7

For some problems, the structured approach to program design will be very effective. Other problems will be better addressed by OOD. For example, if a problem requires manipulating sets of numbers with mathematical functions, you might use the structured design approach and outline the steps required to obtain the solution. The C++ library supplies a wealth of functions that you can use effectively to manipulate numbers. On the other hand, if you want to write a program that would make a juice machine operational, the OOD approach is more effective. C++ was designed especially to implement OOD.

QUICK REVIEW

1. A computer is an electronic device capable of performing arithmetic and logical operations.
2. A computer system has two components: hardware and software.
3. The central processing unit (CPU) and the main memory are examples of hardware components.
4. The control unit (CU) controls a program's overall execution. It is one of several components of the CPU.
5. The arithmetic logic unit (ALU) is the component of the CPU that performs arithmetic and logical operations.
6. The instructor register (IR) holds the instruction currently being executed.

0

7. The program counter (PC) points to the next instruction to be executed.

8. All programs must be brought into main memory before they can be executed.

9. When the power is switched off, everything in main memory is lost.

10. Secondary storage provides permanent storage for information. Hard disks, flash drives, 3.5-inch disks, Zip disks, CD-ROMs, and tapes are examples of secondary storage.

11. Input to the computer is done via an input device. Two common input devices are the keyboard and the mouse.

12. The computer sends its output to an output device such as the computer screen.

13. Software consists of programs run by the computer.

14. The operating system monitors the overall activity of the computer and provides services.

15. The most basic language of a computer is a sequence of 0s and 1s called machine language. Every computer directly understands its own machine language.

16. A bit is a binary digit, 0 or 1.

17. A byte is a sequence of eight bits.

18. A sequence of 0s and 1s is referred to as a binary code or a binary number.

19. One kilobyte (KB) is $2^{10} = 1024$ bytes; one megabyte (MB) is $2^{20} = 1,048,576$ bytes; one gigabyte (GB) is $2^{30} = 1,073,741,824$ bytes; one terabyte (TB) is $2^{40} = 1,099,511,627,776$ bytes; one petabyte (PB) is $2^{50} = 1,125,899,906,842,624$ bytes; one exabyte (EB) is $2^{60} = 1,152,921,504,606,846,976$ bytes; and one zettabyte (ZB) is $2^{70} = 1,180,591,620,717,411,303,424$ bytes.

20. Assembly language uses easy-to-remember instructions called mnemonics.

21. Assemblers are programs that translate a program written in assembly language into machine language.

22. Compilers are programs that translate a program written in a high-level language into machine code, called object code.

23. A linker links the object code with other programs provided by the integrated development environment (IDE) and used in the program to produce executable code.

24. Typically, six steps are needed to execute a C++ program: edit, preprocessor, compile, link, load, and execute.

25. A loader transfers executable code into main memory.

26. An algorithm is a step-by-step problem-solving process in which a solution is arrived at in a finite amount of time.

27. The problem-solving process has three steps: analyze the problem and design an algorithm, implement the algorithm in a programming language, and maintain the program.

28. Programs written using the structured design approach are easier to understand, easier to test and debug, and easier to modify.

29. In structured design, a problem is divided into smaller subproblems. Each subproblem is solved, and the solutions to all the subproblems are then combined to solve the problem.

30. In object-oriented design (OOD), a program is a collection of interacting objects.

31. An object consists of data and operations on those data.

EXERCISES

1. Mark the following statements as true or false.

   a. In ASCII coding, every character is coded as a sequence of seven bits.

   b. A compiler translates a high-level program into assembly language.

   c. The arithmetic logic unit performs arithmetic operations and, if an error is found, it outputs the logical errors.

   d. A loader loads the object code from main memory into the CPU for execution.

   e. Development of a C++ program includes six steps.

   f. The CPU functions under the control of the control unit.

   g. RAM stands for readily available memory.

   h. A program written in a high-level programming language is called a source program.

   i. ZB stands for zero byte.

   j. The first step in the problem-solving process is to analyze the problem.

2. Name some components of the central processing unit.

3. What is the function of the control unit?

4. Name two input devices.

5. Name two output devices.

6. Why is secondary storage needed?

7. What is the function of an operating system?

8. What is a source program?

9. Why do you need a compiler?

10. What kind of errors are reported by a compiler?

11. Why do you need to translate a program written in a high-level language into machine language?

0

12. Why would you prefer to write a program in a high-level language rather than a machine language?

13. What is linking?

14. What are the advantages of problem analysis and algorithm design over directly writing a program in a high-level language?

15. Design an algorithm and write the pseudocode to find the weighted average of four test scores. The four test scores and their respective weights are given in the following format:

```
testscore1 weight1
```
...

Some sample data follows:

```
75 0.20
95 0.35
85 0.15
65 0.30
```

16. Design an algorithm and write the pseudocode to convert the change given in quarters, dimes, nickels, and pennies into pennies.

17. Given the radius, in inches, and price of a pizza, design an algorithm and write the pseudocode to find the price of the pizza per square inch.

18. To make a profit, the prices of the items sold in a furniture store are marked up by 60%. Design an algorithm and write the pseudocode to find the selling price of an item sold at the furniture store. What information do you need to find the selling price?

19. Suppose a, b, and c denote the lengths of the sides of a triangle. The area of the triangle can be calculated using the formula

$$\sqrt{s(s-a)(s-b)(s-c)},$$

where $s = (1/2)(a + b + c)$. Design an algorithm and write the pseudocode that uses this formula to find the area of a triangle. What information do you need to find the area?

20. A triangle ABC is inscribed in a circle, that is, the vertices of the triangle are on the circumference of the circle. Suppose the triangle ABC divides the circumference into lengths of a, b, and c inches. Design an algorithm and write the pseudocode that asks the user to specify the values of a, b, and c and then calculates the radius of the circle. Note that if r is the radius of the circle, then $2\pi r = a + b + c$.

21. The cost of an international call from New York to New Delhi is calculated as follows: connection fee, $1.99; $2.00 for the first three minutes; and $0.45 for each additional minute. Design an algorithm and write the pseudocode that asks the user to enter the number of minutes the call

lasted. The algorithm then uses the number of minutes to calculate the amount due.

22. You are given a list of students' names and their test scores. Design an algorithm and write the pseudocode that does the following:

   a. Calculates the average test score

   b. Determines and prints the names of all the students whose test scores are below the average test score

   c. Determines the highest test score

   d. Prints the names of all the students whose test scores are the same as the highest test score

(*Note:* You must divide this problem into subproblems as follows: The first subproblem determines the average test score. The second subproblem determines and prints the names of all the students whose test scores are below the average test score. The third subproblem determines the highest test score. The fourth subproblem prints the names of all the students whose test scores are the same as the highest test score. The main algorithm combines the solutions of the subproblems.)

BASIC ELEMENTS OF C++

IN THIS CHAPTER, YOU WILL:

- Become familiar with the basic components of a C++ program, including functions, special symbols, and identifiers
- Explore simple data types and examine the string data type
- Discover how to use arithmetic operators
- Examine how a program evaluates arithmetic expressions
- Learn what an assignment statement is and what it does
- Become familiar with the use of increment and decrement operators
- Learn how to output results using `cout` statements
- Learn how to use preprocessor directives and why they are necessary
- Explore how to properly structure a program, including using comments to document a program
- Learn how to write a C++ program
- Learn how to avoid bugs using consistent and proper formatting
- Learn how to do a code walk-through

In this chapter, you will learn the basics of C++. As you begin to learn the C++ programming language, two questions naturally arise: First, what is a computer program? Second, what is programming? A **computer program**, or a program, is a sequence of statements intended to accomplish a task. **Programming** is a process of planning and creating a program. These two definitions tell the truth, but not the whole truth, about programming. It might take an entire book to give a satisfactory definition of programming. An analogy might help you gain a better grasp of the nature of programming, so we'll use a topic about which almost everyone has some knowledge—cooking. A recipe is also a program, and everyone with some cooking experience can agree on the following:

1.   It is usually easier to follow a recipe than to create one.

2.   There are good recipes and there are bad recipes.

3.   Some recipes are easy to follow and some are difficult to follow.

4.   Some recipes produce reliable results and some do not.

5.   You must have some knowledge of how to use cooking tools to follow a recipe to successful completion.

6.   To create good new recipes, you must have significant knowledge and understanding of cooking.

These same six points can also be applied to programming. Let's take the cooking analogy one step further. Suppose you want to teach someone how to become a chef. How would you go about it? Would you introduce the person to good food, hoping the person develops a desire to be able to produce it? Would you have the person follow recipe after recipe in the hope that some of the techniques might rub off? Or, would you first teach the use of the tools, the nature of ingredients and foods and spices, and then explain how these concepts fit together?

Just as there are different ways to learn cooking, there are also different ways to learn programming. However, some fundamentals apply to programming, just as they do to cooking or to other activities such as music.

Learning a programming language is like learning to become a chef or learning to play a musical instrument. All three skills require direct interaction with the tools. You cannot become a good chef just by reading recipes. Similarly, you cannot learn to play musical instruments simply by reading books about musical instruments. The same is true of programming. You cannot learn to program simply by reading books about program-ming. You must write programs and run them on the computer, making sure that the program does what it is supposed to do.

A C++ Program

In this chapter, you will learn the basic elements and concepts of the C++ programming language to create C++ programs. In addition to giving examples to illustrate various concepts, we will also show C++ programs to clarify them. In this section, we provide an example of a C++ program. At this point, you need not be too concerned with the details of this program. You only need to know the effect of an output statement, which is introduced in this program.

Consider the following C++ program:

```
//**********************************************************
// Author: D.S. Malik
//
// This is a C++ program. It displays three lines of text,
// including the sum of two numbers.
//**********************************************************

#include <iostream>

using namespace std;

int main()
{
    cout << "My first C++ program." << endl;
    cout << "The sum of 2 and 3 = " << 5 << endl;
    cout << "7 + 8 = " << 7 + 8 << endl;

    return 0;
}
```

Sample Run: (When you compile and execute, or "run," this program, the following three lines are displayed on the screen.)

```
My first C++ program.
The sum of 2 and 3 = 5
7 + 8 = 15
```

These lines are displayed by the execution of the following three statements:

```
cout << "My first C++ program." << endl;
cout << "The sum of 2 and 3 = " << 5 << endl;
cout << "7 + 8 = " << 7 + 8 << endl;
```

Next, we explain how this happens. Let us first consider the following statement:

```
cout << "My first C++ program." << endl;
```

This is an example of a C++ output statement. It causes the computer to evaluate the expression after the pair of symbols << and to display the result on the screen.

Usually, a C++ program contains various types of expressions such as arithmetic and strings. For example, 7 + 8 is an arithmetic expression. Anything in double quotation marks is a string. For example, "My first C++ program." and "7 + 8 = " are strings. Typically, a string evaluates to itself. Arithmetic expressions are evaluated according to rules of arithmetic operations, which you typically learn in an algebra course.

Also note that in an output statement, `endl` *causes the insertion point to move to the beginning of the next line.* (On the screen, the insertion point is where the cursor is.) Therefore, the preceding statement causes the system to display the following line on the screen:

```
My first C++ program.
```

Let us now consider the following statement:

```
cout << "The sum of 2 and 3 = " << 5 << endl;
```

This output statement consists of two expressions. The first expression (after the first `<<`) is `"The sum of 2 and 3 = "` and the second expression (after the second `<<`) consists of the number 5. The expression `"The sum of 2 and 3 = "` is a string and evaluates to itself. (Notice the space after =.) The second expression, which consists of the number 5, evaluates to 5. Thus, the output of the preceding statement is:

```
The sum of 2 and 3 = 5
```

Let us now consider the following statement:

```
cout << "7 + 8 = " << 7 + 8 << endl;
```

In this output statement, the expression `"7 + 8 = "`, which is a string, evaluates to itself. Let us consider the second expression, 7 + 8. This expression consists of the numbers 7 and 8, and the C++ arithmetic operator +. Therefore, the result of the expression 7 + 8 is the sum of 7 and 8, which is 15. Thus, the output of the preceding statement is:

```
7 + 8 = 15
```

The last statement, that is,

```
return 0;
```

returns the value 0 to the operating system when the program terminates.

In this chapter, until we explain how to properly construct a C++ program, we will use output statements such as the preceding ones to explain various concepts.

Before leaving this section, let us note the following about the preceding C++ program. A C++ program is a collection of functions, one of which is the function `main`. Roughly speaking, a function is a set of statements whose objective is to accomplish something. The preceding program consists of the function `main`.

The first line of the program, that is,

```
#include <iostream>
```

allows us to use the (predefined object) `cout` to generate output and the (manipulator) `endl`. The second line, which is

```
using namespace std;
```

allows you to use `cout` and `endl` without the prefix `std::`. It means that if you do not include this statement, then `cout` should be used as `std::cout`, and `endl` should be used as `std::endl`.

The third line consists of the following line:

```
int main()
```

This is the heading of the function `main`. The fourth line consists of a left brace. This marks the beginning of the (body) of the function `main`. The right brace (at the last line of the program) matches this left brace and marks the end of the body of the function `main`. We will explain the meaning of the other terms, such as the ones shown in blue, later in this book. Note that in C++, `<<` is an operator, called *the stream insertion operator*.

The Basics of a C++ Program

If you have never seen a program written in a programming language, the C++ program given in the previous section might look like a foreign language. To make meaningful sentences in a foreign language, you must learn its alphabet, words, and grammar. The same is true of a programming language. To write meaningful programs, you must learn the programming language's special symbols, words, and syntax rules. The **syntax rules** tell you which statements (instructions) are legal, or accepted by the programming language, and which are not. You must also learn **semantic rules**, which determine the meaning of the instructions. The programming language's rules, symbols, and special words enable you to write programs to solve problems. The syntax rules determine which instructions are valid.

Programming language: A set of rules, symbols, and special words used to construct programs.

In the remainder of this section, you will learn about some of the special symbols of a C++ program. Additional symbols are introduced as other concepts are encountered in later chapters. Similarly, syntax and semantic rules are introduced and discussed throughout the book.

Comments

The program that you write should be clear not only to you, but also to any person reading your program. Part of good programming is the inclusion of comments in the program. Typically, comments are used to do the following:

- Identify the authors of the program
- Give the date when the program is written or modified
- Give a brief explanation of the program
- Explain the meaning of key statements in a program

(For the programs that we write in this book, we will not include the date when the program is written, consistent with the standard convention for writing such books.)

Comments are for the reader, not for the compiler. So when a compiler compiles a program to check for the syntax errors, it completely ignores comments. Throughout this book, comments are shown in green. The program given in the previous section contains the following comments:

```
//*****************************************************
// Author: D.S. Malik
//
// This is a C++ program. It displays three lines of text,
// including the sum of two numbers.
//*****************************************************
```

A C++ program has two common types of comments: single-line comments and multiple-line comments.

Single-line comments begin with // and can be placed anywhere in the line. Everything encountered in that line after // is ignored by the compiler. For example, consider the following statement:

```
cout << "7 + 8 = " << 7 + 8 << endl;
```

You can put comments at the end of this line as follows:

```
cout << "7 + 8 = " << 7 + 8 << endl; //prints: 7 + 8 = 15
```

This comment could be meaningful for a beginning programmer.

Multiple-line comments are enclosed between /* and */. The compiler ignores anything that appears between /* and */. For example, the following is an example of a multiple-line comment:

```
/*
    You can include comments that can
    occupy several lines.
*/
```

Special Symbols

The smallest individual unit of a program written in any language is called a **token**. C++'s tokens are divided into special symbols, word symbols, and identifiers.

Following are some of the special symbols:

```
+       -       *       /
.       ;       ?       ,
<=      !=      ==      >=
```

The first row includes mathematical symbols for addition, subtraction, multiplication, and division. The second row consists of punctuation marks taken from English grammar.

1

Note that the comma is also a special symbol. In C++, commas are used to separate items in a list. Semicolons are used to end a C++ statement. Note that a blank, which is not shown with the symbols, is also a special symbol. You create a blank symbol by pressing the spacebar (only once) on the keyboard. The third row consists of tokens made up of two characters, but which are regarded as a single symbol. No character can come between the two characters in the token, not even a blank.

Reserved Words (Keywords)

A second category of tokens is word symbols called **reserved words**. Some of the reserved words are:

`int, float, double, char, const, void, return`

Reserved words are also called **keywords**. The letters that make up a reserved word are always lowercase. Like the special symbols, each is considered to be a single symbol. Furthermore, word symbols cannot be redefined within any program; that is, they cannot be used for anything other than their intended use. For a complete list of reserved words, see Appendix A.

NOTE   Throughout this book, reserved words are shown in blue.

Identifiers

A third category of tokens is identifiers. Identifiers are names of things that appear in programs, such as variables, constants, and functions. Some identifiers are predefined; others are defined by the user. All identifiers must obey C++'s rules for identifiers.

Identifier: A C++ identifier consists of letters, digits, and the underscore character (_), and must begin with a letter or underscore.

Identifiers can be made of only letters, digits, and the underscore character; no other symbols are permitted to form an identifier.

NOTE   C++ is case sensitive—uppercase and lowercase letters are considered different letters. Thus, the identifier `NUMBER` is not the same as the identifier `number`. Similarly, the identifiers `X` and `x` are different.

In C++, identifiers can be of any length. Two predefined identifiers that you will encounter frequently are `cout`, which is used when generating output, and `cin`, which is used to input data. Unlike reserved words, predefined identifiers can be redefined, but it would not be wise to do so.

EXAMPLE 1-1

The following are legal identifiers in C++: `first`, `conversion`, `payRate`, and `counter1`.

Table 1-1 shows some illegal identifiers and explains why they are illegal.

TABLE 1-1 Examples of Illegal Identifiers

Illegal Identifier	Description
`employee Salary`	There can be no space between `employee` and `Salary`.
`Hello!`	The exclamation mark cannot be used in an identifier.
`one+two`	The symbol + cannot be used in an identifier.
`2nd`	An identifier cannot begin with a digit.

 NOTE Compiler vendors usually begin certain identifiers with an underscore (_). When the linker links the object program with the system resources provided by the integrated development environment (IDE), certain errors can occur. Therefore, it is advisable that you should not begin identifiers in your program with an underscore (_).

White Spaces

Every C++ program contains white spaces. White spaces include blanks, tabs, and newline characters. In a C++ program, white spaces are used to separate special symbols, reserved words, and identifiers. White spaces are nonprintable in the sense that when they are printed on a white sheet of paper, the space between special symbols, reserved words, and identifiers is white. Proper utilization of white spaces in a program is important. They can be used to make the program readable.

Data Types

The objective of a C++ program is to manipulate data. Different programs manipulate different data. A program designed to calculate an employee's paycheck will add, subtract, multiply, and divide numbers, and some of the numbers might represent hours worked and pay rate. Similarly, a program designed to alphabetize a class list will manipulate names. You wouldn't expect a cherry pie recipe to help you bake cookies. Similarly, you wouldn't use a program designed to perform arithmetic calculations to manipulate alpha-

1

betic characters. Furthermore, you wouldn't multiply or subtract names. Reflecting these kinds of underlying differences, C++ categorizes data into different types, and only certain operations can be performed on particular types of data. Although at first it may seem confusing, by being so type-conscious, C++ has built-in checks to guard against errors.

Data type: A set of values together with a set of operations.

C++ data types fall into the following three categories:

1. Simple data type
2. Structured data type
3. Pointers

For the next few chapters, you will be concerned only with simple data types.

Simple Data Types

The simple data type is the fundamental data type in C++ because it becomes a building block for the structured data type, which you start learning about in Chapter 6. There are three categories of simple data:

1. **Integral**, which is a data type that deals with integers, or numbers without a decimal part
2. **Floating-point**, which is a data type that deals with decimal numbers
3. **Enumeration type**, which is a user-defined data type

NOTE   The enumeration type is C++'s method for allowing programmers to create their own simple data types. This data type will be discussed in Chapter 8.

Integral Data Types

Integral data types are further classified into nine categories: `char`, `short`, `int`, `long`, `bool`, `unsigned char`, `unsigned short`, `unsigned int`, and `unsigned long`.

Why are there so many categories of the same data type? Every data type has a different set of values associated with it. For example, the `char` data type is used to represent integers between −128 and 127. The `int` data type is used to represent integers between −2147483648 and 2147483647, and the data type `short` is used to represent integers between −32768 and 32767.

Which data type you use depends on how big a number your program needs to deal with. In the early days of programming, computers and main memory were very expensive. Only a small amount of memory was available to execute programs and manipulate the data. As a result, programmers had to optimize the use of memory. Because writing a program and making it work is already a complicated process, not having to worry about the size of the memory makes for one less thing to think about. Thus, to effectively use memory, a programmer can look at the type of data used in a program and figure out which data type to use. (Memory constraints may still be a concern for programs written for applications such as a wristwatch.)

Newer programming languages have only five categories of simple data types: `integer`, `real`, `char`, `bool`, and the enumeration type. The integral data types used in this book are `int`, `bool`, and `char`.

Table 1-2 gives the range of possible values associated with these three data types and the size of memory allocated to manipulate these values.

TABLE 1-2 Values and Memory Allocation for Three Simple Data Types

Data Type	Values	Storage (in bytes)
int	$-2147483648 (= -2^{31})$ to $2147483647 (= 2^{31} - 1)$	4
bool	true and false	1
char	$-128 (= -2^{7})$ to $127 (= 2^{7} - 1)$	1

 NOTE Use this table only as a guide. Different compilers may allow different ranges of values. Check your compiler's documentation.

int DATA TYPE

This section describes the `int` data type. In fact, this discussion also applies to other integral data types.

Integers in C++, as in mathematics, are numbers such as the following:

`-6728,    -67,   0, 78, 36782, +763`

Note the following two rules from these examples:

1. Positive integers do not need a + sign in front of them.
2. No commas are used within an integer. Recall that in C++, commas are used to separate items in a list. So `36,782` would be interpreted as two integers: `36` and `782`.

bool DATA TYPE

The data type `bool` has only two values: `true` and `false`. Also, `true` and `false` are called the logical (Boolean) values. The central purpose of this data type is to manipulate logical (Boolean) expressions. Logical (Boolean) expressions will be formally defined and discussed in detail in Chapter 3. In C++, `bool`, `true`, and `false` are reserved words.

char DATA TYPE

The data type char is the smallest integral data type. In addition to dealing with small numbers (-128 to 127), the char data type is used to represent characters—letters, digits, and special symbols. Thus, the char data type can represent every key on your keyboard. When using the char data type, you enclose each character represented within single quotation marks. Examples of values belonging to the char data type include the following:

'A', 'a', '0', '*', '+', '$', '&', ' '

Note that a blank space is a character and is written as ' ', with a space between the single quotation marks.

The data type char allows only one symbol to be placed between the single quotation marks. Thus, the value 'abc' is not of the type char. Furthermore, even though '!=' and similar special symbols are considered to be one symbol, they are not regarded as possible values of the data type char. All the individual symbols located on the keyboard that are printable may be considered as possible values of the char data type.

Several different character data sets are currently in use. The most common are the American Standard Code for Information Interchange (ASCII) and Extended Binary-Coded Decimal Interchange Code (EBCDIC). The ASCII character set has 128 values. The EBCDIC character set has 256 values and was created by IBM. Both character sets are described in Appendix C.

Each of the 128 values of the ASCII character set represents a different character. For example, the value 65 represents 'A', and the value 43 represents '+'. Thus, each character has a predefined ordering, which is called a **collating sequence**, in the set. The collating sequence is used when you compare characters. For example, the value representing 'B' is 66, so 'A' is smaller than 'B'. Similarly, '+' is smaller than 'A' because 43 is smaller than 65.

The 14th character in the ASCII character set is called the newline character and is represented as '\n'. (Note that the position of the newline character in the ASCII character set is 13 because the position of the first character is 0.) Even though the newline character is a combination of two characters, it is treated as one character. Similarly, the horizontal tab character is represented in C++ as '\t' and the null character is represented as '\0' (a backslash followed by a zero). Furthermore, the first 32 characters in the ASCII character set are nonprintable. (See Appendix C for a description of these characters.)

Floating-Point Data Types

To deal with decimal numbers, C++ provides the floating-point data type, which we discuss in this section. To facilitate the discussion, let us review a concept from a high school or college algebra course.

You may be familiar with scientific notation. For example:

$$43872918 = 4.3872918 * 10^7$$
$$.0000265 = 2.65 * 10^{-5}$$
$$47.9832 = 4.79832 * 10^1$$

To represent real numbers, C++ uses a form of scientific notation called **floating-point notation**. Table 1-3 shows how C++ might print a set of real numbers using one machine's interpretation of floating-point notation. In the C++ floating-point notation, the letter E stands for the exponent.

TABLE 1-3   Examples of Real Numbers Printed in C++ Floating-Point Notation

Real Number	C++ Floating-Point Notation
75.924	7.592400E1
0.18	1.800000E-1
0.0000453	4.530000E-5
-1.482	-1.482000E0
7800.0	7.800000E3

C++ provides three data types to manipulate decimal numbers: `float`, `double`, and `long double`. As in the case of integral data types, the data types `float`, `double`, and `long double` differ in the set of values.

NOTE   On most newer compilers, the data types `double` and `long double` are the same. Therefore, only the data types `float` and `double` are described here.

`float:` The data type `float` is used in C++ to represent any real number between –3.4E+38 and 3.4E+38. The memory allocated for a value of the `float` data type is four bytes.

`double:` The data type `double` is used in C++ to represent any real number between –1.7E+308 and 1.7E+308. The memory allocated for a value of the `double` data type is eight bytes.

The maximum and minimum values of the data types `float` and `double` are system dependent. To find these values on a particular system, you can check your compiler's documentation or, alternatively, you can run a program given in Appendix E (Header File `cfloat`).

Other than the set of values, there is one more difference between the data types `float` and `double`. The maximum number of significant digits—the number of decimal places—in `float` values is 6 or 7. The maximum number of significant digits in values belonging to the `double` type is 15.

 NOTE For values of the `double` type, for better precision, some compilers might give more than 15 significant digits. Check your compiler's documentation.

The maximum number of significant digits is called the **precision**. Sometimes `float` values are called **single precision**, and values of the type `double` are called **double precision**. If you are dealing with decimal numbers, for the most part you need only the `float` type; if you need accuracy to more than six or seven decimal places, you can use the `double` type.

 NOTE In C++, by default, floating-point numbers are considered of the type `double`. Therefore, if you use the data type `float` to manipulate floating-point numbers in a program, certain compilers might give you a warning message such as "truncation from double to float." To avoid such warning messages, you should use the `double` data type.
For illustration purposes and to avoid such warning messages in programming examples, this book mostly uses the data type `double` to manipulate floating-point numbers.

LITERALS (CONSTANTS)

Some authors call values such as 23 and −67 **integer literals** or **integer constants** or simply **integers**; values such as 12.34 and 25.60 are called **floating-point literals** or **floating-point constants** or simply **floating-point numbers**; and values such as 'a' and '5' are called **character literals**, **character constants**, or simply **characters**.

Arithmetic Operators and Operator Precedence

One of the most important uses of a computer is its ability to calculate. You can use the standard arithmetic operators to manipulate integral and floating-point data types. There are five arithmetic operators:

Arithmetic Operators: + (**addition**), − (**subtraction** or **negation**), * (**multiplication**), / (**division**), % (**mod** [**modulus** or **remainder**])

You can use the operators +, −, *, and / with both integral and floating-point data types. You use % with only the integral data type, to find the remainder in ordinary division. When you use / with the integral data type, it gives the quotient in ordinary division. That is, integral division truncates any fractional part; there is no rounding.

The following examples show how arithmetic operators—especially / and %—work with integral data types. As you can see from these examples, the operator / represents the quotient in ordinary division when used with integral data types.

EXAMPLE 1-2

Arithmetic Expression	Result	Description
2 + 5	7	
45 – 90	-45	
2 * 7	14	
5 / 2	2	In the division 5 / 2, the quotient is 2 and the remainder is 1. Therefore, 5 / 2 with the integral operands evaluates to the quotient, which is 2.
14 / 7	2	
34 % 5	4	In the division 34 / 5, the quotient is 6 and the remainder is 4. Therefore, 34 % 5 evaluates to the remainder, which is 4.
4 % 6	4	In the division 4 / 6, the quotient is 0 and the remainder is 4. Therefore, 4 % 6 evaluates to the remainder, which is 4.

The following C++ program evaluates the preceding expressions:

```
//*******************************************************
// Author: D.S. Malik
//
// This program illustrates how integral expressions are
// evaluated.
//*******************************************************

#include <iostream>

using namespace std;

int main()
{
    cout << "2 + 5 = " << 2 + 5 << endl;
    cout << "45 - 90 = " << 45 - 90 << endl;
    cout << "2 * 7 = " << 2 * 7 << endl;
    cout << "5 / 2 = " << 5 / 2 << endl;
    cout << "14 / 7 = " << 14 / 7 << endl;
    cout << "34 % 5 = " << 34 % 5 << endl;
    cout << "4 % 6 = " << 4 % 6 << endl;

    return 0;
}
```

Sample Run:

```
2 + 5 = 7
45 - 90 = -45
2 * 7 = 14
5 / 2 = 2
14 / 7 = 2
34 % 5 = 4
4 % 6 = 4
```

 NOTE You should be careful when evaluating the mod operator with negative integer operands. You might not get the answer you expect. For example, −34 % 5 = −4, because in the division −34 / 5, the quotient is −6 and the remainder is −4. Similarly, 34 % −5 = 4, because in the division 34 / −5, the quotient is −6 and the remainder is 4. Also −34 % −5 = −4, because in the division −34 / −5, the quotient is 6 and the remainder is −4.

EXAMPLE 1-3

The following C++ program evaluates various floating-point expressions. (The details, of how the expressions are evaluated, are left as an exercise for you.)

```cpp
//***********************************************************
// Author: D.S. Malik
//
// This program illustrates how floating-point expressions
// are evaluated.
//***********************************************************

#include <iostream>

using namespace std;

int main()
{
    cout << "5.0 + 3.5 = " << 5.0 + 3.5 << endl;
    cout << "16.3 - 5.2 = " << 16.3 - 5.2 << endl;
    cout << "4.2 * 2.5 = " << 4.2 * 2.5 << endl;
    cout << "5.0 / 2.0 = " << 5.0 / 2.0 << endl;
    cout << "34.5 / 6.0 = " << 34.5 / 6.0 << endl;
    cout << "34.5 / 6.5 = " << 34.5 / 6.5 << endl;

    return 0;
}
```

Sample Run:

```
5.0 + 3.5 = 8.5
16.3 - 5.2 = 11.1
4.2 * 2.5 = 10.5
5.0 / 2.0 = 2.5
34.5 / 6.0 = 5.75
34.5 / 6.5 = 5.30769
```

Using arithmetic operators and numbers, you can form expressions such as the following:

```
-5,
3 + 4,
2 - 3 * 5,
5.6 + 6.2 * 3,  and
x + 2 * 5 + 6 / y,
```
where x and y are unknown numbers.

These are examples of arithmetic expressions. Formally, an **arithmetic expression** is constructed by using arithmetic operators and numbers. The numbers appearing in the expression are called **operands**. The numbers that are used to evaluate an operator are called the operands for that operator.

Notice that in the expression −5, the symbol − specifies that the number 5 is negative. In this expression, − has only one operand. Operators that have only one operand are called **unary operators**. Similarly, in the expression 3 + 4, the symbol + is used to add 3 and 4. In this expression, + has two operands, 3 and 4. Operators that have two operands are called **binary operators**.

Unary operator: An operator that has only one operand.

Binary operator: An operator that has two operands.

Note that − and + are both unary and binary arithmetic operators. However, as arithmetic operators, *, /, and % are binary and so must have two operands.

Order of Precedence

When more than one arithmetic operator is used in an expression, C++ uses the operator precedence rules to evaluate the expression. According to the order of precedence rules for arithmetic operators,

*, /, %

are at a higher level of precedence than:

+, −

Note that the operators *, /, and % have the same level of precedence. Similarly, the operators + and − have the same level of precedence.

When operators have the same level of precedence, the operations are performed from left to right. To avoid confusion, you can use parentheses to group arithmetic expressions. For example, using the order of precedence rules,

```
3 * 7 - 6 + 2 * 5 / 4
```

means the following:

```
    ((3 * 7) - 6) + ((2 * 5) / 4)
=   (21 - 6) + (10 / 4)      (Evaluate *)
=   (21 - 6) + 2             (Evaluate /. Note that this is an integer division.)
=   15 + 2                   (Evaluate -)
=   17                       (Evaluate +)
```

Note that the use of parentheses in the second example clarifies the order of precedence. You can also use parentheses to override the order of precedence rules.

Because arithmetic operators are evaluated from left to right, unless parentheses are present, the **associativity** of the arithmetic operators is said to be from left to right.

> **NOTE** (**Character Arithmetic**) Because the `char` data type is also an integral data type, C++ allows you to perform arithmetic operations on `char` data. However, you should use this ability carefully. There is a difference between the character `'8'` and the integer 8. The integer value of 8 is 8. The integer value of `'8'` is 56, which is the ASCII collating sequence of the character `'8'`.
>
> When evaluating arithmetic expressions, 8 + 7 = 15; `'8'` + `'7'` = 56 + 55, which yields 111; and `'8'` + 7 = 56 + 7, which yields 63. Furthermore, because `'8'` * `'7'` = 56 * 55 = 3080 and the ASCII character set has only 128 values, `'8'` * `'7'` is undefined in the ASCII character data set.
>
> These examples illustrate that many things can go wrong when you are performing character arithmetic. If you must use arithmetic operations on the `char` type data, do so with caution.

Expressions

To this point, we have discussed only arithmetic operators. In this section, we discuss arithmetic expressions in some detail.

There are three types of arithmetic expressions:

- **Integral expression**—An arithmetic expression in which all operands (that is, numbers) are integers. An integral expression yields an integral result.

- **Floating-point (decimal expression)**—An arithmetic expression in which all operands are floating-point numbers. A floating-point expression yields a floating-point result.

- **Mixed expression**—An expression that has operands of different data types. A mixed expression contains both integers and floating-point numbers.

EXAMPLE 1-4

The following are integral expressions:

```
2 + 3 * 5
3 + x - y / 7
x + 2 * (y - z) + 18, where x, y, and z are integers.
```

EXAMPLE 1-5

The following are floating-point expressions:

```
12.8 * 17.5 - 34.50
x * 10.5 + y - 16.2, where x and y are floating-point numbers.
```

EXAMPLE 1-6

The following expressions are examples of mixed expressions:

```
2 + 3.5
6 / 4 + 3.9
5.4 * 2 - 13.6 + 18 / 2
```

Evaluating an integral or a floating-point expression is straightforward. As before, when operators have the same precedence, the expression is evaluated from left to right. You can always use parentheses to group operands and operators to avoid confusion.

Evaluating Mixed Expressions

Two rules apply when evaluating a mixed expression:

1. When evaluating an operator in a mixed expression:

   a. If the operator has the same types of operands (that is, either both integers or both floating-point numbers), the operator is evaluated according to the type of the operands. Integer operands thus yield an integer result; floating-point numbers yield a floating-point number.

   b. If the operator has both types of operands (that is, one is an integer and the other is a floating-point number), then during calculation the integer is changed to a floating-point number with the decimal part of zero, and the operator is evaluated. The result is a floating-point number.

2. The entire expression is evaluated according to the precedence rules; the multiplication, division, and modulus operators are evaluated before the addition and subtraction operators. Operators having the same level of precedence are evaluated from left to right. Grouping is allowed for clarity.

From these rules, it follows that when evaluating a mixed expression, you concentrate on one operator at a time, using the rules of precedence. If the operator to be evaluated has operands of the same data type, evaluate the operator using Rule 1(a). That is, an operator with integer operands will yield an integer result, and an operator with floating-point operands will yield a floating-point result. If the operator to be evaluated has one integer operand and one floating-point operand, before evaluating this operator, convert the integer operand to a floating-point number with the decimal part of 0. The following examples show how to evaluate mixed expressions.

EXAMPLE 1-7

Mixed Expression	Evaluation	Rule Applied
3 / 2 + 5.5	= 1 + 5.5 = 6.5	3/2 = 1 (integer division; Rule 1(a)) (1 + 5.5 = 1.0 + 5.5 (Rule 1(b)) = 6.5)
15.6 / 2 + 5	= 7.8 + 5	15.6 / 2 = 15.6 / 2.0 (Rule 1(b)) = 7.8
	= 12.8	7.8 + 5 = 7.8 + 5.0 (Rule 1(b)) = 12.8
4 + 5 / 2.0	= 4 + 2.5	5 / 2.0 = 5.0 / 2.0 (Rule 1(b)) = 2.5
	= 6.5	4 + 2.5 = 4.0 + 2.5 (Rule 1(b)) = 6.5
4 * 3 + 7 / 5 − 25.5	= 12 + 7 / 5 − 25.5 = 12 + 1 − 25.5	4 * 3 = 12; (Rule 1(a)) 7 / 5 = 1 (integer division; Rule 1(a))
	= 13 − 25.5	12 + 1 = 13; (Rule 1(a))
	= −12.5	13 − 25.5 = 13.0 − 25.5 (Rule 1(b)) = −12.5

The following C++ program evaluates the preceding expressions:

```cpp
//*********************************************************
// Author: D.S. Malik
//
// This program illustrates how mixed expressions are
// evaluated.
//*********************************************************

#include <iostream>

using namespace std;

int main()
{
    cout << "3 / 2 + 5.5 = " << 3 / 2 + 5.5 << endl;
    cout << "15.6 / 2 + 5 = " << 15.6 / 2 + 5 << endl;
    cout << "4 + 5 / 2.0 = " << 4 + 5 / 2.0 << endl;
    cout << "4 * 3 + 7 / 5 - 25.5 = "
         << 4 * 3 + 7 / 5 - 25.5
         << endl;

    return 0;
}
```

Sample Run:

```
3 / 2 + 5.5 = 6.5
15.6 / 2 + 5 = 12.8
4 + 5 / 2.0 = 6.5
4 * 3 + 7 / 5 - 25.5 = -12.5
```

These examples illustrate that an integer is not converted to a floating-point number unless the operator to be evaluated has one integer and one floating-point operand.

Type Conversion (Casting)

In the previous section, you learned that when evaluating an arithmetic expression, if the operator has mixed operands, the integer value is changed to a floating-point value with a zero decimal part. When a value of one data type is automatically changed to another data type, an **implicit type coercion** is said to have occurred. As the examples in the preceding section illustrate, if you are not careful about data types, implicit type coercion can generate unexpected results.

To avoid implicit type coercion, C++ provides for explicit type conversion through the use of a cast operator. The **cast operator**, also called **type conversion** or **type casting**, takes the following form:

```cpp
static_cast<dataTypeName>(expression)
```

First, the expression is evaluated. Its value is then converted to a value of the type specified by dataTypeName. In C++, static_cast is a reserved word.

When converting a floating-point (decimal) number to an integer using the cast operator, you simply drop the decimal part of the floating-point number. That is, the floating-point number is truncated. Example 1-8 shows how cast operators work. Be sure you understand why the last two expressions evaluate as they do.

EXAMPLE 1-8

Expression	Evaluates to
static_cast<int>(7.9)	7
static_cast<int>(3.3)	3
static_cast<double>(25)	25.0
static_cast<double>(5 + 3)	= static_cast<double>(8) = 8.0
static_cast<double>(15) / 2	= 15.0 / 2
	(because static_cast<double>(15) = 15.0)
	= 15.0 / 2.0 = 7.5
static_cast<double>(15 / 2)	= static_cast<double>(7)
	(because 15 / 2 = 7)
	= 7.0
static_cast<int>(7.8 + static_cast<double>(15) / 2)	= static_cast<int>(7.8 + 7.5)
	= static_cast<int>(15.3)
	= 15
static_cast<int>(7.8 + static_cast<double>(15 / 2))	= static_cast<int>(7.8 + 7.0)
	= static_cast<int>(14.8)
	= 14

The following C++ program evaluates the preceding expressions:

```cpp
//**************************************************************
// Author: D.S. Malik
//
// This program illustrates how explicit type conversion works.
//**************************************************************

#include <iostream>

using namespace std;

int main()
{
    cout << "static_cast<int>(7.9) = " << static_cast<int>(7.9)
        << endl;
    cout << "static_cast<int>(3.3) = " << static_cast<int>(3.3)
        << endl;
```

```cpp
    cout << "static_cast<double>(25) = " << static_cast<double>(25)
         << endl;
    cout << "static_cast<double>(5 + 3) = "
         << static_cast<double>(5 + 3)
         << endl;
    cout << "static_cast<double>(15) / 2 = "
         << static_cast<double>(15) / 2
         << endl;
    cout << "static_cast<double>(15 / 2) = "
         << static_cast<double>(15 / 2)
         << endl;
    cout << "static_cast<int>(7.8 + static_cast<double>(15) / 2) = "
         << static_cast<int>(7.8 + static_cast<double>(15) / 2)
         << endl;
    cout << "static_cast<int>(7.8 + static_cast<double>(15 / 2)) = "
         << static_cast<int>(7.8 + static_cast<double>(15 / 2))
         << endl;

    return 0;
}
```

Sample Run:

```
static_cast<int>(7.9) = 7
static_cast<int>(3.3) = 3
static_cast<double>(25) = 25
static_cast<double>(5 + 3) = 8
static_cast<double>(15) / 2 = 7.5
static_cast<double>(15 / 2) = 7
static_cast<int>(7.8 + static_cast<double>(15) / 2) = 15
static_cast<int>(7.8 + static_cast<double>(15 / 2)) = 14
```

Note that the value of the expression static_cast<double>(25) is 25.0. However, it is output as 25 rather than 25.0. This is because we have not yet discussed how to output decimal numbers with 0 decimal parts to show the decimal point and the trailing zeros. Chapter 2 explains how to output decimal numbers in a desired format. Similarly, the output of other decimal numbers with zero decimal parts is output without the decimal point and the 0 decimal part.

NOTE   In C++, the cast operator can also take the form dataType(expression). This form is called C-like casting. For example, double(5) = 5.0 and int(17.6) = 17. However, static_cast is more stable than C-like casting.

You can also use cast operators to explicitly convert char data values into int data values, and int data values into char data values. To convert char data values into int data values, you use a collating sequence. For example, in the ASCII character set, static_cast<int>('A') is 65 and static_cast<int>('8') is 56. Similarly, static_cast<char>(65) is 'A' and static_cast<char>(56) is '8'.

Before leaving the discussion of data types, let us discuss one more data type—string.

string Type

In the preceding sections, we discussed simple types to deal with data consisting of numbers and characters. What about data values such as a person's name? A person's name contains more than one character. Such values are called **strings**. Most often, we process strings as a single unit. To process strings effectively, C++ provides the type string. The type string contains various operations to manipulate a string. You will see this type used throughout the book.

A **string** is a sequence of zero or more characters. Strings in C++ are enclosed in double quotation marks (not in single quotation marks, as are the char data types). A string containing no characters is called a **null** or **empty** string. The following are examples of strings. Note that "" is the empty string.

```
"William Jacob"
"Mickey"
""
```

A string, such as "hello", sometimes is called a **character string** or **string literal** or **string constant**. However, if no confusion arises, we refer to sequences of characters between double quotation marks simply as strings.

Every character in a string has a relative position in the string. The position of the first character is 0, the position of the second character is 1, and so on. The length of a string is the number of characters in it.

EXAMPLE 1-9

String	Position of a Character in the String	Length of the String
"William Jacob"	Position of 'W' is 0. Position of the first 'i' is 1. Position of ' ' (the space) is 7. Position of 'J' is 8. Position of 'b' is 12.	13

When determining the length of a string, you must also count any spaces in the string. For example, the length of the following string is 22:

```
"It is a beautiful day."
```

Technically speaking, the type string is not a simple type, despite its common and frequent usage. In fact, the type string is a programmer-defined data type. It is not directly available for use in a program like the simple data types discussed earlier. To use this data type, you need to access program components from the library, which will be discussed later in this chapter.

Named Constants, Variables, and Assignment Statements

The main objective of a C++ program is to perform calculations and manipulate data. Recall that data must be loaded into main memory before it can be manipulated. In this section, you will learn how to put data into the computer's memory. Storing data in the computer's memory is a two-step process:

1. Instruct the computer to allocate memory.
2. Include statements in the program to put data into the allocated memory.

Allocating Memory with Named Constants and Variables

When you instruct the computer to allocate memory, you tell it not only what names to use for each memory location, but also what type of data to store in those memory locations. Knowing the location of data is essential, because data stored in one memory location might be needed at several places in the program. As you saw earlier, knowing what data type you have is crucial for performing accurate calculations. It is also critical to know whether your data needs to remain fixed throughout program execution or whether it should change.

Some data must stay the same throughout a program. For example, the pay rate is usually the same for all part-time employees. A conversion formula that converts inches into centimeters is fixed because 1 inch is always equal to **2.54** centimeters. When stored in memory, this type of data needs to be protected from accidental changes during program execution. In C++, you can use a **named constant** to instruct a program to mark those memory locations in which data is fixed throughout program execution.

Named constant: A memory location whose content is not allowed to change during program execution.

To allocate memory, we use C++'s declaration statements. The syntax to declare a named constant is:

```
const dataType identifier = value;
```

In C++, `const` is a reserved word.

EXAMPLE 1-10

Consider the following C++ statements:

```
const double CONVERSION = 2.54;
const int NO_OF_STUDENTS = 20;
const char BLANK = ' ';
const double PAY_RATE = 15.75;
```

The first statement tells the compiler to allocate memory (eight bytes), to store a value of the type double, to call this memory space `CONVERSION`, and to store the value `2.54` in it. Throughout a program that uses this statement, whenever the conversion formula is needed, the memory space `CONVERSION` can be accessed. The meaning of the other statements is similar.

Note that the identifier for a named constant is in uppercase letters. Even though there are no written rules, C++ programmers typically prefer to use uppercase letters to name a named constant. Moreover, if the name of a named constant is a combination of more than one word, called a run-together word, then the words are separated using an underscore. For example, in the preceding example, `PAY_RATE` is a run-together word.

> **NOTE** As noted earlier, the default type of floating-point numbers is `double`. Therefore, if you declare a named constant of the type `float`, then you must specify that the value is of the type `float` as follows:
>
> `const float PAY_RATE = 15.75f;`
>
> otherwise, the compiler will generate an error message. Notice that `15.75f` says that it is a `float` value. Recall that the memory size for `float` values is four bytes; for `double` values, eight bytes. Because memory size is rarely a concern, as indicated earlier we will mostly use the type `double` to work with floating-point values.

Using a named constant to store fixed data, rather than using the data value itself, has one major advantage. If the fixed data changes, you do not need to edit the entire program and change the old value to the new value wherever the old value is used. Instead, you can make the change at just one place, recompile the program, and execute it using the new value throughout. In addition, by storing a value and referring to that memory location whenever the value is needed, you avoid typing the same value again and again and prevent typos. If you misspell the name of the constant value's location, the computer will warn you through an error message, but it will not warn you if the value is mistyped.

In some programs, data needs to be modified during program execution. For example, after each test, the average test score and the number of tests taken change. Similarly, after each pay increase, the employee's salary changes. This type of data must be stored in those memory cells whose contents can be modified during program execution. In C++, memory cells whose contents can be modified during program execution are called variables.

Variable: A memory location whose content may change during program execution.

The syntax for declaring one variable or multiple variables is:

```
dataType identifier, identifier, . . .;
```

EXAMPLE 1-11

Consider the following statements:

```
double amountDue;
char ch;
int num1, num2;
string name;
```

The first statement tells the compiler to allocate enough memory to store a value of the type double and call it amountDue. The second statement has a similar convention. The third statement tells the compiler to allocate two different memory spaces, each large enough to store a value of the type int; to name the first memory space num1; and to name the second memory space num2. The fourth statement tells the compiler to allocate memory space to store a string and call it name.

As in the case of naming named constants, there are no written rules for naming variables. However, C++ programmers typically use lowercase letters to declare variables. If a variable name is a combination of more than one word, then the first letter of each word, except the first word, is uppercase. (For example, see the variable amountDue in the preceding example.)

From now on, when we say "variable," we mean a variable memory location.

 NOTE In C++, you must declare all identifiers before you can use them. If you refer to an identifier without declaring it, the compiler will generate an error message (syntax error), indicating that the identifier is not declared. Therefore, to use either a named constant or a variable, you must first declare it.

Now that data types, variables, and constants have been defined and discussed, it is possible to offer a formal definition of simple data types. A data type is called **simple** if the variable or named constant of that type can store only one value at a time. For example, if x is an int variable, at a given time only one value can be stored in x.

Putting Data into Variables

Now that you know how to declare variables, the next question is: How do you put data into those variables? In C++, you can place data into a variable in two ways:

1. Use C++'s assignment statement.
2. Use input (read) statements.

Assignment Statement

The assignment statement takes the following form:

```
variable = expression;
```

In an assignment statement, the value of the **expression** should match the data type of the **variable**. The expression on the right side is evaluated, and its value is assigned to the variable (and thus to a memory location) on the left side.

A variable is said to be **initialized** the first time a value is placed in the variable.

In C++, = is called the **assignment operator**.

EXAMPLE 1-12

Suppose you have the following variable declarations:

```
int num1, num2;
double sale;
char first;
string str;
```

Now consider the following assignment statements:

```
num1 = 4;
num2 = 4 * 5 - 11;
sale = 0.02 * 1000;
first = 'D';
str = "It is a sunny day.";
```

For each of these statements, the computer first evaluates the expression on the right and then stores that value in a memory location named by the identifier on the left. The first statement stores the value 4 in num1, the second statement stores 9 in num2, the third statement stores 20.00 in sale, and the fourth statement stores the character D in first. The fifth statement stores the string "It is a sunny day." in the variable str.

The following C++ program shows the effect of the preceding statements:

```
//*************************************************************
// Author: D.S. Malik
//
// This program illustrates how data in the variables is
// manipulated.
//*************************************************************

#include <iostream>
#include <string>

using namespace std;

int main()
{
    int num1, num2;
    double sale;
    char first;
    string str;
```

```
num1 = 4;
cout << "num1 = " << num1 << endl;

num2 = 4 * 5 - 11;
cout << "num2 = " << num2 << endl;

sale = 0.02 * 1000;
cout << "sale = " << sale << endl;

first = 'D';
cout << "first = " << first << endl;

str = "It is a sunny day.";
cout << "str = " << str << endl;

return 0;
}
```

Sample Run:

```
num1 = 4
num2 = 9
sale = 20
first = D
str = It is a sunny day.
```

For the most part, the preceding program is straightforward. Let us take a look at the output statement:

```
cout << " num1 = " << num1 << endl;
```

This output statement consists of the string " num1 = ", the operator <<, and the variable num1. Here first the value of the string " num1 = " is output, and then the value of the variable num1 is output. The meaning of the other output statements is similar.

A C++ statement such as

```
num = num + 2;
```

means "evaluate whatever is in num, add 2 to it, and assign the new value to the memory location num." The expression on the right side must be evaluated first; that value is then assigned to the memory location specified by the variable on the left side. Thus, the sequence of C++ statements

```
num = 6;
num = num + 2;
```

and the statement

```
num = 8;
```

both assign 8 to num. Note that the statement num = num + 2 is meaningless if num has not been initialized.

The statement num = 5; is read as "num becomes 5" or "num gets 5" or "num is assigned the value 5." Reading the statement as "num equals 5" is incorrect, especially for statements such as num = num + 2;. Each time a new value is assigned to num, the old value is overwritten.

EXAMPLE 1-13

Suppose that num1, num2, and num3 are int variables and the following statements are executed in sequence.

1. num1 = 18;

2. num1 = num1 + 27;

3. num2 = num1;

4. num3 = num2 / 5;

5. num3 = num3 / 4;

The following shows the values of the variables after the execution of each statement. A ? (question mark) indicates that the value is unknown. The orange color in a box shows that the value of that variable is changed.

	Values of the Variables			Explanation
Before Statement 1	? num1	? num2	? num3	
After Statement 1	18 num1	? num2	? num3	
After Statement 2	45 num1	? num2	? num3	num1 + 27 = 18 + 27 = 45. This value is assigned to num1, which replaces the old value of num1.
After Statement 3	45 num1	45 num2	? num3	Copy the value of num1 into num2.
After Statement 4	45 num1	45 num2	9 num3	num2 / 5 = 45 / 5 = 9. This value is assigned to num3. So num3 = 9.
After Statement 5	45 num1	45 num2	2 num3	num3 / 4 = 9 / 4 = 2. This value is assigned to num3, which replaces the old value of num3.

Thus, after the execution of the statement in Line 5, num1 = 45, num2 = 45, and num3 = 2.

Tracing values through a sequence, called a **walk-through**, is a valuable tool to learn and practice. Try it in the preceding sequence. You will learn more about how to walk through a sequence of C++ statements later in this chapter.

The Web Site accompanying this book contains the program `Example1_13.cpp` that shows the effect of the five statements listed at the beginning of Example 1-13.

NOTE   Suppose that **x**, **y**, and **z** are `int` variables. The following is a legal statement in C++:

```
x = y = z;
```

In this statement, first the value of **z** is assigned to **y**, and then the new value of **y** is assigned to **x**. Because the assignment operator, =, is evaluated from right to left, the **associativity** of the **assignment operator** is said to be from right to left.

Earlier, you learned that if a variable is used in an expression, the expression will yield a meaningful value only if the variable has first been initialized. You also learned that after declaring a variable, you can use an assignment statement to initialize it. It is possible to initialize and declare variables at the same time. Before we discuss how to use an input (read) statement, we address this important issue.

Declaring and Initializing Variables

When a variable is declared, C++ may not automatically put a meaningful value in it. In other words, C++ may not automatically initialize variables. For example, the `int` and `double` variables may not be initialized to 0, as happens in some programming languages. This does not mean, however, that there is no value in a variable after its declaration. When a variable is declared, memory is allocated for it.

If you declare a variable and then use it in an expression without first initializing it, when you compile the program you are likely to get a warning or an error message. To avoid these pitfalls, C++ allows you to initialize variables while they are being declared. For example, consider the following C++ statements in which variables are first declared and then initialized:

```
int first;
char ch;
double x;

first = 13;
ch = ' ';
x = 12.6;
```

You can declare and initialize these variables at the same time using the following C++ statements:

```
int first = 13;
char ch = ' ';
double x = 12.6;
```

The first C++ statement declares the `int` variable `first` and stores 13 in `first`. The meaning of the other statements is similar.

In reality, not all variables are initialized during declaration. It is the nature of the program or the programmer's choice that dictates which variables should be initialized during declaration. The key point is that all variables must be initialized before they are used.

Increment and Decrement Operators

Now that you know how to declare a variable and enter data into a variable, in this section you will learn about two more operators: the **increment** and **decrement operators**. These operators are used frequently by C++ programmers and are useful programming tools.

Suppose `count` is an `int` variable. The statement

```
count = count + 1;
```

increments the value of `count` by 1. To execute this assignment statement, the computer first evaluates the expression on the right, which is `count + 1`. It then assigns this value to the variable on the left, which is `count`.

As you will see in later chapters, such statements are frequently used to keep track of how many times certain things have happened. To expedite the execution of such statements, C++ provides the **increment operator**, `++`, which increases the value of a variable by 1, and the **decrement operator**, `--`, which decreases the value of a variable by 1. Increment and decrement operators each have two forms, pre and post. The syntax of the increment operator is:

Pre-increment:	`++variable`
Post-increment:	`variable++`

The syntax of the decrement operator is:

Pre-decrement:	`--variable`
Post-decrement:	`variable--`

Let's look at some examples. The statement

```
++count;
```

or

```
count++;
```

increments the value of `count` by 1. Similarly, the statement

```
--count;
```

or

```
count--;
```

decrements the value of `count` by 1.

Because both the increment and decrement operators are built into C++, the value of the variable is quickly incremented or decremented without having to use the form of an assignment statement.

As you can see from these examples, both the pre- and post-increment operators increment the value of the variable by 1. Similarly, the pre- and post-decrement operators decrement the value of the variable by 1. The difference between the pre and post forms of these operators is shown in the following example:

EXAMPLE 1-14

Suppose that **x** and **y** are `int` variables. If **++x** is used in an expression, first the value of **x** is incremented by 1, and then the new value of **x** is used to evaluate the expression. On the other hand, if **x++** is used in an expression, first the current value of **x** is used in the expression, and then the value of **x** is incremented by 1. For example, consider the following statements:

```
x = 5;
y = ++x;
```

The first statement assigns the value 5 to **x**. To evaluate the second statement, which uses the pre-increment operator, first the value of **x** is incremented to 6, and then this value, 6, is assigned to **y**. After the second statement executes, both **x** and **y** have the value 6.

Now consider the following statements:

```
x = 5;
y = x++;
```

As before, the first statement assigns 5 to **x**. In the second statement, the post-increment operator is applied to **x**. To execute the second statement, first the value of **x**, which is 5, is used to evaluate the expression, and then the value of **x** is incremented to 6. Finally, the value of the expression, which is 5, is stored in **y**. After the second statement executes, the value of **x** is 6, and the value of **y** is 5.

EXAMPLE 1-15

Suppose a and b are `int` variables and:

```
a = 5;
b = 2 + (++a);
```

The first statement assigns 5 to a. To execute the second statement, first the expression 2 + (++a) is evaluated. Because the pre-increment operator is applied to a, first the value of a is incremented to 6. Then 2 is added to 6 to get 8, which is then assigned to b. Therefore, after the second statement executes, a is 6 and b is 8.

On the other hand, after the execution of the statements

```
a = 5;
b = 2 + (a++);
```

the value of a is 6 while the value of b is 7.

1

This book will most often use the increment and decrement operators with a variable in a stand-alone statement. That is, the variable using the increment or decrement operator will not be part of any expression.

Output

In the preceding sections, we explained how to put data into the computer's memory and how to manipulate that data. We also used certain output statements to show the results. This section explains in some detail how to use output statements further to generate the desired results.

In C++, output on the standard output device is accomplished via the use of cout and the operator <<. The general syntax of cout together with << is the following:

```
cout << expression or manipulator << expression or manipulator...;
```

This is called an **output statement**. In C++, << is called the **stream insertion operator**.

 NOTE The standard output device is usually the screen.

 NOTE In a syntax, the shading indicates the part of the definition that is optional. Furthermore, throughout this book, the syntax is enclosed in yellow boxes.

Generating output with cout uses the following two rules:

1. The expression is evaluated and its value is printed at the current insertion point on the output device.

2. A manipulator is used to format the output. The simplest manipulator is endl (the last character is the letter el), which causes the insertion point to move to the beginning of the next line.

 NOTE On the screen, the insertion point is where the cursor is.

The next example illustrates how an output statement works. In an output statement, a string or an expression involving only one variable or a single value evaluates to itself.

NOTE When an output statement outputs **char** values, it outputs only the character without the single quotation marks (unless the single quotation marks are part of the output statement).

For example, suppose ch is a **char** variable and ch = **'A';**. The statement:

```
cout << ch; or cout << 'A';
```

outputs:

A

Similarly, when an output statement outputs the value of a string, it outputs only the string without the double quotation marks (unless you include double quotation marks as part of the output).

EXAMPLE 1-16

Consider the following statements. The output is shown to the right of each statement.

	Statement	Output
1	`cout << 29 / 4 << endl;`	7
2	`cout << "Hello there." << endl;`	Hello there.
3	`cout << 12 << endl;`	12
4	`cout << "4 + 7" << endl;`	4 + 7
5	`cout << 4 + 7 << endl;`	11
6	`cout << 'A' << endl;`	A
7	`cout << "4 + 7 = " << 4 + 7 << endl;`	4 + 7 = 11
8	`cout << 2 + 3 * 5 << endl;`	17
9	`cout << "Hello \nthere." << endl;`	Hello
		there.

Look at the output of statement 9. Recall that in C++, the newline character is '\n'; it causes the insertion point to move to the beginning of the next line before printing there. Therefore, when \n appears in a string in an output statement, it causes the insertion point to move to the beginning of the next line on the output device. This fact explains why Hello and there. are printed on separate lines.

NOTE In C++, \ is called the escape character, and \n is called the newline escape sequence.

Recall that all variables must be properly initialized; otherwise, the value stored in them may not make much sense. Also recall that C++ does not automatically initialize variables. If num is an **int** variable, then the output of the C++ statement

```
cout << num << endl;
```

is meaningful provided that num has been given a value. For example, the sequence of the C++ statements

```
num = 45;
cout << num << endl;
```

will produce the output 45.

Let us now take a close look at the newline character, `'\n'`. Consider the following C++ statements:

```
cout << "Hello there. ";
cout << "My name is James.";
```

If these statements are executed in sequence, the output is the following:

```
Hello there. My name is James.
```

Now consider the following C++ statements:

```
cout << "Hello there.\n";
cout << "My name is James.";
```

The output of these C++ statements is:

```
Hello there.
My name is James.
```

When \n is encountered in the string, the insertion point is positioned at the beginning of the next line. Note also that \n may appear anywhere in the string. For example, the output of the statement

```
cout << "Hello \nthere. \nMy name is James.";
```

is:

```
Hello
there.
My name is James.
```

Also, note that the output of the statement

```
cout << '\n';
```

is the same as the output of the statement

```
cout << "\n";
```

which is equivalent to the output of the statement

```
cout << endl;
```

Thus, the output of the sequence of statements

```
cout << "Hello there.\n";
cout << "My name is James.";
```

is equivalent to the output of the sequence of statements

```
cout << "Hello there." << endl;
cout << "My name is James.";
```

EXAMPLE 1-17

Suppose that you want to output the following sentence in one line as part of a message:

```
It is sunny, warm, and not a windy day. We can go golfing.
```

Obviously, you will use an output statement to produce this output. However, in the programming code, this statement may not fit in one line as part of the output statement. Of course, you can use multiple output statements, as follows:

```
cout << "It is sunny, warm, and not a windy day. ";
cout << "We can go golfing." << endl;
```

Note the semicolon at the end of the first statement and the identifier `cout` at the beginning of the second statement. Also note that there is no manipulator `endl` at the end of the first statement. Here, two output statements are used to output the sentence in one line. Equivalently, you can use the following output statement to output the following sentence:

```
cout << "It is sunny, warm, and not a windy day. "
     << "We can go golfing." << endl;
```

In this statement, note that there is no semicolon at the end of the first line, and the identifier `cout` does not appear at the beginning of the second line. Because there is no semicolon at the end of the first line, this output statement continues at the second line. Also, note the double quotation marks at the beginning and end of the sentences on each line. The string is broken into two strings, but both strings are part of the same output statement.

If a string appearing in an output statement is long and you want to output the string in one line, you can break the string by using either of the previous two methods. However, the following statement would be incorrect:

```
cout << "It is sunny, warm, and not a windy day.
       We can go golfing." << endl;          //illegal
```

In other words, the return (or Enter) key on your keyboard cannot be part of the string. That is, in programming code, a string cannot be broken into more than one line by using the return (Enter) key on your keyboard.

Recall that the newline character is \n, which causes the insertion point to move to the beginning of the next line. There are many escape sequences in C++ that allow you to control the output. Table 1-4 lists some of the commonly used escape sequences.

TABLE 1-4 Commonly Used Escape Sequences

	Escape Sequence	Description
\n	Newline	Cursor moves to the beginning of the next line
\t	Tab	Cursor moves to the next tab stop
\b	Backspace	Cursor moves one space to the left
\r	Return	Cursor moves to the beginning of the current line (not the next line)
\\	Backslash	Backslash is printed
\'	Single quotation	Single quotation mark is printed
\"	Double quotation	Double quotation mark is printed

The following example shows the effect of some of these escape sequences.

EXAMPLE 1-18

The output of the statement

```
cout << "The newline escape sequence is \\n" << endl;
```

is

```
The newline escape sequence is \n
```

The output of the statement

```
cout << "The tab character is represented as \'\\t\'" << endl;
```

is

```
The tab character is represented as '\t'
```

Note that the single quotation mark can also be printed without using the escape sequence. Therefore, the preceding statement is equivalent to the following output statement:

```
cout << "The tab character is represented as '\\t'" << endl;
```

The output of the statement

```
cout << "The string \"Sunny\" contains five characters." << endl;
```

is

```
The string "Sunny" contains five characters.
```

 NOTE The Web site accompanying this book contains the C++ program that shows the effect of the statements in Example 1-18. The program is named `Example1_18.cpp`.

Preprocessor Directives

Only a small number of operations, such as arithmetic and assignment operations, are explicitly defined in C++. Many of the functions and symbols needed to run a C++ program are provided as a collection of libraries. Every library has a name and is referred to by a header file. For example, the descriptions of the functions needed to perform input/output (I/O) are contained in the header file `iostream`. Similarly, the descriptions of some very useful mathematical functions, such as power, absolute, and sine, are contained in the header file `cmath`. If you want to use I/O or math functions, you need to tell the computer where to find the necessary code. You use preprocessor directives and the names of header files to tell the computer the locations of the code provided in libraries. Preprocessor directives are processed by a program called a **preprocessor**.

Preprocessor directives are commands supplied to the preprocessor that cause the preprocessor to modify the text of a C++ program before it is compiled. All preprocessor commands begin with **#**. There are no semicolons at the end of preprocessor commands because they are not C++ statements. To use a header file in a C++ program, use the preprocessor directive `include`.

The general syntax to include a header file (provided by the IDE) in a C++ program is:

```
#include <headerFileName>
```

For example, the following statement includes the header file `iostream` in a C++ program:

```
#include <iostream>
```

Preprocessor directives to include header files are placed as the first line of a program so that the identifiers declared in those header files can be used throughout the program. (Recall that in C++, identifiers must be declared before they can be used.)

1

Certain header files are required to be provided as part of C++. Appendix E describes some of the commonly used header files. Individual programmers can also create their own header files, which is discussed in the Chapter 7, "Classes and Data Abstraction."

Note that the preprocessor commands are processed by the preprocessor before the program goes through the compiler.

From Figure 0-4 (Chapter 0), we can conclude that a C++ system has three basic components: the program development environment, the C++ language, and the C++ library. All three components are integral parts of the C++ system. The program development environment consists of the six steps shown in Figure 0-4. As you learn the C++ language throughout this book, we will discuss components of the C++ library as we need them.

namespace and Using cout in a Program

Earlier, you learned that cout is a predefined identifier. This identifier is declared in the header file iostream, but within a namespace. The name of this namespace is std. (The namespace mechanism will be formally defined and discussed in detail in Chapter 8. For now, you need to know only how to use cout, and, in fact, any other identifier from the header file iostream.)

There are several ways you can use an identifier declared in the namespace std. One way to use cout is to refer to it as std::cout throughout the program. Another option is to include the following statement in your program:

```
using namespace std;
```

This statement appears after the statement #include <iostream>. You can then refer to cout without using the prefix std::. To simplify the use of cout, this book uses the second form. That is, to use cout in a program, the program will contain the following two statements:

```
#include <iostream>
```

```
using namespace std;
```

In C++, namespace and using are reserved words.

Using the string Data Type in a Program

Recall that the string data type is a programmer-defined data type and is not directly available for use in a program. To use the string data type, you need to access its definition from the header file string. Therefore, to use the string data type in a program, you must include the following preprocessor directive:

```
#include <string>
```

Creating a C++ Program

In previous sections, you learned enough C++ concepts to write meaningful programs. You are now ready to create a complete C++ program.

A C++ program is a collection of functions, one of which is the function `main`. Therefore, if a C++ program consists of only one function, then it must be the function `main`. Moreover, a function is a set of instructions designed to accomplish a specific task. Until Chapter 5, you will deal mainly with the function `main`.

The statements to declare variables, the statements to manipulate data (such as assignments), and the statements to input and output data are placed within the function `main`. The statements to declare named constants are usually placed outside of the function `main`.

The syntax of the function `main` used throughout this book has the following form:

```
int main()
{
    statement1
        .
        .
        .
    statementn

    return 0;
}
```

In the syntax of the function `main`, each statement (`statement1`, ..., `statementn`) is usually either a declarative statement or an executable statement. The statement `return 0;` must be included in the function `main` and must be the last statement. If the statement `return 0;` is misplaced in the body of the function `main`, the results generated by the program may not be to your liking. The meaning of the statement `return 0;` will be discussed in Chapter 5. In C++, `return` is a reserved word.

A C++ program might use the resources provided by the IDE, such as the necessary code to input the data, which would require your program to include certain header files. You can, therefore, divide a C++ program into two parts: preprocessor directives and the program. The preprocessor directives tell the compiler which header files to include in the program. The program contains statements that accomplish meaningful results. Taken together, the preprocessor directives and the program statements constitute the C++ **source code**. Recall that to be useful, source code must be saved in a file with the file extension `.cpp`. For example, if the source code is saved in the file `firstProgram`, then the complete name of this file is `firstProgram.cpp`. The file containing the source code is called the **source code file** or **source file**.

When the program is compiled, the compiler generates the **object code**, which is saved in a file with the file extension `.obj`. When the object code is linked with the system resources, the **executable code** is produced and saved in a file with the file extension `.exe`. Typically, the name of the file containing the object code and the name of the file containing the executable code are the same as the name of the file containing the source code. For example, if the source code is located in a file named `firstProg.cpp`, the name of the file containing the object code is `firstProg.obj`, and the name of the file containing the executable code is `firstProg.exe`.

The extensions as given in the preceding paragraph—that is, **.cpp**, **.obj**, and **.exe**—are system dependent. Moreover, some IDEs maintain programs in the form of projects. The name of the project and the name of the source file need not be the same. It is possible that the name of the executable file is the name of the project, with the extension **.exe**. To be certain, check your system or IDE documentation. The Web site accompanying this book illustrates how to use some of the IDEs such as Microsoft Visual Studio .NET.

In skeleton form, a C++ program looks like the following:

```
preprocessor directives to include header files

using statement

declare named constants, if necessary

int main()
{
    statement1
        .
        .
        .
    statementn

    return 0;
}
```

The C++ program in Example 1-19 shows where include statements, declaration statements, executable statements, and so on typically appear in the program.

EXAMPLE 1-19

```
//************************************************************
// Author: D.S. Malik
//
// This program shows where the include statements, using
// statement, named constants, variable declarations, assignment
// statements, and output statements typically appear.
//************************************************************

#include <iostream>                              //Line 1

using namespace std;                             //Line 2

const int NUMBER = 12;                           //Line 3
```

```cpp
int main()                                          //Line 4
{                                                   //Line 5
    int firstNum;                                   //Line 6
    int secondNum;                                  //Line 7

    firstNum = 18;                                  //Line 8

    cout << "Line 9: firstNum = " << firstNum
         << endl;                                   //Line 9

    secondNum = firstNum + 2 * NUMBER;              //Line 10

    cout << "Line 11: secondNum = " << secondNum
         << endl;                                   //Line 11

    return 0;                                       //Line 12
}                                                   //Line 13
```

Sample Run:

```
Line 9: firstNum = 18
Line 11: secondNum = 42
```

The preceding program works as follows: The statement in Line 1 includes the header file iostream so that the program can perform input/output. The statement in Line 2 uses the using namespace statement so that identifiers declared in the header file iostream, such as cin, cout, and endl, can be used without using the prefix std::. The statement in Line 3 declares the named constant NUMBER and sets its value to 12. The statement in Line 4 contains the heading of the function main, and the left brace in Line 5 marks the beginning of the function main. The statements in Lines 6 and 7 declare the variables firstNum and secondNum.

The statement in Line 8 sets the value of firstNum to 18, and the statement in Line 9 outputs the value of firstNum. Next, the statement in Line 10 evaluates the expression

```cpp
firstNum + 2 * NUMBER
```

and assigns the value of this expression to the variable secondNum, which is 42 in the sample run. The statement in Line 11 outputs the new value of secondNum. The statement in Line 12 contains the return statement. The right brace in Line 13 marks the end of the function main.

Syntax, Semantics, and Errors

In previous sections, you learned enough C++ concepts to write meaningful programs. Before beginning to write programs, however, you need to learn their proper structure, among other things. Using the proper structure for a C++ program makes it easier to understand and subsequently modify the program. There is nothing more frustrating than trying to follow, and perhaps modify, a program that is syntactically correct but has no structure.

In addition, every C++ program must satisfy certain rules of the language. A C++ program must contain the function **main**. It must also follow the syntax rules, which, like grammar rules, tell what is right and what is wrong, and what is legal and what is illegal in the language. Other rules serve the purpose of giving precise meaning to the language; that is, they support the language's semantics.

The following sections are designed to help you learn how to use the C++ programming elements you have learned so far to create a functioning program. These sections cover the syntax; the use of blanks; the use of semicolons, brackets, and commas; semantics; naming identifiers; and form and style.

Syntax

The syntax rules of a language tell what is legal and what is not legal. Errors in syntax are detected during compilation. For example, consider the following C++ statements:

```
int x;          //Line 1
int y           //Line 2
double z;       //Line 3

y = w + x;      //Line 4
```

When these statements are compiled, a compilation error will occur at Line 2 because the semicolon is missing after the declaration of the variable **y**. A second compilation error will occur at Line 4 because the identifier **w** is used but has not been declared.

When a program is typed, errors are almost unavoidable. Therefore, when the program is compiled, you most likely will see syntax errors. It is possible that a syntax error at a particular place might lead to syntax errors in several subsequent statements. It is common for the omission of a single character to cause four or five error messages. However, when the first syntax error is removed and the program is recompiled, subsequent syntax errors caused by the first syntax error may disappear. Therefore, you should correct syntax errors in the order in which the compiler lists them. As you become more experienced with C++, you will learn how to spot and fix syntax errors quickly. Compilers not only discover syntax errors, but also provide hints and sometimes tell the user where the syntax errors are and how to fix them.

Use of Semicolons, Braces, and Commas

In C++, a semicolon is used to terminate a statement. The semicolon is also called a **statement terminator**.

Braces, { and } , are not C++ statements, even though they often appear on a line with no other code. You can regard braces as delimiters because they enclose the body of a function and set it off from other parts of the program. (Braces have other uses, which are explained in Chapter 3.)

Recall that commas are used to separate items in a list. For example, you use commas when you declare more than one variable following a data type.

Semantics

The set of rules that gives meaning to a language is called **semantics**. For example, the order-of-precedence rules for arithmetic operators are semantic rules.

If a program contains syntax errors, the compiler will warn you. What happens when a program contains semantic errors? It is quite possible to eradicate all syntax errors in a program and still not have it run. And if it runs, it may not do what you meant it to do. For example, the following two lines of code are both syntactically correct expressions, but they have different meanings:

```
2 + 3 * 5
```

and

```
(2 + 3) * 5
```

If you substitute one of these lines of code for the other in a program, you will not get the same results—even though the numbers are the same, the semantics are different. You will learn about semantics throughout this book.

Naming Identifiers

Consider the following two sets of statements:

```
const double A = 2.54;    //conversion constant
double x;                 //variable to hold centimeters
double y;                 //variable to hold inches

x = y * A;
```

and

```
const double CENTIMETERS_PER_INCH = 2.54;
double centimeters;
double inches;

centimeters = inches * CENTIMETERS_PER_INCH;
```

The identifiers in the second set of statements, such as CENTIMETERS_PER_INCH, are usually called **self-documenting** identifiers. As you can see, self-documenting identifiers can make comments less necessary.

Consider the self-documenting identifier annualsale. This identifier is called a **run-together word**. In using self-documenting identifiers, you may inadvertently include run-together words, which may lessen the clarity of your documentation. You can make run-together words easier to understand by either capitalizing the beginning of each new word or by inserting an underscore just before a new word. For example, you could use either `annualSale` or `annual_sale` to create an identifier that is clearer.

Recall that earlier in this chapter we specified the general rules for naming named constants and variables. For example, an identifier used to name a named constant is all uppercase. If this identifier is a run-together word, then the words are separated with the underscore character.

Form and Style

You might be thinking that C++ has too many rules. However, in practice, the rules give C++ a great degree of freedom. For example, consider the following two ways of declaring variables:

```
int feet, inch;
double x, y;
```

and

```
int feet,inches;double x,y;
```

The computer would have no difficulty understanding either of these formats, but the first form is easier to read and follow. Of course, the omission of a single comma or semicolon in either format may lead to all sorts of strange error messages.

What about blank spaces? Where are they significant and where are they meaningless? Consider the following two statements:

```
int a;
```

and:

```
int     a;
```

Both of these declarations mean the same thing. Here the blanks between the identifiers in the second statement are meaningless. On the other hand, consider the following statement:

```
inta;
```

This statement contains a syntax error. The lack of a blank space between `int` and the identifier `a` changes the reserved word `int` and the identifier `a` into a new identifier, `inta`.

The clarity of the rules of syntax and semantics frees you to adopt formats that are pleasing to you and easier to understand.

The following example further elaborates on this.

EXAMPLE 1-20

Consider the following C++ program:

```
//********************************************
// Author: D.S. Malik
//
// An improperly formatted C++ program.
//********************************************

#include <iostream>
#include <string>

using namespace std;

int main()
{
int num; double height;
string name;
num=10; cout<<"num: "<<num
<<endl;
name="John Smith";height = 5.8;
cout<<"Name: "<<name<<endl;cout<<"Height: "
<<height<<endl;return 0;
}
```

This program is syntactically correct; the C++ compiler would have no difficulty reading and compiling this program. However, this program is very hard to read. The program that you write should be properly indented and formatted. Note the difference when the program is reformatted:

```
//********************************************
// Author: D.S. Malik
//
// A properly formatted C++ program.
//********************************************

#include <iostream>
#include <string>

using namespace std;

int main()
{
    int num;
    double height;
    string name;

    num = 10;
```

```cpp
    cout << "num: " << num << endl;

    name = "John Smith";
    height = 5.8;

    cout << "Name: " << name << endl;
    cout << "Height: " << height <<endl;

    return 0;
}
```

As you can see, this program is easier to read. Your programs should be properly indented and formatted. To document the variables, programmers typically declare one variable per line. Also, always put a space before and after an operator.

Avoiding Bugs: Consistent, Proper Formatting

Consistent, proper formatting of a report, term paper, or dissertation helps an author communicate her or his message. Consistent, proper formatting is just as important when you are writing programs. Using consistent, proper formatting makes it easier to develop, debug, and maintain programs. In all the examples presented in this book, you will see consistent and predictable use of blanks, tabs, and newline characters to separate the elements of these programs. You will also see consistent, predictable use of uppercase letters and lowercase letters. This makes it easy to discover the nature and function of the elements of a program and how they fit together. In addition to learning how the examples behave, observe how they are formatted and carefully copy this style in the programs you create.

Debugging: Code Walk-Throughs

As you write programs, you will create unintentional bugs. Every programmer creates bugs. Bugs are aspects of programs that cause the programs to do other than what you intended. The C++ compiler will find the aspects of your program that violate C++'s syntax rules so that you can correct them. Sometimes a syntactically correct program (one that compiles successfully) has other problems that cause it to produce incorrect results or even to crash. Almost all the time, these problems are due to bugs in the program.

Programmers usually try to find and fix these problems themselves. They do so by walking carefully through their programs—identifying what actually is done and comparing it with what should be done at each step and in each section of the program. Often this approach reveals the problem so the programmer can fix it. Sometimes, however, especially after multiple readings of a program in search of the bug, the programmer begins to gloss over sections of code, one of which may contain the elusive bug. At this point, it can be advantageous to invite the assistance of someone else who is learning to program or who has learned to program already. Before you invite someone to examine your program, you'll probably make sure that it is formatted properly, that you have used uppercase letters and lowercase letters correctly, and that you have chosen good names for identifiers. In the process, you may find the bug. If not, as you explain your program to this person, you will not be able to gloss over sections of code as you might have done when you were reading your program to yourself. As you explain your program to someone else, you will be surprised how often you find the problem, even with the other person just listening. Finally, the person looking at your program will hear your explanation of what you intended to do while looking at what you actually wrote your program to do. The person may be able to detect the inconsistency between what you intended to code and what you actually coded. Each of these processes (the private examination of your code, the preparation of your code for review by another person, and the review of your code with another person) is a walk-through. A presentation to a larger group, such as your study group, also is called a walk-through. A walk-through can be helpful for all phases of the software development process.

QUICK REVIEW

1. A C++ program is a collection of functions.
2. Every C++ program has a function called `main`.
3. A single-line comment starts with the pair of symbols // anywhere in the line.
4. Multiple-line comments are enclosed between /* and */.
5. The compiler skips comments.
6. In C++, << is called the stream insertion operator.
7. In an output statement, `endl` positions the insertion point at the beginning of the next line on an output device.
8. Reserved words cannot be used as identifiers in a program.
9. All reserved words in C++ consist of lowercase letters (see Appendix A).
10. In C++, identifiers are names of things.
11. A C++ identifier consists of letters, digits, and underscores, and must begin with a letter or underscore.
12. The most common character sets are ASCII, which has 128 values, and EBCDIC, which has 256 values.
13. The collating sequence of a character is its preset number in the character data set.
14. The arithmetic operators in C++ are addition (+), subtraction (-), multiplication (*), division (/), and modulus (%).
15. The modulus operator, %, takes only integer operands.
16. Arithmetic expressions are evaluated using the precedence rules and the associativity of the arithmetic operators.

1

17. All operands in an integral expression, or integer expression, are integers, and all operands in a floating-point expression are decimal numbers.

18. A mixed expression is an expression that consists of both integers and decimal numbers.

19. When evaluating an operator in an expression, an integer is converted to a floating-point number, with a decimal part of 0, only if the operator has mixed operands.

20. You can use the cast operator to explicitly convert values from one data type to another.

21. During program execution, the contents of a named constant cannot be changed.

22. A named constant is declared by using the reserved word `const`.

23. A named constant is initialized when it is declared.

24. All variables must be declared before they can be used.

25. C++ does not automatically initialize variables.

26. Every variable has a name, a value, a data type, and a size.

27. When a new value is assigned to a variable, the old value is destroyed.

28. An assignment statement can change the value of a variable.

29. Outputting or accessing the value of a variable in an expression does not destroy or modify the contents of the variable.

30. When the binary operator `<<` is used with an output stream object, such as `cout`, it is called the stream insertion operator. The left-side operand of `<<` must be an output stream variable, such as `cout`; the right-side operand of `<<` must be an expression or a manipulator.

31. To use `cout`, the program must include the header file `iostream` and either include the statement `using namespace std;` or refer to this identifier as `std::cout`.

32. All preprocessor commands start with the symbol `#`.

33. The preprocessor commands are processed by the preprocessor before the program goes through the compiler.

34. The preprocessor command `#include <iostream>` instructs the preprocessor to include the header file `iostream` in the program.

35. All C++ statements end with a semicolon. The semicolon in C++ is called the statement terminator.

36. Standard libraries are not part of the C++ language. They contain functions to perform operations such as mathematical operations.

37. A file containing a C++ program usually ends with the extension `.cpp`.

EXERCISES

1. Mark the following statements as true or false.

    a. An identifier can be any sequence of digits and letters.

    b. In C++, there is no difference between a reserved word and a predefined identifier.

    c. A C++ identifier can start with a digit.

    d. The operands of the modulus operator must be integers.

    e. If a = 4;, and b = 3;, then after the statement a = b;, the value of b is still 3.

    f. In an output statement, the newline character may be a part of the string.

    g. The following is a legal C++ program:

        ```
        int main()
        {
            return 0;
        }
        ```

    h. In a mixed expression, all the operands are converted to floating-point numbers.

    i. Suppose x = 5. After the statement y = x++; executes, y is 5 and x is 6.

    j. Suppose a = 5. After the statement ++a; executes, the value of a is still 5 because the value of the expression is not saved in another variable.

2. Which of the following are valid C++ identifiers?

    a. `myFirstProgram`

    b. `MIX-UP`

    c. `C++Program2`

    d. `quiz7`

    e. `ProgrammingLecture2`

    f. `1footEquals12Inches`

    g. `Mike'sFirstAttempt`

    h. `Update Grade`

    i. `4th`

    j. `New_Student`

3. Which of the following is (are) reserved in C++?

    a.   `Const`

    b.   `include`

    c.   `Char`

    d.   `void`

    e.   `int`

    f.   `Return`

4. Evaluate the following expressions:

    a.   `13 / 4`

    b.   `2 + 12 / 4`

    c.   `21 % 5`

    d.   `3 - 5 % 7`

    e.   `17.0 / 4`

    f.   `8 - 5 * 2.0`

    g.   `14 + 5 % 2 - 3`

    h.   `15.0 + 3.0 / 2.0`

5. If $x = 5$, $y = 6$, $z = 4$, and $w = 3.5$, evaluate each of the following statements, if possible. If it is not possible, state the reason.

    a.   `(x + z) % y`

    b.   `(x + y) % w`

    c.   `(y + w) % x`

    d.   `(x + y) * w`

    e.   `(x % y) % z`

    f.   `(y % z) % x`

    g.   `(x * z) % y`

    h.   `((x * y) * w) * z`

6. What is the output of each of the following C++ statements?

    a.   `cout << "C++ is a high-level language." << endl;`

    b.   `cout << "Enter the distance traveled: " << endl;`

    c.   `cout << "The difference of 7 and 3 = " << 7 - 3 << endl;`

7. What is the output of the following C++ program?

```cpp
#include <iostream>

using namespace std;

int main()
{
    cout << "This is Exercise 7." << endl;
    cout << "In C++, the multiplication symbol is *."
        << endl;
    cout << "2 + 3 * 5 = " << 2 + 3 * 5 << endl;

    return 0;
}
```

8. Given:

```cpp
int num1, num2, newNum;
double x, y;
```

which of the following assignments are valid? If an assignment is not valid, state the reason. When not given, assume that each variable is declared.

a. num1 = 15;

b. num2 = num1 - 18;

c. num1 = 5; num2 = 2 + 6; num1 = num2 / 3;

d. num1 + num2 = newNum;

e. x = 12 * num1 - 15.3;

f. num1 * 2 = newNum;

g. x / y = x * y;

h. num2 = num1 % 1.0;

i. newNum = static_cast<int> (x) % 5;

j. x = x + 5;

k. newNum = num1 + static_cast<int> (4.6 / 2);

9. Do a walk-through to find the value assigned to e. Assume that all variables are properly declared.

```cpp
a = 3;
b = 4;
c = (a % b) * 6;
d = c / b;
e = (a + b + c + d) / 4;
```

10. Which of the following variable declarations are correct? If a variable declaration is not correct, give the reason(s) and provide the correct variable declaration.

```
n = 12;                  //Line 1
char letter = ;          //Line 2
int one = 5, two;        //Line 3
double x, y, z;          //Line 4
```

1

11. Which of the following are valid C++ assignment statements? Assume that i, x, and percent are double variables.

   a. i = i + 5;

   b. x + 2 = x;

   c. x = 2.5 * x;

   d. percent = 10%;

12. Write C++ statements that accomplish the following:

   a. Declare int variables x and y. Initialize x to 25 and y to 18.

   b. Declare and initialize an int variable temp to 10 and a char variable ch to 'A'.

   c. Update the value of an int variable x by adding 5 to it.

   d. Declares and initializes a double variable payRate to 12.50.

   e. Copy the value of an int variable firstNum into an int variable tempNum.

   f. Swap the contents of the int variables x and y. (Declare additional variables, if necessary.)

   g. Suppose x and y are double variables. Output the contents of x, y, and the expression x + 12 / y - 18.

   h. Declares a char variable grade and sets the value of grade to 'A'.

   i. Declares int variables to store four integers.

   j. Copies the value of a double variable z to the nearest integer into an int variable x.

13. Write each of the following as a C++ expression:

   a. -10 times a

   b. The character that represents 8

   c. $(b^2 - 4ac) / 2a$

   d. $(-b + (b^2 - 4ac)) / 2a$

14. Suppose x, y, z, and w are int variables. What value is assigned to each of these variables after the last statement executes?

```
x = 5; z = 3;
y = x - z;
z = 2 * y + 3;
w = x - 2 * y + z;
z = w - x;
w++;
```

15. Suppose x, y, and z are **int** variables, and w and t are **double** variables. What value is assigned to each of these variables after the last statement executes?

    ```
    x = 17;
    y = 15;
    x = x + y / 4;
    z = x % 3 + 4;
    w = 17 / 3 + 6.5;
    t = x / 4.0 + 15 % 4 - 3.5;
    ```

16. Suppose x, y, and z are **int** variables and x = 2, y = 5, and z = 6. What is the output of each of the following statements?

    a. `cout << "x = " << x << ", y = " << y << ", z = " << z << endl;`

    b. `cout << "x + y = " << x + y << endl;`

    c. `cout << "Sum of " << x << " and " << z << " is " << x + z << endl;`

    d. `cout << "z / x = " << z / x << endl;`

    e. `cout << "2 times " << x << " = " << 2 * x << endl;`

17. What is the output of the following statements? Suppose a and b are **int** variables, c is a **double** variable, and a = 13, b = 5, and c = 17.5.

    a. `cout << a + b - c << endl;`

    b. `cout << 15 / 2 + c << endl;`

    c. `cout << a / static_cast<double> (b) + 2 * c << endl;`

    d. `cout << 14 % 3 + 6.3 + b / a << endl;`

    e. `cout << static_cast<int> (c) % 5 + a - b << endl;`

    f. `cout << 13.5 / 2 + 4.0 * 3.5 + 18 << endl;`

18. Give meaningful identifiers for the following variables:

    a. A variable to store the first name of a student

    b. A variable to store the discounted price of an item

    c. A variable to store the number of juice bottles

    d. A variable to store the number of miles traveled

    e. A variable to store the highest test score

19. Write C++ statements that accomplish the following:

    a. Outputs the newline character.

    b. Outputs the tab character.

    c. Outputs double quotation mark.

20. Which of the following are correct C++ statements?

    a. `cout << "Hello There!" << endl;`

    b. `cout << "Hello";`
       `    << " There!" << endl;`

    c. `cout << "Hello"`
       `    << " There!" << endl;`

    d. `cout << 'Hello There!' << endl;`

21. Write C++ statements to do the following.

    a. Declare `int` variable `num1` and `num2`.

    b. Prompt the user to input two numbers.

    c. Input the first number in `num1` and the second number in `num2`.

    d. Output `num1`, `num2`, and 2 times `num1` minus `num2`. Your output must identify each number and the expression.

22. The following two programs have syntax mistakes. Correct them. On each successive line, assume that any preceding error has been corrected.

    a.
```
#include <iostream>

const int SECRET_NUM = 11,213;
const PAY_RATE = 18.35

main()
{
    int one, two;
    double first, second;

    one = 18;
    two = 11;

    first = 25;
    second = first * three;

    second = 2 * SECRET_NUM;
    SECRET_NUM = SECRET_NUM + 3;
    cout << first << " " << second << SECRET_NUM << endl;

    paycheck = hoursWorked * PAY_RATE

    cout << "Wages = " << paycheck << endl;
    return 0;
}
```

```
b.  const char = STAR = '*'
    const int PRIME = 71;

    int main
    {
        int count, sum;
        double x;

        count = 1;
        sum = count + PRIME;
        x := 25.67;
        newNum = count * ONE + 2;
        sum + count = sum;
        x = x + sum * COUNT;
        cout << " count = " << count << ", sum = " << sum
             << ", PRIME = " << Prime << endl;
    }
```

PROGRAMMING EXERCISES

1. Write a program that produces the following output:

```
**********************************
*      Programming Assignment 1   *
*        Computer Programming I    *
*            Author: ???           *
*      Due Date: Thursday, Jan. 24 *
**********************************
```

In your program, replace ??? with your own name. If necessary, adjust the positions and the number of the stars to produce a rectangle.

2. Write a program that produces the following output:

```
CCCCCCCCC          ++                      ++
CC                 ++                      ++
CC            ++++++++++++++    ++++++++++++++
CC            ++++++++++++++    ++++++++++++++
CC                 ++                      ++
CCCCCCCCC          ++                      ++
```

3. Write a program that prints the following banner:

```
****************************
****************************
********  WELCOME *********
============================
============================
********   HOME    *********
****************************
****************************
```

1

4. Consider the following program segment:

```
//include statement(s)
//using namespace statement

int main()
{
    //variable declaration

    //executable statements

    //return statement
}
```

  a. Write a C++ statement that includes the header file iostream.

  b. Write a C++ statement that allows you to use cin, cout, and endl without the prefix std::.

  c. Write C++ statements that declare the following variables: num1, num2, and num3, and average of type int.

  d. Write C++ statements that store 125 into num1, 28 into num2, and –25 into num3.

  e. Write a C++ statement that stores the average of num1, num2, and num3 into average.

  f. Write C++ statements that output the values of num1, num2, num3, and average.

  g. Compile and run your program.

5. Repeat Exercise 4 by declaring num1, num2, and num3, and average of type double. Store 75.35 into num1, –35.56 into num2, and 15.76 into num3.

6. Consider the following program segment:

```
//include statement(s)
//using namespace statement

int main()
{
    //variable declaration

    //executable statements

    //return statement
}
```

a. Write C++ statements that include the header files `iostream` and `string`.

b. Write a C++ statement that allows you to use `cout` and `endl` without the prefix `std::`.

c. Write C++ statements that declare the following variables: `name` of type `string` and `studyHours` of type `double`.

d. Write C++ statements that store the string `"Donald Smith"` into `name` and store `4.5` into `studyHours`.

e. Write a C++ statement that outputs the values of `name` and `studyHours` with the appropriate text. A sample output is the following:

```
Hello, Donald Smith! On Saturday, you need to study
4.5 hours for the exam.
```

f. Compile and run your program.

7. Consider the following program segment:

```
//include statement(s)
//using namespace statement

int main()
{
    //variable declaration

    //executable statements

    //return statement
}
```

a. Write C++ statements that include the header files `iostream` and `string`.

b. Write a C++ statement that allows you to use `cin`, `cout`, and `endl` without the prefix `std::`.

c. Write C++ statements that declare and initialize the following named constants: `SECRET` of the type `int` initialized to `11`, and `RATE` of the type `double` initialized to `12.50`.

d. Write C++ statements that declare the following variables: `num1`, `num2`, and `newNum` of the type `int`; `name` of the type `string`; and `hoursWorked` and `wages` of the type `double`.

e. Write C++ statements that store `15` into `num1` and `28` into `num2`.

f. Write a C++ statement(s) that outputs the following line:

```
The value of num1 = 15 and the value of num2 = 28.
```

g. Write a C++ statement that multiplies that value of `num1` by 2, adds the value of `num2` to it, and then stores the result in `newNum`. Then, write a C++ statement that outputs the value of `newNum`.

h. Write a C++ statement that updates the value of `newNum` by adding the value of the named constant `SECRET`. Then, write a C++ statement that outputs the value of `newNum` with an appropriate message.

i. Write a C++ statement that stores `"Cynthia Jacobson"` into `name`.

j. Write a C++ statement that stores `45.50` into `hoursWorked`.

k. Write a C++ statement that multiplies the value of the named constant `RATE` by the value of `hoursWorked` and stores the result into the variable `wages`.

l. Write C++ statements that produce the following output:

```
Name:            //output the value of the variable name
Pay Rate: $      //output the value of the variable RATE
Hours Worked:    //output the value of the variable hoursWorked
Salary: $        //output the value of the variable wages
```

For the data given in the program, the output is:

```
Name: Cynthia Jacobson
Pay Rate: $12.5
Hours Worked: 45.5
Salary: $568.75
```

INPUT/OUTPUT

IN THIS CHAPTER, YOU WILL:

- Discover how to input data into memory using input statements
- Explore how to read data from the standard input device
- Learn how to debug a program using `cout` statements
- Learn how to debug a program by understanding error messages
- Explore how to use the input stream functions `get`, `ignore`, and `clear`
- Become familiar with input failure
- Learn how to perform input and output operations with the `string` data type
- Learn how to format output using the manipulators `fixed`, `showpoint`, `setprecision`, `setw`, `left`, and `right`
- Become familiar with file input and output

Input (Read) Statement

In the previous chapter, you learned how to put data into variables using the assignment statement. In this section, you learn how to put data into variables from the standard input device using C++'s input (or read) statements.

 NOTE   In most cases, the standard input device is the keyboard.

When the program gets the data from the keyboard, the user is said to be interacting with the program.

Putting data into variables from the standard input device is accomplished through the use of `cin` and the operator `>>`. The syntax of `cin` together with `>>` is:

```
cin >> variable >> variable ...;
```

This is called an **input (read)** statement. In C++, `>>` is called the **stream extraction operator**.

 NOTE   Recall that in a syntax, the shading indicates the part of the definition that is optional.

EXAMPLE 2-1

Suppose that `miles` is a variable of the data type `double`. Further suppose that the input is `73.65`. Consider the following statement:

```
cin >> miles;
```

This statement causes the computer to get the input, which is `73.65`, from the standard input device, and store it in the variable `miles`. That is, after this statement executes, the value of the variable `miles` is `73.65`.

To use `cin` in a program, the program must include the header file `iostream`. Like the identifier `cout`, the identifier `cin` is also declared in the header file `iostream`, but within the namespace `std`. Therefore, after including this header file and the statement, `using namespace std;`, we can refer to `cin` without using the prefix `std::`.

Example 2-2 further explains how to input numeric data into a program.

EXAMPLE 2-2

Suppose we have the following statements:

```
int feet;
int inches;
```

Suppose the input is:

23 7

Next, consider the following statement:

```
cin >> feet >> inches;
```

This statement first stores the number 23 into the variable feet and then the number 7 into the variable inches. Notice that when these numbers are entered via the keyboard, they are separated with a blank. In fact, they can be separated with one or more blanks or lines or even the tab character.

The following C++ program shows the effect of the preceding input statements:

```
//******************************************************
// Author: D.S. Malik
//
// This program illustrates how input statements work.
//******************************************************

#include <iostream>

using namespace std;

int main()
{
    int feet;
    int inches;

    cout << "Enter two integers separated by spaces: ";
    cin >> feet >> inches;
    cout << endl;

    cout << "Feet = " << feet << endl;
    cout << "Inches = " << inches << endl;

    return 0;
}
```

Sample Run: (In this sample run, the user input is shaded.)

Enter two integers separated by spaces: 23 7

Feet = 23
Inches = 7

The C++ program in Example 2-3 illustrates how to read strings and numeric data.

EXAMPLE 2-3

```
//*************************************************************
// Author D.S. Malik
//
// This program illustrates how to read strings and numeric data.
//*************************************************************

#include <iostream>                                          //Line 1
#include <string>                                            //Line 2

using namespace std;                                         //Line 3

int main()                                                   //Line 4
{                                                            //Line 5
    string firstName;                                        //Line 6
    string lastName;                                         //Line 7
    int age;                                                 //Line 8
    double weight;                                           //Line 9

    cout << "Enter first name, last name, age, "
         << "and weight, separated by spaces."
         << endl;                                            //Line 10

    cin >> firstName >> lastName;                            //Line 11
    cin >> age >> weight;                                    //Line 12

    cout << "Name: " << firstName << " " << lastName
         << endl;                                            //Line 13

    cout << "Age: " << age << endl;                          //Line 14
    cout << "Weight: " << weight << endl;                    //Line 15

    return 0;                                                //Line 16
}                                                            //Line 17
```

Sample Run: (In this sample run, the user input is shaded.)

```
Enter first name, last name, age, and weight, separated by spaces.
Sheila Mann 23 120.5
Name: Sheila Mann
Age: 23
Weight: 120.5
```

The preceding program works as follows: The statements in Lines 6 to 9 declare the variables firstName and lastName of type string; age of type int; and weight of type double. The statement in Line 10 is an output statement and tells the user what to do. (Such output statements are called prompt lines.) As shown in the sample run, the input to the program is:

```
Sheila Mann 23 120.5
```

The statement in Line 11 first reads and stores the string `Sheila` into the variable `firstName` and then skips the space after `Sheila` and reads and stores the string `Mann` into the variable `lastName`. Next, the statement in Line 12 first skips the blank after `Mann` and reads and stores `23` into the variable `age` and then skips the blank after `23` and reads and stores `120.5` into the variable `weight`.

The statements in Lines 13, 14, and 15 produce the third, fourth, and fifth lines of the sample run.

2

 NOTE During programming execution, if more than one value is entered in a line, these values must be separated by at least one blank or tab. Alternately, one value per line can be entered.

Variable Initialization

Remember, there are two ways to initialize a variable: by using the assignment statement and by using a read statement. Consider the following declaration:

```
int feet;
```

You can initialize the variable `feet` to a value of `35` either by using the assignment statement

```
feet = 35;
```

or by executing the following statement and entering `35` during program execution:

```
cin >> feet;
```

If you use the assignment statement to initialize `feet`, then you are stuck with the same value each time the program runs unless you edit the source code, change the value, recompile, and run. By using an input statement each time the program runs, you are prompted to enter a value, and the value entered is stored into `feet`. Therefore, a read statement is much more versatile than an assignment statement.

Sometimes it is necessary to initialize a variable by using an assignment statement. This is especially true if the variable is used only for internal calculation and not for reading and storing data.

Recall that C++ does not automatically initialize variables when they are declared. Some variables can be initialized when they are declared, whereas others must be initialized using either an assignment statement or a read statement.

 NOTE When the program is compiled, some of the newer IDEs might give warning messages if the program uses the value of a variable without first properly initializing that variable. In this case, if you ignore the warning and execute the program, the program might terminate abnormally with an error message.

NOTE Suppose you want to store a character into a **char** variable using an input statement. During program execution, when you enter the character, you do not include the single quotation marks. For example, suppose that ch is a **char** variable. Consider the following input statement:

```
cin >> ch;
```

If you want to store K into ch using this statement, during program execution you only enter K. Similarly, if you want to store a string into a variable of type **string** using an input statement, during program execution you enter only the string without the double quotation marks.

EXAMPLE 2-4

This example further illustrates how assignment statements and input statements manipulate variables. Consider the following declarations:

```
int firstNum, secondNum;
double z;
char ch;
string name;
```

Also, suppose that the following statements execute in the order given.

```
 1.   firstNum = 4;
 2.   secondNum = 2 * firstNum + 6;
 3.   z = (firstNum + 1) / 2.0;
 4.   ch = 'A';
 5.   cin >> secondNum;
 6.   cin >> z;
 7.   firstNum = 2 * secondNum + static_cast<int>(z);
 8.   cin >> name;
 9.   secondNum = secondNum + 1;
10.   cin >> ch;
11.   firstNum = firstNum + static_cast<int>(ch);
12.   z = firstNum - z;
```

In addition, suppose the input is

```
8 16.3 Jenny D
```

This line has four values, 8, 16.3, Jenny, and D, and each value is separated from the others by a blank.

Let's now determine the values of the declared variables after the last statement executes. To explicitly show how a particular statement changes the value of a variable, the values of the variables after each statement executes are shown. A question mark (?) in a box indicates that the value in the box is unknown.

Before statement 1 executes, all variables are uninitialized, as shown in Figure 2-1.

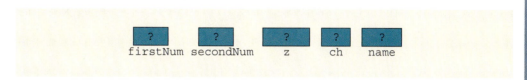

FIGURE 2-1 Variables before statement 1 executes

Next, we show the values of the variables after the execution of each statement.

After St.	Values of the Variables	Explanation
1	firstNum **4**, secondNum ?, z ?, ch ?, name ?	Store 4 into firstNum.
2	firstNum 4, secondNum **14**, z ?, ch ?, name ?	$2 * \text{firstNum} + 6 = 2 * 4 + 6 = 14$. Store 14 into secondNum.
3	firstNum 4, secondNum 14, z **2.5**, ch ?, name ?	$(\text{firstNum} + 1) / 2.0 = (4 + 1) / 2.0 = 5 / 2.0 = 2.5$. Store 2.5 into z.
4	firstNum 4, secondNum 14, z 2.5, ch **A**, name ?	Store 'A' into ch.
5	firstNum 4, secondNum **8**, z 2.5, ch A, name ?	Read a number from the keyboard (which is 8) and store it into secondNum. This statement replaces the old value of secondNum with this new value.
6	firstNum 4, secondNum 8, z **16.3**, ch A, name ?	Read a number from the keyboard (which is 16.3) and store this number into z. This statement replaces the old value of z with this new value.

After St.	Values of the Variables	Explanation
7	firstNum: 32, secondNum: 8, z: 16.3, ch: A, name: ?	$2 *$ secondNum $+$ static_cast<int>(z) $=$ $2 * 8 +$ static_cast<int>(16.3) $= 16 + 16 = 32$. Store 32 into firstNum. This statement replaces the old value of firstNum with this new value.
8	firstNum: 32, secondNum: 8, z: 16.3, ch: A, name: Jenny	Read the next input, Jenny, from the keyboard and store it into name.
9	firstNum: 32, secondNum: 9, z: 16.3, ch: A, name: Jenny	secondNum $+ 1 = 8 + 1 = 9$. Store 9 into secondNum.
10	firstNum: 32, secondNum: 9, z: 16.3, ch: D, name: Jenny	Read the next input from the keyboard (which is D) and store it into ch. This statement replaces the old value of ch with the new value.
11	firstNum: 100, secondNum: 9, z: 16.3, ch: D, name: Jenny	firstNum $+$ static_cast<int>(ch) $= 32 +$ static_cast<int>('D') $= 32 + 68 = 100$. Store 100 into firstNum.
12	firstNum: 100, secondNum: 9, z: 83.7, ch: D, name: Jenny	firstNum $-$ z $= 100 - 16.3 = 100.0 - 16.3 = 83.7$. Store 83.7 into z.

NOTE When something goes wrong in a program and the results it generates are not what you expected, you should do a walk-through of the statements that assign values to your variables. Example 2-4 illustrates how to do a walk-through of your program. This is a very effective debugging technique. The Web site accompanying this book contains a C++ program that shows the effect of the 12 statements listed at the beginning of Example 2-4. The program is named **Example2_4.cpp**.

NOTE If you assign the value of an expression that evaluates to a floating-point value—without using the cast operator—to a variable of type **int**, the fractional part is dropped. In this case, the compiler most likely will issue a warning message about the implicit type conversion.

Creating a C++ Program (Revisited)

In Chapter 1, you learned how to create a C++ program. In this chapter, you have learned how to input data in a program using the standard output device. To input data in a program, you use the identifier cin, which requires you to include the header file iostream. Thus, in skeleton form, a C++ program looks like the following:

```
preprocessor directives to include header files

using statement

declare named constants, if necessary

int main()
{
    variable declaration

    statements

    return 0;
}
```

The C++ program in Example 2-5 shows where include statements, declaration statements, executable statements, and so on typically appear in the program.

EXAMPLE 2-5

```cpp
//*************************************************************
// Author: D.S. Malik
//
// This program shows where the include statements, using
// statement, named constants, variable declarations, assignment
// statements, and input and output statements typically appear.
//*************************************************************

#include <iostream>                                     //Line 1

using namespace std;                                    //Line 2

const int NUMBER = 12;                                  //Line 3

int main()                                              //Line 4
{                                                       //Line 5
    int firstNum;                                       //Line 6
    int secondNum;                                      //Line 7

    firstNum = 18;                                      //Line 8
    cout << "Line 9: firstNum = " << firstNum
        << endl;                                        //Line 9
```

```
    cout << "Line 10: Enter an integer: ";       //Line 10
    cin >> secondNum;                            //Line 11
    cout << endl;                                //Line 12

    cout << "Line 13: secondNum = " << secondNum
         << endl;                                //Line 13

    firstNum = firstNum + NUMBER + 2 * secondNum;  //Line 14

    cout << "Line 15: The new value of "
         << "firstNum = " << firstNum << endl;   //Line 15

    return 0;                                    //Line 16
}                                                //Line 17
```

Sample Run: In this sample run, the user input is shaded.

```
Line 9: firstNum = 18
Line 10: Enter an integer: 15

Line 13: secondNum = 15
Line 15: The new value of firstNum = 60
```

The preceding program works as follows: The statement in Line 1 includes the header file `iostream` so that the program can perform input/output. The statement in Line 2 uses the `using namespace` statement so that identifiers declared in the header file `iostream`, such as `cin`, `cout`, and `endl`, can be used without using the prefix `std::`. The statement in Line 3 declares the named constant `NUMBER` and sets its value to `12`. The statement in Line 4 contains the heading of the function `main`, and the left brace in Line 5 marks the beginning of the function `main`. The statements in Lines 6 and 7 declare the variables `firstNum` and `secondNum`.

The statement in Line 8 sets the value of `firstNum` to `18`, and the statement in Line 9 outputs the value of `firstNum`. Next, the statement in Line 10 prompts the user to enter an integer. The statement in Line 11 reads and stores the integer into the variable `secondNum`, which is `15` in the sample run. The statement in Line 12 positions the cursor on the screen at the beginning of the next line. The statement in Line 13 outputs the value of `secondNum`. The statement in Line 14 evaluates the expression

```
firstNum + NUMBER + 2 * secondNum
```

and assigns the value of this expression to the variable `firstNum`, which is `60` in the sample run. The statement in Line 15 outputs the new value of `firstNum`. The statement in Line 16 contains the `return` statement. The right brace in Line 17 marks the end of the function `main`.

Programming Style and Form (Revisited)

In Chapter 1, you learned about syntax, semantics, errors, and how to format a program properly. In this section, we extend our capabilities to include prompt lines in a program.

Prompt Lines

Part of good documentation is the use of clearly written prompts so that users will know what to do when they interact with a program. It is frustrating for a user to sit in front of a running program and not have the foggiest notion of whether to enter something, and if so, what to enter. **Prompt lines** are executable statements that tell the user what to do to interact with the program. Consider the following C++ statements, in which `num` is an `int` variable:

```
cout << "Please enter a number between 1 and 10 and then "
     << " press Enter." << endl;
cin >> num;
```

When these two statements execute in the order given, first the output statement causes the following line of text to appear on the screen:

```
Please enter a number between 1 and 10 and then press Enter.
```

After seeing this line, an example of a prompt line, users know that they must enter a number and press the `Enter` key. The preceding output statement is an example of a prompt line.

In a program, whenever users must provide input, you should include the necessary prompt lines to assist them. The prompt lines should include sufficient information about what input is acceptable. For example, the preceding prompt line not only tells the user to input a number, but also informs the user that the number should be between `1` and `10` (inclusive), followed by pressing the `Enter` key.

Debugging – Sprinkling with couts

Consider the following program designed to convert Fahrenheit temperatures to Celsius temperatures using the formula:

Celsius temperature = 5 / 9 * (*Fahrenheit temperature* − 32)

```
#include <iostream>                              //Line 1

using namespace std;                             //Line 2

int main(String[] args)                          //Line 3
{                                                //Line 4
    int fahrenheit = 32;                         //Line 5
    int celsius = 5 / 9 * (fahrenheit - 32);     //Line 6
```

```cpp
    cout << fahrenheit << " degrees "
         << "Fahrenheit is " << celsius
         << " degrees " << "Celsius. " << endl;    //Line 7

    fahrenheit = 212;                               //Line 8
    celsius = 5 / 9 * (fahrenheit - 32);            //Line 9

    cout << fahrenheit << " degrees "
         << "Fahrenheit is " << celsius
         << " degrees " << "Celsius.");             //Line 10

    return 0;                                        //Line 11
}                                                    //Line 12
```

Sample Run:

```
32 degrees Fahrenheit is 0 degrees Celsius.
212 degrees Fahrenheit is 0 degrees Celsius.
```

The first calculation looks correct, but the second calculation clearly is not correct, even though the same formula is used. A private walk-through, preparation for a walk-through with another person, and the actual walk-through with another person may fail to reveal the problem. So, to discover the problem, you could insert a temporary cout statement immediately following line 7 to print the value of fahrenheit, and another temporary cout statement immediately following line 10 to print the value of celsius, but the cout statement on line 10 already prints these values. Hence, the problem must be somewhere on the right side of the assignment operator on line 9. The program can be modified temporarily to print the two operands associated with the multiplication operation.

```cpp
#include <iostream>                                 //Line 1

using namespace std;                                //Line 2

int main(String[] args)                             //Line 3
{                                                    //Line 4
    int fahrenheit = 32;                            //Line 5
    int celsius = 5 / 9 * (fahrenheit - 32);        //Line 6

    cout << fahrenheit << " degrees "
         << "Fahrenheit is " << celsius
         << " degrees " << "Celsius. " << endl;    //Line 7

    cout << "5 / 9 is " << 5 / 9
         << " and fahrenheit - 32 is "
         << fahrenheit - 32 << endl;                //Line 7a

    fahrenheit = 212;                               //Line 8
    celsius = 5 / 9 * (fahrenheit - 32);            //Line 9
```

```
    cout << fahrenheit << " degrees "
         << "Fahrenheit is " << celsius
         << " degrees " << "Celsius.");          //Line 10

    cout << "5 / 9 is " << 5 / 9
         << " and fahrenheit - 32 is "
         << fahrenheit - 32 << endl;             //Line 10a

    return 0;                                    //Line 11
}                                                //Line 12
```

Sample Run:

```
32 degrees Fahrenheit is 0 degrees Celsius.
5/9 is 0 and fahrenheit - 32 is 0
212 degrees Fahrenheit is 0 degrees Celsius.
5/9 is 0 and fahrenheit - 32 is 180
```

Now is it easy to see that the problem is the result of integer division. The problem can be corrected by changing the integer 5 to the floating-point value 5.0 or by changing the integer 9 to the floating-point value 9.0, but this will cause the result to be a floating-point value. A better solution is to interchange the operands to the multiplication operation on lines 6 and 9:

```
celsius = (fahrenheit - 32) * 5 / 9;
```

By "sprinkling" part of the code with couts, we were able to find the problem. After correcting the problem, the sprinkled couts are removed.

PROGRAMMING EXAMPLE: Convert Length

Write a program that takes as input given lengths expressed in feet and inches. The program should then convert and output the lengths in centimeters. Assume that the given lengths in feet and inches are integers.

Input   Length in feet and inches

Output   Equivalent length in centimeters

PROBLEM ANALYSIS AND ALGORITHM DESIGN

The lengths are given in feet and inches, and you need to find the equivalent length in centimeters. One inch is equal to 2.54 centimeters. The first thing the program needs to do is convert the length given in feet and inches to all inches. Then you can use the conversion formula, 1 inch = 2.54 centimeters, to find the equivalent length in centimeters. To convert the length from feet and inches to inches, you multiply the number of feet by 12, because 1 foot is equal to 12 inches, and add the given inches.

For example, suppose the input is 5 feet and 7 inches. You then find the total inches as follows:

```
totalInches = (12 * feet) + inches
            = 12 * 5 + 7
            = 67
```

You can then apply the conversion formula, 1 inch = 2.54 centimeters, to find the length in centimeters:

```
centimeters = totalInches * 2.54
            = 67 * 2.54
            = 170.18
```

Based on this analysis of the problem, you can design an algorithm as follows:

1. Get the length in feet and inches.
2. Convert the length into total inches.
3. Convert total inches into centimeters.
4. Output centimeters.

Variables   The input for the program is two numbers: one for feet and one for inches. Thus, you need two variables: one to store feet and the other to store inches. Because the program will first convert the given length into inches, you need another variable to store the total inches. You also need a variable to store the equivalent length in centimeters. In summary, you need the following variables:

```
int feet;              //variable to hold given feet
int inches;            //variable to hold given inches
int totalInches;       //variable to hold total inches
double centimeters;    //variable to hold length in centimeters
```

Named Constant   To calculate the equivalent length in centimeters, you need to multiply the total inches by 2.54. Instead of using the value 2.54 directly in the program, you will declare this value as a named constant. Similarly, to find the total inches, you need to multiply the feet by 12 and add the inches. Instead of using 12 directly in the program, you will also declare this value as a named constant. Using a named constant makes it easier to modify the program later.

```
const double CENTIMETERS_PER_INCH = 2.54;
const int INCHES_PER_FOOT = 12;
```

MAIN ALGORITHM   In the preceding sections, we analyzed the problem and determined the formulas to do the calculations. We also determined the necessary variables and named constants. We can now expand the algorithm given in the section Problem Analysis and Algorithm Design to solve the problem given at the beginning of this programming example.

1. Prompt the user for the input. (Without a prompt line, the user will be staring at a blank screen and will not know what to do.)
2. Get the data.
3. Echo the input—that is, output what the program read as input. (Without this step, after the program has executed, you will not know what the input was.)
4. Find the length in inches.
5. Output the length in inches.
6. Convert the length to centimeters.
7. Output the length in centimeters.

Putting It Together

Now that the problem has been analyzed and the algorithm has been designed, the next step is to translate the algorithm into C++ code. To write the complete program, let's review the necessary steps in sequence.

The program will begin with comments that document its purpose and functionality. As there is both input to this program (the length in feet and inches) and output (the equivalent length in centimeters), the program must include the header file `iostream`. Thus, the first statement of the program, after the comments as described earlier, will be the preprocessor directive to include this header file.

This program requires two types of memory locations for data manipulation: named constants and variables. Depending on the nature of a named constant, it can be placed before the function `main` or within the function `main`. If a named constant is to be used throughout the program, then it is typically placed before the function `main`. We will comment further on where to put named constants within a program in Chapter 5, when we discuss user-defined functions in general. Until then, usually, we will place named constants before the function `main` so that they can be used throughout the program.

This program has only one function, the function `main`, which will contain all of the programming instructions in its body. In addition, the program needs variables to manipulate data, and these variables will be declared in the body of the function `main`. The reasons for declaring variables in the body of the function `main` are explained in Chapter 5. The body of the function `main` will also contain the C++ statements that implement the algorithm. Therefore, the body of the function `main` has the following form:

```
int main()
{
    declare variables

    statements

    return 0;
}
```

To write the complete length conversion program, follow these steps:

1. Begin the program with comments for documentation.
2. Include header files, if any are used in the program.
3. Declare named constants, if any.
4. Write the definition of the function main.

COMPLETE PROGRAM LISTING

```
//**********************************************************
// Author: D.S. Malik
//
// Program Convert Measurements: This program converts
// measurements in feet and inches into centimeters using
// the formula that 1 inch is equal to 2.54 centimeters.
//**********************************************************

    //header file
#include <iostream>

using namespace std;

    //named constants
const double CENTIMETERS_PER_INCH = 2.54;
const int INCHES_PER_FOOT = 12;

int main()
{
        //declare variables
    int feet, inches;
    int totalInches;
    double centimeters;

        //Statements: Step 1 - Step 7
    cout << "Enter two integers, one for feet and "
         << "one for inches: ";                          //Step 1
    cin >> feet >> inches;                               //Step 2
    cout << endl;
```

```
cout << "The numbers you entered are " << feet
     << " for feet and " << inches
     << " for inches. " << endl;                    //Step 3

totalInches = INCHES_PER_FOOT * feet + inches;      //Step 4

cout << "The total number of inches = "
     << totalInches << endl;                        //Step 5

centimeters = CENTIMETERS_PER_INCH * totalInches;   //Step 6

cout << "The number of centimeters = "
     << centimeters << endl;                        //Step 7

    return 0;
}
```

Sample Run: In this sample run, the user input is shaded:

```
Enter two integers, one for feet, one for inches: 15 7

The numbers you entered are 15 for feet and 7 for inches.
The total number of inches = 187
The number of centimeters = 474.98
```

Debugging – Understanding Error Messages

The C++ compiler will find syntactic errors in your program and will provide messages describing the errors. These messages do not always describe the problem exactly, nor do they always describe all the syntactic problems in your program at once, but they provide a good indication of where to look for the problem(s). Look carefully in the immediate vicinity of the reported error for anything that might be causing the problem. Often, correcting a single syntactic error will result in the reporting of multiple new syntactic errors, but there is no need for concern. Finding and reporting errors is like peeling away layers of an onion. By finding and correcting the sources of errors as they are reported, ultimately you will be able to find and correct all the syntactic errors in your program.

More on Input

Suppose that the input is 2. How does the extraction operator >> distinguish between the character 2 and the number 2? The right-side operand of the extraction operator >> makes this distinction. If the right-side operand is a variable of the data type **char**, the input 2 is treated as the character 2, and, in this case, the ASCII value of 2 is stored. If the right-side operand is a variable of the data type `int` or `double`, the input 2 is treated as the number 2.

Next, consider the input 25 and the statement:

```
cin >> var;
```

where `var` is a variable of some simple data type. If `var` is of the data type `char`, only the single character 2 is stored in `var`. If `var` is of the data type `int`, 25 is stored in `var`. If `var` is of the data type `double`, the input 25 is converted to the decimal number `25.0`. Table 2-1 summarizes this discussion by showing the valid input for a variable of the simple data type.

TABLE 2-1   Valid Input for a Variable of the Simple Data Type

Data Type of `var`	Valid Input for `var`
`char`	One printable character except the blank.
`int`	An integer, possibly preceded by a + or − sign.
`double`	A decimal number, possibly preceded by a + or − sign. If the actual data input is an integer, the input is converted to a decimal number with the zero decimal part.

When reading data into a `char` variable, after skipping any leading whitespace characters, the extraction operator >> finds and stores only the next character; reading stops after a single character. To read data into an `int` or `double` variable, after skipping all leading whitespace characters and reading the plus or minus sign (if any), the extraction operator >> reads the digits of the number, including the decimal point for floating-point variables, and stops when it finds a whitespace character or a character other than a digit.

EXAMPLE 2-6

Suppose you have the following variable declarations:

```
int a, b;
double z;
char ch, ch1, ch2;
```

The following statements show how the extraction operator >> works.

	Statement	Input	Value Stored in Memory
1	cin >> ch;	A	ch = 'A'
2	cin >> ch;	AB	ch = 'A', 'B' is held for later input
3	cin >> a;	48	a = 48
4	cin >> a;	46.35	a = 46, .35 is held for later input
5	cin >> z;	74.35	z = 74.35
6	cin >> z;	39	z = 39.0
7	cin >> z >> a;	65.78 38	z = 65.78, a = 38
8	cin >> a >> b;	4 60	a = 4, b = 60
9	cin >> a >> ch >> z;	57 A 26.9	a = 57, ch = 'A', z = 26.9
10	cin >> a >> ch >> z;	57 A 26.9	a = 57, ch = 'A', z = 26.9
11	cin >> a >> ch >> z;	57 A 26.9	a = 57, ch = 'A', z = 26.9
12	cin >> a >> ch >> z;	57A26.9	a = 57, ch = 'A', z = 26.9
13	cin >> z >> ch >> a;	36.78B34	z = 36.78, ch = 'B', a = 34
14	cin >> z >> ch >> a;	36.78 B34	z = 36.78, ch = 'B', a = 34
15	cin >> a >> b >> z;	11 34	a = 11, b = 34, computer waits for the next number
16	cin >> a >> z;	46 32.4 68	a = 46, z = 32.4, 68 is held for later input
17	cin >> a >> z;	78.49	a = 78, z = 0.49
18	cin >> ch >> a;	256	ch = '2', a = 56
19	cin >> a >> ch;	256	a = 256, computer waits for the input value for ch
20	cin >> ch1 >> ch2;	A B	ch1 = 'A', ch2 = 'B'

 NOTE Recall that, during program execution, when entering character data such as letters, you do not enter the single quotation marks around the character.

What happens if the input stream has more data items than required by the program? After the program terminates, any values left in the input stream are discarded. When you enter data for processing, the data values should correspond to the data types of the variables in the input statement. Recall that when entering a number for a `double` variable, it is not necessary for the input number to have a decimal part. If the input number is an integer and has no decimal part, it is converted to a decimal value. The computer, however, does not tolerate any other kind of mismatch. For example, entering a `char` value into an `int` or `double` variable causes serious errors, called **input failure**. Input failure is discussed later in this chapter.

What happens when you try to read a non-numeric character into an `int` variable? Example 2-10 (given later in this chapter) illustrates this situation.

The extraction operator, when scanning for the next input in the input stream, skips whitespace such as blanks and the newline character. However, there are situations when these characters must also be stored and processed. For example, if you are processing text in a line-by-line fashion, you must know where in the input stream the newline character is located. Without identifying the position of the newline character, the program would not know where one line ends and another begins. The next section teaches you how to input data into a program using the input functions `get` and `ignore`. These functions are associated with the data type `istream` and are called **istream functions**. I/O functions such as `get` are typically called **stream member functions** or **stream functions**.

cin and the get Function

As you have seen, the extraction operator skips all leading whitespace characters when scanning for the next input value. Consider the variable declarations

```
char ch1, ch2;
int num;
```

and the input

```
A 25
```

Now consider the following statement:

```
cin >> ch1 >> ch2 >> num;
```

When the computer executes this statement, `'A'` is stored in `ch1`, the blank is skipped by the extraction operator `>>`, the character `'2'` is stored in `ch2`, and 5 is stored in `num`. However, what if you intended to store `'A'` in `ch1`, the blank in `ch2`, and 25 in `num`? It is clear that you cannot use the extraction operator `>>` to input this data.

As stated earlier, sometimes you need to process the entire input, including whitespace characters, such as blanks and the newline character. For example, suppose you want to process the entered data on a line-by-line basis. Because the extraction operator `>>` skips the newline character and unless the program captures the newline character, the computer does not know where one line ends and the next begins.

The variable `cin` can access the stream function `get`, which is used to read character data. The `get` function inputs the very next character, including whitespace characters, from the input stream and stores it in the memory location indicated by its argument. The function `get` comes in many forms. Next, we discuss the one that is used to read a character.

The syntax of `cin`, together with the `get` function to read a character, follows:

```
cin.get(varChar);
```

2

In the `cin.get` statement, `varChar` is a `char` variable. `varChar`, which appears in parentheses following the function name, is called the **argument** or **parameter** of the function. The effect of the preceding statement would be to store the next input character in the variable `varChar`.

Now consider the following input again:

```
A 25
```

To store `'A'` in `ch1`, the blank in `ch2`, and `25` in `num`, you can effectively use the `get` function as follows:

```
cin.get(ch1);
cin.get(ch2);
cin >> num;
```

Because this form of the `get` function has only one argument and reads only one character, and you need to read two characters from the input stream, you need to call this function twice. Notice that you cannot use the `get` function to read data into the variable `num`, because `num` is an `int` variable. The preceding form of the `get` function reads values of only the `char` data type.

The preceding set of `cin.get` statements is equivalent to the following statements:

```
cin >> ch1;
cin.get(ch2);
cin >> num;
```

 NOTE   The function `get` has other forms, one of which you will study in Chapter 6. For the next few chapters, you need only the form of the function `get` introduced here.

`cin` and the `ignore` Function

When you want to process only partial data (say, within a line), you can use the stream function `ignore` to discard a portion of the input. The syntax to use the function `ignore` is:

```
cin.ignore(intExp, chExp);
```

Here `intExp` is an integer expression yielding an integer value, and `chExp` is a `char` expression yielding a `char` value. In fact, the value of the expression `intExp` specifies the maximum number of characters to be ignored in a line.

Suppose `intExp` yields a value, say `100`. This statement says to ignore the next `100` characters or ignore the input until `cin` encounters the character specified by `chExp`, whichever comes first. To be specific, consider the following statement:

```
cin.ignore(100, '\n');
```

When this statement executes, it ignores either the next 100 characters or all characters until the newline character is found, whichever comes first. For example, if the next 120 characters do not contain the newline character, then only the first 100 characters are discarded, and the next input data is the character 101. However, if the seventy-fifth character is the newline character, then the first 75 characters are discarded, and the next input data is the 76th character. Similarly, the execution of the statement

```
cin.ignore(100, 'A');
```

results in ignoring the first 100 characters or all characters until the character 'A' is found, whichever comes first.

EXAMPLE 2-7

Consider the declaration

```
int a, b;
```

and the input

```
25 67 89 43 72
12 78 34
```

Now consider the following statements:

```
cin >> a;
cin.ignore(100, '\n');
cin >> b;
```

The first statement, cin >> a;, stores 25 in a. The second statement, cin.ignore(100, '\n');, discards all of the remaining numbers in the first line. The third statement, cin >> b;, stores 12 (from the next line) in b.

EXAMPLE 2-8

Consider the declaration

```
char ch1, ch2;
```

and the input

```
Hello there. My name is Mickey.
```

Now consider the following statements:

```
cin >> ch1;
cin.ignore(100, '.');
cin >> ch2;
```

2

The first statement, `cin >> ch1;`, stores `'H'` in ch1. The second statement, `cin.ignore(100, '.' );`, results in discarding all characters until the . (period). The third statement, `cin >> ch2;`, stores the character `'M'` (from the same line) in ch2. (Remember that the extraction operator `>>` skips all leading whitespace characters. Thus, the extraction operator skips the space after the . (period) and stores `'M'` in ch2.)

Input Failure

Many things can go wrong during program execution. A program that is syntactically correct might produce incorrect results. For example, suppose that a part-time employee's paycheck is calculated by using the following formula:

```
wages = payRate * hoursWorked;
```

If you accidentally type + in place of *, the calculated wages would be incorrect, even though the statement containing the + is syntactically correct.

What about an attempt to read invalid data? For example, what would happen if you tried to input a letter into an `int` variable? If the input data did not match the corresponding variables, the program would run into problems. For example, trying to read a letter into an `int` or `double` variable would result in an **input failure**. Consider the following statements:

```
int a, b, c;
double x;
```

If the input is

```
W 54
```

then the statement

```
cin >> a >> b;
```

would result in an input failure, because you are trying to input the character `'W'` into the `int` variable a. If the input were

```
35 67.93 48 78
```

then the input statement

```
cin >> a >> x >> b;
```

would result in storing 35 in a, 67.93 in x, and 48 in b.

Now consider the following read statement with the previous input (the input with three values):

```
cin >> a >> b >> c;
```

This statement stores 35 in a and 67 in b. The reading stops at the **.** (the decimal point). Because the next variable c is of type **int,** the computer tries to read **.** into c, which is an error. The input stream then enters a state called the **fail state**.

What actually happens when the input stream enters the fail state? Once an input stream enters a fail state, all further I/O statements using that stream are ignored. Unfortunately, the program quietly continues to execute with whatever values are stored in variables, and produces incorrect results. The program in Example 2-9 illustrates an input failure. This program on your system may produce different results.

EXAMPLE 2-9

```cpp
//************************************************************
// Author: D.S. Malik
//
// Input Failure program
// This program illustrates input failure.
//************************************************************

#include <iostream>                                    //Line 1

using namespace std;                                   //Line 2

int main()                                             //Line 3
{                                                      //Line 4
    int a = 10;                                        //Line 5
    int b = 20;                                        //Line 6
    int c = 30;                                        //Line 7
    int d = 40;                                        //Line 8

    cout << "Line 9: Enter four integers: ";           //Line 9
    cin >> a >> b >> c >> d;                            //Line 10
    cout << endl;                                      //Line 11

    cout << "Line 12: The numbers you entered are:"
         << endl;                                      //Line 12
    cout << "Line 13: a = " << a << ", b = " << b
         << ", c = " << c << ", d = " << d << endl;    //Line 13

    return 0;                                          //Line 14
}                                                      //Line 15
```

Sample Runs: In these sample runs, the user input is shaded.

Sample Run 1

Line 9: Enter four integers: 34 K 67 28

Line 12: The numbers you entered are:
Line 13: a = 34, b = 20, c = 30, d = 40

The statements in Lines 5, 6, 7, and 8 declare and initialize the variables a, b, c, and d to 10, 20, 30, and 40, respectively. The statement in Line 9 prompts the user to enter four integers; the statement in Line 10 inputs these four integers into variables a, b, c, and d.

In this sample run, the second input value is the character 'K'. The cin statement tries to input this character into the variable b. However, because b is an int variable, the input stream enters the fail state. Note that the values of b, c, and d are unchanged, as shown by the output of the statement in Line 13.

Sample Run 2

```
Line 9: Enter four integers: 37 653.89 23 76

Line 12: The numbers you entered are:
Line 13: a = 37, b = 653, c = 30, d = 40
```

In this **sample** run, the cin statement in Line 10 inputs 37 into a, and 653 into b, and then tries to input the decimal point into c. Because c is an int variable, the decimal point is regarded as a character, so the input stream enters the fail state. In this sample run, the values of c and d are unchanged, as shown by the output of the statement in Line 13.

The clear Function

When an input stream enters the fail state, the system ignores all further I/O using that stream. You can use the stream function clear to restore the input stream to a working state.

The syntax to use the function clear is:

```
istreamVar.clear();
```

Here istreamVar is an input stream variable, such as cin.

After using the function clear to return the input stream to a working state, you still need to clear the rest of the garbage from the input stream. This can be accomplished by using the function ignore. Example 2-10 illustrates this situation.

EXAMPLE 2-10

```
//*************************************************************
// Author: D.S. Malik
//
// Input failure and the function clear
// This program illustrates how to use the function clear.
//*************************************************************
```

```cpp
#include <iostream>                                      //Line 1

using namespace std;                                     //Line 2

int main()                                               //Line 3
{                                                        //Line 4
    int a = 23;                                          //Line 5
    int b = 34;                                          //Line 6

    cout << "Line 7: Enter a number followed"
         << " by a character: ";                         //Line 7
    cin >> a >> b;                                       //Line 8
    cout << endl << "Line 9: a = " << a
         << ", b = " << b << endl;                       //Line 9

    cin.clear();                //Restore input stream; Line 10

    cin.ignore(200,'\n');          //Clear the buffer; Line 11

    cout << "Line 12: Enter two numbers: ";              //Line 12
    cin >> a >> b;                                       //Line 13
    cout << endl << "Line 14: a = " << a
         << ", b = " << b << endl;                       //Line 14

    return 0;                                            //Line 15
}                                                        //Line 16
```

Sample Run: In this sample run, the user input is shaded.

```
Line 7: Enter a number followed by a character: 78 d

Line 9: a = 78, b = 34
Line 12: Enter two numbers: 65 88

Line 14: a = 65, b = 88
```

The statements in Lines 5 and 6 declare and initialize the variables a and b to 23 and 34, respectively. The statement in Line 7 prompts the user to enter a number followed by a character; the statement in Line 8 inputs this number into the variable a and then tries to input the character into the variable b. Because b is an int variable, an attempt to input a character into b causes the input stream to enter the fail state. The value of b is unchanged, as shown by the output of the statement in Line 9.

The statement in Line 10 restores the input stream by using the function clear, and the statement in Line 11 ignores the rest of the input. The statement in Line 12 prompts the user to input two numbers; the statement in Line 13 stores these two numbers into a and b. Next, the statement in Line 14 outputs the values of a and b.

Input/Output and the **string** Type

You can use an input stream variable, such as `cin`, and the extraction operator `>>` to read a string into a variable of the data type `string`. For example, if the input is the string `"Shelly"`, the following code stores this input into the `string` variable `name`:

```
string name;    //variable declaration
cin >> name;    //input statement
```

2

Recall that the extraction operator skips any leading whitespace characters and that reading stops at a whitespace character. As a consequence, you cannot use the extraction operator to read strings that contain blanks. For example, suppose that `name` is the `string` variable as defined earlier. If the input is

```
Alice Wonderland
```

then after the statement

```
cin >> name;
```

executes, the value of the variable `name` is `"Alice"`.

To read a string containing blanks, you can use the function `getline`. The syntax to use the function `getline` is

```
getline(istreamVar, strVar);
```

where `istreamVar` is an input stream variable, and `strVar` is a variable of type `string`. The reading is delimited by the newline character, `'\n'`.

The function `getline` reads until it reaches the end of the current line. The newline character is also read but not stored in the `string` variable.

Consider the following statement:

```
string myString;
```

If the input is 29 characters,

```
bbbbHello there. How are you?
```

where b represents a blank, after executing the statement

```
getline(cin, myString);
```

the value of `myString` is

```
myString =  "    Hello there. How are you? "
```

All 29 characters, including the first four blanks, are stored into `myString`.

Similarly, you can use an output stream variable, such as `cout`, and the insertion operator `<<` to output the contents of a variable of the data type `string`.

Formatting Output

Other than writing efficient programs, generating the desired output is one of a programmer's highest priorities. In the previous sections, you learned how to use the insertion operator << and the manipulator endl to display results on the standard output device. However, there is a lot more to output than just displaying results. Sometimes floating-point numbers must be output in a specific way. For example, a paycheck must be printed to two decimal places, whereas the results of a scientific experiment might require the output of floating-point numbers to six, seven, or perhaps even ten decimal places. Also, you might like to align the numbers in specific columns. In this section, you will learn about various output functions and manipulators that allow you to format your output in a desired way.

setprecision Manipulator

You use the manipulator setprecision to control the output of floating-point numbers. The default output of floating-point numbers is scientific notation. Some IDEs might use a maximum of six decimal places for the default output of floating-point numbers. However, when an employee's paycheck is printed, the desired output is a maximum of two decimal places. To print floating-point output to two decimal places, you use the setprecision manipulator to set the precision to 2.

The general syntax of the setprecision manipulator is

```
setprecision(n)
```

where n is the number of decimal places.

You use the setprecision manipulator with cout and the extraction operator. For example, the statement

```
cout << setprecision(2);
```

formats the output of decimal numbers to two decimal places, until a similar subsequent statement changes the precision. Notice that the number of decimal places, or the precision value, is passed as an argument to setprecision.

To use the manipulator setprecision, the program must include the header file iomanip. Thus, the following include statement is required:

```
#include <iomanip>
```

fixed Manipulator

To further control the output of floating-point numbers, you can use other manipulators. To output floating-point numbers in a fixed decimal format, you use the manipulator fixed. The following statement sets the output of floating-point numbers in a fixed decimal format on the standard output device:

```
cout << fixed;
```

After the preceding statement executes, all floating-point numbers are displayed in the fixed decimal format until the manipulator `fixed` is disabled. You can disable the manipulator `fixed` by using the stream member function `unsetf`. For example, to disable the manipulator `fixed` on the standard output device, you use the following statement:

```
cout.unsetf(ios::fixed);
```

After the manipulator `fixed` is disabled, the output of the floating-point numbers returns to their default settings. The manipulator `scientific` is used to output floating-point numbers in scientific format.

showpoint Manipulator

Suppose that the decimal part of a decimal number is zero. In this case, when you instruct the computer to output the decimal number in a fixed decimal format, the output may not show the decimal point and the decimal part. To force the output to show the decimal point and trailing zeros, you use the manipulator `showpoint`. The following statement sets the output of decimal numbers with a decimal point and trailing zeros on the standard input device:

```
cout << showpoint;
```

Of course, the following statement sets the output of a floating-point number in a fixed decimal format with the decimal point and trailing zeros on the standard output device:

```
cout << fixed << showpoint;
```

The program in Example 2-11 illustrates how to use the manipulators `setprecision`, `fixed`, and `showpoint`.

EXAMPLE 2-11

```
//***********************************************************
// Author: D.S. Malik
//
// This program illustrates how to use the manipulators
// setprecision, fixed, and showpoint.
//***********************************************************

#include <iostream>                          //Line 1
#include <iomanip>                           //Line 2

using namespace std;                         //Line 3

int main()                                   //Line 4
{                                            //Line 5
    double x = 15.674;                       //Line 6
    double y = 235.73;                       //Line 7
    double z = 9525.9864;                    //Line 8
```

```cpp
cout << fixed << showpoint;                           //Line 9

cout << setprecision(2)
     << "Line 10: setprecision(2)" << endl;           //Line 10
cout << "Line 11: x = " << x << endl;                 //Line 11
cout << "Line 12: y = " << y << endl;                 //Line 12
cout << "Line 13: z = " << z << endl;                 //Line 13

cout << setprecision(3)
     << "Line 14: setprecision(3)" << endl;           //Line 14
cout << "Line 15: x = " << x << endl;                 //Line 15
cout << "Line 16: y = " << y << endl;                 //Line 16
cout << "Line 17: z = " << z << endl;                 //Line 17

cout << setprecision(4)
     << "Line 18: setprecision(4)" << endl;           //Line 18
cout << "Line 19: x = " << x << endl;                 //Line 19
cout << "Line 20: y = " << y << endl;                 //Line 20
cout << "Line 21: z = " << z << endl;                 //Line 21

return 0;                                             //Line 22
}                                                     //Line 23
```

Sample Run:

```
Line 10: setprecision(2)
Line 11: x = 15.67
Line 12: y = 235.73
Line 13: z = 9525.99
Line 14: setprecision(3)
Line 15: x = 15.674
Line 16: y = 235.730
Line 17: z = 9525.986
Line 18: setprecision(4)
Line 19: x = 15.6740
Line 20: y = 235.7300
Line 21: z = 9525.9864
```

The statements in Lines 6, 7, and 8 declare and initialize x, y, and z to 15.674, 235.73, and 9525.9864, respectively. The statement in Line 9 sets the output of floating-point numbers in a fixed decimal format with a decimal point and trailing zeros. The statement in Line 10 sets the output of floating-point numbers to two decimal places.

The statements in Lines 11, 12, and 13 output the values of x, y, and z to two decimal places. Note that the printed value of z in Line 13 is rounded. The statement in Line 14 sets the output of floating-point numbers to three decimal places; the statements in Lines 15, 16, and 17 output the values of x, y, and z to three decimal places. Note that the value of y, in Line 16, is output to three decimal places. Because the number stored in y has only two decimal places, a 0 is printed as the third decimal place.

The statement in Line 18 sets the output of floating-point numbers to four decimal places; the statements in Lines 19, 20, and 21 output the values of x, y, and z to four decimal places. Note that in Line 19, the printed value of **x** contains a 0 in the fourth decimal place. The printed value of **y**, in Line 20, contains a 0s in the third and fourth decimal places.

setw

The manipulator **setw** is used to output the value of an expression in a specific number of columns. The value of the expression can be either a string or a number. The expression **setw(n)** outputs the value of the next expression in n columns. The output is right-justified. Thus, if you specify the number of columns to be 8, for example, and the output requires only 4 columns, the first four columns are left blank. Furthermore, if the number of columns specified is less than the number of columns required by the output, the output automatically expands to the required number of columns; the output is not truncated. For example, if **x** is an **int** variable, the following statement outputs the value of **x** in five columns on the standard output device:

```
cout << setw(5) << x << endl;
```

To use the manipulator **setw**, the program must include the header file **iomanip**. Thus, the following include statement is required:

```
#include <iomanip>
```

Unlike **setprecision**, which controls the output of all floating-point numbers until it is reset, **setw** controls the output of only the next expression.

EXAMPLE 2-12

```
//***********************************************************
// Author: D.S. Malik
//
// This program illustrates how to use the manipulator setw.
//***********************************************************

#include <iostream>                                    //Line 1
#include <iomanip>                                     //Line 2

using namespace std;                                   //Line 3

int main()                                             //Line 4
{                                                      //Line 5
    int x = 19;                                        //Line 6
    int a = 345;                                       //Line 7
    double y = 76.384;                                 //Line 8

    cout << fixed << showpoint;                        //Line 9

    cout << "12345678901234567890" << endl;            //Line 10
```

```
cout << setw(5) << x << endl;                          //Line 11
cout << setw(5) << a << setw(5) << "Hi"
     << setw(5) << x << endl << endl;                  //Line 12

cout << setprecision(2);                               //Line 13
cout << setw(6) << a << setw(6) << y
     << setw(6) << x << endl;                          //Line 14
cout << setw(6) << x << setw(6) << a
     << setw(6) << y << endl << endl;                  //Line 15

cout << setw(5) << a << x << endl;                     //Line 16
cout << setw(2) << a << setw(4) << x << endl;          //Line 17

return 0;                                              //Line 18
}                                                      //Line 19
```

Sample Run:

```
12345678901234567890
   19
  345    Hi     19


  345 76.38      19
   19    345 76.38


  34519
345   19
```

The statements in Lines 6, 7, and 8 declare the variables x, a, and y and initialize these variables to 19, 345, and 76.384, respectively. The statement in Line 9 sets the output of floating-point numbers in a fixed decimal format with a decimal point and trailing zeros. The output of the statement in Line 10 shows the column positions when the specific values are printed; it is the first line of output.

The statement in Line 11 outputs the value of x in five columns. Because x has only two digits, only two columns are needed to output its value. Therefore, the first three columns are left blank in the second line of output. The statement in Line 12 outputs the value of a in the first five columns, the string "Hi" in the next five columns, and then the value of x in the following five columns. Because the string "Hi" contains only two characters, and five columns are set to output these two characters, the first three columns are left blank. See the third line of output. The fourth line of output is blank because the manipulator endl appears twice in the statement in Line 12.

The statement in Line 13 sets the output of floating-point numbers to two decimal places. The statement in Line 14 outputs the values of a in the first six columns, y in the next six columns, and x in the following six columns, creating the fifth line of output. The output of the statement in Line 15 (which is the sixth line of output) is similar to the output of the statement in Line 14. Notice how the numbers are nicely aligned in the outputs of the statements in Lines 14 and 15. The seventh line of output is blank because the manipulator endl appears twice in the statement in Line 15.

The statement in Line 16 first outputs the value of **a** in five columns and then outputs the value of **x**. Note that the manipulator `setw` in the statement in Line 16 controls only the output of **a**. Thus, after the value of **a** is printed, the value of **x** is printed at the current cursor position (see the eighth line of output).

In the `cout` statement in Line 17, only two columns are assigned to output the value of **a**. However, the value of **a** has three digits, so the output is expanded to three columns. The value of **x** is then printed in four columns. Because the value of **x** contains only two digits, only two columns are required to output the value of **x**. Therefore, because four columns are allocated to output the value of **x**, the first two columns are left blank (see the ninth line of output).

2

`left` and `right` Manipulators

Recall that if the number of columns specified in the `setw` manipulator exceeds the number of columns required by the next expression, the default output is right-justified. Sometimes you might want the output to be left-justified. To left-justify the output, you use the manipulator `left`. The syntax to set the manipulator `left` is

```
ostreamVar << left;
```

where `ostreamVar` is an output stream variable. For example, the following statement sets the output to be left-justified on the standard output device:

```
cout << left;
```

The syntax to set the manipulator `right` is

```
ostreamVar << right;
```

where `ostreamVar` is an output stream variable. For example, the following statement sets the output to be right-justified on the standard output device:

```
cout << right;
```

The program in Example 2-13 illustrates the effect of the manipulators `left` and `right`.

EXAMPLE 2-13

```cpp
//*************************************************************
// Author: D.S. Malik
//
// Left justification
// This program illustrates how to left-align the output.
//*************************************************************
```

```
#include <iostream>                                    //Line 1
#include <iomanip>                                     //Line 2

using namespace std;                                   //Line 3

int main()                                             //Line 4
{                                                      //Line 5
    int x = 15;                                        //Line 6
    int y = 7634;                                      //Line 7

    cout << left;                                      //Line 8

    cout << "12345678901234567890" << endl;            //Line 9
    cout << setw(5) << x << setw(7) << y
         << setw(8) << "Warm" << endl;                 //Line 10

    cout << right;                                     //Line 11

    cout << setw(5) << x << setw(7) << y
         << setw(8) << "Warm" << endl;                 //Line 12

    return 0;                                          //Line 13
}                                                      //Line 14
```

Sample Run:

```
12345678901234567890
15    7634    Warm
   15    7634      Warm
```

The statement in Line 8 sets the output to be left-justified. The statement in Line 10 outputs the values of x, y, and the string **"Warm"** left-justified; see the second line of output. The statement in Line 11 sets the output to be right-justified. The statement in Line 12 outputs the values of x, y, and the string **"Warm"** right-justified; see the third line of output.

 NOTE This chapter discusses several stream functions and stream manipulators. To use stream functions such as get, ignore, and clear in a program, the program must include the header file iostream. There are two types of manipulators: those with parameters and those without parameters. Manipulators with parameters are called **parameterized stream manipulators**. For example, manipulators such as setprecision and setw are parameterized. On the other hand, manipulators such as endl, fixed, scientific, showpoint, and left do not have parameters. To use a parameterized stream manipulator in a program, you must include the header file iomanip. Manipulators without parameters are part of the iostream header file and, therefore, do not require inclusion of the header file iomanip.

File Input/Output

The previous sections discussed in some detail how to get input from the keyboard (standard input device) and send output to the screen (standard output device). However, getting input from the keyboard and sending output to the screen have several limitations. Inputting data in a program from the keyboard is comfortable as long as the amount of input is very small. Sending output to the screen works well if the amount of data is small (no larger than the size of the screen), and you do not want to distribute the output in a printed format to others.

If the amount of input data is large, however, it is inefficient to type it at the keyboard each time you run a program. In addition to the inconvenience of typing large amounts of data, typing can generate errors, and typos cause erroneous results. You must have some way to get data into the program from other sources. By using alternative sources of data, you can prepare the data before running a program, and the program can access the data each time it runs.

Suppose you want to present the output of a program in a meeting. Distributing printed copies of the program output is a better approach than showing the output on a screen. For example, you might give a printed report to each member of a committee before an important meeting. Furthermore, output must sometimes be saved so that the output produced by one program can be used as an input to other programs.

This section discusses how to obtain data from other input devices, such as a disk (that is, secondary storage), and how to save the output to a disk. C++ allows a program to get data directly from, and save output directly to, secondary storage. A program can use the file I/O and read data from or write data to a file. Formally, a file is defined as follows:

File: An area in secondary storage used to hold information.

The standard I/O header file, `iostream`, contains data types and variables that are used only for input from the standard input device and output to the standard output device. In addition, C++ provides a header file called `fstream`, which is used for file I/O. Among other things, the `fstream` header file contains the definitions of two data types: `ifstream`, which means input file stream and is similar to `istream`, and `ofstream`, which means output file stream and is similar to `ostream`.

The variables `cin` and `cout` are already defined and associated with the standard input/output devices. In addition, `>>`, `get`, and `ignore` can be used with `cin`, while `<<`, `setprecision`, `fixed`, `showpoint`, and `setw` can be used with `cout`. These same operators and functions are also available for file I/O, but the header file `fstream` does not declare variables to use them. You must declare variables called **file stream variables**, which include `ifstream` variables for input and `ofstream` variables for output. You then use these variables together with `>>`, `<<`, or other functions for I/O. Remember that C++ does not automatically initialize user-defined variables. Once you declare the `fstream` variables, you must associate these file variables with the input/output sources.

File I/O is a five-step process:

1. Include the header file `fstream` in the program.
2. Declare file stream variables.
3. Associate the file stream variables with the input/output sources.
4. Use the file stream variables with >>, <<, or other input/output functions.
5. Close the files.

We will now describe these five steps in detail. A skeleton program then shows how the steps might appear in a program.

Step 1 requires that the header file `fstream` be included in the program. The following statement accomplishes this task:

```
#include <fstream>
```

Step 2 requires you to declare file stream variables. Consider the following statements:

```
ifstream inData;
ofstream outData;
```

The first statement declares `inData` to be an input file stream variable. The second statement declares `outData` to be an output file stream variable.

Step 3 requires you to associate file stream variables with the input/output sources. This step is called **opening the files**. The stream member function `open` is used to open files. The syntax for opening a file is:

```
fileStreamVariable.open(sourceName);
```

Here `fileStreamVariable` is a file stream variable, and `sourceName` is the name of the input/output file.

Suppose you include the declaration from Step 2 in a program. Further suppose that the input data is stored in a file called `prog.dat`. The following statements associate `inData` with `prog.dat` and `outData` with `prog.out`. That is, the file `prog.dat` is opened for inputting data, and the file `prog.out` is opened for outputting data.

```
inData.open("prog.dat");   //open the input file;  Line 1
outData.open("prog.out"); //open the output file; Line 2
```

2

 NOTE IDEs such as Visual Studio .Net manage programs in the form of projects. That is, first you create a project and then add source files to the project. The statement in Line 1 assumes that the file `prog.dat` is in the same directory (subdirectory) as your project. However, if this is in a different directory (subdirectory), then you must specify the path where the file is located, along with the name of the file. For example, suppose that the file `prog.dat` is on a storage device in drive A. Then the statement in Line 1 should be modified as follows:

`inData.open("a:\\prog.dat");`

Note that there are two slashes (`\\`) after `a:`. Recall from Chapter 1 that in C++, the `\` is the escape character. Therefore, to produce a `\` within a string, you need `\\`. (To be absolutely sure about specifying the source where the input file is stored, such as the drive `a:\\`, check your system's documentation.)

Similar conventions apply for the statement in Line 2.

 NOTE Suppose that a program reads data from a file. Because different computers label drives differently, for simplicity, throughout the book we assume that the file containing the data and the program reading data from the file are in the same directory (subdirectory).

Step 4 typically works as follows. You use the file stream variables with >>, <<, or other input/output functions. The syntax for using >> or << with file stream variables is exactly the same as the syntax for using `cin` and `cout`. Instead of using `cin` and `cout`, however, you use the file stream variable names that were declared. For example, the statement

`inData >> payRate;`

reads the data from the file `prog.dat` and stores it in the variable `payRate`. The statement

`outData << "The paycheck is: $" << pay << endl;`

stores the output—`The paycheck is: $565.78`—in the file `prog.out`. This statement assumes that the `pay` was calculated as `565.78`.

Once the I/O is completed, Step 5 requires closing the files. Closing a file means that the file stream variables are disassociated from the storage area and are freed. Once these variables are freed, they can be reused for other file I/O. Moreover, closing an output file ensures that the entire output is sent to the file, that is, the buffer is emptied. You close files by using the stream function `close`. For example, assuming the program includes the declarations listed in Steps 2 and 3, the statements for closing the files are

`inData.close();`
`outData.close();`

NOTE On some systems, it is not necessary to close the files. When the program terminates, the files are closed automatically. Nevertheless, it is a good practice to close the files yourself. Also, if you want to use the same file stream variable to open another file, you must close the first file opened with that file stream variable.

In skeleton form, a program that uses file I/O usually takes the following form:

```
#include <fstream>

//Add additional header files you use

using namespace std;

int main()
{
        //Declare file stream variables such as the following
    ifstream inData;
    ofstream outData;
    .
    .
    .

        //Open the files
    inData.open("prog.dat");   //open the input file
    outData.open("prog.out"); //open the output file

        //Code for data manipulation

        //Close files
    inData.close();
    outData.close();

    return 0;
}
```

Recall that Step 3 requires the file to be opened for file I/O. Opening a file associates a file stream variable declared in the program with a physical file at the source, such as a disk. In the case of an input file, the file must exist before the **open** statement executes. If the file does not exist, the **open** statement fails and the input stream enters the fail state. An output file does not have to exist before it is opened; if the output file does not exist, the computer prepares an empty file for output. If the designated output file already exists, by default the old contents are erased when the file is opened.

 NOTE To add the output at the end of an existing file, you can use the option `ios::app` as follows. Suppose that `outData` is declared as before, and you want to add the output at the end of the existing file, say `firstProg.out`. The statement to open this file is:

`outData.open("firstProg.out", ios::app);`

If the file `firstProg.out` does not exist, then the system creates an empty file.

2

PROGRAMMING EXAMPLE: Student Grade

Write a program that reads a student name followed by five test scores. The program should output the student name, the five test scores, and the average test score. Output the average test score with two decimal places.

The data to be read is stored in a file called `test.txt`. The output should be stored in a file called `testavg.out`.

Input   A file containing the student name and the five test scores. A sample input is

Andrew Miller 87.50 89 65.75 37 98.50

Output   The student name, the five test scores, and the average of the five test scores, saved to a file.

PROBLEM
ANALYSIS
AND
ALGORITHM
DESIGN

To find the average of the five test scores, you add the five test scores and divide the sum by 5. The input data is in the following form: the student name followed by the five test scores. Therefore, you must read the student name first and then read the five test scores. This problem analysis translates into the following algorithm:

1.   Read the student name and the five test scores.
2.   Output the student name and the five test scores.
3.   Calculate the average.
4.   Output the average.

You output the average test score in the fixed decimal format with two decimal places.

Variables   The program needs to read a student's first and last name and five test scores. Therefore, you need two variables to store the student name and five variables to store the five test scores.

To find the average, you must add the five test scores and then divide the sum by 5. Thus, you need a variable to store the average test score. Furthermore, because the input data is in a file, you need an `ifstream` variable to open the input file. Because the program output will be stored in a file, you need an `ofstream` variable to open the output file. The program, therefore, needs at least the following variables:

```
ifstream inFile;      //input file stream variable
ofstream outFile;     //output file stream variable

double test1, test2, test3, test4, test5; //variables to
                              //read the five test scores
double average;       //variable to store the average test score
string firstName;     //variable to store the first name
string lastName;      //variable to store the last name
```

MAIN ALGORITHM

In the preceding sections, we analyzed the problem and determined the formulas to perform the calculations. We also determined the necessary variables. We can now expand the previous algorithm to solve the problem given at the beginning of this programming example.

1. Declare the variables.
2. Open the input file.
3. Open the output file.
4. To output the floating-point numbers in a fixed decimal format with a decimal point and trailing zeros, set the manipulators `fixed` and `showpoint`. Also, to output the floating-point numbers with two decimal places, set the precision to two decimal places.
5. Read the student name.
6. Output the student name.
7. Read the five test scores.
8. Output the five test scores.
9. Find the average test score.
10. Output the average test score.
11. Close the input and output files.

Because this program reads data from a file and outputs data to a file, it must include the header file `fstream`. Because the program outputs the average test score to two decimal places, you need to set the precision to two decimal places. Therefore, the program uses the manipulator `setprecision`, which requires you to include the header file `iomanip`. Because `firstName` and `lastName` are `string` variables, we must include the header file `string`. The program also includes the header file `iostream` to print a message on the screen so that you will not stare at a blank screen while the program executes.

COMPLETE PROGRAM LISTING

```
//******************************************************
// Author: D.S. Malik
//
// Program to calculate the average test score.
// Given a student's name and five test scores, this program
// calculates the average test score. The student's name, the
// five test scores, and the average test score are stored in
// the file testavg.out. The data is input from the file
// test.txt.
//******************************************************
```

```cpp
#include <iostream>
#include <fstream>
#include <iomanip>
#include <string>

using namespace std;

int main()
{
        //Declare variables;                            Step 1
    ifstream inFile; //input file stream variable
    ofstream outFile; //output file stream variable

    double test1, test2, test3, test4, test5;
    double average;

    string firstName;
    string lastName;

    inFile.open("test.txt");                        //Step 2
    outFile.open("testavg.out");                    //Step 3

    outFile << fixed << showpoint;                  //Step 4
    outFile << setprecision(2);                     //Step 4

    cout << "Processing data" << endl;

    inFile >> firstName >> lastName;                //Step 5
    outFile << "Student name: " << firstName
            << " " << lastName << endl;             //Step 6

    inFile >> test1 >> test2 >> test3
           >> test4 >> test5;                       //Step 7
    outFile << "Test scores: " << setw(6) << test1
            << setw(6) << test2 << setw(6) << test3
            << setw(6) << test4 << setw(6) << test5
            << endl;                                //Step 8

    average = (test1 + test2 + test3 + test4
              + test5) / 5.0;                       //Step 9

    outFile << "Average test score: " << setw(6)
            << average << endl;                     //Step 10

    inFile.close();                                 //Step 11
    outFile.close();                                //Step 11

    return 0;
}
```

Sample Run

Input File (contents of the file `test.txt`):

Andrew Miller 87.50 89 65.75 37 98.50

Output File (contents of the file `testavg.out`):

```
Student name: Andrew Miller
Test scores:   87.50 89.00 65.75 37.00 98.50
Average test score:   75.55
```

NOTE   The preceding program uses five variables—test1, test2, test3, test4, and test5—to read the five test scores and then find the average test score. The Web site accompanying this book contains a modified version of this program that uses only one variable, testScore, to read the test scores and another variable, sum, to find the sum of the test scores. The program is named Ch2_AverageTestScoreVersion2.cpp.

QUICK REVIEW

1. In C++, >> is called the stream extraction operator.
2. Input from the standard input device is accomplished by using `cin` and the stream extraction operator >>.
3. When data is input in a program, the data items, such as numbers, are usually separated by blanks, lines, or tabs.
4. When inputting data into a variable, the operator >> skips all leading whitespace characters.
5. To use `cin`, the program must include the header file `iostream`.
6. Prompt lines are executable statements that tell the user what to do.
7. The function `get` is used to read data on a character-by-character basis and does not skip any whitespace characters.
8. The function `ignore` is used to skip data in a line.
9. Attempting to read invalid data into a variable causes the input stream to enter the fail state.
10. Once an input failure has occurred, you use the function `clear` to restore the input stream to a working state.
11. The manipulator `setprecision` formats the output of floating-point numbers to a specified number of decimal places.

2

12. The manipulator `fixed` outputs floating-point numbers in the fixed decimal format.

13. The manipulator `showpoint` outputs floating-point numbers with a decimal point and trailing zeros.

14. The manipulator `setw` formats the output of an expression in a specific number of columns; the default output is right-justified.

15. If the number of columns specified in the argument of `setw` is less than the number of columns needed to print the value of the expression, the output is not truncated and the output of the expression expands to the required number of columns.

16. If the number of columns specified in the `setw` manipulator exceeds the number of columns required by the next expression, the output is right-justified. To left-justify the output, you use the manipulator `left`.

17. To use the stream functions `get`, `ignore`, `clear`, and `unsetf` for standard I/O, the program must include the header file `iostream`.

18. To use the manipulators `setprecision` and `setw`, the program must include the header file `iomanip`.

19. The header file `fstream` contains the definitions of `ifstream` and `ofstream`.

20. For file I/O, you must use the statement `#include <fstream>` to include the header file `fstream` in the program. You must also do the following: declare variables of type `ifstream` for file input and of type `ofstream` for file output; use open statements to open input and output files; and use `<<`, `>>`, `get`, `ignore`, or `clear` with file stream variables.

21. To close a file as indicated by the `ifstream` variable `inFile`, you use the statement `inFile.close();`. To close a file as indicated by the `ofstream` variable `outFile`, you use the statement `outFile.close();`.

EXERCISES

1. Mark the following statements as true or false.

   a. In the statement `cin >> y;`, y can only be a variable of type `int` or `double`.

   b. The extraction operator `>>` skips all leading whitespace characters when searching for the next data in the input stream.

   c. In the statement `cin >> x;`, x must be a variable.

   d. The statement `cin >> x >> y;` requires the input values for x and y to appear on the same line.

   e. The statement `cin >> num;` is equivalent to the statement `num >> cin;`.

f. You generate the newline character by pressing the Enter (return) key on the keyboard.

g. The function `ignore` is used to skip certain input in a line.

2. What is printed by the following program? Suppose the input is 20 15.

```cpp
#include <iostream>

using namespace std;

const int NUM = 10;
const double X = 20.5;

int main()
{
    int a, b;
    double z;
    char grade;

    a = 25;

    cout << "a = " << a << endl;

    cout << "Enter two integers : ";
    cin >> a >> b;
    cout << endl;

    cout << "The numbers you entered are "
         << a << " and " << b << endl;

    z = X + 2 * a - b;
    cout << "z = " << z << endl;

    grade = 'A';
    cout << "Your grade is " << grade << endl;

    a = 2 * NUM + z;
    cout << "The value of a = " << a << endl;

    return 0;
}
```

3. What is printed by the following program? Suppose the input is the following:

```
Miller
34
340
```

```cpp
#include <iostream>
#include <string>

using namespace std;
```

```cpp
const int PRIME_NUM = 11;

int main()
{
    const int SECRET = 17;

    string name;
    int id;
    int num;
    int mysteryNum;

    cout << "Enter last name: ";
    cin >> name;
    cout << endl;

    cout << "Enter a two-digit number: ";
    cin >> num;
    cout << endl;

    id = 100 * num + SECRET;

    cout << "Enter a positive integer less than 1000: ";
    cin >> num;
    cout << endl;

    mysteryNum = num * PRIME_NUM - 3 * SECRET;

    cout << "Name: " << name << endl;
    cout << "Id: " << id << endl;
    cout << "Mystery number: " << mysteryNum << endl;

    return 0;
}
```

4. Rewrite the following program so that it is properly formatted.

```cpp
#include <iostream>
#include <string>
using namespace std;
const double X = 13.45;const int Y=34;
const char BLANK= ' ';
int main()
{string firstName,lastName;int num;
double salary;
cout<<"Enter first name: "; cin>> firstName; cout<<endl;
cout<<"Enter last name: "; cin
>>lastName;cout<<endl;
    cout<<"Enter a positive integer less than 70:";
cin>>num;cout<<endl; salary=num*X;
 cout<<"Name: "<<firstName<<BLANK<<lastName<<endl;cout
<<"Wages: $"<<salary<<endl; cout<<"X = "<<X<<endl;
 cout<<"X+Y = " << X+Y << endl; return 0;
}
```

5. What type of input does the following program require, and in what order does the input need to be provided?

    ```cpp
    #include <iostream>

    using namespace std;

    int main()
    {
        int age;
        double weight;
        string firstName, lastName;

        cin >> firstName >> lastName;
        cin >> age >> weight;

        return 0;
    }
    ```

6. Suppose x and y are int variables and ch is a char variable. Consider the following input:

    ```
    5 28 36
    ```

    What value (if any) is assigned to x, y, and ch after each of the following statements executes? (Use the same input for each statement.)

    a. `cin >> x >> y >> ch;`

    b. `cin >> ch >> x >> y;`

    c. `cin >> x >> ch >> y;`

    d. `cin >> x >> y;`
        `cin.get(ch);`

7. Suppose x and y are int variables and z is a double variable. Assume the following input data:

    ```
    37 86.56 32
    ```

    What value (if any) is assigned to x, y, and z after each of the following statements executes? (Use the same input for each statement.)

    a. `cin >> x >> y >> z;`

    b. `cin >> x >> z >> y;`

    c. `cin >> z >> x >> y;`

8. Suppose x and y are int variables and ch is a char variable. Assume the following input data:

    ```
    13 28 D
    14 E 98
    A B 56
    ```

    What value (if any) is assigned to x, y, and ch after each of the following statements executes? (Use the same input for each statement.)

2

a. ```
    cin >> x >> y;
    cin.ignore(50, '\n');
    cin >> ch;
    ```

b.  ```
    cin >> x;
    cin.ignore(50, '\n');
    cin >> y;
    cin.ignore(50, '\n');
    cin.get(ch);
    ```

c. ```
    cin >> y;
    cin.ignore(50, '\n');
    cin >> x >> ch;
    ```

d.  ```
    cin.get(ch);
    cin.ignore(50, '\n');
    cin >> x;
    cin.ignore(50, 'E');
    cin >> y;
    ```

9. Given the input

   ```
   46 A 49
   ```

   and the C++ code

   ```
   int x = 10, y = 18;
   char z = 'A';
   cin >> x >> y >> z;
   cout << x << " " << y << " " << z;
   ```

   what is the output?

10. Suppose that age is a variable of type int, and name is a variable of type string. What are the values of age and name after the following input statements execute?

    ```
    cin >> age;
    getline(cin, name);
    ```

    if the input is:

    a. 35 Mickey Balto

    b. 35
        Mickey Balto

11. Suppose that age is a variable of type int, ch is a variable of type char, and name is a variable of type string. What are the values of age and name after the following input statements execute?

    ```
    cin >> age;
    cin.get(ch);
    getline(cin, name);
    ```

    if the input is:

    a. 35 Mickey Balto

    b. 35
        Mickey Balto

12. The following program is supposed to read two numbers from a file named `input.dat`, and write the sum of the numbers to a file named `output.dat`. However, it fails to do so. Rewrite the program so that it accomplishes what it is intended to do. (Also, include statements to close the files.)

```cpp
#include <iostream>
#include <fstream>
using namespace std;

int main()
{
    int num1, num2;
    ifstream infile;

    outfile.open("output.dat");
    infile >> num1 >> num2;
    outfile << "Sum = " << num1 + num2 << endl;
    return 0;
}
```

13. What may cause an input stream to enter the fail state? What happens when an input stream enters the fail state?

14. A program reads data from a file called `inputFile.dat` and, after doing some calculations, writes the results to a file called `outFile.dat`. Answer the following questions:

    a. After the program executes, what are the contents of the file `inputFile.dat`?

    b. After the program executes, what are the contents of the file `outFile.dat` if this file was empty before the program executed?

    c. After the program executes, what are the contents of the file `outFile.dat` if this file contained 100 numbers before the program executed?

    d. What would happen if the file `outFile.dat` did not exist before the program executed?

PROGRAMMING EXERCISES

1. Consider the following program segment:

```cpp
//include statement(s)
//using namespace statement

int main()
{
    //variable declaration

    //executable statements

    //return statement
}
```

a. Write C++ statements that include the header files `iostream` and `string`.

b. Write a C++ statement that allows you to use `cin`, `cout`, and `endl` without the prefix `std::`.

c. Write C++ statements that declare and initialize the following named constants: `SECRET` of type `int` initialized to `11`, and `RATE` of type `double` initialized to `12.50`.

d. Write C++ statements that declare the following variables: `num1`, `num2`, and `newNum` of type `int`; `name` of type `string`; and `hoursWorked` and `wages` of type `double`.

e. Write C++ statements that prompt the user to input two integers and store the first number in `num1` and the second number in `num2`.

f. Write a C++ statement(s) that outputs the values of `num1` and `num2`, indicating which is `num1` and which is `num2`. For example, if `num1` is 8 and `num2` is 5, then the output is:

```
The value of num1 = 8 and the value of num2 = 5.
```

g. Write a C++ statement that multiplies the value of `num1` by 2, adds the value of `num2` to it, and then stores the result in `newNum`. Then write a C++ statement that outputs the value of `newNum`.

h. Write a C++ statement that updates the value of `newNum` by adding the value of the named constant `SECRET`. Then write a C++ statement that outputs the value of `newNum` with an appropriate message.

i. Write C++ statements that prompt the user to enter a person's last name and then store the last name into the variable `name`.

j. Write C++ statements that prompt the user to enter a decimal number between 0 and 70 and then store the number entered into `hoursWorked`.

k. Write a C++ statement that multiplies the value of the named constant `RATE` with the value of `hoursWorked`, and then stores the result into the variable `wages`.

l. Write C++ statements that produce the following output:

```
Name:          //output the value of the variable name
Pay Rate: $    //output the value of the variable RATE
Hours Worked:  //output the value of the variable hoursWorked
Salary: $      //output the value of the variable wages
```

For example, if the value of `name` is `"Rainbow"` and `hoursWorked` is `45.50`, then the output is:

```
Name: Rainbow
Pay Rate: $12.5
Hours Worked: 45.5
Salary: $568.75
```

m. Write a C++ program that tests each of the C++ statements that you wrote in parts a through l. Place the statements at the appropriate place in the previous C++ program segment. Test-run your program (twice) on the following input data:

    i. `num1 = 13, num2 = 28; name = "Jacobson"; hoursWorked = 48.30.`

    ii. `num1 = 32, num2 = 15; name = "Crawford"; hoursWorked = 58.45.`

2. Write a program that prompts the user to input a decimal number and outputs the number rounded to the nearest integer.

3. Write a program that prompts the user to input the length and width of a rectangle and then prints the rectangle's area and perimeter. (Assume that the length and the width are decimal numbers.)

4. Write a program that prompts the user to enter five test scores and then prints the average test score. (Assume that the test scores are decimal numbers.)

5. Write a program that prompts the user to input five decimal numbers. The program should then add the five decimal numbers, convert the sum to the nearest integer, and print the result.

6. Write a program that does the following:

    a. Prompts the user to input five decimal numbers

    b. Prints the five decimal numbers

    c. Converts each decimal number to the nearest integer

    d. Adds the five integers

    e. Prints the sum and average of the five integers

7. Write a C++ program that prompts the user to input the elapsed time for an event in seconds. The program then outputs the elapsed time in hours, minutes, and seconds. (For example, if the elapsed time is 9630 seconds, then the output is `2:40:30`.)

8. To make a profit, a local store marks up the prices of its items by a certain percentage. Write a C++ program that reads the original price of the item sold, the percentage of the marked-up price, and the sales tax rate. The program then outputs the original price of the item, the percentage of the mark-up, the store's selling price of the item, the sales tax rate, the sales tax, and the final price of the item. (The final price of the item is the selling price plus the sales tax.)

9. Write a program that prompts the user to input a length expressed in centimeters. The program should then convert the length to inches (to the nearest inch) and output the length expressed in yards, feet, and inches, in that order. For example, suppose the input for centimeters is 312. To the nearest inch, 312 centimeters is equal to 123 inches. 123 inches would thus be output as:

`3 yard(s), 1 feet (foot), and 3 inch(es)`

10. Write a program to implement and test the algorithm that you designed for Exercise 20 of Chapter 0. (You may assume that the value of $\pi = 3.141593$. In your program, declare a named constant PI to store this value.)

11. A milk carton can hold 3.78 liters of milk. Each morning, a dairy farm ships cartons of milk to a local grocery store. The cost of producing one liter of milk is $0.38, and the profit on each carton of milk is $0.27. Write a program that does the following:

   a. Prompts the user to enter the total amount of milk produced in the morning.

   b. Outputs the number of milk cartons needed to hold the milk. (Round your answer to the nearest integer.)

   c. Outputs the cost of producing the milk.

   d. Outputs the profit for producing the milk.

12. Redo Programming Exercise 11 so that the user can also input the cost of producing one liter of milk and the profit on each carton of milk.

13. You found an exciting summer job for five weeks. It pays $15.50 per hour. Suppose that the total tax you pay on your summer job income is 14%. After paying the taxes, you spend 10% of your net income to buy new clothes and other accessories for the next school year and 1% to buy school supplies. After buying clothes and school supplies, you use 25% of the remaining money to buy savings bonds. For each dollar you spend to buy savings bonds, your parents spend $0.50 to buy additional savings bonds for you. Write a program that prompts the user to enter the pay rate for an hour and the number of hours you worked each week. The program then outputs the following:

   a. Your income before and after taxes from your summer job.

   b. The money you spend on clothes and other accessories.

   c. The money you spend on school supplies.

   d. The money you spend to buy savings bonds.

   e. The money your parents spend to buy additional savings bonds for you.

14. A permutation of three objects, a, b, and c, is any arrangement of these objects in a row. For example, some of the permutations of these objects are abc, bca, and cab. The number of permutations of three objects is 6. Suppose that these three objects are strings. Write a program that prompts the user to enter three strings. The program then outputs the six permutations of those strings.

15. Consider the following incomplete C++ program:

```
#include <iostream>

int main()
{
    ...
}
```

a. Write a statement that includes the header files `fstream`, `string`, and `iomanip` in this program.

b. Write statements that declare `inFile` to be a variable of type `ifstream` and `outFile` to be a variable of type `ofstream`.

c. The program will read data from the file `inData.txt` and write output to the file `outData.txt`. Write statements to open both these files, to associate `inFile` with `inData.txt`, and to associate `outFile` with `outData.txt`.

d. Suppose that the file `inData.txt` contains the following data:

```
10.20 5.35
15.6
Randy Gill 31
18500 3.5
A
```

The numbers in the first line represent the length and width, respectively, of a rectangle. The number in the second line represents the radius of a circle. The third line contains the first name, last name, and the age of a person. The first number in the fourth line is the savings account balance at the beginning of the month, and the second number is the interest rate per year. (Assume that $\pi = 3.1416$.) The fifth line contains an uppercase letter between `A` and `Y` (inclusive). Write statements so that after the program executes, the contents of the file `outData.txt` are as shown below. If necessary, declare additional variables. Your statements should be general enough so that if the content of the input file changes and the program is run again (without editing and recompiling), it outputs the appropriate results.

```
Rectangle:
Length = 10.20, width = 5.35, area = 54.57, parameter = 31.10

Circle:
Radius = 15.60, area = 764.54, circumference = 98.02

Name: Randy Gill, age: 31
Beginning balance = 18500.00, interest rate = 3.50
Balance at the end of the month = 18553.96

The character that comes after A in the ASCII set is B
```

e. Write statements that close the input and output files.

f. Write a C++ program that tests the statements in parts a through e.

16. The manager of a football stadium wants you to write a program that calculates the total ticket sales after each game. There are four types of tickets—box, sideline, premium, and general admission. After each game, data is stored in a file in the following form:

```
ticketPrice    numberOfTicketsSold
...
```

Sample data are :

```
250 5750
100 28000
 50 35750
 25 18750
```

The first line indicates that the ticket price is $250 and that 5750 tickets were sold at that price. Output the number of tickets sold and the total sale amount. Format your output with two decimal places.

17. Write a program to calculate property tax. Property tax is calculated on 92% of the assessed value of the property. For example, if the assessed value is $200,000, the property tax is on $184,000. Assume that the property tax rate is $1.05 for each $100 of the assessed value. Your program should prompt the user to enter the assessed value of the property. Store the output in a file in the following format. (Here is a sample output.)

```
Assessed Value:                    200000.00
Taxable Amount:                    184000.00
Tax Rate for each $100.00:              1.05
Property Tax:                       1932.00
```

Format your output to have two decimal places. (Note that the left column is left-justified, and the right column is right-justified.)

18. Three employees in a company are up for a special pay increase. You are given a file, say Ch2_Ex18Data.txt, with the following data:

```
Miller Andrew 65789.87 5
Green Sheila 75892.56 6
Sethi Amit 74900.50 6.1
```

Each input line consists of an employee's last name, first name, current salary, and percent pay increase. For example, in the first input line, the last name of the employee is Miller, the first name is Andrew, the current salary is 65789.87, and the pay increase is 5%. Write a program that reads data from the specified file and stores the output in the file Ch2_Ex18Output.dat. For each employee, the data must be output in the following form: firstName lastName updatedSalary. Format the output of decimal numbers to two decimal places.

19. Write a program that accepts as input the mass, in grams, and density, in grams per cubic centimeters, and outputs the volume of the object using the formula: *volume = mass / density*. Format your output to two decimal places.

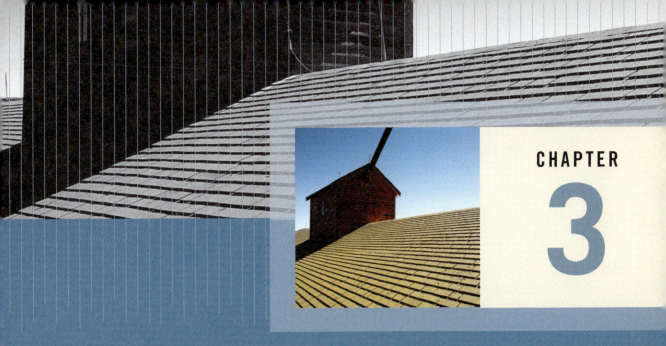

CONTROL STRUCTURES I (SELECTION)

IN THIS CHAPTER, YOU WILL:

- Learn about control structures
- Examine relational and logical operators
- Explore how to form and evaluate logical (Boolean) expressions
- Discover how to use the selection control structures `if`, `if...else`, and `switch` in a program
- Learn how to avoid bugs by avoiding partially understood concepts and techniques

Chapter 1 defined a program as a sequence of statements whose objective is to accomplish some task. The programs you have examined so far were simple and straightforward. To process a program, the computer begins at the first executable statement and executes the statements in order until it comes to the end. In this chapter and Chapter 4, you will learn how to tell a computer that it does not have to follow a simple sequential order of statements; it can also make decisions and repeat certain statements over and over until certain conditions are met.

Control Structures

A computer can process a program in one of the following ways: in sequence; selectively, by making a choice, which is also called a branch; repetitively, by executing a statement over and over, using a structure called a loop; or by calling a function. Figure 3-1 illustrates the first three types of program flow. (In Chapter 5, we will show how function calls work.) The programming examples in Chapters 1 and 2 included simple sequential programs. With such a program, the computer starts at the beginning and follows the statements in order. No choices are made; there is no repetition. Control structures provide alternatives to sequential program execution and are used to alter the sequential flow of execution. The two most common control structures are selection and repetition. In *selection*, the program executes particular statements depending on some condition(s). In *repetition*, the program repeats particular statements a certain number of times based on some condition(s).

Branching: Altering the flow of program execution by making a selection or choice.

Looping: Altering the flow of program execution by the repetition of statement(s).

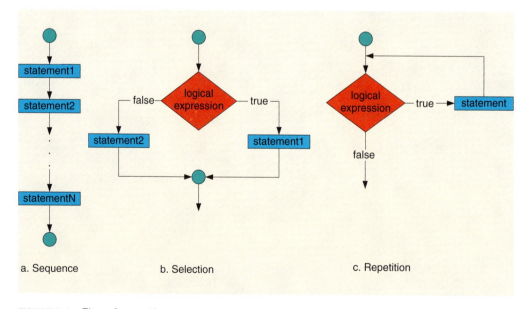

a. Sequence   b. Selection   c. Repetition

FIGURE 3-1 Flow of execution

Before you can learn about selection and repetition, you must understand the nature of conditional statements and how to use them. Consider the following three statements:

1. `if (score is greater than or equal to 90)`
   `grade is A`

2. `if (hours worked are less than or equal to 40)`
   `wages = rate * hours`
   `otherwise`
   `wages = (rate * 40) + 1.5 * (rate * (hours - 40))`

3. `if (temperature is greater than 70 degrees and it is not raining)`
   `print Go golfing!`

These statements are examples of conditional statements. You can see that certain statements are to be executed only if certain conditions are met. A condition is met if it evaluates to **true**. For example, in statement 1

`score is greater than or equal to 90`

is **true** if the value of `score` is greater than or equal to 90; it is **false** otherwise. For example, if the value of `score` is 95, the statement evaluates to **true**. Similarly, if the value of `score` is 86, the statement evaluates to **false**.

It would be useful if the computer could recognize these types of statements to be true for appropriate values. Furthermore, in certain situations, the truth or falsity of a statement could depend on more than one condition. For example, in statement 3, both `temperature is greater than 70 degrees` and `it is not raining` must be true to recommend golfing.

As you can see, for the computer to make decisions and repeat statements, it must be able to react to conditions that exist when the program executes. The next few sections discuss how to represent and evaluate conditional statements in C++.

Relational Operators

To make decisions, you must be able to express conditions and make comparisons. For example, the interest rate and service charges on a checking account might depend on the balance at the end of the month. If the balance is less than some minimum balance, not only is the interest rate lower, but there is also usually a service charge. Therefore, to determine the interest rate, you must be able to state the minimum balance (a condition) and compare the account balance with the minimum balance. The premium on an insurance policy is also determined by stating conditions and making comparisons. For example, to determine an insurance premium, you must be able to check the smoking status of the policyholder. Nonsmokers (the condition) receive lower premiums than smokers. Both of these examples involve comparing items. Certain items are compared for equality against a particular condition; others are compared for inequality (greater than or less than) against a particular condition.

In C++, a condition is represented by a logical (Boolean) expression. An expression that has a value of either **true** or **false** is called a **logical (Boolean) expression**. Moreover, **true** and **false** are **logical (Boolean) values**. Suppose i and j are integers. Consider the following expression:

```
i > j
```

If this expression is a logical expression, it will have the value **true** if the value of i is greater than the value of j; otherwise, it will have the value **false**. The symbol > is called a relational operator. A **relational operator** allows you to make comparisons in a program.

C++ includes six relational operators that allow you to state conditions and make comparisons. Table 3-1 lists the relational operators.

TABLE 3-1   Relational Operators in C++

Operator	Description
==	equal to
!=	not equal to
<	less than
<=	less than or equal to
>	greater than
>=	greater than or equal to

NOTE   In C++, the symbol ==, which consists of two equals signs, is called the equality operator. Recall that the symbol = is called the assignment operator. Remember that the equality operator, ==, determines whether two expressions are equal, whereas the assignment operator, =, assigns the value of an expression to a variable.

Each of the relational operators is a binary operator; that is, it requires two operands. Because the result of a comparison is **true** or **false**, expressions using these operators evaluate to **true** or **false**.

Relational Operators and Simple Data Types

You can use the relational operators with all three simple data types. For example, the following expressions use both integers and real numbers:

Expression	Meaning	Value
8 < 15	8 is less than 15	true
6 != 6	6 is not equal to 6	false
2.5 > 5.8	2.5 is greater than 5.8	false
5.9 <= 7.5	5.9 is less than or equal to 7.5	true

Comparing Floating-Point Numbers for Equality

Comparison of floating-point numbers for equality may not behave as you would expect; see Example 3-1.

EXAMPLE 3-1

```
//************************************************************
// Author: D.S. Malik
//
// This program illustrates that the equality of floating-
// point numbers may not yield the desired result.
//************************************************************

#include <iostream>
#include <iomanip>

using namespace std;

int main()
{
    cout << fixed << showpoint << setprecision(17);

    cout << "3.0 / 7.0 = " << (3.0 / 7.0) << endl;
    cout << "2.0 / 7.0 = " << (2.0 / 7.0) << endl;
    cout << "3.0 / 7.0 + 2.0 / 7.0 + 2.0 / 7.0 = "
         << (3.0 / 7.0 + 2.0 / 7.0 + 2.0 / 7.0) << endl;

    return 0;
}
```

Sample Run:

```
3.0 / 7.0 = 0.42857142857142855
2.0 / 7.0 = 0.28571428571428570
3.0 / 7.0 + 2.0 / 7.0 + 2.0 / 7.0 = 0.99999999999999989
```

From the output, it follows that the following equality of floating-point numbers would evaluate to `false`.

```
1.0 == 3.0 / 7.0 + 2.0 / 7.0 + 2.0 / 7.0
```

The preceding program and its output show that you should be careful when comparing floating-point numbers for equality. One way to check whether two floating-point numbers are equal is to check whether the absolute value of their difference is less than a certain tolerance. For example, suppose `x` and `y` are floating-point numbers and the tolerance is `0.000001`. Then `x` and `y` are equal if the absolute value of `(x - y)` is less than `0.000001`. To find the absolute value, you can use the function `fabs` of the header file `cmath`. For example, the expression `fabs(x - y)` gives the absolute value of `x - y`. Therefore, the expression `fabs(x - y) < 0.000001` determines whether the absolute value of `(x - y)` is less than `0.000001`. See the program `Example3-1A.cpp` at the Web site accompanying this book.

Comparing Characters

For `char` values, whether an expression using relational operators evaluates to `true` or `false` depends on a machine's collating sequence. Table 3-2 shows how expressions using the ASCII data set are evaluated.

TABLE 3-2 Evaluating Expressions Using Relational Operators and the ASCII Collating Sequence

Expression	Value	Explanation
`' ' < 'a'`	`true`	The ASCII value of `' '` is 32, and the ASCII value of `'a'` is 97. Because 32 < 97 is `true`, it follows that `' ' < 'a'` is `true`.
`'R' > 'T'`	`false`	The ASCII value of `'R'` is 82, and the ASCII value of `'T'` is 84. Because 82 > 84 is `false`, it follows that `'R' > 'T'` is `false`.
`'+' < '*'`	`false`	The ASCII value of `'+'` is 43, and the ASCII value of `'*'` is 42. Because 43 < 42 is `false`, it follows that `'+' < '*'` is `false`.
`'6' <= '>'`	`true`	The ASCII value of `'6'` is 54, and the ASCII value of `'>'` is 62. Because 54 <= 62 is `true`, it follows that `'6' <= '>'` is `true`.

Comparing values of different data types may produce unpredictable results. For example, the following expression compares an integer and a character:

8 < '5'

In this expression, on a particular machine, 8 would be compared with the collating sequence of '5', which is 53. That is, 8 is compared with 53, which makes this particular expression evaluate to true.

Expressions such as 4 < 6 and 'R' > 'T' are examples of **logical (Boolean) expressions**. When C++ evaluates a logical expression, it returns an integer value of 1 if the logical expression evaluates to true; it returns an integer value of 0 otherwise. In C++, any nonzero value is treated as true.

3

NOTE Chapter 1 introduced the data type bool. Recall that the data type bool has two values, true and false. In C++, true and false are reserved words. The identifier true is set to 1, and the identifier false is set to 0. For readability, whenever logical expressions are used, the identifiers true and false will be used here as the value of the logical expression.

Relational Operators and the string Type

The relational operators can be applied to variables of type string. Variables of type string are compared character-by-character, starting with the first character and using the ASCII collating sequence. The character-by-character comparison continues until either a mismatch is found or the last characters have been compared and are equal. Consider the following declarations:

```
string str1 = "Hello";
string str2 = "Hi";
string str3 = "Air";
string str4 = "Bill";
string str5 = "Big";
```

Using these variable declarations, Table 3-3 shows how various logical expressions are evaluated.

TABLE 3-3 Evaluating Logical Expressions with `string` Variables

Expression	Value	Explanation
str1 < str2	true	str1 = "Hello" and str2 = "Hi". The first character of str1 and str2 is the same, but the second character 'e' of str1 is less than the second character 'i' of str2. Therefore, str1 < str2 is true.
str1 > "Hen"	false	str1 = "Hello". The first two characters of str1 and "Hen" are the same, but the third character 'l' of str1 is less than the third character 'n' of "Hen". Therefore, str1 > "Hen" is false.
str3 < "An"	true	str3 = "Air". The first characters of str3 and "An" are the same, but the second character 'i' of "Air" is less than the second character 'n' of "An". Therefore, str3 < "An" is true.
str1 == "hello"	false	str1 = "Hello". The first character 'H' of str1 is less than the first character 'h' of "hello" because the ASCII value of 'H' is 72, and the ASCII value of 'h' is 104. Therefore, str1 == "hello" is false.
str3 <= str4	true	str3 = "Air" and str4 = "Bill". The first character 'A' of str3 is less than the first character 'B' of str4. Therefore, str3 <= str4 is true.
str2 > str4	true	str2 = "Hi" and str4 = "Bill". The first character 'H' of str2 is greater than the first character 'B' of str4. Therefore, str2 > str4 is true.

If two strings of different lengths are compared and the character-by-character comparison is equal until it reaches the last character of the shorter string, the shorter string is evaluated as less than the larger string. Table 3-4 illustrates this concept.

TABLE 3-4 Evaluating Logical Expressions with `string` Variables

Expression	Value	Explanation
str4 >= "Billy"	false	str4 = "Bill". It has four characters and "Billy" has five characters. Therefore, str4 is the shorter string. All four characters of str4 are the same as the corresponding first four characters of "Billy", and "Billy" is the larger string. Therefore, str4 >= "Billy" is false.
str5 <= "Bigger"	true	str5 = "Big". It has three characters and "Bigger" has six characters. Therefore, str5 is the shorter string. All three characters of str5 are the same as the corresponding first three characters of "Bigger", and "Bigger" is the larger string. Therefore, str5 <= "Bigger" is true.

Logical (Boolean) Operators and Logical Expressions

This section describes how to form and evaluate logical expressions that are combinations of other logical expressions. **Logical (Boolean) operators** enable you to combine logical expressions. C++ has three logical (Boolean) operators, as shown in Table 3-5.

TABLE 3-5 Logical (Boolean) Operators in C++

Operator	Description
!	not
&&	and
||	or

Logical operators take only logical values as operands and yield only logical values as results. The operator ! is unary, so it has only one operand. The operators && and || are binary operators. Tables 3-6, 3-7, and 3-8 define these operators.

Table 3-6 defines the operator ! (not). When you use the ! operator, !`true` is `false` and !`false` is `true`. Putting ! in front of a logical expression reverses the value of that logical expression.

TABLE 3-6   The ! (Not) Operator

Expression	!(Expression)
`true` (nonzero)	`false` (0)
`false` (0)	`true` (1)

EXAMPLE 3-2

Expression	Value	Explanation
`!('A' > 'B')`	`true`	Because `'A' > 'B'` is `false`, `!('A' > 'B')` is `true`.
`!(6 <= 7)`	`false`	Because `6 <= 7` is `true`, `!(6 <= 7)` is `false`.

Table 3-7 defines the operator `&&` (and). From this table, it follows that `Expression1 && Expression2` is `true` if and only if both `Expression1` and `Expression2` are `true`; otherwise, `Expression1 && Expression2` evaluates to `false`.

TABLE 3-7   The `&&` (And) Operator

Expression1	Expression2	Expression1 `&&` Expression2
`true` (nonzero)	`true` (nonzero)	`true` (1)
`true` (nonzero)	`false` (0)	`false` (0)
`false` (0)	`true` (nonzero)	`false` (0)
`false` (0)	`false` (0)	`false` (0)

EXAMPLE 3-3

Expression	Value	Explanation
(14 >= 5) && ('A' < 'B')	true	Because (14 >= 5) is true, ('A' < 'B') is true, and true && true is true, the expression evaluates to true.
(24 >= 35) && ('A' < 'B')	false	Because (24 >= 35) is false, ('A' < 'B') is true, and false && true is false, the expression evaluates to false.

Table 3-8 defines the operator || (or). From this table, it follows that Expression1 || Expression2 is true if and only if at least one of the expressions, Expression1 or Expression2, is true; otherwise, Expression1 || Expression2 evaluates to false.

TABLE 3-8 The || (Or) Operator

Expression1	Expression2	Expression1 || Expression2
true (nonzero)	true (nonzero)	true (1)
true (nonzero)	false (0)	true (1)
false (0)	true (nonzero)	true (1)
false (0)	false (0)	false (0)

EXAMPLE 3-4

Expression	Value	Explanation
(14 >= 5) || ('A' > 'B')	true	Because (14 >= 5) is true, ('A' > 'B') is false, and true || false is true, the expression evaluates to true.
(24 >= 35) || ('A' > 'B')	false	Because (24 >= 35) is false, ('A' > 'B') is false, and false || false is false, the expression evaluates to false.
('A' <= 'a') || (7 != 7)	true	Because ('A' <= 'a') is true, (7 != 7) is false, and true || false is true, the expression evaluates to true.

Order of Precedence

Complex logical expressions can be difficult to evaluate. Consider the following logical expression:

```
11 > 5 || 6 < 15 && 7 >= 8
```

This logical expression yields different results, depending on whether `||` or `&&` is evaluated first. If `||` is evaluated first, the expression evaluates to **false**. If `&&` is evaluated first, the expression evaluates to **true**.

An expression might contain arithmetic, relational, and logical operators, as in the expression

```
5 + 3 <= 9 && 2 > 3.
```

To work with complex logical expressions, there must be some priority scheme for evaluating operators. Table 3-9 shows the order of precedence of some C++ operators, including the arithmetic, relational, and logical operators. (See Appendix B for the precedence of all C++ operators.)

TABLE 3-9   Precedence of Operators

Operators	Precedence
`!, +, -` (unary operators)	first
`*, /, %`	second
`+, -`	third
`<, <=, >=, >`	fourth
`==, !=`	fifth
`&&`	sixth
`||`	seventh
`=` (assignment operator)	last

NOTE   In C++, `&` and `|` are also operators. The meaning of these operators is different from the meaning of `&&` and `||`. Using `&` in place of `&&` or `|` in place of `||`—as might result from a typographical error—would produce very strange results.

Using the precedence rules in an expression, relational and logical operators are evaluated from left to right. Because relational and logical operators are evaluated from left to right, the **associativity** of these operators is said to be from left to right.

Example 3-5 illustrates how logical expressions consisting of variables are evaluated.

EXAMPLE 3-5

Suppose you have the following declarations:

```
bool found = true;
bool flag = false;
int num = 20;
double x = 5.2;
int a = 5, b = 8;
char ch = 'B';
```

Consider the following expressions:

Expression	Value	Explanation
!found	false	Because found is true, !found is false.
!num	false	Because num is 20, which is nonzero, num is true, so !num is false.
!found && (x >= 0)	false	In this expression, !found is false. Also, because x is 5.2 and 5.2 >= 0 is true, x >= 0 is true. Therefore, the value of the expression !found && (x >= 0) is false && true, which evaluates to false.
!(found && (x >= 0))	false	In this expression, found && (x >= 0) is true && true, which evaluates to true. Therefore, the value of the expression !(found && (x >= 0)) is !true, which evaluates to false.
(num >= 0) && (num <= 100)	true	Here num is 20. Because 20 >= 0 is true, num >= 0 is true. Also, because 20 <= 100 is true, num <= 100 is true. Therefore, the value of the expression (num >= 0) && (num <= 100) is true && true, which evaluates to true.
('A' <= ch && ch <= 'Z')	true	In this expression, the value of ch is 'B'. Because 'A' <= 'B' is true, 'A' <= ch evaluates to true. Also, because 'B' <= 'Z' is true, ch <= 'Z' evaluates to true. Therefore, the value of the expression ('A' <= ch && ch <= 'Z') is true && true, which evaluates to true.

3

Expression	Value	Explanation
`(a + 2 <= b) && !flag`	`true`	Now `a + 2 = 5 + 2 = 7` and b is 8. Because `7 <= 8` is `true`, the expression `a + 2 <= b` evaluates to `true`. Also, because `flag` is `false`, `!flag` is `true`. Therefore, the value of the expression `(a + 2 <= b) && !flag` is `true && true`, which evaluates to `true`.

The following program evaluates and outputs the values of these logical expressions. Note that if a logical expression evaluates to `true`, the corresponding output is 1; if the logical expression evaluates to `false`, the corresponding output is 0, as shown in the output at the end of the program. (Recall that if the value of a logical expression is `true`, it evaluates to 1, and if the value of the logical expression is `false`, it evaluates to 0.)

```cpp
//************************************************************
// Author: D.S. Malik
//
// Program to illustrate how logical operators work.
//************************************************************

#include <iostream>

using namespace std;

int main()
{
    bool found = true;
    bool flag = false;
    int num = 20;
    double x = 5.2;
    int a = 5, b = 8;
    char ch = 'B';

    cout << "!found evaluates to " << !found << endl;

    cout << "!num evaluates to " << !num << endl;

    cout << "!found && (x >= 0) evaluates to "
         << (!found && (x >= 0)) << endl;

    cout << "!(found && (x >= 0)) evaluates to "
         << (!(found && (x >= 0))) << endl;

    cout << "(num >= 0) && (num <= 100) evaluates to "
         << ((num >= 0) && (num <= 100)) << endl;

    cout << "('A' <= ch && ch <= 'Z') evaluates to "
         << ('A' <= ch && ch <= 'Z') << endl;
```

```
    cout << "(a + 2 <= b)  && !flag evaluates to "
         << ((a + 2 <= b)  && !flag) << endl;

    return 0;
}
```

Sample Run:

```
!found evaluates to 0
!num evaluates to 0
!found && (x >= 0) evaluates to 0
!(found && (x >= 0)) evaluates to 0
(num >= 0) && (num <= 100) evaluates to 1
('A' <= ch && ch <= 'Z') evaluates to 1
(a + 2 <= b) && !flag evaluates to 1
```

You can insert parentheses into an expression to clarify its meaning. You can also use parentheses to override the precedence of operators. Using the standard order of precedence, the expression

```
11 > 5 || 6 < 15 && 7 >= 8
```

is equivalent to the following:

```
11 > 5 || (6 < 15 && 7 >= 8)
```

In this expression, 11 > 5 is **true**, 6 < 15 is **true**, and 7 >= 8 is **false**. Substitute these values in the expression 11 > 5 || (6 < 15 && 7 >= 8) to get **true** || (**true** && **false**) = **true** || **false** = **true**. Therefore, the expression 11 > 5 || (6 < 15 && 7 >= 8) evaluates to **true**.

EXAMPLE 3-6

Evaluate the following expression:

```
(17 < 4 * 3 + 5) || (8 * 2 == 4 * 4) && !(3 + 3 == 6)
```

Now,

```
      (17 < 4 * 3 + 5) || (8 * 2 == 4 * 4) && !(3 + 3 == 6)
   =  (17 < 12 + 5) || (16 == 16) && !(6 == 6)
   =  (17 < 17) || true && !(true)
   =  false || true && false
   =  false || false   (Because true && false is false)
   =  false
```

Therefore, the value of the original logical expression is **false**—that is, 0.

Short-Circuit Evaluation

Logical expressions in C++ are evaluated using a highly efficient algorithm. This algorithm is illustrated with the help of the following statements:

```
(x > y) || (x == 5)        //Line 1
(a == b) && (x >= 7)       //Line 2
```

In the statement in Line 1, the two operands of the operator || are the expressions (x > y) and (x == 5). This expression evaluates to true if either the operand (x > y) is true or the operand (x == 5) is true. With short-circuit evaluation, the computer evaluates the logical expression from left to right. As soon as the value of the entire logical expression is known, the evaluation stops. For example, in the statement in Line 1, if the operand (x > y) evaluates to true, then the entire expression evaluates to true because true || true is true and true || false is true. Therefore, the value of the operand (x == 5) has no bearing on the final outcome.

Similarly, in the statement in Line 2, the two operands of the operator && are (a == b) and (x >= 7). If the operand (a == b) evaluates to false, then the entire expression evaluates to false because false && true is false and false && false is false.

Short-circuit evaluation (of a logical expression): A process in which the computer evaluates a logical expression from left to right and stops as soon as the value of the expression is known.

EXAMPLE 3-7

Consider the following expressions:

```
(age >= 21) || (x == 5)        //Line 1
(grade == 'A') && (x >= 7)     //Line 2
```

For the expression in Line 1, suppose that the value of age is 25. Because (25 >= 21) is true and the logical operator used in the expression is ||, the expression evaluates to true. Due to short-circuit evaluation, the computer does not evaluate the expression (x == 5). Similarly, for the expression in Line 2, suppose that the value of grade is 'B'. Because ('B' == 'A') is false and the logical operator used in the expression is &&, the expression evaluates to false. The computer does not evaluate (x >= 7).

bool Data Type and Logical (Boolean) Expressions

In C++, logical (Boolean) expressions can be manipulated using bool variables. Recall that in C++, bool, true, and false are reserved words. Now consider the following declaration:

```
bool legalAge;
int age;
```

The statement

```
legalAge = true;
```

sets the value of the variable `legalAge` to `true`. The statement

```
legalAge = (age >= 21);
```

assigns the value `true` to `legalAge` if the value of `age` is greater than or equal to `21`. This statement assigns the value `false` to `legalAge` if the value of `age` is less than `21`. For example, if the value of `age` is `25`, the value assigned to `legalAge` is `true`. Similarly, if the value of `age` is `16`, the value assigned to `legalAge` is `false`.

Formatting Logical (Boolean) Expressions: A Precaution

Sometimes logical expressions do not behave as you might expect. Suppose, for example, that `num` is an `int` variable. Further suppose that you want to write a logical expression that evaluates to `true` if the value of `num` is between 0 and 10, including 0 and 10, and that evaluates to `false` otherwise. The following expression appears to represent a comparison of 0, `num`, and 10 that will yield the desired result:

```
0 <= num <= 10
```

Although this statement is a legal C++ expression, you will not get the desired result. Let us evaluate this expression for certain values of `num`. Suppose that the value of `num` is 5. Then:

```
0 <= num <= 10  = 0 <= 5 <= 10
                = (0 <= 5) <= 10    (Because relational operators are evaluated
                                    from left to right)
                = 1 <= 10           (Because 0 <= 5 is true, 0 <= 5
                = 1 (true)          evaluates to 1)
```

Now suppose that `num` = 20. Then:

```
0 <= num <= 10  = 0 <= 20 <= 10
                = (0 <= 20) <= 10   (Because relational operators are evaluated
                                    from left to right)
                = 1 <= 10           (Because 0 <= 20 is true, 0 <= 20
                = 1 (true)          evaluates to 1)
```

Clearly, this answer is incorrect. Because `num` is 20, it is not between 0 and 10, and 0 <= 20 <= 10 should not evaluate to `true`. Note that this expression will always evaluate to `true`, no matter what `num` is. This is because the expression 0 <= `num` evaluates to either 0 or 1, and 0 <= 10 is `true` and 1 <= 10 is `true`. So what is wrong with the expression 0 <= `num` <= 10? It is missing the logical operator `&&`. A correct way to write this expression in C++ is:

```
0 <= num && num <= 10
```

You must take care when formulating logical expressions. When creating a complex logical expression, you must use the proper logical operators.

Selection: `if` and `if...else`

Although there are only two logical values, `true` and `false`, they turn out to be extremely useful because they permit programs to incorporate decision making that alters the processing flow. The remainder of this chapter discusses ways to incorporate decisions into a program. In C++, there are three selections, or branch control structures: `if` statements, `if...else` statements, and the `switch` structure. This section discusses how `if` and `if...else` statements can be used to create one-way selection, two-way selection, and multiple selections. The `switch` structure is discussed later in this chapter.

One-Way Selection

A bank would like to send a notice to a customer if her or his checking account balance falls below the required minimum balance. That is, if the account balance is below the required minimum balance, it should send a notice to the customer; otherwise, it should do nothing. Similarly, if the policyholder of an insurance policy is a nonsmoker, the company would like to apply a 10% discount to the policy premium. Both of these examples involve one-way selection. In C++, one-way selections are incorporated using the `if` statement. The syntax of one-way selection is the following:

```
if (expression)
    statement
```

Note the elements of this syntax. It begins with the reserved word `if`, followed by an **expression** contained within parentheses, followed by a **statement**. Note that the parentheses around the **expression** are part of the syntax. The **expression** is sometimes called a **decision maker** because it decides whether to execute the **statement** that follows it. The **expression** is usually a logical expression. If the value of the **expression** is `true`, the **statement** executes. If the value is `false`, the **statement** does not execute, and the computer goes on to the next statement in the program. The **statement** following the **expression** is sometimes called the **action statement**. Figure 3-2 shows the flow of execution of the `if` statement (one-way selection).

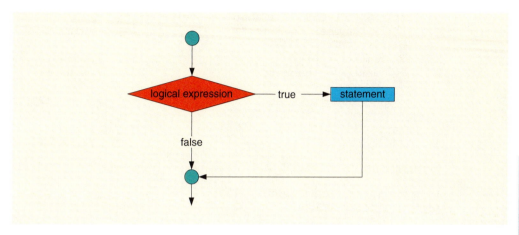

FIGURE 3-2 One-way selection

EXAMPLE 3-8

```
if (score >= 60)
    grade = 'P';
```

In this code, if the expression (`score >= 60`) evaluates to **true**, the assignment statement, `grade = 'P';`, executes. If the expression evaluates to **false**, the statements (if any) following the `if` structure execute. For example, if the value of `score` is 65, the value assigned to the variable `grade` is `'P'`.

EXAMPLE 3-9

The following C++ program finds the absolute value of an integer:

```
//**************************************************************
// Author: D.S. Malik
//
// This program determines the absolute value of an int value.
//**************************************************************

#include <iostream>                              //Line 1

using namespace std;                             //Line 2

int main()                                       //Line 3
{                                                //Line 4
    int number;                                  //Line 5

    cout << "Line 6: Enter an integer: ";        //Line 6
    cin >> number;                               //Line 7
    cout << endl;                                //Line 8
```

3

```
    cout << "Line 9: The absolute value of "
         << number << " is ";                    //Line 9

    if (number < 0)                              //Line 10
        number = -number;                        //Line 11

    cout << number << endl;                      //Line 12

    return 0;                                     //Line 13
}                                                 //Line 14
```

Sample Run: In this sample run, the user input is shaded.

```
Line 6: Enter an integer: -6734
Line 9: The absolute value of -6734 is 6734
```

The statement in Line 6 prompts the user to enter an integer; the statement in Line 7 inputs the number into the variable `number`. The statement in Line 10 checks whether `number` is negative. If `number` is negative, the statement in Line 11 changes `number` to a positive number. The statements in Line 9 and 12 output the number and its absolute value.

EXAMPLE 3-10

Consider the following statement:

```
if score >= 60        //syntax error
   grade = 'P';
```

This statement illustrates an incorrect version of an `if` statement. The parentheses around the logical expression are missing, which is a syntax error.

Putting a semicolon after the parentheses following the **expression** in an `if` statement (that is, before the **statement**) is a semantic error. If the semicolon immediately follows the closing parenthesis, the `if` statement will operate on the empty statement.

EXAMPLE 3-11

Consider the following C++ statements:

```
if (score >= 60);        //Line 1
    grade = 'P';         //Line 2
```

Because there is a semicolon at the end of the expression (see Line 1), the `if` statement in Line 1 terminates. The action of this `if` statement is null, and the statement in Line 2 is not part of the `if` statement in Line 1. Hence, the statement in Line 2 executes regardless of how the `if` statement evaluates.

Two-Way Selection

There are many programming situations in which you must choose between two alternatives. For example, if a part-time employee works overtime, the paycheck is calculated using the overtime payment formula; otherwise, the paycheck is calculated using the regular formula. This is an example of two-way selection. To choose between two alternatives—that is, to implement two-way selections—C++ provides the `if...else` statement. Two-way selection uses the following syntax:

```
if (expression)
    statement1
else
    statement2
```

Take a moment to examine this syntax. It begins with the reserved word `if`, followed by a logical expression contained within parentheses, followed by a statement, followed by the reserved word `else`, followed by a second statement. Statements 1 and 2 are any valid C++ statements. In a two-way selection, if the value of the `expression` is `true`, statement1 executes. If the value of the `expression` is `false`, statement2 executes. Figure 3-3 shows the flow of execution of the `if...else` statement (two-way selection).

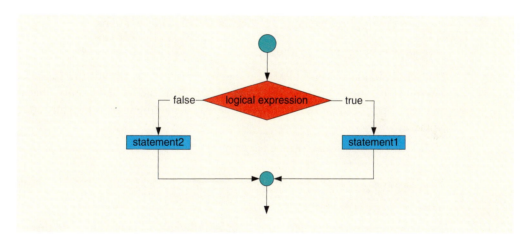

FIGURE 3-3 Two-way selection

EXAMPLE 3-12

Consider the following statements:

```
if (hours > 40.0)                          //Line 1
    wages = 40.0 * rate +
            1.5 * rate * (hours - 40.0);   //Line 2
else                                       //Line 3
    wages = hours * rate;                  //Line 4
```

If the value of the variable `hours` is greater than `40.0`, then the `wages` include overtime payment. Suppose that `hours` is `50`. The expression in the `if` statement, in Line 1, evaluates to `true`, so the statement in Line 2 executes. On the other hand, if `hours` is `30`, or any number less than or equal to `40`, the expression in the `if` statement, in Line 1, evaluates to `false`. In this case, the program skips the statement in Line 2 and executes the statement in Line 4—that is, the statement following the reserved word `else` executes.

In a two-way selection statement, putting a semicolon after the `expression` and before `statement1` creates a syntax error. If the `if` statement ends with a semicolon, `statement1` is no longer part of the `if` statement, and the `else` part of the `if...else` statement stands all by itself. There is no stand-alone `else` statement in C++. That is, it cannot be separated from the `if` statement.

EXAMPLE 3-13

The following statements show an example of a syntax error:

```
if (hours > 40.0);                           //Line 1
    wages = 40.0 * rate +
            1.5 * rate * (hours - 40.0);     //Line 2
else                                         //Line 3
    wages = hours * rate;                    //Line 4
```

The semicolon at the end of the `if` statement (see Line 1) ends the `if` statement, so the statement in Line 2 separates the `else` clause from the `if` statement. That is, `else` is all by itself. Because there is no stand-alone `else` statement in C++, this code generates a syntax error.

EXAMPLE 3-14

The following program determines an employee's weekly wages. If the hours worked exceed `40`, wages include overtime payment.

```
//*************************************************************
// Author: D.S. Malik
//
// This program computes and outputs the weekly wages of an
// employee.
//*************************************************************

#include <iostream>                          //Line 1
#include <iomanip>                           //Line 2

using namespace std;                         //Line 3
```

```
int main()                                              //Line 4
{                                                       //Line 5
    double wages, rate, hours;

    cout << fixed << showpoint << setprecision(2);      //Line 6
    cout << "Line 7: Enter working hours and rate: ";   //Line 7
    cin >> hours >> rate;                               //Line 8

    if (hours > 40.0)                                   //Line 9
        wages = 40.0 * rate +
                1.5 * rate * (hours - 40.0);            //Line 10
    else                                                //Line 11
        wages = hours * rate;                           //Line 12

    cout << endl;                                       //Line 13
    cout << "Line 14: The wages are $" << wages
         << endl;                                       //Line 14

    return 0;                                           //Line 15
}                                                       //Line 16
```

Sample Run: In this sample run, the user input is shaded.

```
Line 7: Enter working hours and rate: 56.45 12.50
Line 14: The wages are $808.44
```

The statement in Line 6 sets the output of the floating-point numbers in a fixed decimal format, with a decimal point, trailing zeros, and two decimal places. The statement in Line 7 prompts the user to input the number of hours worked and the pay rate. The statement in Line 8 inputs these values into the variables **hours** and **rate**, respectively. The statement in Line 9 checks whether the value of the variable **hours** is greater than **40.0**. If **hours** is greater than **40.0**, then the wages are calculated by the statement in Line 10, which includes overtime payment. Otherwise, the wages are calculated by the statement in Line 12. The statement in Line 14 outputs the wages.

Let us now consider more examples of `if` statements and examine some of the semantic errors that can occur.

EXAMPLE 3-15

Consider the following statements:

```
if (score >= 60)
    grade = 'P';
    cout << "The grade is " << grade << endl;
```

These statements contain a semantic error. The `if` statement acts on only one statement, which is `grade = 'P';`. The `cout` statement executes regardless of whether (`score >= 60`) is `true` or `false`.

Example 3-16 illustrates another common mistake.

EXAMPLE 3-16

Consider the following statements:

```
if (score >= 60)                  //Line 1
    cout << "Passing" << endl;    //Line 2
    cout << "Failing" << endl;    //Line 3
```

If the expression (score >= 60) evaluates to **false**, the output statement in Line 2 does not execute. So the output would be **Failing**. That is, this set of statements performs the same action as an **if...else** statement. It will execute the output statement in Line 3 rather than the output statement in Line 2. For example, if the value of score is 50, these statements will output the following line:

```
Failing
```

However, if the expression (score >= 60) evaluates to **true**, the program will execute both the output statements, giving a very unsatisfactory result. For example, if the value of score is 70, these statements will output the following lines:

```
Passing
Failing
```

The **if** statement controls the execution of only the statement in Line 2. The statement in Line 3 always executes.

The correct code to print **Passing** or **Failing**, depending on the value of score, is:

```
if (score >= 60)
    cout << "Passing" << endl;
else
    cout << "Failing" << endl;
```

Compound (Block of) Statements

The **if** and **if...else** structures control only one statement at a time. Suppose, however, that you want to execute more than one statement if the **expression** in an **if** or **if...else** statement evaluates to **true**. To permit more complex statements, C++ provides a structure called a **compound statement** or a **block of statements**. A compound statement takes the following form:

```
{
    statement1
    statement2
        .
        .
        .
    statementn
}
```

That is, a compound statement consists of a sequence of statements enclosed in curly braces, { and }. In an `if` or `if...else` structure, a compound statement functions as if it were a single statement. Thus, instead of having a simple two-way selection similar to

```
if (age >= 18)
    cout << "Eligible to vote." << endl;
else
    cout << "Not eligible to vote." << endl;
```

you could include compound statements, similar to the following code:

```
if (age >= 18)
{
    cout << "Eligible to vote." << endl;
    cout << "No longer a minor." << endl;
}
else
{
    cout << "Not eligible to vote." << endl;
    cout << "Still a minor." << endl;
}
```

The compound statement is very useful and will be used in most of the structured statements in this chapter.

Multiple Selections: Nested `if`

In the previous sections, you learned how to implement one-way and two-way selections in a program. Some problems require the implementation of more than two alternatives. For example, suppose that if the checking account balance is more than $50,000, the interest rate is 7%; if the balance is between $25,000 and $49,999.99, the interest rate is 5%; if the balance is between $1000 and $24,999.99, the interest rate is 3%; otherwise, the interest rate is 0%. This particular problem has four alternatives—that is, multiple selection paths. You can include multiple selection paths in a program by using an `if...else` structure, if the action statement itself is an `if` or `if...else` statement. When one control statement is located within another, it is said to be **nested**.

Example 3-17 illustrates how to incorporate multiple selections using a nested `if...else` structure.

EXAMPLE 3-17

Suppose that `balance` and `interestRate` are variables of type `double`. The following statements determine the `interestRate` depending on the value of the `balance`:

```
if (balance > 50000.00)            //Line 1
    interestRate = 0.07;           //Line 2
else                               //Line 3
    if (balance >= 25000.00)       //Line 4
        interestRate = 0.05;       //Line 5
```

```
    else                            //Line 6
        if (balance >= 1000.00)     //Line 7
            interestRate = 0.03;    //Line 8
        else                        //Line 9
            interestRate = 0.00;    //Line 10
```

A nested `if...else` structure demands the answer to an important question: How do you know which `else` is paired with which `if`? Recall that in C++ there is no stand-alone `else` statement. Every `else` must be paired with an `if`. The rule to pair an `else` with an `if` is as follows:

Pairing an `else` with an `if`: In a nested `if` statement, C++ associates an `else` with the most recent incomplete `if`—that is, the most recent `if` that has not been paired with an `else`.

Using this rule, in Example 3-17, the `else` in Line 3 is paired with the `if` in Line 1. The `else` in Line 6 is paired with the `if` in Line 4, and the `else` in Line 9 is paired with the `if` in Line 7.

To avoid excessive indentation, the code in Example 3-17 can be rewritten as follows:

```
if (balance > 50000.00)              //Line 1
    interestRate = 0.07;             //Line 2
else if (balance >= 25000.00)        //Line 3
    interestRate = 0.05;             //Line 4
else if (balance >= 1000.00)         //Line 5
    interestRate = 0.03;             //Line 6
else                                 //Line 7
    interestRate = 0.00;             //Line 8
```

Examples 3-18 through 3-22 will help you to see the various ways in which you can use nested `if` structures to implement multiple selection.

EXAMPLE 3-18

Assume that `score` is a variable of type `int`. Based on the value of `score`, the following code outputs the grade:

```
if (score >= 90)
    cout << "The grade is A." << endl;
else if (score >= 80)
    cout << "The grade is B." << endl;
else if (score >= 70)
    cout << "The grade is C." << endl;
else if (score >= 60)
    cout << "The grade is D." << endl;
else
    cout << "The grade is F." << endl;
```

EXAMPLE 3-19

Assume that all variables are properly declared, and consider the following statements:

```
if (temperature >= 50)                                  //Line 1
    if (temperature >= 80)                              //Line 2
        cout << "Good day for swimming." << endl;       //Line 3
    else                                                //Line 4
        cout << "Good day for golfing." << endl;        //Line 5
else                                                    //Line 6
    cout << "Good day to play tennis." << endl;         //Line 7
```

In this C++ code, the else in Line 4 is paired with the if in Line 2, and the else in Line 6 is paired with the if in Line 1. Note that the else in Line 4 cannot be paired with the if in Line 1. If you pair the else in Line 4 with the if in Line 1, the if in Line 2 becomes the action statement part of the if in Line 1, leaving the else in Line 6 dangling. Also, the statements in Lines 2 though 5 form the statement part of the if in Line 1. The indentation does not determine the pairing, but it should be used to communicate the pairing.

To clarify the pairing of an else with an if, you can write the preceding code as follows:

```
if (temperature >= 50)                                  //Line 1
{                                                       //Line 2
    if (temperature >= 80)                              //Line 3
        cout << "Good day for swimming." << endl;       //Line 4
    else                                                //Line 5
        cout << "Good day for golfing." << endl;        //Line 6
}                                                       //Line 7
else                                                    //Line 8
    cout << "Good day to play tennis." << endl;         //Line 9
```

EXAMPLE 3-20

Assume that all variables are properly declared, and consider the following statements:

```
if (temperature >= 70)                                  //Line 1
    if (temperature >= 80)                              //Line 2
        cout << "Good day for swimming." << endl;       //Line 3
    else                                                //Line 4
        cout << "Good day for golfing." << endl;        //Line 5
```

In this code, the else in Line 4 is paired with the if in Line 2. Note that for the else in Line 4, the most recent incomplete if is in Line 2. In this code, the if in Line 1 has no else and is a one-way selection. Once again, the indentation does not determine the pairing, but it communicates the pairing.

EXAMPLE 3-21

Assume that all variables are properly declared, and consider the following statements:

```
if (GPA >= 2.0)                                           //Line 1
    if (GPA >= 3.9)                                       //Line 2
        cout << "Dean\'s Honor List." << endl;            //Line 3
else                                                      //Line 4
    cout << "Current GPA below graduation requirement. "
         << "\nSee your academic advisor." << endl;    //Line 5
```

This code is awkward. Following the rule of pairing an else with an if, the else in Line 4 is paired with the if in Line 2. However, this pairing produces an unsatisfactory result. Suppose that GPA is 3.8. The expression in the if in Line 1 evaluates to true, and the statement part of the if, which is an if...else structure, executes. Because GPA is 3.8, the expression in the if in Line 2 evaluates to false, and the else associated with this if executes, producing the following output:

```
Current GPA below graduation requirement.
See your academic advisor.
```

However, a student with a GPA of 3.8 would graduate with some type of honor. In fact, the code intended to print the message

```
Current GPA below graduation requirement.
See your academic advisor.
```

only if the GPA is less than 2.0, and the message

```
Dean's Honor List.
```

if the GPA is greater than or equal to 3.9. To achieve that result, the else in Line 4 needs to be paired with the if in Line 1. To pair the else in Line 4 with the if in Line 1, you need to use a compound statement as follows:

```
if (GPA >= 2.0)                                           //Line 1
{                                                         //Line 2
    if (GPA >= 3.9)                                       //Line 3
        cout << "Dean\'s Honor List." << endl;            //Line 4
}                                                         //Line 5
else                                                      //Line 6
    cout << "Current GPA below graduation requirement. "
         << "\nSee your academic advisor." << endl;    //Line 7
```

In cases such as this one, the general rule is that you cannot look inside a block (that is, inside the braces) to pair an else with an if. The else in Line 6 cannot be paired with the if in Line 3 because the if statement in Line 3 is enclosed within braces, and the else in Line 6 cannot look inside those braces. Therefore, the else in Line 6 is paired with the if in Line 1.

EXAMPLE 3-22

Assume that all variables are properly declared, and consider the following statements:

```
if (gender == 'M')                   //Line 1
    if (age < 21 )                   //Line 2
        policyRate = 0.05;           //Line 3
    else                             //Line 4
        policyRate = 0.35;           //Line 5
else if (gender == 'F')              //Line 6
    if (age < 21 )                   //Line 7
        policyRate = 0.04;           //Line 8
    else                             //Line 9
        policyRate = 0.30;           //Line 10
```

In this code, the `else` in Line 4 is paired with the `if` in Line 2. Note that for the `else` in Line 4, the most recent incomplete `if` is the `if` in Line 2. The `else` in Line 6 is paired with the `if` in Line 1. The `else` in Line 9 is paired with the `if` in Line 7. Once again, the indentation does not determine the pairing, but it communicates the pairing.

Comparing `if...else` Statements with a Series of `if` Statements

Consider the following C++ program segments, all of which accomplish the same task:

```
a. if (month == 1)                        //Line 1
       cout << "January" << endl;         //Line 2
   else if (month == 2)                   //Line 3
       cout << "February" << endl;        //Line 4
   else if (month == 3)                   //Line 5
       cout << "March" << endl;           //Line 6
   else if (month == 4)                   //Line 7
        cout << "April" << endl;          //Line 8
   else if (month == 5)                   //Line 9
       cout << "May" << endl;             //Line 10
   else if (month == 6)                   //Line 11
       cout << "June" << endl;            //Line 12

b. if (month == 1)
       cout << "January" << endl;
   if (month == 2)
       cout << "February" << endl;
   if (month == 3)
       cout << "March" << endl;
   if (month == 4)
       cout << "April" << endl;
   if (month == 5)
       cout << "May" << endl;
   if (month == 6)
       cout << "June" << endl;
```

Program segment (a) is written as a sequence of `if...else` statements; program segment (b) is written as a series of `if` statements. Both program segments accomplish the same thing. If `month` is 3, then both program segments output `March`. If `month` is 1, then in program segment (a), the expression in the `if` statement in Line 1 evaluates to `true`. The statement (in Line 2) associated with this `if` then executes; the rest of the structure, which is the `else` of this `if` statement, is skipped; and the remaining `if` statements are not evaluated. In program segment (b), the computer has to evaluate the expression in each `if` statement because there is no `else` statement. As a consequence, program segment (b) executes more slowly than does program segment (a).

A second reason to use `if-else if` rather than a sequence of `if`s is that sometimes more than one condition will be true, but only the consequent for the "first" of the `true` conditions should be executed. For example, in Example 3-18, if `score` is 95, then expressions in all the `if` statements are `true`, but only the first `cout` statement should be executed.

Input Failure and the `if` Statement

In Chapter 2, you saw that an attempt to read invalid data causes the input stream to enter a fail state. Once an input stream enters a fail state, all subsequent input statements associated with that input stream are ignored, and the computer continues to execute the program, which produces erroneous results. You can use `if` statements to check the status of an input stream variable and, if the input stream enters the fail state, include instructions that stop program execution.

In addition to reading invalid data, other events can cause an input stream to enter the fail state. Two additional common causes of input failure are the following:

- Attempting to open an input file that does not exist
- Attempting to read beyond the end of an input file

One way to address these causes of input failure is to check the status of the input stream variable. You can check the status by using the input stream variable as the logical expression in an `if` statement. If the last input succeeded, the input stream variable evaluates to `true`, if the last input failed, it evaluates to `false`.

The statement

```
if (cin)
    cout << "Input is OK." << endl;
```

prints

```
Input is OK.
```

if the last input from the standard input device succeeded. Similarly, if `infile` is an `ifstream` variable, the statement

```
if (!infile)
    cout << "Input failed." << endl;
```

prints

```
Input failed.
```

if the last input associated with the stream variable `infile` failed.

Suppose an input stream variable tries to open a file for inputting data into a program. If the input file does not exist, you can use the value of the input stream variable, in conjunction with the **return** statement, to terminate the program.

Recall that the last statement included in the function `main` is:

```
return 0;
```

This statement returns a value of 0 to the operating system when the program terminates. A value of 0 indicates that the program terminated normally and that no error occurred during program execution. Values of type **int** other than 0 can also be returned to the operating system via the **return** statement. The return of any value other than 0, however, indicates that something went wrong during program execution.

The **return** statement can appear anywhere in the program. Whenever a **return** statement executes, it immediately exits the function in which it appears. In the case of the function `main`, the program terminates when the **return** statement executes. You can use these properties of the **return** statement to terminate the function `main` whenever the input stream fails. This technique is especially useful when a program tries to open an input file. Consider the following statements:

```
ifstream infile;

infile.open("inputdat.dat");   //open inputdat.dat

if (!infile)
{
    cout << "Cannot open the input file. "
         << "The program terminates." << endl;
    return 1;
}
```

Suppose that the file `inputdat.dat` does not exist. The operation to open this file fails, causing the input stream to enter the fail state. As a logical expression, the file stream variable `infile` then evaluates to **false**. Because `infile` evaluates to **false**, the expression `!infile` (in the **if** statement) evaluates to **true**, and the body of the **if** statement executes. The message

```
Cannot open the input file. The program terminates.
```

is printed on the screen, and the **return** statement terminates the program by returning a value of 1 to the operating system.

Let's now use the code that responds to input failure by including these features in the Programming Example: Student Grade from Chapter 2. Recall that this program calculates the average test score based on data from an input file and then outputs the results to another file. The following programming code is the same as the code from Chapter 2, except that it includes statements to exit the program if the input file does not exist:

```cpp
//***************************************************************
// Author: D.S. Malik
//
// This program reads a student's name and the test scores from
// a file and determines the average test score. If the input
// file does not exist, the program is terminated.
//***************************************************************

#include <iostream>
#include <fstream>
#include <iomanip>
#include <string>

using namespace std;

int main()
{
    ifstream inFile;   //input file stream variable
    ofstream outFile;  //output file stream variable

    double test1, test2, test3, test4, test5;
    double average;

    string firstName;
    string lastName;

    inFile.open("test.txt"); //open the input file

    if (!inFile)
    {
        cout << "Cannot open the input file. "
             << "The program terminates." << endl;
        return 1;
    }

    outFile.open("testavg.out");   //open the output file

    outFile << fixed << showpoint;
    outFile << setprecision(2);

    cout << "Processing data" << endl;

    inFile >> firstName >> lastName;
    outFile << "Student name: " << firstName
            << " " << lastName << endl;

    inFile >> test1 >> test2 >> test3
           >> test4 >> test5;
```

```
outFile << "Test scores: " << setw(4) << test1
        << setw(4) << test2 << setw(4) << test3
        << setw(4) << test4 << setw(4) << test5
        << endl;

average = (test1 + test2 + test3 + test4 + test5) / 5.0;

outFile << "Average test score: " << setw(6)
        << average << endl;

inFile.close();
outFile.close();

return 0;
}
```

Confusion Between the Equality Operator (==) and the Assignment Operator (=)

Recall that if the decision-making expression in the `if` statement evaluates to `true`, the `statement` part of the `if` statement executes. In addition, the `expression` is usually a logical expression. However, C++ allows you to use *any* expression that can be evaluated to either `true` or `false` as an `expression` in the `if` statement. Consider the following statement:

```
if (x = 5)
    cout << "The value is five." << endl;
```

The `expression`—that is, the decision maker—in the `if` statement is x = 5. The expression x = 5 is called an assignment expression because the operator = appears in the expression and there is no semicolon at the end.

This expression is evaluated as follows. First, the right side of the operator = is evaluated, which evaluates to 5. The value 5 is then assigned to x. Moreover, the value 5—that is, the new value of x—also becomes the value of the expression in the `if` statement—that is, the value of the assignment expression. Because 5 is nonzero, the expression in the `if` statement evaluates to `true`, so the statement part of the `if` statement outputs the following: The value is five.

No matter how experienced a programmer is, almost everyone makes the mistake of using = in place of == at one time or another. One reason these two operators are often confused is that most programming languages use = as an equality operator. Thus, experience with other programming languages can create confusion. Sometimes the error is merely typographical, which is another reason to be careful when typing code. Another reason people confuse = and == is that the = is the equality sign in conventional mathematical usage.

Despite the fact that an assignment expression can be used as an expression, using the assignment operator in place of the equality operator can cause serious problems in a program. For example, suppose that the discount on a car insurance policy is based on the insured's driving record. A driving record of 1 means that the driver is accident-free and he or she will receive a 25% discount on the policy. The statement

```
if (drivingCode == 1)
    cout << "The discount on the policy is 25%." << endl;
```

outputs

```
The discount on the policy is 25%.
```

only if the value of `drivingCode` is 1. However, the statement

```
if (drivingCode = 1)
    cout << "The discount on the policy is 25%." << endl;
```

always outputs

```
The discount on the policy is 25%.
```

because the right side of the assignment expression evaluates to 1, which is nonzero and so evaluates to **true**. Therefore, the expression in the **if** statement evaluates to **true**, outputting the following line of text: `The discount on the policy is 25%.` Also, the value 1 is assigned to the variable `drivingCode`. Suppose that before the **if** statement executes, the value of the variable `drivingCode` is 4. After the **if** statement executes, not only is the output wrong, but the new value also replaces the old driving code.

The appearance of = in place of == resembles a *silent killer*. It is not a syntax error, so the compiler does not warn you of an error. Rather, it is a logical error.

 NOTE   Using = in place of == can cause serious problems, especially if it happens in a looping statement. Chapter 4 discusses looping structures.

The appearance of the equality operator in place of the assignment operator can also cause errors in a program. For example, suppose **x**, **y**, and **z** are **int** variables. The statement

```
x = y + z;
```

assigns the value of the expression **y + z** to **x**. The statement

```
x == y + z;
```

compares the value of the expression **y + z** with the value of **x**; the value of **x** remains the same, however. If somewhere else in the program you are counting on the value of **x** being **y + z**, a logic error will occur, the program output will be incorrect, and you will receive no warning of this situation from the compiler. The compiler provides feedback only about syntax errors, not logic errors. For this reason, you must use extra care when working with the equality operator and the assignment operator.

Conditional Operator (?:) (Optional)

Certain `if...else` statements can be written in a more concise way by using C++'s conditional operator. The **conditional operator**, written as `? :`, is a **ternary operator**, which means that it takes three arguments. The syntax for using the conditional operator is:

```
expression1 ? expression2 : expression3
```

This type of statement is called a **conditional expression**. The conditional expression is evaluated as follows: If `expression1` evaluates to a nonzero integer (that is, to `true`), the result of the conditional expression is `expression2`. Otherwise, the result of the conditional expression is `expression3`.

Consider the following statements:

```
if (a >= b)
    max = a;
else
    max = b;
```

You can use the conditional operator to simplify the writing of this `if...else` statement as follows:

```
max = (a >= b) ? a : b;
```

`switch` Structures

Recall that there are three selection, or branch, structures in C++. The first two selection structures, which are implemented with `if` and `if...else` statements, usually require the evaluation of a (logical) expression. The third selection structure, which does not require the evaluation of a logical expression, is called the **switch structure**. C++'s `switch` structure gives the computer the power to choose from among many alternatives.

A general syntax of the `switch` statement is:

```
switch (expression)
{
case value1:
    statements1
    break;

case value2:
    statements2
    break;
    .
    .
    .
case valuen:
    statementsn
    break;

default:
    statements
}
```

In C++, `switch`, `case`, `break`, and `default` are reserved words. In a `switch` structure, first the `expression` is evaluated. The value of the `expression` is then used to perform the actions specified in the statements that follow the reserved word `case`. Recall that, in a syntax, shading indicates an optional part of the definition.

Although it need not be, the `expression` is usually an identifier. Whether it is an identifier or an expression, the value can be only integral, such as `int` or `char`. The `expression` is sometimes called the **selector**. Its value determines which statement is selected for execution. A particular `case` value should appear only once. One or more statements may follow a `case` label, so you do not need to use braces to turn multiple statements into a single compound statement. The `break` statement may or may not appear after each statement. Figure 3-4 shows the flow of execution of the `switch` statement.

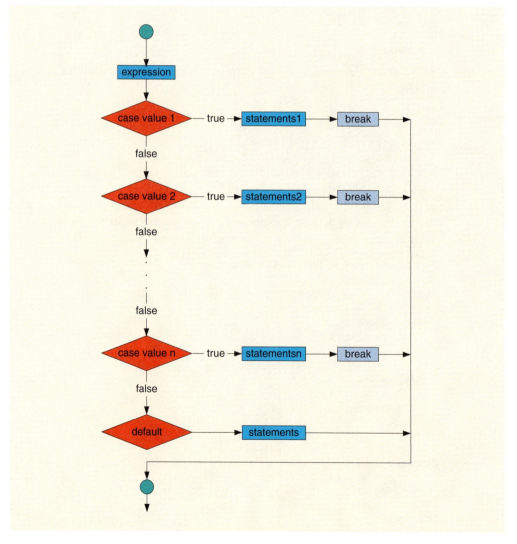

FIGURE 3-4 `switch` statement

The `switch` statement executes according to the following rules:

1. When the value of the `expression` is matched against a `case` value (also called a label), the statements execute until either a `break` statement is found or the end of the `switch` structure is reached.

2. If the value of the `expression` does not match any of the `case` values, the statements following the `default` label execute. If the `switch` structure has no `default` label, and if the value of the `expression` does not match any of the `case` values, the entire `switch` statement is skipped. Note that although `default`s aren't required in a `switch` statement, it's good practice to include them, even if you think they'll never be needed. If nothing else, they are a useful debugging aid.

3. A `break` statement causes an immediate *exit* from the `switch` structure.

EXAMPLE 3-23

Consider the following statements, where `grade` is a variable of type `char`:

```
switch (grade)
{
case 'A':
    cout << "The grade is 4.0.";
    break;

case 'B':
    cout << "The grade is 3.0.";
    break;

case 'C':
    cout << "The grade is 2.0.";
    break;

case 'D':
    cout << "The grade is 1.0.";
    break;

case 'F':
    cout << "The grade is 0.0.";
    break;

default:
    cout << "The grade is invalid.";
}
```

In this example, the expression in the `switch` statement is a variable identifier. The variable `grade` is of type `char`, which is an integral type. The possible values of `grade` are `'A'`, `'B'`, `'C'`, `'D'`, and `'F'`. Each `case` label specifies a different action to take, depending on the value of `grade`. If the value of `grade` is `'A'`, the output is:

```
The grade is 4.0.
```

EXAMPLE 3-24

The following program illustrates the effect of the **break** statement. It asks the user to input a number between 0 and 7.

```cpp
//*************************************************************
// Author: D.S. Malik
//
// This program shows the effect of break statements in a
// switch structure.
//*************************************************************

#include <iostream>                                    //Line 1

using namespace std;                                   //Line 2

int main()                                             //Line 3
{                                                      //Line 4
    int num;                                           //Line 5

    cout << "Enter an integer between 0 and 7: ";      //Line 6
    cin >> num;                                        //Line 7
    cout << endl;                                      //Line 8

    cout << "The number you entered is " << num
         << endl;                                      //Line 9

    switch (num)                                       //Line 10
    {                                                  //Line 11
    case 0:                                            //Line 12
    case 1:                                            //Line 13
        cout << "Learning to use ";                    //Line 14
    case 2:                                            //Line 15
        cout << "C++'s ";                              //Line 16
    case 3:                                            //Line 17
        cout << "switch structure." << endl;           //Line 18
        break;                                         //Line 19

    case 4:                                            //Line 20
        break;                                         //Line 21

    case 5:                                            //Line 22
        cout << "This program shows the effect ";      //Line 23
    case 6:                                            //Line 24
    case 7:                                            //Line 25
        cout << "of the break statement." << endl;     //Line 26
        break;                                         //Line 27

    default:                                           //Line 28
        cout << "The number is out of range." << endl; //Line 29
    }                                                  //Line 30
```

```
    cout << "Out of the switch structure." << endl;      //Line 31

    return 0;                                             //Line 32
}                                                         //Line 33
```

Sample Runs: These outputs were obtained by executing the preceding program several times. In each of these outputs, the user input is shaded.

Sample Run 1:

```
Enter an integer between 0 and 7: 0

The number you entered is 0
Learning to use C++'s switch structure.
Out of the switch structure.
```

Sample Run 2:

```
Enter an integer between 0 and 7: 2

The number you entered is 2
C++'s switch structure.
Out of the switch structure.
```

Sample Run 3:

```
Enter an integer between 0 and 7: 4

The number you entered is 4
Out of the switch structure.
```

Sample Run 4:

```
Enter an integer between 0 and 7: 7

The number you entered is 7
of the break statement.
Out of the switch structure.
```

A walk-through of this program, using certain values of the `switch` expression, num, can help you understand how the `break` statement functions. If the value of num is 0, the value of the `switch` expression matches the `case` value 0. All statements following `case` 0: execute until a `break` statement appears.

The first `break` statement appears in Line 19, just before the `case` value of 4. Even though the value of the `switch` expression does not match any of the `case` values (that is, 1, 2, or 3), the statements following these values execute.

When the value of the `switch` expression matches a `case` value, *all* statements execute until a `break` is encountered, and the program skips all `case` labels in between. Similarly, if the value of num is 3, it matches the `case` value of 3 and the statements following this label execute until the **break** statement is encountered in Line 19. If the value of num is 4, it matches the **case** value of 4. In this situation, the action is empty because only the **break** statement, in Line 21, follows the **case** value of 4.

EXAMPLE 3-25

Although a **switch** structure's **case** values (labels) are limited, the **switch** statement **expression** can be as complex as necessary. For example, consider the following **switch** statement:

```
switch (score / 10)
{
case 0:
case 1:
case 2:
case 3:
case 4:
case 5:
     grade = 'F';
     break;

case 6:
     grade = 'D';
     break;

case 7:
     grade = 'C';
     break;

case 8:
     grade = 'B';
     break;

case 9:
case 10:
     grade = 'A';
     break;

default:
     cout << "Invalid test score." << endl;
}
```

Assume that **score** is an **int** variable with values between 0 and 100. If **score** is 75, then **score** / 10 = 75 / 10 = 7, and the grade assigned is **'C'**. If the value of **score** is between 0 and 59, then the grade is **'F'**. If **score** is between 0 and 59, **score** / 10 is 0, 1, 2, 3, 4, or 5. Each of these values corresponds to the grade **'F'**.

Therefore, in this **switch** structure, the action statements of **case** 0, **case** 1, **case** 2, **case** 3, **case** 4, and **case** 5 are all the same. Rather than write the statement **grade = 'F';** followed by the **break** statement for each of the **case** values of 0, 1, 2, 3, 4, and 5, you can simplify the programming code by first specifying all of the case values (as shown in the preceding code) and then specifying the desired action statement. The **case** values of 9 and 10 follow similar conventions.

In addition to being a variable identifier or a complex expression, the **switch** expression can evaluate to a logical value.

```
switch (age >= 18)
{
case true:
    cout << "Old enough to be drafted." << endl;
    cout << "Old enough to vote." << endl;
    break;

case false:
    cout << "Not old enough to be drafted." << endl;
    cout << "Not old enough to vote." << endl;
}
```

If the value of **age** is 25, the expression **age >= 18** evaluates to **true**. If the **expression** evaluates to **true**, the statements following the **case** label **true** execute. If the value of **age** is 14, the expression **age >= 18** evaluates to **false**—and the statements following the **case** label **false** execute.

Note that the preceding **switch** structure does not include the **default** label, because the expression in the **switch** expression evaluates only to 0 (**false**) or 1 (**true**), that is, the **default** label will not be reachable.

As you can see from the preceding examples, the **switch** statement is an elegant way to implement multiple selections. You will see the use of a **switch** statement in the programming example at the end of this chapter. Even though no fixed rules exist that can be applied to decide whether to use an **if...else** structure or a **switch** structure to implement multiple selections, the following considerations should be remembered. If multiple selections involve a range of values, you should use either an **if...else** structure or a **switch** structure, wherein you convert each range to a finite set of values.

For instance, in Example 3-25, the value of **grade** depends on the value of **score**. If **score** is between 0 and 59, **grade** is **'F'**. Because **score** is an **int** variable, 60 values correspond to the grade of **'F'**. If you list all 60 values as **case** values, the **switch** statement could be very long. However, dividing by 10 reduces these 60 values to only 6 values: 0, 1, 2, 3, 4, and 5.

If the range of values consists of infinitely many values and you cannot reduce them to a set containing a finite number of values, you must use the **if...else** structure. For example, if **score** happens to be a **double** variable, the number of values between 0 and 60 is infinite. However, you can use the expression **static_cast<int>(score) / 10** and still reduce this infinite number of values to just six values.

Avoiding Bugs by Avoiding Partially Understood Concepts and Techniques

By now you've probably written enough programs to realize that even small errors can prevent a program from running correctly or from running at all. For example, the omission of parentheses around the condition associated with an `if` statement, such as

```
if score >= 90
```

or an unintended semicolon following the condition of an `if` statement, such as

```
if (hours > 40.0);
```

can prevent successful compilation or correct execution. As a C++ programmer, it is not sufficient to be mostly correct in your use of concepts and techniques. Even though there are many ways to solve a problem, the approach you take must make correct use of concepts and techniques. If you fail to do so, either you will have no solution at all, or your solution will be deficient. If you have a partial understanding of a concept or technique, don't use that concept or technique until your understanding is complete.

The problem of using partially understood concepts and techniques can be illustrated with the `switch` structure that you just learned. Recall Example 3-25 and consider the following statements where we assume again that `grade` is an `int` variable:

```
switch (grade)
{
case 5:
    cout << "The grade is A." << endl;

case 4:
    cout << "The grade is B." << endl;

case 3:
    cout << "The grade is C." << endl;

case 2:
    cout << "The grade is D." << endl;

case 1:
    cout << "The grade is F." << endl;

default:
    cout << "The grade is invalid." << endl;
}
```

If the value of `grade` is of type `int` with a value other than 5, 4, 3, 2, or 1, these statements will produce correct results, but if the value of `grade` is 5, 4, 3, 2, or 1, these statements will produce incorrect results. Can you see why?

Let's suppose that the value of `grade` is 4. The value of `grade` does not match case label 5, but it does match case label 4. So, as we intended

```
The grade is B.
```

is printed. However,

```
The grade is C.
The grade is D.
The grade is F.
The grade is invalid.
```

also are printed. But why? It seems clear that only one `cout` statement is associated with each case label. The problem is a result of having only a partial understanding of how the `switch` structure works. Specifically, when no `break` statement is included, after executing the statement(s) associated with the matching case label, execution continues with the statement(s) associated with the next case label. In this example, this execution continues with all the remaining statements in the `switch` structure, resulting in the printing of four unintended lines.

The concepts and techniques associated with the C++ programming language are simple enough to be understood completely when they are learned one at a time and in a logical order, as we present them in this book. By taking time to understand each concept and technique completely before using it, you will save yourself hours of debugging time.

PROGRAMMING EXAMPLE: Cable Company Billing

This programming example demonstrates a program that calculates a customer's bill for a local cable company. There are two types of customers: residential and business. There are two rates for calculating a cable bill: one for residential customers and one for business customers. For residential customers, the following rates apply:

- Bill-processing fee: $4.50
- Basic service fee: $20.50
- Premium channels: $7.50 per channel

For business customers, the following rates apply:

- Bill-processing fee: $15.00
- Basic service fee: $75.00 for first 10 connections, $5.00 for each additional connection
- Premium channels: $50.00 per channel for any number of connections

The program should ask the user for an account number (an integer) and a customer code. Assume that R or r stands for a residential customer, and B or b stands for a business customer.

Input   The customer's account number, customer code, number of premium channels to which the user subscribes, and, in the case of business customers, number of basic service connections

Output   Customer's account number and the billing amount

PROBLEM
ANALYSIS
AND
ALGORITHM
DESIGN

The purpose of this program is to calculate and print the billing amount. To calculate the billing amount, you need to know the customer for whom the billing amount is calculated (whether the customer is residential or business) and the number of premium channels to which the customer subscribes. In the case of a business customer, you also need to know the number of basic service connections and the number of premium channels. Other values needed to calculate the bill, such as the bill-processing fees and the cost of a premium channel, are known quantities. The program should print the billing amount to two decimal places, which is standard for monetary amounts. This problem analysis translates into the following algorithm:

1. Set the precision to two decimal places.
2. Prompt the user for the account number and customer type.
3. Based on the customer type, determine the number of premium channels and basic service connections, compute the bill, and print the bill.

   a. If the customer type is R or r, do the following:
      i.   Prompt the user for the number of premium channels.
      ii. Compute the bill.
      iii. Print the bill.

   b. If the customer type is B or b, do the following:
      i.   Prompt the user for the number of basic service connections and number of premium channels.
      ii. Compute the bill.
      iii. Print the bill.

Variables   Because the program will ask the user to input the customer account number, customer code, number of premium channels, and number of basic service connections, you need variables to store all of this information. Also, because the program will calculate the billing amount, you need a variable to store the billing amount. Thus, the program needs at least the following variables to compute and print the bill:

```
int accountNumber;     //variable to store the customer's
                       //account number
char customerType;     //variable to store the customer code
int numOfPremChannels; //variable to store the number
                       //of premium channels to which the
                       //customer subscribes
```

```
int numOfBasicServConn;  //variable to store the
                         //number of basic service connections
                         //to which the customer subscribes
double amountDue;    //variable to store the billing amount
```

Named Constants

As you can see, the bill-processing fees, the cost of a basic service connection, and the cost of a premium channel are fixed, and these values are needed to compute the bill. Although these values are constants in the program, the cable company can change them with little warning. To simplify the process of modifying the program later, instead of using these values directly in the program, you should declare them as named constants. Based on the problem analysis, you need to declare the following named constants:

```
    //Named constants - residential customers
const double RES_BILL_PROC_FEES = 4.50;
const double RES_BASIC_SERV_COST = 20.50;
const double RES_COST_PREM_CHANNEL = 7.50;

    //Named constants - business customers
const double BUS_BILL_PROC_FEES = 15.00;
const double BUS_BASIC_SERV_COST = 75.00;
const double BUS_BASIC_CONN_COST = 5.00;
const double BUS_COST_PREM_CHANNEL = 50.00;
```

Formulas

The program uses several formulas to compute the billing amount. To compute the residential bill, you need to know only the number of premium channels to which the user subscribes. The following statement calculates the billing amount for a residential customer:

```
amountDue = RES_BILL_PROC_FEES + RES_BASIC_SERV_COST
            + numOfPremChannels * RES_COST_PREM_CHANNEL;
```

To compute the business bill, you need to know the number of basic service connections and the number of premium channels to which the user subscribes. If the number of basic service connections is less than or equal to 10, the cost of the basic service connections is fixed. If the number of basic service connections exceeds 10, you must add the cost for each connection over 10. The following statement calculates the business billing amount:

```
if (numOfBasicServConn <= 10)
    amountDue = BUS_BILL_PROC_FEES + BUS_BASIC_SERV_COST
                + numOfPremChannels * BUS_COST_PREM_CHANNEL;
else
    amountDue = BUS_BILL_PROC_FEES + BUS_BASIC_SERV_COST
            + (numOfBasicServConn - 10)
                * BUS_BASIC_CONN_COST
          + numOfPremChannels * BUS_COST_PREM_CHANNEL;
```

3

MAIN ALGORITHM

Based on the preceding discussion, you can now write the main algorithm.

1. To output floating-point numbers in a fixed decimal format with a decimal point and trailing zeros, set the manipulators `fixed` and `showpoint`. Also, to output floating-point numbers with two decimal places, set the precision to two decimal places. Recall that to use these manipulators, the program must include the header file `iomanip`.

2. Prompt the user to enter the account number.

3. Get the customer account number.

4. Prompt the user to enter the customer code.

5. Get the customer code.

6. If the customer code is `r` or `R`, do the following:
   a. Prompt the user to enter the number of premium channels.
   b. Get the number of premium channels.
   c. Calculate the billing amount.
   d. Print the account number and the billing amount.

7. If the customer code is `b` or `B`, do the following:
   a. Prompt the user to enter the number of basic service connections.
   b. Get the number of basic service connections.
   c. Prompt the user to enter the number of premium channels.
   d. Get the number of premium channels.
   e. Calculate the billing amount.
   f. Print the account number and the billing amount.

8. If the customer code is something other than `r`, `R`, `b`, or `B`, output an error message.

For Steps 6 and 7, the program uses a `switch` statement to calculate the bill for the selected customer.

COMPLETE PROGRAM LISTING

```
//****************************************************
// Author: D.S. Malik
//
// Program: Cable Company Billing
// This program calculates and prints a customer's bill for a
// local cable company. The program processes two types of
// customers: residential and business.
//****************************************************
```

```cpp
#include <iostream>
#include <iomanip>

using namespace std;

        //Named constants - residential customers
const double RES_BILL_PROC_FEES = 4.50;
const double RES_BASIC_SERV_COST = 20.50;
const double RES_COST_PREM_CHANNEL = 7.50;

        //Named constants - business customers
const double BUS_BILL_PROC_FEES = 15.00;
const double BUS_BASIC_SERV_COST = 75.00;
const double BUS_BASIC_CONN_COST = 5.00;
const double BUS_COST_PREM_CHANNEL = 50.00;

int main()
{
        //Variable declaration
    int accountNumber;
    char customerType;
    int numOfPremChannels;
    int numOfBasicServConn;
    double amountDue;

    cout << fixed << showpoint << setprecision(2);  //Step 1

    cout << "This program computes a cable bill." << endl;

    cout << "Enter account number (an integer): ";  //Step 2
    cin >> accountNumber;                            //Step 3
    cout << endl;

    cout << "Enter customer type: "
         << "R or r (Residential), "
         << "B or b (Business):  ";                  //Step 4
    cin >>  customerType;                            //Step 5
    cout << endl;

    switch (customerType)
    {
    case 'r':                                        //Step 6
    case 'R':
        cout << "Enter the number"
             << " of premium channels: ";            //Step 6a
        cin >> numOfPremChannels;                    //Step 6b
        cout << endl;

        amountDue = RES_BILL_PROC_FEES               //Step 6c
                  + RES_BASIC_SERV_COST
                  + numOfPremChannels *
                    RES_COST_PREM_CHANNEL;
```

3

```cpp
        cout << "Account number: "
             << accountNumber
             << endl;                                    //Step 6d
        cout << "Amount due: $"
             << amountDue
             << endl;                                    //Step 6d
        break;

    case 'b':                                            //Step 7
    case 'B':
        cout << "Enter the number of basic "
             << "service connections: ";                 //Step 7a
        cin >> numOfBasicServConn;                       //Step 7b
        cout << endl;

        cout << "Enter the number"
             << " of premium channels: ";                //Step 7c
        cin >> numOfPremChannels;                        //Step 7d
        cout << endl;

        if (numOfBasicServConn <= 10)                    //Step 7e
            amountDue = BUS_BILL_PROC_FEES
                      + BUS_BASIC_SERV_COST
                      + numOfPremChannels *
                        BUS_COST_PREM_CHANNEL;
        else
            amountDue = BUS_BILL_PROC_FEES
                      + BUS_BASIC_SERV_COST
                      + (numOfBasicServConn - 10) *
                        BUS_BASIC_CONN_COST
                      + numOfPremChannels *
                        BUS_COST_PREM_CHANNEL;

        cout << "Account number: "
             << accountNumber << endl;                   //Step 7f
        cout << "Amount due: $" << amountDue
             << endl;                                     //Step 7f
        break;

    default:
        cout << "Invalid customer type." << endl;   //Step 8
    }//end switch

    return 0;
}
```

Sample Run: In this sample run, the user input is shaded.

```
This program computes a cable bill.
Enter account number (an integer): 12345

Enter customer type: R or r (Residential), B or b (Business): b

Enter the number of basic service connections: 16

Enter the number of premium channels: 8

Account number: 12345
Amount due: $520.00
```

3

QUICK REVIEW

1. Control structures alter the normal flow of control.

2. The two most common control structures are selection and repetition.

3. Selection structures incorporate decisions in a program.

4. The relational operators are == (equality), < (less than), <= (less than or equal to), > (greater than), >= (greater than or equal to), and != (not equal to).

5. Including a space between the relational operators ==, <=, >=, and != creates a syntax error.

6. Characters are compared using a machine's collating sequence.

7. Logical expressions evaluate to 1 (or a nonzero value) or 0. The logical value 1 (or any nonzero value) is treated as **true**; the logical value 0 is treated as **false**.

8. In C++, **bool** variables can be used to store the value of a logical expression.

9. In C++, the logical operators are ! (not), && (and), and || (or).

10. There are three selection structures in C++.

11. One-way selection takes the following form:

    ```
    if (expression)
        statement
    ```

    If expression is **true**, the **statement** executes; otherwise, the computer executes the **statement** following the **if** statement.

12. Two-way selection takes the following form:

    ```
    if (expression)
        statement1
    else
        statement2
    ```

    If expression is **true**, then **statement1** executes; otherwise, **statement2** executes.

13. The expression in an `if` or `if...else` structure is usually a logical expression.

14. Including a semicolon before the `statement` in a one-way selection creates a semantic error. In this case, the action of the `if` statement is empty.

15. Including a semicolon before `statement1` in a two-way selection creates a syntax error.

16. There is no stand-alone `else` statement in C++. Every `else` has a related `if`.

17. An `else` is paired with the most recent `if` that has not been paired with any other `else`.

18. A sequence of statements enclosed between curly braces, { and } , is called a compound statement or block of statements. A compound statement is treated as a single statement.

19. You can use the input stream variable in an `if` statement to determine the state of the input stream.

20. Using the assignment operator in place of the equality operator creates a semantic error. This can cause serious errors in the program.

21. The `switch` structure is used to handle multiway selection.

22. The execution of a `break` statement in a `switch` statement immediately exits the `switch` structure.

EXERCISES

1. Mark the following statements as true or false.

    a. The result of a logical expression cannot be assigned to a `bool` variable.

    b. In a one-way selection, if a semicolon is placed after the expression in an `if` statement, the expression in the `if` statement is always `true`.

    c. Every `if` statement must have a corresponding `else`.

    d. The expression in the `if` statement

    ```
    if (score = 30)
        grade = 'A';
    ```

    always evaluates to `true`.

    e. The expression

    ```
    (ch >= 'A' && ch <= 'Z')
    ```

    evaluates to `false` if either ch < 'A' or ch >= 'Z'.

    f. Suppose the input is 5. The output of the code

    ```
    cin >> num;
    if (num > 5)
        cout << num;
        num = 0;
    else
        cout << "Num is zero." << endl;
    ```

    is: Num is zero.

g. The expression in a `switch` statement should evaluate to a value of the simple data type.

h. The expression `!(x > 0)` is `true` only if `x` is a negative number.

i. In C++, both `!` and `!=` are logical operators.

j. The order in which statements execute in a program is called the flow of control.

2. Circle the best answer.

a.
```
if (6 < 2 * 5)
    cout << "Hello";
    cout << " There";
```

outputs the following:

(i) `Hello There`   (ii) `Hello`   (iii) `Hello`   (iv) `There`
                                           `There`

b.
```
if ('a' > 'b' || 66 > static_cast<int>('A'))
    cout << "#*#" << endl;
```

outputs the following:

(i) `#*#`   (ii) `#`   (iii) `*`   (iv) none of these
                 `*`
                 `#`

c.
```
if (7 <= 7)
    cout << 6 - 9 * 2 / 6 << endl;
```

outputs the following:

(i) `-1`   (ii) `3`   (iii) `3.0`   (iv) none of these

d.
```
if (7 < 8)
{
    cout << "2 4 6 8" << endl;
    cout << "1 3 5 7" << endl;
}
```

outputs the following:

(i) `2 4 6 8`   (ii) `1 3 5 7`   (iii) none of these
    `1 3 5 7`

e.
```
if (5 < 3)
    cout << "*";
else if (7 == 8)
    cout << "&";
else
    cout << "$";
```

outputs the following:

(i) *   (ii) &   (iii) $ (iv) none of these

3. What is the output of the following C++ code?

```
x = 100;
y = 200;
if (x > 100 && y <= 200)
    cout << x << " " << y << " " << x + y << endl;
else
    cout << x << " " << y << " " << 2 * x - y << endl;
```

4. Write C++ statements that output `Male` if the `gender` is `'M'`, `Female` if the `gender` is `'F'`, and `invalid gender` otherwise.

5. Correct the following code so that it prints the correct message.

```
if (score >= 60)
    cout << "You pass." << endl;
else;
    cout << "You fail." << endl;
```

6. State whether the following are valid `switch` statements. If not, explain why. Assume that n and `digit` are `int` variables.

a.
```
switch (n <= 2)
{
case 0:
    cout << "Draw." << endl;
    break;

case 1:
    cout << "Win." << endl;
    break;

case 2:
    cout << "Lose." << endl;
    break;
}
```

b.
```
switch (digit / 4)
{
case 0,
case 1:
    cout << "low." << endl;
    break;

case 1,
case 2:
    cout << "middle." << endl;
    break;

case 3:
    cout << "high." << endl;
}
```

c.
```
switch (n % 6)
{
case 1:
case 2:
case 3:
case 4:
case 5:
    cout << n;
    break;

case 0:
    cout << endl;
    break;
}
```

d.
```
switch (n % 10)
{
case 2:
case 4:
case 6:
case 8:
    cout << "Even";
    break;

case 1:
case 3:
case 5:
case 7:
    cout << "Odd";
    break;
}
```

7. Suppose the input is 5. What is the value of alpha after the following C++ code executes?

```
cin >> alpha;
switch (alpha)
{
case 1:
case 2:
    alpha = alpha + 2;
    break;

case 4:
    alpha++;
case 5:
    alpha = 2 * alpha;
case 6:
    alpha = alpha + 5;
    break;

default:
    alpha--;
}
```

3

8. Suppose the input is 3. What is the value of `beta` after the following C++ code executes?

```cpp
cin >> beta;
switch (beta)
{
case 3:
    beta = beta + 3;
case 1:
    beta++;
    break;

case 5:
    beta = beta + 5;
case 4:
    beta = beta + 4;
}
```

9. Suppose the input is 6. What is the value of `a` after the following C++ code executes?

```cpp
cin >> a;
if (a > 0)
    switch (a)
    {
    case 1:
        a = a + 3;
    case 3:
        a++;
        break;

    case 6:
        a = a + 6;
    case 8:
        a = a * 8;
        break;

    default:
        a--;
    }
else
    a = a + 2;
```

10. In the following code, correct any errors that would prevent the program from compiling or running.

```cpp
include <iostream>

main ()
{
    int a, b;
    bool found;
    cout << "Enter two integers: ;
    cin >> a >> b;
```

```
    if  a > a*b  &&  10 < b
        found = 2 * a > b;
    else
    {
        found = 2 * a < b;
        if found
            a = 3;
            c = 15;
            if b
            {
                b = 0;
                a = 1;
            }
    }
}
```

3

11. The following program contains errors. Correct them so that the program
will run and output w = 21.

```
#include <iostream>

using namespace std;

const int SECRET = 5

main ()
{
    int x, y, w, z;
    z = 9;

    if z > 10
        x = 12; y = 5, w = x + y + SECRET;
    else
        x = 12; y = 4, w = x + y + SECRET;

    cout << "w = " << w << endl;
}
```

PROGRAMMING EXERCISES

1. Write a program that prompts the user to input a number. The program
should then output the number and a message saying whether the number is
positive, negative, or zero.

2. Write a program that prompts the user to input three numbers. The program
should then output the numbers in ascending order.

3. In a right triangle, the square of the length of one side is equal to the sum of
the squares of the lengths of the other two sides. Write a program that
prompts the user to enter the lengths of three sides of a triangle and then
outputs a message indicating whether the triangle is a right triangle.

4. A box of cookies can hold 24 cookies, and a container can hold 75 boxes of cookies. Write a program that prompts the user to enter the total number of cookies, the number of cookies in a box, and the number of cookie boxes in a container. The program then outputs the number of boxes and the number of containers needed to ship the cookies. Note that each box must contain the specified number of cookies, and each container must contain the specified number of boxes. If the last box of cookies contains fewer than the specified number of cookies, you can discard it, and output the number of leftover cookies. Similarly, if the last container contains fewer than the number of specified boxes, you can discard it, and output the number of leftover boxes.

5. The roots of the quadratic equation $ax^2 + bx + c = 0$, $a \neq 0$ are given by the following formula:

$$\frac{-b \pm \sqrt{b^2 - 4ac}}{2a}$$

   In this formula, the term $b^2 - 4ac$ is called the **discriminant**. If $b^2 - 4ac = 0$, then the equation has a single (repeated) root. If $b^2 - 4ac > 0$, the equation has two real roots. If $b^2 - 4ac < 0$, the equation has two complex roots. Write a program that prompts the user to input the value of a (the coefficient of x^2), b (the coefficient of x), and c (the constant term), and outputs the type of roots of the equation. Furthermore, if $b^2 - 4ac \geq 0$, the program should output the roots of the quadratic equation. (*Hint:* Use the function *sqrt* from the header file `cmath` to calculate the square root of a nonnegative real number. For example *sqrt*(4.0) = 2.0.)

6. Write a program that mimics a calculator. The program should take as input two integers and the operation to be performed. It should then output the numbers, the operator, and the result. (For division, if the denominator is zero, output an appropriate message.) Some sample outputs follow:

```
3 + 4 = 7
13 * 5 = 65
```

7. Redo Exercise 6 to handle floating-point numbers. (Format your output to two decimal places.)

8. Redo Programming Exercise 13 of Chapter 2, taking into account that your parents buy additional savings bonds for you as follows:

   a. If you do not spend any money to buy savings bonds, then because you had a summer job, your parents buy savings bonds for you in an amount equal to 1% of the money you save after paying taxes, buying clothes and other accessories, and buying school supplies.

   b. If you spend up to 25% of your net income to buy savings bonds, your parents spend $0.25 for each dollar you spend to buy savings bonds, plus money equal to 1% of the money you save after paying taxes, buying clothes and other accessories, and buying school supplies.

c. If you spend more than 25% of your net income to buy savings bonds, your parents spend $0.40 for each dollar you spend to buy savings bonds, plus money equal to 2% of the money you save after paying taxes, buying clothes and other accessories, and buying school supplies.

9. A bank in your town updates its customers' accounts at the end of each month. The bank offers two types of accounts: savings and checking. Every customer must maintain a minimum balance. If a customer's balance falls below the minimum balance, there is a service charge of $10.00 for savings accounts and $25.00 for checking accounts. If the balance at the end of the month is at least the minimum balance, the account receives interest as follows:

a. Savings accounts receive 4% interest.

b. Checking accounts with balances of up to $5000 more than the minimum balance receive 3% interest; otherwise, the interest is 5%.

Write a program that reads a customer's account number (**int** type), account type (**char**; s for savings, c for checking), minimum balance that the account should maintain, and current balance. The program should then output the account number, account type, current balance, and an appropriate message. Test your program by running it five times, using the following data:

```
46728 S 1000 2700
87324 C 1500 7689
79873 S 1000 800
89832 C 2000 3000
98322 C 1000 750
```

10. Write a program that implements the algorithm given in Example 0-2 (Chapter 0), which determines the sales tax and the price of an item sold in a particular state.

11. The number of lines that can be printed on a paper depends on the paper size, the point size of each character in a line, whether lines are double-spaced or single-spaced, the top and bottom margins, and the left and right margins of the paper. Assume that all characters are of the same point size and all lines are either single-spaced or double-spaced. Note that 1 inch = 72 points. Moreover, assume that the lines are printed along the width of the paper. For example, if the length of the paper is 11 inches and the width is 8.5 inches, then the maximum length of a line is 8.5 inches. Write a program that calculates the number of characters in a line and the number of lines that can be printed on a paper, based on the following input from the user:

a. The length and width, in inches, of the paper

b. The top, bottom, left, and right margins

c. The point size of a line

d. If the lines are double-spaced, then double the point size of each character.

3

12. You have several pictures of different sizes that you would like to frame. A local picture-framing store offers two types of frames—regular and fancy. The frames are available in white and can be ordered in any color the customer desires. Suppose that each frame is 1 inch wide. The cost of coloring the frame is $0.10 per inch. The cost of a regular frame is $0.15 per inch, and the cost of a fancy frame is $0.25 per inch. The cost of putting cardboard behind the picture is $0.02 per square inch, and the cost of putting glass on top of the picture is $0.07 per square inch. The customer can also choose to put crowns on the corners, which costs $0.35 per crown. Write a program that prompts the user to input the following information and then outputs the cost of framing the picture.

   a. The length and width, in inches, of the picture

   b. The type of the frame

   c. Customer's choice of color for the frame

   d. If the user wants to add the crowns, then the number of crowns

CONTROL STRUCTURES II (REPETITION)

IN THIS CHAPTER, YOU WILL:

- Learn about repetition (looping) control structures
- Explore how to construct and use count-controlled, sentinel-controlled, flag-controlled, and EOF-controlled repetition structures
- Examine **break** statements
- Discover how to form and use nested control structures
- Learn how to avoid bugs by avoiding patches

In Chapter 3, you saw how decisions are incorporated in programs. In this chapter, you learn how repetitions are incorporated into programs.

Why Is Repetition Needed?

Suppose you want to add three numbers to find their average. From what you have learned so far, you know that you could proceed as follows (assume that all variables are properly declared):

```
cin >> num1 >> num2 >> num3;   //read three numbers
sum = num1 + num2 + num3;      //add the numbers
average = sum / 3;             //find the average
```

But suppose you want to add and average 100, or 1000, or more numbers. You would have to declare that many variables and list them again in `cin` statements and, perhaps, again in the output statements. This takes an exorbitant amount of space and time. Also, if you want to run this program again with different values, or with a different number of values, you have to rewrite the program.

Suppose you want to add the following numbers:

5 3 7

Consider the following statements, in which `sum` and `num` are variables of the type `int`.

1. `sum = 0;`
2. `cin >> num;`
3. `sum = sum + num;`

The first statement initializes `sum` to 0. Let us execute statements 2 and 3. Statement 2 stores 5 in `num`; statement 3 updates the value of `sum` by adding `num` to it. After statement 3, the value of `sum` is 5.

Let us repeat statements 2 and 3. After statement 2 (after the programming code reads the next number),

num = 3

After statement 3,

sum = sum + num = 5 + 3 = 8

At this point, `sum` contains the sum of the first two numbers. Let us again repeat statements 2 and 3 (third time). After statement 2 (after the code reads the next number),

```
num = 7
```

After statement 3,

```
sum = sum + num = 8 + 7 = 15
```

Now `sum` contains the sum of the first three numbers.

If you want to add 10 numbers, you can repeat statements 2 and 3 ten times. And if you want to add 100 numbers, you can repeat statements 2 and 3 one hundred times. In either case, you do not have to declare any additional variables, as you did in the first code. You can use this C++ code to add any set of numbers, whereas the earlier code requires you to drastically change the code.

There are many other situations where it is necessary to repeat a set of statements. For example, for each student in a class, the formula for determining the course grade is the same. C++ has three repetition, or looping, structures that let you repeat statements over and over until certain conditions are met. This chapter introduces all three looping (repetition) structures. The next section discusses the first repetition structure, called the `while` loop.

while Repetition (Looping) Structure

In the previous section, you saw that sometimes it is necessary to repeat a set of statements several times. One way to repeat a set of statements is to type the set of statements in the program over and over. For example, if you want to repeat a set of statements 100 times, you type the set of statements 100 times in the program. However, this solution of repeating a set of statements is impractical, if not impossible. Fortunately, there is a better way to repeat a set of statements. As noted earlier, C++ has three repetition, or looping, structures that allow you to repeat a set of statements until certain conditions are met. This section discusses the first looping structure, called a `while` **loop**.

The general form of the `while` statement is:

```
while (expression)
    statement
```

In C++, `while` is a reserved word. Of course, the `statement` can be either a simple or compound statement. The `expression` acts as a **decision maker** and is usually a logical expression. The `statement` is called the body of the loop. Note that the parentheses around the `expression` are part of the syntax. Figure 4-1 shows the flow of execution of a `while` loop.

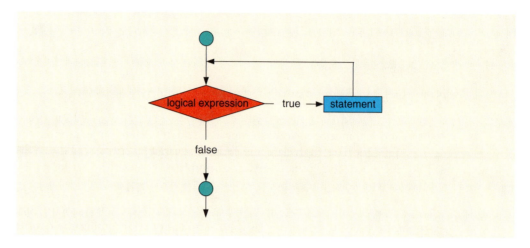

FIGURE 4-1 `while` loop

The `expression` provides an entry condition. If it initially evaluates to `true`, the `statement` executes. The loop condition—the `expression`—is then reevaluated. If it again evaluates to `true`, the `statement` executes again. The `statement` (body of the loop) continues to execute until the `expression` is no longer `true`. A loop that continues to execute endlessly is called an **infinite loop**. To avoid an infinite loop, make sure that the loop's body contains statement(s) that ensure that the exit condition—the expression in the `while` statement—will eventually be `false`.

EXAMPLE 4-1

Consider the following C++ program segment:

```
int i = 0;                //Line 1

while (i <= 20)           //Line 2
{                         //Line 3
    cout << i << " ";     //Line 4
    i = i + 5;            //Line 5
}                         //Line 6

cout << endl;             //Line 7
```

Sample Run:

```
0 5 10 15 20
```

Line 1 declares and initializes the variable `i` to 0. The `expression` in the `while` statement (in Line 2), `i <= 20`, is evaluated. Because the expression `i <= 20` evaluates to `true`, the body of the `while` loop executes next. The body of the `while` loop consists of the statements in Lines 4 and 5. The statement in Line 4 outputs the value of i, which is 0. The statement in Line 5 changes the value of i to 5. After executing the statements in Lines 4 and 5, the **expression** in the **while** loop (Line 2) is evaluated again. Because i is 5, the expression i <= 20 evaluates to **true** and the body of the **while** loop executes again. This process of evaluating the **expression** and executing the body of the **while** loop continues until the **expression**, i <= 20 (in Line 2), no longer evaluates to **true**.

The variable i (in Line 2, Example 4-1) in the expression is called the **loop control variable**.

Note the following from Example 4-1:

a. Within the loop i becomes 25 but is not printed because the entry condition is **false**.

b. If you omit the statement:

```
i = i + 5;
```

from the body of the loop, you will have an infinite loop, continually printing rows of zeros.

c. You must initialize the loop control variable i before you execute the loop. If the statement:

```
i = 0;
```

(at Line 1) is omitted, the loop may not execute at all. (Recall that variables in C++ are not automatically initialized.)

d. In Example 4-1, if the two statements in the body of the loop are interchanged, it may drastically alter the result. For example, consider the following statements:

```
int i = 0;

while (i <= 20)
{
    i = i + 5;
    cout << i << " ";
}

cout << endl;
```

Here the output is:

```
5 10 15 20 25
```

Typically, this would be a semantic error because you rarely want a condition to be true for i <= 20 and yet produce results for i > 20.

4

e. If you put a semicolon at the end of the `while` loop (after the logical expression), then the action of the `while` loop is empty or null. For example, the action of the following `while` loop is empty:

```
int i = 0;

while (i <= 20);
{
    i = i + 5;
    cout << i <<   " ";
}

cout << endl;
```

The statements within the braces do not form the body of the `while` loop.

Designing `while` Loops

As in Example 4-1, the body of a `while` executes only when the **expression** in the `while` statement evaluates to **true**. Typically, the **expression** checks whether a variable(s), called the loop control variable (**LCV**), satisfies certain conditions. For example, in Example 4-1, the **expression** in the `while` statement checks whether i <= 20. The LCV must be properly initialized before the `while` loop, and it should eventually make the **expression** evaluate to **false**. We do this by updating or reinitializing the LCV in the body of the `while` loop. Therefore, typically, `while` loops are written in the following form:

```
//initialize the loop control variable(s)

while (expression)   //expression tests the LCV
{
    .
    .
    .
    //update the loop control variable(s)
    .
    .
    .

}
```

For instance, in Example 4-1, the statement in Line 1 initializes the LCV i to 0. The expression, i <= 20, in Line 2, checks whether i is less than or equal to 20, and the statement in Line 5 updates the value of i.

EXAMPLE 4-2

Consider the following C++ program segment:

```cpp
int i = 20;                //Line 1

while (i < 20)             //Line 2
{                          //Line 3
    cout << i << " ";      //Line 4
    i = i + 5;             //Line 5
}                          //Line 6
cout << endl;              //Line 7
```

It is easy to overlook the difference between this example and Example 4-1. In this example, at Line 1, i is set to 20. Because i is 20, the expression i < 20 in the while statement (Line 2) evaluates to false. Because initially the loop entry condition, i < 20, is false, the body of the while loop never executes. Hence, no values are output and the value of i remains 20.

The next few sections describe the various forms of while loops.

Case 1: Counter-Controlled while Loops

Suppose you know exactly how many times certain statements need to be executed. For example, suppose you know exactly how many pieces of data (or entries) need to be read. In such cases, the while loop assumes the form of a **counter-controlled while loop**. Suppose that a set of statements needs to be executed N times. You can set up a counter (initialized to 0 before the while statement) to track how many items have been read. Before executing the body of the while statement, the counter is compared with N. If counter < N, the body of the while statement executes. The body of the loop continues to execute until the value of counter >= N. Thus, inside the body of the while statement, the value of counter increments after it reads a new item. In this case, the while loop might look like the following:

```cpp
counter = 0;          //initialize the loop control variable

while (counter < N) //test the loop control variable
{
    .
    .
    .
    counter++;           //update the loop control variable
    .
    .
    .
}
```

If N represents the number of data items in a file, then the value of N can be determined several ways. The program can prompt you to specify the number of items in the file; an input statement can read the value; or you can specify the first item in the file as the number of items in the file, so that you need not remember the number of input values (items). This is useful if someone other than the programmer enters the data. Consider Example 4-3.

EXAMPLE 4-3

Suppose the input is:

8 9 2 3 90 38 56 8 23 89 7 2

Suppose you want to add these numbers and find their average. Consider the following program.

```cpp
//*************************************************************
// Author: D.S. Malik
//
// Counter-controlled while loop
// This program illustrates how a counter-controlled loop works.
// It prompts the user to enter the number of integers to be
// added. It adds the numbers and also finds the average.
//*************************************************************

#include <iostream>                                      //Line 1

using namespace std;                                     //Line 2

int main()                                               //Line 3
{                                                        //Line 4
    int limit;     //store the number of data items         Line 5
    int number;    //variable to store the number           Line 6
    int sum;       //variable to store the sum              Line 7
    int counter;   //loop control variable                  Line 8

    cout << "Line 9: Enter the number of "
         << "integers in the list: ";                    //Line 9
    cin >> limit;                                        //Line 10
    cout << endl;                                        //Line 11

    sum = 0;                                             //Line 12
    counter = 0;                                         //Line 13

    cout << "Line 14: Enter " << limit
         << " integers." << endl;                        //Line 14
```

```
    while (counter < limit)                           //Line 15
    {                                                 //Line 16
        cin >> number;                                //Line 17
        sum = sum + number;                           //Line 18
        counter++;                                     //Line 19
    }                                                 //Line 20

    cout << "Line 21: The sum of the " << limit
         << " numbers = " << sum << endl;             //Line 21

    if (counter != 0)                                 //Line 22
        cout << "Line 23: The average = "
             << sum / counter << endl;                //Line 23
    else                                              //Line 24
        cout << "Line 25: No input." << endl;         //Line 25

    return 0;                                         //Line 26
}                                                     //Line 27
```

Sample Run: In this sample run, the user input is shaded.

```
Line 9: Enter the number of integers in the list: 12

Line 14: Enter 12 integers.
8 9 2 3 90 38 56 8 23 89 7 2
Line 21: The sum of the 12 numbers = 335
Line 23: The average = 27
```

This program works as follows. The statement in Line 9 prompts the user to input the number of data items. The statement in Line 10 reads the next input and stores it in the variable `limit`. The value of `limit` indicates the number of items in the list. The statements in Lines 12 and 13 initialize the variables `sum` and `counter` to 0. (The variable `counter` is the loop control variable.) The statement in Line 14 prompts the user to input numbers. (In this sample run, the user is prompted to enter 12 integers.) The `while` statement in Line 15 checks the value of `counter` to determine how many items have been read. If `counter` is less than `limit`, the `while` loop proceeds for the next iteration. The statement in Line 17 reads the next number and stores it in the variable `number`. The statement in Line 18 updates the value of `sum` by adding the value of `number` to the previous value, and the statement in Line 19 increments the value of `counter` by 1. The statement in Line 21 outputs the sum of the numbers; the statements in Lines 22 through 25 output the average.

Note that `sum` is initialized to 0 in Line 12 in this program. In Line 18, after reading a number at Line 17, the program adds it to the sum of all the numbers scanned before the current number. The first number read will be added to zero (because `sum` is initialized to 0), giving the correct sum of the first number. To find the average, divide `sum` by `counter`. If `counter` is 0, then dividing by zero will terminate the program and you will get an error message. Therefore, before dividing `sum` by `counter`, you must check whether or not `counter` is 0.

Notice that in this program, the statement in Line 13 initializes the LCV `counter` to 0. The expression `counter < limit` in Line 15 evaluates whether `counter` is less than `limit`. The statement in Line 19 updates the value of `counter`.

Case 2: Sentinel-Controlled `while` Loops

You do not always know how many pieces of data (or entries) need to be read, but you may know that the last entry is a special value, called a **sentinel**. In this case, you read the first item before the `while` statement. If this item does not equal the sentinel, the body of the `while` statement executes. The `while` loop continues to execute as long as the program has not read the sentinel. Such a `while` loop is called a **sentinel–controlled while loop**. In this case, a `while` loop might look like the following:

```
cin >> variable;              //initialize the loop control variable

while (variable != sentinel)  //test the loop control variable
{
    .
    .
    .
    cin >> variable;          //update the loop control variable
    .
    .
    .
}
```

EXAMPLE 4-4

Suppose you want to read some positive integers and average them, but you do not have a preset number of data items in mind. Suppose the number –999 marks the end of the data. You can proceed as follows.

```
//************************************************************
// Author: D.S. Malik
//
// Sentinel-controlled while loop
// This program illustrates how a sentinel-controlled loop works.
// It prompts the user to enter the number of integers to be
// added. It adds the numbers and finds the average.
//************************************************************

#include <iostream>                                    //Line 1

using namespace std;                                   //Line 2

const int SENTINEL = -999;                             //Line 3
```

```
int main()                                                   //Line 4
{                                                            //Line 5
    int number;       //variable to store the number           Line 6
    int sum = 0;      //variable to store the sum              Line 7
    int count = 0;    //variable to store the total
                      //numbers read                           Line 8

    cout << "Line 9: Enter integers ending with "
         << SENTINEL << endl;                                //Line 9
    cin >> number;                                          //Line 10

    while (number != SENTINEL)                              //Line 11
    {                                                       //Line 12
        sum = sum + number;                                 //Line 13
        count++;                                            //Line 14
        cin >> number;                                      //Line 15
    }                                                       //Line 16

    cout << "Line 17: The sum of the " << count
         << " numbers is " << sum << endl;                  //Line 17

    if (count != 0)                                         //Line 18
        cout << "Line 19: The average is "
             <<  sum / count << endl;                       //Line 19
    else                                                    //Line 20
        cout << "Line 21: No input." << endl;               //Line 21

    return 0;                                               //Line 22
}                                                           //Line 23
```

Sample Run: In this sample run, the user input is shaded.

```
Line 9: Enter integers ending with -999
34 23 9 45 78 0 77 8 3 5 -999
Line 17: The sum of the 10 numbers is 282
Line 19: The average is 28
```

This program works as follows. The statement in Line 9 prompts the user to enter numbers ending with -999. The statement in Line 10 reads the first number and stores it in number. The while statement in Line 11 checks whether number is not equal to SENTINEL. (The variable number is the loop control variable.) If number is not equal to SENTINEL, the body of the while loop executes. The statement in Line 13 updates the value of sum by adding number to it. The statement in Line 14 increments the value of count by 1; the statement in Line 15 reads and stores the next number in number. The statements in Lines 13 through 15 repeat until the program reads the SENTINEL. The statement in Line 17 outputs the sum of the numbers, and the statements in Lines 18 through 21 output the average of the numbers.

Notice that the statement in Line 10 initializes the LCV number. The expression number != SENTINEL in Line 11 checks whether the value of number is equal to SENTINEL. The statement in Line 15 reinitializes the LCV number.

Case 3: Flag-Controlled `while` Loops

A **flag-controlled** `while` **loop** uses a `bool` variable to control the loop. Suppose `found` is a `bool` variable. The flag-controlled `while` loop takes the following form:

```
found = false;      //initialize the loop control variable

while (!found)       //test the loop control variable
{
   .
   .
   .
   if (expression)
      found = true; //update the loop control variable
   .
   .
   .
}
```

The variable `found`, which is used to control the execution of the `while` loop, is called a **flag variable**.

Example 4-5 further illustrates the use of a flag-controlled `while` loop.

EXAMPLE 4-5 NUMBER GUESSING GAME

The following program randomly generates an integer greater than or equal to 0 and less than 100. The program then prompts the user to guess the number. If the user guesses the number correctly, the program outputs an appropriate message. Otherwise, the program checks whether the guessed number is less than the random number. If the guessed number is less than the random number generated by the program, the program outputs the message "Your guess is lower than the number. Guess again!"; otherwise, the program outputs the message "Your guess is higher than the number. Guess again!" The program then prompts the user to enter another number. The user is prompted to guess the random number until the user enters the correct number.

The program uses the function `rand` of the header file `cstdlib` to generate a random number. To be specific, the expression:

```
rand()
```

returns an `int` value between 0 and 32767. To convert it to an integer greater than or equal to 0 and less than 100, we use the following expression:

```
rand() % 100
```

It is possible that every time you run your program, the function `rand` gives the same random number. In this case, you can use the function `time` of the header file `ctime` to include the time. The following expression generates a random integer greater than or equal to 0 and less than 100:

```
(rand() + time(0)) % 100;
```

(Note how the function time is used. It is used with an argument, that is, parameter, which is 0.) The program uses the **bool** variable isGuessed to control the loop. The **bool** variable isGuessed is initialized to **false**. It is set to **true** when the user guesses the correct number.

```cpp
//***********************************************************
// Author: D.S. Malik
//
// Flag-controlled while loop
// This program illustrates how a flag-controlled loop works.
// It randomly generates an integer between 0 (inclusive) and 100
// and then prompts the user to guess the number. The program
// continues to execute until the user has entered the correct
// number.
//***********************************************************

#include <iostream>                              //Line 1
#include <cstdlib>                               //Line 2
#include <ctime>                                 //Line 3

using namespace std;                             //Line 4

int main()                                       //Line 5
{                                                //Line 6
    int num;     //variable to store the random number    Line 7
    int guess;   //variable to store the number
                 //guessed by the user                    Line 8

    bool isGuessed;  //loop control variable               Line 9

    num = (rand() + time(0)) % 100;              //Line 10

    isGuessed = false;                           //Line 11

    while (!isGuessed)                           //Line 12
    {                                            //Line 13
        cout << "Enter an integer greater than or "
             << " equal to 0 and less than 100: ";   //Line 14

        cin >> guess;                            //Line 15
        cout << endl;                            //Line 16

        if (guess == num)                        //Line 17
        {                                        //Line 18
            cout << "You guessed the correct number."
                 << endl;                        //Line 19
            isGuessed = true;                    //Line 20
        }                                        //Line 21
        else if (guess < num)                    //Line 22
            cout << "Your guess is lower than the "
                 << "number.\n Guess again!"
                 << endl;                        //Line 23
```

4

```
        else                                        //Line 24
            cout << "Your guess is higher than "
                 << "the number.\n Guess again!"
                 << endl;                            //Line 25
    } //end while                                    //Line 26

    return 0;                                        //Line 27
}                                                    //Line 28
```

Sample Run: In this sample run, the user input is shaded.

```
Enter an integer greater than or equal to 0 and less than 100: 25

Your guess is higher than the number.
Guess again!
Enter an integer greater than or equal to 0 and less than 100: 5

Your guess is lower than the number.
Guess again!
Enter an integer greater than or equal to 0 and less than 100: 10

Your guess is higher than the number.
Guess again!
Enter an integer greater than or equal to 0 and less than 100: 8

Your guess is higher than the number.
Guess again!
Enter an integer greater than or equal to 0 and less than 100: 6

Your guess is lower than the number.
Guess again!
Enter an integer greater than or equal to 0 and less than 100: 7

You guessed the correct number.
```

The preceding program works as follows: The statement in Line 10 creates an integer greater than or equal to 0 and less than 100 and stores this number in the variable num. The statement in Line 11 sets the **bool** variable isGuessed to **false**. The **while** loop starts at Line 12 and ends at Line 26. The expression in the **while** loop at Line 12 evaluates the expression !isGuessed. If isGuessed is **false**, then !isGuessed is **true** and the body of the **while** loop executes; if isGuessed is **true**, then !isGuessed is **false**, so the **while** loop terminates.

The statement in Line 14 prompts the user to enter an integer greater than or equal to 0 and less than 100. The statement in Line 15 stores the number entered by the user in the variable guess. The expression in the **if** statement in Line 17 determines whether the value of guess is the same as num, that is, if the user guessed the number correctly. If the value of guess is the same as num, then the statements in Lines 19 and 20 execute. The statement in Line 19 outputs the following message:

```
You guessed the correct number.
```

The statement in Line 20 sets the variable isGuessed to true. The control then goes back to Line 12. Because done is true, !isGuessed is false and the while loop terminates.

If the expression in Line 17 evaluates to false, then the else statement in Line 22 executes. The statement part of this else is an if...else statement, ending at Line 25. The if statement in Line 22 determines whether the value of guess is less than num. In this case, the statement in Line 23 outputs the following message:

```
Your guess is lower than the number.
Guess again!
```

If the expression in the if statement in Line 22 evaluates to false, then the statement in Line 25 executes, which outputs the following message:

```
Your guess is higher than the number.
Guess again!
```

The program then prompts the user to enter an integer greater than or equal to 0 and less than 100.

4

Case 4: EOF-Controlled `while` Loops

If the data file is frequently altered (for example, if data is frequently added or deleted), it's best not to read the data with a sentinel value. Someone might accidentally erase the sentinel value or add data after the sentinel, especially if the programmer and the data-entry person are different people. Also, the programmer sometimes does not know what the sentinel is. In such situations, you can use an **EOF (end of file)-controlled** **while loop**.

Until now, we have used an input stream variable, such as cin, and the extraction operator, >>, to read and store data into variables. However, the input stream variable can also return a value after reading data, as follows:

1. If the program has reached the end of the input data, the input stream variable returns the logical value false.

2. If the program reads any faulty data (such as a char value into an int variable), the input stream enters the fail state. Once a stream enters the fail state, any further I/O operations using that stream are considered to be null operations; that is, they have no effect. Unfortunately, the computer does not halt the program or give any error messages. It just continues executing the program, silently ignoring each additional attempt to use that stream. In this case, the input stream variable returns the value false.

3. In cases other than (1) and (2), the input stream variable returns the logical value true.

You can use the value returned by the input stream variable to determine whether the program has reached the end of the input data. Because the input stream variable returns the logical value `true` or `false`, in a `while` loop, it can be considered a logical expression.

The following is an example of an EOF-controlled `while` loop.

```
cin >> variable;        //initialize the loop control variable

while (cin)             //test the loop control variable
{
    .
    .
    .
    cin >> variable; //update the loop control variable
    .
    .
    .
}
```

Notice that here the variable `cin` acts as the loop control variable.

eof Function

In addition to checking the value of an input stream variable, such as `cin`, to determine whether the end of the file has been reached, C++ provides a function that you can use with an input stream variable to determine the end-of-file status. This function is called eof. Like the I/O functions—such as `get` and `ignore`, discussed in Chapter 2—the function eof is of the data type `istream`.

The syntax to use the function eof is:

`istreamVar.eof()`

where `istreamVar` is an input stream variable, such as `cin`.

Suppose you have the following declaration:

`ifstream infile;`

Further suppose that you opened a file using the variable `infile`. Consider the expression:

`infile.eof()`

This is a logical (Boolean) expression. The value of this expression is `true` if the program has read past the end of the input file, `infile`; otherwise, the value of this expression is `false`.

Suppose you have the declaration:

```
ifstream infile;
char ch;

infile.open("inputDat.dat");
```

The following `while` loop continues to execute as long as the program has not reached the end of the file.

```
infile.get(ch);

while (!infile.eof())
{
    cout << ch;
    infile.get(ch);
}
```

As long as the program has not reached the end of the input file, the expression:

```
infile.eof()
```

is `false` and so the expression:

```
!infile.eof()
```

in the `while` statement is `true`. When the program reads past the end of the input file, the expression:

```
infile.eof()
```

becomes `true` and so the expression:

```
!infile.eof()
```

in the `while` statement becomes `false` and the loop terminates.

EXAMPLE 4-6

The following code uses an EOF-controlled `while` loop to find the sum of a set of numbers:

```
int sum = 0;
int num;

cin >> num;

while (cin)
{
    sum = sum + num;     //Add the number to sum
    cin >> num;          //Get the next number
}

cout << "Sum = " << sum << endl;
```

EXAMPLE 4-7

Suppose we are given a file consisting of students' names and their test scores, a number between 0 and 100 (inclusive). Each line in the file consists of a student name followed by the test score. We want a program that outputs each student's name followed by the test score followed by the grade. The program also needs to output the average test score for the class. Consider the following program:

```cpp
//****************************************************************
// Author: D.S. Malik
//
// This program reads data from a file consisting of students'
// names and their test scores. The program outputs each student's
// name followed by the test score followed by the grade. The
// program also outputs the average test score for all the students.
//****************************************************************

#include <iostream>                                    //Line 1
#include <fstream>                                     //Line 2
#include <string>                                      //Line 3
#include <iomanip>                                     //Line 4

using namespace std;                                   //Line 5

int main()                                             //Line 6
{                                                      //Line 7
        //Declare variables to manipulate data
    string firstName;                                  //Line 8
    string lastName;                                   //Line 9
    double testScore;                                  //Line 10
    char grade = ' ';                                  //Line 11
    double sum = 0;                                    //Line 12
    int count = 0;                                     //Line 13

        //Declare stream variables
    ifstream inFile;                                   //Line 14
    ofstream outFile;                                  //Line 15

        //Open input file
    inFile.open("Ch4_stData.txt");                     //Line 16

    if (!inFile)                                       //Line 17
    {                                                  //Line 18
        cout << "Cannot open input file. "
             << "Program terminates!" << endl;         //Line 19
        return 1;                                      //Line 20
    }                                                  //Line 21
        //Open output file
    outFile.open("Ch4_stData.out");                    //Line 22

    outFile << fixed << showpoint << setprecision(2);  //Line 23
```

```
inFile >> firstName >> lastName;  //read the name    Line 24
inFile >> testScore;          //read the test score   Line 25

while (inFile)                                        //Line 26
{                                                     //Line 27
    sum = sum + testScore;  //update sum              Line 28
    count++;                //increment count          Line 29

        //determine the grade
    switch (static_cast<int> (testScore) / 10)        //Line 30
    {                                                 //Line 31
    case 0:                                           //Line 32
    case 1:                                           //Line 33
    case 2:                                           //Line 34
    case 3:                                           //Line 35
    case 4:                                           //Line 36
    case 5:                                           //Line 37
        grade = 'F';                                  //Line 38
        break;                                        //Line 39

    case 6:                                           //Line 40
        grade = 'D';                                  //Line 41
        break;                                        //Line 42

    case 7:                                           //Line 43
        grade = 'C';                                  //Line 44
        break;                                        //Line 45

    case 8:                                           //Line 46
        grade = 'B';                                  //Line 47
        break;                                        //Line 48

    case 9:                                           //Line 49
    case 10:                                          //Line 50
        grade = 'A';                                  //Line 51
        break;                                        //Line 52

    default:                                          //Line 53
        cout << "Invalid score." << endl;             //Line 54
    }//end switch                                     //Line 55

    outFile << left << setw(12) << firstName
            << setw(12) << lastName
            << right << setw(4) << testScore
            << setw(2) << grade << endl;              //Line 56

    inFile >> firstName >> lastName; //read the name Line 57
    inFile >> testScore;         //read the test score Line 58
}//end while                                          //Line 59

outFile << endl;                                      //Line 60
```

```
    if (count != 0)                                    //Line 61
        outFile << "Class Average: " << sum / count
                << endl;                               //Line 62
    else                                               //Line 63
        outFile << "No data." << endl;                 //Line 64

    inFile.close();                                    //Line 65
    outFile.close();                                   //Line 66

    return 0;                                          //Line 67
}                                                      //Line 68
```

Sample Run:

Input File:

```
Steve Gill 89
Rita Johnson 91.5
Randy Brown 85.5
Seema Arora 76.5
Samir Mann 73
Samantha McCoy 88.5
```

Output File:

```
Steve        Gill         89.00 B
Rita         Johnson      91.50 A
Randy        Brown        85.50 B
Seema        Arora        76.50 C
Samir        Mann         73.00 C
Samantha     McCoy        88.50 B

Class Average: 84.00
```

The preceding program works as follows. The statements in Lines 8 to 13 declare and initialize variables needed by the program. The statements in Lines 14 and 15 declare `inFile` to be an `ifstream` variable and `outFile` to be an `ofstream` variable. The statement in Line 16 opens the input file using the variable `inFile`. If the input file does not exist, the statements in Lines 17 to 21 output an appropriate message and terminate the program. The statement in Line 22 opens the output file using the variable `outFile`. The statement in Line 23 sets the output of floating-point numbers to two decimal places in a fixed form with trailing zeros.

The statements in Lines 24 and 25 and the **while** loop in Line 26 read each student's first name, last name, test score, and then output the name followed by the test score followed by the grade. Specifically, the statement in Lines 24 and 57 reads the first and last name; the statement in Lines 25 and 58 reads the test score. The statement in Line 28 updates the value of `sum`. (After reading all the data, the value of `sum` stores the sum of all the test scores.) The statement in Line 29 updates the value of `count`. (The variable `count` stores the number of students in the class.) The **switch** statement from Lines 30 to 55 determines the grade from `testScore` and stores it in the variable **grade**. The statement in Line 56 outputs a student's first name, last name, test score, and grade.

The **if...else** statement in Line 61 to 64 outputs the class average and the statements in Lines 65 and 66 close the files.

More on Expressions in `while` Statements

In the examples of the previous sections, the expression in the **while** statement is quite simple. In other words, the **while** loop is controlled by a single variable. However, there are situations when the expression in the **while** statement may be more complex.

For example, the program in Example 4-5 uses a flag-controlled **while** loop to implement the Number Guessing Game. However, the program gives as many tries as the user needs to guess the number. Suppose you want to give the user, say, no more than five tries to guess the number. If the user does not guess the number correctly within five tries, then the program outputs the random number generated by the program as well as a message that you have lost the game. In this case, you can write the **while** loop as follows (assume that **numOfGuesses** is an **int** variable initialized to 0):

```
while ((numOfGuesses < 5) && (!isGuessed))
{
    cout << "Enter an integer greater than or equal to 0 and "
         << "less than 100: ";
    cin >> guess;
    cout << endl;

    numOfGuesses++;

    if (guess == num)
    {
        cout << "Winner!. You guessed the correct number."
             << endl;
        isGuessed = true;
    }
    else if (guess < num)
        cout << "Your guess is lower than the number.\n"
             << "Guess again!" << endl;
    else
        cout << "Your guess is higher than the number.\n"
             << "Guess again!" << endl;
}//end while
```

You also need the following code, to be included after the **while** loop, in case the user cannot guess the correct number in five tries.

```
if (!isGuessed)
    cout << "You lose! The correct number is " << num << endl;
```

Programming Exercise 13 at the end of this chapter asks you to write a complete C++ program to implement the Number Guessing Game in which the user has at most five tries to guess the number.

As you can see from the preceding `while` loop, the expression in a `while` statement can be complex. The main objective of a `while` loop is to repeat certain statement(s) until certain conditions are met.

PROGRAMMING EXAMPLE: Fibonacci Number

So far, you have seen several examples of loops. Recall that in C++, `while` loops are used when a certain statement(s) must be executed repeatedly until certain conditions are met. Following is a C++ program that uses a `while` loop to find a **Fibonacci number**.

Consider the following sequence of numbers:

1, 1, 2, 3, 5, 8, 13, 21, 34, ...

Given the first two numbers of the sequence (say, a_1 and a_2), the nth number a_n, $n >= 3$, of this sequence is given by:

$$a_n = a_{n-1} + a_{n-2}$$

Thus, $a_3 = a_2 + a_1 = 1 + 1 = 2$, $a_4 = a_3 + a_2 = 2 + 1 = 3$, and so on.

Such a sequence is called a **Fibonacci sequence**. In the preceding sequence, $a_2 = 1$ and $a_1 = 1$. However, given any first two numbers, using this process, you can determine the nth number, a_n, $n >= 3$, of the sequence. The number determined this way is called the **nth Fibonacci number**. Suppose $a_2 = 6$ and $a_1 = 3$.

Then:

$$a_3 = a_2 + a_1 = 6 + 3 = 9; a_4 = a_3 + a_2 = 9 + 6 = 15.$$

Next, we write a program that determines the nth Fibonacci number, given the first two numbers.

Input   The first two Fibonacci numbers and the desired Fibonacci number.

Output   The nth Fibonacci number.

PROBLEM ANALYSIS AND ALGORITHM DESIGN

To find, say, the tenth Fibonacci number of a sequence, you must first find a_9 and a_8, which requires you to find a_7 and a_6 and so on. Therefore, to find a_{10}, you must first find $a_3, a_4, a_5, \ldots, a_9$. This discussion translates into the following algorithm:

1. Get the first two Fibonacci numbers.

2. Get the desired Fibonacci number. That is, get the position, n, of the Fibonacci number in the sequence.

3. Calculate the next Fibonacci number by adding the previous two elements of the Fibonacci sequence.

4. Repeat Step 3 until the *n*th Fibonacci number is found.

5. Output the *n*th Fibonacci number.

Note that the program assumes that the first number of the Fibonacci sequence is less than or equal to the second number of the Fibonacci sequence, and both numbers are nonnegative. Moreover, the program also assumes that the user enters a valid value for the position of the desired number in the Fibonacci sequence; that is, it is a positive integer. (See Programming Exercise 12 at the end of this chapter.)

Variables Because the last two numbers must be known in order to find the current Fibonacci number, you need the following variables: two variables—say, `previous1` and `previous2`—to hold the previous two numbers of the Fibonacci sequence; and one variable—say, `current`—to hold the current Fibonacci number. The number of times that Step 2 of the algorithm repeats depends on the position of the Fibonacci number you are calculating. For example, if you want to calculate the tenth Fibonacci number, you must execute Step 3 eight times. (Remember—the user gives the first two numbers of the Fibonacci sequence.) Therefore, you need a variable to store the number of times that Step 3 should execute. You also need a variable to track the number of times that Step 3 has executed the loop control variable. You therefore need five variables for the data manipulation:

```
int previous1;   //variable to store the first Fibonacci number
int previous2;   //variable to store the second Fibonacci number
int current;     //variable to store the current
                 //Fibonacci number
int counter;     //loop control variable
int nthFibonacci; //variable to store the desired
                 //Fibonacci number
```

To calculate the third Fibonacci number, add the values of `previous1` and `previous2` and store the result in `current`. To calculate the fourth Fibonacci number, add the value of the second Fibonacci number (that is, `previous2`) and the value of the third Fibonacci number (that is, `current`). Thus, when the fourth Fibonacci number is calculated, you no longer need the first Fibonacci number. Instead of declaring additional variables, which could be too many, after calculating a Fibonacci number to determine the next Fibonacci number, `current` becomes `previous2` and `previous2` becomes `previous1`. Therefore, you can again use the variable `current` to store the next Fibonacci number. This process is repeated until the desired Fibonacci number is calculated. Initially, `previous1` and `previous2` are the first two elements of the sequence, supplied by the user. From the preceding discussion, it follows that you need five variables.

1. Prompt the user for the first two numbers—that is, `previous1` and `previous2`.

2. Read (input) the first two numbers into `previous1` and `previous2`.

3. Output the first two Fibonacci numbers. (Echo input.)

4. Prompt the user for the position of the desired Fibonacci number.

5. Read the position of the desired Fibonacci number into `nthFibonacci`.

6. a. `if (nthFibonacci == 1)`

   the desired Fibonacci number is the first Fibonacci number. Copy the value of `previous1` into `current`.

   b. `else if (nthFibonacci == 2)`

   the desired Fibonacci number is the second Fibonacci number. Copy the value of `previous2` into `current`.

   c. `else calculate` the desired Fibonacci number as follows:

   Because you already know the first two Fibonacci numbers of the sequence, start by determining the third Fibonacci number.

   c.1. Initialize `counter` to 3, to keep track of the calculated Fibonacci numbers.

   c.2. Calculate the next Fibonacci number, as follows:

   ```
   current = previous2 + previous1;
   ```

   c.3. Assign the value of `previous2` to `previous1`.

   c.4. Assign the value of `current` to `previous2`.

   c.5. Increment `counter`.

   Repeat Steps c.2 through c.5 until the Fibonacci number you want is calculated.

   The following `while` loop executes Steps c.2 through c.5 and determines the *n*th Fibonacci number.

   ```
   while (counter <= nthFibonacci)
   {
       current = previous2 + previous1;
       previous1 = previous2;
       previous2 = current;
       counter++;
   }
   ```

7. Output the `nthFibonacci` number, which is current.

COMPLETE PROGRAM LISTING

```cpp
//******************************************************
// Author: D.S. Malik
//
// Program: nth Fibonacci number
// Given the first two numbers of a Fibonacci sequence, this
// determines and outputs the desired number of the Fibonacci
// sequence.
//******************************************************

#include <iostream>

using namespace std;

int main()
{
        //Declare variables
    int previous1;
    int previous2;
    int current;
    int counter;
    int nthFibonacci;

    cout << "Enter the first two Fibonacci "
        << "numbers: ";                            //Step 1
    cin >> previous1 >> previous2;                 //Step 2
    cout << endl;

    cout << "The first two Fibonacci numbers are "
        << previous1 << " and " << previous2
        << endl;                                   //Step 3

    cout << "Enter the position of the desired "
        << "Fibonacci number: ";                   //Step 4
    cin >> nthFibonacci;                           //Step 5
    cout << endl;

    if (nthFibonacci == 1)                         //Step 6.a
        current = previous1;
    else if (nthFibonacci == 2)                    //Step 6.b
        current = previous2;
    else                                           //Step 6.c
    {
        counter = 3;                               //Step 6.c.1
```

4

```
                        //Steps 6.c.2 - 6.c.5
        while (counter <= nthFibonacci)
        {
                current = previous2 + previous1;     //Step 6.c.2
                previous1 = previous2;               //Step 6.c.3
                previous2 = current;                 //Step 6.c.4
                counter++;                           //Step 6.c.5
        }//end while
    }//end else

        cout << "The Fibonacci number at position "
             << nthFibonacci << " is " << current
             << endl;                                //Step 7

        return 0;
}//end main
```

Sample Runs: In these sample runs, the user input is shaded.

```
Enter the first two Fibonacci numbers: 12 16

The first two Fibonacci numbers are 12 and 16
Enter the position of the desired Fibonacci number: 10

The Fibonacci number at position 10 is 796
```

`for` Looping (Repetition) Structure

The `while` loop discussed in the previous section is general enough to implement most forms of repetitions. The C++ `for` looping structure discussed here is a specialized form of the `while` loop. Its primary purpose is to simplify the writing of count-controlled loops. For this reason, the `for` loop is typically called a counted or indexed `for` loop.

The general form of the `for` statement is:

```
for (initial statement; loop condition; update statement)
    statement
```

The `initial statement`, `loop condition`, and `update statement` (called `for` **loop control statements**) enclosed within the parentheses control the body (`statement`) of the `for` statement. Figure 4-2 shows the flow of execution of a `for` loop.

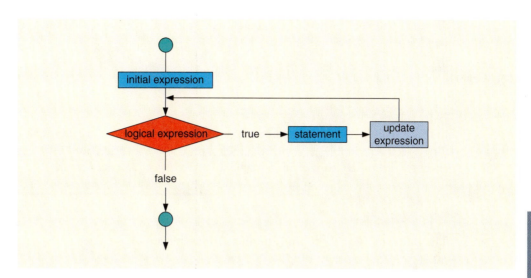

FIGURE 4-2 for loop

The **for** loop executes as follows:

1. The `initial statement` executes.
2. The `loop condition` is evaluated. If the `loop condition` evaluates to **true**
   i. Execute the **for** loop `statement`.
   ii. Execute the `update statement` (the third expression in the parentheses).
3. Repeat Step 2 until the `loop condition` evaluates to **false**.

The `initial statement` usually initializes a variable (called the **for loop control**, or **for indexed, variable**).

In C++, **for** is a reserved word.

NOTE   As the name implies, the `initial expression` in the **for** loop is the first statement to execute; it executes only once.

Primarily, **for** loops are used to implement counter-controlled loops. For this reason, the **for** loop typically is called a **counted** or **indexed** **for** loop. Next, we give various examples to illustrate how a **for** loop works. Before giving examples, let's note the following:

In C++, a variable can be declared anywhere, and it must be declared before it can be used. Typically, C++ programmers prefer to declare a **for** loop control variable within the `for` statement as part of the initial expression. For example, consider the following `for` loop:

```
for (int i = 0; i < 10; i++)
.
.
.
```

In this `for` loop, the initial expression declares the `int` variable i and initializes it to 0. In this case, the variable i is valid (visible) only for the `for` loop. After the `for` loop executes, if you try to use this variable i, you will get a syntax error.

EXAMPLE 4-8

The following `for` loop prints the first 10 nonnegative integers:

```
for (int i = 0; i < 10; i++)
    cout << i << " ";
cout << endl;
```

The `initial statement`, `int i = 0;`, declares and initializes the `int` variable i to 0. Next, the loop condition, `i < 10`, is evaluated. Because `0 < 10` is `true`, the print statement executes and outputs 0. The `update statement`, `i++`, then executes, which sets the value of i to 1. Once again, the `loop condition` is evaluated and is still `true`, and so on. When i becomes 10, the `loop condition` evaluates to `false`, the `for` loop terminates, and the statement following the `for` loop executes.

A `for` loop can have either a simple or compound statement.

The following examples further illustrate how a `for` loop executes.

EXAMPLE 4-9

The following `for` loop outputs `Hello!` and a star (on separate lines) five times:

```
for (int i = 1; i <= 5; i++)
{
    cout << "Hello!" << endl;
    cout << "*" << endl;
}
```

The following `for` loop illustrates a common mistake:

```
for (int i = 1; i <= 5; i++)
    cout << "Hello!" << endl;
    cout << "*" << endl;
```

This loop outputs the word Hello five times and the star only once. In this case, the for loop controls only the first output statement because the two output statements are not part of a compound statement enclosed in braces. Therefore, the first output statement executes five times because the for loop executes five times. After the for loop executes, the second output statement executes only once. The indentation, which is ignored by the compiler, is misleading.

The following for loop executes five empty statements:

```
for (int i = 0; i < 5; i++);        //Line 1
    cout << "*" << endl;            //Line 2
```

The semicolon at the end of the for statement (before the output statement in Line 2) terminates the for loop. The action of this for loop is empty. The statement in Line 2 outputs a star, and the program proceeds to whatever may follow Line 2.

The preceding examples show that care is required in getting a for loop to perform the desired action.

The following are some comments on for loops:

- If the loop condition is initially false, the loop body does not execute.

- The update expression, when executed, changes the value of the loop control variable (initialized by the initial expression), which eventually sets the value of the loop condition to false. The for loop body executes indefinitely if the loop condition is always true.

- C++ allows you to use fractional values for loop control variables of the double type (or any real data type). Because different computers can give these loop control variables different results, you should avoid using such variables.

- A semicolon at the end of the for statement (just before the body of the loop) is a semantic error. In this case, the action of the for loop is empty.

- In the for statement, if the loop condition is omitted, it is assumed to be true.

- In a for statement, you can omit all three statements—initial statement, loop condition, and update statement. The following is a legal for loop:

```
for (;;)
    cout << "Hello" << endl;
```

This is an infinite for loop, continuously printing the word Hello.

Following are more examples of **for** loops.

EXAMPLE 4-10

You can count backward using a **for** loop if the **for** loop control expressions are set correctly. For example, consider the following **for** loop:

```
for (int i = 10; i >= 1; i--)
    cout << " " << i;
cout << endl;
```

The output is

```
10 9 8 7 6 5 4 3 2 1
```

In this **for** loop, the variable i is initialized to 10. After each iteration of the loop, i is decremented by 1. The loop continues to execute as long as i >= 1.

EXAMPLE 4-11

You can increment (or decrement) the loop control variable by any fixed number. In the following **for** loop, the variable is initialized to 1; at the end of the **for** loop, i is incremented by 2. This **for** loop outputs the first 10 positive odd integers.

```
for (int i = 1; i <= 20; i = i + 2)
    cout << " " << i;
cout << endl;
```

EXAMPLE 4-12

1. Consider the following **for** loop.

   ```
   for (int i = 10; i <= 9; i++)
       cout << i << " ";
   cout << endl;
   ```

   In this **for** loop, the initial statement sets i to 10. Because initially the loop condition (i <= 9) is **false**, nothing happens.

2. Consider the following **for** loop.

   ```
   for (int i = 9; i >= 10; i--)
       cout << i << " ";
   cout << endl;
   ```

In this **for** loop, the initial statement sets i to 9. Because initially the loop condition (i >= 10) is **false**, nothing happens.

3. Consider the following **for** loop.

```
for (int i = 10; i <= 10; i++)    //Line 1
    cout << i << " ";             //Line 2
cout << endl;                     //Line 3
```

In this **for** loop, the initial statement sets i to 10. The loop condition (i <= 10) evaluates to **true**, so the output statement in Line 2 executes, which outputs 10. Next the update statement increments the value of i by 1, so the value of i becomes 11. Now the loop condition evaluates to **false** and the **for** loop terminates. Note that the output statement in Line 2 executes only once.

4. Consider the following **for** loop.

```
for (int i = 1; ; i++)
    cout << i << " ";
cout << endl;
```

In this **for** loop, because the **loop condition** is omitted from the **for** statement, the **loop condition** is always **true**. This is an infinite loop.

4

EXAMPLE 4-13

In this example, a **for** loop reads five numbers and finds their sum and average. Consider the following program code, in which newNum, sum, and average are **int** variables.

```
sum = 0;
for (int i = 1; i <= 5; i++)
{
    cin >> newNum;
    sum = sum + newNum;
}

average = sum / 5;
cout << "The sum is " << sum << endl;
cout << "The average is " << average << endl;
```

In the preceding **for** loop, after reading a newNum, this value is added to the previously calculated (partial) sum of all the numbers read before the current number. The variable sum is initialized to 0 before the **for** loop. Thus, after the program reads the first number and adds it to the value of sum, the variable sum holds the correct sum of the first number.

NOTE The syntax of the `for` loop, which is

```
for (initial expression; logical expression; update expression)
    statement
```

is functionally equivalent to the following `while` statement:

```
initial expression
while (expression)
{
      statement
      update expression
}
```

For example, the following `for` and `while` loops are equivalent:

```
for (int i = 0; i < 10; i++)
    cout << i <<  " ";
cout << endl;
```

```
int i = 0;
while (i < 10)
{
     cout << i <<  " ";
     i++;
}
cout << endl;
```

If the number of iterations of a loop is known or can be determined in advance, typically programmers use a `for` loop.

EXAMPLE 4-14 (FIBONACCI NUMBER PROGRAM: REVISITED)

The programming example Fibonacci Number given in the previous section uses a `while` loop to determine the desired Fibonacci number. You can replace the `while` loop with an equivalent `for` loop as follows:

```
for (int counter = 3; counter <= nthFibonacci; counter++)
{
    current = previous2 + previous1;
    previous1 = previous2;
    previous2 = current;
    counter++;
//end for
```

The complete program listing of the program that uses a `for` loop to determine the desired Fibonacci number is given at the Web site accompanying this book. The program is named `Ch4_FibonacciNumberUsingAForLoop.cpp`.

do...while Looping (Repetition) Structure

This section describes the third type of looping or repetition structure, called a do...while loop. The general form of a do...while statement is as follows:

```
do
    statement
while (expression);
```

Of course, statement can be either a simple or compound statement. If it is a compound statement, enclose it between braces. Figure 4-3 shows the flow of execution of a do...while loop.

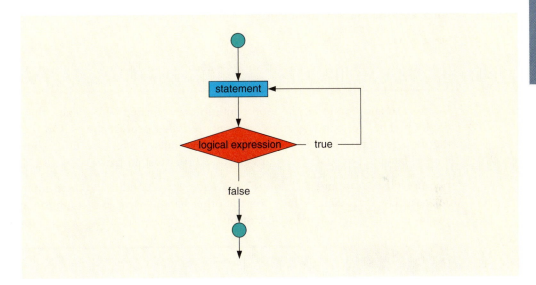

FIGURE 4-3 do...while loop

In C++, do is a reserved word.

The statement executes first, and then the expression is evaluated. If the expression evaluates to true, the statement executes again. As long as the expression in a do...while statement is true, the statement executes. To avoid an infinite loop, you must, once again, make sure that the loop body contains a statement that ultimately makes the expression false and ensures that it exits properly.

EXAMPLE 4-15

```
int i = 0;

do
{
    cout << i << " ";
    i = i + 5;
}
while (i <= 20);
```

The output of this code is:

0 5 10 15 20

After 20 is output, the statement:

```
i = i + 5;
```

changes the value of i to 25 and so i <= 20 becomes **false**, which halts the loop.

In a **while** and **for** loop, the loop condition is evaluated before executing the body of the loop. Therefore, **while** and **for** loops are called **pretest loops**. On the other hand, the loop condition in a do...while loop is evaluated after executing the body of the loop. Therefore, do...while loops are called **posttest loops**.

Because the **while** and **for** loops both have entry conditions, these loops may never activate. The do...while loop, on the other hand, has an exit condition and therefore always executes the statement at least once.

EXAMPLE 4-16

Consider the following two loops:

```
a.  i = 11;
    while (i <= 10)
    {
        cout << i << " ";
        i = i + 5;
    }
    cout << endl;
b.  i = 11;
    do
    {
        cout << i << " ";
        i = i + 5;
    }
    while (i <= 10);

    cout << endl;
```

In (a), the `while` loop produces nothing. In (b), the `do...while` loop outputs the number 11 and also changes the value of `i` to 16.

A `do...while` loop can be used for input validation. Consider a program which prompts a user to enter a test score, which must be at least 12 but not more than 36. If the user enters a score less than 12 or greater than 36, the user should be prompted to reenter the score. The following `do...while` loop can be used to accomplish this objective:

```
int score;

do
{
    cout << "Enter a score between 12 and 36: ";
    cin >> score;
    cout << endl;
}
while (score < 12 || score > 36);
```

Choosing the Right Looping Structure

All three loops have a place in C++. If you know or the program can determine in advance the number of repetitions needed, the `for` loop is the correct choice. If you do not know, and the program cannot determine in advance the number of repetitions needed, and it could be zero, the `while` loop is the right choice. If you do not know, and the program cannot determine in advance, the number of repetitions needed, and it is at least one, the `do...while` loop is the right choice.

Loops and the break Statement

The `break` statement, when executed in a `switch` structure, provides an immediate exit from the `switch` structure. Similarly, you can use the `break` statement in `while`, `for`, and `do...while` loops. When the `break` statement executes in a repetition structure, it immediately exits from the structure. The `break` statement is typically used for two purposes:

- To exit early from a loop
- To skip the remainder of the `switch` structure

After the `break` statement executes, the program continues to execute with the first statement after the structure.

The use of a `break` statement in a loop can eliminate the use of certain (flag) variables. The following C++ code segment helps illustrate this idea. (Assume that all variables are properly declared.)

```
sum = 0;
isNegative = false;

cin >> num;

while (cin && !isNegative)
{
    if (num < 0)    //if num is negative, terminate the loop
                    //after this iteration
    {
        cout << "Negative number found in the data." << endl;
        isNegative = true;
    }
    else
    {
        sum = sum + num;
        cin >> num;
    }
}
```

This `while` loop is supposed to find the sum of a set of positive numbers. If the data set contains a negative number, the loop terminates with an appropriate error message. This `while` loop uses the flag variable `isNegative` to accomplish the desired result. The variable `isNegative` is initialized to `false` before the `while` loop. Before adding `num` to `sum`, check whether `num` is negative. If `num` is negative, an error message appears on the screen and `isNegative` is set to `true`. In the next iteration, when the expression in the `while` statement is evaluated, it evaluates to `false` because `!isNegative` is `false`. (Note that because `isNegative` is `true`, `!isNegative` is `false`.)

The following `while` loop is written without using the variable `isNegative`:

```
sum = 0;
cin >> num;

while (cin)
{
    if (num < 0)    //if num is negative, terminate the loop
    {
        cout << "Negative number found in the data." << endl;
        break;
    }

    sum = sum + num;
    cin >> num;
}
```

In this form of the `while` loop, when a negative number is found, the expression in the `if` statement evaluates to `true`; after printing an appropriate message, the `break` statement terminates the loop. (After the execution of the `break` statement in a loop, the remaining statements in the loop are discarded.)

NOTE The **break** statement is an effective way to avoid extra variables to control a loop and produce an elegant code. However, **break** statements must be used very sparingly within a loop. Excessive use of these statements in a loop will produce spaghetti-code (loops with many exit conditions) and can be very hard to understand and manage. You should be extra careful in using break statements and ensure that the use of the break statements makes the code more readable, and not less readable. If you're not sure, don't use break statements.

Nested Control Structures

In this section, we give examples that illustrate how to use nested loops to achieve useful results and process data.

EXAMPLE 4-17

Suppose you want to create the following pattern:

```
*
**
***
****
*****
```

Clearly, you want to print five lines of stars. In the first line, you want to print one star, in the second line, two stars, and so on. Because five lines will be printed, start with the following **for** statement:

```cpp
for (int i = 1; i <= 5; i++)
```

The value of i in the first iteration is 1, in the second iteration it is 2, and so on. You can use the value of i as the limiting condition in another **for** loop nested within this loop to control the number of stars in a line. A little more thought produces the following code:

```cpp
for (int i = 1; i <= 5; i++)        //Line 1
{                                    //Line 2
    for (int j = 1; j <= i; j++)    //Line 3
        cout << "*";                 //Line 4
    cout << endl;                    //Line 5
}                                    //Line 6
```

A walk-through of this code shows that the **for** loop, in Line 1, starts with i = 1. When i is 1, the inner **for** loop, in Line 3, outputs one star and the insertion point moves to the next line. Then i becomes 2, the inner **for** loop outputs two stars, and the output statement in Line 5 moves the insertion point to the next line, and so on. This process continues until i becomes 6 and the loop stops.

What pattern does this code produce if you replace the **for** statement, in Line 1, with the following?

```cpp
for (int i = 5; i >= 1; i--)
```

EXAMPLE 4-18

Suppose you want to create the following grid of numbers:

```
1 2 3 4 5
2 3 4 5 6
3 4 5 6 7
4 5 6 7 8
5 6 7 8 9
```

There are five lines in this grid. Therefore, as in Example 4-17, we use a `for` statement to output these lines as follows:

```
for (int i = 1; i <= 5; i++)
    //output a line of numbers
```

In the first line, we want to print the numbers 1 through 5, in the second line, we want to print the numbers 2 through 6, and so on. Notice that the first line starts with 1 and when this line is printed, i is 1. Similarly, the second line starts with 2 and when this line is printed, the value of i is 2, and so on. If i is 1, i + 4 is 5; if i is 2, i + 4 is 6; and so on. Therefore, to print a line of numbers, we can use the value of i as the starting number and the value of i + 4 as the limiting value. That is, consider the following `for` loop:

```
for (int j = i; j <= i + 4; j++)
    cout << j << " ";
```

Let us take a look at this `for` loop. Suppose i is 1. Then we are printing the first line of the grid. Also, j goes from 1 to 5 and so this `for` loop outputs the numbers 1 through 5, which is the first line of the grid. Similarly, if i is 2, we are printing the second line of the grid. Also, j goes from 2 to 6 and so this `for` loop outputs the numbers 2 through 6, which is the second line of the grid, and so on.

The following nested loops output the desired grid:

```
for (int i = 1; i <= 5; i++)            //Line 1
{                                       //Line 2
    for (int j = i; j <= i + 4; j++)    //Line 3
        cout << j << " ";               //Line 4
    cout << endl;                       //Line 5
}                                       //Line 6
```

EXAMPLE 4-19

Consider the following data:

```
65 78 65 89 25 98 -999
87 34 89 99 26 78 64 34 -999
23 99 98 97 26 78 100 63 87 23 -999
62 35 78 99 12 93 19 -999
```

The number -999 at the end of each line acts as a sentinel and therefore is not part of the data. Our objective is to find the sum of the numbers in each line and output the sum. Moreover, assume that this data is to be read from a file, say, Exp_4_19.txt. We assume that the input file has been opened using the input file stream variable infile.

This particular data set has four lines of input. So we can use a **for** loop or a counter-controlled **while** loop to process each line of data. Let us use a **for** loop to process these four lines. The **for** loop takes the following form:

```
for (int counter = 0; counter < 4; counter++)      //Line 1
{                                                   //Line 2
    //process the line
    //output the sum
}
```

Let us now concentrate on processing a line. Each line has a varying number of data items. For example, the first line has 6 numbers, the second line has 8 numbers, and so on. Because each line ends with -999, we can use a sentinel-controlled **while** loop to find the sum of the numbers in each line. Consider the following **while** loop:

```
sum = 0;                    //Line 3
infile >> num;              //Line 4

while (num != -999)         //Line 5
{                           //Line 6
    sum = sum + num;        //Line 7
    infile >> num;          //Line 8
}                           //Line 9
```

The statement in Line 3 initializes sum to 0, and the statement in Line 4 reads and stores the first number of the line into num. The Boolean expression, num != -999, in Line 5, checks whether the number is -999. If num is not -999, the statements in Lines 7 and 8 execute. The statement in Line 7 updates the value of sum; the statement in Line 8 reads and stores the next number into num. The loop continues to execute as long as num is not -999.

It now follows that the nested loop to process the data is as follows. (Assume that all variables are properly declared.)

```
for (int counter = 0; counter < 4; counter++)      //Line 1
{                                                   //Line 2
    sum = 0;                                        //Line 3
    infile >> num;                                  //Line 4
    while (num != -999)                             //Line 5
    {                                               //Line 6
        sum = sum + num;                            //Line 7
        infile >> num;                              //Line 8
    }                                               //Line 9

    cout << "Line " << counter + 1
        << ": Sum = " << sum << endl;               //Line 10
    counter++;                                       //Line 11
}                                                   //Line 12
```

EXAMPLE 4-20

Consider the following data:

```
101
John Smith
65 78 65 89 25 98 -999
102
Peter Gupta
87 34 89 99 26 78 64 34 -999
103
Buddy Friend
23 99 98 97 26 78 100 63 87 23 -999
104
Doctor Miller
62 35 78 99 12 93 19 -999
...
```

The number -999 at the end of a line acts as a sentinel and therefore is not part of the data. Assume that this is the data of certain candidates seeking the student council's presidential seat. For each candidate, the data is in the following form:

```
ID
Name
Votes
```

The objective is to find the total number of votes received by the candidate. We assume that the data is input from the file, **Exp_4_20.txt**, of unknown size. We also assume that the input file has been opened using the input file stream variable **infile**.

Because the input file is of an unspecified length, we use an EOF-controlled **while** loop. For each candidate, the first data item is the **ID** of the type **int** on a line by itself; the second data item is the name, which may consist of more than one word; and the third line contains the votes received from the various departments.

To read the **ID**, we use the extraction operator **>>**; to read the name, we use the stream function **getline**. Notice that after reading the **ID**, the reading marker is after the **ID** and the character after the **ID** is the newline character. Therefore, after reading the **ID**, the reading marker is after the **ID** and before the newline character (of the line containing the **ID**.)

The function **getline** reads until the end of the line. Therefore, if we read the name immediately after reading the **ID**, then what is stored in the variable name is the newline character (after the **ID**). It follows that to read the name, we must read and discard the newline character after the **ID**, which we can accomplish by using the stream function **get**. Therefore, the statements to read the **ID** and name are as follows:

```
infile >> ID;              //read the ID
infile.get(ch);            //read the newline character after the ID
getline(infile, name);     //read the name
```

(Assume that ch is a variable of the type **char**.) The general loop to process the data is:

```
infile >> ID;                              //Line 1
while (infile)                             //Line 2
{                                          //Line 3
    infile.get(ch);                        //Line 4
    getline(infile, name);                 //Line 5

    //process the numbers in each line     //Line 6
    //output the name and total votes
    infile >> ID;      //begin processing the next line
}
```

The code to read and sum up the voting data is the same as in Example 4-19. That is, the required **while** loop is:

```
sum = 0;                     //Line 6
infile >> num;               //Line 7; read the first number
while (num != -999)          //Line 8
{                            //Line 9
    sum = sum + num;         //Line 10; update sum
    infile >> num;           //Line 11; read the next number
}                            //Line 12
```

We can now write the following nested loop to process data:

```
infile >> ID;                        //Line 1
while (infile)                       //Line 2
{                                    //Line 3
    infile.get(ch);                  //Line 4
    getline(infile, name);           //Line 5
    sum = 0;                         //Line 6
    infile >> num;                   //Line 7; read the first number
    while (num != -999)              //Line 8
    {                                //Line 9
        sum = sum + num;             //Line 10; update sum
        infile >> num;               //Line 11; read the next number
    }

    cout << "Name: " << name
         << ", Votes: " << sum
         << endl;                    //Line 12

    infile >> ID;      //Line 13; begin processing the next line
}
```

Avoiding Bugs by Avoiding Patches

A software patch is a piece of code written on top of an existing piece of code and intended to remedy a deficiency in the original code. Determining and correcting the original deficiency is a much better approach.

Consider, for example, the following lines of code, originally intended to print three rows of stars, with one star on the first row, two stars on the second row, and three stars on the third row.

```
for (int i = 0; i <= 3; i++)        //Line 1
{                                    //Line 2
    for (int j = 0; j <= i; j++)     //Line 3
        cout << "*";                 //Line 4

    cout << endl;                    //Line 5
}                                    //Line 6
```

These lines of code produce the following output:

```
*
**
***
****
```

The output consists of four rows of stars rather than three rows of stars, as intended originally.

Instead of addressing the problem, some programmers address the symptom of the problem by adding a software patch. The following example illustrates a software patch that might be produced by a beginning programmer:

```
for (int i = 0; i <= 3; i++)            //Line 1
{                                        //Line 2
    if (i == 3)                          //Line p1
        break;                           //Line p2
    else                                 //Line p3
        for (int j = 0; j <= i; j++)     //Line 3
            cout << "*";                 //Line 4

    cout << endl;                        //Line 5
}                                        //Line 6
```

Here, the programmer has observed a symptom of the problem, namely the printing of an extra row of stars. Instead of addressing the problem, he has addressed the symptom by exiting the outer **for** loop during its fourth repetition. The patch on Lines p1, p2, and p3 eliminates the symptom, but it represents poor programming practice. Instead, the programmer should find and fix the problem. Here, the code allows four values of the loop control variable i, in this case 0, 1, 2, and 3. This is an example of the classic "off by one" problem. The problem can be eliminated by allowing i to range from 0 to 2. The problem also can be eliminated by allowing i to range from 1 to 3, but this necessitates initializing j to 1 (rather than 0) in the inner **for** loop. However, the code becomes clearer by allowing i to range from 1 to 3 with j initialized to 1, so this is the better solution even though it requires more changes:

```
for (int i = 1; i <= 3; i++)          //Line 1
{                                       //Line 2
    for (int j = 1; j <= i; j++)       //Line 3
        cout << "*"; << endl;          //Line 4

    cout << endl;                       //Line 5
}                                       //Line 6
```

This piece of code fixes the original problem without using a software patch and represents good programming practice.

QUICK REVIEW

1. C++ has three looping (repetition) structures: `while`, `for`, and `do...while`.

2. The syntax of the `while` statement is:

    ```
    while (expression)
        statement
    ```

3. In C++, `while` is a reserved word.

4. In the `while` statement, the parentheses around the **expression** (the decision maker) are important; they mark the beginning and end of the expression.

5. The `statement` is called the body of the loop.

6. The body of the `while` loop must contain a statement that eventually sets the expression to `false`.

7. A counter-controlled `while` loop uses a counter to control the loop.

8. In a counter-controlled `while` loop, you must initialize the counter before the loop, and the body of the loop must contain a statement that changes the value of the counter variable.

9. A sentinel is a special value that marks the end of the input data. The sentinel must be similar to, yet differ from, all the data items.

10. A sentinel-controlled `while` loop uses a sentinel to control the `while` loop. The `while` loop continues to execute until the sentinel is read.

11. An EOF-controlled `while` loop continues to execute until the program detects the end-of-file marker.

12. A `for` loop simplifies the writing of a count-controlled `while` loop.

13. In C++, `for` is a reserved word.

14. The syntax of the `for` loop is:

    ```
    for (initialize statement; loop condition; update statement)
        statement
    ```

    statement is called the body of the `for` loop.

15. Putting a semicolon at the end of the `for` loop (before the body of the `for` loop) is a semantic error. In this case, the action of the `for` loop is empty.

16. The syntax of the `do...while` statement is:

```
do
      statement
while (expression);
```

`statement` is called the body of the `do...while` loop.

17. Both `while` and `for` loops are called pretest loops. A `do...while` loop is called a posttest loop.

18. The `while` and `for` loops may not execute at all, but the `do...while` loop always executes at least once.

19. Executing a `break` statement in the body of a loop immediately terminates the loop.

EXERCISES

1. Mark the following statements as true or false.

a. In a counter-controlled `while` loop, it is not necessary to initialize the loop control variable.

b. It is possible that the body of a `while` loop may not execute at all.

c. In an infinite `while` loop, the `while` expression (the decision maker) is initially false, but after the first iteration it is always true.

d. The `while` loop:

```
int j = 0;
while (j <= 10)
    j++;
```

terminates if j > 10.

e. A sentinel-controlled `while` loop is an event-controlled `while` loop whose termination depends on a special value.

f. A loop is a control structure that causes certain statements to execute over and over.

g. To read data from a file of an unspecified length, an EOF-controlled loop is a good choice.

h. When a `while` loop terminates, the control first goes back to the statement just before the `while` statement, and then the control goes to the statement immediately following the `while` loop.

2. What is the output of the following C++ code?

```
int count = 1;
int y = 100;
while (count < 100)
{
    y = y - 1;
    count++;
}
cout << " y = " << y << " and count = " << count << endl;
```

3. What is the output of the following C++ code?

```
int num = 5;
while (num > 5)
    num = num + 2;
cout << num << endl;
```

4. What is the output of the following C++ code?

```
int num = 1;
while (num < 10)
{
    cout << num << " ";
    num = num + 2;
}
cout << endl;
```

5. When does the following `while` loop terminate?

```
char ch = 'D';
while ('A' <= ch && ch <= 'Z')
    ch = static_cast<char>(static_cast<int>(ch) + 1);
```

6. Suppose that the input is 38 45 71 4 −1. What is the output of the following code? Assume all variables are properly declared.

```
cin >> sum;
cin >> num;

for (int j = 1; j <= 3; j++)
{
    cin >> num;
    sum = sum + num;
}
cout << "Sum = " << sum << endl;
```

7. Suppose that the input is 38 45 71 4 −1. What is the output of the following code? Assume all variables are properly declared.

```
cin >> sum;
cin >> num;

while (num != -1)
{
    sum = sum + num;
    cin >> num;
}
cout << "Sum = " << sum << endl;
```

8. Suppose that the input is 38 45 71 4 −1. What is the output of the following code? Assume all variables are properly declared.

```
cin >> num;
sum = num;
```

4

```
while (num != -1)
{
    cin >> num;
    sum = sum + num;
}
cout << "Sum = " << sum << endl;
```

9. Suppose that the input is 38 45 71 4 -1. What is the output of the following code? Assume all variables are properly declared.

```
sum = 0;
cin >> num;

while (num != -1)
{
    sum = sum + num;
    cin >> num;
}
cout << "Sum = " << sum << endl;
```

10. Correct the following code so that it finds the sum of 10 numbers.

```
sum = 0;

while (count < 10)
    cin >> num;
    sum = sum + num;
    count++;
```

11. What is the output of the following program?

```
#include <iostream>

using namespace std;

int main()
{
    int  x, y, z;

    x = 4;    y = 5;
    z = y + 6;

    while (((z - x) % 4) != 0)
    {
        cout << z << " ";
        z = z + 7;
    }
    cout << endl;

    return 0;
}
```

12. Suppose that the input is: 58 23 46 75 98 150 12 176 145 -999

What is the output of the following program?

```cpp
#include <iostream>

using namespace std;

int main()
{
    int num;

    cin >> num;

    while (num != -999)
    {
      cout << num % 25 << " ";
      cin >> num;
    }

    cout << endl;

    return 0;
}
```

13. Given the following:

```cpp
for (int i = 12; i <= 25; i++)
    cout << i;
```

a. The seventh integer printed is _____.

b. The statement produces _____ lines of output.

c. If i++ were changed to i--, a compilation error would result. True or false?

14. Given that the following code is correctly inserted into a program, state its entire output as to content and form.

```cpp
int num = 0;
for (int i = 1; i <= 4; i++)
{
    num = num + 10 * (i - 1);
    cout << num << " ";
}
cout << endl;
```

15. Given that the following code is correctly inserted into a program, state its entire output as to content and form.

```cpp
int j = 2;
for (int i = 0; i <= 5; i++)
{
    cout << j << " ";
    j = 2 * j + 3;
}
cout << j << " " << endl;
```

16. Assume that the following code is correctly inserted into a program:

```
int s = 0;
int i;
for (i = 0; i < 5; i++)
{
    s = 2 * s + i;
    cout << s << " ";
}
cout << endl;
```

a. What is the final value of s?

   i.   11   ii.   4   iii.   26   iv.   none of these

b. If a semicolon is inserted after the right parenthesis in the **for** loop statement, what is the final value of s?

   i.   0   ii.   1   iii.   2   iv.   5   v.   none of these

c. If the 5 is replaced with a 0 in the **for** loop control expression, what is the final value of s?

   i.   0   ii.   1   iii.   2   iv.   none of these

17. State what output, if any, results from each of the following statements:

a.
```
for (int i = 1; i <= 1; i++)
    cout << "*";
cout << endl;
```

b.
```
for (int i = 2; i >= 1; i++)
    cout << "*";
cout << endl;
```

c.
```
for (int i = 1; i <= 1; i--)
    cout << "*";
cout << endl;
```

d.
```
for (int i = 12; i >= 9; i--)
    cout << "*";
cout << endl;
```

e.
```
for (int i = 0; i <= 5; i++)
    cout << "*";
cout << endl;
```

f.
```
for (int i = 1; i <= 5; i++)
{
    cout << "*";
    i = i + 1;
}
cout << endl;
```

18. Write a **for** statement to add all the multiples of 3 between 1 and 100.

19. Suppose that the input is **5 3 8**. What is the output of the following code? Assume all variables are properly declared.

```
cin >> a >> b >> c;
for (int j = 1; j < a; j++)
{
    d = b + c;
    b = c;
    c = d;
    cout << c << " ";
}
cout << endl;
```

20. The following program has more than five mistakes that prevent it from compiling and/or running. Correct all such mistakes.

```
#include <iostream>

using namespace std;
const int N = 2,137;

main ()
{
    int a, b, c, d:

    a := 3;
    b = 5;
    c = c + d;
    N = a + n;
    for (i = 3; i <= N; i++)
    {
        cout << setw(5) << i;
        i = i + 1;
    }

    return 0;
}
```

4

21. Which of the following apply to the **while** loop only? To the **do...while** loop only? To both?

a. It is considered a conditional loop.

b. The body of the loop executes at least once.

c. The logical expression controlling the loop is evaluated before the loop is entered.

d. The body of the loop may not execute at all.

22. How many times will each of the following loops execute? What is the output in each case?

    a. ```
        x = 5;   y = 50;
        do
             x = x + 10;
        while (x < y);
        cout << x << " " << y << endl;
        ```

    b.  ```
        x = 5;   y = 80;
        do
              x = x * 2;
        while (x < y);
        cout << x << " " << y << endl;
        ```

    c. ```
        x = 5;   y = 20;
        do
             x = x + 2;
        while (x >= y);
        cout << x << " " << y << endl;
        ```

    d.  ```
        x = 5;   y = 35;
        while (x < y)
              x = x + 10;
        cout << x << " " << y << endl;
        ```

    e. ```
        x = 5;   y = 30;
        while (x <= y)
             x = x * 2;
        cout << x << " " << y << endl;
        ```

    f.  ```
        x = 5;   y = 30;
        while (x > y)
              x = x + 2;
        cout << x << " " << y << endl;
        ```

23. The do...while loop in the following program is supposed to read some numbers until it reaches a sentinel (in this case, -1). It is supposed to add all of the numbers except for the sentinel. If the data looks like:

    12   5   30   48   -1

    the program does not add the numbers correctly. Correct the program so that it adds the numbers correctly.

    ```
    #include <iostream>

    using namespace std;

    int main()
    {
        int total = 0;
        int count = 0;
        int number;
    ```

```
    do
    {
        cin >> number;
        total = total + number;
        count++;
    }
    while (number != -1);

    cout << "The number of data read is " << count << endl;
    cout << "The sum of the numbers entered is  " << total
        << endl;

    return 0;
}
```

24. Using the same data as in Exercise 23, the following two loops also fail. Correct them.

   a.
```
    cin >> number;
    while (number != -1)
        total =  total + number;
        cin >> number;
        cout << endl;
        cout << total << endl;
```

   b.
```
    cin >> number;
    while (number != -1)
        {
        cin >> number;
        total = total + number;
    }
    cout << endl;
    cout << total << endl;
```

25. Given the following program segment:

```
for (int number = 1; number <= 10; number++)
    cout << setw(3) << number;
```

   write a while loop and a do...while loop that have the same output.

26. Given the following program segment:

```
int j = 2;
for (int i = 1; i <= 5; i++);
{
    cout << setw(4) << j;
    j = j + 5;
}
cout << endl;
```

   write a while loop and a do...while loop that have the same output.

27. What is the output of the following program?

```cpp
#include <iostream>

using namespace std;

int main()
{
    int x, y, z;
    x = 4;    y = 5;
    z = y + 6;
    do
    {
        cout << z << " ";
        z = z + 7;
    }
    while (((z - x) % 4) != 0);

    cout << endl;

    return 0;
}
```

28. Do a walk-through of the following program segments and determine, in each case, the exact output.

a.
```cpp
for (int i = 1; i <= 5; i++)
{
    for (int j = 1; j <= 5; j++)
        cout << setw(3) << i * j;
    cout << endl;
}
```

b.
```cpp
for (int i = 1; i <= 5; i++)
{
    for (int j = 1; j <= 5; j++)
        cout << setw(3) << i;
    cout << endl;
}
```

c.
```cpp
for (int i = 1; i <= 5; i++)
{
    for (int j = (i + 1); j <= 5; j++)
        cout << setw(5) << j;
    cout << endl;
}
```

d.
```cpp
for (int i = 1; i <= 5; i++)
{
    for (int j = 1; j <= i; j++)
        cout << setw(3) << j;
    cout << endl;
}
```

e.
```cpp
const int M = 10;
const int N = 10;
```

```
        for (int i = 1; i <= M; i++)
        {
             for (int j = 1; j <= N; j++)
                 cout << setw(3) << M * (i - 1) + j;
             cout << endl;
        }
f.      for (int i = 1; i <= 9; i++)
        {
             for (int j = 1; j <= (9 - i); j++)
                 cout << " ";
             for (int j = 1; j <= i; j++)
                 cout << setw(1) << j;
             for (int j = (i - 1); j >= 1; j--)
                 cout << setw(1) << j;
             cout << endl;
        }
```

4

PROGRAMMING EXERCISES

1. Write a program that prompts the user to input an integer and then outputs both the individual digits of the number and the sum of the digits. For example, it should output the individual digits of 3456 as 3 4 5 6, output the individual digits of 8030 as 8 0 3 0, output the individual digits of 2345526 as 2 3 4 5 5 2 6, output the individual digits of 4000 as 4 0 0 0, and output the individual digits of −2345 as 2 3 4 5.

2. Write a program that prompts the user to input an integer and then outputs the number with the digits reversed. For example, if the input is 12345, the output should be 54321. Your program must also output 5000 as 0005 and 980 as 089.

3. Write a program that prompts the user to enter an uppercase letter. The program outputs the corresponding telephone digit.

4. The program in Exercise 3 outputs only telephone digits that correspond to uppercase letters. Rewrite the program so that it processes both uppercase and lowercase letters and outputs the corresponding telephone digit. If the input is other than an uppercase or lowercase letter, the program outputs an appropriate error message.

5. To make telephone numbers easier to remember, some companies use letters to show their telephone number. For example, using letters, the telephone number 438-5626 can be shown as GET LOAN. In some cases, to make a telephone number meaningful, companies might use more than seven letters. For example, 224-5466 can be displayed as CALL HOME, which uses eight letters. Write a program that prompts the user to enter a telephone number expressed in letters and outputs the corresponding telephone number in digits. If the user enters more than seven letters, then process only the first seven letters. Also output the - (hyphen) after the third digit. Allow the user

to use both uppercase and lowercase letters as well as spaces between words. Moreover, your program should process as many telephone numbers as the user wants.

6. Write a program that reads a set of integers, and then finds and prints the sums of the even and odd integers.

7. Write a program that prompts the user to input a positive integer. It should then output a message indicating whether the number is a prime number. (*Note:* An even number is prime if it is 2. An odd integer is prime if it is not divisible by any odd integer less than or equal to the square root of the number. You can use the function `sqrt` from the header file `cmath` to find the square root of a nonnegative real number. For example, `sqrt(2.25) = 1.5`.).

8. Let $n = a_k a_{k-1} a_{k-2} \ldots a_1 a_0$ be an integer. Let $s = a_k + a_{k-1} + a_{k-2} + \ldots + a_1 + a_0$ be the sum of the digits of n. It has been proved that n is divisible by 3 and 9 if s is divisible by 3 and 9. In other words, an integer is divisible by 3 and 9 if and only if the sum of its digits is divisible by 3 and 9. For example, suppose $n = 27193257$. Then $s = 2 + 7 + 1 + 9 + 3 + 2 + 5 + 7 = 36$. Because 36 is divisible by both 3 and 9, it follows that 27193257 is divisible by both 3 and 9. Write a program that prompts the user to enter a positive integer and then uses this criterion to determine whether the number is divisible by 3 and/or 9.

9. Write a program that uses `while` loops to perform the following steps:

   a. Prompt the user to input two integers: `firstNum` and `secondNum` (`firstNum` must be less than `secondNum`).

   b. Output all odd numbers between `firstNum` and `secondNum` (inclusive).

   c. Output the sum of all even numbers between `firstNum` and `secondNum`.

   d. Output the numbers and their squares between 1 and 10.

   e. Output the sum of the square of the odd numbers between `firstNum` and `secondNum`.

   f. Output all uppercase letters.

10. Redo Exercise 9 using `for` loops.

11. Redo Exercise 9 using `do...while` loops.

12. The program in the Programming Example Fibonacci Number does not check whether the first number entered by the user is less than or equal to the second number and whether both the numbers are nonnegative. Also, the program does not check whether the user entered a valid value for the position of the desired number in the Fibonacci sequence. Rewrite that program so that it checks for these things.

13. The program in Example 4-5 implements the Number Guessing Game. However, in that program the user is given as many tries as needed to guess

the correct number. Rewrite the program so that the user has no more than five tries to guess the correct number. Your program should print an appropriate message, such as "You win!" or "You lose!"

14. Example 4-5 implements the Number Guessing Game program. If the guessed number is not correct, the program outputs a message indicating whether the guess is low or high. Modify the program as follows: Suppose that the variables num and guess are as declared in Example 4-5 and diff is an int variable. Let diff = the absolute value of (num – guess). If diff is 0, then guess is correct and the program outputs a message indicating that the user guessed the correct number. Suppose diff is not 0. Then the program outputs the message as follows:

   a. If diff is greater than or equal to 50, the program outputs the message indicating that the guess is very high (if guess is greater than num) or very low (if guess is less than num).

   b. If diff is greater than or equal to 30 and less than 50, the program outputs the message indicating that the guess is high (if guess is greater than num) or low (if guess is less than num).

   c. If diff is greater than or equal to 15 and less than 30, the program outputs the message indicating that the guess is moderately high (if guess is greater than num) or moderately low (if guess is less than num).

   d. If diff is greater than 0 and less than 15, the program outputs the message indicating that the guess is somewhat high (if guess is greater than num) or somewhat low (if guess is less than num).

   As in Programming Exercise 13, give the user no more than five tries to guess the number. (To find the absolute value of num – guess, use the expression abs(num – guess). The function abs is from the header file cstdlib.

15. A high school has 1000 students and 1000 lockers, one locker for each student. On the first day of school, the principal plays the following game: She asks the first student to go and open all the lockers. She then asks the second student to go and close all the even numbered lockers. The third student is asked to check every third locker. If it is open, the student closes it; if it is closed, the student opens it. The fourth student is asked to check every fourth locker. If it is open, the student closes it; if it is closed, the student opens it. The remaining students continue this game. In general, the *n*th student checks every *n*th locker. If the locker is open, the student closes it; if it is closed, the student opens it. After all the students have taken their turn, some of the lockers are open and some are closed. Write a program that prompts the user to enter the number of lockers in a school. After the game is over, the program outputs the number of lockers that are open. Test run your program for the following inputs: 1000, 5000, 10000. Do you see any pattern developing?

(*Hint*: Consider locker number 100. This locker is visited by student numbers 1, 2, 4, 5, 10, 20, 25, 50, and 100. These are the positive divisors of 100. Similarly, locker number 30 is visited by student numbers 1, 2, 3, 5, 6, 10, 15, and 30. Notice that if the number of positive divisors of a locker number is odd, then at the end of the game the locker is opened. If the number of positive divisors of a locker number is even, then at the end of the game the locker is closed.)

16. When you borrow money to buy a house or a car, or for some other purpose, you repay the loan by making periodic payments over a certain time. Of course the lending company will charge interest on the loan. Every periodic payment consists of the interest on the loan and the payment toward the principal amount. To be specific, suppose that you borrow $1000 at the interest rate of 7.2% per year and the payments are monthly. Suppose that your monthly payment is $25. The interest is 7.2% per year and the payments are monthly, so the interest rate per month is $7.2/12 = 0.6\%$. The first month's interest on $1000 is $1000 * 0.006 = 6$. Because the payment is $25 and interest for the first month is $6, the payment toward the principal amount is $25 - 6 = 19$. This means that after making the first payment, the loan amount is $1000 - 19 = 981$. For the second payment, the interest is calculated on $981. So the interest for the second month is $981 * 0.006 = 5.886$, that is, approximately $5.89. This implies that the payment toward the principal is $25 - 5.89 = 19.11$, and the remaining balance after the second payment is $981 - 19.11 = 961.89$. This process is repeated until the loan is paid. Write a program that accepts as input, the loan amount, the interest rate per year, and the monthly payment. (Enter the interest rate as a percentage. For example, if the interest rate is 7.2% per year, then enter 7.2.) The program then outputs the number of months it would take to repay the loan. (Note that if the monthly payment is less then the first month's interest, then after each payment, the loan amount will increase. In this case, the program must warn the borrower that the monthly payment is too low and with this monthly payment the loan amount could not be repaid.)

17. Enhance your program from Exercise 16 by first telling the user the minimum monthly payment and then prompting the user to enter the monthly payment. The last payment might be more than the remaining loan amount and interest on it. In this case, output the loan amount before the last payment and the actual amount of the last payment. Also, output the total interest paid.

18. Write a complete program to test the code in Example 4-17.

19. Write a complete program to test the code in Example 4-18.

20. Write a complete program to test the code in Example 4-19.

21. Write a complete program to test the code in Example 4-20.

22. (**Apartment Problem**) A real estate office handles, say, 50 apartment units. When the rent is, say, $600 per month, all the units are occupied. However, for each, say, $40 increase in rent, one unit becomes vacant. Moreover, each occupied unit requires an average of $27 per month for maintenance. Write a program that prompts the user to enter the following:

   a. The number of apartments

   b. The rent to occupy all the units

   c. The increase in rent that results in a vacant unit

   d. The amount to maintain a rented unit

   The program then outputs the number of units to be rented to maximize the profit.

4

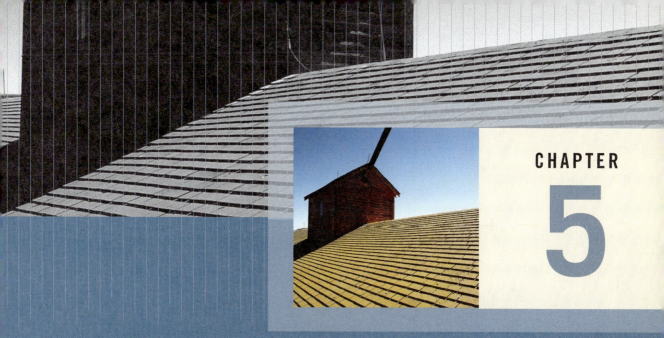

USER-DEFINED FUNCTIONS

IN THIS CHAPTER, YOU WILL:

■ Learn about standard (predefined) functions and discover how to use them in a program

■ Learn about user-defined functions

■ Examine value-returning functions, including actual and formal parameters

■ Explore how to construct and use a value-returning, user-defined function in a program

■ Learn how to construct and use void functions in a program

■ Discover the difference between value and reference parameters

■ Explore reference parameters and value-returning functions

■ Learn about the scope of an identifier

■ Examine the difference between local and global identifiers

■ Discover static variables

■ Learn function overloading

■ Explore functions with default parameters

In Chapter 1, you learned that a C++ program is a collection of functions. One such function is `main`. The programs in Chapters 1 through 4 use only the function `main`; the programming instructions are packed into one function. This technique, however, is good only for short programs. For large programs, it is not practical (although it is possible) to put the entire programming instructions into one function, as you will soon discover. You must learn to break the problem into manageable pieces. This chapter first discusses the previously defined functions and then discusses user-defined functions.

Let us imagine an automobile factory. When an automobile is manufactured, it is not made from basic raw materials; it is put together from previously manufactured parts. Some parts are made by the company itself; others are made by different companies.

Functions are like building blocks. They let you divide complicated programs into manageable pieces. They have other advantages, too:

- While working on one function, you can focus on just that part of the program and construct it, debug it, and perfect it.
- Different people can work on different functions simultaneously.
- If a function is needed in more than one place in a program, or in different programs, you can write it once and use it many times.
- Using functions greatly enhances the program's readability because it reduces the complexity of the function `main`.

Functions are often called **modules**. They are like miniature programs; you can put them together to form a larger program. Functions also make programs conceptually easier to understand. Not only is `main` simplified, but the overall program is simplified by grouping tasks into functions. When user-defined functions are discussed, you will see that this is the case. This ability is less apparent with predefined functions because their programming code is not available to us. However, because predefined functions are already written for us, you will learn these first so that you can use them when needed.

Predefined Functions

Before formally discussing predefined functions in C++, let us review a concept from a college algebra course. In algebra, a function can be considered a rule or correspondence between values, called the function's arguments, and the unique value of the function associated with the arguments. Thus, if $f(x) = 2x + 5$, then $f(1) = 7$, $f(2) = 9$, and $f(3) = 11$, where 1, 2, and 3 are the arguments of f, and 7, 9, and 11 are the corresponding values of the function f.

In C++, the concept of a function, either predefined or user-defined, is similar to that of a function in algebra. For example, every function has a name and, depending on the values specified by the user, it does some computation. This section discusses various predefined functions.

Some of the predefined mathematical functions are `pow(x, y)`, `sqrt(x)`, and `floor(x)`.

The *power* function, `pow(x, y)`, calculates x^y; that is, the value of `pow(x, y)` $= x^y$. For example, `pow(2, 3)` $= 2^3 = 8.0$, and `pow(2.5, 3)` $= 2.5^3 = 15.625$. Because the value of pow(x, y) is of type double, we say that the function pow is of type double or that the function pow returns a value of type double. Moreover, x and y are called the parameters of the function pow. Function pow has two parameters.

The *square root* function, sqrt(x), calculates the nonnegative square root of x for x >= 0.0. For example, sqrt(2.25) is 1.5. The function sqrt is of type double and has only one parameter.

The *floor* function, floor(x), calculates the largest whole number that is less than or equal to x. For example, floor(48.79) is 48.0. The function floor is of type double and has only one parameter.

In C++, predefined functions are organized into separate libraries. For example, the header file iostream contains I/O functions, and the header file cmath contains math functions. Table 5-1 lists some of the predefined functions, the name of the header file in which each function's specification can be found, the data type of the parameters, and the function type. The function type is the data type of the final value returned by the function. (For a list of additional predefined functions, see Appendix E.)

5

TABLE 5-1 Predefined Functions

Function	Header File	Purpose	Parameter(s) Type	Result
abs(x)	<cstdlib>	Returns the absolute value of its argument: abs(-7) = 7	int	int
ceil(x)	<cmath>	Returns the smallest whole number that is not less than x: ceil(56.34) = 57.0	double	double
cos(x)	<cmath>	Returns the cosine of angle x: cos(0.0) = 1.0	double (radians)	double
exp(x)	<cmath>	Returns e^x, where e = 2.718: exp(1.0) = 2.71828	double	double
fabs(x)	<cmath>	Returns the absolute value of its argument: fabs(-5.67) = 5.67	double	double
floor(x)	<cmath>	Returns the largest whole number that is not greater than x: floor(45.67) = 45.00	double	double

TABLE 5-1   Predefined Functions (continued)

Function	Header File	Purpose	Parameter(s) Type	Result
pow(x, y)	<cmath>	Returns x^y; If x is negative, y must be a whole number: pow(0.16, 0.5) = 0.4	double	double
sqrt(x)	<cmath>	Returns the square root of x if x is a nonnegative real number: sqrt(4.0)=2.0	double	double
tolower(x)	<cctype>	Returns the lowercase value of x if x is uppercase; otherwise, returns x	int	int
toupper(x)	<cctype>	Returns the uppercase value of x if x is lowercase; otherwise, returns x	int	int

To use predefined functions in a program, you must include the header file that contains the function's specification via the include statement. For example, to use the function pow, the program must include:

```
#include <cmath>
```

Example 5-1 shows you how to use some of the predefined functions.

EXAMPLE 5-1

```
//********************************************************
// Author: D.S. Malik
//
// This program shows how to use predefined functions.
//********************************************************

#include <iostream>                                    //Line 1
#include <cmath>                                        //Line 2
#include <cctype>                                       //Line 3
#include <cstdlib>                                      //Line 4

using namespace std;                                    //Line 5
```

```
int main()                                          //Line 6
{                                                   //Line 7
    int    x;                                       //Line 8
    double u, v;                                    //Line 9

    cout << "Line 10: Uppercase a is "
         << static_cast<char>(toupper('a'))
         << endl;                                   //Line 10

    u = 4.2;                                        //Line 11
    v = 3.0;                                        //Line 12
    cout << "Line 13: " << u << " to the power of "
         << v << " = " << pow(u, v) << endl;        //Line 13

    cout << "Line 14: 5.0 to the power of 4 = "
         << pow(5.0, 4) << endl;                    //Line 14

    u = u + pow(3.0, 3);                            //Line 15
    cout << "Line 16: u = " << u << endl;           //Line 16

    x = -15;                                        //Line 17
    cout << "Line 18: Absolute value of " << x
         << " = " << abs(x) << endl;                //Line 18

    return 0;                                       //Line 19
}                                                   //Line 20
```

Sample Run:

```
Line 10: Uppercase a is A
Line 13: 4.2 to the power of 3 = 74.088
Line 14: 5.0 to the power of 4 = 625.0
Line 16: u = 31.2
Line 18: Absolute value of -15 = 15
```

This program works as follows. The statement in Line 10 outputs the uppercase letter that corresponds to 'a', which is A. Note that the function toupper returns an int value. Therefore, the value of the expression toupper('a') is 65, which is the ASCII value of 'A'. To print A rather than 65, you need to apply the cast operator as shown in the statement in Line 10. In the statement in Line 13, the function pow is used to output u^v. In C++ terminology, it is said that the function pow is called with the parameters u and v. In this case, the values of u and v are passed to the function pow. The other statements have similar meanings.

User-Defined Functions

As Example 5-1 illustrates, using functions in a program greatly enhances the program's readability because it reduces the complexity of the function main. Also, once you write and properly debug a function, you can use it in the program (or different programs) again and again without having to rewrite the same code repeatedly. For instance, in Example 5-1, the function pow is used more than once.

Because C++ does not provide every function that you will ever need, and designers cannot possibly know a user's specific needs, you must learn to write your own functions.

User-defined functions in C++ are classified into two categories:

- **Value-returning functions**—Functions that have a return data type. These functions return a value of a specific data type using the `return` statement, which we will explain shortly.
- **Void functions**—Functions that do not have a return type. These functions *do not* use a `return` statement to return a value.

Next, we discuss value-returning functions. Many of the concepts discussed regarding value-returning functions also apply to void functions.

Value-Returning Functions

The previous section introduced some predefined C++ functions such as `pow`, `abs`, `tolower`, and `toupper`. These are examples of value-returning functions. To use these functions in your programs, you must know the name of the header file that contains the functions' specification. You need to include this header file in your program using the include statement and know the following items:

1. The name of the function
2. The number of **parameters**, if any
3. The data type of each parameter
4. The data type of the value computed (that is, the value returned) by the function, called the type of the function

Because the value returned by a value-returning function is unique, the natural thing for you to do is to use the value in one of three ways:

- Save the value for further calculation.
- Use the value in some calculation.
- Print the value.

This suggests that a value-returning function is used:

- In an assignment statement
- In an output statement
- As a parameter in a function call

That is, a value-returning function is used (called) in an expression.

Before we look at the syntax of a user-defined, value-returning function, let us consider the things associated with such functions. In addition to the four properties described previously, the following fifth item is associated with functions (both value-returning and void):

5. The code required to accomplish the task

The first four properties form what is called the **heading** of the function (also called the **function header**); the fifth property is called the **body** of the function. Together, these five properties form what is called the **definition** of the function. For example, for the function `abs`, the heading might look like the following:

```
int abs(int number)
```

Similarly, the function `abs` might have the following definition:

```
int abs(int number)
{
    if (number < 0)
        number = -number;

    return number;
}
```

The variable declared in the heading of the function `abs` is called the **formal parameter** of the function `abs`. Thus, the formal parameter of `abs` is `number`.

The program in Example 5-1 contains several statements that use the function `pow`. That is, in C++ terminology, the function `pow` is called several times. Later in this chapter, we discuss what happens when a function is called.

Suppose that the heading of the function `pow` is:

```
double pow(double base, double exponent)
```

From the heading of the function `pow`, it follows that the formal parameters of `pow` are `base` and `exponent`. Consider the following statements:

```
double u = 2.5;
double v = 3.0;
double x, y, w;

x = pow(u, v);        //Line 1
y = pow(2.0, 3.2);    //Line 2
w = pow(u, 7);        //Line 3
```

In Line 1, the function `pow` is called with the parameters `u` and `v`. In this case, the values of `u` and `v` are passed to the function `pow`. In fact, the value of `u` is copied into `base`, and the value of `v` is copied into `exponent`. The variables `u` and `v` that appear in the call to the function `pow` in Line 1 are called the actual parameters of that call. In Line 2, the function `pow` is called with the parameters `2.0` and `3.2`. In this call, the value `2.0` is copied into `base`, and `3.2` is copied into `exponent`. Moreover, in this call of the function `pow`, the actual parameters are `2.0` and `3.2`, respectively. Similarly, in Line 3, the actual parameters of the function `pow` are `u` and `7`, the value of `u` is copied into `base`, and `7.0` is copied into `exponent`.

We can now formally present two definitions:

Formal Parameter: A variable declared in the function heading.

Actual Parameter: A variable or expression listed in a call to a function.

For predefined functions, you need to be concerned only with the first four properties. Software companies do not give out the actual source code, which is the body of the function. Otherwise, software costs would be exorbitant.

SYNTAX: VALUE-RETURNING FUNCTION

The syntax of a value-returning function is

```
functionType functionName(formal parameter list)
{
    statements
}
```

where statements are usually declaration statements and/or executable statements. In this syntax, `functionType` is the type of the value that the function returns. The `functionType` is also called the **data type** or the **return type** of the value-returning function. Moreover, statements enclosed between curly braces form the body of the function.

SYNTAX: FORMAL PARAMETER LIST

The syntax of the formal parameter list is:

```
dataType identifier, dataType identifier, ...
```

FUNCTION CALL

The syntax to call a value-returning function is:

```
functionName(actual parameter list)
```

SYNTAX: ACTUAL PARAMETER LIST

The syntax of the actual parameter list is:

```
expression or variable, expression or variable, ...
```

(In this syntax, `expression` can be a single constant value.) Thus, to call a value-returning function, you use its name, with the actual parameters (if any) in parentheses.

A function's formal parameter list *can* be empty. However, if the formal parameter list is empty, the parentheses are still needed. The function heading of the value-returning function thus takes, if the formal parameter list is empty, the following form:

```
functionType functionName()
```

If the formal parameter list of a value-returning function is empty, in a function call the actual parameter is also empty. In this case (that is, an empty formal parameter list), in a function call the empty parentheses are still needed. Thus, a call to a value-returning function with an empty formal parameter list is:

```
functionName()
```

In a function call, the number of actual parameters, together with their data types, must match with the formal parameters in the order given. That is, actual and formal parameters have a one-to-one correspondence.

As stated previously, a value-returning function is called in an expression. The expression can be part of either an assignment statement or an output statement, or a parameter in a function call. A function call in a program causes the body of the called function to execute.

5

`return` **Statement**

Once a value-returning function computes the value, the function returns this value via the `return` statement. In other words, it passes this value outside the function via the `return` statement.

SYNTAX: `return` STATEMENT

The `return` statement has the following syntax

```
return expr;
```

where `expr` is a variable, constant value, or expression. The `expr` is evaluated and its value is returned. The data type of the value that `expr` computes must match the function type.

In C++, `return` is a reserved word.

When a `return` statement executes in a function, the function immediately terminates and the control goes back to the caller. Moreover, the function call statement is replaced by the value returned by the `return` statement. When a `return` statement executes in the function `main`, the program terminates.

To put the ideas in this discussion to work, let us write a function that determines the larger of two numbers. Because the function compares two numbers, it follows that this function has two parameters and that both parameters are numbers. Let us assume that the data type of these numbers is floating-point (decimal)—say `double`. Because the larger number is of type `double`, the function's data type is also `double`. Let us name this function `larger`. The only thing you need to complete this function is the body of the function. Thus, following the syntax of a function, you can write this function as follows:

```
double larger(double x, double y)
{
    double max;

    if (x >= y)
        max = x;
    else
        max = y;

    return max;
}
```

You can also write this function as follows:

```
double larger(double x, double y)
{
    if (x >= y)
        return x;
    else
        return y;
}
```

Because the execution of a `return` statement in a function terminates the function, the preceding function `larger` can also be written (without the word `else`) as follows:

```
double larger(double x, double y)
{
    if (x >= y)
        return x;

    return y;
}
```

The first form of the function `larger` requires that you use an additional variable `max` (called a **local declaration**, where `max` is a variable local to the function `larger`); the second form does not require use of an additional variable.

NOTE

1. In the definition of the function `larger`, x and y are formal parameters.

2. The `return` statement can appear anywhere in the function. Recall that once a `return` statement executes, all subsequent statements are skipped. Thus, it's a good idea to return the value as soon as it is computed.

EXAMPLE 5-2

Now that the function `larger` is written, the following C++ code illustrates how to use it.

```
double firstNum = 13;
double secondNum = 36;
double maxNum;
```

Consider the following statements:

```
cout << "The larger of 5 and 6 is " << larger(5, 6)
     << endl;                                              //Line 1

cout << "The larger of " << firstNum << " and "
     << secondNum << " is "
     << larger(firstNum, secondNum) << endl;               //Line 2

cout << "The larger of " << firstNum << " and 29 is "
     << larger(firstNum, 29) << endl;                      //Line 3

maxNum = larger(38.45, 56.78);                             //Line 4
```

- The expression `larger(5, 6)`, in Line 1, is a function call, and 5 and 6 are actual parameters. This statement outputs the larger of 5 and 6.

- The expression `larger(firstNum, secondNum)`, in Line 2, is a function call. Here, `firstNum` and `secondNum` are actual parameters. This statement outputs the larger of `firstNum` and `secondNum`.

- The expression `larger(firstNum, 29)`, in Line 3, is also a function call. Here, `firstNum` and 29 are actual parameters.

- The expression `larger(38.45, 56.78)`, in Line 4, is a function call. In this call, the actual parameters are `38.45` and `56.78`. In this statement, the value returned by the function `larger` is assigned to the variable `maxNum`.

NOTE   In a function call, you specify only the actual parameter, not its data type. For example, in Example 5-2, the statements in Lines 1, 2, 3, and 4 show how to call the function `larger` with the actual parameters. However, the following statements contain incorrect calls to the function larger and would result in syntax errors. (Assume that all variables are properly declared.)

```
x = larger(int one, 29);            //illegal
y = larger(int one, int 29);        //illegal
cout << larger(int one, int two);   //illegal
```

Function Prototype

Now that you have some idea of how to write and use functions in a program, the next question relates to the order in which user-defined functions should appear in a program. For example, do you place the function `larger` before or after the function `main`? Following the rule that you must declare an identifier before you can use it, and knowing that the function `main` uses the identifier `larger`, logically you must place `larger` before `main`.

In reality, C++ programmers customarily place the function `main` before all other user-defined functions. However, this organization could produce a compilation error because functions are compiled in the order in which they appear in the program. For example, if the function `main` is placed before the function `larger`, the identifier `larger` is undefined when the function `main` is compiled. To work around this problem of undeclared identifiers, we place **function prototypes** before any function definition (including the definition of `main`).

Function Prototype: The function heading without the body of the function.

SYNTAX: FUNCTION PROTOTYPE

The general syntax of the function prototype of a value-returning function is:

```
functionType functionName(parameter list);
```

(Note that the function prototype ends with a semicolon.)

For the function `larger`, the prototype is:

```
double larger(double x, double y);
```

 NOTE When writing the function prototype, you do not have to specify the variable name in the parameter list. However, you must specify the data type of each parameter.

You can rewrite the function prototype of the function `larger` as follows:

```
double larger(double, double);
```

FINAL PROGRAM

You now know enough to write the entire program, compile it, and run it. The program in the following example uses the functions `larger` and `main` to determine the larger/largest of two or three numbers.

EXAMPLE 5-3

```cpp
//**********************************************************
// Author: D.S. Malik
//
// This program shows how to use the function larger.
//**********************************************************

#include <iostream>                                  //Line 1

using namespace std;                                 //Line 2

double larger(double x, double y);                   //Line 3

int main()                                           //Line 4
{                                                    //Line 5
    double one, two;                                 //Line 6

    cout << "Line 7: The larger of 5 and 10 is "
         << larger(5, 10) << endl;                   //Line 7

    cout << "Line 8: Enter two numbers: ";           //Line 8
    cin >> one >> two;                               //Line 9
    cout << endl;                                    //Line 10

    cout << "Line 11: The larger of " << one
         << " and " << two << " is "
         << larger(one, two) << endl;                //Line 11

    cout << "Line 2: The largest of 23, 34, and "
         << "12 is " << larger(larger(23, 34), 12)
         << endl;                                    //Line 12

    return 0;                                        //Line 13
}                                                    //Line 14

double larger(double x, double y)                    //Line 15
{                                                    //Line 16
    if (x >= y)                                      //Line 17
        return x;                                    //Line 18
    else                                             //Line 19
        return y;                                    //Line 20
} //end larger                                       Line 21
```

Sample Run: In this sample run, the user input is shaded.

```
Line 5: The larger of 5 and 10 is 10
Line 8: Enter two numbers: 25 73

Line 11: The larger of 25 and 73 is 73
Line 12: The largest of 23, 34, and 12 is 34
```

Note that the expression `larger(larger(23, 34), 12)`, in Line 12, first determines the larger of 23 and 34, which is then compared with 12. Thus, this expression determines the largest of the numbers 23, 34, and 12.

Once a function is written, you can use it anywhere in the program. The function `larger` compares two numbers and returns the larger of the two. Let us now write another function that uses this function to determine the largest of three numbers. We call this function `compareThree`.

```
double compareThree(double x, double y, double z)
{
    return larger(larger(x, y), z);
}
```

In the function heading, `x`, `y`, and `z` are formal parameters.

Let us take a look at the expression

```
larger(larger(x, y), z)
```

in the definition of the function `compareThree`. This expression has two calls to the function `larger`. The actual parameters to the outer call are `larger(x, y)` and `z`; the actual parameters to the inner call are `x` and `y`. It follows that first the expression `larger(x, y)` is evaluated, that is, the inner call executes first, which gives the larger of `x` and `y`. Suppose that `larger(x, y)` evaluates to, say, t. (Notice that t is either `x` or `y`.) Next, the outer call determines the larger of t and `z`. Finally, the **return** statement returns the largest number. It thus follows that to execute a function call, the parameters are evaluated first. For example, the actual parameter `larger(x, y)` of the outer call evaluates first.

Value-Returning Functions: Some Peculiarity

A value-returning function must return a value. Consider the following function, `secret`, that takes as a parameter an **int** value. If the value of the parameter, `x`, is greater than 5, it returns twice the value of `x`; otherwise, the value of `x` remains unchanged.

```
int secret(int x)        //Line 1
{                        //Line 2
    if (x > 5)           //Line 3
        return 2 * x;    //Line 4
}                        //Line 5
```

Because this is a value-returning function of type **int**, it must return a value of type **int**. Suppose the value of `x` is 10. Then the expression, `x > 5`, in Line 3, evaluates to **true**. So the **return** statement in Line 4 returns the value 20. Now suppose that `x` is 3. The expression, `x > 5`, in Line 3, now evaluates to **false**. The **if** statement therefore fails, and the **return** statement in Line 4 *does not* execute. However, there are no more statements to be executed in the body of the function. In this case, the function returns a strange value. It thus follows that if the value of **x** is less than or equal to 5, the function does not contain any valid **return** statements to return the value of **x**.

A correct definition of the function **secret** is:

```
int secret(int x)          //Line 1
{                          //Line 2
    if (x > 5)             //Line 3
        return 2 * x;      //Line 4

    return x;              //Line 5
}                          //Line 6
```

Here, if the value of **x** is less than or equal to 5, the **return** statement in Line 5 executes, which returns the value of **x**. On the other hand, if the value of **x** is, say, 10, the **return** statement in Line 4 executes, which returns the value 20 and also terminates the function.

Recall that in a value-returning function, the **return** statement returns the value. Consider the following **return** statement:

```
return x, y;   //only the value of y will be returned
```

This is a legal **return** statement. You might think that this **return** statement is returning the values of **x** and **y**. However, this is not the case. Remember, a **return** statement returns only one value, even if the **return** statement contains more than one expression. If a **return** statement contains more than one expression, *only the value of the last expression is returned*. Therefore, in the case of the preceding **return** statement, the value of **y** is returned. The following example further illustrates this concept.

EXAMPLE 5-4

```
//**********************************************************
// Author: D.S. Malik
//
// This program illustrates that a value-returning function returns
// only one value, even if the return statement contains more than
// one expression.
//**********************************************************

#include <iostream>                              //Line 1

using namespace std;                             //Line 2

int funcRet1();                                  //Line 3
int funcRet2();                                  //Line 4
int funcRet3(int z);                             //Line 5
```

```
int main()                                                //Line 6
{                                                         //Line 7
    int num = 4;

    cout << "Line 8: The value returned by funcRet1: "
         << funcRet1() << endl;                           //Line 8
    cout << "Line 9: The value returned by funcRet2: "
         << funcRet2() << endl;                           //Line 9
    cout << "Line 10: The value returned by funcRet3: "
         << funcRet3(num) << endl;                        //Line 10

    return 0;                                             //Line 11
}                                                         //Line 12

int funcRet1()                                            //Line 13
{                                                         //Line 14
    return 23, 45;    //Only 45 is returned                 Line 15
}                                                         //Line 16

int funcRet2()                                            //Line 17
{                                                         //Line 18
    int x = 5;                                            //Line 19
    int y = 6;                                            //Line 20

    return x, y; //Only the value of y is returned          Line 21
}                                                         //Line 22

int funcRet3(int z)                                       //Line 23
{                                                         //Line 24
    int a = 2;                                            //Line 25
    int b = 3;                                            //Line 26

    return 2 * a + b, z + b; //Only the value of z + b
                             //is returned                  Line 27
}                                                         //Line 28
```

Sample Run:

```
Line 8: The value returned by funcRet1: 45
Line 9: The value returned by funcRet2: 6
Line 10: The value returned by funcRet3: 7
```

EXAMPLE 5-5

In this example, we write the definition of a function, courseGrade, that takes as a parameter an **int** value specifying the score for a course and returns the grade, a value of type **char**, for the course. (We assume that the test score is a value between 0 and 100 inclusive.)

```cpp
char courseGrade(int score)
{
    switch (score / 10)
    {
    case 0:
    case 1:
    case 2:
    case 3:
    case 4:
    case 5:
        return 'F';
    case 6:
        return 'D';
    case 7:
        return 'C';
    case 8:
        return 'B';
    case 9:
    case 10:
        return 'A';
    }
}
```

You can also write an equivalent definition of the function `courseGrade` that uses an `if...else` structure to determine the course grade.

Flow of Execution

As stated earlier, a C++ program is a collection of functions. Recall that functions can appear in any order. The only thing that you have to remember is that you must declare an identifier before you can use it. The program is compiled by the compiler sequentially from beginning to end. Thus, if the function `main` appears before any other user-defined functions, it is compiled first. However, if `main` appears at the end (or middle) of the program, all functions whose definitions (not prototypes) appear before the function `main` are compiled before the function `main`, in the order they are placed.

Function prototypes appear before any function definition, so the compiler translates these first. The compiler can then correctly translate a function call. However, when the program executes, the first statement in the function `main` always executes first, regardless of where in the program the function `main` is placed. Other functions execute only when they are called.

A function call statement transfers control to the first statement in the body of the function. In general, after the last statement of the called function executes, control is passed back to the point immediately following the function call. A value-returning function returns a value. Therefore, after executing the value-returning function, when the control goes back to the caller, the value that the function returns replaces the function call statement. The execution continues at the point immediately following the function call.

Void Functions

Void functions and value-returning functions have similar structures. Both have a heading and a body. You can place user-defined void functions either before or after the function `main`. However, the program execution always begins with the first statement in the function `main`. If you place user-defined void functions after the function `main`, you should place the function prototype before the function `main`. A void function does not have a data type. Therefore, `functionType`, that is, the return type, in the heading part and the return statement in the body of the void functions are meaningless. However, in a void function, you can use the return statement without any value; it is typically used to exit the function early. Like value-returning functions, void functions may or may not have formal parameters.

Because void functions do not have a data type, they are not used (called) in an expression. A call to a void function is a stand-alone statement. Thus, to call a void function, you use the function name together with the actual parameters (if any) in a stand-alone statement. Before giving examples of void functions, next we give the syntax of a void function.

FUNCTION DEFINITION

The function definition of void functions with parameters has the following syntax:

```
void functionName(formal parameter list)
{
    statements
}
```

where `statements` are usually declaration and/or executable statements. The formal parameter list may be empty, in which case, in the function heading, the empty parentheses are still needed.

FORMAL PARAMETER LIST

The formal parameter list has the following syntax:

```
dataType& variable, dataType& variable, ...
```

You must specify both the data type and the variable name in the formal parameter list. The symbol `&` after `dataType` has a special meaning; it is used only for certain formal parameters and is discussed later in this chapter.

FUNCTION CALL

The function call has the following syntax:

```
functionName(actual parameter list);
```

ACTUAL PARAMETER LIST

The actual parameter list has the following syntax:

```
expression or variable, expression or variable, ...
```

where **expression** can consist of a single constant value. As with value-returning functions, in a function call the number of actual parameters together with their data types must match the formal parameters in the order given. Actual and formal parameters have a one-to-one correspondence. A function call results in the execution of the body of the called function.

Example 5-6 shows a void function with parameters.

EXAMPLE 5-6

```cpp
void funExp(int a, double b, char c, int x)
{
    .
    .
    .
}
```

The function **funExp** has four parameters.

Parameters provide a communication link between the calling function (such as **main**) and the called function. They enable functions to manipulate different data each time they are called. In general, there are two types of formal parameters: **value parameters** and **reference parameters**.

Value parameter: A formal parameter that receives a copy of the content of the corresponding actual parameter.

Reference parameter: A formal parameter that receives the location (memory address) of the corresponding actual parameter.

When you attach **&** after the **dataType** in the formal parameter list of a function, the variable following that **dataType** becomes a reference parameter.

Example 5-7 shows a void function with value and reference parameters.

EXAMPLE 5-7

```cpp
void expfun(int one, int& two, char three, double& four)
{
    .
    .
    .
}
```

5

The function `expfun` has four parameters: (1) `one`, a value parameter of the type `int`, (2) `two`, a reference parameter of the type `int`, (3) `three`, a value parameter of the type `char`, and (4) `four`, a reference parameter of the type `double`.

EXAMPLE 5-8

We write a program to print a pattern (a triangle of stars) similar to the following:

The first line has one star with some blanks before the star, the second line has two stars, some blanks before the stars, and a blank between the stars, and so on. Let's write the method `printStars` that has two parameters: a parameter to specify the number of blanks before the stars in a line and the second parameter to specify the number of stars in a line. To be specific, the definition of the method `printStars` is:

```
void printStars(int blanks, int starsInLine)
{
        //print the number of blanks before the stars in a line
    for (int count = 1; count <= blanks; count++)
        cout << ' ';

        //print the number of stars with a blank between stars
    for (int count = 1; count <= starsInLine; count++)
        cout << " *";

    cout << endl;
} //end printStars
```

The first parameter, `blanks`, determines how many blanks to print preceding the star(s); the second parameter, `starsInLine`, determines how many stars to print in a line. If the value of the parameter `blanks` is 30, for instance, then the first `for` loop in the method `printStars` executes 30 times and prints 30 blanks. Also, because you want to print spaces between the stars, every iteration of the second `for` loop in the method `printStars` prints the string `" *"`—a blank followed by a star.

Next consider the following statements:

```
int numberOfLines = 15;
int numberOfBlanks = 30;

for (int counter = 1; counter <= numberOfLines; counter++)
{
    printStars(numberOfBlanks, counter);
    numberOfBlanks--;
}
```

The **for** loop calls the function `printStars`. Every iteration of this **for** loop specifies the number of blanks followed by the number of stars to print in a line, using the variables `numberOfBlanks` and `counter`. Every invocation of the function `printStars` receives one fewer blank and one more star than the previous call. For example, the first iteration of the **for** loop in the method `main` specifies 30 blanks and 1 star (which are passed as the parameters, `numberOfBlanks` and `counter`, to the function `printStars`). The **for** loop then decrements the number of blanks by 1 by executing the statement, `numberOfBlanks--;`. At the end of the **for** loop, the number of stars is incremented by 1 for the next iteration. This is done by executing the update statement, `counter++`, in the **for** statement, which increments the value of the variable `counter` by 1. In other words, the second call of the function `printStars` receives 29 blanks and 2 stars as parameters. Thus, the previous statements will print a triangle of stars consisting of 15 lines.

The following C++ program prints a triangle of stars:

```
//************************************************************
// Author: D.S. Malik
//
// Program: Print a triangle of stars
// This program prints a triangle of stars. The input to the
// program is the number of lines in the triangle of stars.
//************************************************************

#include <iostream>

using namespace std;

void printStars(int blanks, int starsInLine);

int main()
{
    int numberOfLines;
    int counter;
    int numberOfBlanks;

    cout << "Enter the number of star lines (1 to 20) "
         << "to be printed: ";
    cin >> numberOfLines;

    while (numberOfLines < 0 || numberOfLines > 20)
    {
        cout << "Number of star lines should be "
             << "between 1 and 20"<<endl;
        cout << "Enter the number of star lines "
             << "(1 to 20) to be printed: ";
        cin >> numberOfLines;
    }
```

5

```
        cout << endl << endl;
        numberOfBlanks = 30;

        for (counter = 1; counter <= numberOfLines; counter++)
        {
            printStars(numberOfBlanks, counter);
            numberOfBlanks--;
        }

        return 0;
}

void printStars(int blanks, int starsInLine)
{
    for (int count = 1; count <= blanks; count++)
        cout << ' ';
    for (int count = 1; count <= starsInLine; count++)
        cout << " *";
    cout << endl;
}
```

Sample Run: In this sample run, the user input is shaded.

Enter the number of star lines (1 to 20) to be printed: 10

In the function `main`, the user is first asked to specify how many lines of stars to print. (In this program, the user is restricted to 20 lines because a triangular grid of up to 20 lines fits nicely on the screen.) Because the program is restricted to only 20 lines, the `while` loop in the function `main` ensures that the program prints the triangular grid of stars only if the number of lines is between 1 and 20.

Value Parameters

The previous section defined two types of parameters—value parameters and reference parameters. Example 5-8 shows a program that uses a function with parameters. Before considering more examples of void functions with parameters, let us make the following observation about value and reference parameters. When a function is called, the value of the actual parameter is copied into the corresponding formal parameter. If the formal parameter is a value parameter, then after copying the value of the actual parameter, there is no connection between the formal parameter and actual parameter; that is, the formal parameter has its own copy of the data. Therefore, during program execution, the formal parameter manipulates the data stored in its own memory space. The program in Example 5-9 further illustrates how a value parameter works.

EXAMPLE 5-9

The following program shows how a formal parameter of a simple data type works.

```cpp
//**********************************************************
// Author: D.S. Malik
//
// This program illustrates how a value parameter works.
//**********************************************************

#include <iostream>                                   //Line 1

using namespace std;                                  //Line 2

void funcValueParam(int num);                         //Line 3

int main()                                            //Line 4
{                                                     //Line 5
    int number = 6;                                   //Line 6

    cout << "Line 7: Before calling the function "
         << "funcValueParam, number = " << number
         << endl;                                     //Line 7

    funcValueParam(number);                           //Line 8

    cout << "Line 9: After calling the function "
         << "funcValueParam, number = " << number
         << endl;                                     //Line 9

    return 0;                                         //Line 10
} //end main                                          Line 11

void funcValueParam(int num)                          //Line 12
{                                                     //Line 13
    cout << "Line 14: In the function funcValueParam, "
         << "before changing, num = " << num
         << endl;                                     //Line 14

    num = 15;                                         //Line 15

    cout << "Line 16: In the function funcValueParam, "
         << "after changing, num = " << num
         << endl;                                     //Line 16
} //end funcValueParam                                Line 17
```

5

Sample Run:

```
Line 7: Before calling the function funcValueParam, number = 6
Line 14: In the function funcValueParam, before changing, num = 6
Line 16: In the function funcValueParam, after changing, num = 15
Line 9: After calling the function funcValueParam, number = 6
```

This program works as follows. The execution begins at the function main. The statement in Line 6 declares and initializes the **int** variable number. The statement in Line 7 outputs the value of number before calling the function funcValueParam; the statement in Line 8 calls the function funcValueParam. The value of the variable number is then passed to the formal parameter num. Control now transfers to the function funcValueParam.

The statement in Line 14 outputs the value of num before changing its value. The statement in Line 15 changes the value of num to 15; the statement in Line 16 outputs the value of num. After this statement executes, the function funcValueParam exits and control goes back to the function main.

The statement in Line 9 outputs the value of number after calling the function funcValueParam. The sample run shows that the value of number (Lines 7 and 9) remains the same even though the value of its corresponding formal parameter num was changed within the function funcValueParam.

The output shows the sequence in which the statements execute.

After copying data, a value parameter has no connection with the actual parameter, so a value parameter cannot pass any result back to the calling function. When the function executes, any changes made to the formal parameters do not in any way affect the actual parameters. The actual parameters have no knowledge of what is happening to the formal parameters. Thus, value parameters cannot pass information outside the function. Value parameters provide only a one-way link between actual parameters and formal parameters. Hence, functions with only value parameters have limitations.

Reference Variables as Parameters

The program in Example 5-9 illustrates how a value parameter works. On the other hand, suppose that a formal parameter is a reference parameter. Because a reference parameter receives the address (memory location) of the actual parameter, reference parameters can pass one or more values from a function and can change the value of the actual parameter.

Reference parameters are useful in three situations:

- When you want to return more than one value from a function
- When the value of the actual parameter needs to be changed
- When passing the address would save memory space and time relative to copying a large amount of data

The first two situations are illustrated throughout this book. Chapters 6 and 7 discuss the third situation, when arrays and classes are introduced.

Recall that, when you attach & after the dataType in the formal parameter list of a function, the variable following that dataType becomes a reference parameter.

NOTE You can declare a reference (formal) parameter as a constant by using the keyword const. Chapters 6 and 7 discuss constant reference parameters. Until then, the reference parameters that you use will be nonconstant as defined in this chapter. From the definition of a reference parameter, it follows that a constant value or an expression cannot be passed to a nonconstant reference parameter. If a formal parameter is a nonconstant reference parameter, during a function call, its corresponding actual parameter must be a variable.

EXAMPLE 5-10 CALCULATE GRADE

5

The following program takes a course score (a value between 0 and 100) and determines a student's course grade. This program has three functions: main, getScore, and printGrade, as follows:

1. main
    a. Get the course score.
    b. Print the course grade.

2. getScore
    a. Prompt the user for the input.
    b. Get the input.
    c. Print the course score.

3. printGrade
    a. Calculate the course grade.
    b. Print the course grade.

The complete program follows.

```
//**********************************************************
// Author: D.S. Malik
// This program reads a course score and prints the associated
// course grade.
//**********************************************************

#include <iostream>                                       //Line 1

using namespace std;                                      //Line 2

void getScore(int& score);                                //Line 3
void printGrade(int score);                               //Line 4
```

```
int main()                                                //Line 5
{                                                         //Line 6
    int courseScore;                                      //Line 7

    cout << "Line 8: Based on the course score, \n"
         << "         this program computes the "
         << "course grade." << endl;                      //Line 8

    getScore(courseScore);                                //Line 9

    printGrade(courseScore);                              //Line 10

    return 0;                                             //Line 11
}                                                         //Line 12

void getScore(int& score)                                 //Line 13
{                                                         //Line 14
    cout << "Line 15: Enter course score: ";              //Line 15
    cin >> score;                                         //Line 16
    cout << endl << "Line 17: Course score is "
         << score << endl;                                //Line 17
} //end getScore                                             Line 18

void printGrade(int cScore)                               //Line 19
{                                                         //Line 20
    cout << "Line 21: Your grade for the course is ";     //Line 21

    if (cScore >= 90)                                     //Line 22
        cout << "A." << endl;                             //Line 23
    else if (cScore >= 80)                                //Line 24
        cout << "B." << endl;                             //Line 25
    else if(cScore >= 70)                                 //Line 26
        cout << "C." << endl;                             //Line 27
    else if (cScore >= 60)                                //Line 28
        cout << "D." << endl;                             //Line 29
    else                                                  //Line 30
        cout << "F." << endl;                             //Line 31
} //end printGrade                                           Line 32
```

Sample Run: In this sample run, the user input is shaded.

```
Line 8: Based on the course score,
        this program computes the course grade.
Line 15: Enter course score: 85

Line 17: Course score is 85
Line 21: Your grade for the course is B.
```

This program works as follows. The program starts to execute at Line 8, which prints the first line of the output (see the sample run). The statement in Line 9 calls the function getScore with the actual parameter courseScore (a variable declared in main). Because the formal parameter score of the function getScore is a reference parameter, the address (that is, the memory location of the variable `courseScore`) passes to `score`. Thus, both `score` and `courseScore` refer to the same memory location, which is `courseScore` (see Figure 5-1).

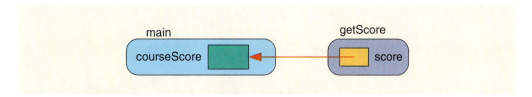

FIGURE 5-1   Variable `courseScore` and the parameter `score`

Any changes made to `score` immediately change the value of `courseScore`.

Control is then transferred to the function `getScore`, and the statement in Line 15 executes, printing the second line of output. This statement prompts the user to enter the course `score`. The statement at Line 16 reads and stores the value entered by the user (85 in the sample run) in `score`, which is actually `courseScore` (because `score` is a reference parameter). Thus, at this point, the value of the variables `score` and `courseScore` is 85 (see Figure 5-2).

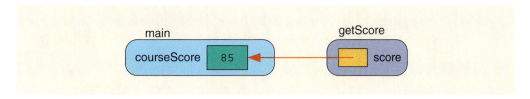

FIGURE 5-2   Variable `courseScore` and the parameter `score` after the statement in Line 16 executes

Next, the statement in Line 17 outputs the value of `score`, as shown by the third line of the sample run. After Line 17 executes, control goes back to the function `main` (see Figure 5-3).

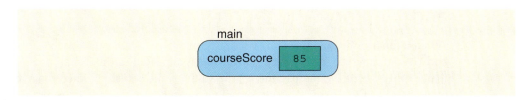

FIGURE 5-3   Variable `courseScore` after the statement in Line 17 is executed and control goes back to `main`

The statement in Line 10 executes next. It is a function call to the function `printGrade` with the actual parameter `courseScore`. Because the formal parameter `cScore` of the function `printScore` is a value parameter, the parameter `cScore` receives the value of the corresponding actual parameter `courseScore`. Thus, the value of `cScore` is 85. After copying the value of `courseScore` into `cScore`, no communication exists between `cScore` and `courseScore` (see Figure 5-4).

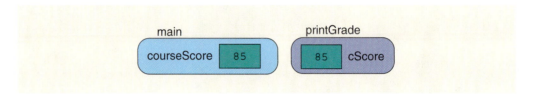

FIGURE 5-4 Variable `courseScore` and the parameter `cScore`

The program then executes the statement in Line 21, which outputs the fourth line except the grade. The `if...else` statement in Line 22 determines and outputs the grade for the course. Because the output statement in Line 21 does not contain the newline character or the manipulator `endl`, the output of the `if...else` statement is part of the fourth line of the output. After the `if...else` statement executes, control goes back to the function `main`. Because the next statement to execute in the function `main` is the last statement of the function `main`, the program terminates.

In this program, the function `main` first calls the function `getScore` to obtain the course score from the user. The function `main` then calls the function `printGrade` to calculate and print the grade based on this course score. The course score is retrieved by the function `getScore`; later, this course score is used by the function `printGrade`. Because the value retrieved by the `getScore` function is used later in the program, the function `getScore` must pass this value outside. Thus, the formal parameter that holds this value must be a reference parameter.

Value and Reference Parameters and Memory Allocation

When a function is called, memory for its formal parameters and variables declared in the body of the function (called **local variables**) is allocated in the function data area. Recall that, in the case of a value parameter, the value of the actual parameter is copied into the memory cell of its corresponding formal parameter. In the case of a reference parameter, the address of the actual parameter passes to the formal parameter. That is, the content of the formal parameter is an address. During data manipulation, the content of the formal parameter directs the computer to manipulate the data of the memory cell indicated by its content. Thus, in the case of a reference parameter, both the actual and formal parameters refer to the same memory location. Consequently, during program execution, changes made by the formal parameter permanently change the value of the actual parameter.

 NOTE Stream variables (for example, `ifstream` and `ofstream`) should be passed by reference to a function. After opening the input/output file or after reading and/or outputting data, the state of the input and/or output stream can then be passed outside the function.

Because parameter passing is fundamental to any programming language, Example 5-11 further illustrates this concept.

EXAMPLE 5-11

```cpp
//*************************************************************
// Author: D.S. Malik
//
// The program shows how reference and value parameters work.
//*************************************************************

#include <iostream>                              //Line 1

using namespace std;                             //Line 2

void funOne(int a, int& b, char v);              //Line 3

int main()                                       //Line 4
{                                                //Line 5
    int num1, num2;                              //Line 6
    char ch;                                     //Line 7

    num1 = 10;                                   //Line 8
    num2 = 15;                                   //Line 9
    ch = 'A';                                    //Line 10

    cout << "Line 11: Inside main: num1 = " << num1
         << ", num2 = " << num2 << ", and ch = "
         << ch << endl;                          //Line 11

    funOne(num1, num2, ch);                      //Line 12

    cout << "Line 13: After funOne: num1 = " << num1
         << ", num2 = " << num2 << ", and ch = "
         << ch << endl;                          //Line 13

    return 0;                                    //Line 14
} //end main                                     Line 15
```

5

```cpp
void funOne (int a, int& b, char v)              //Line 16
{                                                 //Line 17
    int one;                                      //Line 18

    one = a;                                      //Line 19
    a++;                                          //Line 20
    b = b * 2;                                    //Line 21
    v = 'B';                                      //Line 22

    cout << "Line 23: Inside funOne: a = " << a
         << ", b = " << b << ", v = " << v
         << ", and one = " << one << endl;        //Line 23
} //end funOne                                    Line 24
```

Sample Run:

```
Line 11: Inside main: num1 = 10, num2 = 15, and ch = A
Line 23: Inside funOne: a = 11, b = 30, v = B, and one = 10
Line 13: After funOne: num1 = 10, num2 = 30, and ch = A
```

Let us walk through this program. The values of the variables are shown before and/or after each statement executes.

Just before the statement in Line 8 executes, memory is allocated only for the variables of the function `main`; this memory is not initialized. After the statement in Line 10 executes, the variables are as shown in Figure 5-5.

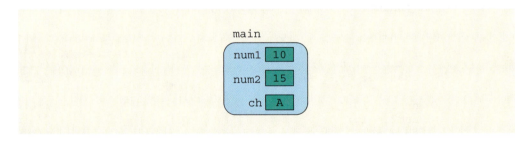

FIGURE 5-5 Values of the variables after the statement in Line 10 executes

The statement in Line 11 produces the following output:

```
Line 11: Inside main: num1 = 10, num2 = 15, and ch = A
```

The statement in Line 12 is a function call to the function `funOne`. Now function `funOne` has three parameters and one local variable. Memory for the parameters and the local variable of function `funOne` is allocated. Because the formal parameter `b` is a reference parameter, it receives the address (memory location) of the corresponding actual parameter, which is `num2`. The other two formal parameters are value parameters, so they copy the values of their corresponding actual parameters. Just before the statement in Line 19 executes, the variables are as shown in Figure 5-6.

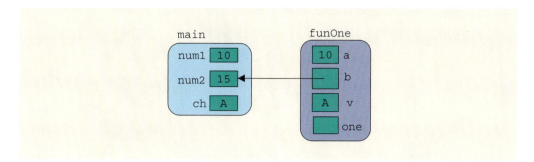

FIGURE 5-6   Values of the variables just before the statement in Line 19 executes

After the statement in Line 19, `one = a;`, executes, the variables are as shown in Figure 5-7.

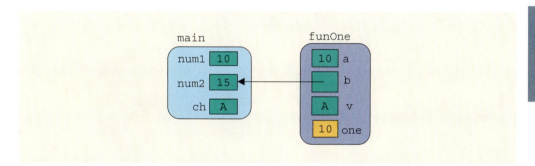

FIGURE 5-7   Values of the variables after the statement in Line 19 executes

After the statement in Line 20, `a++;`, executes, the variables are as shown in Figure 5-8.

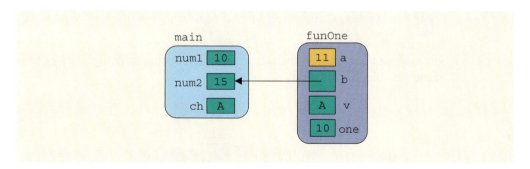

FIGURE 5-8   Values of the variables after the statement in Line 20 executes

After the statement in Line 21, `b = b * 2;`, executes, the variables are as shown in Figure 5-9. (Note that the variable `b` changed the value of `num2`.)

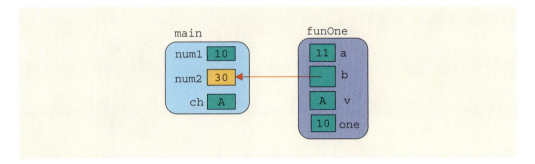

FIGURE 5-9 Values of the variables after the statement in Line 21 executes

After the statement in Line 22, v = 'B'; , executes, the variables are as shown in Figure 5-10.

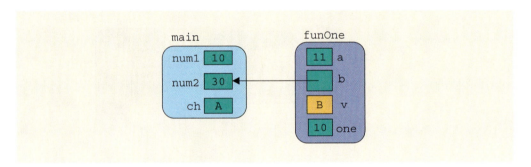

FIGURE 5-10 Values of the variables after the statement in Line 22 executes

The statement in Line 23 produces the following output:

```
Line 23: Inside funOne: a = 11, b = 30, v = B, and one = 10
```

After the statement in Line 23 executes, control goes back to Line 13, and the memory allocated for the variables of function funOne is deallocated. Figure 5-11 shows the values of the variables of the function main.

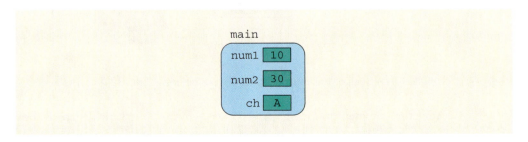

FIGURE 5-11 Values of the variables when control goes back to Line 13

Line 13 produces the following output:

```
Line 13: After funOne: num1 = 10, num2 = 30, and ch = A
```

After the statement in Line 14 executes, the program terminates.

Reference Parameters and Value-Returning Functions

Earlier in this chapter, in the discussion of value-returning functions, you learned how to use value parameters only. You can also use reference parameters in a value-returning function, although this approach is not recommended. By definition, a value-returning function returns a single value; this value is returned via the return statement. If a function needs to return more than one value, you should change it to a void function and use the appropriate reference parameters to return the values.

Scope of an Identifier

The previous sections presented several examples of programs with user-defined functions. Identifiers are declared in a function heading, within a block, or outside a block. A question naturally arises: Are you allowed to access any identifier anywhere in the program? The answer is no. You must follow certain rules to access an identifier. The **scope** of an identifier refers to where in the program an identifier is accessible (visible). Recall that an identifier is the name of something in C++, such as a variable or function name.

This section examines the scope of an identifier. First, we define the following two terms:

Local identifier: Identifier declared within a function (or block).

Local identifiers are not accessible outside of the function (block).

Global identifier: Identifier declared outside of every function definition.

In general, the following rules apply when an identifier is accessed.

1. Global identifiers (such as variables) are accessible by a function or a block if:
   a. The identifier is declared before the function definition (block)
   b. The function name is different from the identifier
   c. All parameters of the function have names different from the name of the identifier
   d. All local identifiers (such as local variables) have names different from the name of the identifier

2. **Nested Block:** An identifier declared within a block is accessible:

    a. Only within the block from the point at which it is declared until the end of the block

    b. By those blocks that are nested within that block if the nested block does not have an identifier with the same name as that of the outside block (the block that encloses the nested block)

3. The scope of a function name is similar to the scope of an identifier declared outside any block. That is, the scope of a function name is the same as the scope of a global variable. (Note that C++ *does not* allow the nesting of functions. That is, you cannot include the definition of one function in the body of another function.)

Before considering an example to explain these scope rules, first note the scope of the identifier declared in the `for` statement. Recall that C++ allows the programmer to declare a variable in the initialization statement of the `for` statement. For example, the following `for` statement

```
for (int count = 1; count < 10; count++)
    cout << count << endl;
```

declares the variable `count` and initializes it to 1. The scope of the variable `count` is limited to only the body of the `for` loop.

EXAMPLE 5-12

The following C++ program helps illustrate the scope rules:

```
#include <iostream>

using namespace std;

const double rate = 10.50;
int z;
double t;

void one(int x, char y);
void two(int a, int b, char x);
void three(int one, double y, int z);

int main()
{
    int num, first;
    double x, y, z;
    char name, last;
        .
        .
        .
    return 0;
}
```

```
void one(int x, char y)
{
     .
     .
     .
}

int w;

void two(int a, int b, char x)
{
   int count;
     .
     .
     .
}

void three(int one, double y, int z)
{
     char ch;
     int a;
       .
       .
   //Block four
     {
         int x;
         char a;
           .
           .
     }//end Block four
       .
       .
}
```

Table 5-2 summarizes the scope (visibility) of the identifiers.

TABLE 5-2 Scope (Visibility) of the Identifiers

Identifier	Visibility in one	Visibility in two	Visibility in three	Visibility in Block four	Visibility in main
rate (before main)	Y	Y	Y	Y	Y
z (before main)	Y	Y	N	N	N
t (before main)	Y	Y	Y	Y	Y
main	Y	Y	Y	Y	Y
local variables of main	N	N	N	N	Y

TABLE 5-2 Scope (Visibility) of the Identifiers (continued)

Identifier	Visibility in one	Visibility in two	Visibility in three	Visibility in Block four	Visibility in main
one (function name)	Y	Y	N	N	Y
x (one's formal parameter)	Y	N	N	N	N
y (one's formal parameter)	Y	N	N	N	N
w (before function two)	N	Y	Y	Y	N
two (function name)	Y	Y	Y	Y	Y
a (two's formal parameter)	N	Y	N	N	N
b (two's formal parameter)	N	Y	N	N	N
x (two's formal parameter)	N	Y	N	N	N
local variables of two	N	Y	N	N	N
three (function name)	Y	Y	Y	Y	Y
one (three's formal parameter)	N	N	Y	Y	N
y (three's formal parameter)	N	N	Y	Y	N
z (three's formal parameter)	N	N	Y	Y	N
ch (three's local variable)	N	N	Y	Y	N
a (three's local variable)	N	N	Y	N	N
x (Block four's local variable)	N	N	N	Y	N
a (Block four's local variable)	N	N	N	Y	N

Note that function three cannot call function one, because function three has a formal parameter named one. Similarly, the block marked four in function three cannot use the `int` variable a, which is declared in function three, because block four has an identifier named a.

Before closing this section, let us note the following about global variables:

1. Chapter 1 stated that C++ does not automatically initialize variables. Some compilers initialize global variables to their default values. For example, if a global variable is of the type `int`, `char`, or `double`, it is initialized to zero. However, if you are working with a compiler that automatically initializes global variables, you should still explicitly initialize global variables.

2. In C++, `::` is called the **scope resolution operator**. By using the scope resolution operator, a global variable declared before the definition of a function (block) can be accessed by the function (or block) even if the function (or block) has an identifier with the same name as the variable. In the preceding program, by using the scope resolution operator, the function `main` can refer to the global variable z as `::z`. Similarly, suppose that a global variable `t` is declared before the definition of the function—say, `funExample`. Then `funExample` can access the variable t using the scope resolution operator even if `funExample` has an identifier t. Using the scope resolution operator, `funExample` refers to the variable t as `::t`. Also, in the preceding program, using the scope resolution operator, function `three` can call function `one`.

3. C++ provides a way to access a global variable declared after the definition of a function. In this case, the function must not contain any identifier with the same name as the global variable. In the preceding program, the global variable w is declared after the definition of function `one`. The function `one` does not contain any identifier named w; therefore, w can be accessed by function `one` only if you declare w as an **external variable** inside one. To declare w as an external variable inside function `one`, the function `one` must contain the following statement:

   ```
   extern int w;
   ```

   In C++, `extern` is a reserved word. The word `extern` in the preceding statement announces that w is a global variable declared elsewhere. Thus, when function `one` is called, no memory for w, as declared inside one, is allocated. In C++, external declaration also has another use, but it is not discussed in this book. The Web site accompanying this book contains the program `Ch5_externVar.cpp`, which shows the effect of an external variable.

Global Variables, Named Constants, and Side Effects

A C++ program can contain global variables. Using global variables, however, has side effects. If more than one function uses the same global variable and something goes wrong, it is difficult to discover what went wrong and where. Problems caused by global variables in one area of a program might be misunderstood as problems caused in another area. For example, consider the program given in Example 5-13.

EXAMPLE 5-13

```cpp
//*************************************************************
// Author: D.S. Malik
//
// Global variable.
//*************************************************************

#include <iostream>                                    //Line 1

using namespace std;                                   //Line 2

int t;              // global variable                  Line 3

void funOne(int& a);                                   //Line 4

int main()                                             //Line 5
{                                                      //Line 6
    t = 15;                                            //Line 7

    cout << "Line 8: In main: t = " << t << endl;      //Line 8

    funOne(t);                                         //Line 9

    cout << "Line 10: In main after funOne: "
        << " t = " << t << endl;                       //Line 10

    return 0;                                          //Line 11
}                                                      //Line 12

void funOne(int& a)                                    //Line 13
{                                                      //Line 14
    cout << "Line 15: In funOne: a = " << a
        << " and t = " << t << endl;                   //Line 15

    a = a + 12;                                        //Line 16
    cout << "Line 17: In funOne: a = " << a
        << " and t = " << t << endl;                   //Line 17

    t = t + 13;                                        //Line 18

    cout << "Line 19: In funOne: a = " << a
        << " and t = " << t << endl;                   //Line 19
} //end funOne                                          Line 20
```

This program has a variable t that is declared, in Line 3, before the definition of any function. Because none of the functions has an identifier t, the variable t is accessible anywhere in the program. Also, the program consists of a void function with a reference parameter.

In Line 9, the function `main` calls the function `funOne`, and the actual parameter passed to `funOne` is `t`. So, `a`, the formal parameter of `funOne`, receives the address of `t`. Any changes that `a` makes to its value immediately change `t`. Because `t` can be directly accessed anywhere in the program, in Line 18 the function `funOne` changes the value of `t` by using `t` itself. Thus, you can manipulate the value of `t` by using either a reference parameter or `t` itself.

In the previous program, if the last value of `t` is incorrect, it would be difficult to determine what went wrong and in which part of the program. We strongly recommend that you do not use global variables; instead, use the appropriate parameters.

In the programs given in this book, we typically placed named constants before the function `main`, outside of every function definition. That is, the named constants we used are *global named constants*. Unlike global variables, global named constants have no side effects because during program execution their values cannot be changed. Moreover, placing a named constant in the beginning of the program can increase readability, even if it is used only in one function. If you need to later modify the program and change the value of a named constant, it will be easier to find if it is placed in the beginning of the program.

Avoiding Bugs: Using "Stubs" as Appropriate

Sometimes a function can be tested in isolation. Other times, for example, when one function relies on another function, testing in isolation is not possible until the other function is written. Does this dictate the order in which the completed pieces of a program must be written? Not necessarily. A **function stub** is a function that is not fully coded. Sometimes a function stub consists of only a function header and a set of empty braces, `{}`, which is sufficient to permit it to be called, at least for a void method. Sometimes a stub merely produces a plausible return value. For example, a stub for function `calculateCost` that accepts `item` as a parameter might simply return 100.00, independent of the value associated with `item`. This permits function `calculateCost` to be called while the program is being coded. To complete the coding of the program, the stub for function `calculateCost` ultimately is replaced with a function that properly calculates cost based on the value of `item` passed in as a parameter. In the meantime, the function stub permits work to progress on other parts of the solution that call method `calculateCost`.

Static and Automatic Variables (Optional)

The variables discussed so far have followed two simple rules:

1. Memory for global variables remains allocated as long as the program executes.
2. Memory for a variable declared within a block is allocated at block entry and deallocated at block exit. For example, memory for the formal parameters and local variables of a function is allocated when the function is called and deallocated when the function exits.

A variable for which memory is allocated at block entry and deallocated at block exit is called an **automatic variable**. A variable for which memory remains allocated as long as the program executes is called a **static variable**. Global variables are static variables and, by default, variables declared within a block are automatic variables. You can declare a static variable within a block by using the reserved word `static`. The syntax for declaring a static variable is:

```
static dataType identifier;
```

The statement

```
static int x;
```

declares `x` to be a static variable of the type `int`.

Static variables declared within a block are local to the block, and their scope is the same as that of any other local identifier of that block.

Most compilers initialize `static` variables to their default values. For example, `static int` variables are initialized to 0. However, it is a good practice to initialize `static` variables yourself, especially if the initial value is not the default value. In this case, `static` variables are initialized when they are declared. The statement

```
static int x = 0;
```

declares `x` to be a static variable of the type `int` and initializes `x` to 0.

EXAMPLE 5-14

The following program shows how static and automatic variables behave.

```cpp
//************************************************************
// Author: D.S. Malik
//
// This program illustrates how static and automatic variables
// work.
//************************************************************

#include <iostream>

using namespace std;

void test();

int main()
{
    for (int count = 1; count <= 5; count++)
        test();

    return 0;
}
```

```
void test()
{
    static int x = 0;
    int y = 10;

    x = x + 2;
    y = y + 1;

    cout << "Inside test x = " << x << " and y = " << y << endl;
} //end test
```

Sample Run:

```
Inside test x = 2 and y = 11
Inside test x = 4 and y = 11
Inside test x = 6 and y = 11
Inside test x = 8 and y = 11
Inside test x = 10 and y = 11
```

In the function `test`, `x` is a `static` variable initialized to 0, and `y` is an automatic variable initialized to 10. The function `main` calls the function `test` five times. Memory for the variable `y` is allocated every time the function `test` is called and deallocated when the function exits. Thus, every time the function `test` is called, it prints the same value for `y`. However, because `x` is a static variable, memory for `x` remains allocated as long as the program executes. The variable `x` is initialized once to 0. The subsequent calls of the function `test` use the current value of `x`.

Because memory for static variables remains allocated between function calls, static variables allow you to use the value of a variable from one function call to another function call. Even though you can use global variables if you want to use certain values from one function call to another, the local scope of a static variable prevents other functions from manipulating that static variable's value.

Before we look at some programming examples, another concept about functions is worth mentioning: function overloading.

Function Overloading (Optional)

In a C++ program, several functions can have the same name. This is called **function overloading** or **overloading a function name**. Before we state the rules to overloading a function, let us define the following:

Two functions are said to have **different formal parameter lists** if both functions have:

- A different number of formal parameters, or
- If the number of formal parameters is the same, then the data type of the formal parameters, in the order you list them, must differ in at least one position.

For example, consider the following function headings:

```
void functionOne(int x)
void functionTwo(int x, double y)
void functionThree(double y, int x)
int functionFour(char ch, int x, double y)
int functionFive(char ch, int x, string name)
```

These functions all have different formal parameter lists.

Now consider the following function headings:

```
void functionSix(int x, double y, char ch)
void functionSeven(int one, double u, char firstCh)
```

The functions functionSix and functionSeven both have three formal parameters, and the data type of the corresponding parameters is the same. Therefore, these functions have the same formal parameter list.

To overload a function name, any two definitions of the function must have different formal parameter lists.

Function overloading: Creating several functions with the same name.

The **signature** of a function consists of the function name and its formal parameter list. Two functions have different signatures if they have either different names or different formal parameter lists. (Note that the signature of a function does not include the return type of the function.)

If a function's name is overloaded, then all the functions in the set have the same name. Therefore, all the functions in the set have different signatures if they have different formal parameter lists. Thus, the following function headings correctly overload the function functionXYZ:

```
void functionXYZ()
void functionXYZ(int x, double y)
void functionXYZ(double one, int y)
void functionXYZ(int x, double y, char ch)
```

Consider the following function headings to overload the function functionABC:

```
void functionABC(int x, double y)
int functionABC(int x, double y)
```

Both of these function headings have the same name and same formal parameter list. Therefore, these function headings to overload the function functionABC are incorrect. In this case, the compiler will generate a syntax error. (Notice that the return types of these function headings are different.)

If a function is overloaded, then in a call to that function, the signature—that is, the formal parameter list of the function—determines which function to execute.

NOTE Some authors define the signature of a function as the formal parameter list, and some consider the entire heading of the function as its signature. However, in this book, the signature of a function, consists of the function's heading and its formal parameter list. If the functions, names are different, then, of course, the compiler would have no problem identifying which function is called, and it will correctly translate the code. However, if a function's name is overloaded, then, as noted, the function's formal parameter list determines which function's body executes.

Suppose you need to write a function that determines the larger of two items. Both items can be integers, floating-point numbers, characters, or strings. You could write several functions as follows:

```
int largerInt(int x, int y);
char largerChar(char first, char second);
double largerDouble(double u, double v);
string largerString(string first, string second);
```

The function `largerInt` determines the larger of two integers; the function `largerChar` determines the larger of two characters, and so on. All of these functions perform similar operations. Instead of giving different names to these functions, you can use the same name—say, `larger`—for each function; that is, you can overload the function `larger`. Thus, you can write the previous function prototypes simply as follows:

```
int larger(int x, int y);
char larger(char first, char second);
double larger(double u, double v);
string larger(string first, string second);
```

If the call is `larger(5, 3)`, for example, the first function is executed. If the call is `larger('A', '9')`, the second function is executed, and so on.

Function overloading is used when you have the same action for different sets of data. Of course, for function overloading to work, you must give the definition of each function.

Functions with Default Parameters (Optional)

This section discusses functions with default parameters. Recall that when a function is called, the number of actual and formal parameters must be the same. C++ relaxes this condition for functions with default parameters. You specify the value of a default parameter when the function name appears for the first time, such as in the prototype. In general, the following rules apply for functions with default parameters:

- If you do not specify the value of a default parameter, the default value is used for that parameter.

- All of the default parameters must be the rightmost parameters of the function.

- Suppose a function has more than one default parameter. In a function call, if a value to a default parameter is not specified, then you must omit all of the arguments to its right.

- Default values can be constants, global variables, or function calls.

- The caller has the option of specifying a value other than the default for any default parameter.

- You cannot assign a constant value as a default value to a reference parameter.

Consider the following function prototype:

```
void funcExp(int x, int y, double t, char z = 'A', int u = 67,
             char v = 'G', double w = 78.34);
```

The function `funcExp` has seven parameters. The parameters z, u, v, and w are default parameters. If no values are specified for z, u, v, and w in a call to the function `funcExp`, their default values are used.

Suppose you have the following statements:

```
int a, b;
char ch;
double d;
```

The following function calls are legal:

1. `funcExp(a, b, d);`
2. `funcExp(a, 15, 34.6, 'B', 87, ch);`
3. `funcExp(b, a, 14.56, 'D');`

In statement 1, the default values of z, u, v, and w are used. In statement 2, the default value of z is replaced by 'B', the default value of u is replaced by 87, the default value of v is replaced by the value of ch, and the default value of w is used. In statement 3, the default value of z is replaced by 'D', and the default values of u, v, and w are used.

The following function calls are illegal:

1. `funcExp(a, 15, 34.6, 46.7);`
2. `funcExp(b, 25, 48.76, 'D', 4567, 78.34);`

In statement 1, because the value of z is omitted, all other default values must be omitted. In statement 2, because the value of v is omitted, the value of w should be omitted, too.

The following are illegal function prototypes with default parameters:

1. `void funcOne(int x, double z = 23.45, char ch, int u = 45);`

2. `int funcTwo(int length = 1, int width, int height = 1);`

3. `void funcThree(int x, int& y = 16, double z = 34);`

In statement 1, because the second parameter z is a default parameter, all other parameters after z must be default parameters. In statement 2, because the first parameter is a default parameter, all parameters must be the default parameters. In statement 3, a constant value cannot be assigned to y because y is a reference parameter.

Example 5-15 further illustrates functions with default parameters.

EXAMPLE 5-15

```cpp
//*************************************************************
// Author: D.S. Malik
//
// This program illustrates how functions with default parameters
// work.
//*************************************************************

#include <iostream>                                    //Line 1
#include <iomanip>                                     //Line 2

using namespace std;                                   //Line 3

int volume(int l = 1, int w = 1, int h = 1);           //Line 4
void funcOne(int& x, double y = 12.34, char z = 'B');  //Line 5

int main()                                             //Line 6
{                                                      //Line 7
    int a = 23;                                        //Line 8
    double b = 48.78;                                  //Line 9
    char ch = 'M';                                     //Line 10

    cout << fixed << showpoint << setprecision(2);     //Line 11

    cout << "Line 12: a = " << a << ", b = "
         << b  << ", ch = " << ch << endl;             //Line 12
    cout << "Line 13: Volume = " << volume() << endl;  //Line 13
    cout << "Line 14: Volume = " << volume(5, 4) << endl; //Line 14
    cout << "Line 15: Volume = " << volume(34) << endl;   //Line 15
    cout << "Line 16: Volume = " << volume(6, 4, 5)
         << endl;                                      //Line 16
```

5

```
    funcOne(a);                                              //Line 17
    funcOne(a, 42.68);                                       //Line 18
    funcOne(a, 34.65, 'Q');                                  //Line 19

    cout << "Line 20: a = " << a << ", b = " << b
         << ", ch = " << ch << endl;                         //Line 20

    return 0;                                                //Line 21
} //end main                                                 //Line 22

int volume(int l, int w, int h)                              //Line 23
{                                                            //Line 24
    return l * w * h;                                        //Line 25
} //end volume                                               //Line 26

void funcOne(int& x, double y, char z)                       //Line 27
{                                                            //Line 28
    x = 2 * x;                                               //Line 29
    cout << "Line 30: x = " << x << ", y = "
         << y << ", z = " << z << endl;                      //Line 30
} //end funcOne                                              //Line 31
```

Sample Run:

```
Line 12: a = 23, b = 48.78, ch = M
Line 13: Volume = 1
Line 14: Volume = 20
Line 15: Volume = 34
Line 16: Volume = 120
Line 30: x = 46, y = 12.34, z = B
Line 30: x = 92, y = 42.68, z = B
Line 30: x = 184, y = 34.65, z = Q
Line 20: a = 184, b = 48.78, ch = M
```

 NOTE   In programs in this book, the definition of the function `main` is placed before the definition of any user-defined functions. You must therefore specify the default value for a parameter in the function prototype, and in the function prototype only, *not* in the function definition.

PROGRAMMING EXAMPLE: Classify Numbers

This program reads a given set of integers and then prints the number of odd and even integers. It also outputs the number of zeros.

The program reads 20 integers, but you can easily modify it to read any set of numbers. In fact, you can modify the program so that it first prompts the user to specify how many integers are to be read.

Input   20 integers—positive, negative, or zeros.

Output   The number of zeros, even numbers, and odd numbers.

PROBLEM
ANALYSIS
AND
ALGORITHM
DESIGN

After reading a number, you need to check whether it is even or odd. Suppose the value is stored in **number**. Divide **number** by 2 and check the remainder. If the remainder is 0, **number** is even. Increment the even count and then check whether **number** is 0. If it is, increment the zero count. If the remainder is not 0, increment the odd count.

The program uses a **switch** statement to decide whether **number** is odd or even. Suppose that **number** is odd. Dividing by 2 gives the remainder 1 if **number** is positive and the remainder –1 if it is negative. If **number** is even, dividing by 2 gives the remainder 0 whether **number** is positive or negative. You can use the mod operator, %, to find the remainder. For example,

```
6 % 2 = 0; -4 % 2 = 0; -7 % 2 = -1; 15 % 2 = 1.
```

Repeat the preceding process of analyzing a number for each number in the list.

This discussion translates into the following algorithm:

1. For each number in the list, do the following:
    a. Get the number.
    b. Analyze the number.
    c. Increment the appropriate count.
2. Print the results.

Variables

Because you want to count the number of zeros, even numbers, and odd numbers, you need three variables of the type **int**—say, **zeros**, **evens**, and **odds**—to track the counts. You also need a variable—say, **number**—to read and store the number to be analyzed, and another variable—say, **counter**—to count the numbers analyzed. Therefore, you need the following variables in the program:

```
int counter;    //loop control variable
int number;     //variable to store the number read
int zeros;      //variable to store the zero count
int evens;      //variable to store the even count
int odds;       //variable to store the odd count
```

Clearly, you must initialize the variables zeros, evens, and odds to zero. You can initialize these variables when you declare them. You can use a for loop to count, read, and process the numbers. So the variable counter can be declared within the for loop.

The main parts of the program are: initialize the variables, read and classify the numbers, and then output the results. To simplify the function main and further illustrate parameter passing, the program includes the following:

- A function, getNumber, to get the number.
- A function, classifyNumber, to determine whether the number is odd or even (and whether it is also zero). This function also increments the appropriate count.
- A function, printResults, to print the results.

Let us now describe each of these functions.

getNumber The function getNumber reads a number and then passes this number to the function main. Because you need to pass only one number, this function has only one parameter. The formal parameter of this function must be a reference parameter because the number read is passed outside the function. Essentially this function is:

```
void getNumber(int& num)
{
    cin >> num;
}
```

You can also write the function getNumber as a value-returning function. See the note at the end of this programming example.

classifyNumber The function classifyNumber determines whether the number is odd or even, and, if the number is even, it also checks whether the number is zero. It also updates the values of some of the variables, zeros, odds, and evens. This function needs to know the number to be analyzed; therefore, the number must be passed as a parameter. Because this function also increments the appropriate count, the variables (that is, zeros, odds, and evens declared in main) holding the counts must be passed as parameters to this function. Thus, this function has four parameters.

Because the number will only be analyzed, you need to pass only its value. Thus, the formal parameter corresponding to this variable is a value parameter. After analyzing the number, this function increments the values of some of the variables, zeros, odds, and evens. Therefore, the formal parameters corresponding to these variables must be reference parameters. The algorithm to analyze the number and increment the appropriate count is the same as before. The definition of this function is:

```
void classifyNumber(int num, int& zeroCount, int& oddCount,
                    int& evenCount)
{
    switch (num % 2)
    {
    case 0:
        evenCount++;
        if (num == 0)
            zeroCount++;
        break;

    case 1:
    case -1:
        oddCount++;
    } //end switch
} //end classifyNumbers
```

printResults The function `printResults` prints the final results. To print the results (that is, the number of zeros, odds, and evens), this function must have access to the values of the variables `zeros`, `odds`, and `evens`, declared in the function `main`. Therefore, this function has three parameters. Because this function prints only the values of the variables, the formal parameters are value parameters. The definition of this function is:

```
void printResults(int zeroCount, int oddCount, int evenCount)
{
    cout << "There are " << evenCount << " evens, "
         << "which includes " << zeroCount << " zeros"
         << endl;

    cout << "The number of odd numbers is: " << oddCount
         << endl;
} //end printResults
```

We now give the main algorithm and show how the function `main` calls these functions.

MAIN ALGORITHM

1. Declare and, if needed, initialize the variables.
2. Prompt the user to enter 20 numbers.
3. For each number in the list, do the following:
   a. Call the function `getNumber` to read a number.
   b. Output the number.
   c. Call the function `classifyNumber` to classify the number and increment the appropriate count.
4. Call the function `printResults` to print the final results.

COMPLETE PROGRAM LISTING

```cpp
//************************************************************
// Author: D.S. Malik
//
// Program: Classify Numbers
// This program reads 20 numbers and outputs the number of
// zeros, odd numbers, and even numbers.
//************************************************************

#include <iostream>
#include <iomanip>

using namespace std;

const int N = 20;

    //Function prototypes
void getNumber(int& num);
void classifyNumber(int num, int& zeroCount, int& oddCount,
                    int& evenCount);
void printResults(int zeroCount, int oddCount, int evenCount);

int main ()
{
        //Step 1: variable declaration
    int number;
    int zeros = 0;    //initialize
    int odds = 0;     //initialize
    int evens = 0;    //initialize

    cout << "Please enter " << N << " integers."
         << endl;                                      //Step 2
    cout << "The numbers you entered are: "
         << endl;

    for (int counter = 1; counter <= N; counter++)   //Step 3
    {
        getNumber(number);                            //Step 3a
        cout << number << " ";                        //Step 3b
        classifyNumber(number, zeros, odds, evens); //Step 3c
    } // end for loop

    cout << endl;

    printResults(zeros, odds, evens);                 //Step 4

    return 0;
}

void getNumber(int& num)
{
    cin >> num;
}
```

```
void classifyNumber(int num, int& zeroCount, int& oddCount,
                    int& evenCount)
{
    switch (num % 2)
    {
    case 0:
        evenCount++;
        if (num == 0)
            zeroCount++;
        break;
    case 1:
    case -1:
        oddCount++;
    } //end switch
} //end classifyNumbers

void printResults(int zeroCount, int oddCount, int evenCount)
{
    cout << "There are " << evenCount << " evens, "
         << "which includes " << zeroCount << " zeros"
         << endl;

    cout << "The number of odd numbers is: " << oddCount
         << endl;
} //end printResults
```

Sample Run: In this sample run, the user input is shaded.

```
Please enter 20 integers.
The numbers you entered are:
0 0 12 23 45 7 -2 -8 -3 -9 4 0 1 0 -7 23 -24 0 0 12
0 0 12 23 45 7 -2 -8 -3 -9 4 0 1 0 -7 23 -24 0 0 12
There are 12 evens, which includes 6 zeros
The number of odd numbers is: 8
```

 NOTE In the previous program, because the data is assumed to be input from the standard input device (the keyboard) and the function getNumber returns only one value, you can also write the function getNumber as a value-returning function. If written as a value-returning function, the definition of the function getNumber is:

```
int getNumber()
{
    int num;

    cin >> num;

    return num;
}
```

5

In this case, the statement (function call)

```
getNumber(number);
```

in the function `main` should be replaced by the following statement:

```
number = getNumber();
```

Of course, you also need to change the function prototype.

PROGRAMMING EXAMPLE: Data Comparison

This programming example illustrates:

- How to read data from more than one file in the same program
- How to send output to a file
- How to generate bar graphs
- With the help of functions and parameter passing, how to use the same program segment on different (but similar) sets of data
- How to use structured design to solve a problem and how to perform parameter passing

This program is broken into two parts. First, you learn how to read data from more than one file. Second, you learn how to generate bar graphs.

Two groups of students at a local university are enrolled in certain special courses during the summer semester. The courses are offered for the first time and are taught by different teachers. At the end of the semester, both groups are given the same tests for the same courses and their scores are recorded in separate files. The data in each file is in the following form:

```
courseNo  score1 score2 ... scoreN -999
courseNo  score1 score2 ... scoreM -999
.
.
.
```

Let us write a program that finds the average course score for each course for each group. The output is of the following form:

```
Course No    Group No     Course Average
   CSC          1            83.71
                2            80.82
   ENG          1            82.00
                2            78.20
```

.
.
.

```
Avg for group 1: 82.04
Avg for group 2: 82.01
```

Input   Because the data for the two groups is recorded in separate files, the input data appears in two separate files.

Output   As shown previously.

PROBLEM
ANALYSIS
AND
ALGORITHM
DESIGN

Reading input data from both files is straightforward. Suppose the data is stored in the file **group1.txt** for group 1 and the file **group2.txt** for group 2. After processing the data for one group, we can process the data for the second group for the same course, and continue until we run out of data. Processing data for each course is similar and is the following two-step process:

1. a. Sum the scores for the course.
   b. Count the number of students in the course.
   c. Divide the total score by the number of students to find the course average.
2. Output the results.

We are comparing only the averages of the corresponding courses in each group, and the data in each file is ordered according to course ID. To ensure that only the averages of the corresponding courses are compared, we compare the course IDs for each group. If the corresponding course IDs are not the same, we output an error message and terminate the program.

This discussion suggests that we should write a function, **calculateAverage**, to find the course average. We should also write another function, **printResults**, to output the data in the form given. By passing the appropriate parameters, we can use the same functions, **calculateAverage** and **printResults**, to process each course's data for both groups. (In the second part of the program, we modify the function **printResults**.)

The preceding discussion translates into the following algorithm:

1. Initialize the variables.
2. Get the course IDs for group 1 and group 2.
3. If the course IDs are different, print an error message and exit the program.

4. Calculate the course averages for group 1 and group 2.

5. Print the results in the form given earlier.

6. Repeat Steps 2 through 5 for each course.

7. Print the final results.

Variables (Function main) The preceding discussion suggests that the program needs the following variables for data manipulation in the function `main`:

```
string courseId1;       //course ID for group 1
string courseId2;       //course ID for group 2
int numberOfCourses;
double avg1;            //average for a course in group 1
double avg2;            //average for a course in group 2
double avgGroup1;       //average group 1
double avgGroup2;       //average group 2
ifstream group1;        //input stream variable for group 1
ifstream group2;        //input stream variable for group 2
ofstream outfile;       //output stream variable
```

Next, we discuss the functions `calculateAverage` and `printResults`. Then we will put the function `main` together.

calculate Average This function calculates the average for a course. Because the input is stored in a file and the input file is opened in the function `main`, we must pass the `ifstream` variable associated with the input file to this function. Furthermore, after calculating the course average, this function must pass the course average to the function `main`. Therefore, this function has two parameters, and both parameters must be reference parameters.

To find the course average, we must first find the sum of all scores for the course and the number of students who took the course, and then divide the sum by the number of students. Thus, we need a variable to find the sum of the scores, a variable to count the number of students, and a variable to read and store a score. Of course, we must initialize the variable to find the sum and the variable to count the number of students to zero.

Local Variables (Function calculate Average) In the previous discussion of data manipulation, we identified the following three variables for the function `calculateAverage`:

```
double totalScore = 0.0;
int numberOfStudents = 0;
int score;
```

The preceding discussion translates into the following algorithm for the function calculateAverage:

1. Declare and initialize variables.
2. Get the (next) course score, score.
3. while the score is not -999

    a. Update totalScore by adding the course score.
    b. Increment numberOfStudents by 1.
    c. Get the (next) course score, score.

4. courseAvg = totalScore / numberOfStudents;

We are now ready to write the definition of the function calculateAverage.

```
void calculateAverage(ifstream& inp, double& courseAvg)
{
    double totalScore = 0.0;
    int numberOfStudents = 0;
    int score;

    inp >> score;
    while (score != -999)
    {
        totalScore = totalScore + score;
        numberOfStudents++;
        inp >> score;
    } //end while

    courseAvg = totalScore / numberOfStudents;
} //end calculate Average
```

(Note that the definition of the function calculateAverage assumes that every course has at least one value.)

printResults The function printResults prints the group's course ID, group number, and course average. The output is stored in a file. So we must pass four parameters to this function: the ofstream variable associated with the output file, the group number, the course ID, and the course average for the group. The ofstream variable must be passed by reference. Because the function uses only the values of the other variables, the remaining three parameters should be value parameters. Also, from the output, it is clear that we print the course ID only before group 1. In pseudocode, the algorithm is:

```
if (group number == 1)
    print course ID
else
    print a blank

print group number and course average
```

5

The definition of the function `printResults` follows:

```
void printResults(ofstream& outp, string courseID, int groupNo,
                  double avg)
{
    if (groupNo == 1)
        outp << "  " << courseID << "    ";
    else
        outp << "            ";

    outp << setw(8) << groupNo << setw(17) << avg << endl;
} //end printResults
```

Now that we have designed and defined the functions `calculateAverage` and `printResults`, we can describe the algorithm for the function `main`. Before outlining the algorithm, however, we note the following: It is quite possible that in both input files the data is ordered according to the course IDs, but one file might have fewer courses than the other. We do not discover this error until after we have processed both files and discover that one file has unprocessed data. Make sure to check for this error before printing the final answer—that is, the averages for group 1 and group 2.

Main Algorithm:
Function `main`

1. Declare the variables (local declaration).
2. Open the input files.
3. Print a message if you are unable to open a file, and terminate the program.
4. Open the output file.
5. To output floating-point numbers in a fixed-decimal format with the decimal point and trailing zeros, set the manipulators `fixed` and `showpoint`. Also, to output floating-point numbers to two decimal places, set the precision to two decimal places.
6. Initialize the course average for group 1 to `0.0`.
7. Initialize the course average for group 2 to `0.0`.
8. Initialize the number of courses to `0`.
9. Print the heading.
10. Get the course ID, `courseId1`, for group 1.
11. Get the course ID, `courseId2`, for group 2.
12. For each course in group 1 and group 2,
    a. `if (courseId1 != courseId2)`
    ```
    {
        cout << "Data error: Course IDs do not match.\n";
        return 1;
    }
    ```

b. `else`
   `{`

     i. Calculate the course average for group 1 (call the function `calculateAverage` and pass the appropriate parameters).

     ii. Calculate the course average for group 2 (call the function `calculateAverage` and pass the appropriate parameters).

     iii. Print the results for group 1 (call the function `printResults` and pass the appropriate parameters).

     iv. Print the results for group 2 (call the function `printResults` and pass the appropriate parameters).

     v. Update the average for group 1.

     vi. Update the average for group 2.

     vii. Increment the number of courses.

   `}`

c. Get the course ID, `courseId1`, for group 1.

d. Get the course ID, `courseId2`, for group 2.

13. a. `if` not_end_of_file on group 1 and end_of_file on group 2

    print "Ran out of data for group 2 before group 1"

b. `else if` end_of_file on group 1 and not_end_of_file on group 2

    print "Ran out of data for group 1 before group 2"

c. `else`

    print the average of group 1 and group 2.

14. Close the input and output files.

COMPLETE PROGRAM LISTING

```
//*************************************************************
// Author: D.S. Malik
//
// Program: Comparison of Class Averages
// This program computes and compares the class averages of
// two groups of students.
//*************************************************************

#include <iostream>
#include <iomanip>
#include <fstream>
#include <string>
```

```cpp
using namespace std;

    //Function prototypes
void calculateAverage(ifstream& inp, double& courseAvg);
void printResults(ofstream& outp, string courseId,
                  int groupNo, double avg);

int main ()
{
        //Step 1
    string courseId1;       //course ID for group 1
    string courseId2;       //course ID for group 2
    int numberOfCourses;
    double avg1;            //average for a course in group 1
    double avg2;            //average for a course in group 2
    double avgGroup1;       //average group 1
    double avgGroup2;       //average group 2
    ifstream group1;        //input stream variable for group 1
    ifstream group2;        //input stream variable for group 2
    ofstream outfile;       //output stream variable

    group1.open("group1.txt");                  //Step 2
    group2.open("group2.txt");                  //Step 2

    if (!group1 || !group2)                     //Step 3
    {
        cout << "Unable to open files." << endl;
        cout << "Program terminates." << endl;
        return 1;
    }

    outfile.open("student.out");                //Step 4
    outfile << fixed << showpoint;              //Step 5
    outfile << setprecision(2);                 //Step 5

    avgGroup1 = 0.0;                            //Step 6
    avgGroup2 = 0.0;                            //Step 7
    numberOfCourses = 0;                        //Step 8

    outfile << "Course No   Group No    "
            << "Course Average" << endl;        //Step 9

    group1 >> courseId1;                        //Step 10
    group2 >> courseId2;                        //Step 11
    while (group1 && group2)                    //Step 12
    {
        if (courseId1 != courseId2)             //Step 12a
        {
            cout << "Data error: Course IDs "
                 << "do not match." << endl;
```

```
                    cout << "Program terminates." << endl;
                    return 1;
            }
            else                                        //Step 12b
            {
                    calculateAverage(group1, avg1);      //Step 12b.i
                    calculateAverage(group2, avg2);      //Step 12b.ii
                    printResults(outfile, courseId1,
                            1, avg1);                    //Step 12b.iii
                    printResults(outfile, courseId2,
                            2, avg2);                    //Step 12b.iv
                    avgGroup1 = avgGroup1 + avg1;         //Step 12b.v
                    avgGroup2 = avgGroup2 + avg2;         //Step 12b.vi
                    outfile << endl;
                    numberOfCourses++;                   //Step 12b.vii
            }

            group1 >> courseId1;                         //Step 12c
            group2 >> courseId2;                         //Step 12d
    } //end while

    if (group1 && !group2)                               //Step 13a
        cout << "Ran out of data for group 2 "
             << "before group 1." << endl;
    else if (!group1 && group2)                          //Step 13b
        cout << "Ran out of data for group 1 "
             << "before group 2." << endl;
    else                                                 //Step 13c
    {
        outfile << "Avg for group 1: "
                << avgGroup1 / numberOfCourses
                << endl;
        outfile << "Avg for group 2: "
                << avgGroup2 / numberOfCourses
                << endl;
    }

    group1.close();                                      //Step 14
    group2.close();                                      //Step 14
    outfile.close();                                     //Step 14

    return 0;
}

void calculateAverage(ifstream& inp, double& courseAvg)
{
    double totalScore = 0.0;
    int numberOfStudents = 0;
    int score;
```

```
        inp >> score;
        while (score != -999)
        {
            totalScore = totalScore + score;
            numberOfStudents++;
            inp >> score;
        }//end while

        courseAvg = totalScore / numberOfStudents;
} //end calculate Average

void printResults(ofstream& outp, string courseID, int groupNo,
                 double avg)
{
    if (groupNo == 1)
        outp << "  " << courseID << "    ";
    else
        outp << "          ";

    outp << setw(8) << groupNo << setw(17) << avg << endl;
} //end printResults
```

Sample Run:

```
Course No    Group No      Course Average
   CSC          1              83.71
                2              80.82

   ENG          1              82.00
                2              78.20

   HIS          1              77.69
                2              84.15

   MTH          1              83.57
                2              84.29

   PHY          1              83.22
                2              82.60
Avg for group 1: 82.04
Avg for group 2: 82.01
```

Input Data Group 1

```
CSC 80 100 70 80 72 90 89 100 83 70 90 73 85 90 -999
ENG 80 90 80 94 90 74 78 63 83 80 90 -999
HIS 90 70 80 70 90 50 89 83 90 68 90 60 80 -999
MTH 74 80 75 89 90 73 90 82 74 90 84 100 90 79 -999
PHY 100 83 93 80 63 78 88 89 75 -999
```

Input Data Group 2

```
CSC 90 75 90 75 80 89 100 60 80 70 80 -999
ENG 80 80 70 68 70 78 80 90 90 76 -999
HIS 100 80 80 70 90 76 88 90 90 75 90 85 80 -999
MTH 80 85 85 92 90 90 74 90 83 65 72 90 84 100 -999
PHY 90 93 73 85 68 75 67 100 87 88 -999
```

BAR GRAPH

In the business world, company executives often like to see results in a visual form, such as a bar graph. Many currently available software packages can analyze data in several forms and then display the results in a visual form such as bar graphs or pie charts. The second part of this program aims to display the results found earlier in the form of bar graphs, as shown below:

```
Course          Course Average
   ID    0   10   20   30   40   50   60   70   80   90   100
         |....|....|....|....|....|....|....|....|....|....|
   CSC   ******************************************
         ^^^^^^^^^^^^^^^^^^^^^^^^^^^^^^^^^^^^^^^^^^

   ENG   ******************************************
         ^^^^^^^^^^^^^^^^^^^^^^^^^^^^^^^^^^^^^^^^^^

   .
   .
   .

Group 1 -- ***
Group 2 -- ^^^
Avg for group 1: 82.04
Avg for group 2: 82.01
```

Each symbol (* or ^) in the bar graph represents 2 points. If a course average is less than 2, no symbol is printed.

Because the output is in the form of a bar graph, we need to modify the function printResults.

printResults

The function printResults prints the course ID and the bar graph representing the average for a course. The output is stored in a file. So we must pass five parameters to this function: the ofstream variable associated with the output file, the course ID, the group number (to print * or ^), the symbol (* or ^) to print, and the course average for the department. To print the bar graph, we can use a loop to print a symbol for each two points. If the average is 78.45, for example, we must print 39 symbols to represent this average. To find the number of symbols to print, we can use integer division as follows:

numOfSymbols = static_cast<int>(average) / 2;

For example, static_cast<int>(78.45) / 2 = 78 / 2 = 39.

Following this discussion, the definition of the function printResults is:

```cpp
void printResults(ofstream& outp, string courseID,
                  int groupNo, char sym, double avg)
{
    int numOfSymbols;
    int count;

    if (groupNo == 1)
        outp << setw(4) << courseID << "     ";
    else
        outp << "            ";

    numOfSymbols = static_cast<int>(avg)/2;

    for (count = 1; count <= numOfSymbols; count++)
        outp << sym;

    outp << endl;
}//end printResults
```

We also include a function, printHeading, to print the first two lines of the output. The definition of this function is:

```cpp
void printHeading(ofstream& outp)
{
    outp << "Course          Course Average" << endl;
    outp << "  ID    0   10   20   30   40   50   60   70"
         << "   80   90   100" << endl;
    outp << "         |....|....|....|....|....|....|....|"
         << "....|....|....|"<<endl;
}//end printHeading
```

Replace the function printResults in the preceding program, include the appropriate statement in the function main to call this function, include the function printHeading, include the statements to output — Group 1 -- *** and Group 2 -- ^^^ — , and then rerun the program. The output for the previous data is as follows:

Sample Run:

```
Course          Course Average
  ID    0   10   20   30   40   50   60   70   80   90   100
         |....|....|....|....|....|....|....|....|....|....|
  CSC    *************************************
         ^^^^^^^^^^^^^^^^^^^^^^^^^^^^^^^^^^^^^^^


  ENG    ****************************************
         ^^^^^^^^^^^^^^^^^^^^^^^^^^^^^^^^^^^^^^^^


  HIS    ***********************************
         ^^^^^^^^^^^^^^^^^^^^^^^^^^^^^^^^^^^^^^^^^^^
```

```
MTH     *****************************************
        ^^^^^^^^^^^^^^^^^^^^^^^^^^^^^^^^^^^^^^^^^^^

PHY     *****************************************
        ^^^^^^^^^^^^^^^^^^^^^^^^^^^^^^^^^^^^^^^^^^

Group 1 -- ***
Group 2 -- ^^^
Avg for group 1: 82.04
Avg for group 2: 82.01
```

The complete program listing is available at the Web site accompanying this book.

QUICK REVIEW

1. Functions are like miniature programs and are called modules.

2. Functions enable you to divide a program into manageable tasks.

3. The C++ system provides the standard (predefined) functions.

4. To use a standard function, you must:

    i. Know the name of the header file that contains the function's specification

    ii. Include that header file in the program

    iii. Know the name and type of the function, and know the number and types of the parameters (arguments)

5. There are two types of user-defined functions: value-returning functions and void functions.

6. Variables defined in a function heading are called formal parameters.

7. Expressions, variables, or constant values used in a function call are called actual parameters.

8. In a function call, the number of actual parameters and their types must match with the formal parameters in the order given.

9. To call a function, use its name together with the actual parameter list.

10. A value-returning function returns a value. Therefore, a value-returning function is used (called) in either an expression or an output statement, or as a parameter in a function call.

11. The general syntax of a user-defined function is:

```
functionType  functionName(formal parameter list)
{
    statements
}
```

5

12. The line `functionType functionName(formal parameter list)` is called the function heading (or function header). Statements enclosed between braces { and } are called the body of the function.

13. The function heading and the body of the function are called the definition of the function.

14. If a function has no parameters, you still need the empty parentheses in both the function heading and the function call.

15. A value-returning function returns its value via the `return` statement.

16. A function can have more than one `return` statement. However, whenever a `return` statement executes in a function, the remaining statements are skipped and the function exits.

17. A `return` statement returns only one value.

18. A function prototype is the function heading without the body of the function; the function prototype ends with the semicolon.

19. A function prototype announces the function type, as well as the type and number of parameters, used in the function.

20. In a function prototype, the names of the variables in the formal parameter list are optional.

21. Function prototypes help the compiler correctly translate each function call.

22. In a program, function prototypes are placed before every function definition, including the definition of the function `main`.

23. When you use function prototypes, user-defined functions can appear in any order in the program.

24. When the program executes, the execution always begins with the first statement in the function `main`.

25. User-defined functions execute only when they are called.

26. A call to a function transfers control from the caller to the called function.

27. In a function call statement, you specify only the actual parameters, not their data type or the function type.

28. When a function exits, the control goes back to the caller.

29. A function that does not have a data type is called a void function.

30. A return statement without any value can be used in a void function. If a return statement is used in a void function, it is typically used to exit the function early.

31. The heading of a void function starts with the word `void`.

32. In C++, `void` is a reserved word.

33. A void function may or may not have parameters.

34. A call to a void function is a stand-alone statement.

35. To call a void function, you use the function name together with the actual parameters in a stand-alone statement.

36. There are two types of formal parameters: value parameters and reference parameters.

37. A value parameter receives a copy of its corresponding actual parameter.

38. A reference parameter receives the address (memory location) of its corresponding actual parameter.

39. The corresponding actual parameter of a value parameter is an expression, a variable, or a constant value.

40. A constant value cannot be passed to a reference parameter.

41. The corresponding actual parameter of a reference parameter must be a variable.

42. When you include the & after the data type of a formal parameter, the formal parameter becomes a reference parameter.

43. The stream variables should be passed by reference to a function.

44. If a formal parameter needs to change the value of an actual parameter, you must declare this formal parameter as a reference parameter in the function heading.

45. The scope of an identifier refers to those parts of the program where the identifier is accessible.

46. Variables declared within a function (or block) are called local variables.

47. Variables declared outside of every function definition (and block) are called global variables.

48. The scope of a function name is the same as the scope of an identifier declared outside of any block.

49. See the scope rules in this chapter (in the "Scope of an Identifier" section).

50. C++ does not allow the nesting of function definitions.

51. An automatic variable is a variable for which memory is allocated on function (or block) entry and deallocated on function (or block) exit.

52. A static variable is a variable for which memory remains allocated throughout the execution of the program.

53. By default, global variables are static variables.

54. In C++, a function can be overloaded.

55. Two functions are said to have different formal parameter lists if both functions have:

    - A different number of formal parameters, or

    - If the number of formal parameters is the same, then the data type of the formal parameters, in the order you list them, must differ in at least one position.

56. The signature of a function consists of the function name and its formal parameter list. Two functions have different signatures if they have either different names or different formal parameter lists.

57. If a function is overloaded, then in a call to that function, the signature, that is, the formal parameter list of the function, determines which function to execute.

58. C++ allows functions to have default parameters.

59. If you do not specify the value of a default parameter, the default value is used for that parameter.

60. All of the default parameters must be the rightmost parameters of the function.

61. Suppose a function has more than one default parameter. In a function call, if a value to a default parameter is not specified, then you must omit all arguments to its right.

62. Default values can be constants, global variables, or function calls.

63. The calling function has the option of specifying a value other than the default for any default parameter.

64. You cannot assign a constant value as a default value to a reference parameter.

EXERCISES

1. Mark the following statements as true or false.

   a. To use a predefined function in a program, you need to know only the name of the function and how to use it.

   b. A value-returning function returns only one value.

   c. Parameters allow you to use different values each time the function is called.

   d. When a `return` statement executes in a user-defined function, the function immediately exits.

   e. A value-returning function returns only integer values.

   f. A function that changes the value of a reference parameter also changes the value of the actual parameter.

   g. A variable name cannot be passed to a value parameter.

   h. If a C++ function does not use parameters, parentheses around the empty parameter list are still required.

   i. In C++, the names of the corresponding formal and actual parameters must be the same.

   j. Whenever the value of a reference parameter changes, the value of the actual parameter changes.

   k. In C++, function definitions can be nested; that is, the definition of one function can be enclosed in the body of another function.

l. Using global variables in a program is a better programming style than using local variables, because extra variables can be avoided.

m. In a program, global constants are as dangerous as global variables.

n. The memory for a static variable remains allocated between function calls.

2. Which of the following function headings are valid? If they are invalid, explain why.

a. one (int a, int b)

b. int thisone (char x)

c. char another (int a, b)

d. double yetanother

3. Consider the following statements.

```
double num1, num2, num3;
int int1, int2, int3;
int value;

num1 = 5.0; num2 = 6.0; num3 = 3.0;
int1 = 4; int2 = 7; int3 = 8;
```

and the following function prototype:

```
double cube (double a, double b, double c);
```

Which of the following statements are valid? If they are invalid, explain why.

a. value = cube (num1, 15.0, num3);

b. cout << cube (num1, num3, num2) << endl;

c. cout << cube (6.0, 8.0, 10.5) << endl;

d. cout << cube (num1, num3) << endl;

e. value = cube (num1, int2, num3);

f. value = cube (7, 8, 9);

g. value = cube (int1, int2, int3);

4. Consider the following functions:

```
int secret (int x)
{
    int i, j;

    i = 2 * x;

    if (i > 10)
        j = x / 2;
    else
        j = x / 3;

    return j - 1;
}
```

```
int another(int a, int b)
{
    int i, j;

    j = 0;

    for (i = a; i <= b; i++)
        j = j + i;

    return j;
}
```

What is the output of each of the following program segments?

a.
```
x = 10;
cout << secret(x) << endl;
```

b.
```
x = 5; y = 8;
cout << another(x, y) << endl;
```

c.
```
x = 10; k = secret(x);
cout << x << " " << k << " " << another(x, k) << endl;
```

d.
```
x = 5; y = 8;
cout << another(y, x) << endl;
```

5. Consider the following function prototypes:

```
int test(int, char, double, int);
double two(double, double);
char three(int, int, char, double);
```

Answer the following questions.

a. How many parameters does the function test have? What is the type of the function test?

b. How many parameters does the function two have? What is the type of the function two?

c. How many parameters does the function three have? What is the type of the function three?

d. How many actual parameters are needed to call the function test? What is the type of each actual parameter, and in what order should you use these parameters in a call to the function test?

e. Write a C++ statement that prints the value returned by the function test with the actual parameters 5, 5, 7.3, and 'z'.

f. Write a C++ statement that prints the value returned by the function two with the actual parameters 17.5 and 18.3, respectively.

g. Write a C++ statement that prints the next character returned by the function three. (Use your own actual parameters.)

6. Consider the following function:

```cpp
int mystery(int x, double y, char ch)
{
    int u;

    if ('A' <= ch && ch <= 'R')
        return (2 * x + static_cast<int>(y));
    else
        return (static_cast<int>(2 * y) - x);
}
```

What is the output of the following C++ statements?

a. `cout << mystery(5, 4.3, 'B') << endl;`

b. `cout << mystery(4, 9.7, 'v') << endl;`

c. `cout << 2 * mystery(6, 3.9, 'D') << endl;`

7. Consider the following function:

```cpp
int secret(int one)
{
    int prod = 1;
    for (int i = 1; i <= 3; i++)
        prod = prod * one;
    return prod;
}
```

a. What is the output of the following C++ statements?

   i. `cout << secret(5) << endl;`

   ii. `cout << 2 * secret(6) << endl;`

b. What does the function secret do?

8. What is the output of the following C++ program?

```cpp
#include <iostream>
#include <cmath>

using namespace std;

int main()
{
    for (int counter = 1; counter <= 100; counter++)
        if (pow(floor(sqrt(counter + 0.0)), 2) == counter)
            cout << counter << " ";

    cout << endl;

    return 0;
}
```

5

9. Show the output of the following program.

```cpp
#include <iostream>

using namespace std;

int mystery(int);

int main()
{
    for (int n = 1; n <= 5; n++)
        cout << mystery(n) << endl;

    return 0;
}

int mystery(int k)
{
    int y;

    y = k;

    for (int x = 1; x <= (k - 1); x++)
        y = y * (k - x);

    return y;
}
```

10. Show the output of the following program.

```cpp
#include <iostream>

using namespace std;

bool strange(int);

int main()
{
    int num = 0;

    while (num <= 29)
    {
        if (strange(num))
            cout << "True" << endl;
        else
            cout << "False" << endl;

        num = num + 4;
    }

    return 0;
}
```

```
bool strange(int n)
{
    if (n % 2 == 0 && n % 3 == 0)
        return true;
    else
        return false;
}
```

11. Explain the difference between an actual and a formal parameter.

12. Identify items a. through d. in the programming code that follows item d.:

a. Function prototype, function heading, function body, and function definitions

b. Function call statements, formal parameters, and actual parameters

c. Value parameters and reference parameters

d. Local variables and global variables

```
#include <iostream>                              //Line 1

using namespace std;                             //Line 2

int one;                                         //Line 3

void hello(int&, double, char);                  //Line 4

int main()                                       //Line 5
{                                                //Line 6
    int x;                                       //Line 7
    double y;                                    //Line 8
    char z;                                      //Line 9
    .
    .
    .
    hello(x, y, z);                              //Line 10
    .
    .
    .
    hello(x, y - 3.5, 'S');                      //Line 11
    .
    .
    .
}                                                //Line 12

void hello(int& first, double second, char ch) //Line 13
{                                                //Line 14
    int num;                                     //Line 15
    double y;                                    //Line 16
    int u ;                                      //Line 17
    .
    .
    .
}                                                //Line 18
```

5

13. Explain the difference between a value and a reference parameter.

14. Explain the difference between a local and a global variable.

15. Explain the difference between an automatic and a static variable.

16. What is the output of the following program?

```cpp
#include <iostream>
#include <iomanip>

using namespace std;

void test(int first, int& second);

int main()
{
    int num;
    num = 5;

    test(24, num);
    cout << num << endl;

    test(num, num);
    cout << num << endl;

    test(num * num, num);
    cout << num << endl;

    test(num + num, num);
    cout << num << endl;

    return 0;
}

void test(int first, int& second)
{
    int third;

    third = first + second * second + 2;
    first = second - first;
    second = 2 * second;

    cout << first << "  " << second << "  "
         << third << endl;
}
```

17. Assume the following input values:

```
7 3 6 4
2 6 3 5
```

Show the output of the following program:

```cpp
#include <iostream>
```

```
using namespace std;

void goofy(int&, int&, int, int&);

int main()
{
    int first, second, third, fourth;

    first = 3; second = 4; third = 20; fourth = 78;
    cout << first << "  " << second << "  " << third << "  "
        << fourth << endl;

    goofy(first, second, third, fourth);
    cout << first << "  " << second << "  " << third << "  "
        << fourth << endl;

    fourth = first * second + third - fourth;
    goofy(fourth, third, first, second);

    cout << first << "  " << second << "  " << third << "  "
        << fourth << endl;

    return 0;
}

void goofy(int& a, int& b, int c, int& d)
{
    cin >> a >> b >> c >> d;
    c = a * b + d - c;
    c = 2 * c;
}
```

18. What is the output of the following program?

```
#include <iostream>
using namespace std;

int x;

void mickey(int&, int);
void minnie(int, int&);

int main()
{
    int first;
    int second = 5;
    x = 6;

    mickey(first, second);
    cout << first << " " << second << " " << x << endl;
```

```
        minnie(first, second);
        cout << first << " " << second << " " << x << endl;
        return 0;
}

void mickey(int& a, int b)
{
        int first;
        first = b + 12;
        a = 2 * b;
        b = first + 4;
}

void minnie(int u, int& v)
{
        int second;
        second = x;
        v = second + 4;
        x = u + v;
}
```

19. In the following program, number the marked statements to show the order
    in which they will execute (the logical order of execution). Use the blanks
    to the left of the statements to write the number.

```
#include <iostream>

using namespace std;

void func(int val1, int val2);

int main()
{
        int num1, num2;
_____   cout << "Please enter two integers." << endl;
_____   cin >> num1 >> num2;
_____   func (num1, num2);
_____   cout << " The two integers are " << num1
                << ", " << num2 << endl;
_____   return 0;
}

void func (int val1, int val2)
{
        int val3, val4;
_____   val3 = val1 + val2;
_____   val4 = val1 * val2;
_____   cout << "The sum and product are " << val3
                << " and " << val4 << endl;
}
```

20. Consider the following program. What is its exact output? Show the values of the variables after each line executes, as in Example 5-11.

```cpp
#include <iostream>                                      //Line 1
using namespace std;                                     //Line 2

void funOne(int& a);                                     //Line 3

int main()                                               //Line 4
{                                                        //Line 5
    int num1, num2;

    num1 = 10;                                           //Line 6
    num2 = 20;                                           //Line 7

    cout << "Line 8: In main: num1 = " << num1
         << ", num2 = " << num2 << endl;                 //Line 8

    funOne(num1);                                        //Line 9

    cout << "Line 10: In main after funOne: num1 = "
         << num1 << ", num2 = " << num2 << endl;         //Line 10

    return 0;                                            //Line 11
}                                                        //Line 12

void funOne(int& a)                                      //Line 13
{
    int x = 12;                                          //Line 14
    int z;                                               //Line 15

    z = a + x;                                           //Line 16

    cout << "Line 17: In funOne: a = " << a
         << ", x = " << x
         << ", and z = " << z << endl;                   //Line 17

    x = x + 5;                                           //Line 18

    cout << "Line 19: In funOne: a = " << a << ", x = "
         << x << ", and z = " << z << endl;              //Line 19

    a = a + 8;                                           //Line 20

    cout << "Line 21: In funOne: a = " << a
         << ", x = " << x
         << ", and z = " << z << endl;                   //Line 21
}                                                        //Line 22
```

5

21. What is the output of the following code fragment? (*Note:* `alpha` and `beta` are `int` variables.)

```
alpha = 5;
beta = 10;
if (beta >= 10)
{
    int alpha = 10;
    beta = beta + alpha;
    cout << alpha << ' ' << beta << endl;
}
cout << alpha << ' ' << beta << endl;
```

22. a. What is function overloading?

    b. What is the signature of a function?

23. Consider the following function prototype:

```
void testDefaultParam(int a, int b = 7, char z = '*');
```

Which of the following function calls is correct?

   a. `testDefaultParam(5);`

   b. `testDefaultParam(5, 8);`

   c. `testDefaultParam(6, '#');`

   d. `testDefaultParam(0, 0, '*');`

24. Consider the following function definition:

```
void defaultParam(int u, int v = 5, double z = 3.2)
{
    int a;
    u = u + static_cast<int>(2 * v + z);
    a = u + v * z;
    cout << "a = " << a << endl;
}
```

What is the output of the following function calls?

   a. `defaultParam(6);`

   b. `defaultParam(3, 4);`

   c. `defaultParam(3, 0, 2.8);`

PROGRAMMING EXERCISES

1. Write a value-returning function, `isVowel`, that returns the value **true** if a given character is a vowel and otherwise returns **false**. Also write a program to test your function.

2. Write a program that prompts the user to input a sequence of characters and outputs the number of vowels. (Use the function `isVowel` written in Programming Exercise 1.)

3. Write a function, `reverseDigit`, that takes an integer as a parameter and returns the number with its digits reversed. For example, the value of `reverseDigit(12345)` is `54321`; the value of `reverseDigit(5600)` is `65`; the value of `reverseDigit(7008)` is `8007`; and the value of `reverseDigit(-532)` is `-235`.

4. The formula to find the distance between two points (x_1, y_1) and (x_2, y_2) in the Cartesian plane is $\sqrt{(x_2 - x_1)^2 + (y_2 - y_1)^2}$. Given the center and a point on a circle, you can use this formula to find the radius of the circle. Write a program that prompts the user to enter the center and a point on the circle. The program should then output the circle's radius, diameter, circumference, and area. Your program must have at least the following functions:

   a. `distance`: This function takes as its parameters four numbers that represent two points in the plane and returns the distance between them.

   b. `radius`: This function takes as its parameters four numbers that represent the center and a point on the circle, calls the function `distance` to find the radius of the circle, and returns the circle's radius.

   c. `circumference`: This function takes as its parameter a number that represents the radius of the circle and returns the circle's circumference. (If r is the radius, the circumference is $2\pi r$.)

   d. `area`: This function takes as its parameter a number that represents the radius of the circle and returns the circle's area. (If r is the radius, the area is πr^2.)

   Assume that $\pi = 3.1416$.

5. Write a program that takes as input five numbers and outputs the mean (average) and standard deviation of the numbers. If the numbers are x_1, x_2, x_3, x_4, and x_5, then the mean is $x = (x_1 + x_2 + x_3 + x_4 + x_5) / 5$ and the standard deviation is:

$$s = \sqrt{\frac{(x_1 - x)^2 + (x_2 - x)^2 + (x_3 - x)^2 + (x_4 - x)^2 + (x_5 - x)^2}{5}}$$

   Your program must contain at least the following functions: a function that calculates and returns the mean and a function that calculates the standard deviation.

6. Consider the definition of the function `main`:

```
int main()
{
    int x, y;
    char z;
    double rate, hours;
    double amount;
    .
    .
    .
}
```

The variables x, y, z, rate, and hours referred to in items a through f, below, are the variables of the function main. Each of the functions described must have the appropriate parameters to access these variables.

a. Write the definition of the function initialize that initializes x and y to 0, and z to the blank character.

b. Write the definition of the function getHoursRate that prompts the user to input the hours worked and rate per hour to initialize the variables hours and rate of the function main.

c. Write the definition of the value-returning function payCheck that calculates and returns the amount to be paid to an employee based on the hours worked and rate per hour. The hours worked and rate per hour are stored in the variables hours and rate, respectively, of the function main. The formula for calculating the amount to be paid is as follows: For the first 40 hours, the rate is the given rate; for hours over 40, the rate is 1.5 times the given rate.

d. Write the definition of the function printCheck that prints the hours worked, rate per hour, and the amount due.

e. Write the definition of the function funcOne that prompts the user to input a number. The function then changes the value of x by assigning the value of the expression 2 times the (old) value of x plus the value of y minus the value entered by the user.

f. Write the definition of the function nextChar that sets the value of z to the next character stored in z.

g. Write the definition of a function main that tests each of these functions.

7. The function printGrade in Example 5-10 is written as a **void** function to compute and output the course grade. The course score is passed as a parameter to the function printGrade. Rewrite the function printGrade as a value-returning function so that it computes and returns the course grade. (The course grade must be output in the function main.) Also, change the name of the function to calculateGrade.

8. In this exercise, you are to modify the Classify Numbers programming example in this chapter. As written, the program inputs the data from the standard input device (keyboard) and outputs the results on the standard output device (screen). The program can process only 20 numbers. Rewrite the program to incorporate the following requirements:

a. Data to the program is input from a file of an unspecified length; that is, the program does not know in advance how many numbers are in the file.

b. Save the output of the program in a file.

c. Modify the function getNumber so that it reads a number from the input file (opened in the function main), outputs the number to the output file (opened in the function `main`), and sends the number read to the function `main`. Print only 10 numbers per line.

d. Have the program find the sum and average of the numbers.

e. Modify the function `printResults` so that it outputs the final results to the output file (opened in the function `main`). Other than outputting the appropriate counts, this new definition of the function `printResults` should also output the sum and average of the numbers.

9. For research purposes and to better help students, the admissions office of your local university wants to know how well female and male students perform in certain courses. You receive a file that contains female and male student GPAs for certain courses. Due to confidentiality, the letter code f is used for female students and m is used for male students. Every file entry consists of a letter code followed by a GPA. Each line has one entry. The number of entries in the file is unknown. Write a program that computes and outputs the average GPA for both female and male students. Format your results to two decimal places. Your program should use the following functions:

a. Function `openFiles`: This function opens the input and output files, and sets the output of the floating-point numbers to two decimal places in a fixed-decimal format with a decimal point and trailing zeros.

b. Function `initialize`: This function initializes variables such as `countFemale`, `countMale`, `sumFemaleGPA`, and `sumMaleGPA`.

c. Function `sumGrades`: This function finds the sum of the female and male students' GPAs.

d. Function `averageGrade`: This function finds the average GPA for female and male students.

e. Function `printResults`: This function outputs the relevant results.

f. There can be no global variables. Use the appropriate parameters to pass information in and out of functions.

10. Write a program that prints the day number of the year, given the date in the form month-day-year. For example, if the input is 1-1-2010, the day number is 1; if the input is 12-25-2010, the day number is 359. The program should check for a leap year. A year is a leap year if it is divisible by 4 but not divisible by 100. For example, 1992 and 2008 are divisible by 4, but not by 100. A year that is divisible by 100 is a leap year if it is also divisible by 400. For example, 1600 and 2000 are divisible by 400. However, 1800 is not a leap year because 1800 is not divisible by 400.

11. Write a progam that reads a string and outputs the number of times each lowercase vowel appears in it. Your program must contain a function with one of its parameters being a string and return the number of times each lowercase vowel appears in it. Also write a program to test your function. (Note that if `str` is a variable of type `string`, then `str.at(i)` returns the character at the

ith position. The position of the first character is 0. Also, `str.length()` returns length of `str`, that is, the number of characters in `str`.)

12. Redo Programming Exercise 11 as follows: Write a progam that reads a string and outputs the number of times each lowercase vowel appears in it. Your program must contain a function with one of its parameters being a character, and if that character is a vowel, it increments that vowel's count.

13. Write a function that takes as a parameter an integer (as a **long** value) and returns the number of odd, even, and zero digits. Also write a program to test your function. (If a digit is 0, then it is counted as an even digit as well as a zero.)

14. Write a program that reads a student's name together with his or her test scores. The program should then compute the average test score for each student and assign the appropriate grade. The grade scale is as follows: 90–100, A; 80–89, B; 70–79, C; 60–69, D; 0–59, F.

Your program must use the following functions:

a. A void function, `calculateAverage`, to determine the average of the five test scores for each student. Use a loop to read and sum the five test scores. (This function does not output the average test score. That task must be done in the function `main`.)

b. A value-returning function, `calculateGrade`, to determine and return each student's grade. (This function does not output the grade. That task must be done in the function `main`.)

Test your program on the following data. Read the data from a file and send the output to a file. Do not use any global variables. Use the appropriate parameters to pass values in and out of functions.

```
Johnson 85 83 77 91 76
Aniston 80 90 95 93 48
Cooper 78 81 11 90 73
Gupta 92 83 30 69 87
Blair 23 45 96 38 59
Clark 60 85 45 39 67
Kennedy 77 31 52 74 83
Bronson 93 94 89 77 97
Sunny 79 85 28 93 82
Smith 85 72 49 75 63
```

The output should be of the following form: (Fill in the last two columns and the last line showing the class average.)

Student	Test1	Test2	Test3	Test4	Test5	Average	Grade
Johnson	85	83	77	91	76		
Aniston	80	90	95	93	48		
Cooper	78	81	11	90	73		
Gupta	92	83	30	69	87		
Blair	23	45	96	38	59		
Clark	60	85	45	39	67		

Kennedy	77	31	52	74	83
Bronson	93	94	89	77	97
Sunny	79	85	28	93	82
Smith	85	72	49	75	63

Class Average =

15. Write a program to process text files. The program should read a text file and output the data in the file as is. The program should also output the number of words, number of lines, and number of paragraphs. (When you create the input file, insert a blank line between paragraphs. See part d.) You must write and use the following functions:

a. initialize: This function initializes all the variables of the function main.

b. processBlank: This function reads and writes blanks. Whenever it hits a nonblank (except whitespace characters), it increments the number of words in a line. The number of words in a line is set back to zero in the function updateCount. The function exits after processing the blanks.

c. copyText: This function reads and writes the nonblank characters. Whenever it hits a blank, it exits.

d. updateCount: This function takes place at the end of each line. It updates the total word count, increments the number of lines, and sets the number of words on a line back to zero. If there are no words in a line, it increments the number of paragraphs. One blank line (between paragraphs) is used to distinguish paragraphs and should not be counted with the number of lines.

e. printTotal: This function outputs the number of words, number of lines, and number of paragraphs.

Your program should read data from a file and send output to a file. Do not use any global variables. Use the appropriate parameters to pass values in and out of the functions just described. Test your program using the following function main.

```
int main()
{
    variables declaration
    open files

    read a character
    while (not end of file)
    {
        while (not end of line)
        {
            processBlank(parameters);
            copyText(parameters);
        }
```

```
        updateCount(parameters);
        read a character;
            .
            .
            .
    }
    printTotal(parameters);
    close files;

    return 0;
}
```

16. (**The box problem**) You have been given a flat piece of cardboard having an area of, say, 70 square inches, to make an open box by cutting a square from each corner and folding the sides. See Figure 5-12. Your objective is to determine the dimensions, that is, the length and width, and the side of the square to be cut from the corners, so that the resulting box is of maximum volume.

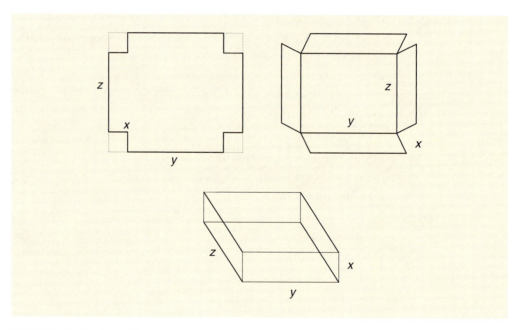

FIGURE 5-12 Cardboard box

Write a program that prompts the user to enter the area of the flat cardboard. The program then outputs the length and width of the cardboard and the length of the side of the square to be cut from the corner so that the resulting box is of maximum volume. Calculate your answer to three decimal places. Your program must contain a function that takes as input the length and width of the cardboard and returns the side of the square that should be cut to maximize the volume. The function also returns the maximum volume.

ARRAYS

IN THIS CHAPTER, YOU WILL:

- Learn about arrays
- Explore how to declare and manipulate data into arrays
- Understand the meaning of "array index out of bounds"
- Become familiar with the restrictions on array processing
- Discover how to pass an array as a parameter to a function
- Learn about c-strings
- Examine the use of string functions to process c-strings
- Discover how to input data into—and output data from—a c-string
- Learn about parallel arrays
- Discover how to manipulate data in a two-dimensional array
- Learn about multidimensional arrays

In previous chapters, you worked with simple data types. In Chapter 1, you learned that C++ data types fall into three categories. One of these categories is the structured data type. This chapter focuses on a commonly used structured data type—an array.

Recall that a data type is called **simple** if variables of that type can store only one value at a time. In contrast, in a **structured data type**, each data item is a collection of other data items. Simple data types are building blocks of structured data types. The structured data type that we will discuss is an array.

Before formally defining an array, let us consider the following problem. We want to write a C++ program that reads five numbers, finds their sum, and prints the numbers in reverse order.

In Chapter 4, you learned how to read numbers, print them, and find the sum. The difference here is that we want to print the numbers in reverse order. This means we cannot print the first four numbers until we have printed the fifth, and so on. To do this, we need to store all the numbers before we start printing them in reverse order. From what we have learned so far, the following program accomplishes this task.

```cpp
//***********************************************************
// Author: D.S. Malik
//
// This program reads five numbers, finds their sum, and prints
// the numbers in reverse order.
//***********************************************************

#include <iostream>

using namespace std;

int main()
{
    int item0, item1, item2, item3, item4;
    int sum;

    cout << "Enter five integers: ";
    cin >> item0 >> item1 >> item2 >> item3 >> item4;
    cout << endl;

    sum = item0 + item1 + item2 + item3 + item4;

    cout << "The sum of the numbers = " << sum << endl;
    cout << "The numbers in the reverse order are: ";
    cout << item4 << " " << item3 << " " << item2 << " "
         << item1 << " " << item0 << endl;

    return 0;
}
```

This program works fine. However, if you need to read 100 (or more) numbers and print them in reverse order, you would have to declare 100 variables and write many cin and cout statements. Thus, for large amounts of data, this type of program is not desirable.

Note the following in the previous program:

1. Five variables must be declared because the numbers are to be printed in reverse order.

2. All variables are of type `int`—that is, of the same data type.

3. The way in which these variables are declared indicates that the variables to store these numbers all have the same name—except the last character, which is a digit.

Statement 1 tells you that you have to declare five variables. Statement 3 tells you that it would be convenient if you could somehow put the last character, which is a digit, into a counter variable and use one `for` loop to count from 0 to 4 for reading and another `for` loop to count from 4 to 0 for printing. Finally, because all variables are of the same type, you should be able to specify how many variables must be declared—and their data type—with a simpler statement than the one we used earlier.

The data structure that lets you do all of these things in C++ is called an array.

6

Arrays

An **array** is a collection of a fixed number of components all of the same data type. A **one-dimensional array** is an array in which the components are arranged in a list form. This section discusses only one-dimensional arrays. Arrays of two dimensions or more are discussed later in this chapter.

The general form for declaring a one-dimensional array is

```
dataType arrayName[intExp];
```

where `intExp` is any constant expression that evaluates to a positive integer. Also, `intExp` specifies the number of components in the array.

EXAMPLE 6-1

The statement:

```
int num[5];
```

declares an array `num` of 5 components. Each component is of type `int`. The components are `num[0]`, `num[1]`, `num[2]`, `num[3]`, and `num[4]`. Figure 6-1 illustrates the array `num`.

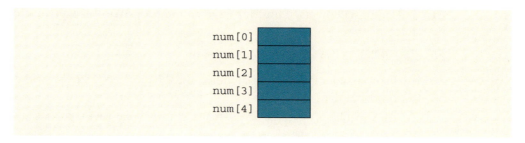

FIGURE 6-1 Array num

NOTE To save space, we also draw an array as shown in Figure 6-2(a) or 6-2(b).

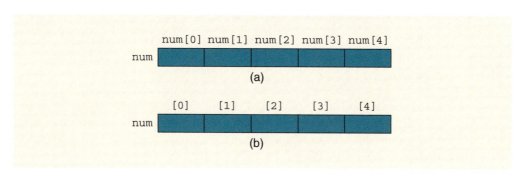

FIGURE 6-2 Array num

Accessing Array Components

The general form (syntax) used for accessing an array component is

```
arrayName[indexExp]
```

where `indexExp`, called the **index**, is any expression whose value is a nonnegative integer. The index value specifies the position of the component in the array.

In C++, `[ ]` is an operator, called the **array subscripting operator**. Moreover, in C++, the array index starts at 0.

Consider the following statement:

```
int list[10];
```

This statement declares an array `list` of 10 components. The components are `list[0]`, `list[1]`, ..., and `list[9]`. In other words, we have declared 10 variables. (See Figure 6-3.)

Arrays | 341

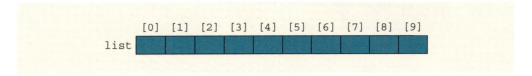

FIGURE 6-3 Array list

The assignment statement

```
list[5] = 34;
```

stores 34 in list[5], which is the sixth component of the array list. (See Figure 6-4.)

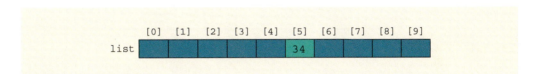

FIGURE 6-4 Array list after execution of the statement list[5]= 34;

6

Suppose i is an **int** variable. Then the statements

```
i = 3;
list[i] = 63;
```

store 63 into list[3]. Similarly, if i is 4, then the statement

```
list[2 * i - 3] = 58;
```

stores 58 in list[5] because 2 * i - 3 evaluates to 5. The index expression is evaluated first, giving the position of the component in the array.

Next, consider the following statements:

```
list[3] = 10;
list[6] = 35;
list[5] = list[3] + list[6];
```

The first statement stores 10 in list[3], the second statement stores 35 in list[6], and the third statement adds the contents of list[3] and list[6] and stores the result in list[5]. (See Figure 6-5.)

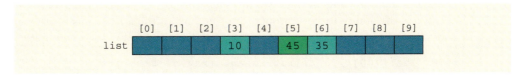

FIGURE 6-5 Array list after execution of the statements list[3]= 10;, list[6]= 35;, and list[5] = list[3] + list[6];

EXAMPLE 6-2

You can also declare arrays as follows:

```
const int ARRAY_SIZE = 10;
int list[ARRAY_SIZE];
```

That is, you can first declare a named constant and then use the value of the named constant to declare an array and specify its size. Declaring and using a named constant is useful, especially if you need to declare several arrays of the same size. Later, if the sizes of those arrays change, then you only need to change the value of the named constant specifying the sizes of the array, recompile, and rerun the program.

NOTE When you declare an array, its size must be known. For example, you cannot do the following:

```
int arraySize;                                  //Line 1

cout << "Enter the size of the array: "; //Line 2
cin >> arraySize;                              //Line 3
cout << endl;                                  //Line 4

int list[arraySize];                           //Line 5; not allowed
```

The statement in Line 2 asks the user to enter the size of the array when the program executes. The statement in Line 3 inputs the size of the array into `arraySize`.
When the compiler compiles Line 1, the value of the variable `arraySize` is unknown. Thus, when the compiler compiles Line 5, the size of the array is unknown, and the compiler will not know how much memory space to allocate for the array. In Chapter 9, you will learn how to specify the size of an array during program execution and then declare an array of that size using pointers. Arrays that are created by using pointers during program execution are called **dynamic arrays**. For now, whenever you declare an array, its size must be known.

Processing One-Dimensional Arrays

Some of the basic operations performed on a one-dimensional array are initializing, inputting data, outputting data stored in an array, and finding the largest and/or smallest element. Moreover, if the data is numeric, some other basic operations performed are finding the sum and average of the elements of the array. Each of these operations requires the ability to step through the elements of the array. This is easily accomplished using a loop. For example, suppose that we have the following statements:

```
int list[100];    //list is an array of size 100
```

The following **for** loop steps through each element of the array **list**, starting at the first element of **list**:

```
for (int i = 0; i < 100; i++) //Line 1
    //process list[i]            //Line 2
```

If processing the list requires inputting data into **list**, the statement in Line 2 takes the form of an input statement, such as the **cin** statement. For example, the following statements read 100 numbers from the keyboard and store the numbers in **list**:

```
for (int i = 0; i < 100; i++) //Line 1
    cin >> list[i];              //Line 2
```

Similarly, if processing **list** requires outputting the data, then the statement in Line 2 takes the form of an output statement. Example 6-3 further illustrates how to process one-dimensional arrays.

EXAMPLE 6-3

This example shows how loops are used to process arrays. The following declaration is used throughout this example:

```
double sales[10];
double largestSale, sum, average;
```

The first statement declares an array **sales** of 10 components, with each component being of type **double**. The meaning of the other statements is clear.

   a. **Initializing an array:** The following loop initializes every component of the array **sales** to 0.0:

```
for (int index = 0; index < 10; index++)
    sales[index] = 0.0;
```

   b. **Reading data into an array:** The following loop inputs the data into the array **sales**. For simplicity, we assume that the data is entered at the keyboard.

```
for (int index = 0; index < 10; index++)
    cin >> sales[index];
```

   c. **Printing an array:** The following loop outputs the array **sales**. For simplicity, we assume that the output goes to the screen.

```
for (int index = 0; index < 10; index++)
    cout << sales[index] << " ";
```

   d. **Finding the sum and average of an array:** Because the array **sales**, as its name implies, represents certain sales data, it is natural to find the total sale and average sale amounts. The following C++ code finds the sum of the elements of the array **sales** and the average sale amount:

6

```
sum = 0;
for (int index = 0; index < 10; index++)
    sum = sum + sales[index];

average = sum / 10;
```

e. **Largest element in the array:** We now discuss the algorithm to find the (first occurrence of the) largest element in an array—that is, the first array component with the largest value. However, in general, the user is more interested in determining the location of the largest element in the array. Of course, if you know the location (that is, the index of the largest element in the array), you can easily determine the value of the largest element in the array. So let us describe the algorithm to determine the index of the first occurrence of the largest element in an array—in particular, the index of the first occurrence of the largest sale amount in the array `sales`. We will use the index of the largest element in the array to find the largest sale.

We assume that `maxIndex` will contain the index of the first occurence of the largest element in the array `sales`. The general algorithm is straightforward. Initially, we assume that the first element in the list is the largest element, and so `maxIndex` is initialized to 0. We then compare the element to which `maxIndex` points with every subsequent element in the list. Whenever we find an element in the array larger than the element to which `maxIndex` points, we update `maxIndex` so that it points to the new larger element. The algorithm is as follows:

```
maxIndex = 0;
for (int index = 1; index < 10; index++)
    if (sales[maxIndex] < sales[index])
        maxIndex = index;

largestSale = sales[maxIndex];
```

Let us demonstrate how this algorithm works with an example. Suppose the array `sales` is as given in Figure 6-6.

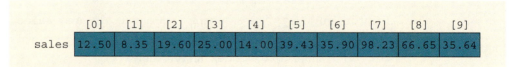

	[0]	[1]	[2]	[3]	[4]	[5]	[6]	[7]	[8]	[9]
sales	12.50	8.35	19.60	25.00	14.00	39.43	35.90	98.23	66.65	35.64

FIGURE 6-6 Array `sales`

Here, we determine the largest element in the array `sales`. Before the `for` loop begins, `maxIndex` is initialized to 0, and the `for` loop initializes `index` to 1. In the following, we show the values of `maxIndex`, `index`, and certain array elements during each iteration of the `for` loop:

index	maxIndex	sales[maxIndex]	sales[index]	sales[maxIndex] < sales[index]
1	0	12.50	8.35	12.50 < 8.35 is false
2	0	12.50	19.60	12.50 < 19.60 is true; maxIndex = 2
3	2	19.60	25.00	19.60 < 25.00 is true; maxIndex = 3
4	3	25.00	14.00	25.00 < 14.00 is false
5	3	25.00	39.43	25.00 < 39.43 is true; maxIndex = 5
6	5	39.43	35.90	39.43 < 35.90 is false
7	5	39.43	98.23	39.43 < 98.23 is true; maxIndex = 7
8	7	98.23	66.65	98.23 < 66.65 is false
9	7	98.23	35.64	98.23 < 35.64 is false

After the `for` loop executes, `maxIndex = 7`, giving the index of the largest element in the array `sales`. Thus, `largestSale = sales[maxIndex] = 98.23`.

NOTE You can write an algorithm to find the first occurrence of the smallest element in the array that is similar to the algorithm for finding the largest element in an array. (See Programming Exercise 2 at the end of this chapter.)

Now that we know how to declare and process arrays, let us rewrite the program that we discussed in the beginning of this chapter. Recall that this program reads five numbers, finds the sum, and prints the numbers in reverse order.

EXAMPLE 6-4

```cpp
//************************************************************
// Author: D.S. Malik
//
// This program reads five numbers, finds their sum, and prints
// the numbers in reverse order. The numbers are stored in an
// array and loops are used to read the numbers, find their sum,
// and print the numbers in reverse order.
//************************************************************

#include <iostream>

using namespace std;

int main()
{
    int item[5];   //Declare an array item of five components
    int sum;

    cout << "Enter five numbers: ";

    sum = 0;

    for (int counter = 0; counter < 5; counter++)
    {
        cin >> item[counter];
        sum = sum + item[counter];
    }

    cout << endl;

    cout << "The sum of the numbers is: " << sum << endl;
    cout << "The numbers in reverse order are: ";

        //Print the numbers in reverse order.
    for (int counter = 4; counter >= 0; counter--)
        cout << item[counter] << " ";

    cout << endl;

    return 0;
}
```

Sample Run: In this sample run, the user input is shaded.

Enter five numbers: 12 76 34 52 89

The sum of the numbers is: 263
The numbers in reverse order are: 89 52 34 76 12

Array Index Out of Bounds

Consider the following declaration:

```
double num[10];
int i;
```

The component `num[i]` is valid, that is, `i` is a valid index if `i = 0, 1, 2, 3, 4, 5, 6, 7, 8, or 9`.

The index—say, `index`—of an array is **in bounds** if `index >= 0` and `index <= ARRAY_SIZE - 1`. If either `index < 0` or `index > ARRAY_SIZE - 1`, then we say that the index is **out of bounds**.

Unfortunately, in C++, there is no guard against out-of-bound indices. Thus, C++ does not check whether the index value is within range—that is, between 0 and `ARRAY_SIZE - 1`. If the index goes out of bounds and the program tries to access the component specified by the index, then whatever memory location is indicated by the index is accessed. This situation can result in altering or accessing the data of a memory location that you never intended. Consequently, if during execution the index goes out of bounds, several strange things can happen. It is solely the programmer's responsibility to make sure that the index is within bounds.

A loop such as the following can set the index out of bounds:

```
for (int i = 0; i <= 10; i++)
    list[i] = 0;
```

Here, we assume that `list` is an array of 10 components. When `i` becomes 10, the loop test condition `i <= 10` evaluates to `true` and the body of the loop executes, which results in storing 0 in `list[10]`. Logically, `list[10]` does not exist.

NOTE On some new compilers, if an array index goes out of bounds in a progam, it is possible that the program will terminate with an error message. For example, see the programs `Example_ArrayIndexOutOfBoundsA.cpp` and `Example_ArrayIndexOutOfBoundsB.cpp` at the Web site accompanying this book.

Array Initialization During Declaration

Like any other simple variable, an array can also be initialized while it is being declared. For example, the following C++ statement declares an array, `sales`, of five components and initializes these components:

```
double sales[5] = {12.25, 32.50, 16.90, 23, 45.68};
```

The values are placed between curly braces and separated by commas. Here, `sales[0] = 12.25`, `sales[1] = 32.50`, `sales[2] = 16.90`, `sales[3] = 23.00`, and `sales[4] = 45.68`.

When initializing arrays as they are declared, it is not necessary to specify the size of the array. The size is determined by the number of initial values in the braces. However, you must include the brackets following the array name. The previous statement is therefore equivalent to the following:

```
double sales[] = {12.25, 32.50, 16.90, 23, 45.68};
```

Although it is not necessary to specify the size of the array if it is initialized during declaration, it is a good practice to do so.

PARTIAL INITIALIZATION OF ARRAYS DURING DECLARATION

When you declare and initialize an array simultaneously, you do not need to initialize all components of the array. This procedure is called **partial initialization of an array during declaration**. However, if you partially initialize an array during declaration, you must exercise some caution. The following examples help explain what happens when you declare and partially initialize an array.

The statement

```
int list[10] = {0};
```

declares `list` to be an array of 10 components and initializes all the components to 0. The statement

```
int list[10] = {8, 5, 12};
```

declares `list` to be an array of 10 components, initializes `list[0]` to 8, `list[1]` to 5, `list[2]` to 12, and all other components to 0. Thus, if all the values are not specified in the initialization statement, the array components for which the values are not specified are initialized to 0. Note that here the size of the array in the declaration statement does matter. For example, the statement

```
int list[] = {5, 6, 3};
```

declares `list` to be an array of 3 components and initializes `list[0]` to 5, `list[1]` to 6, and `list[2]` to 3. In contrast, the statement:

```
int list[25] = {4, 7};
```

declares `list` to be an array of 25 components. The first two components are initialized to 4 and 7, respectively, and all other components are initialized to 0.

Some Restrictions on Array Processing

Consider the following statements:

```
int myList[5] = {0, 4, 8, 12, 16};   //Line 1
int yourList[5];                      //Line 2
```

The statement in Line 1 declares and initializes the array `myList`, and the statement in Line 2 declares the array `yourList`. Note that these arrays are of the same type and have the same number of components. Suppose that you want to copy the elements of `myList` into the corresponding elements of `yourList`. The following statement is illegal:

```
yourList = myList;   //illegal
```

In fact, this statement will generate a syntax error. C++ does not allow aggregate operations on an array. An **aggregate operation** on an array is any operation that manipulates the entire array as a single unit.

To copy one array into another array, you must copy it component-wise—that is, one component at a time. This can be done using a loop such as the following:

```
for (int index = 0; index < 5; index ++)
    yourList[index] = myList[index];
```

Next, suppose that you want to read data into the array `yourList`. The following statement is illegal and in fact would generate a syntax error:

```
cin >> yourList;   //illegal
```

To read data into `yourList`, you must read one component at a time, using a loop such as the following:

```
for (int index = 0; index < 5; index ++)
    cin >> yourList[index];
```

Similarly, determining whether two arrays have the same elements and printing the contents of an array must be done component-wise. Note that the following statements are illegal in the sense that they do not generate a syntax error, but do not give the desired results.

```
cout << yourList;

if (myList <= yourList)
.
.
.
```

We will comment on these statements in the section "Base Address of an Array and an Array in Computer Memory," later in this chapter.

Arrays as Parameters to Functions

Now that you have seen how to work with arrays, a question naturally arises: How are arrays passed as parameters to functions?

By reference only: In C++, arrays as parameters to functions are passed by reference only.

Because arrays are passed by reference only, you *do not* use the symbol `&` when declaring an array as a formal parameter.

A major reason to pass arrays by reference only, and not by value, is that if an array is allowed to be passed by value to a function, then when the function is called, the function must allocate memory to copy the data stored in the actual array and spend computer time to copy the data. This could be very expensive in terms of both computer time and memory, especially if the actual array is very large. Thus, the cost in time and memory is a major reason arrays are passed by refrence only.

When declaring a one-dimensional array as a formal parameter, the size of the array is usually omitted. If you specify the size of a one-dimensional array when it is declared as a formal parameter, the size is ignored by the compiler.

EXAMPLE 6-5

Consider the following function:

```
void funcArrayAsParam(int listOne[], double listTwo[])
{
    .
    .
    .
}
```

The function `funcArrayAsParam` has two formal parameters: (1) `listOne`, a one-dimensional array of type `int` (that is, the component type is `int`), and (2) `listTwo`, a one-dimensional array of type `double`. In this declaration, the size of both arrays is unspecified.

Sometimes the number of elements in the array might be less than the size of the array. For example, the number of elements in an array storing student data might increase or decrease as students drop or add courses. In such situations, we want to process only the components of the array that hold actual data. Furthermore, when writing the definition of a function that has an array as a formal parameter, you may not know the actual size of the array, or there may not be a global named constant that the function can use to determine the array capacity. To write a function to process such arrays, in addition to declaring an array as a formal parameter, we declare another formal parameter specifying the number of elements in the array, as in the following function:

```
void initialize(int list[], int listSize)
{
    for (int count = 0; count < listSize; count++)
        list[count] = 0;
}
```

The first parameter of the function `initialize` is an `int` array of any size. When the function `initialize` is called, the size of the actual array is passed as the second parameter of the function `initialize`.

CONSTANT ARRAYS AS FORMAL PARAMETERS

Recall that when a formal parameter is a reference parameter, then whenever the formal parameter changes, the actual parameter changes as well. However, even though an array is always passed by reference, you can still prevent the function from changing the actual parameter. You do so by using the reserved word `const` in the declaration of the formal parameter. Consider the following function:

```
void example(int x[], const int y[], int sizeX, int sizeY)
{
    .
    .
    .
}
```

Here, the function `example` can modify the array `x`, but not the array `y`. Any attempt to change `y` results in a compile-time error. It is a good programming practice to declare an array to be constant as a formal parameter if you do not want the function to modify the array.

EXAMPLE 6-6

6

This example shows how to write functions for array processing and declare an array as a formal parameter.

```
    //Function to initialize an int array to 0.
    //The array to be initialized and its size are passed
    //as parameters. The parameter listSize specifies the
    //number of elements to be initialized.
void initializeArray(int list[], int listSize)
{
    for (int index = 0; index < listSize; index++)
        list[index] = 0;
}


    //Function to read and store the data into an int array.
    //The array to store the data and its size are passed as
    //parameters. The parameter listSize specifies the number
    //of elements to be read.
void fillArray(int list[], int listSize)
{
    for (int index = 0; index < listSize; index++)
        cin >> list[index];
}


    //Function to print the elements of an int array.
    //The array to be printed and the number of elements
    //are passed as parameters. The parameter listSize
    //specifies the number of elements to be printed.
```

```cpp
void printArray(const int list[], int listSize)
{
    for (int index = 0; index < listSize; index++)
        cout << list[index] << " ";
}


    //Function to find and return the sum of the
    //elements of an int array. The parameter listSize
    //specifies the number of elements to be added.
int sumArray(const int list[], int listSize)
{
    int sum = 0;

    for (int index = 0; index < listSize; index++)
        sum = sum + list[index];

    return sum;
}


    //Function to find and return the index of the first
    //largest element in an int array. The parameter listSize
    //specifies the number of elements in the array.
int indexLargestElement(const int list[], int listSize)
{
    int maxIndex = 0; //assume the first element is the largest

    for (int index = 1; index < listSize; index++)
        if (list[maxIndex] < list[index])
            maxIndex = index;

    return maxIndex;
}


    //Function to copy one array into another array.
    //The elements of listOne are copied into listTwo.
    //The array listTwo must be at least as large as the
    //number of elements to be copied. The parameter
    //listOneSize specifies the number of elements of
    //listOne to be copied into listTwo.
void copyArray(const int listOne[], int listTwo[],
               int listOneSize)
{
    for (int index = 0; index < listOneSize; index++)
        listTwo[index] = listOne[index];
}
```

Note that for the function copyArray to work correctly, the array listTwo must be at least as large as the array listOne.

BASE ADDRESS OF AN ARRAY AND AN ARRAY IN COMPUTER MEMORY

The **base address** of an array is the address (that is, memory location) of the first array component. For example, if `list` is a one-dimensional array, then the base address of `list` is the address of the component `list[0]`.

Consider the following statement:

```
int myList[5];          //Line 1
```

This statement declares `myList` to be an array of five components of type `int`. The components are `myList[0]`, `myList[1]`, `myList[2]`, `myList[3]`, and `myList[4]`. The computer allocates five memory spaces, each large enough to store an `int` value, for these components. Moreover, the five memory spaces are contiguous.

The base address of the array `myList` is the address of the component `myList[0]`. Suppose that the base address of the array `myList` is 1000. Then the address of the component `myList[0]` is 1000. Typically, the memory allocated for an `int` variable is four bytes. Recall from Chapter 0 that main memory is an ordered sequence of cells, and each cell has a unique address. Typically, each cell is one byte. Therefore, to store a value into `myList[0]`, starting at the address 1000, the next four bytes are allocated for `myList[0]`. It follows that the starting address of `myList[1]` is 1004, the starting address of `myList[2]` is 1008, and so on (see Figure 6-7).

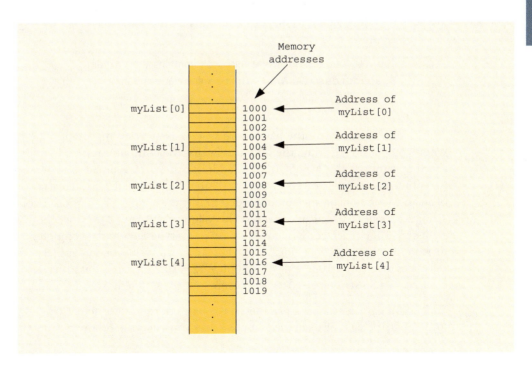

FIGURE 6-7 Array `myList` and the addresses of its components

Now `myList` is the name of an array. There is also a memory space associated with the identifier `myList`, and the base address of the array is stored in that memory space. Consider the following statement:

```
cout << myList << endl;          //Line 2
```

Earlier, we said that this statement won't give the desired result. That is, this statement will not output the values of the *components* of `myList`. In fact, the statement outputs the value of `myList`, which is the base address of the array. This is why the statement will not generate a syntax error.

Suppose that you also have the following statement:

```
int yourList[5];
```

Then, in the statement

```
if (myList <= yourList)          //Line 3
.
.
.
```

the expression `myList <= yourList` evaluates to `true` if the base address of the array `myList` is less than the base address of the array `yourList`, and evaluates to `false` otherwise. It *does not* determine whether the elements of `myList` are less than or equal to the corresponding elements of `yourList`.

NOTE   The Web site accompanying this book contains the program
`BaseAddressOfAnArray.cpp`, which clarifies statements such as those in Lines 2 and 3.

You might wonder why the base address of an array is so important. The reason is that when you declare an array, the only things that the computer remembers about the array are the name of the array, its base address, the data type of each component, and (possibly) the number of components. Using the base address of the array and the index of an array component, the computer determines the address of a particular component. For example, suppose you want to access the value of `myList[3]`. Now, the base address of `myList` is 1000. Each component of `myList` is of type `int`, so the computer uses four bytes to store a value, and the index is 3. To access the value of `myList[3]`, the computer calculates the address 1000 + 4 * 3 = 1000 + 12 = 1012. That is, this is the starting address of `myList[3]`. So starting at 1012, the computer accesses the next four bytes.

When you pass an array as a parameter, the base address of the actual array is passed to the formal parameter. For example, suppose that you have the following function:

```
void arrayAsParameter(int list[], int size)
{
    .
    .
    .
    list[2] = 28;           //Line 4
    .
    .
    .
}
```

Also suppose that you have the following call to this function:

```
arrayAsParameter(myList, 5);   //Line 5
```

In this statement, the base address of `myList` is passed to the formal parameter `list`. Therefore, the base address of `list` is 1000. The definition of the function contains the statement `list[2] = 28;`. This statement stores 28 into `list[2]`. To access `list[2]`, the computer calculates the address as follows: 1000 + 4 * 2 = 1008. So, starting at the address 1008, the computer accesses the next four bytes and stores 28. Note that, in fact, 1008 is the address of `myList[2]` (see Figure 6-7). It follows that during the execution of the statement in Line 5, the statement in Line 4 stores the value 28 into `myList[2]`. It also follows that during the execution of the function call statement in Line 5, `list[index]` and `myList[index]` refer to the same memory space, where 0 <= index and index < 5.

FUNCTIONS CANNOT RETURN A VALUE OF THE TYPE ARRAY

C++ does not allow functions to return a value of the type array. Note that the functions `sumArray` and `largestElement` described earlier return values of type `int`.

PROCESSING ARRAYS

Example 6-7 shows how arrays are passed as parameters to functions and processed.

EXAMPLE 6-7

```
//***************************************************************
// Author: D.S. Malik
//
// This program shows how arrays are passed as parameters to
// functions.
//***************************************************************
```

```
#include <iostream>                                    //Line 1

using namespace std;                                   //Line 2

const int ARRAY_SIZE = 10;                             //Line 3

void initializeArray(int x[], int sizeX);              //Line 4
void fillArray(int x[], int sizeX);                    //Line 5
void printArray(const int x[], int sizeX);             //Line 6
int sumArray(const int x[], int sizeX);                //Line 7
int indexLargestElement(const int x[], int sizeX);     //Line 8
void copyArray(const int x[], int y[], int length);    //Line 9

int main()                                             //Line 10
{
    int listA[ARRAY_SIZE] = {0}; //Declare the array listA
                           //of 10 components and initialize
                           //each component to 0.         Line 11
    int listB[ARRAY_SIZE]; //Declare the array listB
                           //of 10 components.            Line 12

    cout << "Line 13: listA elements: ";               //Line 13

        //Output the elements of listA using
        //the function printArray
    printArray(listA, ARRAY_SIZE);                     //Line 14
    cout << endl;                                      //Line 15

        //Initialize listB using the function
        //initializeArray
    initializeArray(listB, ARRAY_SIZE);                //Line 16

    cout << "Line 17: listB elements: ";               //Line 17

        //Output the elements of listB
    printArray(listB, ARRAY_SIZE);                     //Line 18
    cout << endl << endl;                              //Line 19

    cout << "Line 20: Enter " << ARRAY_SIZE
         << " integers: ";                             //Line 20

        //Input data into listA using the
        //function fillArray
    fillArray(listA, ARRAY_SIZE);                      //Line 21
    cout << endl;                                      //Line 22

    cout << "Line 23: After filling listA, "
         << "the elements are:" << endl;               //Line 23

        //Output the elements of listA
    printArray(listA, ARRAY_SIZE);                     //Line 24
    cout << endl << endl;                              //Line 25
```

```
            //Find and output the sum of the elements
            //of listA
        cout << "Line 26: The sum of the elements of "
            << "listA is: "
            << sumArray(listA, ARRAY_SIZE) << endl
            << endl;                                        //Line 26

            //Find and output the position of the largest
            //element in listA
        cout << "Line 27: The position of the largest "
            << "element in listA is: "
            << indexLargestElement(listA, ARRAY_SIZE)
            << endl;                                        //Line 27

            //Find and output the largest element
            //in listA
        cout << "Line 28: The largest element in "
            << "listA is: "
            << listA[indexLargestElement(listA, ARRAY_SIZE)]
            << endl << endl;                                //Line 28

            //Copy the elements of listA into listB using the
            //function copyArray
        copyArray(listA, listB, ARRAY_SIZE);               //Line 29

        cout << "Line 30: After copying the elements "
            << "of listA into listB," << endl
            << "           listB elements are: ";           //Line 30

            //Output the elements of listB
        printArray(listB, ARRAY_SIZE);                     //Line 31
        cout << endl;                                      //Line 32

        return 0;                                          //Line 33
}                                                          //Line 34
//Place the definitions of the functions initializeArray,
//fillArray, and so on here. Example 6-6 gives the definitions
//of these functions.
```

Sample Run: In this sample run, the user input is shaded.

```
Line 13: listA elements: 0 0 0 0 0 0 0 0 0 0
Line 17: ListB elements: 0 0 0 0 0 0 0 0 0 0

Line 20: Enter 10 integers: 33 77 25 63 56 48 98 39 5 12

Line 23: After filling listA, the elements are:
33 77 25 63 56 48 98 39 5 12

Line 26: The sum of the elements of listA is: 456

Line 27: The position of the largest element in listA is: 6
Line 28: The largest element in listA is: 98
```

```
Line 30: After copying the elements of listA into listB,
         listB elements are: 33 77 25 63 56 48 98 39 5 12
```

The output of this program is straightforward. First we declare the array listA of 10 components and initialize each component of listA to 0. Then we declare the array listB of 10 components. The statement in Line 14 calls the function printArray and outputs the values stored in listA. The statement in Line 21 calls the function fillArray to input the data into listA. The statement in Line 26 calls the function sumArray and outputs the sum of all the elements of listA. Similarly, the statement in Line 28 outputs the value of the largest element in listA.

C-strings (Character Arrays)

Until now, we have avoided discussing character arrays for a simple reason: Character arrays are of special interest, and you process them differently than you process other arrays. C++ provides many (predefined) functions that you can use with character arrays.

Character array: An array whose components are of type char.

Recall that the most widely used character sets are ASCII and EBCDIC. The first character in the ASCII character set is the null character, which is nonprintable. Also recall that in C++, the null character is represented as '\0', a backslash followed by a zero.

The statement

```
ch = '\0';
```

stores the null character in ch, where ch is a char variable.

As you will see, the null character plays an important role in processing character arrays. Because the collating sequence of the null character is 0, the null character is less than any other character in the char data set.

The most commonly used term for character arrays is C-strings. However, there is a subtle difference between character arrays and C-strings. Recall that a string is a sequence of zero or more characters, and strings are enclosed in double quotation marks. In C++, C-strings are null terminated; that is, the last character in a C-string is always the null character. A character array might not contain the null character, but the last character in a C-string is always the null character. As you will see, the null character should not appear anywhere in the C-string except the last position. Also, C-strings are stored in (one-dimensional) character arrays.

The following are examples of C-strings:

```
"John L. Johnson"
"Hello there."
```

From the definition of C-strings, it is clear that there is a difference between `'A'` and `"A"`. The first one is character `A`; the second is C-string `A`. Because C-strings are null terminated, `"A"` represents two characters: `'A'` and `'\0'`. Similarly, the C-string `"Hello"` represents six characters: `'H'`, `'e'`, `'l'`, `'l'`, `'o'`, and `'\0'`. To store `'A'`, we need only one memory cell of type `char`; to store `"A"`, we need two memory cells of type `char`—one for `'A'` and one for `'\0'`. Similarly, to store the C-string `"Hello"` in computer memory, we need six memory cells of type `char`.

Consider the following statement:

```
char name[16];
```

This statement declares an array `name` of `16` components of type `char`. Because C-strings are null terminated and `name` has `16` components, the largest string that can be stored in `name` is of length `15`. If you store a C-string of length `10` in `name`, the first `11` components of `name` are used and the last `5` are left unused.

The statement

```
char name[16] = {'J', 'o', 'h', 'n', '\0'};
```

declares an array `name` containing `16` components of type `char` and stores the C-string `"John"` in it. During `char` array variable declaration, C++ allows the C-string notation to be used in the initialization statement. The preceding statement is, therefore, equivalent to the following:

```
char name[16] = "John";          //Line A
```

Recall that the size of an array can be omitted if the array is initialized during the declaration. The statement

```
char name[] = "John";          //Line B
```

declares a C-string variable `name` of a length large enough—in this case, `5`—and stores `"John"` in it. There is a difference between the last two statements: Both statements store `"John"` in `name`, but the size of `name` in the statement in Line A is `16`, and the size of `name` in the statement in Line B is `5`.

Most rules that apply to other arrays also apply to character arrays. Consider the following statement:

```
char studentName[26];
```

Suppose you want to store `"Lisa L. Johnson"` in `studentName`. Because aggregate operations, such as assignment and comparison, are not allowed on arrays, the following statement is not legal:

```
studentName = "Lisa L. Johnson"; //illegal
```

C++ provides a set of functions that can be used for C-string manipulation. The header file `cstring` describes these functions. We often use three of these functions: `strcpy`

6

(string copy, to copy a C-string into a C-string variable—that is, assignment); `strcmp` (string comparison, to compare C-strings); and `strlen` (string length, to find the length of a C-string). Table 6-1 summarizes these functions.

TABLE 6-1 `strcpy`, `strcmp`, and `strlen` functions

Function	Effect
`strcpy(s1, s2)`	Copies the string s2 into the string variable s1 The length of s1 should be at least as large as s2
`strcmp(s1, s2)`	Returns a value < 0 if s1 is less than s2 Returns 0 if s1 and s2 are the same Returns a value > 0 if s1 is greater than s2
`strlen(s)`	Returns the length of the string s, excluding the null character

To use these functions, the program must include the header file `cstring` via the `include` statement. That is, the following statement must be included in the program:

`#include <cstring>`

String Comparison

In C++, C-strings are compared character-by-character using the system's collating sequence. Let us assume that you use the ASCII character set's collating sequence for character-by-character comparison.

1. The C-string `"Air"` is less than the C-string `"Boat"` because the first character of `"Air"` is less than the first character of `"Boat"`.

2. The C-string `"Air"` is less than the C-string `"An"` because the first character of both strings is the same, but the second character of `"Air"`, `'i'`, is less than the second character of `"An"`, `'n'`.

3. The C-string `"Bill"` is less than the C-string `"Billy"` because the first four characters of `"Bill"` and `"Billy"` are the same, but the fifth character of `"Bill"`, which is `'\0'` (the null character), is less than the fifth character of `"Billy"`, which is `'y'`. (Recall that C-strings in C++ are null terminated.)

4. The ASCII collating sequence of `'H'` is 72, and the collating sequence of `'h'` is 104. So, the C-string `"Hello"` is less than `"hello"` because the first character of the C-string `"Hello"`, `'H'`, is less than the first character of the C-string `"hello"`, `'h'`.

As you can see, the function strcmp compares its first C-string argument with its second C-string argument character-by-character.

EXAMPLE 6-8

Suppose you have the following statements:

```
char studentName[21];
char myname[16];
char yourname[16];
```

The following statements show how string functions work:

Statement	Effect
strcpy(myname, "John Robinson");	myname = "John Robinson"
strlen("John Robinson");	Returns 13, the length of the string "John Robinson"
int len; len = strlen("Sunny Day");	Stores 9 into len
strcpy(yourname, "Lisa Miller"); strcpy(studentName, yourname);	yourname = "Lisa Miller" studentName = "Lisa Miller"
strcmp("Bill", "Lisa");	Returns a value < 0

strcpy(yourname, "Kathy Brown");
strcpy(myname, "Mark G. Clark");
strcmp(myname, yourname);
	yourname = "Kathy Brown"
	myname = "Mark G. Clark"
	Returns a value > 0

6

 NOTE In this chapter, we defined a C-string to be a sequence of zero or more characters. C-strings are enclosed in double quotation marks. We also said that C-strings are null terminated, so the C-string "Hello" has six characters even though only five are enclosed in double quotation marks. Therefore, to store the C-string "Hello" in computer memory, you must use a character array of size 6. The length of a C-string is the number of actual characters enclosed in double quotation marks; for example, the length of the C-string "Hello" is 5. Thus, in a logical sense, a C-string is a sequence of zero or more characters, but in the physical sense (that is, to store the C-string in computer memory), a C-string has at least one character. Because the length of the C-string is the actual number of characters enclosed in double quotation marks, we defined a C-string to be a sequence of zero or more characters. However, you must remember that the null character stored in computer memory at the end of the C-string plays a key role when we compare C-strings, especially C-strings such as "Bill" and "Billy".

Reading and Writing Strings

As mentioned earlier, most rules that apply to arrays apply to C-strings as well. Aggregate operations such as assignment and comparison are not allowed on arrays. Even the input/output of arrays is done component-wise. However, the one place where C++ allows aggregate operations on arrays is the input and output of C-strings (that is, character arrays).

We will use the following declaration for our discussion:

```
char name[31];
```

String Input

Because aggregate operations are allowed for C-string input, the statement

```
cin >> name;
```

stores the next input C-string into `name`. The length of the input C-string must be less than or equal to `30`. If the length of the input string is `4`, the computer stores the four characters that are input and the null character `'\0'`. If the length of the input C-string is more than `30`, then, because there is no check on the array index bounds, the computer continues storing the string in whatever memory cells follow `name`. This process can cause serious problems, because data in the adjacent memory cells will be corrupted.

 NOTE   When you input a C-string using an input device, such as the keyboard, you do not include the double quotation marks around it, unless the double quotation marks are part of the string. For example, the C-string `"Hello"` is entered as `Hello`.

Recall that the extraction operator, `>>`, skips all leading whitespace characters and stops reading data into the current variable as soon as it finds the first whitespace character or invalid data. As a result, C-strings that contain blanks cannot be read using the extraction operator, `>>`. For example, if a first name and last name are separated by blanks, they cannot be read into `name`.

How do you input C-strings with blanks into a character array? Once again, the function `get` comes to our rescue. Recall that the function `get` is used to read character data. Until now, the form of the function `get` that you have used (Chapter 2) reads only a single character. However, the function `get` can also be used to read strings. To read C-strings, you use the form of the function `get` that has two parameters. The first parameter is a C-string variable; the second parameter specifies how many characters to read into the string variable.

To read C-strings, the general form (syntax) of the `get` function, together with an input stream variable such as `cin`, is:

```
cin.get(str, m + 1);
```

This statement stores the next **m** characters, or all characters until the newline character '\n' is found, into str. The newline character is not stored in str. If the input C-string has fewer than **m** characters, then the reading stops at the newline character.

Consider the following statements:

```
char str[31];
cin.get(str, 31);
```

If the input is

```
William T. Johnson
```

then "William T. Johnson" is stored in str. Suppose that the input is:

```
Hello there. My name is Mickey Blair.
```

Then, because str can store at most 30 characters, the C-string "Hello there. My name is Mickey" is stored in str.

Now suppose that we have the statements

```
char str1[26];
char str2[26];
char discard;
```

and the following two lines of input:

```
Summer is warm.
Winter will be cold.
```

Further suppose that we want to store the first C-string in str1 and the second C-string in str2. Both str1 and str2 can store C-strings that are up to 25 characters in length. Because the number of characters in the first line is 15, the reading stops at '\n'. You must read and discard the newline character at the end of the first line to store the second line into str2. The following sequence of statements stores the first line into str1 and the second line into str2:

```
cin.get(str1, 26);
cin.get(discard);
cin.get(str2, 26);
```

String Output

The output of C-strings is another place where aggregate operations on arrays are allowed. You can output C-strings by using an output stream variable, such as cout, together with the insertion operator, <<. For example, the statement

```
cout << name;
```

outputs the contents of name on the screen. The insertion operator, <<, continues to write the contents of name until it finds the null character. Thus, if the length of name is

6

4, the preceding statement outputs only four characters. If name does not contain the null character, then you will see strange output because the insertion operator continues to output data from memory adjacent to name until '\0' is found.

Specifying Input/Output Files at Execution Time

In Chapter 2, you learned how to read data from a file. In subsequent chapters, the name of the input file was included in the open statement. By doing so, the program always received data from the same input file. In real-world applications, the data may actually be collected at several locations and stored in separate files. Also, for comparison purposes, someone might want to process each file separately and then store the output in separate files. To accomplish this task efficiently, the user would prefer to specify the name of the input and/or output file at execution time rather than in the programming code. C++ allows the user to do so.

Consider the following statements:

```
ifstream infile;
ofstream outfile;

char fileName[51];    //assume that the file name is at most
                      //50 characters long
```

The following statements prompt and allow the user to specify the input and output files at execution time:

```
cout << "Enter the input file name: ";
cin >> fileName;

infile.open(fileName);    //open the input file
.
.
.
cout << "Enter the output file name: ";
cin >> fileName;

outfile.open(fileName);   //open the output file
```

THE class string AND INPUT/OUTPUT FILES

In Chapter 1, we introduced the class string. We now want to point out that values (that is, strings) of type string are not null terminated. Variables of type string can also be used to read and store the names of input/output files. However, the argument to the function open must be a null-terminated string—that is, a C-string. Therefore, if we use a variable of type string to read the name of an input/output file and then use this variable to open a file, the value of the variable must (first) be converted to a C-string (that is, a null-terminated string). The header file string contains the function c_str, which converts a value of type string to a null-terminated character array (that is, a C-string). The syntax to use the function c_str is

```
strVar.c_str()
```

where `strVar` is a variable of type `string`.

The following statements illustrate how to use variables of type `string` to read the names of the input/output files during program execution and to open those files:

```
ifstream infile;
string fileName;

cout << "Enter the input file name: ";
cin >> fileName;

infile.open(fileName.c_str());    //open the input file
```

Of course, you must also include the header file `string` in the program. The output file has similar conventions.

Parallel Arrays

Two (or more) arrays are called **parallel** if their corresponding components hold related information.

Suppose you need to keep track of students' course grades, together with their ID numbers, so that their grades can be posted at the end of the semester. Further suppose that there is a maximum of 50 students in a class, and their IDs are 5 digits long. Because there may be 50 students, you need 50 variables to store the students' IDs and 50 variables to store their grades. You can declare two arrays: `studentId` of type `int` and `courseGrade` of type `char`. Each array has 50 components. Furthermore, `studentId[0]` and `courseGrade[0]` will store the ID and course grade of the first student, `studentId[1]` and `courseGrade[1]` will store the ID and course grade of the second student, and so on.

The following statements declare these two arrays:

```
int studentId[50];
char courseGrade[50];
```

Suppose you need to input data into these arrays, and the data is provided in a file in the following form:

```
studentId courseGrade
```

For example, a sample data set is:

```
23456 A
86723 B
22356 C
92733 B
11892 D
.
.
.
```

6

Suppose that the input file is opened using the `ifstream` variable `infile`. Because the size of each array is 50, a maximum of 50 elements can be stored into each array. Moreover, it is possible that there may be fewer than 50 students in the class. Therefore, while reading the data, we also count the number of students and ensure that the array indices do not go out of bounds. The following loop reads the data into the parallel arrays `studentId` and `courseGrade`:

```
int numOfStudents = 0;

infile >> studentId[numOfStudents] >> courseGrade[numOfStudents];

while (infile && numOfStudents < 50)
{
    numOfStudents++;
    infile >> studentId[numOfStudents]
           >> courseGrade[numOfStudents];
}
```

Two-Dimensional and Multidimensional Arrays

The remainder of this chapter discusses two-dimensional arrays and ways to work with multidimensional arrays.

In the previous section, you learned how to use one-dimensional arrays to manipulate data. If the data is provided in a list form, you can use one-dimensional arrays. However, sometimes data is provided in a table form. For example, suppose that you want to track the number of cars in a particular color that are in stock at a local dealership. The dealership sells six types of cars in five different colors. Figure 6-8 shows sample data.

inStock	Red	Brown	Black	White	Gray
GM	10	7	12	10	4
Ford	18	11	15	17	10
Toyota	12	10	9	5	12
BMW	16	6	13	8	3
Nissan	10	7	12	6	4
Volvo	9	4	7	12	11

FIGURE 6-8 Table `inStock`

You can see that the data is in a table format. The table has 30 entries, and every entry is an integer. Because the table entries are all of the same type, you can declare a one-dimensional array of 30 components of type `int`. The first five components of the one-dimensional array can store the data of the first row of the table, the next five components of the one-dimensional array can store the data of the second row of the table, and so on. In other words, you can simulate the data given in a table format in a one-dimensional array.

If you do so, the algorithms to manipulate the data in the one-dimensional array will be somewhat complicated, because you must know where one row ends and another begins. You must also correctly compute the index of a particular element. C++ simplifies the process of manipulating data in a table form with the use of two-dimensional arrays. This section first discusses how to declare two-dimensional arrays and then looks at ways to manipulate data in a two-dimensional array.

Two-dimensional array: A collection of a fixed number of components arranged in rows and columns (that is, in two dimensions), wherein all components are of the same type.

The syntax for declaring a two-dimensional array is

```
dataType   arrayName[intExp1][intExp2];
```

where `intExp1` and `intExp2` are constant expressions yielding positive integer values. The two expressions, `intExp1` and `intExp2`, specify the number of rows and the number of columns, respectively, in the array.

The statement

```
double sales[10][5];
```

declares a two-dimensional array `sales` of 10 rows and 5 columns, where every component is of type `double`. As in the case of a one-dimensional array, the rows are numbered 0...9, and the columns are numbered 0...4. (See Figure 6-9.)

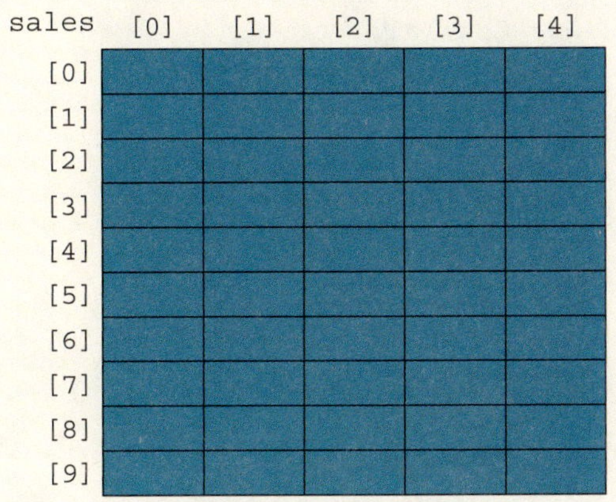

FIGURE 6-9 Two-dimensional array `sales`

Accessing Array Components

To access the components of a two-dimensional array, you need a pair of indices: one for the row position and one for the column position.

The syntax to access a component of a two-dimensional array is

```
arrayName[indexExp1][indexExp2]
```

where `indexExp1` and `indexExp2` are expressions yielding nonnegative integer values. `indexExp1` specifies the row position; `indexExp2` specifies the column position.

The statement

```
sales[5][3] = 25.75;
```

stores 25.75 into row number 5 and column number 3 (that is, the sixth row and the fourth column) of the array `sales`. (See Figure 6-10.)

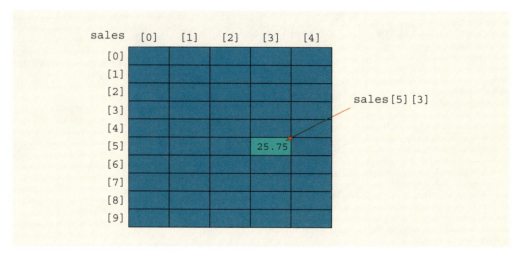

FIGURE 6-10 `sales[5][3]`

Suppose that

```
int i = 5;
int j = 3;
```

Then the previous statement

```
sales[5][3] = 25.75;
```

is equivalent to

```
sales[i][j] = 25.75;
```

So the indices can also be variables.

Two-Dimensional Array Initialization During Declaration

Like one-dimensional arrays, two-dimensional arrays can be initialized when they are declared. The following example helps illustrate this concept.

Consider the following statement:

```
int board[4][3] = {{2, 3, 1},
                   {15, 25, 13},
                   {20, 4, 7},
                   {11, 18, 14}};
```

This statement declares `board` to be a two-dimensional array of `4` rows and `3` columns. The components of the first row are `2`, `3`, and `1`; the components of the second row are `15`, `25`, and `13`; the components of the third row are `20`, `4`, and `7`; and the components of the fourth row are `11`, `18`, and `14`, respectively. Figure 6-11 shows the array `board`.

board	[0]	[1]	[2]
[0]	2	3	1
[1]	15	25	13
[2]	20	4	7
[3]	11	18	14

FIGURE 6-11 Two-dimensional array `board`

To initialize a two-dimensional array when it is declared:

1. The elements of each row are enclosed within curly braces and separated by commas.
2. All rows are enclosed within curly braces.
3. For number arrays, if all components of a row are not specified, the unspecified components are initialized to `0`. In this case, at least one of the values must be given to initialize all the components of a row.

Processing Two-Dimensional Arrays

A two-dimensional array can be processed in three ways:

1. Process the entire array.
2. Process a particular row of the array, called **row processing**.
3. Process a particular column of the array, called **column processing**.

Initializing and printing the array are examples of processing the entire two-dimensional array. Finding the largest element in a row (column) and finding the sum of a row (column) are examples of row (column) processing. We will use the following declaration for our discussion:

```
const int NUMBER_OF_ROWS = 7;      //This can be set to any number.
const int NUMBER_OF_COLUMNS = 6;   //This can be set to any number.

int matrix[NUMBER_OF_ROWS][NUMBER_OF_COLUMNS];
int sum;
int largest;
int temp;
```

Figure 6-12 shows the array `matrix`.

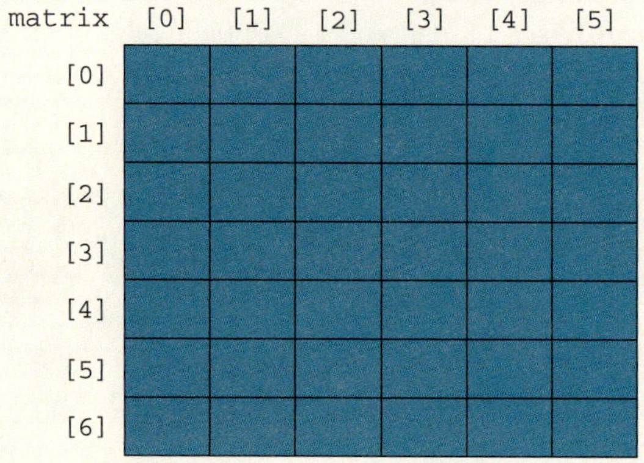

FIGURE 6-12 Two-dimensional array `matrix`

Because the components of a two-dimensional array are of the same type, the components of any row or column are of the same type. This means that each row and each column of a two-dimensional array is a one-dimensional array. Therefore, when processing a particular row or column of a two-dimensional array, we use algorithms similar to those that process one-dimensional arrays. We will further explain this concept with the help of the two-dimensional array `matrix`, as declared previously.

Suppose that we want to process row number 5 of `matrix` (that is, the sixth row of `matrix`). The components of row number 5 of `matrix` are:

```
matrix[5][0], matrix[5][1], matrix[5][2], matrix[5][3], matrix[5][4],
matrix[5][5]
```

We see that in these components the first index (the row position) is fixed at 5. The second index (the column position) ranges from 0 to 5. Therefore, we can use the following **for** loop to process row number 5:

```
for (int col = 0; col < NUMBER_OF_COLUMNS; col++)
    process matrix[5][col]
```

Clearly, this **for** loop is equivalent to the following **for** loop:

```
int row = 5;
for (int col = 0; col < NUMBER_OF_COLUMNS; col++)
    process matrix[row][col]
```

Similarly, suppose that we want to process column number 2 of `matrix`, that is, the third column of `matrix`. The components of this column are:

```
matrix[0][2], matrix[1][2], matrix[2][2], matrix[3][2], matrix[4][2],
matrix[5][2], matrix[6][2]
```

Here the second index (that is, the column position) is fixed at 2. The first index (that is, the row position) ranges from 0 to 6. In this case, we can use the following **for** loop to process column 2 of `matrix`:

```
for (int row = 0; row < NUMBER_OF_ROWS; row++)
    process matrix[row][2]
```

Clearly, this **for** loop is equivalent to the following **for** loop:

```
int col = 2;
for (int row = 0; row < NUMBER_OF_ROWS; row++)
    process matrix[row][col]
```

Next, we discuss specific processing algorithms.

INITIALIZATION

Suppose that you want to initialize row number 4, that is, the fifth row, to 0. As explained earlier, the following **for** loop does this:

```
int row = 4;
for (int col = 0; col < NUMBER_OF_COLUMNS; col++)
    matrix[row][col] = 0;
```

If you want to initialize the entire `matrix` to 0, you can also put the first index (that is, the row position) in a loop. By using the following nested **for** loops, we can initialize each component of `matrix` to 0:

```
for (int row = 0; row < NUMBER_OF_ROWS; row++)
    for (int col = 0; col < NUMBER_OF_COLUMNS; col++)
        matrix[row][col] = 0;
```

PRINT

By using a nested **for** loop, you can output the components of `matrix`. The following nested **for** loops print the components of `matrix`, one row per line:

```
for (int row = 0; row < NUMBER_OF_ROWS; row++)
{
    for (int col = 0; col < NUMBER_OF_COLUMNS; col++)
        cout << setw(5) << matrix[row][col] << " ";

    cout << endl;
}
```

INPUT

The following **for** loop inputs the data into row number 4, that is, the fifth row of **matrix**:

```
int row = 4;
for (int col = 0; col < NUMBER_OF_COLUMNS; col++)
    cin >> matrix[row][col];
```

As before, by putting the row number in a loop, you can input data into each component of **matrix**. The following **for** loop inputs data into each component of **matrix**:

```
for (int row = 0; row < NUMBER_OF_ROWS; row++)
    for (int col = 0; col < NUMBER_OF_COLUMNS; col++)
        cin >> matrix[row][col];
```

SUM BY ROW

The following **for** loop finds the sum of row number 4 of **matrix**; that is, it adds the components of row number 4:

```
sum = 0;
int row = 4;
for (int col = 0; col < NUMBER_OF_COLUMNS; col++)
    sum = sum + matrix[row][col];
```

Once again, by putting the row number in a loop, we can find the sum of each row separately. Following is the C++ code to find the sum of each individual row:

```
    //Sum of each individual row
for (int row = 0; row < NUMBER_OF_ROWS; row++)
{
    sum = 0;
    for (int col = 0; col < NUMBER_OF_COLUMNS; col++)
        sum = sum + matrix[row][col];

    cout << "Sum of row " << row + 1 << " = " << sum << endl;
}
```

SUM BY COLUMN

As in the case of finding the sum by row, the following nested **for** loop finds the sum of each individual column:

```
//Sum of each individual column
for (int col = 0; col < NUMBER_OF_COLUMNS; col++)
{
    sum = 0;
    for (int row = 0; row < NUMBER_OF_ROWS; row++)
        sum = sum + matrix[row][col];

    cout << "Sum of column " << col + 1 << " = " << sum
        << endl;
}
```

LARGEST ELEMENT IN EACH ROW AND EACH COLUMN

As stated earlier, another operation on a two-dimensional array is finding the largest element in each row and each column. Next, we give the C++ code to perform this operation.

The following **for** loop determines the largest element in row number 4:

```
int row = 4;
largest = matrix[row][0]; //Assume that the first element of
                          //the row is the largest.
for (int col = 1; col < NUMBER_OF_COLUMNS; col++)
    if (largest < matrix[row][col])
        largest = matrix[row][col];
```

6

The following C++ code determines the largest element in each row and each column:

```
//Largest element in each row
for (int row = 0; row < NUMBER_OF_ROWS; row++)
{
    largest = matrix[row][0]; //Assume that the first element
                              //of the row is the largest.
    for (int col = 1; col < NUMBER_OF_COLUMNS; col++)
        if (largest < matrix[row][col])
            largest = matrix[row][col];

    cout << "The largest element in row " << row + 1 << " = "
        << largest << endl;
}

//Largest element in each column
for (int col = 0; col < NUMBER_OF_COLUMNS; col++)
{
    largest = matrix[0][col]; //Assume that the first element
                              //of the column is the largest.
    for (int row = 1; row < NUMBER_OF_ROWS; row++)
        if (largest < matrix[row][col])
            largest = matrix[row][col];

    cout << "The largest element in column " << col + 1
        << " = " << largest << endl;
}
```

Passing Two-Dimensional Arrays as Parameters to Functions

Two-dimensional arrays can be passed as parameters to a function, and they are passed by reference. The base address (that is, the address of the first component of the actual parameter) is passed to the formal parameter. If `matrix` is the name of a two-dimensional array, then `matrix[0][0]` is the first component of `matrix`.

When storing a two-dimensional array in the computer's memory, C++ uses the **row order form**. That is, the first row is stored first, followed by the second row, followed by the third row, and so on.

In the case of a one-dimensional array, when declaring it as a formal parameter, we usually omit the size of the array. Because C++ stores two-dimensional arrays in row order form, to compute the address of a component correctly, the compiler must know where one row ends and the next row begins. Thus, when declaring a two-dimensional array as a formal parameter, you can omit the size of the first dimension, but not the second; that is, you must specify the number of columns.

Suppose we have the following declaration:

```
const int NUMBER_OF_ROWS = 6;
const int NUMBER_OF_COLUMNS = 5;
```

Consider the following definition of the function `printMatrix`:

```
void printMatrix(int matrix[][NUMBER_OF_COLUMNS], int numOfRows)
{
    for (int row = 0; row < numOfRows; row++)
    {
        for (int col = 0; col < NUMBER_OF_COLUMNS; col++)
            cout << setw(5) << matrix[row][col] << " ";

        cout << endl;
    }
}
```

This function takes as a parameter a two-dimensional array of an unspecified number of rows, and 5 columns, and outputs the content of the two-dimensional array. During the function call, the number of columns of the actual parameter must match the number of columns of the formal parameter.

Similarly, the following function outputs the sum of the elements of each row of a two-dimensional array whose elements are of type `int`:

```
void sumRows(int matrix[][NUMBER_OF_COLUMNS], int numOfRows)
{
    int sum;

        //Sum of each individual row
    for (int row = 0; row < numOfRows; row++)
    {
        sum = 0;

        for (int col = 0; col < NUMBER_OF_COLUMNS; col++)
            sum = sum + matrix[row][col];

        cout << "Sum of row " << (row + 1) << " = " << sum
             << endl;
    }
}
```

The following function determines the largest element in each row:

```
void largestInRows(int matrix[][NUMBER_OF_COLUMNS], int numOfRows)
{
    int largest;

        //Largest element in each row
    for (int row = 0; row < numOfRows; row++)
    {
        largest = matrix[row][0]; //Assume that the first element
                                  //of the row is the largest.
        for (int col = 1; col < NUMBER_OF_COLUMNS; col++)
            if (largest < matrix[row][col])
                largest = matrix[row][col];

        cout << "The largest element of row " << (row + 1)
             << " = " << largest << endl;
    }
}
```

6

Likewise, you can write a function to find the sum of the elements of each column, read the data into a two-dimensional array, find the largest and/or smallest element in each row or column, and so on.

Example 6-9 shows how the functions printMatrix, sumRows, and largestInRows are used in a program.

EXAMPLE 6-9

```cpp
//************************************************************
// Author: D.S. Malik
//
// This program shows how two-dimensional arrays are passed as
// parameters to functions.
//************************************************************

#include <iostream>                                     //Line 1
#include <iomanip>                                      //Line 2

using namespace std;                                    //Line 3

const int NUMBER_OF_ROWS = 6;                           //Line 4
const int NUMBER_OF_COLUMNS = 5;                        //Line 5

void printMatrix(int matrix[][NUMBER_OF_COLUMNS],
                 int NUMBER_OF_ROWS);                   //Line 6
void sumRows(int matrix[][NUMBER_OF_COLUMNS],
             int NUMBER_OF_ROWS);                       //Line 7
void largestInRows(int matrix[][NUMBER_OF_COLUMNS],
                   int NUMBER_OF_ROWS);                 //Line 8

int main()                                              //Line 9
{                                                       //Line 10
    int board[NUMBER_OF_ROWS][NUMBER_OF_COLUMNS]
                 = {{23, 5, 6, 15, 18},
                    {4, 16, 24, 67, 10},
                    {12, 54, 23, 76, 11},
                    {1, 12, 34, 22, 8},
                    {81, 54, 32, 67, 33},
                    {12, 34, 76, 78, 9}};               //Line 11

    printMatrix(board, NUMBER_OF_ROWS);                 //Line 12
    cout << endl;                                       //Line 13
    sumRows(board, NUMBER_OF_ROWS);                     //Line 14
    cout << endl;                                       //Line 15
    largestInRows(board, NUMBER_OF_ROWS);               //Line 16

    return 0;                                           //Line 17
}                                                       //Line 18

//Place the definitions of the functions printMatrix,
//sumRows, and largestInRows as previously described here.
```

Sample Run:

```
23      5      6     15     18
 4     16     24     67     10
12     54     23     76     11
 1     12     34     22      8
81     54     32     67     33
12     34     76     78      9
```

```
Sum of row 1 = 67
Sum of row 2 = 121
Sum of row 3 = 176
Sum of row 4 = 77
Sum of row 5 = 267
Sum of row 6 = 209
```

```
The largest element in row 1 = 23
The largest element in row 2 = 67
The largest element in row 3 = 76
The largest element in row 4 = 34
The largest element in row 5 = 81
The largest element in row 6 = 78
```

In this program, the statement in Line 11 declares and initializes `board` to be a two-dimensional array of 6 rows and 5 columns. The statement in Line 12 uses the function `printMatrix` to output the elements of `board` (see the first six lines of the sample run). The statement in Line 14 uses the function `sumRows` to calculate and print the sum of each row. The statement in Line 16 uses the function `largestInRows` to find and print the largest element in each row.

Multidimensional Arrays

In this chapter, we defined an array as a collection of a fixed number of elements (called components) of the same type. A one-dimensional array is an array in which the elements are arranged in a list form; in a two-dimensional array, the elements are arranged in a table form. We can also define three-dimensional or larger arrays. In C++, there is no limit on the dimensions of arrays. Following is the general definition of an array:

Array: A collection of a fixed number of elements (called components) arranged in n dimensions ($n >= 1$), also called an n-**dimensional array**.

The general syntax for declaring an n-dimensional array is

```
dataType arrayName[intExp1][intExp2] ... [intExpn];
```

where `intExp1`, `intExp2`, ... , and `intExpn` are constant expressions yielding positive integer values.

The syntax to access a component of an n-dimensional array is

```
arrayName[indexExp1][indexExp2] ... [indexExpn]
```

where indexExp1, indexExp2, ..., and indexExpn are expressions yielding nonnegative integer values. indexExpi gives the position of the array component in the ith dimension.

For example, the statement

```
double carDealers[10][5][7];
```

declares carDealers to be a three-dimensional array. The size of the first dimension is 10, the size of the second dimension is 5, and the size of the third dimension is 7. The first dimension ranges from 0 to 9, the second dimension ranges from 0 to 4, and the third dimension ranges from 0 to 6. The base address of the array carDealers is the address of the first array component—that is, the address of carDealers[0][0][0]. The total number of components in the array carDealers is 10 * 5 * 7 = 350.

The statement

```
carDealers[5][3][2] = 15564.75;
```

sets the value of the component carDealers[5][3][2] to 15564.75.

You can use loops to process multidimensional arrays. For example, the nested for loops

```
for (int i = 0; i < 10; i++)
    for (int j = 0; j < 5; j++)
        for (int k = 0; k < 7; k++)
            carDealers[i][j][k] = 0.0;
```

initialize the entire array to 0.0.

When declaring a multidimensional array as a formal parameter in a function, you can omit the size of the first dimension but not the other dimensions. As parameters, multidimensional arrays are passed by reference only, and a function cannot return a value of the array type. There is no check to determine whether the array indices are within bounds.

PROGRAMMING EXAMPLE: Text Processing

(Line and letter count) Let us now write a program that reads a given text, outputs the text as is, and also prints the number of lines and the number of times each letter appears in the text. An uppercase letter and a lowercase letter are treated as being the same; that is, they are tallied together.

Because there are 26 letters, we use an array of 26 components to perform the letter count. We also need a variable to store the line count.

The text is stored in a file, which we will call `textin.txt`. The output will be stored in a file, which we will call `textout.out`.

Input   A file containing the text to be processed

Output   A file containing the text, number of lines, and the number of times a letter appears in the text

PROBLEM
ANALYSIS
AND
ALGORITHM
DESIGN

Based on the desired output, it is clear that we must output the text as is. That is, if the text contains any whitespace characters, they must be output as well. Furthermore, we must count the number of lines in the text. Therefore, we must know where a line ends, which means that we must trap the newline character. This requirement suggests that we cannot use the extraction operator to process the input file. Because we also need to perform the letter count, we use the `get` function to read the text.

Let us first describe the variables that are necessary to develop the program. This will simplify the discussion that follows.

Variables

We need to store the line count and the letter count. Therefore, we need a variable to store the line count and 26 variables to perform the letter count. We will use an array of `26` components to perform the letter count. We also need a variable to read and store each character in turn, because the input file is to be read character-by-character. Because data is to be read from an input file and output is to be saved in a file, we need an input stream variable to open the input file and an output stream variable to open the output file. These statements indicate that the function `main` needs (at least) the following variables:

```
int lineCount;          //variable to store the line count
int letterCount[26];    //array to store the letter count
char ch;                //variable to store a character
ifstream infile;        //input file stream variable
ofstream outfile;       //output file stream variable
```

In this declaration, `letterCount[0]` stores the A count, `letterCount[1]` stores the B count, and so on. Clearly, the variable `lineCount` and the array `letterCount` must be initialized to 0.

The algorithm for the program is:

1. Declare the variables.
2. Open the input and output files.
3. Initialize the variables.
4. While there is more data in the input file:
   4.1.   For each character in a line:
          4.1.1.   Read and write the character.
          4.1.2.   Increment the appropriate letter count.
   4.2.   Increment the line count.

5. Output the line count and letter counts.

6. Close the files.

To simplify the function `main`, we divide it into four functions:

- Function `initialize`
- Function `characterCount`
- Function `copyText`
- Function `writeTotal`

The following sections describe each of these functions in detail. Then, with the help of these functions, we describe the algorithm for the function `main`.

Initialize This function initializes the variable `lineCount` and the array `letterCount` to 0. It therefore has two parameters: one corresponding to the variable `lineCount` and one corresponding to the array `letterCount`. Clearly, the parameter corresponding to `lineCount` must be a reference parameter. The definition of this function is

```
void initialize(int& lc, int list[])
{
    lc = 0;

    for (int j = 0; j < 26; j++)
        list[j] = 0;
} //end initialize
```

characterCount This function increments the letter count. To increment the appropriate letter count, this function must know what the letter is. Therefore, the `characterCount` function has two parameters: a `char` variable and the array to update the letter count. In pseudocode, this function is

a. Convert the letter to uppercase.

b. Find the index of the array corresponding to this letter.

c. If the index is valid, increment the appropriate count. At this step, we must ensure that the character is a letter. We are counting only letters, so other characters—such as commas, hyphens, and periods—are ignored.

Following this algorithm, the definition of this function is

```
void characterCount(char ch, int list[])
{
    int index;

    ch = toupper(ch);                           //Step a
```

```
        index = static_cast<int>(ch)
                - static_cast<int>('A');        //Step b

    if (0 <= index && index < 26)               //Step c
        list[index]++;
} //end characterCount
```

copyText   This function reads a line and outputs the line. After reading a character, it calls the function `characterCount` to update the letter count. Clearly, this function has four parameters: an input file stream variable, an output file stream variable, a `char` variable, and the array to update the letter count.

Note that the `copyText` function does not perform the letter count, but we still pass the array `letterCount` to it. We take this step because this function calls the function `characterCount`, which needs the array `letterCount` to update the appropriate letter count. Therefore, we must pass the array `letterCount` to the `copyText` function so that it can pass the array to the function `characterCount`.

```
void copyText(ifstream& intext, ofstream& outtext, char& ch,
              int list[])
{
    while (ch != '\n')          //process the entire line
    {
        outtext << ch;          //output the character

        characterCount(ch, list);    //call the function
                                     //characterCount
        intext.get(ch);         //read the next character
    }
    outtext << ch;              //output the newline character
} //end copyText
```

writeTotal   This function outputs the line count and the letter count. It has three parameters: the output file stream variable, the line count, and the array to output the letter count. The definition of this function is

```
void writeTotal(ofstream& outtext, int lc, int list[])
{
    outtext << endl << endl;
    outtext << "The number of lines = " << lc << endl;

    for (int index = 0; index < 26; index++)
        outtext << static_cast<char>(index
                                     + static_cast<int>('A'))
                << " count = " << list[index] << endl;
} //end writeTotal
```

6

We now describe the algorithm for the function `main`.

MAIN
ALGORITHM

1. Declare the variables.

2. Open the input and output files.

3. If the input file does not exist, exit the program.

4. Open the output file.

5. Initialize the variables, such as `lineCount` and the array `letterCount`.

6. Read the first character.

7. While (not end of input file):

   7.1. Process the next line; call the function `copyText`.

   7.2. Increment the line count. (Increment the variable `lineCount`.)

   7.3. Read the next character.

8. Output the line count and letter count. Call the function `writeTotal`.

9. Close the files.

COMPLETE PROGRAM LISTING

```
//***************************************************************
// Author: D.S. Malik
//
// Program: Line and Letter Count
// This program reads a text, outputs the text as is, and also
// prints the number of lines and the number of times each
// letter appears in the text. An uppercase letter and a
// lowercase letter are treated as being the same; that is,
// they are tallied together.
//***************************************************************

#include <iostream>
#include <fstream>
#include <cctype>

using namespace std;

void initialize(int& lc, int list[]);
void characterCount(char ch, int list[]);
void copyText(ifstream& intext, ofstream& outtext, char& ch,
              int list[]);
void writeTotal(ofstream& outtext, int lc, int list[]);
```

```cpp
int main()
{
        //Step 1; Declare variables
    int lineCount;
    int letterCount[26];
    char ch;
    ifstream infile;
    ofstream outfile;

    infile.open("textin.txt");                              //Step 2

    if (!infile)                                            //Step 3
    {
        cout << "Cannot open the input file."
            << endl;
        return 1;
    }

    outfile.open("textout.out");                            //Step 4

    initialize(lineCount, letterCount);                     //Step 5

    infile.get(ch);                                         //Step 6

    while (infile)                                          //Step 7
    {
        copyText(infile, outfile, ch, letterCount); //Step 7.1
        lineCount++;                                        //Step 7.2
        infile.get(ch);                                     //Step 7.3
    }

    writeTotal(outfile, lineCount, letterCount);    //Step 8

    infile.close();                                         //Step 9
    outfile.close();                                        //Step 9

    return 0;
}

void initialize(int& lc, int list[])
{
    lc = 0;

    for (int j = 0; j < 26; j++)
        list[j] = 0;
} //end initialize

void characterCount(char ch, int list[])
{
    int index;

    ch = toupper(ch);                               //Step a
```

```cpp
    index = static_cast<int>(ch)
            - static_cast<int>('A');        //Step b

    if (0 <= index && index < 26)           //Step c
        list[index]++;
} //end characterCount

void copyText(ifstream& intext, ofstream& outtext, char& ch,
            int list[])
{
    while (ch != '\n')          //process the entire line
    {
        outtext << ch;          //output the character

        characterCount(ch, list);   //call the function
                                    //characterCount
        intext.get(ch);         //read the next character
    }
    outtext << ch;              //output the newline character
} //end copyText

void writeTotal(ofstream& outtext, int lc, int list[])
{
    outtext << endl << endl;
    outtext << "The number of lines = " << lc << endl;

    for (int index = 0; index < 26; index++)
        outtext << static_cast<char>(index
                                + static_cast<int>('A'))
                << " count = " << list[index] << endl;
} //end writeTotal
```

Sample Run (`textout.out`)

Today we live in an era where information is processed
almost at the speed of light. Through computers, the
technological revolution is drastically changing the way we
live and communicate with one another. Terms such as
"the Internet," which was unfamiliar just a few years ago, are
very common today. With the help of computers you can send
letters to, and receive letters from, loved ones within
seconds. You no longer need to send a résumé by mail to apply
for a job; in many cases you can simply submit your job
application via the Internet. You can watch how stocks perform
in real time, and instantly buy and sell them. Students
regularly "surf" the Internet and use computers to design
their classroom projects. They also use powerful word
processing software to complete their term papers. Many
people maintain and balance their checkbooks on computers.

```
The number of lines = 15
A count = 53
B count = 7
C count = 30
D count = 19
E count = 81
F count = 11
G count = 10
H count = 29
I count = 41
J count = 4
K count = 3
L count = 31
M count = 26
N count = 50
O count = 59
P count = 21
Q count = 0
R count = 45
S count = 48
T count = 62
U count = 24
V count = 7
W count = 15
X count = 0
Y count = 20
Z count = 0
```

6

QUICK REVIEW

1. A data type is simple if variables of that type can hold only one value at a time.

2. In a structured data type, each data item is a collection of other data items.

3. An array is a structured data type with a fixed number of components. Every component is of the same type, and components are accessed using their relative positions in the array.

4. Elements of a one-dimensional array are arranged in the form of a list.

5. In C++, an array index starts with 0.

6. An array index can be any expression that evaluates to a nonnegative integer. The value of the index must always be less than the size of the array.

7. There are no aggregate operations on arrays, except for the input/output of character arrays (C-strings).

8. There is no check on an array index out of bounds.

9. Arrays can be initialized during their declaration. If there are fewer initial values than the array size, the excess elements are initialized to 0.

10. The base address of an array is the address of the first array component. For example, if `list` is a one-dimensional array, the base address of `list` is the address of `list[0]`.

11. When declaring a one-dimensional array as a formal parameter, you usually omit the array size. If you specify the size of a one-dimensional array in the formal parameter declaration, the compiler will ignore the size.

12. In a function call statement, when passing an array as an actual parameter, you use only its name.

13. As parameters to functions, arrays are passed by reference only.

14. Because, as parameters, arrays are passed by reference only, when declaring an array as a formal parameter, you do not use the symbol `&` after the data type.

15. A function cannot return a value of type array.

16. Although, as parameters, arrays are passed by reference, when declaring an array as a formal parameter, using the reserved word **const** before the data type prevents the function from modifying the array.

17. Individual array components can be passed as parameters to functions.

18. In C++, a string is any sequence of characters enclosed between double quotation marks.

19. In C++, C-strings are null terminated.

20. In C++, the null character is represented as `'\0'`.

21. In the ASCII character set, the collating sequence of the null character is 0.

22. C-strings are stored in character arrays.

23. Character arrays can be initialized during declaration using string notation.

24. Input and output of C-strings is the only place where C++ allows aggregate operations.

25. The header file `cstring` contains the specifications of the functions that can be used for C-string manipulation.

26. Commonly used C-string manipulation functions include `strcpy` (string copy), `strcmp` (string comparison), and `strlen` (string length).

27. C-strings are compared character-by-character.

28. Because C-strings are stored in arrays, individual characters in the C-string can be accessed using the array component access notation.

29. Parallel arrays are used to hold related information.

30. In a two-dimensional array, the elements are arranged in a table form.

31. To access an element of a two-dimensional array, you need a pair of indices: one for the row position and one for the column position.

32. If `matrix` is a two-dimensional array, then the base address of `matrix` is the address of the array component `matrix[0][0]`.

33. In row processing, a two-dimensional array is processed one row at a time.

34. In column processing, a two-dimensional array is processed one column at a time.

35. When declaring a two-dimensional array as a formal parameter, you can omit the size of the first dimension but not the second.

36. When a two-dimensional array is passed as an actual parameter, the number of columns of the actual and formal arrays must match.

37. C++ stores two-dimensional arrays in a row order form in computer memory.

EXERCISES

1. Mark the following statements as true or false.

   a. A `double` type is an example of a simple data type.

   b. A one-dimensional array is an example of a structured data type.

   c. Arrays can be passed as parameters to a function either by value or by reference.

   d. A function can return a value of type array.

   e. The size of an array is determined at compile time.

   f. The only aggregate operations allowable on `int` arrays are the increment and decrement operations.

   g. Given the declaration

      ```
      int list[10];
      ```

      the statement

      ```
      list[5] = list[3] + list[2];
      ```

      updates the content of the fifth component of the array `list`.

   h. If an array index goes out of bounds, the program always terminates in an error.

   i. In C++, some aggregate operations are allowed for strings.

   j. The declaration

      ```
      char name[16] = "John K. Miller";
      ```

      declares `name` to be an array of 15 characters because the string `"John K. Miller"` has only 14 characters.

   k. The declaration

      ```
      char str = "Sunny Day";
      ```

      declares `str` to be a string of an unspecified length.

   l. As parameters, two-dimensional arrays are passed either by value or by reference.

2. Write C++ statements to do the following:

   a. Declare an array `alpha` of 15 components of type `int`.

   b. Output the value of the tenth component of the array `alpha`.

   c. Set the value of the fifth component of the array `alpha` to 35.

   d. Set the value of the ninth component of the array `alpha` to the sum of the sixth and thirteenth components of the array `alpha`.

   e. Set the value of the fourth component of the array `alpha` to three times the value of the eighth component minus 57.

   f. Output `alpha` so that five components per line are printed.

3. Consider the function headings

```
void funcOne(int alpha[], int size);
int funcSum(int x, int y);
void funcTwo(const int alpha[], int beta[]);
```

and the declarations

```
int list[50];
int aList[60];
int num;
```

Write C++ statements that do the following:

   a. Call the function `funcOne` with the actual parameters, `list`, and 50, respectively.

   b. Print the value returned by the function `funcSum` with the actual parameters, 50, and the fourth component of `list`, respectively.

   c. Print the value returned by the function `funcSum` with the actual parameters, the thirtieth, and the tenth components of `list`, respectively.

   d. Call the function `funcTwo` with the actual parameters, `list`, and `aList`, respectively.

4. Suppose `list` is an array of five components of type `int`. What is stored in `list` after the following C++ code executes?

```
for (int i = 0; i < 5; i++)
{
    list[i] = 2 * i + 5;
    if (i % 2 == 0)
        list[i] = list[i] - 3;
}
```

5. Suppose `list` is an array of six components of type `int`. What is stored in `list` after the following C++ code executes?

```
list[0] = 5;
for (int i = 1; i < 6; i++)
{
    list[i] = i * i + 5;
    if (i > 2)
        list[i] = 2 * list[i] - list[i - 1];
}
```

6. Given the declaration

   ```
   char string15[16];
   ```

   mark the following statements as valid or invalid. If a statement is invalid, explain why.

   a. `strcpy(string15, "Hello there");`

   b. `strlen(string15);`

   c. `string15 = "Jacksonville";`

   d. `cin >> string15;`

   e. `cout << string15;`

   f. ```
      if (string15 >= "Nice day")
            cout << string15;
      ```

   g. `string15[6] = 't';`

7. Given the declaration

   ```
   char str1[15];
   char str2[15] = "Good day";
   ```

   mark the following statements as valid or invalid. If a statement is invalid, explain why.

   a. `str1 = str2;`

   b. ```
      if (str1 == str2)
            cout << " Both strings are of the same length." << endl;
      ```

   c. ```
      if (strlen(str1) >= strlen(str2))
            str1 = str2;
      ```

   d. ```
      if (strcmp(str1, str2) < 0)
            cout << "str1 is less that str2." << endl;
      ```

8. Given the declaration:

   ```
   char name[8] = "Shelly";
   ```

   mark the following statements as "Yes" if they output Shelly. Otherwise, mark the statement as "No" and explain why it does not output Shelly.

   a. `cout << name;`

   b. ```
      for (int j = 0; j < 6; j++)
            cout << name[j];
      ```

   c. ```
      int j = 0;
      while (name[j] != '\0')
            cout << name[j++];
      ```

   d. ```
      int j = 0;
      while (j < 8)
            cout << name[j++];
      ```
      ```

9. Given the declaration

```
char str1[21];
char str2[21];
```

   a. Write a C++ statement that stores "Sunny Day" in str1.

   b. Write a C++ statement that stores the length of str1 into the int variable length.

   c. Write a C++ statement that copies the value of name into str2.

   d. Write C++ code that outputs str1 if str1 is less than or equal to str2, and otherwise outputs str2.

10. Assume the following declarations:

```
char name[21];
char yourName[21];
char studentName[31];
```

   Mark the following statements as valid or invalid. If a statement is invalid, explain why.

   a. `cin >> name;`

   b. `cout << studentName;`

   c. `yourName[0] = '\0';`

   d. `yourName = studentName;`

   e. `if (yourName == name)`
      `    studentName = name;`

   f. `int x = strcmp(yourName, studentName);`

   g. `strcpy(studentName, name);`

   h. `for (int j = 0; j < 21; j++)`
      `    cout << name[j];`

11. What is the output of the following program?

```
#include <iostream>

using namespace std;

int main()
{
    int alpha[5];

    alpha[0] = 5;
    for (int count = 1; count < 5; count++)
    {
        alpha[count] = 5 * count + 10;
        alpha[count - 1] = alpha[count] - 4;
    }
```

```
        cout << "List elements: ";
        for (int count = 0; count < 5; count++)
            cout << alpha[count] << " ";
        cout << endl;

        return 0;
    }
```

12. What is the output of the following program?

```
#include <iostream>

using namespace std;

int main()
{
    int one[5];
    int two[10];

    for (int j = 0; j < 5; j++)
        one[j] = 5 * j + 3;

    cout << "One contains: ";
    for (int j = 0; j < 5; j++)
        cout << one[j] << " ";
    cout << endl;
    for (int j = 0; j < 5; j++)
    {
        two[j] = 2 * one[j] - 1;
        two[j + 5] = one[4 - j] + two [j];
    }

    cout << "Two contains: ";
    for (int j = 0; j < 10; j++)
        cout << two[j] << " ";
    cout << endl;

    return 0;
}
```

13. Consider the following declarations:

```
const int CAR_TYPES = 5;
const int COLOR_TYPES = 6;

double sales[CAR_TYPES][COLOR_TYPES];
```

a. How many components does the array sales have?

b. What is the number of rows in the array sales?

c. What is the number of columns in the array sales?

d. To sum the sales by CAR_TYPES, what kind of processing is required?

e. To sum the sales by COLOR_TYPES, what kind of processing is required?

14. Write C++ statements that do the following:

   a. Declare an array `alpha` of 10 rows and 20 columns of type `int`.

   b. Initialize the array `alpha` to 0.

   c. Store 1 in the first row and 2 in the remaining rows.

   d. Store 5 in the first column, and make sure that the value in each subsequent column is twice the value in the previous column.

   e. Print the array `alpha` one row per line.

   f. Print the array `alpha` one column per line.

15. Consider the following declaration:

```
int beta[3][3];
```

   What is stored in `beta` after each of the following statements executes?

   a.
```
for (int i = 0; i < 3; i++)
    for (int j = 0; j < 3; j++)
        beta[i][j] = 0;
```

   b.
```
for (int i = 0; i < 3; i++)
    for (int j = 0; j < 3; j++)
        beta[i][j] = i + j;
```

   c.
```
for (int i = 0; i < 3; i++)
    for (int j = 0; j < 3; j++)
        beta[i][j] = i * j;
```

   d.
```
for (int i = 0; i < 3; i++)
    for (int j = 0; j < 3; j++)
        beta[i][j] =  2 * (i + j) % 4;
```

PROGRAMMING EXERCISES

1. Write a C++ program that declares an array `alpha` of 50 components of type `double`. Initialize the array so that the first 25 components are equal to the square of the index variable, and the last 25 components are equal to three times the index variable. Output the array so that 10 elements per line are printed.

2. Write a C++ function, `smallestIndex`, that takes as parameters an `int` array and its size, and returns the index of the first occurrence of the smallest element in the array. Also, write a program to test your function.

3. Write a C++ function, `lastLargestIndex`, that takes as parameters an `int` array and its size, and returns the index of the last occurrence of the largest element in the array. Also, write a program to test your function.

4. Write a program that reads a file consisting of students' test scores in the range 0–200. It should then determine the number of students having scores in each of the following ranges: 0–24, 25–49, 50–74, 75–99, 100–124, 125–149, 150–174, and 175–200. Output the score ranges and the number of students. (Run your program with the following input data: 76, 89, 150, 135, 200, 76, 12, 100, 150, 28, 178, 189, 167, 200, 175, 150, 87, 99, 129, 149, 176, 200, 87, 35, 157, 189.)

5. Write a program that prompts the user to input a string and outputs the string in uppercase letters. (Use a character array to store the string.)

6. The history teacher at your school needs help in grading a True/False test. The students' IDs and test answers are stored in a file. The first entry in the file contains answers to the test in the form:

   TFFTFFTTTTFFTFTFTT

   Every other entry in the file is the student ID, followed by a blank, followed by the student's responses. For example, the entry

   ABC54301 TFTFTFTT TFTFTFFTTFT

   indicates that the student ID is ABC54301 and the answer to question 1 is True, the answer to question 2 is False, and so on. This student did not answer question 9. The exam has 20 questions, and the class has more than 150 students. Each correct answer is awarded two points, each wrong answer gets −1 point, and no answer gets 0 points. Write a program that processes the test data. The output should be the student's ID, followed by the answers, followed by the test score, followed by the test grade. Assume the following grade scale: 90%–100%, A; 80%–89.99%, B; 70%–79.99%, C; 60%–69.99%, D; and 0%–59.99%, F.

7. Write a program that allows the user to enter the last names of five candidates in a local election and the number of votes received by each candidate. The program should then output each candidate's name, the number of votes received, and the percentage of the total votes received by the candidate. Your program should also output the winner of the election. A sample output is:

Candidate	Votes Received	% of Total Votes
Johnson	5000	25.91
Miller	4000	20.72
Duffy	6000	31.09
Robinson	2500	12.95
Ashtony	1800	9.33
Total	19300	

The Winner of the Election is Duffy.

8. Consider the following function `main`:

```
int main()
{
    int inStock[10][4];
    int alpha[20];
    int beta[20];
    int gamma[4] = {11, 13, 15, 17};
    int delta[10] = {3, 5, 2, 6, 10, 9, 7, 11, 1, 8};
    .
    .
    .
}
```

a. Write the definition of the function `setZero` that initializes any one-dimensional array of type `int` to 0.

b. Write the definition of the function `inputArray` that prompts the user to input 20 numbers and stores the numbers into `alpha`.

c. Write the definition of the function `doubleArray` that initializes the elements of `beta` to two times the corresponding elements in `alpha`. Make sure that you prevent the function from modifying the elements of `alpha`.

d. Write the definition of the function `copyGamma` that sets the elements of the first row of `inStock` to `gamma` and the remaining rows of `inStock` to three times the previous row of `inStock`. Make sure that you prevent the function from modifying the elements of `gamma`.

e. Write the definition of the function `copyAlphaBeta` that stores `alpha` into the first five rows of `inStock` and `beta` into the last five rows of `inStock`. Make sure that you prevent the function from modifying the elements of `alpha` and `beta`.

f. Write the definition of the function `printArray` that prints any one-dimensional array of type `int`. Print 15 elements per line.

g. Write the definition of the function `setInStock` that prompts the user to input the elements for the first column of `inStock`. The function should then set the elements in the remaining columns to two times the corresponding element in the previous column, minus the corresponding element in `delta`.

h. Write C++ statements that call each of the functions in parts a through g.

i. Write a C++ program that tests the function `main` and the functions discussed in parts a through g. (Add additional functions, such as printing a two-dimensional array, as needed.)

9. Write a program that uses a two-dimensional array to store the highest and lowest temperatures for each month of the year. The program should output the average high, average low, and the highest and lowest temperatures for the year. Your program must consist of the following functions:

a.   Function `getData`: This function reads and stores data in the two-dimensional array.

b.   Function `averageHigh`: This function calculates and returns the average high temperature for the year.

c.   Function `averageLow`: This function calculates and returns the average low temperature for the year.

d.   Function `indexHighTemp`: This function returns the index of the highest high temperature in the array.

e.   Function `indexLowTemp`: This function returns the index of the lowest low temperature in the array.
(These functions must all have the appropriate parameters.)

10. **(Adding Large Integers)** In C++, the largest `int` value is 2147483647. An integer larger than this cannot be stored and processed as an integer. Similarly, if the sum or product of two positive integers is greater than 2147483647, then the result will be incorrect. One way to store and manipulate large integers is to store each individual digit of the number in an array. Write a program that inputs two positive integers of at most 20 digits and outputs the sum of the numbers. If the sum of the numbers has more than 20 digits, output the sum with an appropriate message. Your program must, at least, contain a function to read and store a number into an array and another function to output the sum of the numbers. (*Hint:* Read numbers as strings and store the digits of the numbers in the reverse order.)

11. **(Airplane Seating Assignment)** Write a program that can be used to assign seats for a commercial airplane. The airplane has 13 rows, with 6 seats in each row. Rows 1 and 2 are first class, rows 3 through 7 are business class, and rows 8 through 13 are economy class. Your program must prompt the user to enter the following information:

a.   Ticket type (first class, business class, or economy class)

b.   Desired seat

6

Output the seating plan in the following form:

	A	B	C	D	E	F
Row 1	*	*	X	*	X	X
Row 2	*	X	*	X	*	X
Row 3	*	*	X	X	*	X
Row 4	X	*	X	*	X	X
Row 5	*	X	*	X	*	*
Row 6	*	X	*	*	*	X
Row 7	X	*	*	*	X	X
Row 8	*	X	*	X	X	*
Row 9	X	*	X	X	*	X
Row 10	*	X	*	X	X	X
Row 11	*	*	X	*	X	*
Row 12	*	*	X	X	*	X
Row 13	*	*	*	*	X	*

Here, * indicates that the seat is available; x indicates that the seat is occupied. Make this a menu-driven program; show the user's choices and allow the user to make the appropriate choices.

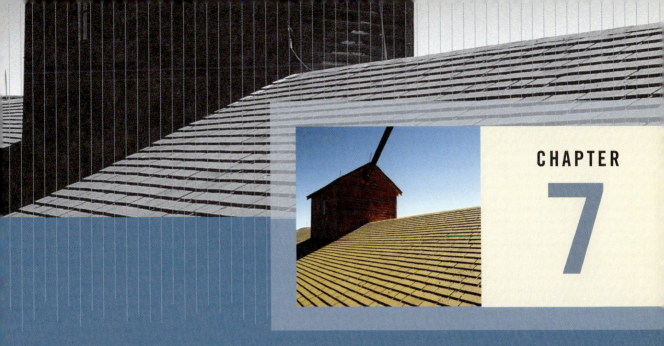

CHAPTER
7

CLASSES AND DATA ABSTRACTION

Chapter 0 introduced the problem-solving methodology called **object-oriented design (OOD)**. In OOD, the first step is to identify the components, called **objects**. An object combines data and the operations on that data in a single unit. In C++, the mechanism that allows you to combine data and the operations on that data in a single unit is called a class. Now that you know how to store and manipulate data in computer memory and how to construct your own functions, you are ready to learn how objects are constructed. This and subsequent chapters develop and implement programs using OOD. This chapter first explains how to define a class and use it in a program.

Classes

A **class** is a collection of a fixed number of components. The components of a class are called the **members** of the class.

The general syntax for defining a class is:

```
class classIdentifier
{
    classMembersList
};
```

where `classMembersList` consists of variable declarations and/or functions. That is, a member of a `class` can be either a variable (to store data) or a function.

- If a member of a class is a variable, you declare it just like any other variable. Also, in the definition of the class, you cannot initialize a variable when you declare it.

- If a member of a class is a function, you typically use the function prototype to declare that member.

- If a member of a class is a function, it can (directly) access any member of the class—data members (variables) and member functions. That is, when you write the definition of a member function, you can directly access any data members (variable) of the class without passing it as a parameter. The only obvious condition is that you must declare an identifier before you can use it.

In C++, `class` is a reserved word, and it defines only a data type; no memory is allocated. It announces the declaration of a class. Moreover, note the semicolon (`;`) after the right brace. The semicolon is part of the syntax. A missing semicolon, therefore, will result in a syntax error.

The members of a `class` are classified into three categories: `private`, `public`, and `protected`. This chapter mainly discusses the first two types, `private` and `public`.

In C++, `private`, `protected`, and `public` are reserved words, and are called member access specifiers.

Following are some facts about `public` and `private` members of a class:

- By default, all members of a class are `private`.
- If a member of a class is `private`, you cannot access it outside the class. (Example 7-1 illustrates this concept.)
- A `public` member is accessible outside the `class`. (Example 7-1 illustrates this concept.)
- To make a member of a class `public`, you use the member access specifier `public` with a colon, `:`.

Suppose that we want to define a class to implement the time of day in a program. Because a clock gives the time of day, let us call this `class` `clockType`. To represent time in computer memory, we use three `int` variables: one to represent the hours, one to represent the minutes, and one to represent the seconds. Suppose these three variables are `hr`, `min`, and `sec`.

We also want to perform the following operations on the time:

1. Set the time.
2. Retrieve the time.
3. Print the time.
4. Increment the time by one second.
5. Increment the time by one minute.
6. Increment the time by one hour.
7. Compare the two times for equality.

To implement these seven operations, we will write seven functions—`setTime`, `getTime`, `printTime`, `incrementSeconds`, `incrementMinutes`, `incrementHours`, and `equalTime`.

From this discussion, it is clear that the `class` `clockType` has 10 members: three data members (variables) and seven member functions.

Some members of the `class` `clockType` will be `private`; others will be `public`. Deciding which member to make `public` and which to make `private` depends on the nature of the member. The general rule is that any member that needs to be accessed outside the class is declared `public`; any member that should not be accessed directly by the user should be declared `private`. For example, the user should be able to set the time and print the time. Therefore, the members that set the time and print the time should be declared `public`.

Similarly, the members to increment the time, and compare the time for equality, should be declared `public`. On the other hand, users should not control the *direct* manipulation of the data members (variables) `hr`, `min`, and `sec`, so we declare them `private`. If the user has direct access to `hr`, `min`, and `sec`, functions such as `setTime` are not needed.

However, in general, the user should never be provided with direct access to the data members (variables).

The following statements define the **class** clockType:

```
class clockType
{
public:
    void setTime(int, int, int);
    void getTime(int&, int&, int&) const;
    void printTime() const;
    void incrementSeconds();
    void incrementMinutes();
    void incrementHours();
    bool equalTime(const clockType&) const;

private:
    int hr;
    int min;
    int sec;
};
```

The data members (variabes) such as hr, min, and sec are called **instance variables**. (Note that these variables are declared without using the keyword static. Later in this chapter, we will discuss static members of a class.)

In this definition:

- The class clockType has seven member functions: setTime, getTime, printTime, incrementSeconds, incrementMinutes, incrementHours, and equalTime. It has three instance variables: hr, min, and sec.

- The three instance variables—hr, min, and sec—are private to the class and cannot be accessed outside the class. (Example 7-1 illustrates this concept.)

- The seven member functions—setTime, getTime, printTime, incrementSeconds, incrementMinutes, incrementHours, and equalTime—can directly access the instance variables (hr, min, and sec). In other words, when we write the definitions of these functions, we do not pass these instance variables as parameters to the member functions.

- In the function equalTime, the formal parameter is a constant reference parameter. That is, in a call to the function equalTime, the formal parameter receives the address of the actual parameter, but the formal parameter cannot modify the value of the actual parameter. You could have declared the formal parameter as a value parameter, but that would require the formal parameter to copy the value of the actual parameter, which could result in poor performance. (See the section "Reference Parameters and Class Objects (Variables)" in this chapter for an explanation.)

- The word `const` at the end of the member functions `getTime`, `printTime`, and `equalTime` specifies that these functions cannot modify the instance variables of a variable of type `clockType`.

NOTE The `private` and `public` members can appear in any order. If you want, you can declare the `private` members first and then declare the `public` ones. The section "Order of `public` and `private` Members of a Class" in this chapter discusses this issue.

NOTE In the definition of the `class clockType`, all instance variables are `private` and all member functions are `public`. However, a member function can also be `private`. For example, if a member function is used only to implement other member functions of the class, and the user does not need to access this function, you make it `private`. Similarly, an instance variable of a class can also be `public`.

Note that we have not yet written the definitions of the member functions of the class. You will learn how to write them shortly.

The function `setTime` sets the three instance variables—`hr`, `min`, and `sec`—to a given value. The given values are passed as parameters to the function `setTime`. The function `printTime` prints the time, that is, the values of `hr`, `min`, and `sec`. The function `incrementSeconds` increments the time by one second, the function `incrementMinutes` increments the time by one minute, the function `incrementHours` increments the time by one hour, and the function `equalTime` compares two times for equality.

Note that the function `equalTime` has only one parameter, although you need two things to make a comparison. We will explain this point with the help of an example in the section "Implementation of Member Functions" later in this chapter.

Before writing the definitions of the member functions, we introduce another important concept related to classes—constructors.

Constructors

Recall that C++ does not automatically initialize variables when they are declared. Therefore, when an object is instantiated, there is no guarantee that the data members of the object will be initialized. To guarantee that the instance variables of a class are initialized, you use constructors. There are two types of constructors: with parameters and without parameters. The constructor without parameters is called the **default constructor**.

Constructors have the following properties:

- The name of a constructor is the same as the name of the class.

- A constructor, even though it is a function, has no type. That is, it is neither a value-returning function nor a `void` function.

- A class can have more than one constructor. However, all constructors of a class have the same name.

- If a class has more than one constructor, the constructors must have different formal parameter lists. That is, either they have a different number of formal parameters or, if the number of formal parameters is the same, then the data type of the formal parameters, in the order you list, must differ in at least one position.

- Constructors execute automatically when a class object enters its scope. Because they have no types, they cannot be called like other functions.

- Which constructor executes depends on the types of values passed to the class object when the class object is declared.

Let us extend the definition of the **class** clockType by including two constructors.

```
class clockType
{
public:
    void setTime(int, int, int);
    void getTime(int&, int&, int&) const;
    void printTime() const;
    void incrementSeconds();
    void incrementMinutes();
    void incrementHours();
    bool equalTime(const clockType&) const;
    clockType(int, int, int);  //constructor with parameters
    clockType();  //default constructor

private:
    int hr;
    int min;
    int sec;
};
```

Note that the default constructor will initialize the instance variables to 0 and the constructor with parameters will initialize the instance variables to the values specified by the parameters.

Unified Modeling Language Class Diagrams

A class and its members can be described graphically using a notation known as the **Unified Modeling Language** (UML) notation. For example, Figure 7-1 shows the UML class diagram of the **class** clockType.

FIGURE 7-1 UML class diagram of the **class** clockType

The top box contains the name of the class. The middle box contains the instance variables and their data types. The last box contains the member function name, parameter list, and the return type of the function. A + (plus) sign in front of a member name indicates that this member is a **public** member; a – (minus) sign indicates that this is a **private** member. The symbol # before the member name indicates that the member is a **protected** member.

VARIABLE (OBJECT) DECLARATION

Once a class is defined, you can declare variables of that type. In C++ terminology, a class variable is called a **class object** or **class instance**. To help you become familiar with this terminology, from now on we will use the term class object, or simply **object**, for a class variable.

A class can have both types of constructors—default constructor and constructors with parameters. Therefore, when you declare a class object, either the default constructor executes or the constructor with parameters executes. The general syntax for declaring a class object that invokes the default constructor is:

```
className   classObjectName;
```

For example, the statement:

```
clockType myClock;
```

declares myClock to be an object of type clockType. In this case, the default constructor executes and the instance variables of myClock are initialized to 0.

NOTE If you declare an object and want the default constructor to be executed, the empty parentheses after the object name are not required in the object declaration statement. In fact, if you accidentally include the empty parentheses, the compiler generates a syntax error message. For example, the following statement used to declare the object `myClock` is illegal:

```
clockType myClock();    //illegal object declaration
```

The general syntax for declaring a class object that invokes a constructor with a parameter is:

```
className classObjectName(argument1, argument2, ...);
```

where each of `argument1`, `argument2`, and so on is either a variable or an expression.

Note the following:

- The number of arguments and their type should match the formal parameters (in the order given) of one of the constructors.

- If the type of the arguments does not match the formal parameters of any constructor (in the order given), C++ uses type conversion and looks for the best match. For example, an integer value might be converted to a floating-point value with a zero decimal part. Any ambiguity will result in a compile-time error.

Consider the following statement:

```
clockType myClock(5, 12, 40);
```

This statement declares the object `myClock` of type `clockType`. Here, we are passing three values of type `int`, which matches the type of the formal parameters of the constructor with a parameter. Therefore, the constructor with parameters of the **class** `clockType` executes and the three instance variables of the object `myClock` are set to 5, 12, and 40.

Consider the following statements that declare two objects of type `clockType`:

```
clockType myClock(8, 12, 30);
clockType yourClock(12, 35, 45);
```

Each object has 10 members: seven member functions and three instance variables. Each object has separate memory allocated for `hr`, `min`, and `sec`.

In actuality, memory is allocated only for the instance variables of each class object. The C++ compiler generates only one physical copy of a member function of a class, and each class object executes the same copy of the member function. Therefore, whenever we draw the figure of a class object, we will show only the instance variables. As an example,

Figure 7-2 shows the objects `myClock` and `yourClock` with values in their instance variables.

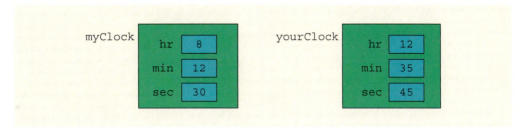

FIGURE 7-2 Objects `myClock` and `yourClock`

ACCESSING CLASS MEMBERS

Once an object of a class is declared, it can access the members of the class. The general syntax for an object to access a member of a class is:

```
classObjectName.memberName
```

In C++, the dot, . (period), is an operator called the **member access operator**.

The class members that a class object can access depend on where the object is declared.

- If the object is declared in the definition of a member function of the class, then the object can access both the **public** and **private** members. (We will elaborate on this when we write the definition of the member function **equalTime** of the **class** **clockType** in the section "Implementation of Member Functions," later in this chapter.)
- If the object is declared elsewhere (for example, in a user's program), then the object can access *only* the **public** members of the class.

Example 7-1 illustrates how to access the members of a class.

EXAMPLE 7-1

Suppose we have the following declaration (say, in a user's program):

```
clockType myClock;
clockType yourClock;
```

Consider the following statements:

```
myClock.setTime(5, 2, 30);
myClock.printTime();
yourClock.setTime(x, y, z);    //assume x, y, and z are
                               //variables of type int
```

7

```
if (myClock.equalTime(yourClock))
    .
    .
    .
```

These statements are legal; that is, they are syntactically correct.

In the first statement, myClock.setTime(5, 2, 30);, the member function setTime is executed. The values 5, 2, and 30 are passed as parameters to the function setTime, and the function uses these values to set the values of the three instance variables hr, min, and sec of myClock to 5, 2, and 30, respectively. Similarly, the second statement executes the member function printTime and outputs the contents of the three instance variables of myClock. In the third statement, the values of the variables x, y, and z are used to set the values of the three instance variables of yourClock.

In the fourth statement, the member function equalTime executes and compares the three instance variables of myClock to the corresponding instance variables of yourClock. Because in this statement equalTime is a member of the object myClock, it has direct access to the three instance variables of myClock. So it needs one more object, which in this case is yourClock, to compare. This explains why the function equalTime has only one parameter.

The objects myClock and yourClock can access only **public** members of the class. Thus, the following statements are illegal because hr and min are declared as **private** members of the **class** clockType and, therefore, cannot be accessed by the objects myClock and yourClock:

```
myClock.hr = 10;                 //illegal
myClock.min = yourClock.min;     //illegal
```

Implementation of Member Functions

When we defined the **class** clockType, we included only the function prototype for the member functions. For these functions to work properly, we must write the related algorithms. One way to implement these functions is to provide the function definition rather than the function prototype in the class itself. Unfortunately, the class definition would then be long and difficult to comprehend. Another reason for providing function prototypes instead of function definitions relates to information hiding; that is, we want to hide the details of the operations on the data from the user.

Next, let us write the definitions of the member functions of the **class** clockType. That is, we will write the definitions of the functions setTime, getTime, printTime, incrementSeconds, equalTime, and so on. Because the identifiers setTime, printTime, and so forth are local to the class, we cannot reference them (directly) outside the class. To reference these identifiers, we use the **scope resolution operator**, :: (double colon). In the function definition's heading, the name of the function is the name of the class, followed by the scope resolution operator, followed by the function name. For example, the definition of the function setTime is as follows:

```
void clockType::setTime(int hours, int minutes, int seconds)
{
    if (0 <= hours && hours < 24)
        hr = hours;
    else
        hr = 0;

    if (0 <= minutes && minutes < 60)
        min = minutes;
    else
        min = 0;

    if (0 <= seconds && seconds < 60)
        sec = seconds;
    else
        sec = 0;
}
```

Note that the definition of the function setTime checks for the valid values of hours, minutes, and seconds. If these values are out of range, the instance variables hr, min, and sec are initialized to 0. Let us now explain how the member function setTime works when accessed by an object of type clockType.

The member function setTime is a **void** function and has three parameters. Therefore,

- A call to this function is a stand–alone statement.
- We must use three parameters in a call to this function.

Furthermore, recall that, because setTime is a member of the **class** clockType, it can directly access the instance variables hr, min, and sec, as shown in the definition of setTime.

Suppose that myClock is an object of type clockType (as declared previously). The object myClock has three instance variables, as shown in Figure 7-3.

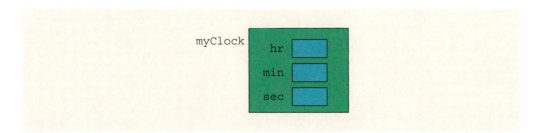

FIGURE 7-3 Object myClock

Consider the following statement:

```
myClock.setTime(3, 48, 52);
```

In the statement `myClock.setTime(3, 48, 52);`, setTime is accessed by the object myClock. Therefore, the three variables—hr, min, and sec—to which the body of the function setTime refers, are the three instance variables of myClock. Thus, the values 3, 48, and 52, which are passed as parameters in the preceding statement, are assigned to the three instance variables of myClock by the function setTime (see the body of the function setTime). After the previous statement executes, the object myClock is as shown in Figure 7-4.

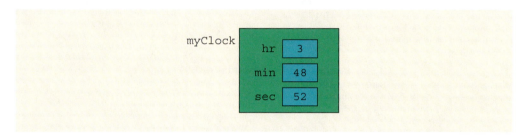

FIGURE 7-4 Object `myClock` after the statement `myClock.setTime(3, 48, 52);` executes

Next, let us give the definitions of the other member functions of the **class** clockType. The definitions of these functions are simple and easy to follow.

```
void clockType::getTime(int& hours, int& minutes,
                        int& seconds) const
{
    hours = hr;
    minutes = min;
    seconds = sec;
}

void clockType::printTime() const
{
    if (hr < 10)
        cout << "0";
    cout << hr << ":";

    if (min < 10)
        cout << "0";
    cout << min << ":";

    if (sec < 10)
        cout << "0";
    cout << sec;
}
```

```
void clockType::incrementHours()
{
    hr++;
    if (hr > 23)
        hr = 0;
}

void clockType::incrementMinutes()
{
    min++;
    if (min > 59)
    {
        min = 0;
        incrementHours(); //increment hours
    }
}

void clockType::incrementSeconds()
{
    sec++;

    if (sec > 59)
    {
        sec = 0;
        incrementMinutes(); //increment minutes
    }
}
```

From the definitions of the functions `incrementMinutes` and `incrementSeconds`, it is clear that a member function of a class can call other member functions of the class.

The function `equalTime` has the following definition:

```
bool clockType::equalTime(const clockType& otherClock) const
{
    return (hr == otherClock.hr
            && min == otherClock.min
            && sec == otherClock.sec);
}
```

(Note that the parameter of the function `equalTime` is `const clockType& otherClock`, which is a constant reference parameter. In the next section, we explain why this parameter is a constant reference parameter.)

Let us see how the member function `equalTime` works.

Suppose that `myClock` and `yourClock` are objects of type `clockType`, as declared previously. Further suppose that we have `myClock` and `yourClock`, as shown in Figure 7-5.

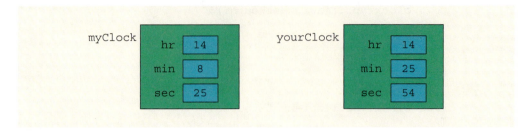

FIGURE 7-5 Objects myClock and yourClock

Consider the following statement:

```
if (myClock.equalTime(yourClock))
   .
   .
   .
```

In the expression

```
myClock.equalTime(yourClock)
```

the object myClock accesses the member function equalTime. Because otherClock is a reference parameter, the address of the actual parameter yourClock is passed to the formal parameter otherClock, as shown in Figure 7-6.

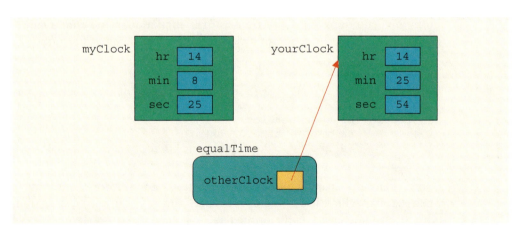

FIGURE 7-6 Object myClock and parameter otherClock

The instance variables hr, min, and sec of otherClock have the values 14, 25, and 54, respectively. In other words, when the body of the function equalTime executes, the value of otherClock.hr is 14, the value of otherClock.min is 25, and the value of otherClock.sec is 54. The function equalTime is a member of myClock. When the function equalTime executes, the variables hr, min, and sec in the body of the function equalTime are the instance variables of the variable myClock. Therefore, the member hr of myClock is compared with otherClock.hr, the member min of myClock is compared with otherClock.min, and the member sec of myClock is compared with otherClock.sec.

Once again, from the definition of the function equalTime, it is clear why this function has only one parameter.

Let us again look at the definition of the function equalTime. Notice that within the definition of this function, the object otherClock accesses the instance variables hr, min, and sec. However, these instance variables are **private**. So is there any violation? The answer is no. The function equalTime is a member of the **class** clockType and hr, min, and sec are the instance variables. Moreover, otherClock is an object of type clockType. Therefore, the object otherClock can access its **private** instance variables within the definition of the function equalTime.

The same is true for any member function of a class. In general, when you write the definition of a member function, say dummyFunction, of a **class**, say dummyClass, and the function uses an object, dummyObject of the **class** dummyClass, then within the definition of dummyFunction, the object dummyObject can access its **private** instance variables (in fact, any **private** member of the class).

This definition of the **class** clockType includes two constructors: one with three parameters and one without any parameters. Let us now write the definitions of these constructors.

```
clockType::clockType()   //default constructor
{
    hr = 0;
    min = 0;
    sec = 0;
}

clockType::clockType(int hours, int minutes, int seconds)
{
    if (0 <= hours && hours < 24)
        hr = hours;
    else
        hr = 0;

    if (0 <= minutes && minutes < 60)
        min = minutes;
    else
        min = 0;

    if (0 <= seconds && seconds < 60)
        sec = seconds;
    else
        sec = 0;
}
```

From the definitions of these constructors, it follows that the default constructor sets the three instance variables—hr, min, and sec—to 0. Also, the constructor with parameters sets the instance variables to whatever values are assigned to the formal parameters. Moreover, we can write the definition of the constructor with parameters by calling the function setTime, as follows:

```
clockType::clockType(int hours, int minutes, int seconds)
{
    setTime(hours, minutes, seconds);
}
```

Once a class is properly defined and implemented, it can be used in a program. A program or software that uses and manipulates the objects of a class is called a **client** of that class.

When you declare objects of the **class** clockType, every object has its own copy of the instance variables hr, min, and sec. In object-oriented terminology, variables such as hr, min, and sec are called **instance variables** of the class because every object has its own instance of the data.

REFERENCE PARAMETERS AND CLASS OBJECTS (VARIABLES)

Recall that when a variable is passed by value, the formal parameter copies the value of the actual parameter. That is, memory to copy the value of the actual parameter is allocated for the formal parameter. As a parameter, a class object can be passed by value.

Suppose that a class has several instance variables requiring a large amount of memory to store data, and you need to pass a variable by value. The corresponding formal parameter then receives a copy of the data of the variable. That is, the compiler must allocate memory for the formal parameter, so as to copy the value of the instance variables of the actual parameter. This operation might require, in addition to a large amount of storage space, a considerable amount of computer time to copy the value of the actual parameter into the formal parameter.

On the other hand, if a variable is passed by reference, the formal parameter receives only the address of the actual parameter. Therefore, an efficient way to pass a variable as a parameter is by reference. If a variable is passed by reference, then when the formal parameter changes, the actual parameter also changes. Sometimes, however, you do not want the function to be able to change the values of the instance variables. In C++, you can pass a variable by reference and still prevent the function from changing its value by using the keyword const in the formal parameter declaration. As an example, consider the following function definition:

```
void testTime(const clockType& otherClock)
{
    clockType dClock;
    .
    .
    .
}
```

The function `testTime` contains a reference parameter, `otherClock`. The parameter `otherClock` is declared using the keyword `const`. Thus, in a call to the function `testTime`, the formal parameter `otherClock` receives the address of the actual parameter, but `otherClock` cannot modify the contents of the actual parameter. For example, after the following statement executes, the value of `myClock` will not be altered:

```
testTime(myClock);
```

Generally, if you want to declare a class object as a value parameter, you declare it as a reference parameter using the keyword `const`, as described previously.

Recall that if a formal parameter is a value parameter, within the function definition you can change the value of the formal parameter. That is, you can use an assignment statement to change the value of the formal parameter (which, of course, would have no effect on the actual parameter). However, if a formal parameter is a constant reference parameter, you cannot use an assignment statement to change its value within the function, nor can you use any other function to change its value. Therefore, within the definition of the function `testTime`, you cannot alter the value of `otherClock`. For example, the following would be illegal in the definition of the function `testTime`:

```
otherClock.setTime(5, 34, 56); //illegal
otherClock = dClock;           //illegal
```

BUILT-IN OPERATIONS ON CLASSES

The two built-in operations that are defined for class objects are member access (`.`) and assignment (`=`). You have seen how to access an individual member of a class by using the name of the class object, then a dot, and then the member name.

We now show how an assignment statement works with the help of an example.

ASSIGNMENT OPERATOR AND CLASSES

Suppose that `myClock` and `yourClock` are variables of type `clockType` as defined previously. Furthermore, suppose that the values of `myClock` and `yourClock` are as shown in Figure 7-7.

FIGURE 7-7 Objects `myClock` and `yourClock`

The statement

```
myClock = yourClock;          //Line 1
```

copies the value of `yourClock` into `myClock`. That is,

- the value of `yourClock.hr` is copied into `myClock.hr`,
- the value of `yourClock.min` is copied into `myClock.min`, and
- the value of `yourClock.sec` is copied into `myClock.sec`.

In other words, the values of the three instance variables of `yourClock` are copied into the corresponding instance variables of `myClock`. Therefore, an assignment statement performs a member-wise copy. After the statement in Line 1 executes, the values of `myClock` and `yourClock` are as shown in Figure 7-8.

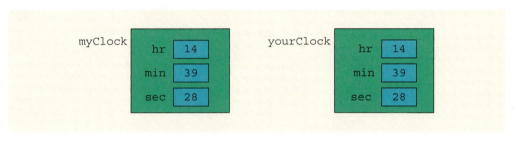

FIGURE 7-8   Objects `myClock` and `yourClock` after the assignment statement
`myClock = yourClock;` executes

Class Scope

A `class` object can be either automatic (that is, created each time the control reaches its declaration, and destroyed when the control exits the surrounding block) or static (that is, created once, when the control reaches its declaration, and destroyed when the program terminates). Also, you can declare an array of `class` objects. A `class` object has the same scope as other variables. A member of a `class` is local to the `class`. You access a `class` member outside the `class` by using the `class` object name and the member access operator (`.`).

Functions and Classes

The following rules describe the relationship between functions and classes:

- Class objects can be passed as parameters to functions and returned as function values.
- As parameters to functions, classes can be passed either by value or by reference.
- If a class object is passed by value, the contents of the instance variables of the actual parameter are copied into the corresponding instance variables of the formal parameter.

Accessor and Mutator Functions

Let us look at the member functions of the **class** clockType. The function setTime sets the values of the instance variables to the values specified by the user. In other words, the function setTime alters or modifies the values of the instance variables. Similarly, the functions incrementSeconds, incrementMinutes, and incrementHours also modify the instance variables. On the other hand, functions such as getTime, printTime, and equalTime only *access* the values of the instance variables. They *do not* modify the instance variables. We can, therefore, categorize the member functions of the **class** clockType into two categories: member functions that modify the instance variables, and member functions that only access, and do not modify, the instance variables.

This is typically true for any class. That is, every class has member functions that only access and do not modify the instance variables, called accessor functions, and member functions that modify the instance variables, called mutator functions.

Accessor function: A member function of a class that only accesses (that is, does not modify) the values of the data members (instance variables).

Mutator function: A member function of a class that modifies the values of the data members (instance variables).

Because an accessor function only accesses the values of the instance variables, as a safeguard we typically include the reserved word **const** at the end of the headings of these functions. Moreover, a constant member function of a class cannot modify the instance variables of that class. For example, see the headings of the member functions getTime, printTime, and equalTime of the **class** clockType.

A member function of a class is called a **constant function** if its heading contains the reserved word **const** at the end. For example, the member functions getTime, printTime, and equalTime of the **class** clockType are constant functions. A constant member function of a class cannot modify the instance variables of that class, and so these are accessor functions. One thing that should be remembered about constant member functions is that a constant member function of a class can *only* call other constant member functions of that class. Therefore, you should be careful when you make a member function constant.

Now that you know how to design a class and write the definitions of the member functions, the next obvious question is how to use a class in a program. To be specific, the question is how to use the **class** clockType. One way to use this class is to put the definition of the class, the definition of the member functions, and the program containing the functions main in one file, and then compile and execute the program. The program Ch7_ClockProg.cpp at the Web site accompanying this book illustrates how how to put the definition of a class, the definitions of the member functions, and the functions main in one file. However, in objected-oriented programming, typically, the definition of the class, the definitions of the member functions, and the program using the class are placed in separate files.

Using the class clockType

To implement `clockType` in a program, the user must declare objects of type `clockType`, and know which operations are allowed and what the operations do. So the user must have access to the specification details. Because the user is not concerned with the implementation details, we must put those details in a separate file, called an **implementation file**. Also, because the specification details can be too long, we must free the user from having to include them directly in the program. However, the user must be able to look at the specification details so that he or she can correctly call the functions, and so forth. We must therefore put the specification details in a separate file. The file that contains the specification details is called the **header file** (or **interface file**).

The implementation file contains the definitions of the functions to implement the operations of an object. This file contains, among other things (such as the preprocessor directives), the C++ statements. Because a C++ program can have only one function, `main`, the implementation file does not contain the function `main`. Only the user program contains the function `main`. Because the implementation file does not contain the function `main`, we cannot produce the executable code from this file. In fact, we produce what is called the object code from the implementation file. The user then links the object code produced by the implementation file with the object code of the program that uses the class to create the final executable code.

Finally, the header file has an extension h, whereas the implementation file has an extension cpp. Suppose that the specification details of the **class** `clockType` are in a file called `clockType`. The complete name of this file should then be `clockType.h`. If the implementation details of the class `clockType` are in a file—say, `clockTypeImp`—the name of this file must be `clockTypeImp.cpp`.

The file `clockTypeImp.cpp` contains only the definitions of the functions, not the definition of the class. Thus, to resolve the problem of an undeclared identifier (such as the function names and variable names), we include the header file `clockType.h` in the file `clockTypeImp.cpp` with the help of the `include` statement. The following `include` statement is required by any program that uses the **class** `clockType`, as well as by the implementation file that defines the operations for the **class** `clockType`:

```
#include "clockType.h"
```

Note that the header file `clockType.h` is enclosed in double quotation marks, not angular brackets. The header file `clockType.h` is called the user-defined header file. Typically, all user-defined header files are enclosed in double quotation marks, whereas the system-provided header files (such as `iostream`) are enclosed between angular brackets.

The implementation contains the definitions of the functions, and these definitions are hidden from the user because the user is typically provided *only* the object code. However, the user of the class should be aware of what a particular function does and how to use it. Therefore, in the specification file with the function prototypes, we include comments that briefly describe the function and specify any preconditions and/or postconditions.

Precondition: A statement specifying the condition(s) that must be true before the function is called.

Postcondition: A statement specifying what is true after the function call is completed.

Following are the specification and implementation files for the `class` clockType:

```cpp
//************************************************************
// Author: D.S. Malik
//
// class clockType.h
// This class specifies the members to implement time in a
// program.
//************************************************************

class clockType
{
public:
    void setTime(int hours, int minutes, int seconds);
      //Function to set the time.
      //The time is set according to the parameters.
      //Postcondition: hr = hours; min = minutes;
      //               sec = seconds;
      //               The function checks whether the
      //               values of hours, minutes, and seconds
      //               are valid. If a value is invalid, the
      //               default value 0 is assigned.

    void getTime(int& hours, int& minutes, int& seconds) const;
      //Function to return the time.
      //Postcondition: hours = hr; minutes = min;
      //               seconds = sec;

    void printTime() const;
      //Function to print the time.
      //Postcondition: The time is printed in the form
      //               hh:mm:ss.

    void incrementSeconds();
      //Function to increment the time by one second.
      //Postcondition: The time is incremented by one second.
      //               If the before-increment time is
      //               23:59:59, the time is reset to 00:00:00.

    void incrementMinutes();
      //Function to increment the time by one minute.
      //Postcondition: The time is incremented by one minute.
      //               If the before-increment time is
      //               23:59:53, the time is reset to 00:00:53.
```

7

```
    void incrementHours();
      //Function to increment the time by one hour.
      //Postcondition: The time is incremented by one hour.
      //                If the before-increment time is
      //                23:45:53, the time is reset to 00:45:53.

    bool equalTime(const clockType& otherClock) const;
      //Function to compare the two times.
      //Postcondition: Returns true if this time is equal to
      //                otherClock; otherwise, returns false.

    clockType(int hours, int minutes, int seconds);
      //Constructor with parameters.
      //The time is set according to the parameters.
      //Postcondition: hr = hours; min = minutes;
      //                sec = seconds;
      //                The constructor checks whether the
      //                values of hours, minutes, and seconds
      //                are valid. If a value is invalid, the
      //                default value 0 is assigned.

    clockType();
      //Default constructor
      //The time is set to 00:00:00.
      //Postcondition: hr = 0; min = 0; sec = 0;

private:
    int hr;  //variable to store the hours
    int min; //variable to store the minutes
    int sec; //variable to store the seconds
};
```

Next, we describe the implementation file, clockTypeImp.cpp, that contains the definitions of member functions of the class clockType.

```
//*********************************************************
// Author: D.S. Malik
//
// Implementation file clockTypeImp.cpp
// This file contains the definitions of the functions to
// implement the operations of the classes clockType.
//*********************************************************

#include <iostream>
#include "clockType.h"

using namespace std;
    .
    .
    .

//Place the definitions of the member functions of the class
//clockType here.
    .
    .
    .
```

NOTE Note that the header file `clockType.h` and the implementation file `clockTypeImp.cpp` are separate files. To save space, we have not provided the complete details of the implementation file. However, you can find this file and the specification (header) file at the Web site accompanying this book.

Next, we describe the user file containing the program that uses the **class** `clockType`. To use the **class** `clockType`, the program must include the header file `clockType.h` via the **include** statement. The following program illustrates how this is done.

```
//************************************************************
// Author: D.S. Malik
//
// This program uses the class clockType to implement time.
//************************************************************

#include <iostream>                                //Line 1
#include "clockType.h"                             //Line 2

using namespace std;                               //Line 3

int main()                                         //Line 4
{                                                  //Line 5
    clockType myClock;                             //Line 6
    clockType yourClock;                           //Line 7

    int hours;                                     //Line 8
    int minutes;                                   //Line 9
    int seconds;                                   //Line 10

    myClock.setTime(5, 4, 30); //Set the time of myClock; Line 11

    cout << "Line 12: myClock: ";                  //Line 12
    myClock.printTime();  //print the time of myClock;   Line 13
    cout << endl;                                  //Line 14

    cout << "Line 15: yourClock: ";                //Line 15
    yourClock.printTime(); //print yourClock         Line 16
    cout << endl;                                  //Line 17

    yourClock.setTime(5, 45, 16); //Set the time of
                                  //yourClock;        Line 18

    cout << "Line 19: After setting, yourClock: ";  //Line 19
    yourClock.printTime(); //print yourClock ;       Line 20
    cout << endl;                                  //Line 21


    if (myClock.equalTime(yourClock)) //Compare myClock
                                      //and yourClock;   Line 22
```

7

```
        cout << "Line 23: Both times are equal."
             << endl;                                    //Line 23
    else                                                 //Line 24
        cout << "Line 25: The two times are not equal."
             << endl;                                    //Line 25

    cout << "Line 26: Enter the hours, minutes, and "
         << "seconds: ";                                 //Line 26
    cin >> hours >> minutes >> seconds;                  //Line 27
    cout << endl;                                        //Line 28


    myClock.setTime(hours, minutes, seconds); //Set the time
                    //of myClock using the value of the variables
                    //hours, minutes, and seconds.       Line 29

    cout << "Line 30: New myClock: ";                    //Line 30
    myClock.printTime();      //print the time of myClock;  Line 31
    cout << endl;                                        //Line 32


    myClock.incrementSeconds();    //Increment the time of
                                   //myClock by one second; Line 33

    cout << "Line 34: After incrementing myClock by "
         << "one second, myClock: ";                     //Line 34
    myClock.printTime();      //print the time of myClock   Line 35
    cout << endl;                                        //Line 36


    myClock.getTime(hours, minutes, seconds);   //Retrieve the
                    //hours, minutes, and seconds of myClock;  Line 37

    cout << "Line 38: hours = " << hours
         << ", minutes = " << minutes
         << ", seconds = " << seconds << endl;           //Line 38

    return 0;                                            //Line 38
}//end main                                              //Line 40
```

Sample Run: In this sample run, the user input is shaded.

```
Line 12: myClock: 05:04:30
Line 15: yourClock: 00:00:00
Line 19: After setting, yourClock: 05:45:16
Line 23: The two times are not equal.
Line 26: Enter the hours, minutes, and seconds: 5 23 59

Line 30: New myClock: 05:23:59
Line 34: After incrementing myClock by one second, myClock: 05:24:00
Line 38: hours = 5, minutes = 24, seconds = 0
```

Executable Code

To use an object in a program, during execution the program must be able to access the implementation details of the object (that is, the algorithms to implement the operations on the object). This section discusses how a client's program obtains access to the implementation details of an object. For illustration purposes, we will use the **class** clockType.

As explained previously, to use the **class** clockType, the program must include the header file clockType.h via the **include** statement. For example, the following program segment includes the header file clockType.h:

```
//Program test.cpp

#include "clockType.h"
  .
  .
  .
int main()
{
    .
    .
    .
}
```

The program test.cpp must include only the header file, not the implementation file. To create the executable code to run the program test.cpp, the following steps are required:

1. We separately compile the file clockTypeImp.cpp and create the object code file clockTypeImp.obj. The object code file contains the machine language code, but the code is not in an executable form. Suppose that the command cc invokes the C++ compiler or linker, or both, on the computer's system command line. The command

   ```
   cc -c clockTypeImp.cpp
   ```

   creates the object code file clockTypeImp.obj.

2. To create the executable code for the source code file test.cpp, we compile the source code file test.cpp, create the object code file test.obj, and then link the files test.obj and clockTypeImp.obj to create the executable file test.exe. The following command on the system command line creates the executable file test.exe:

   ```
   cc test.cpp clockTypeImp.obj
   ```

7

NOTE

1. To link more than one object code file with a source code file, we list all of the object code files on the system command line. For example, to link **A.obj** and **B.obj** with the source code file **test.cpp**, we use the following command:

   `cc test.cpp A.obj B.obj`

2. If a source code file is modified, it must be recompiled.

3. If modifications in one source file affect other files, the other files must be recompiled and relinked.

4. The user must have access to the header file and the object code file. Access to the header file is needed to see what the objects do and how to use them. Access to the object code file is needed so that the user can link the program with the object code to produce an executable code. The user does not need access to the source code file containing the implementation details.

As stated in Chapter 0, various IDE's put the editor, compiler, and linker all into one package. With one command, the program is compiled and linked with the other necessary files. These systems also manage multiple-file programs in the form of a project. Thus, a project consists of several files called the project files. The implementation file, the specification file, and the file containing the main program are added in a single project.

These systems usually have a command, called **build**, **rebuild**, or **make**. (Check your system's documentation.) When the build, rebuild, or make command is applied to a project, the system automatically compiles and links all the files required to create the executable code. When one or more files in the project change, you can use these commands to recompile and relink the files.

Once the executable code is constructed, you use the IDE's appropriate command to execute the program. Because the commands are specific to an IDE, we encourage you to check your system's documentation.

Order of `public` and `private` Members of a Class

C++ has no fixed order in which you declare `public` and `private` members; you can declare them in any order. The only thing you need to remember is that, by default, all members of a class are `private`. You must use the member access specifier `public` to make a member available for `public` access. If you decide to declare the `private` members after the `public` members (as is done in the case of `clockType`), you must use the member access specifier `private` to begin the declaration of the `private` members.

It is a common practice to list all of the `public` members first, and then the `private` members. This way, you can focus your attention on the `public` members.

CONSTRUCTORS AND DEFAULT PARAMETERS (OPTIONAL)

A constructor can also have default parameters. In such cases, the rules for declaring formal parameters are the same as those for declaring default formal parameters in a function. Moreover, actual parameters to a constructor with default parameters are passed according to the rules for functions with default parameters. (Chapter 5 discusses functions with default parameters.) Using the rules for defining default parameters, in the definition of the **class** clockType, you can replace both constructors using the following statement. (Recall that in the function prototype, the name of a formal parameter is optional.)

```
clockType clockType(int = 0, int = 0, int = 0);    //Line 1
```

In the implementation file, the definition of this constructor is the same as the definition of the constructor with parameters.

If you replace the constructors of the **class** clockType with the constructor in Line 1 (the constructor with the default parameters), then you can declare clockType objects with zero, one, two, or three arguments as follows:

```
clockType clock1;                  //Line 2
clockType clock2(5);               //Line 3
clockType clock3(12, 30);          //Line 4
clockType clock4(7, 34, 18);       //Line 5
```

The instance variables of clock1 are initialized to 0. The instance variable hr of clock2 is initialized to 5, and the instance variables min and sec of clock2 are initialized to 0. The instance variable hr of clock3 is initialized to 12, the instance variable min of clock3 is initialized to 30, and the instance variable sec of clock3 is initialized to 0. The instance variable hr of clock4 is initialized to 7, the instance variable min of clock4 is initialized to 34, and the instance variable sec of clock4 is initialized to 18.

Using these conventions, we can say that a constructor that has no parameters, or has all default parameters, is called the **default constructor**.

Classes and Constructors: A Precaution

As discussed in the preceding section, constructors provide guaranteed initialization of the object's instance variables. Typically, the default constructor is used to initialize the instance variables to some default values, and this constructor has no parameters. A constructor with parameters is used to initialize the instance variables to some specific values.

We have seen that if a class has no constructor(s), then the object created is uninitialized because C++ does not automatically initialize variables when they are declared. In reality, if a class has no constructor(s), then C++ automatically provides the default constructor. However, this default constructor does not do anything. The object declared is still uninitialized.

The important things to remember about classes and constructors are the following:

- If a class has no constructor(s), C++ *automatically provides* the default constructor. However, the object declared is still uninitialized.

- On the other hand, suppose a **class**, say dummyClass, includes constructor(s) with parameter(s) and does not include the default constructor. In this case, C++ *does not* provide the default constructor for the **class** dummyClass. Therefore, when an object of the **class** dummyClass is declared, we must include the appropriate arguments in its declaration.

The following code further explains this. Consider the definition of the following class:

```
class dummyClass
{
public:
    void print() const;

    dummyClass(int dX, int dY);

private:
    int x;
    int y;
};
```

The **class** dummyClass *does not* have the default constructor. It has a constructor with parameters. Given this definition of the **class** dummyClass, the following object declaration is legal:

```
dummyClass myObject(10, 25);   //object declaration is legal
```

However, because the **class** dummyClass does not contain the default constructor, the following declaration is incorrect and would generate a syntax error:

```
dummyClass dummyObject;   //incorrect object declaration
```

Therefore, to avoid such pitfalls, if a class has constructor(s), the class should also include the default constructor.

Destructors

Like constructors, destructors are also functions. Moreover, like constructors, a destructor does not have a type. That is, it is neither a value-returning function nor a void function. However, a class can have only one destructor, and the destructor has no parameters. The name of a destructor is the *tilde* character (~), followed by the name of the class. For example, the name of the destructor for the **class** clockType is:

```
~clockType();
```

The destructor automatically executes when the class object goes out of scope. A use of destructors is illustrated in Chapter 9.

Arrays of Class Objects and Constructors

Just as you can declare arrays of simple data types, you can also declare arrays of objects. Now, if a class has constructors and you declare an array of that class's objects, the class should have the default constructor. The default constructor is typically used to initialize each (array) class object.

For example, if you declare an array of 100 class objects, then it is impractical (if not impossible), to specify different constructors for each component. (We will further clarify this at the end of this section.)

Suppose that you have 100 employees who are paid on an hourly basis and you need to keep track of their arrival and departure times. You can declare two arrays—`arrivalTimeEmp` and `departureTimeEmp`—of 100 components each, wherein each component is an object of type `clockType`.

Consider the following statement:

```
clockType arrivalTimeEmp[100];                    //Line 1
```

The statement in Line 1 creates the array of objects `arrivalTimeEmp[0]`, `arrivalTimeEmp[1]`, ..., `arrivalTimeEmp[99]`, as shown in Figure 7-9.

7

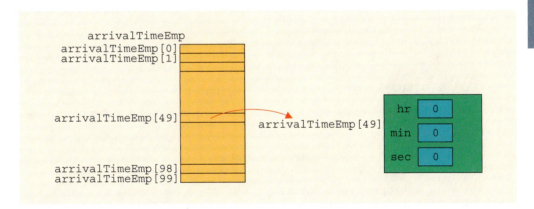

FIGURE 7-9 Array `arrivalTimeEmp`

You can now use the functions of the **class** `clockType` to manipulate the time for each employee. For example, the following statement sets the arrival time, that is, `hr`, `min`, and `sec`, of the 50th employee to `8`, `5`, and `10`, respectively. (See Figure 7-10.)

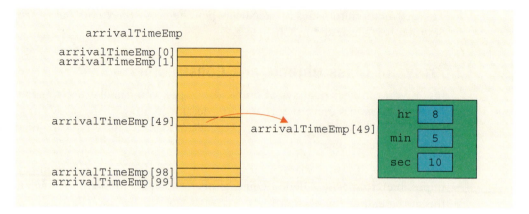

FIGURE 7-10 Array `arrivalTimeEmp` after setting the time of the 50th employee

```
arrivalTimeEmp[49].setTime(8, 5, 10);          //Line 2
```

To output the arrival time of each employee, you can use a loop such as the following:

```
for (int j = 0; j < 100; j++)                   //Line 3
{
    cout << "Employee " << (j + 1)
         << " arrival time: ";
    arrivalTimeEmp[j].printTime();              //Line 4
    cout << endl;
}
```

The statement in Line 4 outputs the arrival time of an employee in the form `hr:min:sec`.

To keep track of the departure time of each employee, you can use the array `departureTimeEmp`.

Similarly, you can use arrays to manage a list of names or other objects.

NOTE   Before leaving our discussion of arrays of class objects, we want to point out the following: The beginning of this section stated that if you declare an array of class objects and the class has constructor(s), then the class should have the default constructor. The compiler uses the default constructor to initialize the array of objects. If the array size is large, then it is impractical to specify a different constructor with parameters for each object. For a small array, we can manage to specify a different constructor with parameters.

For example, the following statement declares clocks to be an array of two components. The member variables of the first component are initialized to 8, 35, and 42, respectively. The member variables of the second component are initialized to 6, 52, and 39, respectively.

```
clockType clocks[2] = {clockType(8, 35, 42), clockType(6, 52, 39)};
```

In fact, the expression `clockType(8, 35, 42)` creates an anonymous object of the `class clockType`; initializes its member variables to 8, 35, and 42, respectively; and then uses a member-wise copy to initialize the object `clocks[0]`.

Consider the following statement, which creates the object `myClock` and initializes its member variables to 10, 45, and 38, respectively. This is how we have been creating and initializing objects. In fact, the statement:

```
clockType myClock(10, 45, 38);
```

is equivalent to the statement:

```
clockType myClock = clockType(10, 45, 38);
```

However, the first statement is more efficient. It does not first require that an anonymous object be created and then member-wise copied in order to initialize `myClock`.

The main point that we are stressing here, as well as having discussed it in the preceding section, is the following: To avoid any pitfalls, if a class has constructor(s), it should also have the default constructor. However, in some cases, default values provided for instance variables by a default constructor might create unintended, unacceptable duplication, in which cases a default constructor can be inappropriate.

7

Debugging—Design Walk-Throughs

In Chapters 1 and 2, you learned about using code walk-throughs to find and remove bugs from programs. The same principles apply to design walk-throughs. Typically, a design walk-through takes place as the design is being finalized and before any code is written.

Except for the syntactic bugs that show up in your program, many of the bugs that you encounter in your programs creep in at design time. Sometimes an important operation is omitted. Sometimes we fail to consider potential future use of the class, and we make a class needlessly specialized. Sometimes too much is expected of a single function, when instead two or more functions should be written to achieve the intended objective. Sometimes not all the data members required by the function are identified and provided. Sometimes the value to be produced and returned by the function is characterized improperly. Sometimes the `public` or `private` status of a member is determined incorrectly. For example, a `public` data member is seldom if ever appropriate. All of these problems can be corrected at design time, before a single line of code is written.

Sometimes, in the interest of generality, programmers provide functions that are unlikely to ever be used. This creates excess baggage that can make it difficult to design, implement, test, and maintain programs. Occasionally, data members are passed into a function even though the function makes no use of them, or a function returns a value that is never used. All of these excesses make programs more difficult to develop. As a programmer, you should take steps to avoid them.

As with a code walk-through, a programmer begins by trying to find and fix these problems herself/himself. The programmer should verify that each intended operation is represented by one or more functions. He/she should verify that each function receives only the data members needed to achieve that function's intended objective. He/she should verify that any intended value is returned by the function. He/she should review the `public` or `private` status of each member. Next, the programmer thinks through the ranges of data that could be passed to each function. By walking through it in his/her mind, the programmer verifies that, in every case, the function performs as intended with each variety of data that could be passed to it.

At this point, it may be prudent for the programmer to repeat the design walk-through process with someone who is learning to design programs or who has learned to design programs already. As always, the programmer should be sure that he/she has prepared his/her design carefully before presenting it to someone else. In the process of doing so, he/she may find and correct one or more bugs that he/she missed during his/her previous design review. As the programmer explains his/her design, both he/she and the intended audience will have an opportunity to look carefully and methodically at each aspect.

As before, avoid the temptation to shortchange the design phase by "cutting to the chase." Deficiencies encountered at design time are much easier to correct than deficiencies encountered after coding has begun.

Data Abstraction, Classes, and Abstract Data Types

For the car that we drive, most of us want to know how to start the car and drive it. Most people are not concerned with the complexity of how the engine works. By separating the design details of a car's engine from its use, the manufacturer helps the driver focus on how to drive the car. Our daily life has other similar examples. For the most part, we are concerned only with how to use certain items, rather than with how they work.

Separating the design details (that is, how the car's engine works) from its use is called **abstraction**. In other words, abstraction focuses on what the engine does and not on how it works. Thus, abstraction is the process of separating the logical properties from the implementation details. Driving the car is a logical property; the construction of the engine constitutes the implementation details. We have an abstract view of what the engine does but are not interested in the engine's actual implementation.

Abstraction can also be applied to data. Earlier sections of this chapter defined a data type `clockType`. The data type `clockType` has three instance variables and the following basic operations:

1. Set the time.
2. Return the time.
3. Print the time.
4. Increment the time by one second.
5. Increment the time by one minute.
6. Increment the time by one hour.
7. Compare two times to see whether they are equal.

The actual implementation of the operations on, that is, the definitions of the member functions of the class, `clockType` was postponed.

Data abstraction is defined as a process of separating the logical properties of the data from its implementation. The definition of `clockType` and its basic operations are the logical properties; storing `clockType` objects in the computer, and the algorithms to perform these operations, are the implementation details of `clockType`.

Abstract data type (ADT): A data type that separates the logical properties from the implementation details.

Like any other data type, an ADT has three things associated with it: the name of the ADT, called the **type name**; the set of values belonging to the ADT, called the **domain**; and the set of **operations** on the data. Following these conventions, we can define the `clockType` ADT as follows:

```
dataTypeName
    clockType

domain
    Each clockType value is a time of day in the form of hours,
    minutes, and seconds.

operations
    Set the time.
    Return the time.
    Print the time.
    Increment the time by one second.
    Increment the time by one minute.
    Increment the time by one hour.
    Compare the two times to see whether they are equal.
```

The next obvious question is how to implement an ADT in a program. To implement an ADT, you must represent the data and write algorithms to perform the operations.

The previous section used classes to group data and functions together. Furthermore, our definition of a class consisted only of the specifications of the operations; functions to implement the operations were written separately. Thus, we see that classes are a convenient way to implement an ADT. In fact, in C++, classes were specifically designed to handle ADTs.

EXAMPLE 7-2

Suppose that we want to define the **class** thermometer to represent the temperature (current, minimum, and maximum) for the day. Also suppose that temperature is represented as an integer. We want to perform the following operations related to the temperature:

1. Set the current temperature.
2. Get the current temperature.
3. Get the maximum temperature.
4. Get the minimum temperature.
5. Print the current, maximum, and minimum temperatures.

To implement these five operations, we write five algorithms, which we implement as functions—five functions to implement five operations. We also include a function to update the temperature. The instance variables are currentTemp, maxTemp, and minTemp. So far, the **class** thermometer has nine members: three instance variables and six functions.

The definition of the **class** thermometer is:

```
//**********************************************************
// Author: D.S. Malik
//
// This class is designed to store the current, maximum, and
// minimum temperatures of the day.
//**********************************************************

class thermometer
{
public:
    void setTemperature(int cTemp);
        //Function to set the current temperature
        //The current temperature is set according to the
        //parameter cTemp. After setting the current temperature,
        //maximum and minimum temperatures also are updated.
        //Postcondition: currentTemp = cTemp;
        //               update maximum and minimum
        //               temperatures

    void updateMaxMinTemp(int currentTemperature);
        //Function to update the maximum and minimum temperatures.
        //This is a private function. It is used by the function
        //setTemperature.
```

```
    int getCurrentTemperature() const;
        //Function to return the current temperature.
        //Postcondition: The value of currentTemp is returned.

    int getMaxTemperature() const;
        //Function to return the maximum temperature.
        //Precondition: A prior call to function setTemperature
        //Postcondition: The value of maxTemp is returned.

    int getMinTemperature() const;
        //Function to return the minimum temperature.
        //Precondition: A prior call to method setTemperature
        //Postcondition: The value of minTemp is returned.

    void print() const;
        //Function to output the temperature.
        //Postcondition: The current, maximum, and minimum
        //               temperatures of the day are printed.

    thermometer();
        //Default constructor
        //Postcondition: maxTemp = Integer.MIN_VALUE;
        //               minTemp = Integer.MAX_VALUE;
        //               currentTemp = 0;

    thermometer(int cTemp);
        //Constructor with parameters, to set the current
        //temperature.
        //The temperature is set according to the parameters
        //Postcondition: currentTemp = cTemp;
        //               maxTemp = cTemp;
        //               minTemp = cTemp;

private:
    int maxTemp;    //store maximum temperature of the day
    int minTemp;    //store minimum temperature of the day
    int currentTemp; //store current temperature of the day
};
```

7

We leave it as an exercise for you to draw the UML class diagram of the **class** thermometer. (See Exercise 10 at the end of this chapter.) Next, we write the definitions of the functions and constructors of the **class** thermometer. The definitions are straightforward and easy to follow. The function definitions are:

```
void thermometer::setTemperature(int cTemp)
{
    currentTemp = cTemp;
    updateMaxMinTemp(currentTemp);
}
```

```cpp
void thermometer::updateMaxMinTemp(int currentTemperature)
{
    if (currentTemp > maxTemp)
        maxTemp = currentTemp;

    if (currentTemp < minTemp)
        minTemp = currentTemp;
}

int thermometer::getCurrentTemperature() const
{
    return currentTemp;
}

int thermometer::getMaxTemperature() const
{
    return maxTemp;
}

int thermometer::getMinTemperature() const
{
    return minTemp;
}

void thermometer::print() const
{
    cout << "Current temperature: " << currentTemp << endl
         << "Maximum temperature: " << maxTemp  << endl
         << "Minimum temperature: " << minTemp << endl;
}
```

The definitions of the constructors are:

```cpp
thermometer::thermometer()
{
    maxTemp = INT_MIN;
    minTemp = INT_MAX;
    currentTemp = 0;
}

thermometer::thermometer(int cTemp)
{
    currentTemp = cTemp;
    maxTemp = cTemp;
    minTemp = cTemp;
}
```

The following program illustrates how to use the **class** thermometer in a program.

```cpp
//*************************************************************
// Author: D.S. Malik
//
// This program tests various operations of the class thermometer.
//*************************************************************
```

```
#include <iostream>                                      //Line 1
#include "thermometer.h"                                 //Line 2

using namespace std;                                     //Line 3

int main()                                               //Line 4
{                                                        //Line 5
    thermometer myThermometer(35);                       //Line 6
    thermometer yourThermometer;                         //Line 7

    int temperature;                                     //Line 8

    cout << "Line 9: myThermometer:" << endl;            //Line 9
    myThermometer.print();                               //Line 10

    cout << "Line 11: yourThermometer:" << endl;         //Line 11
    yourThermometer.print();                             //Line 12

    yourThermometer.setTemperature(34);                  //Line 13

    cout << "Line 14: After setting yourThermometer:"
         << endl;                                        //Line 14
    yourThermometer.print();                             //Line 15

    cout << "Line 16: Enter the current temperature:";   //Line 16
    cin >> temperature;                                  //Line 17
    cout << endl;                                        //Line 18

    myThermometer.setTemperature(temperature);           //Line 19

    cout << "Line 20: myThermometer:" << endl;           //Line 20
    myThermometer.print();                               //Line 21

    return 0;                                            //Line 22
}//end main                                              Line 23
```

7

Sample Run: (In this sample run, the user input is shaded.)

```
Line 9: myThermometer:
Current temperature: 35
Maximum temperature: 35
Minimum temperature: 35
Line 11: yourThermometer:
Current temperature: 0
Maximum temperature: -2147483648
Minimum temperature: 2147483647
Line 14: After setting yourThermometer:
Current temperature: 34
Maximum temperature: 34
Minimum temperature: 34
Line 16: Enter the current temperature: 45
```

```
Line 20: myThermometer:
Current temperature: 45
Maximum temperature: 45
Minimum temperature: 35
```

The preceding program works as follows. The statement in Line 6 creates the object myThermometer and sets the current temperature associated with this object to 35. The statement in Line 7 creates the object yourThermometer and, using the default constructor, sets the current temperature associated with this object to 0. The statement in Line 8 declares the int variable temperature. The statement in Line 10 outputs the temperature associated with the object myThermometer. Similarly, the statement in Line 12 outputs the temperature associated with the object yourThermometer.

The statement in Line 13 sets the current temperature associated with yourThermometer to 34. The statement in Line 15 outputs the temperature associated with the object yourThermometer. The statement in Line 16 prompts the user to enter the value of temperature. The statement in Line 17 stores the value entered by the user in the variable temperature. The statement in Line 19 uses the function setTemperature of the class thermometer to set the current temperature associated with the object myThermometer to the value of the variable temperature. The statement in Line 21 outputs the temperature of the object myThermometer.

The class personType that is designed in Example 7-3 is quite useful; we will use this class in subsequent chapters.

EXAMPLE 7-3

The most common attributes of a person are the person's first name and last name. The typical operations on a person's name are to set the name and print the name. The following statements define a class with these properties.

```
//***********************************************************
// Author: D.S. Malik
//
// class personType
// This class specifies the members to implement a name.
//***********************************************************

#include <string>

using namespace std;

class personType
{
public:
    void print() const;
        //Function to output the first name and last name
        //in the form firstName lastName.
```

```
    void setName(string first, string last);
      //Function to set firstName and lastName according
      //to the parameters.
      //Postcondition: firstName = first; lastName = last

    string getFirstName() const;
      //Function to return the first name.
      //Postcondition: The value of firstName is returned.

    string getLastName() const;
      //Function to return the last name.
      //Postcondition: The value of lastName is returned.

    personType();
      //Default constructor
      //Sets firstName and lastName to null strings.
      //Postcondition: firstName = ""; lastName = "";

    personType(string first, string last);
      //Constructor with parameters.
      //Sets firstName and lastName according to the parameters.
      //Postcondition: firstName = first; lastName = last;

private:
    string firstName; //variable to store the first name
    string lastName;  //variable to store the last name
};
```

Figure 7-11 shows the UML class diagram of the **class** personType.

```
                        personType
─────────────────────────────────────────────
-firstName: string
-lastName: string
─────────────────────────────────────────────
+print(): void
+setName(string, string): void
+getFirstName() const: string
+getLastName() const: string
+personType()
+personType(string, string)
```

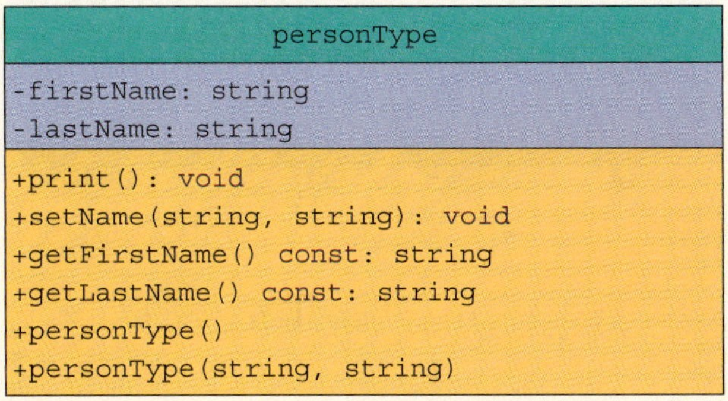

FIGURE 7-11 UML class diagram of the **class** personType

We now give the definitions of the member functions of the **class** personType.

7

```cpp
void personType::print() const
{
    cout << firstName << " " << lastName;
}

void personType::setName(string first, string last)
{
    firstName = first;
    lastName = last;
}

string personType::getFirstName() const
{
    return firstName;
}

string personType::getLastName() const
{
    return lastName;
}

    //Default constructor
personType::personType()
{
    firstName = "";
    lastName = "";
}

    //Constructor with parameters
personType::personType(string first, string last)

{
    firstName = first;
    lastName = last;
}
```

Avoiding Bugs: One-Piece-at-a-Time Coding

Except for the simplest problems, a solution consists of several pieces that work together. In C++, classes and objects—consisting of data, functions, and sometimes inner classes—are the pieces that work together to provide a solution.

After the problem is understood fully, the solution is designed. All design decisions should be made during the design phase, before any code is written. This includes the design of every class needed to solve the problem, the determination of how the classes relate to each other, and often, the determination of the specific objects of each class needed to solve the problem. The design of each class includes the determination of the data elements and functions of each class, including which functions provide services to the user and which functions provide support for other functions.

It would be a mistake to attempt to design all or several pieces at once. Instead, we can begin at level 0, the level of the original problem. We ask ourselves how this problem can be broken down into a few subproblems, which we can call level-1 problems. Chances are, the level-1 problems will need to be broken down into smaller subproblems, which we can call level-2 problems. We do this by picking one of the level-1 problems for further subdivision into level-2 problems. Then we have a choice: we can subdivide one of the level-2 problems, or we can subdivide one of the remaining level-1 problems. A good rule of thumb is to pick a remaining problem whose subdivision is obvious. Subdivision continues in this manner until the solution to each subproblem is so clear that it can be designed directly. By picking a problem for subdivision where the subdivision is obvious, we are tackling a relatively easy task from among the remaining tasks. After tackling a relatively easy task, the solution to one or more of the remaining tasks often becomes clear, and we find that we are able to complete all the tasks without ever encountering a task that seems overly challenging. Designing a solution by starting with the original problem and subdividing it into smaller problems reflects a divide-and-conquer and top-down design approach. Both are proven techniques that work for many kinds of problems, including most or all of the problems you will encounter as a beginning programmer.

Coding proceeds in a similar manner. The function `main` corresponds to level 0 of the problem solution. The function `main` often contains calls to other functions, each of which corresponds to a solution to one of the level-1 problems. Similarly, each of the functions representing the solution to a level-1 problem often contains calls to other functions, each of which represents a solution to one of the level-2 problems, and so on until we reach levels where solutions can be coded directly without further subdivision. The implementation reflects the design exactly.

Again, it would be a mistake to attempt to code all or several pieces at once, so we code a piece at a time. Neither classes nor functions need to be coded in the order used to design them. Nevertheless, the same rule of thumb applies: Pick a remaining task whose implementation is clear and code it. As before, we tackle a relatively easy task from among the remaining tasks. Having done so, the solution to one or more of the remaining tasks often becomes obvious, and we find that we are able to complete all the tasks without encountering a particularly challenging task.

The divide-and-conquer approach really should be called the divide-conquer-and-reassemble approach. If we want to build an automobile, it is not sufficient simply to identify the parts that make up an automobile, and then to build each part, making sure that it is exactly as we intended. It is necessary to make all the parts of the automobile work together. Similarly, it is not sufficient simply to code all the required classes with their data and functions, and to instantiate all the necessary objects. We need to make them work together to provide the intended solution. This is achieved by calling the intended functions at the intended times, as specified in the design, passing the intended parameter(s) when a function is called, returning the intended value from each value-returning function, and manipulating the instance variables of any objects passed to the function, as intended.

The task of building a solution (a program) that consists of several pieces is simplified when we code it a piece at a time. The first version of a solution should be a working program with perhaps only a single feature—generally one that is easy to provide. That program is saved. Then, work continues by adding the next easy-to-provide feature, saving the revised program using a different name. After all, a working program with fewer features is better than a nonworking program with more features; we do not want to overwrite our working program with a nonworking program, even if the nonworking program has more features. This process continues, adding perhaps just one feature at a time until all the intended features are present and the solution is complete.

Static Members of a Class (Optional)

In Chapter 5, we described two types of variables, automatic and `static`. Recall that if a local variable of a function is `static`, it exists between function calls. Similarly to `static` variables, a class can have `static` members, functions, or variables. Let us note the following about the `static` members of a class:

- If a function of a class is `static`, in the class definition it is declared using the keyword `static` in its heading.
- If a data member of a class is `static`, it is declared using the keyword `static`, as discussed in Chapter 5 and also illustrated in Example 7-4.
- A `public static` member, function, or variable of a class can be accessed using the class name and the scope resolution operator.

Example 7-4 clarifies the effect of the keyword `static`.

EXAMPLE 7-4

Consider the following definition of the `class` illustrate:

```
//**********************************************************
// Author: D.S. Malik
//
// The class is designed to show how static members of a class
// are defined.
//**********************************************************

class illustrate
{
public:
    void setX(int a);
        //Function to set x.
        //Postcondition: x = a
```

```
    int getX() const;
        //Function to return the value of the instance variables.
        //Postcondition: The value of x is returned.

    int getCount() const;
        //Function to return the value of the static variable
        //count.
        //Postcondition: The value of count is returned.

    static void incrementCount();
        //Function to increment the value of the private
        //static member count.
        //Postcondition: count is incremented by 1.

    void print() const;
        //Function to print the values of the instance
        //and static variables as a string.
        //Postcondition: The values of x and count
        //                 are printed.

    illustrate();
        //Default constructor
        //Postcondition: x = 0

    illustrate(int a);
        //Constructor with parameters
        //Postcondition: x = a

private:
    int x;
    static int count;
};
```

7

Suppose that the **static** data members (variables), and the definitions of the member functions of the **class** illustrate, are as follows. (These statements are all placed in the implementation file. Also notice that all **static** variables are initialized as shown below.)

```
int illustrate::count = 0;

void illustrate::setX(int a)
{
    x = a;
}

int illustrate::getX() const
{
    return x;
}

int illustrate::getCount() const
{
    return count;
}
```

```
void illustrate::incrementCount()
{
    count++;
}

void illustrate::print( )const
{
    cout << "x = " << x << " and count = " << count << endl;
}

illustrate::illustrate()
{
    x = 0;
}

illustrate::illustrate(int a)
{
    x = a;
}
```

Furthermore, suppose that you have the following declaration:

```
illustrate illusObject;
```

The object illusObject can access any **public** member of the **class** illustrate. So the following statement is legal:

```
illusObject.incrementCount();
```

The function incrementCount is **static** and **public**, so the following statement is legal:

```
illustrate::incrementCount();
```

In essence, **public static** members of a **class** can be accessed either by an object of the **class** type and the dot operator, or by using the **class** name and the scope resolution operator.

Next, we elaborate on **static** data members a bit more. Suppose that you have a **class**, say myClass, with data members (**static** as well as non-**static**). When you create objects of type myClass, only non-**static** data members of the **class** myClass become the data members of each object. For each **static** data member of a **class**, C++ allocates only one memory space. All myClass objects refer to the same memory space. In fact, **static** data members of a **class** *exist* even when no object of that **class** type exists. You can access the **public static** data members outside the **class** as explained in the previous section.

Example 7-5 further clarifies how memory space is allocated for **static** and non-**static** data members of a class.

Suppose that you have the **class** illustrate as given in Example 7-4. Memory space then exists for the **static** variable count.

Consider the following statements:

```
illustrate illusObject1(3);    //Line 1
illustrate illusObject2(5);    //Line 2
```

The statements in Line 1 and Line 2 declare illusObject1 and illusObject2 to be illustrate type objects. (See Figure 7-12.)

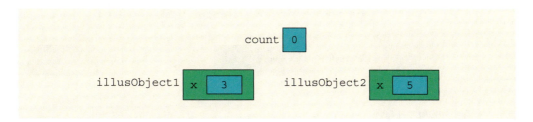

FIGURE 7-12 illusObject1 and illusObject2

Now consider the following statement:

```
illustrate::incrementCount();
```

After this statement executes, the objects and static members are as shown in Figure 7-13.

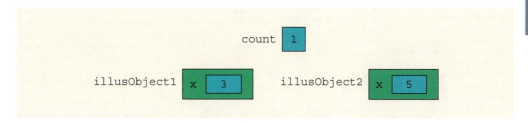

FIGURE 7-13 illusObject1 and illusObject2 after the statement illustrate:: incrementCount(); executes

The output of the statement

```
illusObject1.print();
```

is:

```
x = 3 and count = 1
```

Similarly, the output of the statement

```
illusObject2.print();
```

is:

x = 5 and   count = 1

Now consider the statement:

illusObject1.incrementCount();

After this statement executes, the objects and static members are as shown in Figure 7-14.

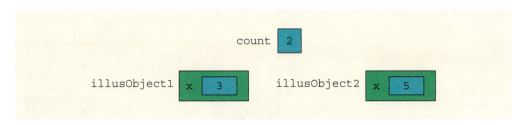

FIGURE 7-14   illusObject1 and illusObject2 after the statement
illusObject1.incrementCount(); executes

The output of the statements

illusObject1.print();
illusObject2.print();

is:

x = 3 and count = 2
x = 5 and count = 2

The program in Example 7-5 further illustrates how **static** members of a class work.

EXAMPLE 7-5

```
//************************************************************
// Author: D.S. Malik
//
// This program shows how static members of a class work.
// ************************************************************

#include <iostream>                              //Line 1
#include "illustrate.h"                          //Line 2

using namespace std;                             //Line 3

int main()                                       //Line 4
{                                                //Line 5
    illustrate illusObject1(3);                  //Line 6
    illustrate illusObject2(5);                  //Line 7
```

```
        cout << "Line 8: ***Increment count using "
            << "the class illustrate***" << endl;          //Line 8

        illustrate::incrementCount();                       //Line 9
        illusObject1.print();                               //Line 10
        illusObject2.print();                               //Line 11

        cout << "Line 12: ***Increment count using "
            << "illusObject1***" << endl;                   //Line 12

        illusObject1.incrementCount();                      //Line 13
        illusObject1.setX(8);                               //Line 14
        illusObject1.print();                               //Line 15
        illusObject2.print();                               //Line 16

        cout << "Line 17: ***Increment count using "
            << "illusObject2***" << endl;                   //Line 17

        illusObject2.incrementCount();                      //Line 18
        illusObject2.setX(23);                              //Line 19
        illusObject1.print();                               //Line 20
        illusObject2.print();                               //Line 21

        return 0;                                           //Line 22
}                                                           //Line 23
```

7

Sample Run:

```
Line 8: ***Increment count using the class illustrate***
x = 3 and count = 1
x = 5 and count = 1
Line 12: ***Increment count using illusObject1***
x = 8 and count = 2
x = 5 and count = 2
Line 17: ***Increment count using illusObject2***
x = 8 and count = 3
x = 23 and count = 3
```

The preceding program works as follows. The **static** variable count is initialized to 0. The statement in Line 6 declares illusObject1 to be an object of the **class** illustrate and initializes its instance variable **x** to 3. The statement in Line 7 declares illusObject2 to be an object of the **class** illustrate and initializes its instance variable **x** to 5.

The statement in Line 9 uses the name of the **class** illustrate and the function incrementCount to increment count. The statements in Lines 10 and 11 output the data stored in the objects illusObject1 and illusObject2. Notice that the value of count for both objects is the same.

The statement in Line 12 is an output statement. The statement in Line 13 uses the object illusObject1 and the function incrementCount to increment count. The statement in Line 14 sets the value of the instanace variable **x** of illusObject1 to 8. Lines 15 and

16 output the data stored in the objects `illusObject1` and `illusObject2`. Notice that the value of `count` for both objects is the same. Also, notice that the statement in Line 14 changes only the value of the instance variable `x` of `illusObject1` because `x` is *not* a `static` member of the **class** `illustrate`.

The statement in Line 18 uses the object `illusObject2` and the function `incrementCount` to increment `count`. The statement in Line 19 sets the value of the instance variable `x` of `illusObject2` to 23. Lines 20 and 21 output the data stored in the objects `illusObject1` and `illusObject2`. Notice that the value of `count` for both objects is the same. Also, notice that the statement in Line 19 changes only the value of the instance variable `x` of `illusObject2`, because `x` is *not* a `static` member of the **class** `illustrate`.

 NOTE Here are some additional comments on `static` members of a class. As you have seen in this section, a `static` member function of a class does not need any object to be invoked. It can be called using the name of the class and the scope resolution operator, as illustrated. Therefore, a `static` member function cannot use anything that depends on a calling object. In other words, in the definition of a `static` member function, you cannot use a non-`static` data member or a non-`static` function, unless there is an object declared locally that accesses the non-`static` data member(s) or the non-`static` member function(s).

Let us again consider the **class** `illustrate`, as defined in Example 7-4. This class contains both `static` and non-`static` data members. When we declare objects of this class, each object has its own copy of the instance variable `x`, which is non-`static`, and all objects share the data member `count`, which is `static`. Earlier in this chapter, we defined the terminology instance variables of a class using the **class** `clockType`. However, at that point, we did not discuss `static` data members of a class. A class can have `static` as well as non-`static` data members. We can, therefore, make the general statement that non-`static` data members of a class are called the *instance variables* of the class.

A **struct** versus a **class**

In this chapter, you learned how to group related values that are of different types. C++ provides another structured data type, called a **struct** (some languages use the term "record") to group related items of different types. The general syntax of a **struct** in C++ is:

```
struct structName
{
    dataType1 identifier1;
    dataType2 identifier2;
        .
        .
        .
    dataTypen identifiern;
};
```

In C++, **struct** is a reserved word. The members of a **struct**, even though enclosed in braces (that is, they form a block), are not considered to form a compound statement. Thus, a semicolon (after the right brace) is essential to end the **struct** statement. A semicolon at the end of the **struct** definition is, therefore, a part of the syntax.

The statement

```
struct studentType
{
    string firstName;
    string lastName;
    char courseGrade;
    int testScore;
    int programmingScore;
    double GPA;
};
```

defines a **struct** studentType with 6 members. The members firstName and lastName are of type string; courseGrade is of type char; testScore and programmingScore are of the type int, and GPA is of the type double.

Once a data type is defined, you can declare variables of that type. Let us first define a **struct** type, studentType, and then declare variables of that type.

```
studentType newStudent;
studentType student;
```

These statements declare two **struct** variables, newStudent and student, of the type studentType. The memory allocated is large enough to store firstName, lastName, courseGrade, testScore, programmingScore, and GPA.

Just as with classes, you use the **struct** variable name together with the member name; these names are separated by a dot (period). Suppose you want to initialize the member GPA of newStudent to 0.0. The following statement accomplishes this task:

```
newStudent.GPA = 0.0;
```

Similarly, the statements:

```
newStudent.firstName = "John";
newStudent.lastName = "Brown";
```

7

store "John" in the member firstName and "Brown" in the member lastName of newStudent.

As noted, a struct is a fixed collection of components, wherein the components can be of different types. This definition of components in a struct included only data members. However, a C++ struct is very similar to a C++ class. As with a class, members of a struct can also be functions, including constructors and a destructor. The only difference between a struct and a class is that, by default, all members of a struct are public, and all members of a class are private. You can use the member access specifier private in a struct to make a member private.

In C, the definition of a struct is similar to the definition of a struct in C++ as given earlier. Because C++ evolved from C, the standard C-structs are perfectly acceptable in C++. However, the definition of a struct in C++ was expanded to include member functions and constructors and destructors. Both C++ classes and structs have the same capabilities. However, most programmers restrict their use of structures to adhere to their C-like structure form, and so do not use them to include member functions. In other words, if all of the data members of a class are public and the class has no member functions, you typically use a struct to group these members.

PROGRAMMING EXAMPLE: Fruit Juice Machine

A new fruit juice machine has been purchased for the cafeteria, and a program is needed to make the machine function properly. The machine dispenses apple juice, orange juice, mango lassi, and fruit punch in recyclable containers. In this programming example, we write a program for the fruit juice machine so that it can be put into operation.

The program should do the following:

1. Show the customer the different products sold by the juice machine.
2. Let the customer make the selection.
3. Show the customer the cost of the item selected.
4. Accept money from the customer.
5. Release the item.

Input   The item selection and the cost of the item.

Output   The selected item.

PROBLEM ANALYSIS AND ALGORITHM DESIGN

A juice machine has two main components: a built-in cash register and several dispensers to hold and release the products.

Cash Register Let us first discuss the properties of a cash register. The cash register has some cash on hand, it accepts the amount from the customer, and if the amount deposited is more than the cost of the item, then—if possible—the cash register returns the change. For simplicity, we assume that the user deposits the exact amount of money for the product. The cash register should also be able to show the juice machine's owner the amount of money in the register at any given time. The following class defines the properties of a cash register.

```cpp
//****************************************************************
// Author: D.S. Malik
//
// class cashRegister
// This class specifies the members to implement a cash register.
//****************************************************************

class cashRegister
{
public:
    int getCurrentBalance() const;
      //Function to show the current amount in the cash
      //register.
      //Postcondition: The value of cashOnHand is returned.

    void acceptAmount(int amountIn);
      //Function to receive the amount deposited by
      //the customer and update the amount in the register.
      //Postcondition: cashOnHand = cashOnHand + amountIn;

    cashRegister();
      //Default constructor
      //Sets the cash in the register to 500 cents.
      //Postcondition: cashOnHand = 500.

    cashRegister(int cashIn);
      //Constructor with a parameter.
      //Sets the cash in the register to a specific amount.
      //Postcondition: cashOnHand = cashIn;

private:
    int cashOnHand;   //variable to store the cash
                      //in the register
};
```

7

Figure 7-15 shows the UML class diagram of the **class** cashRegister.

cashRegister
-cashOnHand: int
+getCurrentBalance() const: int +acceptAmount(int): void +cashRegister() +cashRegister(int)

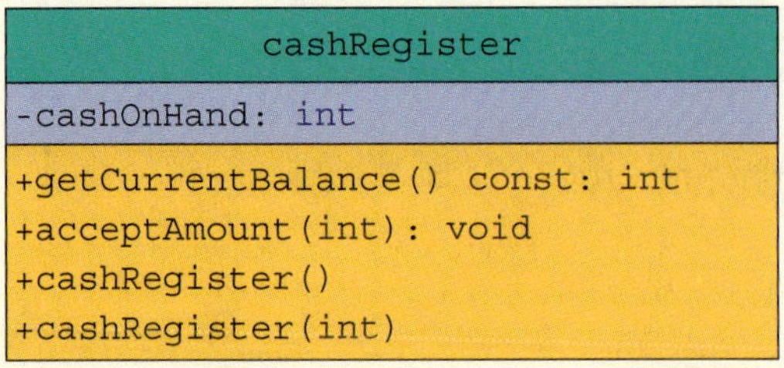

FIGURE 7-15 UML class diagram of the **class** cashRegister

Next, we give the definitions of the functions to implement the operations of the **class** cashRegister. The definitions of these functions are simple and easy to follow.

The function getCurrentBalance shows the current amount in the cash register. It returns the value of the instance variable cashOnHand. So, its definition is the following:

```
int cashRegister::getCurrentBalance() const
{
    return cashOnHand;
}
```

The function acceptAmount accepts the amount of money deposited by the customer. It updates the cash in the register by adding the amount deposited by the customer to the previous amount in the cash register. Essentially, the definition of this function is:

```
void cashRegister::acceptAmount(int amountIn)
{
    cashOnHand = cashOnHand + amountIn;
}
```

The default constructor sets the cashOnHand to 500 and the constructor with a parameter sets the value of cashOnHand to the value specified by the user. The definitions of these constructors are:

```
cashRegister::cashRegister()
{
    cashOnHand = 500;
}
```

```
cashRegister::cashRegister(int cashIn)
{
    if (cashIn >= 0)
        cashOnHand = cashIn;
    else
        cashOnHand = 500;
}
```

Note that the definition of the constructor with a parameter checks for valid values of the parameter `cashIn`. If the value of `cashIn` is less than 0, the value assigned to the instance variable `cashOnHand` is 500.

Dispenser The dispenser releases the selected item if it is not empty. The dispenser should show the number of items in the dispenser and the cost of the item. The following class defines the properties of a dispenser. Let us call this **class dispenserType**.

```cpp
//***********************************************************
// Author: D.S. Malik
//
// class dispenserType
// This class specifies the members to implement a dispenser.
//***********************************************************

class dispenserType
{
public:
    int getNoOfItems() const;
      //Function to show the number of items in the machine.
      //Postcondition: The value of numberOfItems is returned.

    int getCost() const;
      //Function to show the cost of the item.
      //Postcondition: The value of cost is returned.

    void makeSale();
      //Function to reduce the number of items by 1.
      //Postcondition: numberOfItems--;

    dispenserType();
      //Default constructor
      //Sets the cost and number of items in the dispenser
      //to 50.
      //Postcondition: numberOfItems = 50; cost = 50;

    dispenserType(int setNoOfItems, int setCost);
      //Constructor with parameters
      //Sets the cost and number of items in the dispenser
      //to the values specified by the user.
      //Postcondition: numberOfItems = setNoOfItems;
      //               cost = setCost;

private:
    int numberOfItems;   //variable to store the number of
                         //items in the dispenser
    int cost;  //variable to store the cost of an item
};
```

Figure 7-16 shows the UML class diagram of the **class** dispenserType.

```
                    dispenserType
-numberOfItems: int
-cost: int
+getNoOfItems() const: int
+getCost() const: int
+makeSale(): void
+dispenserType()
+dispenserType(int, int)
```

FIGURE 7-16   UML class diagram of the **class** dispenserType

Because the juice machine sells four types of items, we shall declare four objects of type dispenserType. For example, the statement

```
dispenserType appleJuice(100, 50);
```

declares appleJuice to be an object of type dispenserType, and sets the number of apple juice cans in the dispenser to 100 and the cost of each can to 50 cents. (See Figure 7-17.)

FIGURE 7-17   Object appleJuice

Next, we discuss the definitions of the functions to implement the operations of the **class** dispenserType.

The function getNoOfItems returns the number of items of a particular product. Because the number of items currently in the dispenser is stored in the instance variable numberOfItems, the function returns the value of numberOfItems. The definition of this function is:

```
int dispenserType::getNoOfItems() const
{
    return numberOfItems;
}
```

The function `getCost` returns the cost of a product. Because the cost of a product is stored in the instance variable `cost`, the function returns the value of `cost`. The definition of this function is:

```
int dispenserType::getCost() const
{
    return cost;
}
```

When a product is sold, the number of items in that dispenser is reduced by 1. Therefore, the function `makeSale` reduces the number of items in the dispenser by 1. That is, it decrements the value of the instance variable `numberOfItems` by 1. The definition of this function is:

```
void dispenserType::makeSale()
{
    numberOfItems--;
}
```

The default constructor sets the values of the instance variables to 50. The constructor with parameters sets the values of the instance variables to the values specified by the user. The definitions of these constructors are:

```
dispenserType::dispenserType()
{
    numberOfItems = 50;
    cost = 50;
}
```

```
dispenserType::dispenserType(int setNoOfItems, int setCost)
{
    if (setNoOfItems >= 0)
        numberOfItems = setNoOfItems;
    else
        numberOfItems = 50;

    if (setCost >= 0)
        cost = setCost;
    else
        cost = 50;
}
```

MAIN
PROGRAM

When the program executes, it must do the following:

1. Show the different products sold by the juice machine.
2. Show how to select a particular product.
3. Show how to terminate the program.

7

Furthermore, these instructions must be displayed after processing each selection (except exiting the program), so that the user need not remember what to do if he or she wants to buy two or more items. Once the user has made the appropriate selection, the juice machine must act accordingly. If the user has opted to buy a product and if that product is available, the juice machine should show the cost of the product and ask the user to deposit the money. If the amount deposited is at least the cost of the item, the juice machine should sell the item and display an appropriate message.

This discussion translates into the following algorithm:

1. Show the selection to the customer.

2. Get the selection.

3. If the selection is valid and the dispenser corresponding to the selection is not empty, sell the product.

We divide this program into three functions—showSelection, sellProduct, and main.

showSelection This function displays the information necessary to help the user select and buy a product. Essentially, it contains the following output statements. (We assume that the juice machine sells four types of products.)

```
*** Welcome to Shelly's Fruit Juice Shop ***
To select an item, enter
1 for apple juice
2 for orange juice
3 for mango lassi
4 for fruit punch
9 to exit
```

This definition of the function showSelection is:

```cpp
void showSelection()
{
    cout << "*** Welcome to Shelly's Fruit Juice Shop ***" << endl;
    cout << "To select an item, enter " << endl;
    cout << "1 for apple juice" << endl;
    cout << "2 for orange juice" << endl;
    cout << "3 for mango lassi" << endl;
    cout << "4 for fruit punch" << endl;
    cout << "9 to exit" << endl;
}//end showSelection
```

sellProduct This function attempts to sell the product selected by the customer. Therefore, it must have access to the dispenser holding the product. The first thing that this function does is check whether the dispenser holding the product is empty. If the dispenser is empty, the function informs the customer that this product is sold out. If the dispenser is not empty, it tells the user to deposit the necessary amount to buy the product.

If the user does not deposit enough money to buy the product, `sellProduct` tells the user how much additional money must be deposited. If the user fails to deposit enough money, in two tries, to buy the product, then the function simply returns the money. (Programming Exercise 5, at the end of this chapter, asks you to revise the definition of the function `sellProduct` so that it keeps asking the user to enter the additional amount as long as the user has not entered enough money to buy the product.) If the amount deposited by the user is sufficient, it accepts the money and sells the product. Selling the product means to decrement the number of items in the dispenser by 1, and to update the money in the cash register by adding the cost of the product. (Because this program does not return the extra money deposited by the customer, the cash register is updated by adding the money entered by the user.)

From this discussion, it is clear that the function `sellProduct` must have access to the dispenser holding the product (to decrement the number of items in the dispenser by 1 and to show the cost of the item) as well as the cash register (to update the cash). Therefore, this function has two parameters: one corresponding to the dispenser and the other corresponding to the cash register. Furthermore, both parameters must be referenced.

In pseudocode, the algorithm for this function is:

1. If the dispenser is not empty
   a. Show and prompt the customer to enter the cost of the item.
   b. Get the amount entered by the customer.
   c. If the amount entered by the customer is less than the cost of the product
      i. Show and prompt the customer to enter the additional amount.
      ii. Calculate the total amount entered by the customer.
   d. If the amount entered by the customer is at least the cost of the product
      i. Update the amount in the cash register.
      ii. Sell the product—that is, decrement the number of items in the dispenser by 1.
      iii. Display an appropriate message.
   e. If the amount entered by the user is less than the cost of the item, return the amount.
2. If the dispenser is empty, tell the user that this product is sold out.

This definition of the function `sellProduct` is:

```cpp
void sellProduct(dispenserType& product,
                 cashRegister& pCounter)
{
    int amount;   //variable to hold the amount entered
    int amount2;  //variable to hold the extra amount needed

    if (product.getNoOfItems() > 0) //if the dispenser is not
                                    //empty
    {
        cout << "Please deposit " << product.getCost()
             << " cents" << endl;
        cin >> amount;

        if (amount < product.getCost())
        {
            cout << "Please deposit another "
                 << product.getCost()- amount
                 << " cents" << endl;
            cin >> amount2;
            amount = amount + amount2;
        }

        if (amount >= product.getCost())
        {
            pCounter.acceptAmount(amount);
            product.makeSale();
            cout << "Collect your item at the bottom and "
                 << "enjoy." << endl;
        }
        else
            cout << "The amount is not enough. "
                 << "Collect what you deposited." << endl;

        cout << "*-*-*-*-*-*-*-*-*-*-*-*-*-*-*-*-*-*-*-*"
             << endl << endl;
    }
    else
        cout << "Sorry, this item is sold out." << endl;
}//end sellProduct
```

Now that we have described the functions `showSelection` and `sellProduct`, the function `main` is described next.

main The algorithm for the function `main` is as follows:

1. Create the cash register—that is, declare a variable of type `cashRegister`.

2. Create four dispensers—that is, declare four objects of type `dispenserType` and initialize these objects. For example, the statement

   ```
   dispenserType mangoLassi(100, 45);
   ```

   creates a dispenser object, `mangoLassi`, to hold the juice cans. The number of items in the dispenser is 100, and the cost of an item is 45 cents.

3. Declare additional variables as necessary.

4. Show the selection; call the function `showSelection`.

5. Get the selection.

6. While not done (a selection of 9 exits the program)

   a. Sell the product; call the function `sellProduct`.

   b. Show the selection; call the function `showSelection`.

   c. Get the selection.

The definition of the function `main` is as follows:

```cpp
int main()
{
    cashRegister counter;
    dispenserType appleJuice(100, 50);
    dispenserType orangeJuice(100, 65);
    dispenserType mangoLassi(75, 45);
    dispenserType fruitPunch(100, 85);

    int choice;   //variable to hold the selection

    showSelection();
    cin >> choice;

    while (choice != 9)
    {
        switch (choice)
        {
        case 1:
            sellProduct(appleJuice, counter);
            break;

        case 2:
            sellProduct(orangeJuice, counter);
            break;
```

7

```
        case 3:
            sellProduct(mangoLassi, counter);
            break;

        case 4:
            sellProduct(fruitPunch, counter);
            break;

        default:
            cout << "Invalid selection." << endl;
        }//end switch

        showSelection();
        cin >> choice;
    }//end while

    return 0;
}//end main
```

COMPLETE PROGRAM LISTING

In the previous sections, we designed the classes to implement cash registers and dispensers to design a fruit juice machine. In this section, for the sake of completeness, we give complete definitions of the classes, the implementation files, and the user program to create a fruit juice machine.

```
//************************************************************
// Author: D.S. Malik
//
// class cashRegister
// This class specifies the members to implement a cash
// register.
//************************************************************

class cashRegister
{
public:
    int getCurrentBalance() const;
        //Function to show the current amount in the cash
        //register.
        //Postcondition: The value of cashOnHand is returned.

    void acceptAmount(int amountIn);
        //Function to receive the amount deposited by
        //the customer and update the amount in the register.
        //Postcondition: cashOnHand = cashOnHand + amountIn;
```

```cpp
    cashRegister();
        //Default constructor
        //Sets the cash in the register to 500 cents.
        //Postcondition: cashOnHand = 500.

    cashRegister(int cashIn);
        //Constructor with a parameter.
        //Sets the cash in the register to a specific amount.
        //Postcondition: cashOnHand = cashIn;

private:
    int cashOnHand;      //variable to store the cash
                         //in the register
};


//***********************************************************
// Author: D.S. Malik
//
// Implementation file cashRegisterImp.cpp
// This file contains the definitions of the functions to
// implement the operations of the class cashRegister.
//***********************************************************

#include <iostream>
#include "cashRegister.h"

using namespace std;

int cashRegister::getCurrentBalance() const
{
    return cashOnHand;
}

void cashRegister::acceptAmount(int amountIn)
{
    cashOnHand = cashOnHand + amountIn;
}

cashRegister::cashRegister()
{
    cashOnHand = 500;
}

cashRegister::cashRegister(int cashIn)
{
    if (cashIn >= 0)
        cashOnHand = cashIn;
    else
        cashOnHand = 500;
}
```

7

```
//**********************************************************
// Author: D.S. Malik
//
// class dispenserType
// This class specifies the members to implement a dispenser.
//**********************************************************

class dispenserType
{
public:
    int getNoOfItems() const;
      //Function to show the number of items in the machine.
      //Postcondition: The value of numberOfItems is returned.

    int getCost() const;
      //Function to show the cost of the item.
      //Postcondition: The value of cost is returned.

    void makeSale();
      //Function to reduce the number of items by 1.
      //Postcondition: numberOfItems--;

    dispenserType();
      //Default constructor
      //Sets the cost and number of items in the dispenser
      //to 50.
      //Postcondition: numberOfItems = 50; cost = 50;

    dispenserType(int setNoOfItems, int setCost);
      //Constructor with parameters
      //Sets the cost and number of items in the dispenser
      //to the values specified by the user.
      //Postcondition: numberOfItems = setNoOfItems;
      //               cost = setCost;

private:
    int numberOfItems;       //variable to store the number of
                             //items in the dispenser
    int cost;  //variable to store the cost of an item
};


//**********************************************************
// Author: D.S. Malik
//
// Implementation file dispenserTypeImp.cpp
// This file contains the definitions of the functions to
// implement the operations of the class dispenserType.
//**********************************************************
```

```cpp
#include <iostream>
#include "dispenserType.h"

using namespace std;

int dispenserType::getNoOfItems() const
{
    return numberOfItems;
}

int dispenserType::getCost() const
{
    return cost;
}

void dispenserType::makeSale()
{
    numberOfItems--;
}

dispenserType::dispenserType()
{
    numberOfItems = 50;
    cost = 50;
}

dispenserType::dispenserType(int setNoOfItems, int setCost)
{
    if (setNoOfItems >= 0)
        numberOfItems = setNoOfItems;
    else
        numberOfItems = 50;

    if (setCost >= 0)
        cost = setCost;
    else
        cost = 50;
}
```

MAIN PROGRAM

```cpp
//*****************************************************
// Author: D.S. Malik
//
// This program uses the classes cashRegister and
// dispenserType to implement a fruit juice machine.
// *****************************************************

#include <iostream>
#include "cashRegister.h"
#include "dispenserType.h"
```

```cpp
using namespace std;

void showSelection();
void sellProduct(dispenserType& product,
                 cashRegister& pCounter);

int main()
{
    cashRegister counter;
    dispenserType appleJuice(100, 50);
    dispenserType orangeJuice(100, 65);
    dispenserType mangoLassi(75, 45);
    dispenserType fruitPunch(100, 85);

    int choice;   //variable to hold the selection

    showSelection();
    cin >> choice;

    while (choice != 9)
    {
        switch (choice)
        {
        case 1:
            sellProduct(appleJuice, counter);
            break;

        case 2:
            sellProduct(orangeJuice, counter);
            break;

        case 3:
            sellProduct(mangoLassi, counter);
            break;

        case 4:
            sellProduct(fruitPunch, counter);
            break;

        default:
            cout << "Invalid selection." << endl;
        }//end switch

        showSelection();
        cin >> choice;
    }//end while

    return 0;
}//end main
```

```cpp
void showSelection()
{
    cout << "*** Welcome to Shelly's Fruit Juice Shop ***"
         << endl;
    cout << "To select an item, enter " << endl;
    cout << "1 for apple juice" << endl;
    cout << "2 for orange juice" << endl;
    cout << "3 for mango lassi" << endl;
    cout << "4 for fruit punch" << endl;
    cout << "9 to exit" << endl;
}//end showSelection

void sellProduct(dispenserType& product,
                 cashRegister& pCounter)
{
    int amount;   //variable to hold the amount entered
    int amount2;  //variable to hold the extra amount needed

    if (product.getNoOfItems() > 0) //if the dispenser is not
                                    //empty
    {
        cout << "Please deposit " << product.getCost()
             << " cents" << endl;
        cin >> amount;

        if (amount < product.getCost())
        {
            cout << "Please deposit another "
                 << product.getCost()- amount
                 << " cents" << endl;
            cin >> amount2;
            amount = amount + amount2;
        }

        if (amount >= product.getCost())
        {
            pCounter.acceptAmount(amount);
            product.makeSale();
            cout << "Collect your item at the bottom and "
                 << "enjoy." << endl;
        }
        else
            cout << "The amount is not enough. "
                 << "Collect what you deposited." << endl;

        cout << "*-*-*-*-*-*-*-*-*-*-*-*-*-*-*-*-*-*-*"
             << endl << endl;
    }
    else
        cout << "Sorry, this item is sold out." << endl;
}//end sellProduct
```

Sample Run: In this sample run, the user input is shaded.

```
*** Welcome to Shelly's Fruit Juice Shop ***
To select an item, enter
1 for apple juice
2 for orange juice
3 for mango lassi
4 for fruit punch
9 to exit
1
Please deposit 50 cents
50
Collect your item at the bottom and enjoy.
* _* _* _* _* _* _* _* _* _* _* _* _* _* _* _* _* _*

*** Welcome to Shelly's Fruit Juice Shop ***
To select an item, enter
1 for apple juice
2 for orange juice
3 for mango lassi
4 for fruit punch
9 to exit
3
Please deposit 45 cents
45
Collect your item at the bottom and enjoy.
* _* _* _* _* _* _* _* _* _* _* _* _* _* _* _* _* _*

*** Welcome to Shelly's Fruit Juice Shop ***
To select an item, enter
1 for apple juice
2 for orange juice
3 for mango lassi
4 for fruit punch
9 to exit
9
```

Avoiding Bugs: Compiling/Testing Often

Earlier in this chapter, you learned that programs should be coded a piece at a time. The pieces are classes and objects, consisting of data, and functions that work together to provide a solution. You learned to select a piece whose implementation is obvious and code it, doing one piece at a time until no more pieces remain to be coded. You learned that it is not sufficient simply to code all the needed pieces, establishing that each piece works by itself; you also must make all the pieces work together to provide a complete solution.

You learned that the first version of the program should be a working program with perhaps a single feature. This version of the program is saved. Then, your work continues by adding a next feature, saving the revised program using a different name. This process continues, adding perhaps just one feature at a time until all the intended features are present and the solution is complete.

As each new feature is added, the program should be tested not only to verify that the new feature works but also to verify that the previously developed features of the program continue to work. Each time you add a new feature, you should compile and test the program.

During program development, three kinds of testing take place: unit testing, integration testing, and regression testing. A **unit** is the smallest testable piece of a program. A successful **unit test** establishes that a new piece works as intended by itself. A successful integration test establishes that the new piece works as intended together with the previously coded pieces. A complete **integration test** establishes that all the pieces work together to provide a complete solution to the problem.

Occasionally, when a new feature is added to a program, the feature works as intended, but, as an unintended consequence, one or more features coded previously cease to work properly. A successful **regression test** establishes that all the previously coded features still work properly after a new feature is added. **Regression bugs** are discovered by redoing previous tests. A regression bug might be part of the new feature or part of a previous feature that was thought to be correct but that was not fully debugged. The source of the bug must be determined so the bug can be removed.

7

QUICK REVIEW

1. A `class` is a collection of a fixed number of components.
2. Components of a `class` are called the members of the class.
3. Members of a `class` are accessed by name.
4. In C++, `class` is a reserved word.
5. Members of a class are classified into one of three categories: `private`, `protected`, and `public`.
6. The `private` members of a class are not accessible outside the class.
7. The `public` members of a class are accessible outside the class.
8. By default, all members of a class are `private`.
9. The `public` members are declared using the member access specifier `public` and the colon, :.
10. The `private` members are declared using the member access specifier `private` and the colon, :.
11. A member of a class can be a function or a variable.
12. If any member of a class is a function, you usually use the function prototype to declare it.

13. If any member of a class is a variable, it is declared like any other variable.

14. In the definition of a class, you cannot initialize a variable when you declare it.

15. In the Unified Modeling Language (UML) diagram of a class, the top box contains the name of the class. The middle box contains the instance variables and their data types. The last box contains the member function name, parameter list, and the return type of the function. A + (plus) sign in front of a member indicates that this member is a `public` member. A – (minus) sign preceding a member indicates that this is a `private` member. The symbol # before the member name indicates that the member is a `protected` member.

16. In C++, a `class` is a definition. No memory is allocated for the `class` itself; memory is allocated for the class variables when you declare them.

17. In C++, class variables are called class objects or class instances, or simply objects.

18. A class member is accessed using the class variable name, followed by the dot operator (`.`), followed by the member name.

19. The only built-in operations on classes are the assignment and member selection.

20. As parameters to functions, classes can be passed either by value or by reference.

21. A function can return a value of type `class`.

22. Any program (or software) that uses a class is called a client of the class.

23. A member function of a class that only accesses (that is, does not modify) the value(s) of the data members (variables) is called an accessor function.

24. A member function of a class that modifies the value(s) of the data members (variables) is called a mutator function.

25. A member function of a class is called a constant function if its heading contains the reserved word `const` at the end. Moreover, a constant member function of a class cannot modify the data members of the class.

26. A constant member function of a class can only call the other constant member functions of the class.

27. Constructors guarantee that the instance variables are initialized when an object is declared.

28. The name of a constructor is the same as the name of the class.

29. A class can have more than one constructor.

30. A constructor without parameters is called the default constructor.

31. Constructors automatically execute when a class object enters its scope.

32. A precondition is a statement specifying the condition(s) that must be true before the function is called.

33. A postcondition is a statement specifying what is true after the function call is completed.

34. Destructors automatically execute when a class object goes out of scope.

35. A class can have only one destructor, and the destructor has no parameters.

36. The name of a destructor is the tilde (~), followed by the class name (no spaces in between).

37. Constructors and destructors are functions without any type; that is, they are neither value-returning nor void. As a result, they cannot be called like other functions.

38. A data type that separates the logical properties from the implementation details is called an abstract data type (ADT).

39. Classes were specifically designed in C++ to handle ADTs.

40. To implement an ADT, you must represent the data and write related algorithms to implement the operations.

41. A `public static` member, function, or variable of a class can be accessed using the class name and the scope resolution operator.

42. For each `static` variable of a class, C++ allocates only one memory space. All objects of the class refer to the same memory space.

43. `static` data members of a class exist even when no object of the `class` type exists.

44. Non-`static` data members of a class are called the instance variables of the class.

45. In C++, `struct` is a reserved word.

46. A C++ `struct` is quite similar to a C++ `class`.

47. The members of a `struct` can also be functions, including constructors and a destructor.

48. The only difference between a `struct` and a `class` is that, by default, all members of a `struct` are `public`, and all members of a `class` are `private`.

EXERCISES

1. Mark the following statements as true or false.

   a. The instance variables of a class must be of the same type.

   b. The member functions of a class must be `public`.

   c. A class can have more than one constructor.

   d. A class can have more than one destructor.

   e. Both constructors and destructors can have parameters.

   f. All members of a `struct` must be variables.

   g. By default, all members of a `struct` are public.

2. Find the syntax errors in the definitions of the following classes:

a.
```cpp
class AA
{
public:
    void print() const;
    int sum();
    AA();
    int AA(int, int);
private:
    int x;
    int y;
};
```

b.
```cpp
class BB
{
    int one;
    int two;
public:
    bool equal() const;
    print();
    BB(int, int);
}
```

c.
```cpp
class CC
{
public;
    void set(int, int);
    void print() const;
    CC();
    CC(int, int);
    bool CC(int, int);
private:
    int u;
    int v;
};
```

3. Consider the following declarations:

```cpp
class xClass
{
public:
    void func();
    void print() const;
    xClass();
    xClass(int, double);
private:
    int u;
    double w;
};
```

and assume that the following statement is in a user program:

```cpp
xClass x;
```

a. How many members does **class** xClass have?

b. How many **private** members does **class** xClass have?

c. How many constructors does **class** xClass have?

d. Write the definition of the member function func so that u is set to 10 and w is set to 15.3.

e. Write the definition of the member function print that prints the contents of u and w.

f. Write the definition of the default constructor of the **class** xClass so that the instance variables are initialized to 0.

g. Write a C++ statement that prints the values of the instance variables of the object x.

h. Write a C++ statement that declares an object t of type xClass, and initializes the instance variables of t to 20 and 35.0, respectively.

4. Consider the definition of the following class:

```
class CC
{
public:
    CC();                //Line 1
    CC(int);             //Line 2
    CC(int, int);        //Line 3
    CC(double, int);     //Line 4
        .
        .
        .
private:
    int u;
    double v;
};
```

a. Give the line number containing the constructor that is executed in each of the following declarations:

    i.   CC one;

    ii. CC two(5, 6);

    iii. CC three(3.5, 8);

b. Write the definition of the constructor in Line 1 so that the instance variables are initialized to 0.

c. Write the definition of the constructor in Line 2 so that the instance variable u is initialized according to the value of the parameter, and the instance variable v is initialized to 0.

d. Write the definition of the constructors in Lines 3 and 4 so that the instance variables are initialized according to the values of the parameters.

7

5. Consider the definition of the following `class`:

```
class testClass
{
public:
    int sum();
        //Returns the sum of the instance variables
    void print() const;
        //Prints the values of the instance variables
    testClass();
        //Default constructor
        //Initializes the instance variables to 0
    testClass(int a, int b);
        //Constructors with parameters
        //initializes the instance variables to the values
        //specified by the parameters
        //Postcondition: x = a; y = b;
private:
    int x;
    int y;
};
```

a. Write the definitions of the member functions as described in the definition of the `class` `testClass`.

b. Write a test program to test the various operations of the `class` `testClass`.

6. Given the definition of the `class` `clockType` with constructors (as described in this chapter), what is the output of the following C++ code?

```
clockType clock1;
clockType clock2(23, 13, 75);

clock1.printTime();
cout << endl;
clock2.printTime();
cout << endl;

clock1.setTime(6, 59, 39);
clock1.printTime();
cout << endl;

clock1.incrementMinutes();
clock1.printTime();
cout << endl;

clock1.setTime(0, 13, 0);

if (clock1.equalTime(clock2))
    cout << "Clock1 time is the same as clock2 time." << endl;
else
    cout << "The two times are different." << endl;
```

7. Assume the definition of the **class** personType as given in this chapter.

   a. Write a C++ statement that declares student to be a personType object, and initialize its first name to "Buddy" and last name to "Arora".

   b. Write a C++ statement that outputs the data stored in the object student.

   c. Write C++ statements that change the first name of student to "Susan" and the last name to "Gilbert".

8. Write the definition of a class that has the following properties:

   a. The name of the **class** is secretType.

   b. The **class** secretType has four instance variables: name of type string, age and weight of type **int**, and height of type **double**.

   c. The **class** secretType has the following member functions. (Make each accessor function constant.)

print—outputs the data stored in the instance variables with the appropriate titles

setName—function to set the name

setAge—function to set the age

setWeight—function to set the weight

setHeight—function to set the height

getName—value-returning function to return the name

getAge—value-returning function to return the age

getWeight—value-returning function to return the weight

getHeight—value-returning function to return the height

Default constructor—sets name to the empty string and age, weight, and height to 0.

Constructor with parameter—sets the values of the instance variables to the values specified by the user.

   d. Write the definition of the member functions of the **class** secretType as described in Part c.

9. Consider the following definition of the **class** myClass:

```cpp
class myClass
{
public:
    void setX(int a);
        //Function to set the value of x.
        //Postcondition: x := a;
    void printX() const;
        //Function to output x.
```

7

```
    static void printCount();
      //Function to output count.
    static void incrementCount();
      //Function to increment count.
      //Postcondition: count++;
    myClass(int a = 0);
      //constructor with default parameters
      //Postcondition x = a;
      //If no value is specified for a, x = 0;

private:
    int x;
    static int count;
};
```

a. Write a C++ statement that initializes the count to 0.

b. Write a C++ statement that increments the value of count by 1.

c. Write a C++ statement that outputs the value of count.

d. Write the definitions of the functions of the class myClass as described in its definition.

e. Write a C++ statement that declares myObject1 to be a myClass object and initializes its instance variable x to 5.

f. Write a C++ statement that declares myObject2 to be a myClass object and initializes its instance variable x to 7.

g. Which of the following statements are valid? (Assume that myObject1 and myObject2 are as declared in Parts e and f.)

```
myObject1.printCount();      //Line 1
myObject1.printX();          //Line 2
myClass.printCount();        //Line 3
myClass.printX();            //Line 4
myClass::count++;            //Line 5
```

h. Assume that myObject1 and myObject2 are as declared in Parts e and f. What is the output of the following C++ code?

```
myObject1.printX();
cout << endl;
myObject1.incrementCount();
myClass::incrementCount();
myObject1.printCount();
cout << endl;
myObject2.printCount();
cout << endl;
myObject2.printX();
cout << endl;
myObject1.setX(14);
myObject1.incrementCount();
```

```
    myObject1.printX();
    cout << endl;
    myObject1.printCount();
    cout << endl;
    myObject2.printCount();
    cout << endl;
```

10. Draw the UML class diagram of the **class** `thermometer` given in Example 7-2.

PROGRAMMING EXERCISES

1. Write a program that converts a number entered in Roman numerals to decimal. Your program should consist of a **class**, say `romanType`. An object of type `romanType` should do the following:

   a. Store the number as a Roman numeral.

   b. Convert and store the number into decimal form.

   c. Print the number as a Roman numeral or decimal number as requested by the user. (Write two separate functions, one to print the number as a Roman numeral and the other to print the number as a decimal number.)

   The decimal values of the Roman numerals are:

   ```
   M    1000
   D     500
   C     100
   L      50
   X      10
   V       5
   I       1
   ```

   Remember, a larger numeral preceding a smaller numeral means addition, so `LX` is `60`. A smaller numeral preceding a larger numeral means subtraction, so `XL` is `40`. Any place in a decimal number, such as the 1s place, the 10s place, and so on, requires from zero to four Roman numerals.

   d. Test your program using the following Roman numerals: `MCXIV`, `CCCLIX`, and `MDCLXVI`.

2. Write the definition of the **class** `dayType` that implements the day of the week in a program. The **class** `dayType` should store the day, such as `Sun` for Sunday. The program should be able to perform the following operations on an object of type `dayType`:

   a. Set the day.

   b. Print the day.

   c. Return the day.

   d. Return the next day.

e. Return the previous day.

f. Calculate and return the day by adding certain days to the current day. For example, if the current day is Monday and we add 4 days, the day to be returned is Friday. Similarly, if today is Tuesday and we add 13 days, the day to be returned is Monday.

g. Add the appropriate constructors.

3. Write the definitions of the functions to implement the operations for the **class dayType** as defined in Programming Exercise 2. Also, write a program to test various operations on this class.

4. Example 7-3 defined a **class personType** to store the name of a person. The member functions that we included merely print the name and set the name of a person. Redefine the **class personType** so that, in addition to what the existing **class** does, you also can do the following:

a. Set the first name only.

b. Set the last name only.

c. Store and set the middle name.

d. Check whether a given first name is the same as the first name of this person.

e. Check whether a given last name is the same as the last name of this person.

Write the definitions of the member functions to implement the operations for this class. Also, write a program to test various operations on this class.

5. The function **sellProduct** of the Fruit Juice Machine programming example gives the user only two chances to enter enough money to buy the product. Rewrite the definition of the function **sellProduct** so that it keeps prompting the user to enter more money as long as the user has not entered enough money to buy the product. Also, write a program to test your function.

6. The equation of a line in standard form is $ax + by = c$, where a and b both cannot be zero, and a, b, and c are real numbers. If $b \neq 0$, then $-a/b$ is the slope of the line. If $a = 0$, then it is a horizontal line, and if $b = 0$, then it is a vertical line. The slope of a vertical line is undefined. Two lines are parallel if they have the same slope or both are vertical lines. Two lines are perpendicular if either one of the lines is horizontal and another is vertical, or if the product of their slopes is -1. Design the **class lineType** to store a line. To store a line, you need to store the values of a (coefficient of x), b (coefficient of y), and c. Your class must contain the following operations:

a. If a line is nonvertical, then determine its slope.

b. Determine if two lines are equal. (Two lines $a_1x + b_1y = c_1$ and $a_2x + b_2y = c_2$ are equal if either $a_1 = a_2$, $b_1 = b_2$, and $c_1 = c_2$ or $a_1 = ka_2$, $b_1 = kb_2$, and $c_1 = kc_2$ for some real number k.)

c. Deterime if two lines are parallel.

d. Determine if two lines are perpendicular.

e. If two lines are not parallel, then find the point of intersection.

Add appropriate constructors to initialize variables of lineType. Also write a program to test your class.

7. a. Some of the characteristics of a book are the title, author(s), publisher, ISBN, price, and year of publication. Design a **class** bookType that defines the book as an ADT.

    i. Each object of the **class** bookType can hold the following information about a book: title, up to four authors, publisher, ISBN, price, and number of copies in stock. To keep track of the number of authors, add another member variable.

    ii. Include the member functions to perform the various operations on objects of type bookType. For example, the usual operations that can be performed on the title are to show the title, set the title, and check whether a title is the same as the actual title of the book. Similarly, the typical operations that can be performed on the number of copies in stock are to show the number of copies in stock, set the number of copies in stock, update the number of copies in stock, and return the number of copies in stock. Add the appropriate constructors and a destructor (if one is needed).

b. Write the definitions of the member functions of the **class** bookType.

c. Write a program that uses the **class** bookType and tests various operations on the objects of the **class** bookType. Declare an array of 100 components of type bookType. Some of the operations that you should perform are to search for a book by its title, search by ISBN, and update the number of copies of a book.

8. In this exercise, you will design a **class** memberType.

a. Each object of memberType can hold the name of a person, member ID, number of books bought, and amount spent.

b. Include the member functions to perform the various operations on the objects of memberType—for example, modify, set, and show a person's name. Similarly, update, modify, and show the number of books bought and the amount spent.

c. Add the appropriate constructors.

d. Write the definitions of the member functions of memberType.

e. Write a program to test various operations of your **class** memberType.

7

9. Using the classes designed in Programming Exercises 7 and 8, write a program to simulate a bookstore. The bookstore has two types of customers: those who are members of the bookstore, and those who buy books from the bookstore only occasionally. Each member has to pay a $10 yearly membership fee and receives a 5 percent discount on each book purchased. For each member, the bookstore keeps track of the number of books purchased and the total amount spent. For every 11th book that a member buys, the bookstore takes the average of the total amount of the last 10 books purchased, applies this amount as a discount, and then resets the total amount spent to 0.

   Write a program that can process up to 1000 book titles and 500 members. Your program should contain a menu that gives the user different choices to effectively run the program; in other words, your program should be user-driven.

10. (Tic-Tac-Toe) Write a program that allows two players to play the tic-tac-toe game. Your program must contain the **class** ticTacToe to implement a ticTacToe object. Include a 3 by 3 two-dimensional array, as a **private** member variable, to create the board. If needed, include additional member variables. Some of the operations on a ticTacToe object are printing the current board, getting a move, checking if a move is valid, and determining the winner after each move. Add additional operations as needed.

CHAPTER

8

NAMESPACES, THE class string, AND USER-DEFINED SIMPLE DATA TYPES

The statement **using namespace std;** (discussed in Chapter 1) is used in every C++ program. This chapter examines the purpose of the **using namespace std;** statement. In fact, you will learn what the **namespace** mechanism is. You will also learn in some detail about the **class string** and the many useful functions that you can use to effectively manipulate strings. Furthermore, in Chapter 1, you learned that C++'s simple data type is divided into three categories: integral, floating-point, and **enum**. In Chapters 1 through 7, you worked mainly with integral and floating-point data types. In the second half of this chapter, you will learn about the **enum** type.

Namespaces

The programming language C++ evolved from C and was designed by Bjarne Stroustrup at Bell Laboratories in the early 1980s. From the early 1980s through the early 1990s, several C++ compilers were available. Even though all compilers had mostly the same fundamental features of C++, the C++ language was evolving in slightly different ways in different compilers. As a consequence, C++ programs were not always portable from one compiler to another.

To address this problem, in the early 1990s a joint committee of the American National Standards Institute (ANSI) and the International Organization for Standardization (ISO) was established to standardize the syntax of C++. In July 1998, ANSI/ISO Standard C++ was officially approved. Most recent compilers are also compatible with ANSI/ISO Standard C++. (To be absolutely sure, check your compiler's documentation.) The **namespace** mechanism, which was introduced in Chapter 1, is a feature of ANSI/ISO Standard C++.

When a header file, such as **iostream**, is included in a program, the global identifiers in the header file also become the global identifiers in the program. Therefore, if a global identifier in a program has the same name as one of the global identifiers in the header file, the compiler generates a syntax error (such as "identifier redefined"). The same problem can occur if a program uses third-party libraries. To overcome this problem, third-party vendors begin their global identifiers with a special symbol. In Chapter 1, you learned that because compiler vendors begin their global identifier names with an under-score (_), to avoid linking errors you should not begin identifier names in your program with an underscore (_).

ANSI/ISO Standard C++ tries to solve this problem of overlapping global identifier names with the **namespace** mechanism.

The general syntax of the statement **namespace** is

```
namespace namespace_name
{
    members
}
```

where a `member` is usually a named constant, variable declaration, function, or another `namespace`. Note that `namespace_name` is a C++ identifier.

In C++, `namespace` is a reserved word.

EXAMPLE 8-1

The statement

```cpp
namespace globalType
{
    const int n = 10;
    const double rate = 7.50;
    int count = 0;
    void printResult();
}
```

defines `globalType` to be a `namespace` with four members: named constants `n` and `rate`, the variable `count`, and the function `printResult`.

The scope of a `namespace` member is local to the `namespace`. You can usually access a `namespace` member outside the `namespace` in one of two ways, as described next.

The general syntax for accessing a `namespace` member is:

```
namespace_name::identifier
```

Recall that, in C++, `::` is called the scope resolution operator.

To access the member `rate` of the `namespace` `globalType`, the following statement is required:

```
globalType::rate
```

To access the member `printResult` (which is a function), the following statement is required:

```
globalType::printResult();
```

Thus, to access a member of a `namespace`, you use the `namespace_name`, followed by the scope resolution operator, followed by the member name.

To simplify accessing a `namespace` member, C++ provides the use of the statement `using`. The syntax to use the statement `using` is as follows:

8

a. To simplify accessing all **namespace** members:

```
using namespace namespace_name;
```

b. To simplify accessing a specific **namespace** member:

```
using namespace_name::identifier;
```

For example, the **using** statement

```
using namespace globalType;
```

simplifies accessing all members of the **namespace** `globalType`. The statement

```
using globalType::rate;
```

simplifies accessing the member `rate` of the **namespace** `globalType`.

In C++, **using** is a reserved word.

You typically put the **using** statement after the **namespace** declaration. For the **namespace** `globalType`, for example, you usually write the code as follows:

```
namespace globalType
{
    const int n = 10;
    const double rate = 7.50;
    int count = 0;
    void printResult();
}

using namespace globalType;
```

After the **using** statement, to access a **namespace** member, you do not have to put the namespace_name and the scope resolution operator before the **namespace** member. However, if a **namespace** member and a global identifier in a program have the same name, to access this **namespace** member in the program, the namespace_name and the scope resolution operator must precede the **namespace** member. Similarly, if a **namespace** member and an identifier in a block have the same name, to access this **namespace** member in the block, the namespace_name and the scope resolution operator must precede the **namespace** member.

Examples 8-2 through 8-5 help clarify the use of the **namespace** mechanism.

EXAMPLE 8-2

Consider the following C++ code:

```cpp
#include <iostream>

using namespace std;
.
.
.
int main()
{
    .
    .
    .
}
.
.
.
```

In this example, you can refer to the global identifiers of the header file `iostream`, such as `cin`, `cout`, and `endl`, without using the prefix `std::` before the identifier name. The obvious restriction is that the block (or function) that refers to the global identifier (of the header file `iostream`) must not contain any identifier with the same name as this global identifier.

EXAMPLE 8-3

Consider the following C++ code:

```cpp
#include <cmath>

int main()
{
    double x = 15.3;
    double y;

    y = std::pow(x, 2);
    .
    .
    .
}
```

This example accesses the function `pow` of the header file `cmath`.

EXAMPLE 8-4

Consider the following C++ code:

```
#include <iostream>
.
.
.
int main()
{
    using namespace std;
    .
    .
    .
}
.
.
.
```

In this example, the function main can refer to the global identifiers of the header file iostream without using the prefix std:: before the identifier name. The using statement appears inside the function main. Therefore, other functions (if any) should use the prefix std:: before the name of the global identifier of the header file iostream unless the function has a similar using statement.

EXAMPLE 8-5

Consider the following C++ code:

```
#include <iostream>          //Line 1

using namespace std;         //Line 2

int t;                       //Line 3
double u;                    //Line 4

namespace expN               //Line 5
{                            //Line 6
    int x;                   //Line 7
    char t;                  //Line 8
    double u;                //Line 9
    void printResult();      //Line 10
}                            //Line 11
```

```
using namespace expN;           //Line 12

int main()                      //Line 13
{                               //Line 14
    int one;                    //Line 15
    double t;                   //Line 16
    double three;               //Line 17

        .
        .
        .

}


void expN::printResult() //Definition of the function printResult
{
        .
        .
        .

}
```

Note the following in this C++ program:

1. To refer to the variable t at Line 3 in main, use the *scope resolution operator*, which is :: (that is, refer to t as ::t), because the function main has a variable named t (declared at Line 16). For example, to copy the value of x into t, you can use the statement ::t = x;.

2. To refer to the member t (declared at Line 8) of the namespace expN in main, use the prefix expN:: with t (that is, refer to t as expN::t) because there is a global variable named t (declared at Line 3) and a variable named t in main.

3. To refer to the member u (declared at Line 9) of the namespace expN in main, use the prefix expN:: with u (that is, refer to u as expN::u) because there is a global variable named u (declared at Line 4).

4. You can reference the member x (declared at Line 7) of the namespace expN in main as either x or expN::x because there is no global identifier named x, and the function main does not contain any identifier named x.

5. The definition of a function that is a member of a namespace, such as printResult, is usually written outside the namespace, as in the preceding program. To write the definition of the function printResult, the name of the function in the function heading can be either printResult or expN::printResult (because no other global identifier is named printResult).

NOTE The identifiers in the system-provided header files such as `iostream`, `cmath`, and `iomanip` are defined in the **namespace** `std`. For this reason, to simplify the accessing of identifiers from these header files, we have been using the following statement in the programs that we write:

`using namespace` std;

class string

In Chapter 1, you were introduced to the data type **string**, commonly called the **class** **string**. Prior to the ANSI/ISO C++ language standard, the Standard C++ library did not provide a **string** data type. Compiler vendors often supplied their own programmer-defined **string** type, and the syntax and semantics of string operations often varied from vendor to vendor.

The **class** **string** is programmer-defined and is not part of the C++ language; the Standard C++ library supplies it. Before using the **class** string, the program must include the header file **string**, as follows:

`#include <string>`

Recall that, in C++, a string is a sequence of zero or more characters, and strings are enclosed in double quotation marks.

The statement

`string name = "William Jacob";`

declares **name** to be a **string** object and initializes **name** to **"William Jacob"**. The index (position) of the first character, **W**, in **name** is 0; the index of the second character, **i**, is 1; and so on. That is, the index of the first character in a string is 0, not 1.

The object **name** can store (just about) any size string.

Chapter 2 discussed I/O operations on the **string** objects; Chapter 3 explained relational operations on the **string** objects. We recommend that you revisit Chapters 2 and 3 and review the I/O and relational operations on the **string** objects. (The program `Ch8_stringBoolOperation.cpp` on the Web site accompanying this book shows how the string relational operators work.)

Other operators, such as the binary operator + (to allow the string concatenation operation) and the array index (subscript) operator **[]**, have also been defined for the **class** string. Let's see how these operators work on the **class** string.

Suppose you have the following declarations:

```
string str1, str2, str3;
```

The statement

```
str1 = "Hello There";
```

stores the string **"Hello There"** in **str1**. The statement

```
str2 = str1;
```

copies the value of **str1** into **str2**.

If **str1 = "Sunny"**, the statement

```
str2 = str1 + " Day";
```

stores the string **"Sunny Day"** into **str2**.

Suppose **str1 = "Hello"** and **str2 = "There"**. The statement

```
str3 = str1 + " " + str2;
```

stores **"Hello There"** into **str3**. This statement is equivalent to the following statement:

```
str3 = str1 + ' ' + str2;
```

Also, the statement

```
str1 = str1 + " Mickey";
```

updates the value of **str1** by appending the string **" Mickey"** to its old value. Therefore, the new value of **str1** is **"Hello Mickey"**.

NOTE For the operator + to work with **string** objects, one of the operands of + must be a **string** object. For example, the following statements will not work:

```
str1 = "Hello " + "there!"; //Illegal
str2 = "Sunny Day" + '!';    //Illegal
```

If **str1 = "Hello there"**, the statement

```
str1[6] = 'T';
```

replaces the character **t** with the character **T**. Recall that the position of the first character in a string is 0. Therefore, because **t** is the seventh character in **str1**, its position is 6.

In C++, **[]** is called the **array subscript operator**.

As illustrated previously, using the array subscript operator together with the index of the character, you can access an individual character within a string.

EXAMPLE 8-6

The following program shows the effect of the preceding statements.

```cpp
//****************************************************************
// Author: D.S. Malik
//
// This program illustrates how the array subscript operator,
// [], and the string concatenation operator, +, work.
//****************************************************************

#include <iostream>                                       //Line 1
#include <string>                                         //Line 2

using namespace std;                                      //Line 3

int main()                                                //Line 4
{                                                         //Line 5
    string name = "William Jacob";                        //Line 6
    string str1, str2, str3, str4;                        //Line 7

    cout << "Line 8: Name = " << name << endl;            //Line 8

    str1 = "Hello There";                                 //Line 9
    cout << "Line 10: str1 = " << str1 << endl;           //Line 10

    str2 = str1;                                          //Line 11
    cout << "Line 12: str2 = " << str2 << endl;           //Line 12

    str1 = "Sunny";                                       //Line 13
    str2 = str1 + " Day";                                 //Line 14
    cout << "Line 15: str2 = " << str2 << endl;           //Line 15

    str1 = "Hello";                                       //Line 16
    str2 = "There";                                       //Line 17
    str3 = str1 + " " + str2;                             //Line 18
    cout << "Line 19: str3 = " << str3 << endl;           //Line 19

    str3 = str1 + ' ' + str2;                             //Line 20
    cout << "Line 21: str3 = " << str3 << endl;           //Line 21

    str1 = str1 + " Mickey";                              //Line 22
    cout << "Line 23: str1 = " << str1 << endl;           //Line 23

    str1 = "Hello there";                                 //Line 24
    cout << "Line 25: str1[6] = " << str1[6] << endl;     //Line 25

    str1[6] = 'T';                                        //Line 26
    cout << "Line 27: str1 = " << str1 << endl;           //Line 27
```

```
    //String input operations
cout << "Line 28: Enter a string with "
    << "no blanks: ";                                    //Line 28
cin >> str1;                                             //Line 29

char ch;                                                 //Line 30
cin.get(ch);             //Read the newline character;    Line 31
cout << endl;                                            //Line 32

cout << "Line 33: The string you entered = "
    << str1 << endl;                                     //Line 33

cout << "Line 34: Enter a sentence: ";                   //Line 34
getline(cin, str2);                                      //Line 35
cout << endl;                                            //Line 36

cout << "Line 37: The sentence is: " << str2
    << endl;                                             //Line 37

return 0;                                                //Line 38
}                                                        //Line 39
```

Sample Run: In the following sample run, the user input is shaded.

```
Line 8: Name = William Jacob
Line 10: str1 = Hello There
Line 12: str2 = Hello There
Line 15: str2 = Sunny Day
Line 19: str3 = Hello There
Line 21: str3 = Hello There
Line 23: str1 = Hello Mickey
Line 25: str1[6] = t
Line 27: str1 = Hello There
Line 28: Enter a string with no blanks: Programming

Line 33: The string you entered = Programming
Line 34: Enter a sentence: Testing string operations

Line 37: The sentence is: Testing string operations
```

The preceding output is self-explanatory, and its unraveling is left as an exercise for you.

Additional string Operations

The **class** string contains several other functions for string manipulation. The five in which we are interested—length, size, find, substr, and swap—are described in the next five sections.

The **class** string has a data type, string::size_type, and a named constant, string::npos, associated with it, as described in Table 8-1.

TABLE 8-1 The Data Type and a Named Constant Associated with the **class** string

`string::size_type`	An unsigned integer (data) type
`string::npos`	The maximum value of the (data) type `string::size_type`, a number such as 4294967295 on many machines

length FUNCTION

The `length` function returns the number of characters currently in the string. The value returned is an unsigned integer. The syntax to call the `length` function is

```
strVar.length()
```

where `strVar` is a `string` object. The `length` function has no arguments. Also, because `length` is a value-returning function, the function call, typically, appears in an expression.

Consider the following statements:

```
string firstName;
string name;
string str;

firstName = "Elizabeth";
name = firstName + " Jones";
str = "It is sunny.";
```

Statement	Effect
`cout << firstName.length() << endl;`	Outputs 9
`cout << name.length() << endl;`	Outputs 15
`cout << str.length() << endl;`	Outputs 12

Because the function `length` returns an unsigned integer, the value returned can be stored in an integer variable. Also, because the **class** string has the data type `string::size_type` associated with it, the variable to hold the value returned by the `length` function is usually of this type. This prevents you from guessing whether the value returned is of the type unsigned **int** or unsigned **long**.

Suppose you have the previous declaration and the following statement:

```
string::size_type len;
```

Statement	Effect
`len = firstName.length();`	The value of `len` is 9
`len = name.length();`	The value of `len` is 15
`len = str.length();`	The value of `len` is 12

EXAMPLE 8-7

The following program illustrates the use of the `length` function.

```cpp
//****************************************************************
// Author: D.S. Malik
//
// This program illustrates how the string function length works.
//****************************************************************

#include <iostream>                                    //Line 1
#include <string>                                      //Line 2

using namespace std;                                   //Line 3

int main()                                             //Line 4
{                                                      //Line 5
    string name, firstName;                            //Line 6
    string str;                                        //Line 7
    string::size_type len;                             //Line 8

    firstName = "Elizabeth";                           //Line 9
    name = firstName + " Jones";                       //Line 10
    str = "It is sunny and warm.";                     //Line 11

    cout << "Line 12: Length of \"" << firstName << "\" = "
         << static_cast<unsigned int> (firstName.length())
         << endl;                                      //Line 12

    cout << "Line 13: Length of \"" << name << "\" = "
         << static_cast<unsigned int> (name.length())
         << endl;                                      //Line 13

    cout << "Line 14: Length of \"" << str << "\" = "
         << static_cast<unsigned int> (str.length())
         << endl;                                      //Line 14

    len = firstName.length();                          //Line 15
    cout << "Line 16: len = "
         << static_cast<unsigned int> (len)
         << endl;                                      //Line 16

    len = name.length();                               //Line 17
    cout << "Line 18: len = "
         << static_cast<unsigned int> (len) << endl;   //Line 18

    len = str.length();                                //Line 19
    cout << "Line 20: len = "
         << static_cast<unsigned int> (len) << endl;   //Line 20

    return 0;                                          //Line 21
}                                                      //Line 22
```

8

Sample Run:

```
Line 12: Length of "Elizabeth" = 9
Line 13: Length of "Elizabeth Jones" = 15
Line 14: Length of "It is sunny and warm." = 21
Line 16: len = 9
Line 18: len = 15
Line 20: len = 21
```

The output of this program is self-explanatory. The details are left as an exercise for you. Notice that this program uses the static cast operator to output the value returned by the function `length`. This is because the function `length` returns a value of type `string::size_type`. Without the cast operator, some compilers might give the following warning message:

```
conversion from 'size_t' to 'unsigned int', possible loss of data
```

`size` FUNCTION

Some programmers prefer to use the word `size` instead of the word `length`. Thus, to accommodate both terms, the `class string` provides a function named `size` that returns the same value as does the function `length`. The syntax to call the function `size` is

```
strVar.size()
```

where `strVar` is a `string` object. Like the function `length`, the function `size` has no arguments.

`find` FUNCTION

The `find` function searches a string to find the first occurrence of a particular substring and returns an unsigned integer value (of the type `string::size_type`), giving the result of the search. The syntax to call the function `find` is

```
strVar.find(strExp)
```

or

```
strVar.find(strExp, pos)
```

where `strVar` is a `string` object, and `strExp` is a string expression evaluating to a string. The string expression, `strExp`, can also be a character. If the search is successful, the function `find` returns the index in `strVar` where the match begins. For the search to be successful, the match must be exact. If the search is unsuccessful, the function returns the special value `string::npos` ("not a position within the string"). (This value is suitable for "not a valid position" because the string operations do not let any string become this long.) Because the function `find` returns an unsigned integer, the returned value can be stored in an integer variable (usually of the type `string::size_type`). In the second form of the function `find`, `pos` specifies the index (position) in the string where the search should begin.

Suppose `str1` and `str2` are of `string` objects. The following are valid calls to the function `find`:

```
str1.find(str2)
str1.find("the")
str1.find('a')
str1.find(str2 + "xyz")
str1.find(str2 + 'b')
```

Consider the following statements:

```
string sentence;
string str;
string::size_type position;

sentence = "Outside it is cloudy and warm.";
str = "cloudy";
```

Statement	Effect
`cout << sentence.find("is") << endl;`	Outputs 11
`cout << sentence.find("and") << endl;`	Outputs 21
`cout << sentence.find('s') << endl;`	Outputs 3
`cout << sentence.find('o') << endl;`	Outputs 16
`cout << sentence.find(str) << endl;`	Outputs 14
`cout << sentence.find("the") << endl;`	Outputs the value of `string::nops`
`cout << sentence.find('i', 6) << endl;`	Outputs 8
`position = sentence.find("warm");`	Assigns 25 to `position`

Note that the search is case sensitive. Therefore, the position of o (lowercase o) in the string `sentence` is 16.

EXAMPLE 8-8

The following program illustrates how to use the `string` function `find`.

```
//**************************************************************
// Author: D.S. Malik
//
// This program illustrates how the string function find works.
//**************************************************************
```

8

```cpp
#include <iostream>                                    //Line 1
#include <string>                                      //Line 2

using namespace std;                                   //Line 3

int main()                                             //Line 4
{                                                      //Line 5
    string sentence, str;                              //Line 6
    string::size_type position;                        //Line 7

    sentence = "Outside it is cloudy and warm.";       //Line 8
    str = "cloudy";                                    //Line 9

    cout << "Line 10: sentence = \"" << sentence
         << "\"" << endl;                              //Line 10

    cout << "Line 11: The position of \"is\" in sentence = "
         << static_cast<unsigned int> (sentence.find("is"))
         << endl;                                      //Line 11

    cout << "Line 12: The position of \"and\" in sentence = "
         << static_cast<unsigned int> (sentence.find("and"))
         << endl;                                      //Line 12

    cout << "Line 13: The position of 's' in sentence = "
         << static_cast<unsigned int> (sentence.find('s'))
         << endl;                                      //Line 13

    cout << "Line 14: The position of 'o' in sentence = "
         << static_cast<unsigned int> (sentence.find('o'))
         << endl;                                      //Line 14

    cout << "Line 15: The position of \"" << str
         << "\" in sentence = "
         << static_cast<unsigned int> (sentence.find(str))
         << endl;                                      //Line 15

    cout << "Line 16: The position of \"the\" in sentence = "
         << static_cast<unsigned int> (sentence.find("the"))
         << endl;                                      //Line 16

    cout << "Line 17: The first occurrence of \'i\' in "
         << "sentence \n          after position 6 = "
         << static_cast<unsigned int> (sentence.find('i', 6))
         << endl;                                      //Line 17

    position = sentence.find("warm");                  //Line 18
    cout << "Line 19: " << "Position = "
         << static_cast<unsigned int> (position)
         << endl;                                      //Line 19

    return 0;                                          //Line 20
}                                                      //Line 21
```

Sample Run:

```
Line 10: sentence = "Outside it is cloudy and warm."
Line 11: The position of "is" in sentence = 11
Line 12: The position of "and" in sentence = 21
Line 13: The position of 's' in sentence = 3
Line 14: The position of 'o' in sentence = 16
Line 15: The position of "cloudy" in sentence = 14
Line 16: The position of "the" in sentence = 4294967295
Line 17: The first occurrence of 'i' in sentence
         after position 6 = 8
Line 19: Position = 25
```

The output of this program is self-explanatory. The details are left as an exercise for you. Notice that this program uses the static cast operator to output the value returned by the function `find`. This is because the function `find` returns a value of the type `string::size_type`. Without the cast operator, some compilers might give the following warning message:

```
conversion from 'size_t' to 'unsigned int', possible loss of data
```

`substr` FUNCTION

The `substr` function returns a particular substring of a string. The syntax to call the function `substr` is

```
strVar.substr(expr1, expr2)
```

where `strVar` is a `string` object, and `expr1` and `expr2` are expressions evaluating to unsigned integers. The expression `expr1` specifies an index within the string (the starting index of the substring); the expression `expr2` specifies the length of the substring to be returned. If starting at `expr1`, the number of characters (that is, the length of the substring) specified by `expr2` exceeds the length of the string, characters until the end of the string are returned. (For example, in the following, see the fourth output statement, in which `sentence` is a string of length 22, and starting at position 17 we try to extract a substring of length 10. However, starting at position 17, `sentence` has only five characters and so only `warm.` is output.)

Consider the following statements:

```
string sentence;
string str;

sentence = "It is cloudy and warm.";
```

Statement	Effect
`cout << sentence.substr(0, 5) << endl;`	Outputs: `It is`
`cout << sentence.substr(6, 6) << endl;`	Outputs: `cloudy`
`cout << sentence.substr(6, 16) << endl;`	Outputs: `cloudy and warm.`
`cout << sentence.substr(17, 10) << endl;`	Outputs: `warm.`
`cout << sentence.substr(3, 6) << endl;`	Outputs: `is clo`
`str = sentence.substr(0, 8);`	`str = "It is cl"`
`str = sentence.substr(2, 10);`	`str = " is cloudy"`

EXAMPLE 8-9

The following program illustrates how to use the string function substr.

```cpp
//***********************************************************
// Author: D.S. Malik
//
// This program illustrates how the string function substr works.
//***********************************************************

#include <iostream>                                         //Line 1
#include <string>                                           //Line 2

using namespace std;                                        //Line 3

int main()                                                  //Line 4
{                                                           //Line 5
    string sentence;                                        //Line 6
    string str;                                             //Line 7

    sentence = "It is cloudy and warm.";                    //Line 8

    cout << "Line 9: substr(0, 5) in \"" << sentence
         << "\" = \"" << sentence.substr(0, 5)
         << "\"" << endl;                                   //Line 9

    cout << "Line 10: substr(6, 6) in \"" << sentence
         << "\" = \"" << sentence.substr(6, 6)
         << "\"" << endl;                                   //Line 10

    cout << "Line 11: substr(6, 16) in \"" << sentence
         << "\" = " << endl << "          \""
         << sentence.substr(6, 16) << "\"" << endl;         //Line 11

    cout << "Line 12: substr(17, 10) in \"" << sentence
         << "\" = \"" << sentence.substr(17, 10)
         << "\"" << endl;                                   //Line 12
```

```
        cout << "Line 13: substr(3, 6) in \"" << sentence
             << "\" = \"" << sentence.substr(3, 6)
             << "\"" << endl;                                //Line 13

        str = sentence.substr(0, 8);                        //Line 14
        cout << "Line 15: " << "str = \"" << str
             << "\"" << endl;                                //Line 15

        str = sentence.substr(2, 10);                       //Line 16
        cout << "Line 17: " << "str = \"" << str
             << "\"" << endl;                                //Line 17

        return 0;                                           //Line 18
}                                                           //Line 19
```

Sample Run:

```
Line 9: substr(0, 5) in "It is cloudy and warm." = "It is"
Line 10: substr(6, 6) in "It is cloudy and warm." = "cloudy"
Line 11: substr(6, 16) in "It is cloudy and warm." =
        "cloudy and warm."
Line 12: substr(17, 10) in "It is cloudy and warm." = "warm."
Line 13: substr(3, 6) in "It is cloudy and warm." = "is clo"
Line 15: str = "It is cl"
Line 17: str = " is cloudy"
```

The output of this program is self-explanatory. The details are left as an exercise for you.

swap FUNCTION

The **swap** function is used to swap—that is, interchange—the contents of two **string** objects. The syntax to use the **swap** function is

```
strVar1.swap(strVar2);
```

where **strVar1** and **strVar2** are **string** objects. After this statement executes, the contents of **strVar1** and **strVar2** are swapped.

Suppose you have the following statements:

```
string str1 = "Warm";
string str2 = "Cold";
```

After the following statement executes, the value of **str1** is **"Cold"** and the value of **str2** is **"Warm"**.

```
str1.swap(str2);
```

NOTE   Additional **string** functions, such as **empty**, **clear**, **erase**, **insert**, and **replace**, are provided in Appendix E (Header File **string**).

8

PROGRAMMING EXAMPLE: Pig Latin Strings

In this programming example, we write a program that prompts the user to input a string and then outputs the string in the pig Latin form. The rules for converting a string into pig Latin form are as follows:

1. If the string begins with a vowel, add the string `"-way"` at the end of the string. For example, the pig Latin form of the string `"eye"` is `"eye-way"`.

2. If the string does not begin with a vowel, first add `"-"` at the end of the string. Then rotate the string one character at a time; that is, move the first character of the string to the end of the string until the first character of the string becomes a vowel. Then add the string `"ay"` at the end. For example, the pig Latin form of the string `"There"` is `"ere-Thay"`.

3. Strings such as `"by"` contain no vowels. In cases like this, the letter `y` can be considered a vowel. So, for this program, the vowels are `a, e, i, o, u, y, A, E, I, O, U,` and `Y`. Therefore, the pig Latin form of `"by"` is `"y-bay"`.

4. Strings such as `"1234"` contain no vowels. The pig Latin form of the string `"1234"` is `"1234-way"`. That is, the pig Latin form of a string that has no vowels in it is the string followed by the string `"-way"`.

Input   Input to the program is a string.

Output   Output of the program is the string in the pig Latin form.

PROBLEM ANALYSIS AND ALGORITHM DESIGN

Suppose that `str` denotes a string. To convert `str` into pig Latin, check the first character, `str[0]`, of `str`. If `str[0]` is a vowel, add `"-way"` at the end of `str`—that is, `str = str + "-way"`.

Suppose that the first character of `str`, `str[0]`, is not a vowel. First, add `"-"` at the end of the string. Then remove the first character of `str` from `str` and put it at the end of `str`. Now the second character of `str` becomes the first character of `str`. This process of checking the first character of `str` and moving it to the end of `str` if the first character of `str` is not a vowel is repeated until either the first character of `str` is a vowel or all the characters of `str` are processed, in which case `str` does not contain any vowels.

In this program, we write a function `isVowel`, to determine whether a character is a vowel; a function `rotate`, to move the first character of `str` to the end of `str`; and a function `pigLatinString`, to find the pig Latin form of `str`. The previous discussion translates into the following algorithm:

1. Get `str`.
2. Find the pig Latin form of `str` by using the function `pigLatinString`.
3. Output the pig Latin form of `str`.

Before writing the main algorithm, each of these functions is described in detail.

Function isVowel This function takes a character as a parameter and returns `true` if the character is a vowel, and `false` otherwise. The definition of the function `isVowel` is:

```
bool isVowel(char ch)
{
    switch (ch)
    {
    case 'A':
    case 'E':
    case 'I':
    case 'O':
    case 'U':
    case 'Y':
    case 'a':
    case 'e':
    case 'i':
    case 'o':
    case 'u':
    case 'y':
        return true;

    default:
        return false;
    }
} //end isVowel
```

Function rotate This function takes a string as a parameter, removes the first character of the string, and places it at the end of the string. This is done by extracting the substring starting at position 1 (which is the second character) until the end of the string, and then adding the first character of the string. The new string is returned as the value of this function. Essentially, the definition of the function `rotate` is:

```
string rotate(string pStr)
{
    string::size_type len = pStr.length();

    string rStr;

    rStr = pStr.substr(1, len - 1) + pStr[0];

    return rStr;
} //end rotate
```

8

Function pigLatin String

This function takes a string, `pStr`, as a parameter and returns the pig Latin form of `pStr`. Suppose `pStr` denotes the string to be converted to its pig Latin form. There are three possible cases: `pStr[0]` is a vowel; `pStr` contains a vowel, and the first character of `pStr` is not a vowel; or `pStr` contains no vowels. Suppose that `pStr[0]` is not a vowel. Move the first character of `pStr` to the end of `pStr`. This process is repeated until either the first character of `pStr` has become a vowel or all the characters of pStr are checked, in which case `pStr` does not contain any vowels. This discussion translates into the following algorithm:

1. If `pStr[0]` is a vowel, add `"-way"` at the end of `pStr`.
2. Suppose `pStr[0]` is not a vowel.
3. Move the first character of `pStr` to the end of `pStr`. The second character of `pStr` becomes the first character of `pStr`. Now `pStr` may or may not contain a vowel. We use a Boolean variable, `foundVowel`, which is set to `true` if `pStr` contains a vowel, and `false` otherwise.

   a. Suppose that `len` denotes the length of `pStr`.
   b. Initialize `foundVowel` to `false`.
   c. If `pStr[0]` is not a vowel, move `pStr[0]` to the end of `pStr` by calling the function `rotate`.
   d. Repeat Step c until either the first character of `pStr` becomes a vowel or all the characters of `pStr` have been checked.

4. Convert `pStr` into the pig Latin form.
5. Return `pStr`.

The definition of the function `pigLatinString` is:

```
string pigLatinString(string pStr)
{
    string::size_type len;

    bool foundVowel;

    string::size_type counter;

    if (isVowel(pStr[0]))                        //Step 1
        pStr = pStr + "-way";
    else                                         //Step 2
    {
        pStr = pStr + '-';
        pStr = rotate(pStr);                     //Step 3

        len = pStr.length();                     //Step 3.a
        foundVowel = false;                      //Step 3.b
```

```
            for (counter = 1; counter < len - 1;
                            counter++)                  //Step 3.d
                if (isVowel(pStr[0]))
                {
                    foundVowel = true;
                    break;
                }
                else                                    //Step 3.c
                    pStr = rotate(pStr);

            if (!foundVowel)                             //Step 4
                pStr = pStr.substr(1, len) + "-way";
            else
                pStr = pStr + "ay";
        }

        return pStr;                                     //Step 5
} //end pigLatinString
```

MAIN
ALGORITHM

1. Get the string.
2. Call the function `pigLatinString` to find the pig Latin form of the string.
3. Output the pig Latin form of the string.

COMPLETE PROGRAM LISTING

```
//****************************************************************
// Author: D.S. Malik
//
// Program: Pig Latin Strings
// This program reads a string and outputs the pig Latin form
// of the string.
//****************************************************************

#include <iostream>
#include <string>

using namespace std;

bool isVowel(char ch);
string rotate(string pStr);
string pigLatinString(string pStr);
```

8

```cpp
int main()
{
    string str;

    cout << "Enter a string: ";
    cin >> str;
    cout << endl;

    cout << "The pig Latin form of " << str << " is: "
         << pigLatinString(str) << endl;

    return 0;
} //end main

bool isVowel(char ch)
{
    switch (ch)
    {
    case 'A':
    case 'E':
    case 'I':
    case 'O':
    case 'U':
    case 'Y':
    case 'a':
    case 'e':
    case 'i':
    case 'o':
    case 'u':
    case 'y':
        return true;

    default:
        return false;
    }
} //end isVowel

string rotate(string pStr)
{
    string::size_type len = pStr.length();

    string rStr;

    rStr = pStr.substr(1, len - 1) + pStr[0];

    return rStr;
} //end rotate

string pigLatinString(string pStr)
{
    string::size_type len;

    bool foundVowel;
```

```
        string::size_type counter;

        if (isVowel(pStr[0]))                        //Step 1
            pStr = pStr + "-way";
        else                                         //Step 2
        {
            pStr = pStr + '-';
            pStr = rotate(pStr);                     //Step 3

            len = pStr.length();                     //Step 3.a
            foundVowel = false;                      //Step 3.b

            for (counter = 1; counter < len - 1;
                              counter++)             //Step 3.d
                if (isVowel(pStr[0]))
                {
                    foundVowel = true;
                    break;
                }
                else                                 //Step 3.c
                    pStr = rotate(pStr);

            if (!foundVowel)                         //Step 4
                pStr = pStr.substr(1, len) + "-way";
            else
                pStr = pStr + "ay";
        }

        return pStr;                                 //Step 5
    } //end pigLatinString
```

Sample Runs: In these sample runs, the user input is shaded.

Sample Run 1:

```
Enter a string: eye

The pig Latin form of eye is: eye-way
```

Sample Run 2:

```
Enter a string: There

The pig Latin form of There is: ere-Thay
```

Sample Run 3:

```
Enter a string: 123456

The pig Latin form of 123456 is: 123456-way
```

8

Enumeration Type (Optional)

Chapter 1 defined a data type as a set of values together with a set of operations on those values. For example, the **int** data type consists of integers from –2,147,483,648 to 2,147,483,647 and the set of operations on these numbers—namely, the arithmetic operations (+, –, *, /, and %). Because the main objective of a program is to manipulate data, the concept of a data type becomes fundamental to any programming language. By providing data types, you specify what values are legal and tell the user what kinds of operations are allowed on those values. The system thus provides you with built-in checks against errors.

The data types with which you have worked until now were mostly **int**, **bool**, **char**, and **double**. Even though these data types are sufficient to solve just about any problem, situations occur when these data types are not adequate to solve a particular problem. C++ provides a mechanism for users to create their own data types, which greatly enhances the flexibility of the programming language.

In this section, you will learn how to create your own simple data types, known as the enumeration types. To define an **enumeration type**, you need the following items:

- A name for the data type
- A set of values for the data type
- A set of operations on the values

C++ lets you define a new simple data type wherein you specify its name and values, but not the operations. Preventing users from creating their own operations avoids potential system failures.

The values that you specify for the data type must be identifiers.

The syntax to define an enumeration type is

```
enum typeName {value1, value2, ...};
```

where **value1**, **value2**, ... are identifiers called **enumerators**. In C++, **enum** is a reserved word.

By listing all of the values between the braces, you also specify an ordering among the values. That is, **value1 < value2 < value3 <....** Thus, the enumeration type is an ordered set of values. Moreover, the default value assigned to these enumerators starts at 0. That is, the default value assigned to **value1** is 0, the default value assigned to **value2** is 1, and so on. (You can assign different values—other than the default values—for the enumerators when you define the enumeration type.) Also notice that the enumerators **value1**, **value2**, ... are *not* variables.

EXAMPLE 8-10

The statement

```
enum colors {BROWN, BLUE, RED, GREEN, YELLOW};
```

defines a new data type, called `colors`, and the values belonging to this data type are BROWN, BLUE, RED, GREEN, and YELLOW.

EXAMPLE 8-11

The statement

```
enum standing {FRESHMAN, SOPHOMORE, JUNIOR, SENIOR};
```

defines `standing` to be an enumeration type. The values belonging to `standing` are FRESHMAN, SOPHOMORE, JUNIOR, and SENIOR.

EXAMPLE 8-12

Consider the following statements:

```
enum grades {'A', 'B', 'C', 'D', 'F'}; //illegal enumeration type
enum places {1ST, 2ND, 3RD, 4TH};   //illegal enumeration type
```

These are illegal enumeration types because none of the values is an identifier. The following, however, are legal enumeration types:

```
enum grades {A, B, C, D, F};
enum places {FIRST, SECOND, THIRD, FOURTH};
```

If a value has already been used in one enumeration type, it cannot be used by any other enumeration type in the same block. The same rules apply to enumeration types declared outside of any blocks. Example 8-13 illustrates this concept.

EXAMPLE 8-13

Consider the following statements:

```
enum mathStudents {JOHN, BILL, CINDY, LISA, RON};
enum compStudents {SUSAN, CATHY, JOHN, WILLIAM}; //illegal
```

Suppose that these statements are in the same program in the same block. The second enumeration type, `compStudents`, is not allowed because the value JOHN was used in the previous enumeration type `mathStudents`.

Declaring Variables

Once a data type is defined, you can declare variables of that type. The syntax for declaring variables of an **enum** type is the same as before:

```
dataType identifier, identifier,...;
```

The statement

```
enum sports {BASKETBALL, FOOTBALL, HOCKEY, BASEBALL, SOCCER,
             VOLLEYBALL};
```

defines an enumeration type, called **sports**. The statement

```
sports popularSport, mySport;
```

declares `popularSport` and `mySport` to be variables of the type `sports`.

Assignment

Once a variable is declared, you can store values in it. Assuming the previous declaration, the statement

```
popularSport = FOOTBALL;
```

stores FOOTBALL in `popularSport`. The statement

```
mySport = popularSport;
```

copies the value of `popularSport` into `mySport`.

Operations on Enumeration Types

No arithmetic operations are allowed on the enumeration type. So, the following statements are illegal:

```
mySport = popularSport + 2;              //illegal
popularSport = football + SOCCER;        //illegal
popularSport = popularSport * 2;         //illegal
```

Also, the increment and decrement operations are not allowed on enumeration types. So, the following statements are illegal:

```
popularSport++;   //illegal
popularSport--;   //illegal
```

Suppose you want to increment the value of `popularSport` by 1. You can use the cast operator as follows:

```
popularSport = static_cast<sports>(popularSport + 1);
```

When the type name is used, the compiler assumes that the user understands what he or she is doing. Thus, the preceding statement is compiled, and during execution it advances the value of `popularSport` to the next value in the list. Consider the following statements:

```
popularSport = FOOTBALL;
popularSport = static_cast<sports>(popularSport + 1);
```

After the second statement, the value of `popularSport` is HOCKEY. Similarly, the statements

```
popularSport = FOOTBALL;
popularSport = static_cast<sports>(popularSport - 1);
```

result in storing BASKETBALL in `popularSport`.

Relational Operators

Because an enumeration is an ordered set of values, the relational operators can be used with the enumeration type. Once again, suppose you have the enumeration type `sports` and the variables `popularSport` and `mySport` as defined earlier. Then,

```
FOOTBALL <= SOCCER is true
HOCKEY > BASKETBALL is true
BASEBALL < FOOTBALL is false
```

Suppose that:

```
popularSport = SOCCER;
mySport = VOLLEYBALL;
```

Then,

```
popularSport < mySport is true
```

Enumeration Types and Loops

Recall that the enumeration type is an integral type and that, using the cast operator (that is, type name), you can increment, decrement, and compare the values of the enumeration type. Therefore, you can use these enumeration types in loops. Suppose `mySport` is a variable, as declared earlier. Consider the following `for` loop:

```
for (mySport = BASKETBALL; mySport <= SOCCER;
                    mySport = static_cast<sports>(mySport + 1))
    .
    .
    .
```

8

This `for` loop has 5 iterations.

Using enumeration types in loops increases the readability of the program.

Input/Output of Enumeration Types

Because input and output are defined only for built-in data types such as `int`, `char`, `double`, and so on, the enumeration type can be neither input nor output (directly). However, you can input and output enumeration indirectly. Example 8-14 illustrates this concept.

EXAMPLE 8-14

Suppose you have the following statements:

```
enum courses {ALGEBRA, BASIC, CPP, ANALYSIS, CHEMISTRY, HISTORY};
courses registered;
```

The first statement defines an enumeration type, `courses`; the second declares a variable `registered` of the type `courses`. You can read (that is, input) the enumeration type with the help of the `char` data type. Note that you can distinguish between some of the values in the enumeration type `courses` just by reading the first character, and between other values by reading the first two characters. For example, you can distinguish between `ALGEBRA` and `BASIC` just by reading the first character; you can distinguish between `ALGEBRA` and `ANALYSIS` by reading the first two characters. To read these values from, say, the keyboard, you read two characters and then use a selection structure to assign the value to the variable `registered`. Thus, you need to declare two variables of the type `char`.

```
char ch1, ch2;
cin >> ch1 >> ch2; //Read two characters
```

The following `switch` statement assigns the appropriate value to the variable `registered`:

```
switch (ch1)
{
case 'a':
    if (ch2 == 'l')
        registered = ALGEBRA;
    else
        registered = ANALYSIS;
    break;

case 'b':
    registered = BASIC;
    break;

case 'c':
    if (ch2 == 'h')
        registered = CHEMISTRY;
```

```
        else
            registered = CPP;
        break;

case 'h':
    registered = HISTORY;
    break;

default:
    cout << "Illegal input." << endl;
}
```

Similarly, you can output the enumeration type indirectly:

```
switch (registered)
{
case ALGEBRA:
    cout << "Algebra";
    break;

case ANALYSIS:
    cout << "Analysis";
    break;

case BASIC:
    cout << "Basic";
    break;

case CHEMISTRY:
    cout << "Chemistry";
    break;

case CPP:
    cout << "CPP";
    break;

case HISTORY:
    cout << "History";
    break;
}
```

8

 NOTE   If you try to output the value of an enumerator directly, the computer will output the value assigned to the enumerator. For example, suppose that **registered = ALGEBRA;**. The following statement will output the value 0 because the (default) value assigned to ALGEBRA is 0:

```
cout << registered << endl;
```

Similarly, the following statement will output 4:

```
cout << CHEMISTRY << endl;
```

Functions and Enumeration Types

You can pass the enumeration type as a parameter to functions just like any other simple data type—that is, by either value or reference. Also, as with any other simple data type, a function can return a value of the enumeration type. Using this facility, you can use functions to input and output enumeration types.

The following function inputs data from the keyboard and returns a value of the enumeration type. Assume that the enumeration type **courses** is defined as before.

```cpp
courses readCourses()
{
    courses registered;
    char ch1, ch2;

    cout << "Enter the first two letters of the course: "
         << endl;
    cin >> ch1 >> ch2;

    switch (ch1)
    {
    case 'a':
        if (ch2 == 'l')
            registered = ALGEBRA;
        else
            registered = ANALYSIS;
        break;

    case 'b':
        registered = BASIC;
        break;

    case 'c':
        if (ch2 == 'h')
            registered = CHEMISTRY;
        else
            registered = CPP;
        break;

    case 'h':
        registered = HISTORY;
        break;

     default:
        cout << "Illegal input." << endl;
    } //end switch

    return registered;
} //end readCourses
```

The following function outputs an enumeration type value:

```cpp
void printEnum(courses registered)
{
    switch (registered)
    {
    case ALGEBRA:
        cout << "Algebra";
        break;

    case ANALYSIS:
        cout << "Analysis";
        break;

    case BASIC:
        cout << "Basic";
        break;

    case CHEMISTRY:
        cout << "Chemistry";
        break;

    case CPP:
        cout << "CPP";
        break;

    case HISTORY:
        cout << "History";
        break;
    }//end switch
}//end printEnum
```

8

Declaring Variables When Defining the Enumeration Type

In previous sections, you first defined an enumeration type and then declared variables of that type. C++ allows you to combine these two steps into one. That is, you can declare variables of an enumeration type when you define an enumeration type. For example, the statement

```cpp
enum grades {A, B, C, D, F} courseGrade;
```

defines an enumeration type, `grades`, and declares a variable `courseGrade` of the type `grades`.

Similarly, the statement

```cpp
enum coins {PENNY, NICKEL, DIME, HALFDOLLAR, DOLLAR} change, usCoins;
```

defines an enumeration type, `coins`, and declares two variables, `change` and `usCoins`, of the type `coins`.

Anonymous Data Types

A data type wherein you directly specify values in the variable declaration with no type name is called an **anonymous type**. The following statement creates an anonymous type:

```
enum {BASKETBALL, FOOTBALL, BASEBALL, HOCKEY} mySport;
```

This statement specifies the values and declares a variable `mySport`, but no name is given to the data type.

Creating an anonymous type, however, has drawbacks. First, because there is no name for the type, you cannot pass an anonymous type as a parameter to a function, and a function cannot return an anonymous type value. Second, values used in one anonymous type can be used in another anonymous type, but variables of those types are treated differently. Consider the following statements:

```
enum {ENGLISH, FRENCH, SPANISH, GERMAN, RUSSIAN} languages;
enum {ENGLISH, FRENCH, SPANISH, GERMAN, RUSSIAN} foreignLanguages;
```

Even though the variables `languages` and `foreignLanguages` have the same values, the compiler treats them as variables of different types. The following statement is, therefore, illegal:

```
languages = foreignLanguages; //Illegal
```

Even though these facilities are available, use them with care. To avoid confusion, first define an enumeration type and then declare the variables.

We now describe the `typedef` statement in C++.

typedef Statement

In C++, you can create synonyms or aliases to a previously defined data type by using the `typedef` statement. The general syntax of the `typedef` statement is:

```
typedef existingTypeName newTypeName;
```

In C++, `typedef` is a reserved word. Note that the `typedef` statement does not create any new data type; it creates only an alias to an existing data type.

EXAMPLE 8-15

The statement

```
typedef int integer;
```

creates an alias, `integer`, for the data type `int`. Similarly, the statement

```
typedef double real;
```

creates an alias, `real`, for the data type `double`. The statement

```
typedef double decimal;
```

creates an alias, `decimal`, for the data type `double`.

Using the `typedef` statement, you can create your own Boolean data type, as shown in Example 8-16

EXAMPLE 8-16

From Chapter 3, recall that logical (Boolean) expressions in C++ evaluate to 1 or 0, which are, in fact, `int` values. As a logical value, 1 represents `true` and 0 represents `false`. Consider the following statements:

```
typedef int Boolean;          //Line 1
const Boolean True = 1;        //Line 2
const Boolean False = 0;       //Line 3
Boolean flag;                  //Line 4
```

The statement at Line 1 creates an alias, `Boolean`, for the data type `int`. The statements at Lines 2 and 3 declare the named constants `True` and `False` and initialize them to 1 and 0, respectively. The statement at Line 4 declares `flag` to be a variable of the type `Boolean`. Because `flag` is a variable of the type `Boolean`, the following statement is legal:

```
flag = True;
```

8

QUICK REVIEW

1. The **namespace** mechanism is a feature of ANSI/ISO Standard C++.

2. A **namespace** member is usually a named constant, variable, function, or another **namespace**.

3. The scope of a **namespace** member is local to the **namespace**.

4. One way to access a **namespace** member outside the **namespace** is to precede the **namespace** member name with the **namespace** name and scope resolution operator.

5. In C++, **namespace** is a reserved word.

6. To use the **namespace** mechanism, the program must include the header files without the extension h.

7. The **using** statement simplifies accessing **namespace** members.

8. In C++, **using** is a reserved word.

9. The keyword **namespace** must appear in the **using** statement.

10. When accessing a **namespace** member without the **using** statement, the **namespace** name and the scope resolution operator must precede the name of the **namespace** member.

11. To use an identifier declared in the standard header files without the **namespace** name, after including all the necessary header files, the following statement must appear in the program:

    `using namespace std;`

12. A string is a sequence of zero or more characters.

13. Strings in C++ are enclosed in double quotation marks.

14. To use the type **string**, the program must include the header file **string**.

15. The assignment operator can be used with the **string** type.

16. The operator + can be used to concatenate values of **string** objects.

17. Relational operators, discussed in Chapter 3, can be applied to **string** objects.

18. In a string, the position of the first character is 0, the position of the second character is 1, and so on.

19. The length of a string is the number of characters in the string.

20. In C++, **[ ]** is called the array subscript operator.

21. To access an individual character within a string, use the array subscript operator together with the position of the character.

22. The function **length** returns the number of characters currently in the string. The syntax to call the function **length** is

    `strVar.length()`

    where **strVar** is a **string** object.

23. The function **size** returns the number of characters currently in the string. The syntax to call the function **size** is

    `strVar.size()`

    where **strVar** is a **string** object. The function **size** works in the same way as does the **length** function.

24. The function **find** searches a string to locate the first occurrence of a particular substring, and returns an unsigned integer value (of the type **string::size_type**), giving the result of the search. The syntax to call the function **find** is

    `strVar.find(strExp)`

    or

    `strVar.find(strExp, pos)`

where `strVar` is a string object, and `strExp` is a string expression evaluating to a string. In the second form of the function `find`, `pos` specifies the position in the string where the search should begin. The argument of the function `find` (that is, `strExp`) can also be a character. If the search is successful, the function `find` returns the position in `strVar` where the match begins. If the search is unsuccessful, the function `find` returns the `npos` value.

25. The function `substr` returns a particular substring of a string. The syntax to call the function `substr` is

```
strVar.substr(expr1, expr2)
```

where `expr1` and `expr2` are expressions evaluating to unsigned integers. The expression `expr1` specifies a position within the string (the starting position of the substring). The expression `expr2` specifies the length of the substring to be returned.

26. The function `swap` is used to swap the contents of two string variables. The syntax to use the function `swap` is

```
strVar1.swap(strVar2);
```

where `strVar1` and `strVar2` are string variables. This statement swaps the values of `strVar1` and `strVar2`.

27. An enumeration type is a set of ordered values.

28. C++'s reserved word `enum` is used to create an enumeration type.

29. The syntax of `enum` is

```
enum typeName {value1, value2,...};
```

where `value1, value2,...` are identifiers, and `value1 < value2 < ....`.

30. No arithmetic operations are allowed on the enumeration type.

31. Relational operators can be used with `enum` values.

32. Enumeration type values cannot be input or output directly.

33. Enumeration types can be passed as parameters to functions either by value or by reference.

34. A function can return a value of the enumeration type.

35. An anonymous type is one where a variable's values are specified without any type name.

36. C++'s reserved word `typedef` is used to create synonyms or aliases to previously defined data types.

37. Anonymous types cannot be passed as parameters to functions.

8

EXERCISES

1. Mark the following statements as true or false.

    a. You can use the `namespace` mechanism with header files with the extension h.

    b. Suppose `str = "ABCD";`. After the statement `str[1] = 'a';`, the value of `str` is `"aBCD"`.

    c. Suppose `str = "abcd"`. After the statement

    `str = str + "ABCD";`

    the value of `str` is `"ABCD"`.

    d. The following is a valid C++ enumeration type:

    `enum romanNumerals {I, V, X, L, C, D, M};`

    e. Given the declaration

    ```
    enum cars {FORD, GM, TOYOTA, HONDA};
    cars domesticCars = FORD;
    ```

    the statement

    `domesticCars = domesticCars + 1;`

    sets the value of `domesticCars` to GM.

    f. A function can return a value of an enumeration type.

    g. You can input the value of an enumeration type directly from a standard input device.

    h. The only arithmetic operations allowed on the enumeration type are increment and decrement.

    i. The values in the domain of an enumeration type are called enumerators.

    j. The following are legal C++ statements in the same block of a C++ program:

    ```
    enum mathStudents {BILL, JOHN, LISA, RON, CINDY, SHELLY};
    enum historyStudents {AMANDA, BOB, JACK, TOM, SUSAN};
    ```

    k. The following statement creates an anonymous type:

    `enum {A, B, C, D, F} studentGrade;`

2. What is wrong with the following program?

```
#include <iostream>              //Line 1

int main()                       //Line 2
{                                //Line 3
    cout << "Hello World! " << endl;   //Line 4

    return 0;                    //Line 5
}                                //Line 6
```

3. What is wrong with the following program?

```
#include <iostream.h>                          //Line 1

using namespace std;                           //Line 2

int main()                                     //Line 3
{                                              //Line 4
    int x = 0;                                 //Line 5
    cout << "x = " << x << endl;               //Line 6
    return 0;                                  //Line 7
}                                              //Line 8
```

4. What is wrong with the following program?

```
#include <iostream>                                         //Line 1

namespace aaa                                               //Line 2
{                                                           //Line 3
    const int x = 0;                                        //Line 4
    double y;                                               //Line 5
}                                                           //Line 6

using namespace std;                                        //Line 7

int main()                                                  //Line 8
{                                                           //Line 9
    y = 34.50;                                              //Line 10
    cout << "x = " << x << ", y = " << y << endl;           //Line 11
    return 0;                                               //Line 12
}                                                           //Line 13
```

5. What is wrong with the following program?

```
#include <iostream>   //Line 1
#include <cmath>      //Line 2

using std;            //Line 3

int main()            //Line 4
{                     //Line 5
    return 0;         //Line 6
}                     //Line 7
```

6. What is the output of the following program?

```
#include <iostream>
#include <string>

using namespace std;

int main()
{
    string str1 = "Amusement Park";
    string str2 = "Going to";
    string str3 = "the";
    string str;
```

8

```
        cout << str2 + ' '+  str3 + ' ' + str1 << endl;
        cout << str1.length() << endl;
        cout << str1.find('P') << endl;
        cout << str1.substr(1, 5) << endl;

        str = "ABCDEFGHIJK";
        cout << str << endl;
        cout << str.length() << endl;

        str[0] = 'a';
        str[2] = 'd';

        cout << str << endl;

        return 0;
}
```

7. Given

```
enum currencyType {DOLLAR, POUND, FRANK, LIRA, MARK};
currencyType currency;
```

which of the following statements are valid?

a. `currency = DOLLAR;`

b. `cin >> currency;`

c. `currency = static_cast<currencyType>(currency + 1);`

d. `for (currency = DOLLAR; currency <= MARK; currency++)`
   `      cout << "*";`

8. Write C++ statements that do the following:

a. Define an **enum** type, `bookType`, with the values `MATH`, `CSC`, `ENGLISH`, `HISTORY`, `PHYSICS`, and `PHILOSOPHY`.

b. Declare a variable `book` of the type `bookType`.

c. Assign `MATH` to the variable `book`.

d. Advance `book` to the next value in the list.

e. Output the value of the variable `book`.

9. Given

```
enum cropType {WHEAT, CORN, RYE, BARLEY, OATS};
cropType   crop;
```

circle the correct answer for the following statements:

a. `static_cast<int>(WHEAT) is 0`

   i.   true   ii.   false

b. `static_cast<cropType>(static_cast<int>(WHEAT) - 1) is WHEAT`

   i.   true   ii.   false

   c.   `Rye > WHEAT`

       i.   true   ii.   false

   d.
```
for (crop = WHEAT; crop <= OATS; ++crop)
    cout << "*";
  cout << endl;
```

      outputs: *****

      i.   true   ii.   false

PROGRAMMING EXERCISES

1. Redo the Programming Example of Chapter 3 (Cable Company Billing) so that all of the named constants are defined in a `namespace`.

2. The Programming Example: Pig Latin Strings converts a string into the pig Latin form, but it processes only one word. Rewrite the program so that it can be used to process a block of text of an unspecified length. If a word ends with a punctuation mark, in the pig Latin form put the punctuation at the end of the string. For example, the pig Latin form of `Hello!` is `ello-Hay!`. Assume that the text contains the following punctuation marks: `,` (comma), `.` (period), `?` (question mark), `;` (semicolon), and `:` (colon).

3. Write a program that prompts the user to input a string. The program then uses the function `substr` to remove all the vowels from the string. For example, if `str = "There"`, then after removing all the vowels, `str = "Thr"`. After removing all the vowels, output the string. Your program must contain a function to remove all the vowels and a function to determine whether a character is a vowel.

4. **(Fraction Calculator)** Write a program that lets the user perform arithmetic operations on fractions. Fractions are of the form a/b, where a and b are integers and $b \neq 0$. Your program must be menu driven, allowing the user to select the operation (+, -, *, or /) and input the numerator and denominator of each fraction. Furthermore, your program must consist of at least the following functions:

   a. Function `menu`: This function informs the user about the program's purpose, explains how to enter data, and allows the user to select the operation.

   b. Function `addFractions`: This function takes as input four integers representing the numerators and denominators of two fractions, adds the fractions, and returns the numerator and denominator of the result. (Notice that this function has a total of six parameters.)

   c. Function `subtractFractions`: This function takes as input four integers representing the numerators and denominators of two fractions, subtracts the second fraction from the first fraction, and returns the numerator and denominator of the result. (Notice that this function has a total of six parameters.)

8

d. Function multiplyFractions: This function takes as input four integers representing the numerators and denominators of two fractions, multiplies the fractions, and returns the numerators and denominators of the result. (Notice that this function has a total of six parameters.)

e. Function divideFractions: This function takes as input four integers representing the numerators and denominators of two fractions, divides the first fraction by the second fraction, and returns the numerator and denominator of the result. (Notice that this function has a total of six parameters.)

Some sample outputs are the following:

```
3 / 4 + 2 / 5 = 23 / 20
2 / 3 * 3 / 5 = 6 / 15
```

Your answer need not be in the lowest terms.

5. a. Define an enumeration type, triangleType, that has the values SCALENE, ISOSCELES, EQUILATERAL, and NOTRIANGLE.

b. Write a function, triangleShape, that takes as parameters three numbers, each of which represents the length of a side of the triangle. The function should return the shape of the triangle. (*Note:* In a triangle, the sum of the lengths of any two sides is greater than the length of the third side.)

c. Write a program that prompts the user to input the lengths of the sides of a triangle and outputs the shape of the triangle.

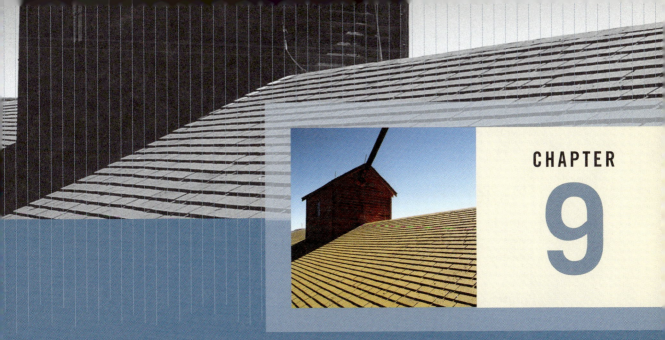

POINTERS

IN THIS CHAPTER, YOU WILL:

- Learn about the pointer data type and pointer variables
- Explore how to declare and manipulate pointer variables
- Learn about the address of operator and the dereferencing operator
- Discover dynamic variables
- Explore how to use the new and delete operators to manipulate dynamic variables
- Learn about pointer arithmetic
- Discover dynamic arrays
- Become aware of the shallow and deep copies

In Chapter 1, you learned that C++'s data types are classified into three categories: simple, structured, and pointers. Until now, you have studied only the first two data types. In this chapter, we discuss the third data type, called the pointer data type. You will first learn how to declare pointer variables (or pointers, for short) and manipulate the data to which they point. Later, you will use these concepts when you study dynamic arrays.

Pointer Data Type and Pointer Variables

The values belonging to pointer data types are the memory addresses of your computer. However, there is no name associated with the pointer data type in C++. Because the domain—that is, the values of a pointer data type—is the addresses (memory locations), a pointer variable is a variable whose content is an address, that is, a memory location.

Pointer variable: A variable whose content is an address (that is, a memory address)

Declaring Pointer Variables

The value of a pointer variable is an address. That is, the value refers to another memory space. The data is typically stored in this memory space. Therefore, when you declare a pointer variable, you also specify the data type of the value to be stored in the memory location to which the pointer variable points.

In C++, you declare a pointer variable by using the asterisk symbol (*) between the data type and the variable name. The general syntax to declare a pointer variable is:

```
dataType *identifier;
```

As an example, consider the following statements:

```
int *p;
char *ch;
```

In these statements, both p and ch are pointer variables. The content of p (when properly assigned) points to a memory location of type `int`, and the content of ch points to a memory location of type `char`. Usually p is called a pointer variable of type `int`, and ch is called a pointer variable of type `char`.

Before discussing how pointers work, let us make the following observations. The following statements to declare p to be a pointer variable of type `int` are equivalent:

```
int *p;
int* p;
int * p;
```

Thus, the character * can appear anywhere between the data type name and the variable name.

Now consider the following statement:

```
int* p, q;
```

In this statement, only p is a pointer variable, not q. Here q is an `int` variable. To avoid confusion, we prefer to attach the character * to the variable name. So the preceding statement is written as:

```
int *p, q;
```

Of course, the statement

```
int *p, *q;
```

declares both p and q to be pointer variables of type `int`.

Now that you know how to declare pointers, next we discuss how to make a pointer point to a memory space and how to manipulate the data stored in these memory locations.

Because the value of a pointer is a memory address, a pointer can store the address of a memory space of the designated type. For example, if p is a pointer of type `int`, p can store the address of any memory space of type `int`. C++ provides two operators—the address of operator (&) and the dereferencing operator (*)—to work with pointers. The next two sections describe these operators.

Address of Operator (&)

In C++, the ampersand, &, called the **address of operator**, is a unary operator that returns the address of its operand. For example, given the statements

```
int x;
int *p;
```

the statement

```
p = &x;
```

assigns the address of x to p. That is, x and the value of p refer to the same memory location.

Dereferencing Operator (*)

Every chapter until this one has used the asterisk character, *, as the binary multiplication operator. C++ also uses * as a unary operator. When *, commonly referred to as the **dereferencing operator** or **indirection operator**, is used as a unary operator, * refers to the object to which the operand of the * (that is, the pointer) points. For example, given the statements

9

```
int x = 25;
int *p;
p = &x;    //store the address of x in p
```

the statement

```
cout << *p << endl;
```

prints the value stored in the memory space to which p points, which is the value of x. Also, the statement

```
*p = 55;
```

stores 55 in the memory location to which p points—that is, 55 is stored in x.

Example 9-1 shows how a pointer variable works.

EXAMPLE 9-1

Let us consider the following statements:

```
int *p;
int num;
```

In these statements, p is a pointer variable of type **int**, and num is a variable of type **int**. Let us assume that memory location 1200 is allocated for p, and memory location 1800 is allocated for num. (See Figure 9-1.)

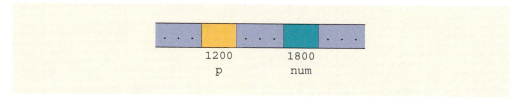

1200   1800
  p   num

FIGURE 9-1 Variables p and num

Consider the following statements:

1. num = 78;
2. p = #
3. *p = 24;

The following shows the values of the variables after the execution of each statement.

After Statement	Values of the Variables	Explanation

1

The statement `num = 78;` stores 78 into `num`.

2

The statement `p = &num;` stores the address of `num`, which is `1800`, into `p`.

3

The statement `*p = 24;` stores 24 into the memory location to which `p` points. Because the value of `p` is `1800`, statement 3 stores 24 into memory location `1800`. Note that the value of `num` is also changed.

Let us summarize the preceding discussion.

1. A declaration such as `int *p;` allocates memory for `p` only, not for `*p`. Later, you will learn how to allocate memory for `*p`.

2. The content of `p` points only to a memory location of type `int`.

3. `&p`, `p`, and `*p` all have different meanings.

4. `&p` means the address of `p`—that is, `1200` (as shown in Figure 9-1).

5. `p` means the content of `p`, which is `1800`, after the statement `p = &num;` executes.

6. `*p` means the content of the memory location to which `p` points. Note that the value of `*p` is 78 after the statement `p = &num;` executes; the value of `*p` is 24 after the statement `*p = 24;` executes.

The program in Example 9-2 further illustrates how a pointer variable works.

EXAMPLE 9-2

```
//********************************************************
// Author: D.S. Malik
//
// This program illustrates how a pointer variable works.
//********************************************************
```

```cpp
#include <iostream>                                  //Line 1

using namespace std;                                 //Line 2

int main()                                           //Line 3
{                                                    //Line 4
    int *p;                                          //Line 5
    int num1 = 5;                                    //Line 6
    int num2 = 8;                                    //Line 7

    p = &num1; //store the address of num1 into p;  Line 8

    cout << "Line 9: &num1 = " << &num1
         << ", p = " << p << endl;                   //Line 9
    cout << "Line 10: num1 = " << num1
         << ", *p = " << *p << endl;                 //Line 10

    *p = 10;                                         //Line 11
    cout << "Line 12: num1 = " << num1
         << ", *p = " << *p << endl << endl;         //Line 12

    p = &num2; //store the address of num2 into p;  Line 13

    cout << "Line 14: &num2 = " << &num2
         << ", p = " << p << endl;                   //Line 14
    cout << "Line 15: num2 = " << num2
         << ", *p = " << *p << endl;                 //Line 15

    *p = 2 * (*p);                                   //Line 16
    cout << "Line 17: num2 = " << num2
         << ", *p = " << *p << endl;                 //Line 17

    return 0;                                        //Line 18
}                                                    //Line 19
```

Sample run:

```
Line 9: &num1 = 0012FF54, p = 0012FF54
Line 10: num1 = 5, *p = 5
Line 12: num1 = 10, *p = 10

Line 14: &num2 = 0012FF48, p = 0012FF48
Line 15: num2 = 8, *p = 8
Line 17: num2 = 16, *p = 16
```

For the most part, the preceding output is straightforward. Let us look at some of these statements. The statement in Line 8 stores the address of num1 into p. The statement in Line 9 outputs the value of &num1, the address of num1, and the value of p. (Note that the values output by Line 9 are machine dependent. When you execute this program on your computer, you are likely to get different values of &num1 and p.) The statement in Line 10 outputs the value of num1 and *p. Because p points to the memory location of num1, *p outputs the value of this memory location, that is, of num1. The statement in Line 11 changes the value of *p to 10. Because p points to the memory location num1, the value of num1 is also changed. The statement in Line 12 outputs the value of num1 and *p.

The statement in Line 13 stores the address of num2 into p. So after the execution of this statement, p points to num2. So, any change that *p makes immediately changes the value of num2. The statement in Line 14 outputs the address of num2 and the value of p. The statement in Line 15 outputs the value of num2 and *p. The statement in Line 16 multplies the value of *p, which is the value of num2, by 2 and stores the new value into *p. This statement also changes the value of num2. The statement in Line 17 outputs the value of num2 and *p.

Initializing Pointer Variables

Because C++ does not automatically initialize variables, pointer variables must be initialized if you do not want them to point to anything. Pointer variables are initialized using the constant value 0, called the **null pointer**. Thus, the statement p = 0; stores the null pointer in p; that is, p points to nothing. Some programmers use the named constant NULL to initialize pointer variables. The following two statements are equivalent:

```
p = NULL;
p = 0;
```

The number 0 is the only number that can be directly assigned to a pointer variable.

Dynamic Variables

In the previous sections, you learned how to declare pointer variables, how to store the address of a variable into a pointer variable of the same type as the variable, and how to manipulate data using pointers. However, you learned how to use pointers to manipulate data only into memory spaces that were created using other variables. In other words, the pointers manipulated data into existing memory spaces. So what is the benefit to using pointers? You can access these memory spaces by working with the variables that were used to create them. In this section, you learn about the power behind pointers. In particular, you will learn how to allocate and deallocate memory during program execution, using pointers.

Variables that are created during program execution are called **dynamic variables**. With the help of pointers, C++ creates dynamic variables. C++ provides two operators, **new** and **delete**, to create and destroy dynamic variables, respectively. When a program requires a new variable, the operator **new** is used. When a program no longer needs a dynamic variable, the operator **delete** is used.

In C++, **new** and **delete** are reserved words.

9

Operator new

The operator **new** has two forms: one to allocate a single variable, and another to allocate an array of variables. The syntax to use the operator **new** is

```
new dataType;          //to allocate a single variable
new dataType[intExp];  //to allocate an array of variables
```

where **intExp** is any expression evaluating to a positive integer.

The operator **new** allocates memory (a variable) of the designated type and returns a pointer to it—that is, the address of this allocated memory. Moreover, the allocated memory is uninitialized.

Consider the following declaration:

```
int *p;
char *q;
int x;
```

The statement

```
p = &x;
```

stores the address of **x** in **p**. However, no new memory is allocated. On the other hand, consider the following statement:

```
p = new int;
```

This statement allocates memory of type **int**, during program execution somewhere in memory, and stores the address of the allocated memory in **p**. The allocated memory is accessed via pointer dereferencing—namely, ***p**. Similarly, the statement

```
q = new char[16];
```

creates an array of 16 components of type **char** and stores the base address of the array in **q**.

Because a dynamic variable is unnamed, it cannot be accessed directly. It is accessed indirectly by the pointer returned by **new**. The following statements illustrate this concept:

```
int *p;         //p is a pointer of type int

p = new int;    //allocates memory of type int and stores the
                //address of the allocated memory in p
*p = 28;        //stores 28 in the allocated memory
```

 NOTE Recall that the operator **new** allocates memory space of a specific type and returns the (starting) address of the allocated memory space. However, if the operator **new** is unable to allocate the required memory space (for example, there is not enough memory space), then the program may terminate with an error message.

Operator `delete`

Suppose you have the following declaration:

```
int *p;
```

This statement declares `p` to be a pointer variable of type `int`. Next, consider the following statements:

```
p = new int;      //Line 1
*p = 54;          //Line 2
p = new int;      //Line 3
*p = 73;          //Line 4
```

Let us see the effect of these statements. The statement in Line 1 allocates memory space of type `int` and stores the address of the allocated memory space into `p`. Suppose that the address of allocated memory space is `1500`. Then, the value of `p` after the execution of this statement is `1500`. (See Figure 9-2.)

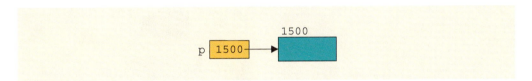

FIGURE 9-2   `p` after the execution of `p = new int;`

In Figure 9-2, the number `1500` on top of the box indicates the address of the memory space. The statement in Line 2 stores `54` into the memory space to which `p` points, which is `1500`. In other words, after execution of the statement in Line 2, the value stored into memory space at location `1500` is `54`. (See Figure 9-3.)

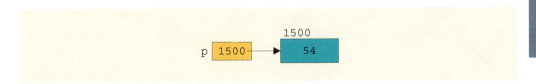

FIGURE 9-3   `p` and `*p` after the execution of `*p = 54;`

Next, the statement in Line 3 executes, which allocates a memory space of type `int` and stores the address of the allocated memory space into `p`. Suppose the address of this allocated memory space is `1800`. It follows that the value of `p` is now `1800`. (See Figure 9-4.)

9

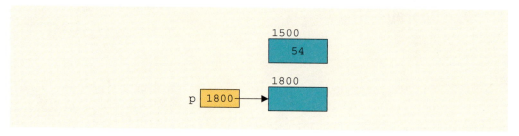

FIGURE 9-4 p after the execution of p = `new int;`

The statement in Line 4 stores **73** into the memory space to which **p** points, which is **1800**. In other words, after execution of the statement in Line 4, the value stored into the memory space at location **1800** is **73**. (See Figure 9-5.)

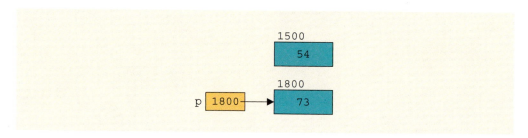

FIGURE 9-5 p after the execution of *p = 73;

Now the obvious question is: What happened to the memory space **1500**, to which **p** was pointing after execution of the statement in Line 3? After execution of the statement in Line 3, **p** points to the new memory space at location **1800**. The previous memory space at location **1500** is now inaccessible. In addition, the memory space **1500** remains marked as allocated. In other words, it cannot be reallocated. This is called **memory leak**. That is, there is an unused memory space that cannot be allocated.

Imagine what would happen if you execute statements such as Line 1 a few thousand times, or a few million times. There will be a good amount of memory leak. The program might then run out of memory space for data manipulation, and eventually result in an abnormal termination of the program.

The question at hand is how to *avoid* memory leak. When a dynamic variable is no longer needed, it can be destroyed; that is, its memory can be deallocated. The C++ operator **delete** is used to destroy dynamic variables. The syntax to use the operator **delete** has the following two forms:

```
delete pointerVariable;        //to deallocate a single
                               //dynamic variable
delete [] pointerVariable;     //to deallocate a dynamically
                               //created array
```

Thus, given the declarations of the previous section, the statements

```
delete p;
delete str;
```

deallocate the memory spaces to which the pointers `p` and `str` point.

Suppose `p` is a pointer variable, as declared previously. Note that an expression such as

```
delete p;
```

only marks as deallocated the memory spaces to which these pointer variables point. Depending on a particular system, after these statements execute, these pointer variables may still contain the addresses of the deallocated memory spaces. In this case, we say that these pointers are **dangling**. Therefore, if you later access the memory spaces via these pointers without properly initializing them, depending on a particular system, either the program will access a wrong memory space, which may result in corrupt data, or the program will terminate with an error message. One way to avoid this pitfall is to set these pointers to `NULL` after the `delete` operation.

The progam in the following example illustrates how to allocate dynamic memory and how to manipulate data into that dynamic memory.

EXAMPLE 9-3

```
//***********************************************************
// Author: D.S. Malik
//
// This program illustrates how to allocate dynamic memory
// using a pointer variable and how to manipulate data into
// that memory location.
//***********************************************************

#include <iostream>                              //Line 1

using namespace std;                             //Line 2

int main()                                       //Line 3
{                                                //Line 4
    int *p;                                      //Line 5
    int *q;                                      //Line 6

    p = new int;                                 //Line 7
    *p = 34;                                     //Line 8
    cout << "Line 9: p = " << p
         << ", *p = " << *p << endl;             //Line 9

    q = p;                                       //Line 10
    cout << "Line 11: q = " << q
         << ", *q = " << *q << endl;             //Line 11
```

9

```
*q = 45;                                        //Line 12
cout << "Line 13: p = " << p
     << ", *p = " << *p << endl;                //Line 13
cout << "Line 14: q = " << q
     << ", *q = " << *q << endl;                //Line 14

p = new int;                                    //Line 15
*p = 18;                                         //Line 16
cout << "Line 17: p = " << p
     << ", *p = " << *p << endl;                //Line 17
cout << "Line 18: q = " << q
     << ", *q = " << *q << endl;                //Line 18

delete q;                                        //Line 19
q = NULL;                                        //Line 20
q = new int;                                     //Line 21
*q = 62;                                         //Line 22
cout << "Line 23: p = " << p
     << ", *p = " << *p << endl;                //Line 23
cout << "Line 24: q = " << q
     << ", *q = " << *q << endl;                //Line 24

return 0;                                         //Line 25
}                                                 //Line 26
```

Sample Run:

```
Line 9: p = 00355620, *p = 34
Line 11: q = 00355620, *q = 34
Line 13: p = 00355620, *p = 45
Line 14: q = 00355620, *q = 45
Line 17: p = 003556C8, *p = 18
Line 18: q = 00355620, *q = 45
Line 23: p = 003556C8, *p = 18
Line 24: q = 00355620, *q = 62
```

The statements in Lines 5 and 6 declare p and q to be pointer variables of type int. The statement in Line 7 allocates memory of type int and stores the address of the allocated memory into p. (See Figure 9-6.)

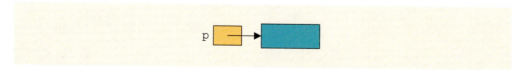

FIGURE 9-6   Pointer p and the memory space to which it points

The box indicates the allocated memory (in this case, of type int), and p together with the arrow indicates that p points to the allocated memory. The statement in Line 8 stores 34 into the memory location to which p points. (See Figure 9-7.)

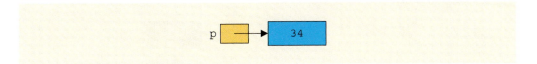

FIGURE 9-7 Pointer p and the value of the memory location to which p points

The statement in Line 9 outputs the value of p and *p. (Note that the values of p and q shown in the sample run are machine dependent. When you execute this program, you are likely to get different values of p and q.)

The statement in Line 10 copies the value of p into q. (See Figure 9-8.)

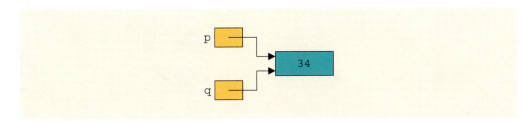

FIGURE 9-8 Pointers p and q and the memory space to which they point after the execution of the statement in Line 10

After the execution of the statement in Line 10, p and q both point to the same memory location. So any changes made into that memory location by q immediately change the value of *p. The statement in Line 11 outputs the value of q and *q. The statement in Line 12 stores 45 into the memory location to which q points. (See Figure 9-9.)

9

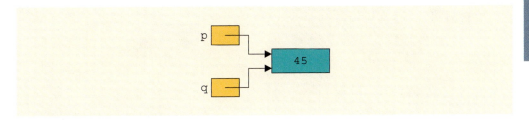

FIGURE 9-9 Pointers p and q and the memory space to which they point after the execution of the statement in Line 12

The statements in Lines 13 and 14 output the values of p, *p, q, and *q.

The statement in Line 15 allocates memory space of type **int** and stores the address of that memory into p. (See Figure 9-10.)

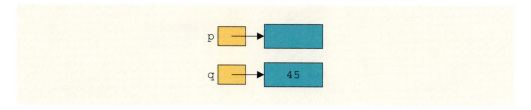

FIGURE 9-10   Pointers p and q and the memory space to which they point after the execution of the statement in Line 15

The statement in Line 16 stores **18** into the memory location to which **p** points. (See Figure 9-11.)

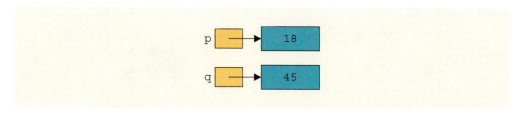

FIGURE 9-11   Pointers p and q and the memory space to which they point after the execution of the statement in Line 16

The statements in Line 17 and 18 output the values of **p**, ***p**, **q**, and ***q**.

The statement in Line 19 deallocates the memory space to which **q** points, and the statement in Line 20 sets the value of **q** to **NULL**. After the execution of the statement in Line 20, **q** does not point to any memory location. (See Figure 9-12.)

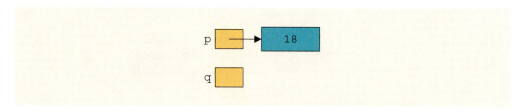

FIGURE 9-12   Pointers p and q and the memory space to which they point after the execution of the statement in Line 20

The statement in Line 21 allocates a memory space of type **int** and stores the address of that memory space into **q**. The statement in Line 22 stores 62 in the memory space to which **q** points. (See Figure 9-13.)

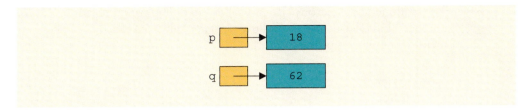

FIGURE 9-13 Pointers p and q and the memory space to which they point after the execution of the statement in Line 22

The statements in Lines 23 and 24 output the values of p, *p, q, and *q.

In the preceding program, omit statements in Lines 19 and 20, rerun the program, and note how the last output statements change.

Operations on Pointer Variables

The operations that are allowed on pointer variables are the assignment and relational operations and some limited arithmetic operations. The value of one pointer variable can be assigned to another pointer variable of the same type. Two pointer variables of the same type can be compared for equality, and so on. Integer values can be added and subtracted from a pointer variable. The value of one pointer variable can be subtracted from another pointer variable.

For example, suppose that we have the following statement:

```
int *p, *q;
```

The statement

```
p = q;
```

copies the value of q into p. After this statement executes, both p and q point to the same memory location. Any changes made to *p automatically change the value of *q, and vice versa.

The expression

```
p == q
```

evaluates to **true** if p and q have the same value—that is, if they point to the same memory location. Similarly, the expression

```
p != q
```

evaluates to **true** if p and q point to different memory locations.

9

The arithmetic operations that are allowed differ from the arithmetic operations on numbers. First, let us use the following statements to explain the increment and decrement operations on pointer variables:

```
int *p;
double *q;
char *chPtr;
```

Recall that the size of the memory allocated for an `int` variable is 4 bytes, a `double` variable is 8 bytes, and a `char` variable is 1 byte.

The statement

```
p++;    or    p = p + 1;
```

increments the value of `p` by 4 bytes because `p` is a pointer of type `int`. Similarly, the statements

```
q++;
chPtr++;
```

increment the value of `q` by 8 bytes and the value of `chPtr` by 1 byte, respectively.

The increment operator increments the value of a pointer variable by the size of the memory to which it is pointing. Similarly, the decrement operator decrements the value of a pointer variable by the size of the memory to which it is pointing.

Moreover, the statement

```
p = p + 2;
```

increments the value of `p` by 8 bytes.

Thus, when an integer is added to a pointer variable, the value of the pointer variable is incremented by the integer times the size of the memory to which the pointer is pointing. Similarly, when an integer is subtracted from a pointer variable, the value of the pointer variable is decremented by the integer times the size of the memory to which the pointer is pointing.

NOTE Pointer arithmetic can be quite dangerous. Using pointer arithmetic, the program can accidentally access the memory locations of other variables and change their content without warning. The programmer is then left to try to find out what went wrong. If a pointer variable tries to access either the memory spaces of other variables or an illegal memory space, some systems might terminate the program with an appropriate error message. Always exercise extra care when doing pointer arithmetic.

Dynamic Arrays

Earlier in this chapter, you learned how to declare and process arrays. The arrays discussed earlier are called static arrays because their size was fixed at compile time. One of the limitations of a static array is that every time you execute the program, the size of the array is fixed, so it might not be possible to use the same array to process different data sets of the same type. One way to handle this limitation is to declare an array that is large enough to process a variety of data sets. However, if the array is big and the data set is small, such a declaration will result in memory waste. On the other hand, it would be helpful if, during program execution, you could prompt the user to enter the size of the array and then create an array of the appropriate size. This approach is especially helpful if you cannot even guess the array size. In this section, you will learn how to create arrays during program execution and how to process such arrays.

An array created during the execution of a program is called a **dynamic array**. To create a dynamic array, we use the second form of the **new** operator.

The statement

```
int *p;
```

declares p to be a pointer variable of type **int**. The statement

```
p = new int[10];
```

allocates 10 contiguous memory locations, each of type **int**, and stores the address of the first memory location into p. In other words, the operator **new** creates an array of 10 components of type **int**, it returns the base address of the array, and the assignment operator stores the base address of the array into p. Thus, the statement

```
*p = 25;
```

stores 25 into the first memory location, and the statements

```
p++;        //p points to the next array component
*p = 35;
```

store 35 into the second memory location. Thus, by using the increment and decrement operations, you can access the components of the array. Of course, after performing a few increment operations, it is possible to lose track of the first array component. C++ allows us to use array notation to access these memory locations. For example, the statements

```
p[0] = 25;
p[1] = 35;
```

store 25 and 35 into the first and second array components, respectively. That is, p[0] refers to the first array component, p[1] refers to the second array component, and so on. In general, p[i] refers to the (i + 1)th array component. After the preceding statements execute, p still points to the first array component. Moreover, the following **for** loop initializes each array component to 0:

9

```
for (int j = 0; j < 10; j++)
    p[j] = 0;
```

When the array notation is used to process the array to which p points, p stays fixed at the first memory location. Moreover, p is a dynamic array, created during program execution.

EXAMPLE 9-4

The following program segment illustrates how to obtain a user's response to get the array size and create a dynamic array during program execution. Consider the following statements:

```
int *intList;                 //Line 1
int arraySize;                //Line 2

cout << "Enter array size: "; //Line 3
cin >> arraySize;             //Line 4
cout << endl;                 //Line 5

intList = new int[arraySize]; //Line 6
```

The statement in Line 1 declares intList to be a pointer of type int, and the statement in Line 2 declares arraySize to be an int variable. The statement in Line 3 prompts the user to enter the size of the array, and the statement in Line 4 inputs the array size into the variable arraySize. The statement in Line 6 creates an array of the size specified by arraySize, and the base address of the array is stored in intList. From this point on, you can treat intList just like any other array. For example, you can use the array notation to process the elements of intList and pass intList as a parameter to the function.

Array Name: A Constant Pointer

The statement

```
int list[5];
```

declares list to be an array of 5 components. Recall that list itself is a variable, and the value stored in list is the base address of the array—that is, it is the address of the first array component. Suppose the address of the first array component is 1000. Figure 9-14 shows list and the array list.

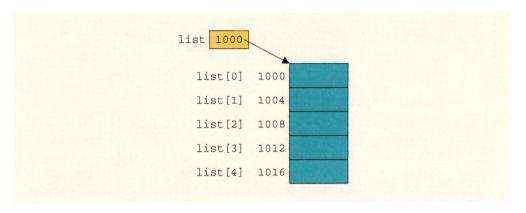

FIGURE 9-14 `list` and array `list`

Because the value of `list`, which is 1000, is a memory address, `list` is a pointer variable. However, the value stored in `list`, which is 1000, *cannot be altered during program execution.* That is, the value of `list` is *constant*. Therefore, the increment and decrement operations cannot be applied to `list`. In fact, any attempt to use the increment or decrement operations on `list` results in a compile-time error.

Notice that here we are *only* saying that the value of `list` cannot be changed. However, the data in the array `list` can be manipulated as before. For example, the statement `list[0] = 25;` stores 25 into the first array component. Similarly, the statement `list[2] = 78` stores 78 into the third component of list. (See Figure 9-15.)

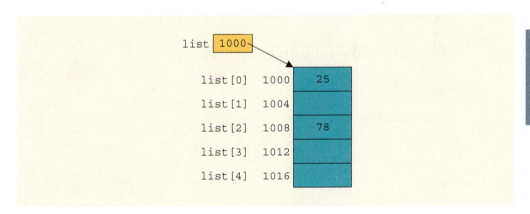

FIGURE 9-15 Array `list` after the execution of the statements `list [0] = 25;` and `list [2] = 78`

If `p` is a pointer variable of type `int`, then the statement

`p = list;`

copies the value of `list`, which is `1000`, the base address of the array, into `p`. We are allowed to perform increment and decrement operations on `p`.

An *array name* is a *constant pointer*.

Functions and Pointers

A pointer variable can be passed as a parameter to a function either by value or by reference. To declare a pointer as a value parameter in a function heading, you use the same mechanism as you use to declare a variable. To make a formal parameter be a reference parameter, you use `&` when you declare the formal parameter in the function heading. Therefore, to declare a formal parameter as a reference parameter, you must use `&`. Between the data type name and the identifier name, you must include `*` to make the identifier a pointer and `&` to make it a reference parameter. The obvious question is: In what order should `&` and `*` appear between the data type name and the identifier to declare a pointer as a reference parameter? In C++, to make a pointer a reference parameter in a function heading, `*` appears before the `&` between the data type name and the identifier. The following example illustrates this concept:

```
void example(int* &p, double *q)
{
     .
     .
     .
}
```

In this example, both `p` and `q` are pointers. The parameter `p` is a reference parameter; the parameter `q` is a value parameter.

Pointers and Function Return Values

In C++, the return type of a function can be a pointer. For example, the return type of the function

```
int* testExp(...)
{
     .
     .
     .
}
```

is a pointer type `int`.

Shallow vs. Deep Copy and Pointers

In an earlier section, we discussed pointer arithmetic and explained that if we are not careful, one pointer might access the data of another (completely unrelated) pointer. This event might result in unsuspected or erroneous results. Here, we discuss another peculiarity of pointers. To facilitate the discussion, we will use diagrams to show pointers and their related memory.

Consider the following statements:

```
int *p;
```

```
p = new int;
```

The first statement declares p to be a pointer variable of type int. The second statement allocates memory of type int, and the address of the allocated memory is stored in p. Figure 9-16 illustrates this situation.

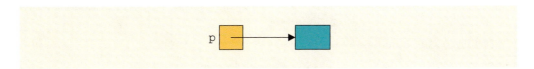

FIGURE 9-16 Pointer p and the memory to which it points

The box indicates the allocated memory (in this case, of type int), and p together with the arrow indicates that p points to the allocated memory. Now consider the following statement:

```
*p = 87;
```

This statement stores 87 in the memory to which p points. Figure 9-17 illustrates this situation.

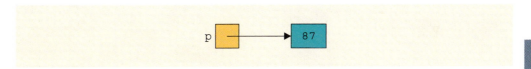

FIGURE 9-17 Pointer p with 87 in the memory to which it points

Suppose that you have the following declarations:

```
int * first;
int * second;
```

Further suppose that **first** points to an **int** array, as shown in Figure 9-18.

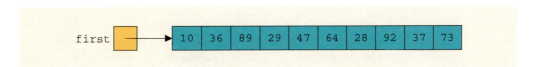

FIGURE 9-18 Pointer first and its array

Next, consider the following statement:

```
second = first;          //Line A
```

This statement copies the value of `first` into `second`. After this statement executes, both `first` and `second` point to the same array, as shown in Figure 9-19.

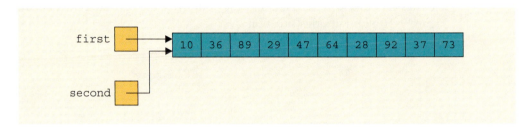

FIGURE 9-19 `first` and `second` after the statement `second = first;` executes

Next, the statement `first[4] = 10;` not only changes the value of `first[4]`, it also changes the value of `second[4]` because they point to the same array.

Let us execute the following statement:

```
delete [] second;
```

After this statement executes, the array to which `second` points is deleted. This action results in Figure 9-20.

FIGURE 9-20 `first` and `second` after the statement `delete [] second;` executes

Because `first` and `second` pointed to the same array, after the statement

```
delete [] second;
```

executes, `first` becomes invalid, that is, `first` (as well as `second`) is now a dangling pointer. Therefore, if the program later tries to access the memory to which `first` pointed, either the program will access the wrong memory or it will terminate in an error. This case is an example of a shallow copy. More formally, in a **shallow copy**, two or more pointers of the same type point to the same memory; that is, they point to the same data.

On the other hand, suppose that instead of the earlier statement, second = first; (in Line A), we have the following statements:

```
second = new int[10];

for (int j = 0; j < 10; j++)
    second[j] = first[j];
```

The first statement creates an array of 10 components of type int, and the base address of the array is stored in second. The second statement copies the array to which first points into the array to which second points. (See Figure 9-21.)

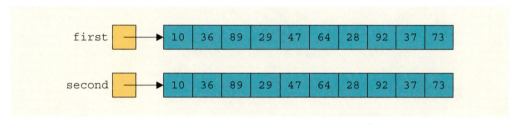

| first | | 10 | 36 | 89 | 29 | 47 | 64 | 28 | 92 | 37 | 73 |

| second | | 10 | 36 | 89 | 29 | 47 | 64 | 28 | 92 | 37 | 73 |

FIGURE 9-21   first and second both pointing to their own data

Both **first** and **second** now point to their own data. If **second** deletes its memory, there is no effect on **first**. This case is an example of a deep copy. More formally, in a **deep copy**, two or more pointers have their own data.

From the preceding discussion, it follows that you must know when to use a shallow copy and when to use a deep copy.

Pointers and Classes

Consider the following statements:

```
string *str;
str = new string;
*str = "Sunny Day";
```

The first statement declares str to be a pointer variable of type string. The second statement allocates memory of type string and stores the address of the allocated memory in str. The third statement stores the string "Sunny Day" in the memory to which str points. Now suppose that you want to use the string function length to find the length of the string "Sunny Day". The statement (*str).length() returns the length of the string. Note the parentheses around *str. The expression (*str).length() is a mixture of pointer dereferencing and the class component selection. In C++, the dot operator, ., has a higher precedence than the dereferencing operator, *. Let us elaborate on this a little more. In the expression (*str).length(), the operator * evaluates first, and so the expression *str evaluates first. Because str is a pointer variable of type string, *str refers to a memory space of type string. Therefore, in the expression

9

(*str).length(), the function length of the **class** string executes. Now consider the expression *str.length(). Let us see how this expression gets evaluated. Because . has a higher precedence than *, the expression str.length() evaluates first. The expression str.length() would result in a syntax error because str is *not* a string object, and so it cannot use the function length of the **class** string.

As you can see, in the expression (*str).length(), the parentheses around *str are important. However, typos are unavoidable. Therefore, to simplify the accessing of **class** or **struct** components via a pointer, C++ provides another operator, called the **member access operator arrow**, ->. The operator -> consists of two consecutive symbols: a hyphen and the "greater than" symbol.

The syntax for accessing a **class** (**struct**) member using the operator -> is

```
pointerVariableName->classMemberName
```

Thus, the expression

(*str).length()

is equivalent to the expression

str->length()

Accessing **class** (**struct**) components via pointers using the operator -> thus eliminates the use both of parentheses and of the dereferencing operator. Because typos are unavoidable and missing parentheses can result in either an abnormal program termination or erroneous results, when accessing **class** (**struct**) components via pointers, this book uses the arrow notation.

PROGRAMMING EXAMPLE: Code Detection

When a message is transmitted in secret code over a transmission channel, it is usually sent as a sequence of bits, that is, 0s and 1s. Due to noise in the transmission channel, the transmitted message may become corrupted. That is, the message received at the destination is not the same as the message transmitted; some of the bits may have been changed. There are several techniques to check the validity of the transmitted message at the destination. One technique is to transmit the same message twice. At the destination, both copies of the message are compared bit by bit. If the corresponding bits are the same, the message received is error-free.

Let us write a program to check whether the message received at the destination is error-free. For simplicity, assume that the secret code representing the message is a sequence of digits (0 to 9). Also, assume that the first number in the message is the length of the message. For example, if the secret code is

7 9 2 7 8 3 5 6

then the message is 7 digits long, and it is transmitted twice.

The preceding message is transmitted as: 7 9 2 7 8 3 5 6 7 9 2 7 8 3 5 6

Input   A secret code and its copy

Output   The secret code, its copy, and a message—if the received code is error-free—in the following form:

```
Code Digit      Code Digit Copy
    9                 9
    2                 2
    7                 7
    8                 8
    3                 3
    5                 5
    6                 6
Message transmitted OK.
```

PROBLEM ANALYSIS AND ALGORITHM DESIGN

Because we have to compare the corresponding digits of the secret code and its copy, we first read the secret code and store it in an array. Then, we read the first digit of the copy and compare it with the first digit of the secret code, and so on. If any corresponding digits are not the same, we indicate this fact by printing a message next to the digits. We use a dynamic array to store the secret code. The first number in the secret code, and in the copy of the secret code, indicates the length of the code. This discussion translates into the following algorithm:

1. Read the length of the secret code.
2. Create an array of appropriate length to store the secret code.
3. Read and store the secret code into an array.
4. Read the length of the copy.
5. If the length of the secret code and its copy are the same, compare the codes. Otherwise, print an error message.

To simplify the function `main`, let us write a function, `readCode`, to read the secret code and another function, `compareCode`, to compare the codes.

readCode

This function first reads the length of the secret code and creates an array to store that secret code. This function then prompts the user to enter the secret code and reads and stores the secret code in the array. Therefore, this function has two parameters: one is a pointer to the array to store the secret code; the other is the length of the code. The definition of the function `readCode` is as follows:

```cpp
void readCode(int* &list, int& length)
{
    int count;
```

9

```
    cout << "Enter the length of the code: ";
    cin >> length;    //get the length of the secret code
    cout << endl;

    list = new int[length];

    cout << "Enter the secret code: ";

        //Get the secret code.
    for (count = 0; count < length; count++)
        cin >> list[count];
    cout << endl;
} //end readCode
```

compare Code This function compares the secret code with its copy. Therefore, it must have access to the array containing the secret code and the length of the secret code. In fact, this function has only two parameters: a pointer to the array containing the secret code and the length of the secret code. The algorithm for the function compareCode is

   a.   Declare the variables.

   b.   Set a bool variable codeOk to true.

   c.   Prompt the user to enter the length of the copy of the secret code and a copy of the secret code.

   d.   Read the length of the copy of the secret code.

   e.   If the length of the secret code and its copy are not the same, output an appropriate error message and terminate the function.

   f.   For each digit in the input file, do the following:

      f.1.   Read the next digit of the copy of the secret code.

      f.2.   Output the corresponding digits from the secret code and the copy of the secret code.

      f.3.   If the corresponding digits are not the same, output an error message and set the bool variable codeOk to false.

   g.   If the bool variable codeOk is true

      Output a message indicating that the secret code was transmitted correctly.

   else

      Output an error message.

Following this algorithm, the definition of the function compareCode is the following:

```
void compareCode(int* list, int length)
{
        //Step a
    int length2;
    int digit;
    int codeOk;
```

```
        codeOk = true;                                    //Step b

        cout << "Enter the length of the copy of the"
            << " secret code \nand a copy of the "
            << "secret code: ";                           //Step c
    cin >> length2;                                       //Step d
    cout << endl;

        if (length != length2)                            //Step e
        {
            cout << "The original code and its copy are not "
                << "of the same length." << endl;
            return;
        }

    cout << "Code Digit     Code Digit Copy" << endl;

        for (int count = 0; count < length; count++)      //Step f
        {
            cin >> digit;                                 //Step f.1
            cout << setw(5) << list[count]
                << setw(17) << digit;                     //Step f.2

            if (digit != list[count])                     //Step f.3
            {
                cout << "  code digits are not the same" << endl;
                codeOk = false;
            }
            else
                cout << endl;
        }

        if (codeOk)                                       //Step g
            cout << "Message transmitted OK." << endl;
        else
            cout << "Error in transmission. Retransmit!!" << endl;
} //end compareCode
```

Following is the algorithm for the function main.

Main Algorithm

1. Declare the variables.
2. Call the function readCode to read the secret code.
3. Call the function compareCode to compare the codes.

PROGRAM LISTING

```cpp
//*********************************************************
// Author: D.S. Malik
//
// This program reads a secret code and determines if the
// secret code is transmitted correctly.
//*********************************************************

#include <iostream>
#include <iomanip>

using namespace std;

void readCode(int* &list, int& length);
void compareCode(int* list, int length);

int main()
{
    int* codeArray = NULL;
    int codeLength;

    readCode(codeArray, codeLength);

    compareCode(codeArray, codeLength);

    return 0;
} //end main

//Place the definitions of the functions readCode and
//compareCode, as described earlier, here.
```

Sample Run: In this sample run, the user input is shaded.

```
Enter the length of the code: 7

Enter the secret code: 9 2 7 8 3 5 6

Enter the length of the copy of the secret code
and a copy of the secret code: 7 9 2 7 8 3 5 6

Code Digit     Code Digit Copy
    9                  9
    2                  2
    7                  7
    8                  8
    3                  3
    5                  5
    6                  6
Message transmitted OK.
```

PROGRAMMING EXAMPLE: Monthly Temperature

The Atmospheric Science Department is looking for someone to write a program to keep track of the daily maximum and minimum temperatures and then analyze the data at the end of the month. In this programming example, we write a program to help the department. Input and output to the program are as follows.

Input The number of days in a month and two arrays, one containing daily maximum temperatures of the month and the other containing daily minimum temperatures of the month, both indexed by the day of the month

Output Maximum, minimum, average maximum, and average minimum temperatures of the entire month

PROBLEM
ANALYSIS
AND
CLASS
DESIGN

In this program, we design the **class temperature** to store the daily maximum and minimum temperatures for a month. This class contains the functions to find the day of the month when the maximum temperature occurred, the day when the minimum temperature occurred, the average maximum temperature, and the average minimum temperature of the month. We use dynamic arrays to store the daily maximum and minimum temperature. Essentially, this class is the following:

```
//************************************************************
// Author: D.S. Malik
//
// This class is used to store the daily maximum and minimum
// temperatures for the month. It also contains functions to
// find the maximum and minimum temperatures of the month
// and average maximum and average minimum temperatures of
// the month.
//************************************************************

class temperature
{
public:
    void setTemp(int* maxT, int* minT, int daysInM);
    //Function to store the daily maximum and minimum
    //temperatures for a month.
    //If the number of days in a month is valid, the instance
    //variables are set according to the parameters.
    //Postcondition: if daysInMonth == daysInM, then
    //               maxTemp = maxT; minTemp = minT.

    int monthMaxTempDay() const;
    //Function to find the day of the maximum temperature.
    //Postcondition: The day of the maximum temperature is
    //               calculated and returned.
```

9

```
int averageMaxTemp() const;
    //Function to find the average maximum temperature.
    //Postcondition: The average maximum temperature is
    //               calculated and returned.

int monthMinTempDay() const;
    //Function to find the day of the mimimum temperature.
    //Postcondition: The day of the mimimum temperature is
    //               calculated and returned.

int averageMinTemp() const;
    //Function to find the average minimum temperature.
    //Postcondition: The average minimum temperature is
    //               calculated and returned.

void print() const;
    //Function to output the maximum, minimum, average maximum,
    //and average minimum temperatures of the month.
    //Postcondition: Maximum, minimum, average maximum, and
    //               average minimum temperatures of the month
    //               are printed.

temperature();
    //Default constructor
    //Postcondition: daysInMonth = 0;
    //               Arrays maxTemp and minTemp of size 31
    //               are created and initialized to 0.

temperature(int* maxT, int* minT, int daysInM);
    //Constructor with parameters.
    //Creates arrays maxTemp and minTemp of sizes specified by
    //the parameter daysInM to store the daily maximum and
    //minimum temperatures for a month.
    //Postcondition: If 0 <= daysInM <= 31, then
    //               create arrays maxTemp and minTemp, and
    //               maxTemp = maxT; minTemp = minT.

private:
    int daysInMonth;
    int* maxTemp;   //pointer to the array to store daily maximum
                    //temperatures
    int* minTemp;   //pointer to the array to store daily minimum
                    //temperatures
};
```

The UML class diagram of the class temperature is shown in Figure 9-22.

temperature
-daysInMonth: int -maxTemp: int* -minTemp: int*
+setTemp(int*, int*, int): void +monthMaxTempDay() const: int +averageMaxTemp() const: int +monthMinTempDay() const: int +averageMinTemp() const: int +print() const: void +temperature() +temperature(int*, int*, int)

FIGURE 9-22 UML class diagram of the `class temperature`

Next, we write the definitions of the functions of the `class temperature`.

The default constructor creates and initializes the arrays `maxTemp` and `minTemp` to `0` and `daysInMonth` to `0`. The constructor with parameters creates the arrays, to store the maximum and minimum daily temperatures for a month, of the sizes specified by the users, and initializes the arrays and the instance variable `daysInMonth` to the values specified by the user.

```
temperature::temperature()
{
    daysInMonth = 0;

    maxTemp = new int[31];
    minTemp = new int[31];

    for (int i = 0; i < 31; i++)
    {
        maxTemp[i] = 0;
        minTemp[i] = 0;
    }
} //end default constructor

temperature::temperature (int* maxT, int* minT, int daysInM)
{
    if (0 <= daysInM &&  daysInM <= 31)
    {
        daysInMonth = daysInM;

        maxTemp = new int[daysInMonth];
        minTemp = new int[daysInMonth];
```

```
                setTemp(maxT, minT, daysInM);
        }
    else
    {
            cout << "Number of days in a month is out of range." << endl;
            daysInMonth = 0;
    }
} //end constructor with parameters
```

The method `setTemp` first checks if the number of days in a month is valid and then makes a deep copy of the arrays containing daily maximum and minimum temperatures for the month. The definition of this function is:

```
void temperature::setTemp(int* maxT, int* minT, int daysInM)
{
    if (daysInMonth == daysInM)
    {
        for (int index = 0; index < daysInMonth; index++)
        {
            maxTemp[index] = maxT[index];
            minTemp[index] = minT[index];
        }
    }
    else
    {
            cout << "Number of days in a month is out of range." << endl;
            daysInMonth = 0;
    }
} //end setTemp
```

The definitions of the remaining functions are straightforward and are given next. Note that the code to find the day of the maximum temperature and the code to find the average maximum and average minimum temperatures are essentially the same as finding the index of the largest element in an array and finding the average of the elements in an array. The code to find the day of the minimum temperature is similar to finding the day of the maximum temperature.

```
int temperature::monthMaxTempDay() const
{
    int day = 0;

    for (int index = 1; index < daysInMonth; index++)
        if (maxTemp[day] < maxTemp[index])
            day = index;

    return day;
} //end monthMaxTempDay
```

```cpp
int temperature::averageMaxTemp() const
{
    int sum = 0;

    for (int index = 0; index < daysInMonth; index++)
        sum = sum + maxTemp[index];

    if (daysInMonth != 0)
        return sum / daysInMonth;
    else
        return -1;
} //end averageMaxTemp

int temperature::monthMinTempDay() const
{
    int day = 0;

    for (int index = 1; index < daysInMonth; index++)
        if (minTemp[day] > minTemp[index])
            day = index;

    return day;
} //end monthMinTempDay

int temperature::averageMinTemp() const
{
    int sum = 0;

    for (int index = 0; index < daysInMonth; index++)
        sum = sum + minTemp[index];

    if (daysInMonth != 0)
        return sum / daysInMonth;
    else
        return -1;
} //end averageMinTemp

void temperature::print() const
{
    cout << "Maximum temperature: "
         << maxTemp[monthMaxTempDay()] << endl
         << "Minimum temperature: "
         << minTemp[monthMinTempDay()] << endl
         << "Average maximum temperature: "
         << averageMaxTemp() << endl
         << "Average minimum temperature: "
         << averageMinTemp()<< endl;

} //end print
```

9

We assume that the definition of the `class` temperature is in the file temperature.h, and the definitions of the functions of this class are in the file temperature Imp.cpp.

MAIN
PROGRAM

```cpp
//*************************************************************
// Author: D.S. Malik
//
// This program tests operations of the class temperature.
//*************************************************************

#include <iostream>
#include "temperature.h"

using namespace std;

int main()
{
    int minT[31];
    int maxT[31];

    cout << "Enter daily maximum temperatures for January" << endl;

    for (int index = 0; index < 31; index++)
        cin >> maxT[index];
    cout << endl;

    cout << "Enter daily minimum temperatures for January" << endl;

    for (int index = 0; index < 31; index++)
        cin >> minT[index];
    cout << endl;

    temperature mthJanuary(maxT, minT, 31);   //Create the object
                        //to store the maximum and minimum daily
                        //temperatures for the January month.

    cout << "January" << endl;
    mthJanuary.print();
} //end main
```

Sample Run: In this sample run, the user input is shaded.

```
Enter daily maximum temperatures for January
25 28 26 32 17 15 10 18 20 30 35 40 28 5 7 10 35 50 48 45 30 15 1 14
20 30 35 27 34 50 40

Enter daily minimum temperatures for January
5 7 3 15 10 -5 -6 -20 5 8 10 20 18 32 10 -8 0 2 20 39 40 41 20 0 -10
5 6 10 20 45 33
```

```
January
Maximum temperature: 50
Minimum temperature: -20
Average maximum temperature: 26
Average minimum temperature: 12
```

 NOTE (**Classes with pointer data members**) Recall that when we use a pointer to allocate dynamic memory and if the dynamic memory is no longer needed, then to avoid memory leak we must use the `delete` operator to deallocate dynamic memory. Now suppose that a class has a pointer variable and when an object is instantiated, it also creates dynamic memory. When the object goes out of scope, how do we ensure that the dynamic memory allocated by the object is deallocated? To accomplish this, we use the destructor. Recall that a class can have a destructor, and the destructor automatically executes when the object goes out of scope. So, to deallocate the dynamic memory created by the object, we put the necessary code in the destructor. For example, the `class temperature` has two pointer variables that are used to create dynamic arrays. In this case, the definition of the destructor of the `class temperature` is the following:

```
temperature::~temperature()
{
        delete [] maxTemp;
        delete [] minTemp;
}
```

The modified definition of the `class temperature` is available at the Web site accompanying this book.

9

QUICK REVIEW

1. Pointer variables contain the addresses of other variables as their values.

2. A pointer variable is declared using an asterisk, *, between the data type and the variable.

3. In C++, & is called the address of operator.

4. The address of operator returns the address of its operand.

5. When used as a unary operator, * is called the dereferencing operator.

6. The memory location indicated by the value of a pointer variable is accessed by using the dereferencing operator, *.

7. Pointer variables are initialized using either 0 (the integer zero), NULL, or the address of a variable of the same type.

8. The only number that can be directly assigned to a pointer variable is 0.

9. The only arithmetic operations allowed on pointer variables are increment (++), decrement (--), addition of an integer to a pointer variable,

subtraction of an integer from a pointer variable, and subtraction of a pointer from another pointer.

10. When an integer is added to a pointer variable, the value of the pointer variable is incremented by the integer times the size of the memory to which the pointer is pointing. Similarly, when an integer is subtracted from a pointer variable, the value of the pointer variable is decremented by the integer times the size of the memory to which the pointer is pointing.

11. Pointer variables can be compared using relational operators.

12. The value of one pointer variable can be assigned to another pointer variable of the same type.

13. A variable created during program execution is called a dynamic variable.

14. The operator `new` is used to create a dynamic variable.

15. The operator `delete` is used to deallocate the memory occupied by a dynamic variable.

16. In C++, both `new` and `delete` are reserved words.

17. The operator `new` has two forms: one to create a single dynamic variable, and another to create an array of dynamic variables.

18. The operator `delete` has two forms: one to deallocate the memory occupied by a single dynamic variable, and another to deallocate the memory occupied by an array of dynamic variables.

19. The array name is a constant pointer. It always points to the same memory location, which is the location of the first array component.

20. To create a dynamic array, the form of the `new` operator that creates an array of dynamic variables is used. For example, if `p` is a pointer of type `int`, the statement

```
p = new int[10];
```

creates an array of 10 components of type `int`. The base address of the array is stored in `p`.

21. Array notation can be used to access the components of a dynamic array. For example, suppose `p` is a dynamic array of 10 components. Then `p[0]` refers to the first array component, `p[1]` refers to the second array component, and so on.

22. An array created during program execution is called a dynamic array.

23. If `p` is a dynamic array, then the statement

```
delete [] p;
```

deallocates the memory occupied by `p`—that is, the components of `p`.

24. In a shallow copy, two or more pointers of the same type point to the same memory space; that is, they point to the same data.

25. In a deep copy, two or more pointers of the same type have their own copies of the data.

EXERCISES

1. Mark the following statements as true or false.

   a. In C++, pointer is a reserved word.

   b. In C++, pointer variables are declared using the word pointer.

   c. The statement **delete** p; deallocates the variable pointer p.

   d. The statement **delete** p; deallocates the dynamic variable to which p points.

   e. Given the declaration

      ```
      int list[10];
      int *p;
      ```

      the statement

      ```
      p = list;
      ```

      is valid in C++.

   f. Given the declaration

      ```
      int *p;
      ```

      the statement

      ```
      p = new int[50];
      ```

      dynamically allocates an array of 50 components of type **int**, and p contains the base address of the array.

   g. The address of operator returns the address and value of its operand.

   h. If p is a pointer variable, then the statement p = p * 2; is valid in C++.

2. Given the declaration

   ```
   int x;
   int *p;
   int *q;
   ```

   mark the following statements as valid or invalid. If a statement is invalid, explain why.

   a. p = q;

   b. *p = 56;

   c. p = x;

   d. *p = *q;

   e. q = &x;

   f. *p = q;

9

3. What is the output of the following C++ code?

```
int x;
int y;
int *p = &x;
int *q = &y;
*p = 35;
*q = 98;
*p = *q;
cout << x << "   " << y << endl;
cout << *p << "   " << *q << endl;
```

4. What is the output of the following C++ code?

```
int x;
int y;
int *p = &x;
int *q = &y;
x = 35;
y = 46;
p = q;
*p = 78;
cout << x << "   " << y << endl;
cout << *p << "   " << *q << endl;
```

5. Given the declaration

```
int num = 6;
int *p = &num;
```

which of the following statements increment(s) the value of num?

a. p++;

b. (*p)++;

c. num++;

d. (*num)++;

6. What is the output of the following code?

```
int *p;
int *q;
p = new int;
q = p;
*p = 46;
*q = 39;
cout << *p << " " << *q << endl;
```

7. What is the output of the following code?

```
int *p;
int *q;
p = new int;
*p = 43;
q = p;
*q = 52;
p = new int;
```

```
*p = 78;
q = new int;
*q = *p;
cout << *p << " " << *q << endl;
```

8. What is wrong with the following code?

```
int *p;                             //Line 1
int *q;                             //Line 2

p = new int;                        //Line 3
*p = 43;                            //Line 4

q = p;                              //Line 5
*q = 52;                            //Line 6

delete q;                           //Line 7

cout << *p << " " << *q << endl;    //Line 8
```

9. What is the output of the following code?

```
int x;
int *p;
int *q;
p = new int[10];
q = p;
*p = 4;

for (int j = 0; j < 10; j++)
{
    x = *p;
    p++;
    *p = x + j;
}

for (int k = 0; k < 10; k++)
{
    cout << *q << " ";
    q++;
}
cout << endl;
```

10. What is the output of the following code?

```
int * secret;

secret = new int[10];
secret[0] = 10;
for (int j = 1; j < 10; j++)
    secret[j] = secret[j - 1] + 5;
for (int j = 0; j < 10; j++)
    cout << secret[j] << " ";
cout << endl;
```

9

11. Explain the difference between a shallow copy and a deep copy of data.

12. What is wrong with the following code?

```
int *p;                              //Line 1
int *q;                              //Line 2

p = new int[5];                      //Line 3
*p = 2;                              //Line 4

for (int i = 1; i < 5; i++)          //Line 5
    p[i] = p[i - 1] + i;             //Line 6

q = p;                               //Line 7

delete [] p;                         //Line 8

for (int j = 0; j < 5; j++)          //Line 9
    cout << q[j] << " ";             //Line 10

cout << endl;                        //Line 11
```

13. What is the output of the following code?

```
int *p;
int *q;

p = new int[5];
p[0] = 5;

for (int i = 1; i < 5; i++)
    p[i] = p[i - 1] + 2 * i;

cout << "Array p: ";
for (int i = 0; i < 5; i++)
    cout << p[i] << " ";
cout << endl;

q = new int[5];

for (int i = 0; i < 5; i++)
    q[i] = p[4 - i];

cout << "Array q: ";
for (int i = 0; i < 5; i++)
    cout << q[i] << " ";

cout << endl;
```

PROGRAMMING EXERCISES

1. Redo Programming Exercise 5 of Chapter 6, using dynamic arrays.

2. Redo Programming Exercise 6 of Chapter 6, using dynamic arrays.

3. Redo Programming Exercise 7 of Chapter 6, using dynamic arrays. You must ask the user for the number of candidates, and then create the appropriate arrays to hold the data.

4. Using dynamic arrays, redo Programming Exercise 10, Chapter 6, so that your program can add two positive integers with any number of digits.

9

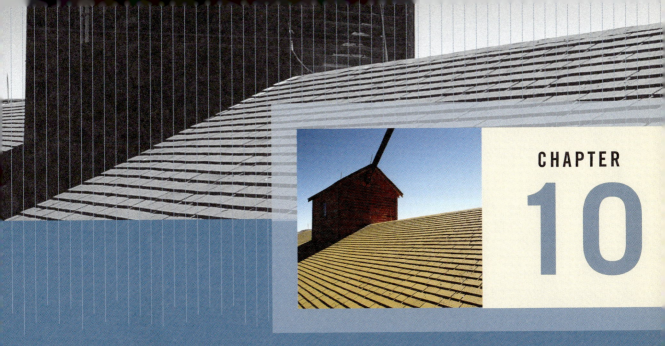

APPLICATIONS OF ARRAYS (SEARCHING AND SORTING) AND THE `class vector`

IN THIS CHAPTER, YOU WILL:

- Explore how to sort an array using the selection sort and insertion sort algorithms
- Learn how to implement the sequential search algorithm
- Learn how to implement the binary search algorithm
- Learn how to avoid bugs by developing test suites in advance
- Become familiar with the class `vector`

Chapter 6 introduced arrays, a structured data type. When the data values are all of the same type, arrays are a convenient way to store and process them. You can effectively use loops for input/output, initialization, and other operations. Moreover, you can pass the entire set of values as a parameter with a single statement. The next section continues our discussion of one-dimensional arrays and shows you how to use them effectively for list processing. We then examine the **vector** type.

List Processing

A **list** is a set of values of the same type. Because all values are of the same type, a convenient place to store a list is in an array, and particularly in a one-dimensional array. The size of a list is the number of elements in the list. Because the size of a list can increase and decrease, the array you use to store the list should be declared as the maximum size of the list.

Basic operations performed on a list include the following:

- Search the list for a given item.
- Sort the list.
- Insert an item in the list.
- Delete an item from the list.

The following sections discuss the sorting and searching algorithms.

Selection Sort

There are many sorting algorithms. This section describes a popular sorting algorithm called the **selection sort**, and uses it to sort a list.

As the name implies, in the **selection sort** algorithm, we rearrange the list by selecting an element in the list and moving it to its proper position. This algorithm finds the location of the smallest element in the unsorted portion of the list, and moves it to the top of the unsorted portion of the list. The first time, we locate the smallest item in the entire list. The second time, we locate the smallest item in the list starting from the second element in the list, and so on.

As an example, suppose that you have the list shown in Figure 10-1.

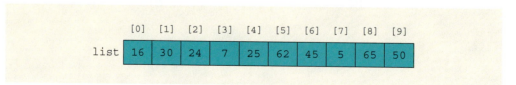

FIGURE 10-1 List of 10 elements

Initially, the entire list is unsorted. So we find the smallest item in the list, which is at position 7, as shown in Figure 10-2.

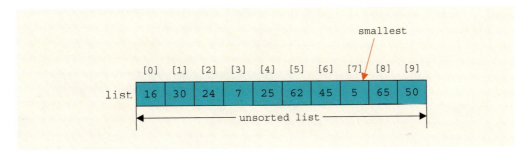

FIGURE 10-2 Smallest element of unsorted `list`

Because this is the smallest item, it must be moved to position 0. We therefore swap 16 (that is, `list[0]`) with 5 (that is, `list[7]`), as shown in Figure 10-3.

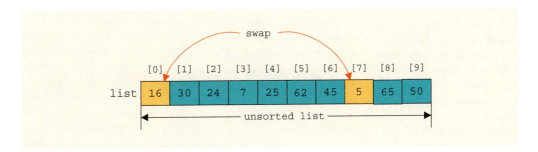

FIGURE 10-3 Swap elements `list[0]` and `list[7]`

After swapping these elements, the resulting list is as shown in Figure 10-4.

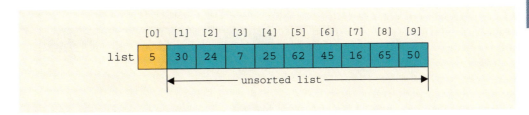

FIGURE 10-4 List after swapping `list[0]` and `list[7]`

10

Now the unsorted list is `list[1]...list[9]`. Next, we find the smallest element in the unsorted portion of the list. The smallest element is at position 3, as shown in Figure 10-5.

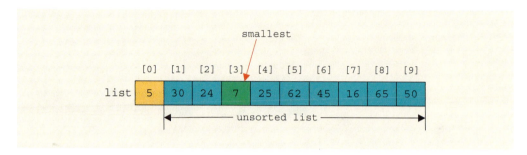

FIGURE 10-5 Smallest element in unsorted portion of `list`

Because the smallest element in the unsorted list is at position 3, it must be moved to position 1. So, we swap 7 (that is, `list[3]`) with 30 (that is, `list[1]`), as shown in Figure 10-6.

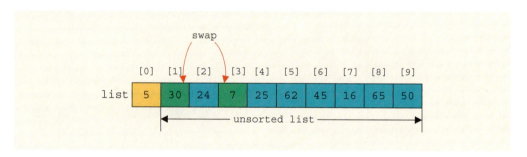

FIGURE 10-6 Swap `list[1]` with `list[3]`

After swapping `list[1]` with `list[3]`, the resulting list is as shown in Figure 10-7.

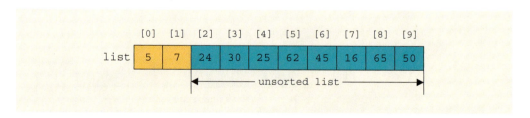

FIGURE 10-7 `list` after swapping `list[1]` with `list[3]`

Now the unsorted list is `list[2]...list[9]`. We repeat this process of finding the (position of the) smallest element in the unsorted portion of the list and moving it to the beginning of the unsorted portion of the list. The selection sort thus involves the following steps:

In the unsorted portion of the list:

    a.   Find the location of the smallest element.

    b.   Move the smallest element to the beginning of the unsorted list.

Initially, the entire list (that is, `list[0]...list[length - 1]`) is the unsorted list. After executing Steps a and b once, the unsorted list is `list[1]...list[length - 1]`. After executing Steps a and b a second time, the unsorted list is `list[2]...list[length - 1]`, and so on. In this way, we can keep track of the unsorted portion of the list and repeat Steps a and b with the help of a **for** loop, as shown in the following pseudo-algorithm:

```
for (int index = 0; index < length - 1; index++)
{
    a. Find the location, smallestIndex, of the smallest element in
       list[index]...list[length - 1].
    b. Swap the smallest element with list[index]. That is, swap
       list[smallestIndex] with list[index].
}
```

The first time through the loop, we locate the smallest element in `list[0]...list[length - 1]` and swap the smallest element with `list[0]`. The second time through the loop, we locate the smallest element in `list[1]...list[length - 1]` and swap the smallest element with `list[1]`, and so on.

Step a is similar to the algorithm of finding the index of the largest item in the list, as discussed in Chapter 6. (Also see Chapter 6, Programming Exercise 2.) Here we find the index of the smallest item in the list. The general form of Step a is the following:

```
smallestIndex = index;   //assume first element is the smallest

for (int minIndex = index + 1; minIndex < length; minIndex++)
    if (list[minIndex] < list[smallestIndex])
        smallestIndex = minIndex;   //current element in the list
                                    //is smaller than the smallest so
                                    //far, so update smallestIndex
```

Step b swaps the contents of `list[smallestIndex]` with `list[index]`. The following statements accomplish this task:

```
temp = list[smallestIndex];
list[smallestIndex] = list[index];
list[index] = temp;
```

It follows that to swap the values, three item assignments are needed. The following function, `selectionSort`, implements the selection sort algorithm.

```
void selectionSort(int list[], int length)
{
    int smallestIndex;
    int temp;
```

10

```
for (int index = 0; index < length - 1; index++)
{
        //Step a
    smallestIndex = index;

    for (int minIndex = index + 1; minIndex < length; minIndex++)
        if (list[minIndex] < list[smallestIndex])
            smallestIndex = minIndex;

        //Step b
    temp = list[smallestIndex];
    list[smallestIndex] = list[index];
    list[index] = temp;
}
} //end selectionSort
```

The program in Example 10-1 illustrates how to use the selection sort algorithm in a program.

EXAMPLE 10-1

```
//**************************************************************
// Author: D.S. Malik
//
// This program shows how to use a selection sort algorithm.
//**************************************************************

#include <iostream>                                        //Line 1

using namespace std;                                       //Line 2

void selectionSort(int list[],  int length);               //Line 3

int main()                                                 //Line 4
{                                                          //Line 5
    int list[] = {2, 56, 34, 25, 73, 46, 89, 10, 5, 16};   //Line 6

    selectionSort(list, 10);                               //Line 7

    cout << "After sorting, the list elements are:"
         << endl;                                          //Line 8

    for (int i = 0; i < 10; i++)                           //Line 9
        cout << list[i] << " ";                            //Line 10

    cout << endl;                                          //Line 11

    return 0;                                              //Line 12
}                                                          //Line 13
```

```
//Place the definition of the function selectionSort given
//previously here.
```

Sample Run:

```
After sorting, the list elements are:
2 5 10 16 25 34 46 56 73 89
```

The statement in Line 6 declares and initializes `list` to be an array of 10 components of type `int`. The statement in Line 7 uses the function `selectionSort` to sort `list`. Notice that both `list` and its length (the number of elements in it, which is 10) are passed as parameters to the function `selectionSort`. The `for` loop in Lines 9 and 10 outputs the elements of `list`.

To illustrate the selection sort algorithm in this program, we declared and initialized the array `list`. However, you can also prompt the user to input the data during program execution.

It is known that for a list of length n, on average a selection sort makes $n(n-1)/2$ key comparisons and $3(n-1)$ item assignments. Therefore, if $n = 1000$, then to sort the list, the selection sort makes about 500,000 key comparisons and about 3000 item assignments. The next section presents the insertion sort algorithm that reduces the number of comparisons.

Insertion Sort

As noted in the previous section, for a list of length 1000, a selection sort makes approximately 500,000 key comparisons, which is quite high. This section describes the sorting algorithm called the insertion sort, which tries to improve—that is, reduce—the number of key comparisons.

The insertion sort algorithm sorts the list by moving each element to its proper place. Consider the list given in Figure 10-8.

	[0]	[1]	[2]	[3]	[4]	[5]	[6]	[7]
list	10	18	25	30	23	17	45	35

FIGURE 10-8 `list`

The length of the list is 8. Moreover, the list elements `list[0]`, `list[1]`, `list[2]`, and `list[3]` are in order. That is, `list[0]...list[3]` is sorted. (See Figure 10-9.)

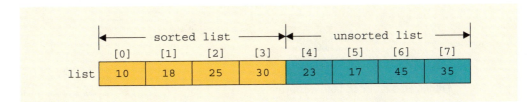

	[0]	[1]	[2]	[3]	[4]	[5]	[6]	[7]
list	10	18	25	30	23	17	45	35

FIGURE 10-9 Sorted and unsorted portions of `list`

Next, we consider the element `list[4]`, the first element of the unsorted list. Because `list[4] < list[3]`, we need to move the element `list[4]` to its proper location. It thus follows that element `list[4]` should be moved to `list[2]`. (See Figure 10-10.)

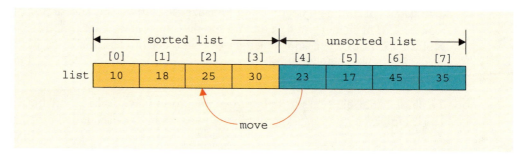

FIGURE 10-10 Move `list[4]` into `list[2]`

To move `list[4]` into `list[2]`, first we copy `list[4]` into `temp`, a temporary memory space. (See Figure 10-11.)

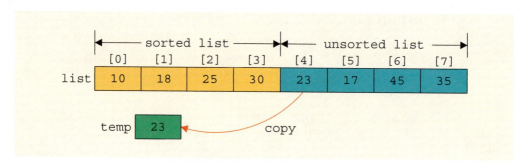

FIGURE 10-11 Copy `list[4]` into `temp`

Next, we copy `list[3]` into `list[4]`, and then `list[2]` into `list[3]`. (See Figure 10-12.)

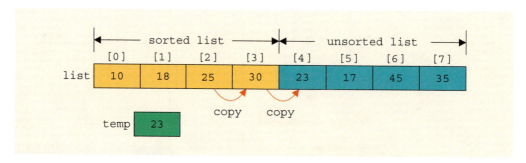

FIGURE 10-12 `list` before copying `list[3]` into `list[4]`, and then `list[2]` into `list[3]`

After copying `list[3]` into `list[4]` and `list[2]` into `list[3]`, the list is as shown in Figure 10-13.

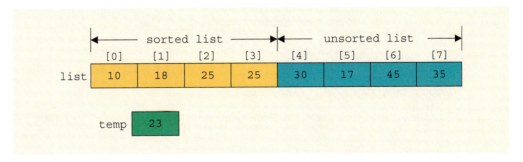

FIGURE 10-13 `list` after copying `list[3]` into `list[4]` and then `list[2]` into `list[3]`

We now copy `temp` into `list[2]`. Figure 10-14 shows the resulting list.

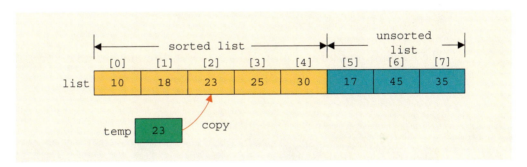

FIGURE 10-14 `list` after copying `temp` into `list[2]`

Now `list[0]...list[4]` is sorted, and `list[5]...list[7]` is unsorted. We repeat this process on the resulting list by moving the first element of the unsorted list into the proper place in the sorted list.

From this discussion, we see that during the sorting phase, the array containing the list is divided into two sublists, upper and lower. Elements in the upper sublist are sorted; elements in the lower sublist are to be moved into their proper places in the upper sublist, one at a time. We use an index—say, `firstOutOfOrder`—to point to the first element in the lower sublist; that is, `firstOutOfOrder` gives the index of the first element in the unsorted portion of the array. Initially, `firstOutOfOrder` is initialized to `1`.

This discussion translates into the following pseudo-algorithm:

```
for (int firstOutOfOrder = 1; firstOutOfOrder < listLength;
                         firstOutOfOrder++)
  if (list[firstOutOfOrder] is less than list[firstOutOfOrder - 1])
  {
      copy list[firstOutOfOrder] into temp

      initialize location to firstOutOfOrder
```

```
    do
    {
        a. copy list[location - 1] into list[location]
        b. decrement location by 1 to consider the next element
           in the sorted portion of the array
    }
    while (location > 0 && the element in the upper list at
                        location - 1 is greater than temp)
}
copy temp into list[location]
```

Let us show a few iterations of this algorithm on the list given in Figure 10-15.

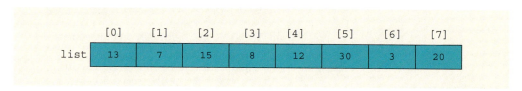

FIGURE 10-15 Unsorted `list`

The length of this list is 8; that is, `length = 8`. We initialize `firstOutOfOrder` to 1. (See Figure 10-16.)

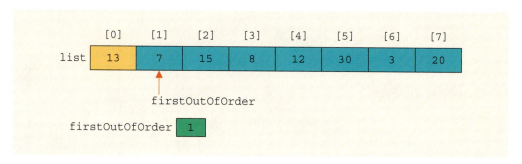

FIGURE 10-16 `firstOutOfOrder = 1`

Now `list[firstOutOfOrder] = 7`, `list[firstOutOfOrder – 1] = 13`, and 7 < 13. The expression in the **if** statement evaluates to **true**, so we execute the body of the **if** statement.

```
temp = list[firstOutOfOrder] = 7
location = firstOutOfOrder = 1
```

Next, we execute the **do...while** loop.

```
list[1] = list[0] = 13    (copy list[0] into list[1])
location = 0              (decrement location)
```

The do...while loop terminates because location = 0. We copy temp into list[location]—that is, into list[0]. Figure 10-17 shows the resulting list.

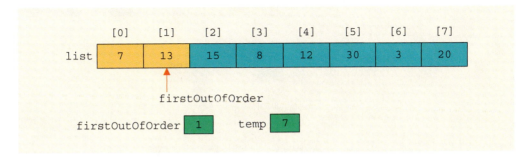

FIGURE 10-17 list after the first iteration of the insertion sort algorithm

Now suppose that we have the list given in Figure 10-18.

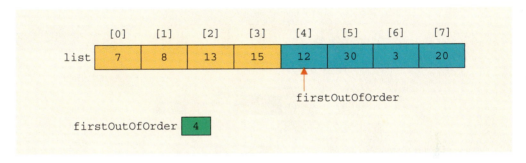

FIGURE 10-18 First out-of-order element is at position 4

Here, list[0]...list[3], or the elements list[0], list[1], list[2], and list[3], are in order. Now firstOutOfOrder = 4. Because list[4] < list[3], the element list[4], which is 12, needs to be moved to its proper location.

As before,

```
temp = list[firstOutOfOrder] = 12
location = firstOutOfOrder   =  4
```

First, we copy list[3] into list[4] and decrement location by 1. Then we copy list[2] into list[3] and again decrement location by 1. Now the value of location is 2. At this point, the list is as shown in Figure 10-19.

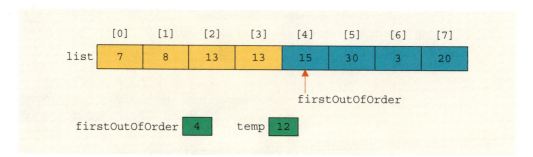

FIGURE 10-19 `list` after copying `list[3]` into `list[4]` and then `list[2]` into `list[3]`

Because `list[1] < temp`, the **do...while** loop terminates. Because at this point `location` is 2, we copy `temp` into `list[2]`. That is, `list[2] = temp = 12`. Figure 10-20 shows the resulting list.

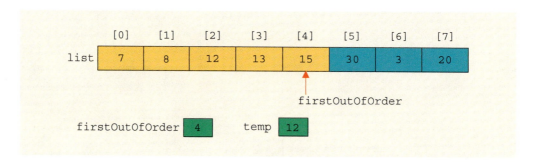

FIGURE 10-20 `list` after copying `temp` into `list[2]`

We can repeat this process for the remaining elements of `list` to sort `list`.

The following C++ function implements the previous algorithm:

```cpp
void insertionSort(int list[], int listLength)
{
    int location;
    int temp;

    for (int firstOutOfOrder = 1; firstOutOfOrder < listLength;
                            firstOutOfOrder++)
        if (list[firstOutOfOrder] < list[firstOutOfOrder - 1])
        {
            temp = list[firstOutOfOrder];
            location = firstOutOfOrder;

            do
            {
                list[location] = list[location - 1];
                location--;
            }
        }
}
```

```
            while (location > 0 && list[location - 1] > temp);

            list[location] = temp;
    }
} //end insertionSort
```

We leave it as an exercise for you to write a program to test the insertion sort algorithm.

It is known that for a list of length n, on average an insertion sort makes about $(n^2 + 3n - 4) / 4$ key comparisons and about $n(n - 1) / 4$ item assignments. Therefore, if $n = 1000$, then to sort the list, an insertion sort makes about 250,000 key comparisons and about 250,000 item assignments.

This chapter has presented two sorting algorithms. In fact, these are not the only sorting algorithms. You might wonder why there are so many different sorting algorithms. The answer is that the performance of each sorting algorithm is different. Some algorithms make more comparisons, while others make fewer item assignments. Also, there are algorithms that make fewer comparisons as well as fewer item assignments. The previous sections give the average number of comparisons and item assignments for the two sorting algorithms covered in this chapter. Analysis of the number of key comparisons and item assignments allows the user to decide which algorithm to use in a particular situation.

Searching

Searching a list for a given item is one of the most common operations performed on a list. To search the list, you need three pieces of information:

1. The list—that is, the array containing the list
2. The length of the list
3. The item for which you are searching

After the search is completed, do the following:

4. If the item is found, then report "success" and the location where the item was found.
5. If the item is not found, then report "failure."

To accommodate 4 and 5, we will write a value-returning function as follows: If the search item is found in the list, the function returns the location in the list where the search item is found; otherwise, it returns –1, indicating an unsuccessful search. From this output, it is clear that the value-returning function we will write has three parameters:

1. The array, `list`, containing the list
2. The length of the list, `listLength` (Note that `listLength <= arraySize`.)
3. The item, `searchItem`, for which you are searching

The search algorithm described here is called a **sequential search** or **linear search**. As the name implies, it sequentially searches the array, starting with the first array component. It compares the `searchItem` with the elements in the array (that is, `list`), starting at position 0, and continues the search until it finds the item, or until no more data is left in the `list` to be compared with the `searchItem`.

Consider the list of seven elements shown in Figure 10-21.

FIGURE 10-21 List of seven elements

Suppose that you want to determine whether 27 is in the list. The sequential search works as follows. First, you compare 27 with `list[0]`—that is, compare 27 with 35. Because `list[0]` ≠ 27, you then compare 27 with `list[1]` (that is, with 12, the second item in the list). Because `list[1]` ≠ 27, you compare 27 with the next element in the list—that is, compare 27 with `list[2]`. Because `list[2]` = 27, the search stops. This is a successful search.

Let us now search for 10. As before, the search starts with the first element in the list—that is, at `list[0]`. This time the search item, which is 10, is compared with every item in the list. Eventually, no more data is left in the list to compare with the search item. This is an unsuccessful search.

It now follows that, as soon as you find an element in the list that is equal to the search item, you must stop the search and report "success." (In this case, you usually also tell the location in the list where the search item was found.) Otherwise, after the search item is compared with every element in the list, you must stop the search and report "failure."

The following function performs a sequential search on a list. To be specific, and for illustration purposes, we assume that the list elements are of type `int`.

```cpp
int seqSearch(const int list[], int listLength, int searchItem)
{
    int loc;
    bool found = false;

    for (loc = 0; loc < listLength; loc++)
        if (list[loc] == searchItem)
        {
            found = true;
            break;
        }
```

```
    if (found)
        return loc;
    else
        return -1;
}
```

If the function `seqSearch` returns a value greater than or equal to 0, it is a successful search; otherwise, it is an unsuccessful search.

As you can see from this algorithm, you start the search by comparing `searchItem` with the first element in the list. If `searchItem` is equal to the first element in `list`, you exit the loop; otherwise, `loc` is incremented by 1 to point to the next element in `list`. You then compare `searchItem` with the next element in `list`, and so on.

The program in Example 10-2 illustrates how to use the function `seqSearch` in a program.

EXAMPLE 10-2

```
//**************************************************************
// Author: D.S. Malik
//
// This program shows how to use a sequential search algorithm.
//**************************************************************

#include <iostream>                                          //Line 1

using namespace std;                                         //Line 2

const int ARRAY_SIZE = 10;                                   //Line 3

int seqSearch(const int list[], int listLength,
              int searchItem);                               //Line 4

int main()                                                   //Line 5
{                                                            //Line 6
    int intList[ARRAY_SIZE];                                 //Line 7
    int number;                                              //Line 8

    cout << "Line 9: Enter " << ARRAY_SIZE
         << " integers." << endl;                            //Line 9

    for (int index  = 0; index < ARRAY_SIZE; index++)        //Line 10
        cin >> intList[index];                               //Line 11

    cout << endl;                                            //Line 12

    cout << "Line 13: Enter the number to be "
         << "searched: ";                                    //Line 13
    cin >> number;                                           //Line 14
    cout << endl;                                            //Line 15
```

10

```
    int pos = seqSearch(intList, ARRAY_SIZE, number);   //Line 16

    if (pos!= -1)                                        //Line 17
        cout <<"Line 18: " << number
            << " is found at position " << pos
            << endl;                                     //Line 18
    else                                                 //Line 19
        cout << "Line 20: " << number
            << " is not in the list." << endl;           //Line 20

    return 0;                                            //Line 21
}                                                        //Line 22
```

```
//Place the definition of the function seqSearch
//given previously here.
```

Sample Run 1: In this sample run, the user input is shaded.

```
Line 9: Enter 10 integers.
2 56 34 25 73 46 89 10 5 16

Line 13: Enter the number to be searched: 25

Line 18: 25 is found at position 3
```

Sample Run 2: In this sample run, the user input is shaded.

```
Line 9: Enter 10 integers.
2 56 34 25 73 46 89 10 5 16

Line 13: Enter the number to be searched: 38

Line 20: 38 is not in the list.
```

In this program, the statement in Line 7 declares `intList` to be an array of 10 components. The `for` loop in Lines 10 and 11 inputs the data into `intList`. The statement in Line 13 prompts the user to enter the search item, and the statement in Line 14 inputs the search item into `number`. The statement in Line 16 uses the function `seqSearch` to search `intList` for the search item. In Sample Run 1, the search item is 25; in Sample Run 2, it is 38. The statements in Lines 17 through 20 output the appropriate message. Notice that the search in Sample Run 1 is successful, and in Sample Run 2 it is unsuccessful.

Suppose that you have a list with 1000 elements. If the search item is the second item in the list, the sequential search makes two **key** (also called **item**) comparisons to determine whether the search item is in the list. Similarly, if the search item is the 900th item in the list, the sequential search makes 900 key comparisons to determine whether the search item is in the list. If the search item is not in the list, the sequential search makes 1000 key comparisons. Therefore, if `searchItem` is always at the bottom of the list, it will take many comparisons to find `searchItem`. Also, if `searchItem` is not in `list`, then we compare `searchItem` with every element in `list`. A sequential search is therefore not very efficient for large lists. In fact, it can be proved that, on average, the number of comparisons (key comparisons, not index comparisons) the sequential search made is equal to half the size of the list. So, for a list size of 1000, on average, the sequential search makes about 500 key comparisons.

The sequential search algorithm does not assume that the list is sorted. If the list is sorted, then you can somewhat improve the search algorithm, which we discuss next.

Binary Search

A sequential search performs somewhat better on a sorted list, but it still is not very efficient for large lists. It typically searches about half the list. However, if the list is sorted, you can use another search algorithm, called the **binary search**. A binary search is much faster than a sequential search. To apply a binary search, *the list must be sorted*.

A binary search uses the "divide and conquer" technique to search the list. First, the search item is compared with the middle element of the list. If the search item is less than the middle element of the list, we restrict the search to the upper half of the list; otherwise, we search the lower half of the list.

Consider the following sorted list of `length = 12`, as shown in Figure 10-22.

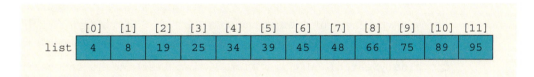

FIGURE 10-22 List of length 12

Suppose that we want to determine whether 75 is in the list. Initially, the entire list is the search list. (See Figure 10-23.)

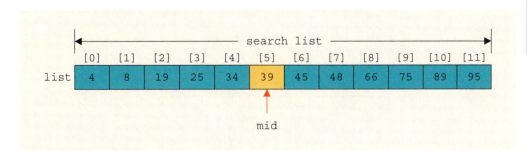

FIGURE 10-23 Search list, `list[0]...list[11]`

First, we compare 75 with the middle element, `list[5]` (which is 39), in the list. Because 75 ≠ `list[5]` and 75 > `list[5]`, we next restrict our search to `list[6]`...`list[11]`, as shown in Figure 10-24.

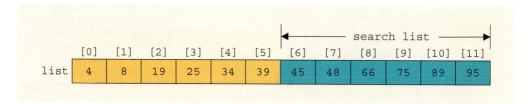

FIGURE 10-24 Search list, `list[6]`...`list[11]`

The preceding process is now repeated on `list[6]`...`list[11]`, which is a list of `length` = 6.

Because we frequently need to determine the middle element of the list, the binary search algorithm is usually implemented for array-based lists. To determine the middle element of the list, we add the starting index, `first`, to the ending index, `last`, of the search list and divide by 2 to calculate its index. That is, $mid = \dfrac{first + last}{2}$. Initially, `first` = 0 and (because array index in C++ starts at 0, and `listLength` denotes the number of elements in the list) `last` = `listLength` - 1.

The following C++ function implements the binary search algorithm. If the item is found in the list, its location is returned. If the search item is not in the list, -1 is returned.

```cpp
int binarySearch(const int list[], int listLength, int searchItem)
{
    int first = 0;
    int last = listLength - 1;
    int mid;

    bool found = false;

    while (first <= last && !found)
    {
        mid = (first + last) / 2;

        if (list[mid] == searchItem)
            found = true;
        else if (list[mid] > searchItem)
            last = mid - 1;
        else
            first = mid + 1;
    }

    if (found)
        return mid;
    else
        return -1;
}//end binarySearch
```

Note that in the binary search algorithm, two key (item) comparisons are made each time through the loop, except in the successful case—the last time through the loop—when only one key comparison is made.

Next, we walk through the binary search algorithm on the list shown in Figure 10-25.

	[0]	[1]	[2]	[3]	[4]	[5]	[6]	[7]	[8]	[9]	[10]	[11]
list	4	8	19	25	34	39	45	48	66	75	89	95

FIGURE 10-25 Sorted list for a binary search

The size of the list in Figure 10-25 is 12, so `length` = 12. Suppose that the item for which we are searching is 89, so `searchItem` = 89. Before the `while` loop executes, `first` = 0, `last` = 11, and `found` = `false`. In the following, we trace the execution of the `while` loop, showing the values of `first`, `last`, and `mid`, and the number of key comparisons during each iteration:

Iteration	first	last	mid	list[mid]	Number of key comparisons
1	0	11	5	39	2
2	6	11	8	66	2
3	9	11	10	89	1 (found is true)

The item is found at location 10, and the total number of key comparisons is 5.

Next, let's search the list for 34, so `searchItem` = 34. Before the `while` loop executes, `first` = 0, `last` = 11, and `found` = `false`. In the following, as before, we trace the execution of the `while` loop, showing the values of `first`, `last`, and `mid`, and the number of key comparisons during each iteration:

Iteration	first	last	mid	list[mid]	Number of key comparisons
1	0	11	5	39	2
2	0	4	2	19	2
3	3	4	3	25	2
4	4	4	4	34	1 (found is true)

The item is found at location 4, and the total number of key comparisons is 7.

Let us now search for 22, so `searchItem` = 22. Before the `while` loop executes, `first` = 0, `last` = 11, and `found` = `false`. In the following, as before, we trace the execution of the `while` loop, showing the values of `first`, `last`, and `mid`, and the number of key comparisons during each iteration:

Iteration	first	last	mid	list[mid]	Number of key comparisons
1	0	11	5	39	2
2	0	4	2	19	2
3	3	4	3	25	2
4	3	2		the loop stops (because `first > last`), unsuccessful search	

This is an unsuccessful search. The total number of key comparisons is 6.

From these tracings of the binary search algorithm, you can see that every time you go through the loop, you cut the size of the sublist by half. That is, the size of the sublist you search the next time through the loop is half the size of the previous sublist.

You can write a program similar to the one in Example 10-2 to test the method `binarySearch`. See Programming Exercise 2 at the end of this chapter.

Performance of Binary Search

Suppose that L is a sorted list of size 1000, and we want to determine if an item x is in L. From the binary search algorithm, it follows that every iteration of the `while` loop cuts the size of the search list by half. Because $1000 \approx 1024 = 2^{10}$, the `while` loop will have, at most, 11 iterations to determine whether x is in L. (Note that the symbol $\approx$ means approximately equal to.) Because every iteration of the `while` loop makes two item (key) comparisons, that is, x is compared twice with the elements of L, the binary search will make, at most, 22 comparisons to determine whether x is in L. On the other hand, recall that a sequential search on average will make 500 comparisons to determine whether x is in L.

To better understand how fast binary search is compared to sequential search, suppose that L is of size 1000000. Because $1000000 \approx 1048576 = 2^{20}$, it follows that the `while` loop in a binary search will have at most 21 iterations to determine whether an element is in L. Every iteration of the `while` loop makes two key (that is, item) comparisons. Therefore, to determine whether an element is in L, a binary search makes at most 42 item comparisons. On the other hand, on average, a sequential search will make 500,000 key (item) comparisons to determine whether an element is in L.

In general, if L is a sorted list of size n, to determine whether an element is in L, the binary search makes at most $2\log_2 n + 2$ key (item) comparisons.

Avoiding Bugs: Developing Test Suites in Advance

It can be tempting to conclude that a program is working correctly when it outputs a correct result for the first time. A program that outputs a correct result is correct for that set of input, but it may be incorrect for other sets of input. However, it is seldom practical to test a program with all possible input sets. So how do we determine that a program is correct without testing every possible input set? We develop an efficient test suite intended to test every kind of input, and we give special attention to boundary values.

For example, suppose we write a program to find the square root of a whole number, but without using the function `sqrt` from the header file `cmath`. In our first attempt to determine if our program is working, we might input the value 16. If our program outputs the value 4, we know that our program works at least for the input value 16, but it may not work for other input values. Next, we might be inclined to try 4 or 25 or 36, because we know the square roots of each of these numbers. But these numbers all are perfect squares (each is the square of some integer). Instead, it might be safe to assume that, if our program works for one perfect square, it probably works for other perfect squares. Hence, we should try our program on a number such as 5, which is not a perfect square. Let us assume it works correctly if the input value is 5. So far, all of the numbers we have tested are positive. We should try our program on one or more negative numbers, to see if our program outputs the correct imaginary number. Then, even though 0 is a perfect square, we ought to try our program on 0. We can say that negative numbers, 0, and positive numbers are different kinds of numbers, and we should make certain that our program works properly on each kind of number. Finally, we should check numbers on the boundaries. The number on the boundary between the negative numbers and 0 is the number −1. The number on the boundary between 0 and the positive numbers is the number 1. Finally, we should try our program on the largest positive integer and the smallest negative integer, which also are boundary values. By checking one number of each kind and at each boundary, we maximize the return on our investment of time to determine if our program is working correctly.

A test suite is a collection of input values (often together with a corresponding set of expected outputs), determined in advance, to be used to verify that a program is working correctly once it is written. At this stage, you are still learning the fundamentals of programming. As you become comfortable with the fundamentals of programming, you should begin to establish test suites as part of the software-development process. A test suite should be established as soon as the requirements are known. After familiarizing yourself with the requirements, you should be able to determine input values (and corresponding output values) that you will use to test your program. At this early development stage, your attention is undiluted by the attention that ultimately you must devote to design and implementation.

Sometimes a programmer establishes a set of objectives for a program, only to realize that the designed and coded program satisfies only a subset of those objectives. Sometimes, in the process of designing and implementing, the programmer even loses track of some of those objectives. Instead of designing and coding program features to satisfy the remaining objectives, the programmer intentionally (or subconsciously) changes the objectives to match what the program actually does. This is seldom, if ever, a suitable approach to programming. By establishing a test suite before beginning to tackle the challenges of design and implementation, the programmer fortifies himself or herself against the temptation to shortchange or to inadvertently omit some of the objectives from the solution.

Let's apply these concepts to determine a test suite for the binary search algorithm. We do so by identifying all the kinds of lists to which the user might apply the binary search algorithm. The list may be empty. Hence, one member of our test suite is the empty list. If the list is not empty, it might consist of a single element (a boundary case), or it could have as many as INT_MAX elements (another boundary case). Further, it might consist of an even number of elements greater than zero or an odd number of elements greater than 1. In each of these cases, the element for which we are searching might or might not be present. If the element is present, it might be the first element in the list, the last element in the list, or it might be neither the first nor the last element in the list. If the element is not present, it might be smaller than the first item in the list, larger than the last element in the list, or, except in the case of a list of only one element, it might be larger than the first element in the list and smaller than the last element in the list. Thus, we have identified nine different kinds of lists on which we should test our binary search algorithm and the method implementing our binary search algorithm. Six of the lists have three subcases each, and one of the lists has two subcases, for a total of 22 different lists on which we should test our binary search algorithm and the method that implements it. The nine lists are:

- An empty list

- A list of one element that is the element for which we are searching

- A list of one element that is not the element for which we are searching, and the element for which we are searching is smaller than the element or larger than the element

- A list with INT_MAX elements that contains the element for which we are searching in the first position, the last position, or in an intermediate position

- A list with INT_MAX elements that does not contain the element for which we are searching, and the element for which we are searching is smaller than the smallest element, larger than the largest element, or neither smaller than the smallest element nor larger than the largest element

- A list with an even number of elements (other than 0) that contains the element for which we are searching in the first position, the last position, or in an intermediate position

- A list with an even number of elements (other than 0) that does not contain the element for which we are searching, and the element for which we are searching is smaller than the smallest element, larger than the largest element, or neither smaller than the smallest element nor larger than the largest element

- A list with an odd number of elements (other than 1 or INT_MAX) that contains the element for which we are searching in the first position, the last position, or in an intermediate position

- A list with an odd number of elements (other than 1 or INT_MAX) that does not contain the element for which we are searching, and the element for which we are searching is smaller than the smallest element, larger than the largest element, or neither smaller than the smallest element nor larger than the largest element

For the most part, test suites are beyond the scope of this text, and are not discussed further. However, to the extent that you include them as part of the software-development process, you will increase your confidence in the quality of the software you develop.

The **class vector** (Optional)

Chapter 6 and the previous sections of this chapter described how arrays can be used to implement and process lists. One of the limitations of arrays discussed so far is that once you create an array, its size remains fixed. This means that only a fixed number of elements can be stored in an array. Also, inserting an element in the array at a specific position could require the elements of the array to be shifted. Similarly, removing an element from the array also could require shifting the elements of the array, because we typically do not leave empty positions between array positions holding some data. Typically, empty array positions are at the end of an array.

In addition to arrays, C++ provides the **class** vector to implement a list. A vector object is called a **vector container** (or a **vector**, or simply an **object**). Unlike an array, the size of a **vector** object can grow and shrink during program execution. Therefore, you do not need to be concerned with the number of data elements.

When you declare a **vector** object, you must specify the type of the element the **vector** object stores. Table 10-1 describes various ways a **vector** object can be declared.

TABLE 10-1 Various Ways to Declare and Initialize a vector Object

Statement	Effect
vector<elemType> vecList;	Creates the empty vector object, vecList, without any elements.
vector<elemType> vecList(otherVecList);	Creates the vector object, vecList, and initializes vecList to the elements of the vector otherVecList. vecList and otherVecList are of the same type.
vector<elemType> vecList(size);	Creates the vector object, vecList, of size size. vecList is initialized using the default values.
vector<elemType> vecList(n, elem);	Creates the vector object, vecList, of size n. vecList is initialized using n copies of the element elem.

In Table 10-1, elemType specifies the data type of the element to be stored in vecList.

EXAMPLE 10-3

a. The following statement declares `intList` to be an empty `vector` object, and the element type is `int`.

    `vector<int> intList;`

b. The following statement declares `intList` to be a `vector` object of size 10, and the element type is `int`. The elements of `intList` are initialized to 0.

    `vector<int> intList(10);`

Now that we know how to declare a **vector** object, let us discuss how to manipulate the data stored in a **vector** object. To do so, we must know the following basic operations:

*   Item insertion
*   Item deletion
*   Stepping through the elements of a vector container

The **class** vector provides various operations to manipulate data stored in a vector object. Each of these operations is defined in the form of a function. Table 10-2 describes some of these functions and how to use them with a vector object. (Assume that **vecList** is a vector object. The name of the function is shown in **bold**.)

TABLE 10-2 Operations on a `vector` Object

Expression	Effect
`vecList.at(index)`	Returns the element at the position specified by `index`.
`vecList[index]`	Returns the element at the position specified by `index`.
`vecList.front()`	Returns the first element. (Does not check whether the object is empty.)
`vecList.back()`	Returns the last element. (Does not check whether the object is empty.)
`vecList.clear()`	Deletes all elements from the object.
`vecList.push_back(elem)`	A copy of `elem` is inserted into `vecList` at the end.

TABLE 10-2 Operations on a `vector` Object (continued)

Expression	Effect
`vecList.pop_back()`	Deletes the last element of `vecList`.
`vecList.empty()`	Returns **true** if the object `vecList` is empty, and **false** otherwise.
`vecList.size()`	Returns the number of elements currently in the object `vecList`. The value returned is an **unsigned int** value.
`vecList.max_size()`	Returns the maximum number of elements that can be inserted into the object `vecList`.

Table 10-2 shows that the elements in a `vector` can be processed just as they are in an array. (Recall that in C++, arrays start at location 0. Similarly, the first element in a `vector` object is at location 0.)

EXAMPLE 10-4

Consider the following statement, which declares `intList` to be a vector of size 5, and the element type is `int`.

```
vector<int> intList(5);
```

You can use a loop, such as the following, to store elements into `intList`.

```
for (int j = 0; j < 5; j++)
    intList[j] = j;
```

Similarly, you can use a **for** loop to output the elements of `intList`.

Example 10-4 uses a **for** loop and the array subscripting operator, `[]`, to access the elements of `intList`. We declare `intList` to be a `vector` object of size 5. Does this mean that we can store only five elements in `intList`? The answer is no. We can, in fact, add more elements to `intList`. However, because when we declared `intList`, we specified the size to be 5, in order to add any elements past position 4, we use the function push_back.

Furthermore, if we initially declare a `vector` object and do not specify its size, then to add elements to the `vector` object, we use the function push_back. Example 10-5 explains how to use this function.

EXAMPLE 10-5

The following statement declares `intList` to be a vector container of size 0.

```
vector<int> intList;
```

To add elements into `intList`, we can use the function `push_back` as follows:

```
intList.push_back(34);
intList.push_back(55);
```

After these statements execute, the size of `intList` is 2, and

```
intList = {34, 55}.
```

In Example 10-5, because `intList` is declared to be of size 0, we use the function `push_back` to add elements to `intList`. However, we can also use the `resize` function to increase the size of `intList`, and then use the array subscripting operator. For example, suppose that `intList` is declared as in Example 10-5. Then the following statement sets the size of `intList` to 10:

```
intList.resize(10);
```

Similarly, the following statement increases the size of `intList` by 10:

```
intList.resize(intList.size() + 10);
```

However, at times, the `push_back` function is more convenient because it does not need to know the size of the vector; it simply adds the elements at the end.

NOTE The name of the header file that contains the **class** vector is `vector`. Therefore, to use the **class** vector, you must include the header file `vector`, that is, include the following statement in your program:

```
#include <vector>
```

The program in Example 10-6 illustrates how to use a **vector** object in a program and how to process the elements of a **vector**.

EXAMPLE 10-6

```
//***********************************************************
// Author: D.S. Malik
//
// This program shows how to process the elements of a vector.
//***********************************************************
```

```cpp
#include <iostream>                                    //Line 1
#include <vector>                                      //Line 2

using namespace std;                                   //Line 3

int main()                                             //Line 4
{                                                      //Line 5
    vector<int> intList;                               //Line 6

    intList.push_back(13);                             //Line 7
    intList.push_back(75);                             //Line 8
    intList.push_back(28);                             //Line 9
    intList.push_back(35);                             //Line 10

    cout << "Line 11: List elements: ";                //Line 11

    for (unsigned int i = 0; i < intList.size(); i++)  //Line 12
        cout << intList[i] << " ";                     //Line 13
    cout << endl;                                      //Line 14

    for (unsigned int i = 0; i < intList.size(); i++)  //Line 15
        intList[i] = intList[i] * 2;                   //Line 16

    cout << "Line 17: List elements: ";                //Line 17

    for (unsigned int i = 0; i < intList.size(); i++)  //Line 18
        cout << intList[i] << " ";                     //Line 19

    cout << endl;                                      //Line 20

    return 0;                                          //Line 21
}                                                      //Line 22
```

Sample Run:

```
Line 11: List elements: 13 75 28 35
Line 17: List elements: 26 150 56 70
```

The statement in Line 6 declares the **vector** object (or **vector** for short), **intList**, of type **int**.

The statements in Lines 7 through 10 use the operation **push_back** to insert four numbers—13, 75, 28, and 35—into **intList**. The statements in Lines 12 and 13 use a **for** loop and the array subscripting operator, **[]**, to output the elements of **intList**. In the output, see the line marked Line 11, which contains the output of Lines 11 through 14 of the program. (Notice that the **for** loop control variable **i** is declared to be an **unsigned int** because, in the **for** loop, we are using the expression **intList.size()**, which returns an **unsigned int** value, to determine the size of **intList**.) The statements in Lines 15 and 16 use a **for** loop to double the value of each element of **intList**; the statements in Lines 18 and 19 output the elements of **intList**. In the output, see the line marked Line 17, which contains the output of Lines 17 through 20 of the program.

PROGRAMMING EXAMPLE: Election Results

The presidential election for the student council of your local university will be held soon. For reasons related to confidentiality, the chair of the election committee wants to computerize the voting. The chair is looking for someone to write a program to analyze the data and report the winner. Let us write a program to help the election committee.

The university has four major divisions, and each division has several departments. For the purpose of the election, the divisions are labeled as Region 1, Region 2, Region 3, and Region 4. Each department in each division manages its own voting process and directly reports the results to the election committee. The voting is reported in the following form:

```
candidateName regionNumber numberOfVotesForTheCandidate
```

The election committee wants the output in the following tabular form:

```
--------------Election Results--------------

Candidate                  Votes
Name        Region1   Region2   Region3   Region4    Total
---------   -------   -------   -------   -------    ------
Ashley           23        89         0       160       272
Donald          110       158         0         0       268
Hamid            25        71        89        97       282
  .
  .
  .


Winner: ???, Votes Received: ???

Total votes polled: ???
```

The names of the candidates in the output must be in alphabetical order.

For this program, we assume that six candidates are running for student council president. This program can be modified to accommodate any number of candidates.

The data is provided in two files. One file, `candData.txt`, consists of the names of candidates. The names in the file are in no particular order. In the second file, `voteData.txt`, each line consists of voting results in the following form:

```
candidateName regionNumber numberOfVotesForTheCandidate
```

That is, each line in the file **voteData.txt** consists of the candidate name, region number, and the votes received by the candidate in this region. There is one entry per line. For example, the input file containing voting data looks like the following:

```
Mia 2 34
Sheila 1 56
Donald 2 56
Mia 1 78
Ravi 2 56
  .
  .
  .
```

The first line indicates that `Mia` received 34 votes from region 2.

Input   Two files, one containing the candidates' names and the other containing the voting data, as described previously

Output   The election results in a tabular form, as described previously, and the winner

PROBLEM ANALYSIS AND ALGORITHM DESIGN

From the output, it is clear that the program must organize the voting data by region, and calculate the total votes both received by each candidate and polled for the election. Furthermore, the names of the candidates must appear in alphabetical order.

The main component of this program is a candidate. Therefore, first we design the `class candidateType` to implement a candidate object. Moreover, in this program, we use an array of `candidateType` object to implement the list of candidates.

Candidate

The main component of this program is the candidate, which is described and implemented in this section. Every candidate has a name and receives votes. Because there are four regions, we declare an array of four components to keep track of the votes for each region. We also need a data member to store the total number of votes received by each candidate. Essentially, the `class candidateType` is the following:

```cpp
//**********************************************************
// Author: D.S. Malik
//
// class candidateType.h
// This class specifies the members to implement a candidate's
// data in a program.
//**********************************************************

#include <string>

using namespace std;

const int NUM_OF_REGIONS = 4;

class candidateType
```

10

```
{
public:
    void setName(string name);
        //Function to set name according to the parameter.
        //Postcondition: candName = name

    string getName() const;
        //Function to return the name.
        //Postcondition: The value of candName is returned.

    void updateVotesByRegion(int region, int votes);
        //Function to update the votes of a candidate for a
        //particular region.
        //Postcondition: Votes for the region specified by
        //               the parameter are updated by adding
        //               the votes specified by the parameter
        //               votes.

    void setVotes(int region, int votes);
        //Function to set the votes of a candidate for a
        //particular region.
        //Postcondition: Votes for the region specified by
        //               the parameter are set to the votes
        //               specified by the parameter votes.

    void calculateTotalVotes();
        //Function to calculate the total votes received by a
        //candidate.
        //Postcondition: The votes in each region are added
        //               and assigned to totalVotes.

    int getTotalVotes() const;
        //Function to return the total votes received by a
        //candidate.
        //Postcondition: The value of totalVotes is returned.

    void printData() const;
        //Function to output the candidate's name, the votes
        //received in each region, and the total votes received.

    candidateType();
        //Default constructor.
        //Postcondition: Candidate's name is initialized to an
        //               empty string, the number of votes in each
        //               region and the total votes are
        //               initialized to 0.
```

```
private:
    string candName; //variable to store name

    int votesByRegion[NUM_OF_REGIONS];    //array to store the
                                          //votes received in
                                          //each region
    int totalVotes; //variable to store the total votes
};
```

We leave the UML class diagram of the **class** candidateType as an exercise for you.

The definitions of the functions of the **class** candidateType are:

```
void candidateType::setName(string name)
{
    candName = name;
}

string candidateType::getName() const
{
    return candName;
}

void candidateType::setVotes(int region, int votes)
{
    votesByRegion[region - 1] = votes;
}

void candidateType::updateVotesByRegion(int region, int votes)
{
    votesByRegion[region - 1] = votesByRegion[region - 1]
                                + votes;
}

void candidateType::calculateTotalVotes()
{

    totalVotes = 0;

    for (int i = 0; i < NUM_OF_REGIONS; i++)
        totalVotes += votesByRegion[i];
}

int candidateType::getTotalVotes() const
{
    return totalVotes;
}
```

```
void candidateType::printData() const
{
    cout << left << setw(9) << candName << "   ";

    cout << right;
    for (int i = 0; i < NUM_OF_REGIONS; i++)
        cout << setw(8) << votesByRegion[i] << "   ";
    cout << setw(6) << totalVotes << endl;
}

candidateType::candidateType()
{
    candName = "";

    for (int i = 0; i < NUM_OF_REGIONS; i++)
        votesByRegion[i] = 0;

    totalVotes = 0;
}
```

Now that the `class candidateType` has been designed and implemented, we focus on designing the main program.

Because there are six candidates, we create a list, `candidatesList`, containing six components of type `candidateType`. The first thing that the program should do is read each candidate's name from the file `candData.txt` into the list `candidatesList`. Next, we sort `candidatesList`.

The next step is to process the voting data from the file `voteData.txt`, which holds the voting data. After processing the voting data, the program should calculate the total votes received by each candidate and print the data as shown previously. Thus, the general algorithm is:

1. Read each candidate's name into `candidatesList`.
2. Sort `candidatesList`.
3. Process the voting data.
4. Calculate the total votes received by each candidate.
5. Print the results.

The following statement creates the array `candidatesList` of six components of type `candidateType`:

```
const int NUM_OF_CANDIDATES = 6;
candidateType candidatesList[NUM_OF_CANDIDATES];
```

Figure 10-26 shows the array `candidatesList`.

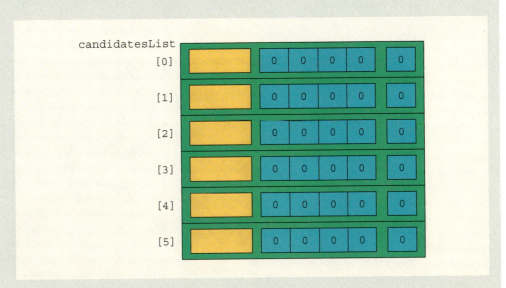

FIGURE 10-26 candidatesList

In Figure 10-26, the array `votesByRegion` and the variable `totalVotes` are initialized to 0 by the default constructor of the **class** `candidateType`.

Function
getCandidatesName

This function reads the data from the input file `candData.txt` and fills the names in the array `candidatesList`. The input file is opened in the function `main`. We see that this function has three parameters: one corresponding to the input file, one corresponding to the array `candidatesName`, and one to pass the number of rows of the array `candidatesName`. Essentially, this function is:

```cpp
void getCandidatesName(ifstream& inp, candidateType cList[],
                       int numOfRows)
{
    string name;

    for (int i = 0; i < numOfRows; i++)
    {
        inp >> name;
        cList[i].setName(name);
    }
}
```

1
0

Figure 10-27 shows the object `candidatesList` after a call to the function `getCandidatesName`.

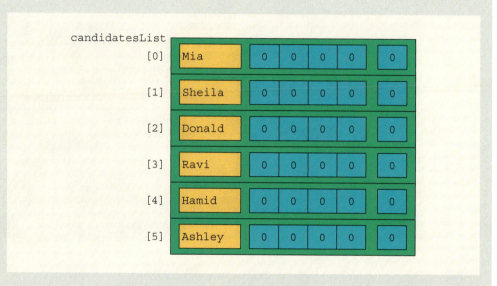

FIGURE 10-27 Array `candidatesList` after a call to the function `getCandidatesName`

Function
sortCandidatesName

This function uses the selection sort algorithm to sort the array `candidatesList`. This function has two parameters: one corresponding to the array `candidatesList`, and a second to pass the number of rows of the array `candidatesList`. Essentially, this function is:

```
void sortCandidatesName(candidateType cList[], int numOfRows)
{
    int min;
    candidateType temp;

        //selection sort
    for (int i = 0; i < numOfRows - 1; i++)
    {
        min = i;

        for (int j = i + 1; j < numOfRows; j++)
            if (cList[j].getName() < cList[min].getName())
                min = j;
```

```
            temp = cList[min];
            cList[min] = cList[i];
            cList[i] = temp;
        }
}
```

After a call to this function, the arrays are as shown in Figure 10-28.

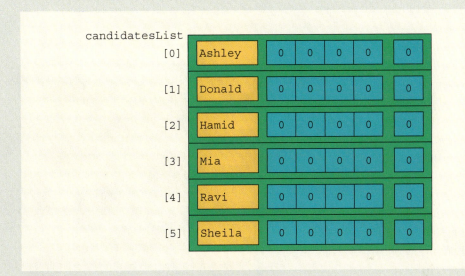

FIGURE 10-28 Array `candidatesList` after calling the function `sortCandidatesName`

Process Voting Data Processing the voting data is quite straightforward. Each entry in the file `voteData.txt` is in the following form:

`candidatesName regionNumber numberOfVotesForThisCandidate`

The general algorithm to process the voting data is shown next. For each entry in the file `voteData.txt`, we do the following:

a. Get a `candidateName`, `regionNumber`, and `numberOfVotesForTheCandidate`.

b. Find the row number in the array `candidatesList` that corresponds to this candidate.

c. Find the column in the array `votesByRegion` that corresponds to the `regionNumber`.

d. Update the appropriate entry in the array `votesByRegion` by adding the `numberOfVotesForTheCandidate`.

Step b requires us to search the array `candidatesList` to find the location (that is, row number) of a particular candidate. Because the array `candidatesList` is sorted, we can use the binary search algorithm to find the row number corresponding to a particular candidate. Therefore, this program also includes a function, `binSearch`, to implement the binary search algorithm on the array `sortCandidatesName`. We will write the definition of the function `binSearch` shortly. First, let us discuss how to update the array `votesByRegion`.

Suppose that the array `candidatesList` is as shown in Figure 10-29.

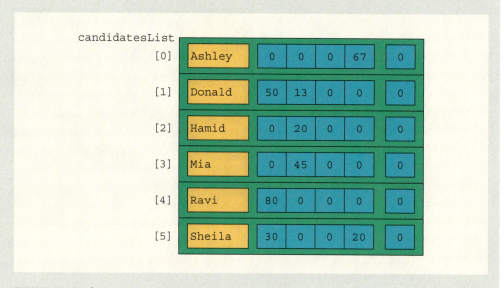

FIGURE 10-29 Array `candidatesList`

Further suppose that the next entry read from the input file is:

`Donald 2 35`

We must locate the row in the grid that corresponds to this candidate. To find the row, we search the array `candidatesList` to find the row that corresponds to this name. `Donald` corresponds to the second row in the array `candidatesList`. (See Figure 10-30.)

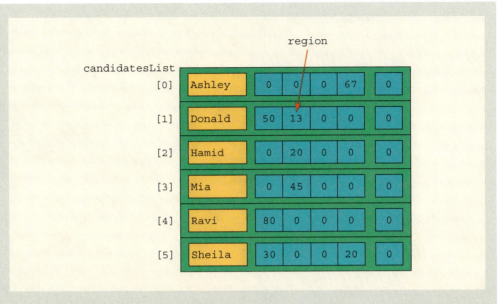

FIGURE 10-30 Position of Donald and region = 2

To process this entry, we access the second row of the array `candidatesList` and use the function `updateVotesByRegion` of the **class** `candidateType`. The following statement accomplishes this task:

```
candidatesList[1].updateVotesByRegion(region, numOfVotes);
```

After processing this entry, the array `candidatesList` is as shown in Figure 10-31.

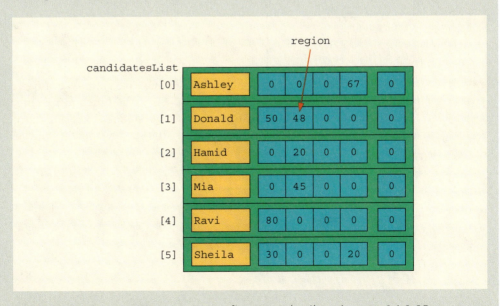

FIGURE 10-31 Array `candidatesList` after processing the entry Donald 2 35

Next, we describe the function `binSearch` and the function `processVotes` to process the voting data.

Function binSearch

This function implements the binary search algorithm on the array `candidatesList`. It is similar to the function `binarySearch` discussed earlier in this chapter. Its definition is:

```
int binSearch(candidateType cList[], int numOfRows, string name)
{
    int first, last, mid;
    bool found;
    first = 0;
    last = numOfRows - 1;
    found = false;

    while (first <= last && !found)
    {
        mid = (first + last) / 2;

        if (cList[mid].getName() == name)
            found = true;
        else if (cList[mid].getName() > name)
            last = mid - 1;
        else
            first = mid + 1;
    }

    if (found)
        return mid;
    else
        return -1;
}
```

Function processVotes

This function processes the voting data. Clearly, it must have access to the array `candidatesList` as well as to the input file `voteData.txt`. We also need to tell this function the number of rows in each array. Thus, the function `processVotes` has three parameters: one to access the input file `voteData.txt`, one corresponding to the array `candidatesList`, and one to pass the number of rows in each array. The definition of this function is:

```
void processVotes(ifstream& inp, candidateType cList[],
                  int numOfRows)
{
    string name;
    int region;
    int numOfVotes;
    int loc;

    inp >> name >> region >> numOfVotes;
```

```
while (inp)
{
    loc =  binSearch(cList, numOfRows, name);

    if (loc != -1)
        cList[loc].updateVotesByRegion(region, numOfVotes);

    inp >> name >> region >> numOfVotes;
}
}
```

Calculate
Total Votes
(Function
addRegionsVote)

After processing the voting data, the next step is to calculate the total votes for each candidate. Suppose that after processing the voting data, the arrays are as shown in Figure 10-32.

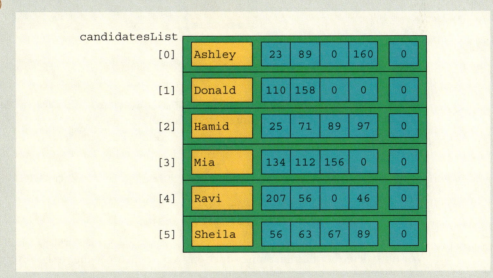

FIGURE 10-32 Array candidatesList after processing the voting data

After calculating the total votes received by each candidate, the array candidatesList is as shown in Figure 10-33.

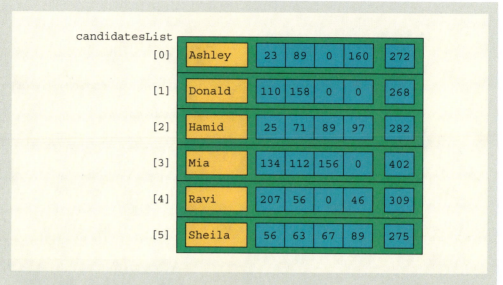

FIGURE 10-33 Array `candidatesList` after calculating total votes received by each candidate

To calculate the total votes received by each candidate, we add the contents of the `votesByRegion` array and then store the sum in the `totalVotes` array. This task is accomplished by the function `addRegionsVote`. The definition of this function is:

```
void addRegionsVote(candidateType cList[], int numOfRows)
{
    for (int i = 0; i < numOfRows; i++)
        cList[i].calculateTotalVotes();
}
```

We now describe the remaining functions required to get the desired output.

Function printHeading

This function outputs the first four lines of input, so it contains certain output statements. The definition of this function is:

```
void printHeading()
{
    cout << "          --------------Election Results----------"
         << "----" << endl << endl;
    cout << "Candidate                       Votes" << endl;
    cout << "Name          Region1   Region2   Region3   "
         << "Region4    Total" << endl;
    cout << "---------    -------   -------   -------    "
         << "-------    ------" << endl;
}
```

Function printResults

This function outputs the remaining lines of the output. Clearly, it must have access to the array `candidatesList`. We must also tell the function the number of rows in each array. Thus, this function has two parameters. The definition of this function is:

```cpp
void printResults(candidateType cList[], int numOfRows)
{
    int largestVotes = 0;
    int winLoc = 0;
    int sumVotes = 0;

    for (int i = 0; i < numOfRows; i++)
    {
        if (largestVotes < cList[i].getTotalVotes())
        {
            largestVotes = cList[i].getTotalVotes();
            winLoc = i;
        }

        sumVotes = sumVotes + cList[i].getTotalVotes();

        cList[i].printData();
    }

    cout << endl << endl << "Winner: " << cList[winLoc].getName()
         << ", Votes Received: " << cList[winLoc].getTotalVotes()
         << endl << endl;
    cout << "Total votes polled: " << sumVotes << endl;
}
```

We now give the main algorithm.

Suppose that the variables in the function `main` are:

```cpp
candidateType candidatesList[NUM_OF_CANDIDATES];
ifstream inFile;
```

Furthermore, suppose that the candidates' names are in the file `candData.txt`, and the voting data is in the file `voteData.txt`.

MAIN ALGORITHM: FUNCTION main

1. Declare the variables.
2. Open the input file `candData.txt`.
3. If the input file does not exist, exit the program.
4. Read the data from the file `candData.txt` into the array `candidatesList`.
5. Sort the array `candidatesList`.
6. Close the file `candData.txt` and clear the input stream.
7. Open the input file `voteData.txt`.

10

8. If the input file does not exist, exit the program.

9. Process the voting data and store the results in the array `candidatesList`.

10. Calculate the number of total votes received by each candidate.

11. Print the heading.

12. Print the results.

13. Close the file `voteData.txt`.

PROGRAM LISTING

```cpp
//**************************************************************
// Author: D.S. Malik
//
// This program uses the class canidateType to process voting
// data for the student council president's post. It outputs
// each candidate's name and the votes he or she received. The
// name of the winner also is printed.
//**************************************************************

#include <iostream>
#include <string>
#include <fstream>
#include "candidateType.h"

using namespace std;

const int NUM_OF_CANDIDATES = 6;

void getCandidatesName(ifstream& inp, candidateType cList[],
                       int numOfRows);
void sortCandidatesName(candidateType cList[], int numOfRows);

int binSearch(candidateType cList[], int numOfRows,
              string name);
void processVotes(ifstream& inp, candidateType cList[],
                  int numOfRows);
void addRegionsVote(candidateType cList[], int numOfRows);
void printHeading();
void printResults(candidateType cList[], int numOfRows);

int main()
{
        //Declare variables; Step 1
    candidateType candidatesList[NUM_OF_CANDIDATES];
    ifstream inFile;

    inFile.open("candData.txt");                        //Step 2
    if (!inFile)                                        //Step 3
```

```
    {
        cout << "Input file (candData.txt) does "
             << "not exist. Program terminates!!"
             << endl;
        return 1;
    }

    getCandidatesName(inFile, candidatesList,
                    NUM_OF_CANDIDATES);                      //Step 4

    sortCandidatesName(candidatesList,
                    NUM_OF_CANDIDATES);                      //Step 5

    inFile.close();                                          //Step 6
    inFile.clear();                                          //Step 6

    inFile.open("voteData.txt");                             //Step 7
    if (!inFile)                                             //Step 8
    {
        cout << "Input file (voteData.txt) does not"
             << " exist. Program terminates!!"
             << endl;
        return 1;
    }

    processVotes(inFile, candidatesList,
                NUM_OF_CANDIDATES);                          //Step 9
    addRegionsVote(candidatesList, NUM_OF_CANDIDATES);       //Step 10
    printHeading();                                          //Step 11
    printResults(candidatesList, NUM_OF_CANDIDATES);         //Step 12
    inFile.close();                                          //Step 13

    return 0;
}

//Place the definitions of the functions getCandidatesName,
//sortCandidatesName, binSearch, processVotes, addRegionsVote,
//printHeading, and printResults here.
```

Sample Run: After placing the definitions of all the functions, as described, into the program, and executing the program:

```
          --------------Election Results--------------

Candidate                    Votes
Name        Region1   Region2   Region3   Region4    Total
---------   -------   -------   -------   -------    ------
Ashley           23        89         0       160       272
Donald          110       158         0         0       268
Hamid            25        71        89        97       282
Mia             134       112       156         0       402
Ravi            207        56         0        46       309
Sheila           56        63        67        89       275
```

1
0

```
Winner: Mia, Votes Received: 402

Total votes polled: 1808
```

Input Files:

candData.txt
```
Mia
Sheila
Donald
Ravi
Hamid
Ashley
```

voteData.txt
```
Mia 2 34
Sheila 1 56
Donald 2 56
Mia 1 78
Ravi 2 56
Hamid 4 29
Ashley 4 78
Sheila 2 63
Donald 1 23
Hamid 1 25
Ravi 4 23
Hamid 4 12
Ashley 4 82
Sheila 3 67
Donald 2 67
Mia 3 67
Ashley 1 23
Mia 1 56
Donald 2 35
Ravi 1 27
Hamid 2 34
Ravi 4 23
Sheila 4 89
Ravi 1 23
Hamid 3 89
Mia 3 89
Ravi 1 67
Hamid 2 37
Ashley 2 89
Mia 2 78
Donald 1 87
Ravi 1 90
Hamid 4 56
```

The complete listing of this program is available at the Web site accompanying this book.

QUICK REVIEW

1. A list is a set of elements of the same type.

2. The length of a list is the number of elements in the list.

3. A one-dimensional array is a convenient place to store and process lists.

4. Selection sorting sorts the list by finding the smallest (or equivalently largest) element in the list and moving it to the beginning (or end) of the list.

5. For a list of length n, on average, a selection sort makes $n(n - 1) / 2$ key comparisons and $3(n-1)$ item assignments.

6. The insertion sort algorithm sorts the list by moving each element to its proper place.

7. For a list of length n, on average, an insertion sort makes $(n^2 + 3n - 4) / 4$ key comparisons and about $n(n - 1) / 4$ item assignments.

8. The sequential search algorithm searches a list for a given item, starting with the first element in the list. It continues to compare the search item with the other elements in the list until either the item is found, or the list has no more elements left to be compared with the search item.

9. On average, the sequential search searches half the list.

10. The sequential search is good only for short lists.

11. The binary search is much faster than the sequential search.

12. The binary search requires that the list elements be in order—that is, the list must be sorted.

13. For a list of length `1024`, to determine whether an item is in the list, the binary search algorithm requires no more than 22 key comparisons.

14. In addition to arrays, C++ provides the **class** vector type.

15. Unlike an array, the size of a `vector` object can increase and decrease during program execution. Therefore, you do not need to be concerned with the number of data elements.

16. When you declare a `vector` object, you must specify the type of element the `vector` object stores.

17. The elements in a `vector` can be processed just as they are in an array. As in an array, the first element in a `vector` object is at location `0`.

18. The following functions can be used to perform various operations on a `vector` object: `at`, `front`, `back`, `clear`, `push_back`, `pop_back`, `empty`, `size`, `resize`, and `max_size`. For a description of these functions, see Table 10-2.

10

EXERCISES

1. Mark the following statements as true or false.

   a. A sequential search of a list assumes that the list is in ascending order.

   b. A binary search of a list assumes that the list is sorted.

   c. A binary search is faster on ordered lists and slower on unordered lists.

   d. A binary search is faster on large lists, but a sequential search is faster on small lists.

   e. When you declare a **vector** object and specify its size as 10, then only 10 elements can be stored in the object.

2. Sort the following list using the selection sort algorithm as discussed in this chapter. Show the list after each iteration of the outer **for** loop.

   36, 55, 17, 35, 63, 85, 12, 48, 3, 66

3. Assume the following list: 5, 18, 21, 10, 55, 20

   The first three keys are in order. To move 10 to its proper position using the insertion sort as described in this chapter, exactly how many key comparisons are executed?

4. Assume the following list: 7, 28, 31, 40, 5, 20

   The first four keys are in order. To move 5 to its proper position using the insertion sort as described in this chapter, exactly how many key comparisons are executed?

5. Assume the following list: 28, 18, 21, 10, 25, 30, 12, 71, 32, 58, 15

   This list is to be sorted using the insertion sort algorithm as described in this chapter. Show the resulting list after six passes of the sorting phase—that is, after six iterations of the **for** loop.

6. Recall the insertion sort algorithm as discussed in this chapter. Assume the following list of keys:

   18, 8, 11, 9, 15, 20, 32, 61, 22, 48, 75, 83, 35, 3

   Exactly how many key comparisons are executed to sort this list using the insertion sort?

7. Consider the following list: 63, 45, 32, 98, 46, 57, 28, 100

   Using a sequential search, how many comparisons are required to determine whether the following items are in the list or not? (Recall that comparisons mean item comparisons, not index comparisons.)

   a. 90

   b. 57

   c. 63

   d. 120

8. Consider the following list: 2, 10, 17, 45, 49, 55, 68, 85, 92, 98, 110

   Using the binary search, how many comparisons are required to determine whether the following items are in the list or not? Show the values of `first`, `last`, and `middle` and the number of comparisons after each iteration of the loop.

   a. 15

   b. 49

   c. 98

   d. 99

9. To use a `vector` object in a program, which header file must be included in the program?

10. What do the following statements do?

    a. `vector<int> list(50);`

    b. `vector<string> namesList;`

11. What is the output of the following C++ code?

```cpp
vector<int> intList(5);

for (int i = 0; i < 5; i++)
    intList[i] = 2 * i + 1;

for (int i = 0; i < 5; i++)
    cout << intList.at(i) << " ";

cout << endl;
```

12. What is the output of the following C++ code?

```cpp
vector<string> classList;

classList.push_back("Nisha");
classList.push_back("Tony");
classList.push_back("Bobby");
classList.push_back("Peter");

for (unsigned int i = 0; i < classList.size(); i++)
    cout << classList[i] << " ";

cout << endl;
```

13. a. Write a C++ statement that declares `secretList` to be a `vector` object to store integers. (Do not specify the size of `secretList`.)

    b. Write C++ statements to store the following values, in the order given, into `secretList`:

       56, 28, 32, 96, 75

    c. Write a `for` loop that outputs the contents of `secretList`. (Use the expression `secretList.size()` to determine the size of `secretList`.)

14. What is the output of the following C++ code?

    ```cpp
    vector<int> intList(10);

    for (int i = 0; i < 10; i++)
        intList[i] = 2 * i + 5;

    cout << intList.front() << " " << intList.back() << endl;
    ```

15. Suppose that you have the following C++ code:

    ```cpp
    vector<int> myList(5);

    unsigned int length;

    myList[0] = 3;
    for (int i = 1; i < 4; i++)
        myList[i] = 2 * myList[i - 1] - 5;

    myList.push_back(46);
    myList.push_back(57);
    myList.push_back(35);
    ```

    a. Write a C++ statement that outputs the first and the last elements of `myList`. (Do not use the array subscripting operator or the index of the elements.)

    b. Write a C++ statement that stores the size of `myList` into `length`.

    c. Write a `for` loop that outputs the elements of `myList`.

PROGRAMMING EXERCISES

1. Write a program to test the insertion sort algorithm as given in this chapter.

2. Write a program to test the function binarySearch. Use either the function selectionSort or `insertionSort` to sort the list before the search.

3. Write a function, `remove`, that takes three parameters: an array of integers, the number of elements in the array, and an integer (say, `removeItem`). The function should find and delete the first occurrence of `removeItem` in the array. If the value does not exist or the array is empty, output an appropriate message. (Note that after deleting the element, the number of elements in the array is reduced by 1.) Assume that the array is unsorted.

4. Write a function, `removeAt`, that takes three parameters: an array of integers, the number of elements in the array, and an integer (say, `index`). The function should delete the array element indicated by `index`. If `index` is out of range or the array is empty, output an appropriate message. (Note that after deleting the element, the number of elements in the array is reduced by 1.) Assume that the array is unsorted.

5. Write a function, `removeAll`, that takes three parameters: an array of integers, the number of elements in the array, and an integer (say, `removeItem`). The function should find and delete all the occurrences of `removeItem` in the array. If the value does not exist or the array is empty, output an appropriate message. (Note that after deleting the element, the number of elements in the array is reduced.) Assume that the array is unsorted.

6. Redo Exercises 3, 4, and 5 for a sorted array.

7. Write a function, `insertAt`, that takes four parameters: an array of integers, the number of elements in the array, an integer (say, `insertItem`), and an integer (say, `index`). The function should insert `insertItem` in the array at the position specified by `index`. If `index` is out of range, output an appropriate message. (Note that `index` must be between 0 and the number of elements in the array; that is, `0 <= index < the number of elements in the array`.) Assume that the array is unsorted.

8. Write a version of the selection sort algorithm that can be used to sort a string `vector` object. Also, write a program to test your algorithm.

9. Write a version of the insertion sort algorithm that can be used to sort a string `vector` object. Also, write a program to test your algorithm.

10. Write a version of the sequential search algorithm that can be used to search a string `vector` object. Also, write a program to test your algorithm.

11. Write a version of the binary search algorithm that can be used to search a string `vector` object. Also, write a program to test your algorithm. (Use the selection sort algorithm you developed in Programming Exercise 8 to sort the vector.)

12. Write a program that reads in a set of positive integers, representing test scores for a class, and outputs how many times a particular number appears in the list. You may assume that the data set has at most 100 numbers, and -999 marks the end of the input data. The numbers must be output in increasing order. For example, for the data

```
55 80 78 92 95 55 78 53 92 65 78 95 85 92 85 95 95
```

the output is:

```
Test Score  Count
   53         1
   55         2
   65         1
   78         3
   80         1
   85         2
   92         3
   95         4
```

1
0

13. Your state is in a process of creating a weekly lottery. Once a week, five distinct random integers between 1 to 40 (inclusive) are drawn. If a player guesses all the numbers correctly, the player wins a certain amount. Write a program that does the following:

    a. Generates five distinct random numbers between 1 and 40 (inclusive) and stores them in an array.

    b. Sorts the array containing the lottery numbers.

    c. Prompts the player to select five distinct integers between 1 and 40 (inclusive) and stores the numbers in an array. The player can select the numbers in any order, and the array containing the numbers need not be sorted.

    d. Determines whether the player guessed the lottery numbers correctly. If the player guessed the lottery numbers correctly, it outputs the message "You win!"; otherwise it outputs the message "You lose!" and outputs the lottery numbers.

    Your program should allow a player to play the game as many times as the player wants to play. Before each play, generate a new set of lottery numbers.

14. Redo the Election Results programming example (in this chapter) so that the array `candidatesList` is created using a pointer.

15. Redo the Election Results programming example (in this chapter) so that the array `candidatesList` is a `vector` object.

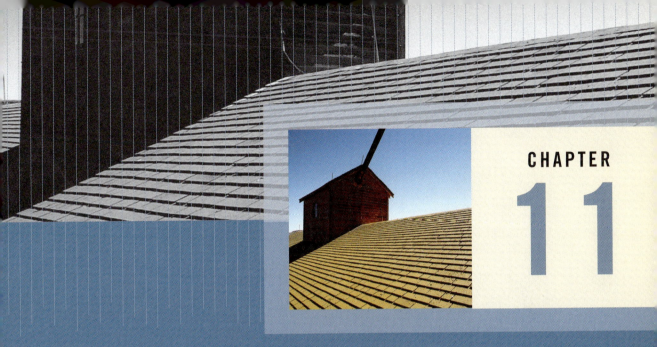

RECURSION

- Learn about recursive definitions
- Explore the base case and the general case of a recursive definition
- Discover what a recursive algorithm does
- Learn about recursive functions
- Explore how to use recursive functions to implement recursive algorithms

In previous chapters, to devise solutions to problems, we used the most common technique, called iteration. For certain problems, however, using the iterative technique to obtain the solution is quite complicated. This chapter introduces another problem-solving technique, called recursion, and provides several examples demonstrating how recursion works.

Recursive Definitions

The process of solving a problem by reducing it to smaller versions of itself is called **recursion**. Recursion is a very powerful way to solve certain problems for which the solution would otherwise be very complicated. Let us consider a problem that is familiar to most everyone.

In mathematics, the factorial of an integer is defined as follows:

$$0! = 1 \qquad\qquad (11\text{-}1)$$

$$n! = n \times (n - 1)! \quad \text{if} \quad n > 0 \qquad (11\text{-}2)$$

In this definition, $0!$ is defined to be 1, and if n is an integer greater than 0, first we find $(n - 1)!$ and then multiply it by n. To find $(n - 1)!$, we apply the definition again. If $(n - 1) > 0$, then we use Equation 11-2; otherwise, we use Equation 11-1. Thus, for an integer n greater than 0, $n!$ is obtained by first finding $(n - 1)!$ (that is, $n!$ is reduced to a smaller version of itself) and then multiplying $(n - 1)!$ by n.

Let us apply this definition to find $3!$. Here, $n = 3$. Because $n > 0$, we use Equation 11-2 to obtain:

$$3! = 3 \times 2!$$

Next, we find $2!$ Here, $n = 2$. Because $n > 0$, we use Equation 11-2 to obtain:

$$2! = 2 \times 1!$$

Now to find $1!$, we again use Equation 11-2 because $n = 1 > 0$. Thus:

$$1! = 1 \times 0!$$

Finally, we use Equation 11-1 to find $0!$, which is 1. Substituting $0!$ into $1!$ gives $1! = 1$. This gives $2! = 2 \times 1! = 2 \times 1 = 2$, which, in turn, gives $3! = 3 \times 2! = 3 \times 2 = 6$.

The solution in Equation 11-1 is direct—that is, the right side of the equation contains no factorial notation. The solution in Equation 11-2 is given in terms of a smaller version of itself. The definition of the factorial given in Equations 11-1 and 11-2 is called a **recursive definition**. Equation 11-1 is called the **base case** (that is, the case for which the solution is obtained directly); Equation 11-2 is called the **general case**.

Recursive definition: A definition in which something is defined in terms of a smaller version of itself.

From the previous example (factorial), it is clear that:

1. Every recursive definition must have one (or more) base cases.
2. The general case must eventually be reduced to a base case.
3. The base case stops the recursion.

The concept of recursion in computer science works similarly. Here we talk about recursive algorithms and recursive functions. An algorithm that finds the solution to a given problem by reducing the problem to smaller versions of itself is called a **recursive algorithm**. The recursive algorithm must have one or more base cases, and the general solution must eventually be reduced to a base case.

A function that calls itself is called a **recursive function**. That is, the body of the recursive function contains a statement that causes the same function to execute again before completing the current call. Recursive algorithms are implemented using recursive functions.

Next, let us write the recursive function that implements the factorial function:

```cpp
int fact(int num)
{
    if (num == 0)
        return 1;
    else
        return num * fact(num - 1);
}
```

Figure 11-1 traces the execution of the following statement:

```cpp
cout << fact(4) << endl;
```

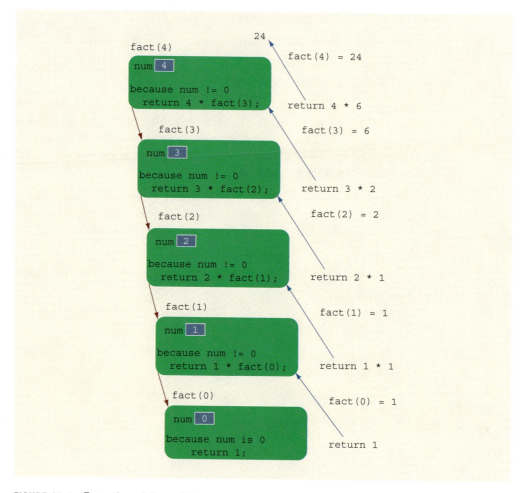

FIGURE 11-1 Execution of `fact(4)`

The output of the previous **cout** statement is:

24

In Figure 11-1, the down arrow represents the successive calls to the function **fact**, and the upward arrows represent the values returned to the caller, that is, the calling function.

Let us note the following from the preceding example, involving the factorial function:

- Logically, you can think of a recursive function as having an unlimited number of copies of itself.

- Every call to a recursive function—that is, every recursive call—has its own code and its own set of parameters and local variables.

- After completing a particular recursive call, control goes back to the calling environment, which is the previous call. The current (recursive) call must execute completely before control goes back to the previous call. The execution in the previous call begins from the point immediately following the recursive call.

Direct and Indirect Recursion

A function is called **directly recursive** if it calls itself. A function that calls another function and eventually results in the original function call is said to be **indirectly recursive**. For example, if a function A calls a function B and function B calls function A, then function A is indirectly recursive. Indirect recursion can be several layers deep. For example, suppose that function A calls function B, function B calls function C, function C calls function D, and function D calls function A. Function A is then indirectly recursive.

Indirect recursion requires the same careful analysis as direct recursion. The base cases must be identified, and appropriate solutions to them must be provided. However, tracing through indirect recursion can be tedious. You must, therefore, exercise extra care when designing indirect recursive functions. For simplicity, the problems in this book involve only direct recursion.

A recursive function in which the last statement executed is the recursive call is called a **tail recursive function**. The function `fact` is an example of a tail recursive function.

Infinite Recursion

Figure 11-1 shows that the sequence of recursive calls eventually reached a call that made no further recursive calls. That is, the sequence of recursive calls eventually reached a base case. On the other hand, if every recursive call results in another recursive call, then the recursive function (algorithm) is said to have infinite recursion. In theory, infinite recursion executes forever. Every call to a recursive function requires the system to allocate memory for the local variables and formal parameters. The system also saves this information so that after completing a call, control can be transferred back to the right caller. Therefore, because computer memory is finite, if you execute an infinite recursive function on a computer, the function executes until the system runs out of memory and results in an abnormal termination of the program.

Recursive functions (algorithms) must be carefully designed and analyzed. You must make sure that every recursive call eventually reduces to a base case. This chapter provides several examples that illustrate how to design and implement recursive algorithms.

To design a recursive function, you must do the following:

a. Understand the problem requirements.
b. Determine the limiting conditions. For example, for a list, the limiting condition is the number of elements in the list.

c. Identify the base cases and provide a direct solution to each base case.

d. Identify the general cases and provide a solution to each general case in terms of smaller versions of itself.

Problem Solving Using Recursion

Examples 11-1 through 11-3 illustrate how recursive algorithms are developed and implemented in C++ using recursive functions.

EXAMPLE 11-1: LARGEST ELEMENT IN AN ARRAY

In Chapter 6, we used a loop to find the largest element in an array. In this example, we use a recursive algorithm to find the largest element in an array. Consider the list given in Figure 11-2.

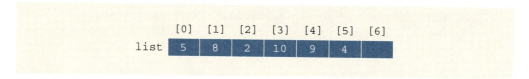

FIGURE 11-2 `list` with six elements

The largest element in the list in Figure 11-2 is 10.

Suppose `list` is the name of the array containing the list elements. Also, suppose that `list[a]...list[b]` stands for the array elements `list[a]`, `list[a + 1]`, ..., and `list[b]`. For example, `list[0]...list[5]` represents the array elements `list[0]`, `list[1]`, `list[2]`, `list[3]`, `list[4]`, and `list[5]`. Similarly, `list[1]...list[5]` represents the array elements `list[1]`, `list[2]`, `list[3]`, `list[4]`, and `list[5]`. To write a recursive algorithm to find the largest element in `list`, let us think in terms of recursion.

If `list` is of length 1, then `list` has only one element, which is the largest element. Suppose the length of `list` is greater than 1. To find the largest element in `list[a]...list[b]`, we first find the largest element in `list[a + 1]...list[b]` and then compare this largest element with `list[a]`. That is, the largest element in `list[a]...list[b]` is given by:

```
maximum(list[a], largest(list[a + 1]...list[b]))
```

Let us apply this formula to find the largest element in the list shown in Figure 11-2. This list has six elements, given by `list[0]...list[5]`. Now the largest element in `list` is:

```
maximum(list[0], largest(list[1]...list[5]))
```

That is, the largest element in `list` is the maximum of `list[0]` and the largest element in `list[1]...list[5]`. To find the largest element in `list[1]...list[5]`, we use the same formula again because the length of this list is greater than 1. The largest element in `list[1]...list[5]` is then:

```
maximum(list[1], largest(list[2]...list[5]))
```

and so on. We see that every time we use the preceding formula to find the largest element in a sublist, the length of the sublist in the next call is reduced by one. Eventually, the sublist is of length 1, in which case the sublist contains only one element, which is the largest element in the sublist. From this point onward, we backtrack through the recursive calls. This discussion translates into the following recursive algorithm, which is presented in pseudocode:

Base Case: The size of the list is 1
          The only element in the list is the largest element

General Case: The size of the list is greater than 1
        To find the largest element in list[a]...list[b]

    a. Find the largest element in list[a + 1]...list[b]
       and call it max
    b. Compare the elements list[a] and max
       if (list[a] >= max)
          the largest element in list[a]...list[b] is list[a]
       otherwise
          the largest element in list[a]...list[b] is max

This algorithm translates into the following C++ function to find the largest element in an array:

```cpp
int largest(const int list[], int lowerIndex, int upperIndex)
{
    int max;

    if (lowerIndex == upperIndex) //size of the sublist is one
        return list[lowerIndex];
    else
    {
        max = largest(list, lowerIndex + 1, upperIndex);

        if (list[lowerIndex] >= max)
            return list[lowerIndex];
        else
            return max;
    }
}
```

Consider the `list` given in Figure 11-3.

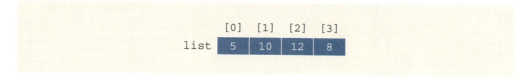

FIGURE 11-3 `list` with four elements

Let us trace the execution of the following statement:

```
cout << largest(list, 0, 3) << endl;
```

Here `upperIndex` = 3, and the list has four elements. Figure 11-4 traces the execution of `largest(list, 0, 3)`.

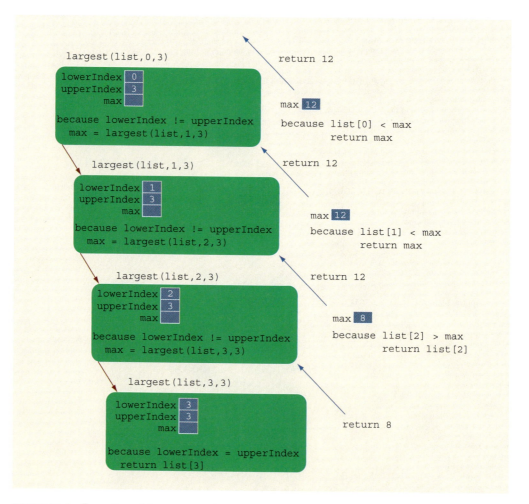

FIGURE 11-4 Execution of `largest(list, 0, 3)`

The value returned by the expression largest(list, 0, 3) is 12, which is the largest element in list.

The following C++ program uses the function largest to determine the largest element in a list:

```cpp
//*************************************************************
// Author: D.S. Malik
//
// This program uses a recursive function to find the largest
// element in a list.
//*************************************************************

#include <iostream>

using namespace std;

int largest(const int list[], int lowerIndex, int upperIndex);

int main()
{
    int intArray[10] = {23, 43, 35, 38, 67, 12, 76, 10, 34, 8};

    cout << "The largest element in intArray: "
         << largest(intArray, 0, 9);
    cout << endl;

    return 0;
}

int largest(const int list[], int lowerIndex, int upperIndex)
{
    int max;

    if (lowerIndex == upperIndex) //size of the sublist is one
        return list[lowerIndex];
    else
    {
        max = largest(list, lowerIndex + 1, upperIndex);

        if (list[lowerIndex] >= max)
            return list[lowerIndex];
        else
            return max;
    }
}
```

Sample Run:

The largest element in intArray: 76

EXAMPLE 11-2: FIBONACCI NUMBER

In Chapter 4, we designed a program to determine the desired Fibonacci number. In this example, we write a recursive function, rFibNum, to determine the desired Fibonacci number. The function rFibNum takes as parameters three numbers representing the first two numbers of the Fibonacci sequence and a number n, the desired nth Fibonacci number. The function rFibNum returns the nth Fibonacci number in the sequence.

Recall that the third Fibonacci number is the sum of the first two Fibonacci numbers. The fourth Fibonacci number in a sequence is the sum of the second and third Fibonacci numbers. Therefore, to calculate the fourth Fibonacci number, we add the second Fibonacci number and the third Fibonacci number (which is itself the sum of the first two Fibonacci numbers). The following recursive algorithm calculates the nth Fibonacci number, where a denotes the first Fibonacci number, b the second Fibonacci number, and n the nth Fibonacci number:

$$rFibNum(a,b,n) = \begin{cases} a & \text{if } n = 1 \\ b & \text{if } n = 2 \quad (11\text{-}3) \\ rFibNum(a,b,n-1) + rFibNum(a,b,n-2) & \text{if } n > 2. \end{cases}$$

Suppose that we want to determine:

rFibNum(2, 5, 4)

Here, $a = 2$, $b = 5$, and $n = 4$. That is, we want to determine the fourth Fibonacci number of the sequence whose first number is 2 and whose second number is 5. Because n is 4 > 2,

1. rFibNum(2, 5, 4) = rFibNum(2, 5, 3) + rFibNum(2, 5, 2)

   Next, we determine rFibNum(2, 5, 3) and rFibNum(2, 5, 2). Let us first determine rFibNum(2, 5, 3). Here, $a = 2$, $b = 5$, and n is 3. Because n is 3,

   1.a. rFibNum(2, 5, 3) = rFibNum(2, 5, 2) + rFibNum(2, 5, 1)

   This statement requires us to determine rFibNum(2, 5, 2) and rFibNum(2, 5, 1). In rFibNum(2, 5, 2), $a = 2$, $b = 5$, and $n = 2$. Therefore, from the definition given in Equation 11-3, it follows that:

   1.a.1. rFibNum(2, 5, 2) = 5

   To find rFibNum(2, 5, 1), note that $a = 2$, $b = 5$, and $n = 1$. Therefore, by the definition given in Equation 11-3,

   1.a.2. rFibNum(2, 5, 1) = 2

   We substitute the values of rFibNum(2, 5, 2) and rFibNum(2, 5, 1) into (1.a) to get:

   rFibNum(2, 5, 3) = 5 + 2 = 7

Next, we determine `rFibNum(2, 5, 2)`. As in (1.a.1), `rFibNum(2, 5, 2)` = 5. We can substitute the values of `rFibNum(2, 5, 3)` and `rFibNum(2, 5, 2)` into (1) to get:

`rFibNum(2, 5, 4)` = 7 + 5 = 12

The following recursive function implements this algorithm:

```
int rFibNum(int a, int b, int n)
{
    if (n == 1)
        return a;
    else if (n == 2)
        return b;
    else
        return rFibNum(a, b, n - 1) + rFibNum(a, b, n - 2);
}
```

Let us trace the execution of the following statement:

```
cout << rFibNum(2, 3, 5) << endl;
```

In this statement, the first number is 2, the second number is 3, and we want to determine the 5th Fibonacci number of the sequence. Figure 11-5 traces the execution of the expression `rFibNum(2,3,5)`. The value returned is 13, which is the 5th Fibonacci number of the sequence whose first number is 2 and second number is 3.

1
1

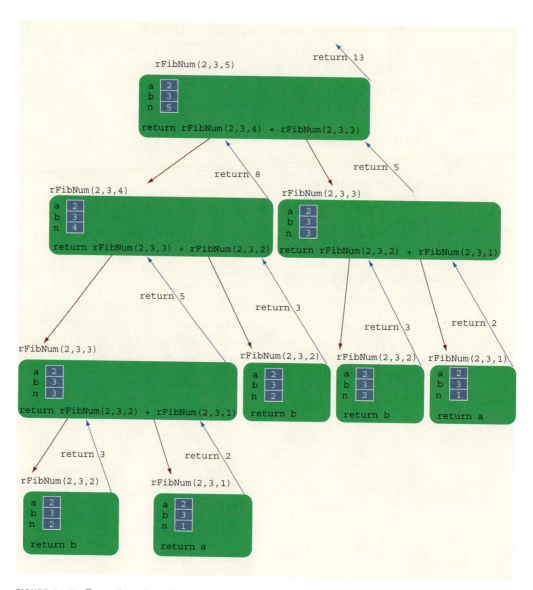

FIGURE 11-5 Execution of `rFibNum(2, 3, 5)`

The following C++ program uses the function `rFibNum`:

```
//*************************************************************
// Author: D.S. Malik
//
// Given the first two numbers of a Fibonacci sequence, this
// program uses a recursive function to determine a specific
// number(s) of a Fibonacci sequence.
//*************************************************************
```

```
#include <iostream>

using namespace std;

int rFibNum(int a, int b, int n);

int main()
{
    int firstFibNum;
    int secondFibNum;
    int nth;

    cout << "Enter the first Fibonacci number: ";
    cin >> firstFibNum;
    cout << endl;

    cout << "Enter the second Fibonacci number: ";
    cin >> secondFibNum;
    cout << endl;

    cout << "Enter the position of the desired Fibonacci number: ";
    cin >> nth;
    cout << endl;

    cout << "The Fibonacci number at position " << nth
         << " is: " << rFibNum(firstFibNum, secondFibNum, nth)
         << endl;

    return 0;
}

int rFibNum(int a, int b, int n)
{
    if (n == 1)
        return a;
    else if (n == 2)
        return b;
    else
        return rFibNum(a, b, n - 1) + rFibNum(a, b, n - 2);
}
```

Sample Runs: In these sample runs, the user input is shaded.

Sample Run 1

Enter the first Fibonacci number: 2

Enter the second Fibonacci number: 5

Enter the position of the desired Fibonacci number: 6

The Fibonacci number at position 6 is: 31

Sample Run 2

```
Enter the first Fibonacci number: 3

Enter the second Fibonacci number: 4

Enter the position of the desired Fibonacci number: 6

The Fibonacci number at position 6 is: 29
```

Sample Run 3

```
Enter the first Fibonacci number: 12

Enter the second Fibonacci number: 18

Enter the position of the desired Fibonacci number: 15

The Fibonacci number at position 15 is: 9582
```

EXAMPLE 11-3: TOWER OF HANOI

In the nineteenth century, a game called the Tower of Hanoi became popular in Europe. This game represents work that is under way in the temple of Brahma. At the creation of the universe, priests in the temple of Brahma were supposedly given three diamond needles, with one needle holding 64 golden disks. Each golden disk is slightly smaller than the disk below it. The priests' task is to move all 64 disks from the first needle to the third needle. The rules for moving the disks are as follows:

1. Only one disk can be moved at a time.
2. The removed disk must be placed on one of the needles.
3. A larger disk cannot be placed on top of a smaller disk.

The priests were told that once they had moved all the disks from the first needle to the third needle, the universe would come to an end.

Our objective is to write a program that prints the sequence of moves needed to transfer the disks from the first needle to the third needle. Figure 11-6 shows the Tower of Hanoi problem with three disks.

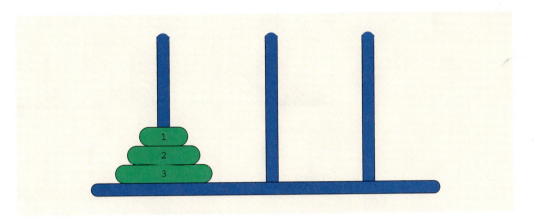

FIGURE 11-6 Tower of Hanoi problem with three disks

As before, we think in terms of recursion. Let us first consider the case when the first needle holds only one disk. In this case, the disk can be moved directly from needle 1 to needle 3. So let us consider the case when the first needle holds only two disks. In this case, first we move the first disk from needle 1 to needle 2, and then we move the second disk from needle 1 to needle 3. Finally, we move the first disk from needle 2 to needle 3. Next, we consider the case when the first needle holds three disks, and then generalize this to the case of 64 disks (in fact, to an arbitrary number of disks).

Suppose that needle 1 holds three disks. To move disk number 3 to needle 3, the top two disks must first be moved to needle 2. Disk number 3 can then be moved from needle 1 to needle 3. To move the top two disks from needle 2 to needle 3, we use the same strategy as before. This time we use needle 1 as the intermediate needle. Figure 11-7 shows a solution to the Tower of Hanoi problem with three disks.

1
1

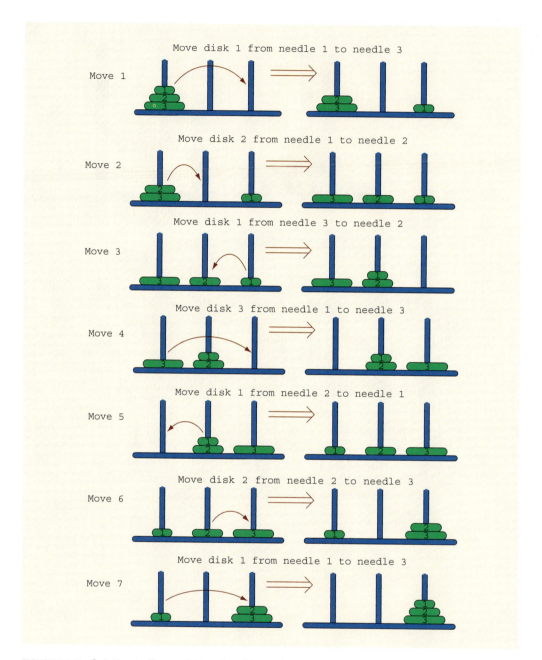

FIGURE 11-7 Solution to Tower of Hanoi problem with three disks

Let us now generalize this problem to the case of 64 disks. To begin, the first needle holds all 64 disks. Disk number 64 cannot be moved from needle 1 to needle 3 unless the top 63 disks are on the second needle. So first we move the top 63 disks from needle 1 to needle 2, and then we move disk number 64 from needle 1 to needle 3. Now the top

63 disks are all on needle 2. To move disk number 63 from needle 2 to needle 3, we first move the top 62 disks from needle 2 to needle 1, and then we move disk number 63 from needle 2 to needle 3. To move the remaining 62 disks, we use a similar procedure. This discussion translates into the following recursive algorithm given in pseudocode. Suppose that needle 1 contains n disks, where $n \geq 1$.

1. Move the top $n - 1$ disks from needle 1 to needle 2, using needle 3 as the intermediate needle.

2. Move disk number n from needle 1 to needle 3.

3. Move the top $n - 1$ disks from needle 2 to needle 3, using needle 1 as the intermediate needle.

This recursive algorithm translates into the following C++ function:

```
void moveDisks(int count, int needle1, int needle3, int needle2)
{
    if (count > 0)
    {
        moveDisks(count - 1, needle1, needle2, needle3);

        cout << "Move disk " << count << " from " << needle1
             << " to " << needle3 << "." << endl;

        moveDisks(count - 1, needle2, needle3, needle1);
    }
}
```

Tower of Hanoi: Analysis

Let us determine how long it would take to move all 64 disks from needle 1 to needle 3. If needle 1 contains three disks, then the number of moves required to move all three disks from needle 1 to needle 3 is $2^3 - 1 = 7$. Similarly, if needle 1 contains 64 disks, then the number of moves required to move all 64 disks from needle 1 to needle 3 is $2^{64} - 1$. Because $2^{10} = 1024 \approx 1000 = 10^3$, we have:

$$2^{64} = 2^4 \times 2^{60} \approx 2^4 \times 10^{18} = 1.6 \times 10^{19}$$

The number of seconds in one year is approximately 3.2×10^7. Suppose the priests move one disk per second and they do not rest. Now:

$$1.6 \times 10^{19} = 5 \times 3.2 \times 10^{18} = 5 \times (3.2 \times 10^7) \times 10^{11} = (3.2 \times 10^7) \times (5 \times 10^{11})$$

The time required to move all 64 disks from needle 1 to needle 3 is roughly 5×10^{11} years. It is estimated that our universe is about 15 billion years old (1.5×10^{10}). Also, $5 \times 10^{11} = 50 \times 10^{10} \approx 33 \times (1.5 \times 10^{10})$. This calculation shows that our universe would last about 33 times as long as it already has.

Assume that a computer can generate 1 billion (10^9) moves per second. Then the number of moves that the computer can generate in one year is:

$(3.2 \times 10^7) \times 10^9 = 3.2 \times 10^{16}$

So the computer time required to generate 2^{64} moves is:

$2^{64} \approx 1.6 \times 10^{19} = 1.6 \times 10^{16} \times 10^3 = (3.2 \times 10^{16}) \times 500$

Thus, it would take about 500 years for the computer to generate 2^{64} moves at the rate of 1 billion moves per second.

Recursive Binary Search

In Chapter 10, you learned how to search a sorted list using a binary search. The algorithm given in Chapter 10 uses a **while** loop to implement a binary search algorithm. In this section, we describe a recursive version of the binary search algorithm. Consider the list shown in Figure 11-8.

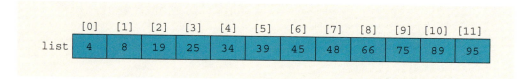

	[0]	[1]	[2]	[3]	[4]	[5]	[6]	[7]	[8]	[9]	[10]	[11]
list	4	8	19	25	34	39	45	48	66	75	89	95

FIGURE 11-8 A sorted list

The length of **list** is 12. Suppose that we want to determine if 25 is in **list**. Also suppose that **first = 0, last = 11**. As before, we find the index of the middle element in **list** using **mid = (first + last) / 2**. So **mid = (0 + 11) / 2 = 5**. Next we compare 25 with **list[5]**. In this case, 25 $\neq$ **list[5]**, and 25 < **list[5]**. So we repeat this process on the list elements **list[0]** ...**list[4]**. The following recursive C++ function implements this process:

```cpp
int recBinSearch(const int list[], int first, int last,
                 int searchItem)
{
    int mid;
    int location = 0;

    if (first <= last)
    {
        mid = (first + last) / 2;

        if (list[mid] == searchItem)
            location = mid;
        else if (list[mid] > searchItem)
            location = recBinSearch(list, first, mid - 1,
                       searchItem);
```

```
        else
            location = recBinSearch(list, mid + 1, last,
                        searchItem);
    }

    if (first > location || last < location)
        location = -1;

    return location;
} //end recBinSearch
```

Figure 11-9 shows the tracing of `recBinarySearch` on the list shown in Figure 11-8.

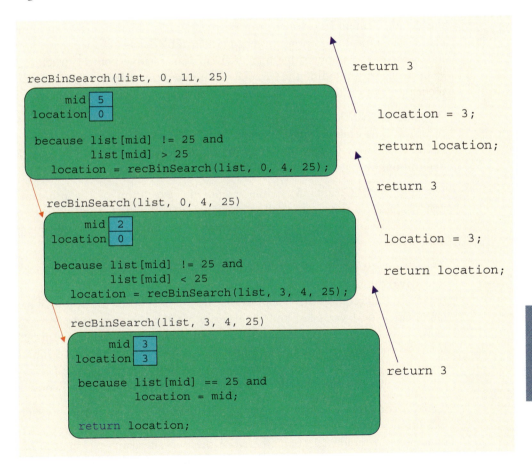

FIGURE 11-9 Tracing the recursive binary search algorithm

The algorithm returns 3. Because 0 <= 3 <= 11, the search item is at location 3.

The Web site accompanying this book, www.course.com, contains the program `Ch11_RecBinarySearch.cpp` that shows how to use the recursive binary search algorithm.

Recursion or Iteration?

In Chapter 4, we designed a program to determine a desired Fibonacci number. That program used a loop to perform the calculation. In other words, the programs in Chapter 4 used an iterative control structure to repeat a set of statements. More formally, **iterative control structures** use a looping structure, such as `while`, `for`, or `do...while`, to repeat a set of statements. In Example 11-2, we designed a recursive function to calculate a Fibonacci number. From the examples here, it follows that in recursion, a set of statements is repeated by having the function call itself. Moreover, a selection control structure is used to control the repeated calls in recursion.

Similarly, in Chapter 6, we used an iterative control structure (a `for` loop) to determine the largest element in a list. In this chapter, we use recursion to determine the largest element in a list. In addition, this chapter began by designing a recursive function to find the factorial of a nonnegative integer. Using an iterative control structure, we can also write an algorithm to find the factorial of a nonnegative integer. The only reason to give a recursive solution to a factorial problem is to illustrate how recursion works.

We thus see that there are usually two ways to solve a particular problem—iteration and recursion. The obvious question is which method is better—iteration or recursion? There is no simple answer. In addition to the nature of the problem, the other key factor in determining the best solution method is efficiency.

Example 5-11 (Chapter 5), while tracing the execution of the problem, showed us that whenever a function is called, memory space for its formal parameters and (automatic) local variables is allocated. When the function terminates, that memory space is deallocated.

This chapter, while tracing the execution of recursive functions, also shows us that every (recursive) call has its own set of parameters and (automatic) local variables. That is, every (recursive) call requires the system to allocate memory space for its formal parameters and (automatic) local variables, and then deallocate the memory space when the function exits. Thus, there is overhead associated with executing a (recursive) function, both in terms of memory space and computer time. Therefore, a recursive function executes more slowly than its iterative counterpart. On slower computers, especially those with limited memory space, the (slow) execution of a recursive function would be visible.

Today's computers, however, are fast and have inexpensive memory. Therefore, the execution of a recursion function is not noticeable. Keeping the power of today's computers in mind, the choice between the two alternatives—iteration or recursion—depends on the nature of the problem. Of course, for problems such as mission control systems, efficiency is absolutely critical and, therefore, the efficiency factor would dictate the solution method.

As a general rule, if you think that an iterative solution is more obvious and easier to understand than a recursive solution, use the iterative solution, which would be more efficient. On the other hand, problems exist for which the recursive solution is more obvious or easier to construct, such as the Tower of Hanoi problem. (In fact, it turns out that it is difficult to construct an iterative solution for the Tower of Hanoi problem.) Keeping the power of recursion in mind, if the definition of a problem is inherently recursive, then you should consider a recursive solution.

PROGRAMMING EXAMPLE: Converting a Number from Binary to Decimal

In Chapter 0, we explained that the language of a computer, called machine language, is a sequence of 0s and 1s. When you press the key **A** on the keyboard, **01000001** is stored in the computer. Also, you know that the collating sequence of **A** in the ASCII character set is **65**. In fact, the binary representation of **A** is **01000001**, and the decimal representation of **A** is **65**.

The numbering system we use is called the decimal system, or base 10 system. The numbering system that the computer uses is called the binary system, or base 2 system. In this and the next programming example, we discuss how to convert a number from base 2 to base 10 and from base 10 to base 2.

Binary to Decimal

To convert a number from base 2 to base 10, we first find the weight of each bit in the binary number. The weight of each bit in the binary number is assigned from right to left. The weight of the rightmost bit is 0. The weight of the bit immediately to the left of the rightmost bit is 1, the weight of the bit immediately to the left of that bit is 2, and so on. Consider the binary number 1001101. The weight of each bit is as follows:

Weight 6 5 4 3 2 1 0

        1 0 0 1 1 0 1

We use the weight of each bit to find the equivalent decimal number. For each bit, we multiply the bit by 2 to the power of its weight, and then we add all of the numbers. For the above binary number, the equivalent decimal number is:

$$1 \times 2^6 + 0 \times 2^5 + 0 \times 2^4 + 1 \times 2^3 + 1 \times 2^2 + 0 \times 2^1 + 1 \times 2^0$$

$$= 64 + 0 + 0 + 8 + 4 + 0 + 1$$

$$= 77$$

To write a program that converts a binary number into the equivalent decimal number, we note two things: (1) the weight of each bit in the binary number must be known, and (2) the weight is assigned from right to left. Because we do not know in advance how many bits are in the binary number, we must process the bits from right to left. After processing a bit, we can add 1 to its weight, giving the weight of the bit immediately to the left of it. Also, each bit must be extracted from the binary number and multiplied by 2 to the power of its weight. To extract a bit, we can use the mod operator. Consider the following recursive algorithm, which is given in pseudocode:

```
if (binaryNumber > 0)
{
    bit = binaryNumber % 10;        //extract the rightmost bit
    decimal = decimal + bit * power(2, weight);
    binaryNumber = binaryNumber / 10; //remove the rightmost
                                      //bit
    weight++;
    convert the binaryNumber into decimal
}
```

This algorithm assumes that the memory locations `decimal` and `weight` have been initialized to 0 before using the algorithm. This algorithm translates to the following C++ recursive function:

```
void binToDec(int binaryNumber, int& decimal, int& weight)
{
    int bit;

    if (binaryNumber > 0)
    {
        bit = binaryNumber % 10;
        decimal = decimal
                    + bit * static_cast<int>(pow(2.0, weight));
        binaryNumber = binaryNumber / 10;
        weight++;
        binToDec(binaryNumber, decimal, weight);
    }
}
```

In this function, both `decimal` and `weight` are reference parameters. The actual parameters corresponding to these reference parameters are initialized to 0. After extracting the rightmost bit, this function updates the decimal number and the weight of the next bit. Suppose `decimalNumber` and `bitWeight` are `int` variables. Consider the following statements:

```
decimalNumber = 0;
bitWeight = 0;
binToDec(1101, decimalNumber, bitWeight);
```

Figure 11-10 traces the execution of the last statement, that is, `binToDec(1101, decimalNumber, bitWeight);`. It shows the content of the variables `decimalNumber` and `bitWeight` next to each function call.

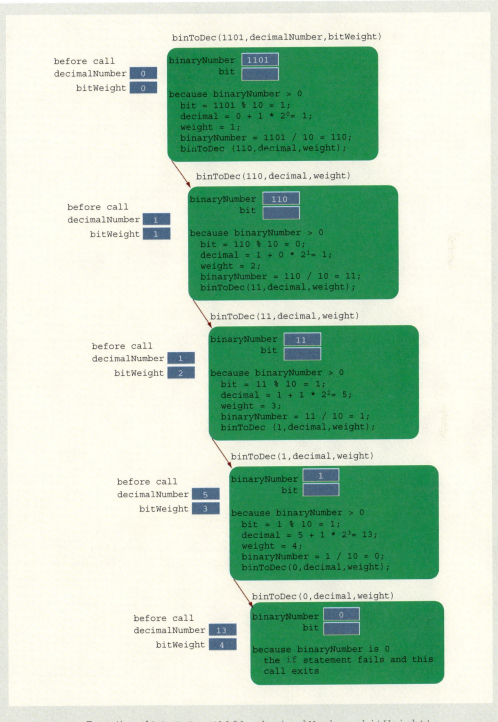

FIGURE 11-10 Execution of `binToDec(1101, decimalNumber, bitWeight);`

In Figure 11-10, each down arrow represents the successive function call. Because the last statement of the function `binToDec` is a function call, after this statement executes, nothing happens. After the statement:

```
binToDec(1101, decimalNumber, bitWeight);
```

executes, the value of the variable `decimalNumber` is 13.

The following C++ program tests the function `binToDec`:

```cpp
//*******************************************************
// Author: D.S. Malik
//
// Program: Binary to decimal
// This program uses recursion to find the decimal
// representation of a binary number.
//*******************************************************

#include <iostream>
#include <cmath>

using namespace std;

void binToDec(int binaryNumber, int& decimal, int& weight);

int main()
{
    int decimalNum;
    int bitWeight;
    int binaryNum;

    decimalNum = 0;
    bitWeight = 0;

    cout << "Enter number in binary: ";
    cin >> binaryNum;
    cout << endl;

    binToDec(binaryNum, decimalNum, bitWeight);
    cout << "Binary " << binaryNum << " = " << decimalNum
         << " decimal" << endl;

    return 0;
}
```

```
void binToDec(int binaryNumber, int& decimal, int& weight)
{
    int bit;

    if (binaryNumber > 0)
    {
        bit = binaryNumber % 10;
        decimal = decimal
                    + bit * static_cast<int>(pow(2.0, weight));
        binaryNumber = binaryNumber / 10;
        weight++;
        binToDec(binaryNumber, decimal, weight);
    }
}
```

Sample Run: In this sample run, the user input is shaded.

```
Enter a number in binary: 11010110

Binary 11010110 = 214 decimal
```

PROGRAMMING EXAMPLE: Converting a Number from Decimal to Binary

The previous programming example discussed and designed a program to convert a number from a binary representation to a decimal format—that is, from base 2 to base 10. This programming example discusses and designs a program that uses recursion to convert a nonnegative integer in decimal format—that is, base 10—into the equivalent binary number—that is, base 2. First, we define some terms.

Let x be an integer. We call the remainder of x after division by 2 the **rightmost bit** of x.

Thus, the rightmost bit of 33 is 1 because 33 % 2 is 1, and the rightmost bit of 28 is 0 because 28 % 2 is 0.

We first illustrate the algorithm to convert an integer in base 10 to the equivalent number in binary format with the help of an example.

Suppose we want to find the binary representation of 35. First, we divide 35 by 2. The quotient is 17, and the remainder—that is, the rightmost bit of 35—is 1. Next, we divide 17 by 2. The quotient is 8, and the remainder—that is, the rightmost bit of 17—is 1. Next, we divide 8 by 2. The quotient is 4, and the remainder—that is, the rightmost bit of 8—is 0. We continue this process until the quotient becomes 0.

The rightmost bit of 35 cannot be printed until we have printed the rightmost bit of 17. The rightmost bit of 17 cannot be printed until we have printed the rightmost bit of 8, and so on. Thus, the binary representation of 35 is the binary representation of 17 (that is, the quotient of 35 after division by 2), followed by the rightmost bit of 35.

Thus, to convert an integer *num* in base 10 into the equivalent binary number, we first convert the quotient *num* / 2 into an equivalent binary number, and then append the rightmost bit of *num* to the binary representation of *num* / 2.

This discussion translates into the following recursive algorithm, where `binary(num)` denotes the binary representation of *num*:

1. `binary(num)` = num if num = 0.
2. `binary(num)` = `binary(num / 2)` followed by num % 2 if num > 0.

The following recursive function implements this algorithm:

```
void decToBin(int num, int base)
{
    if (num > 0)
    {
        decToBin(num / base, base);
        cout << num % base;
    }
}
```

Figure 11-11 traces the execution of the following statement:

```
decToBin(13, 2);
```

where `num` is 13 and `base` is 2.

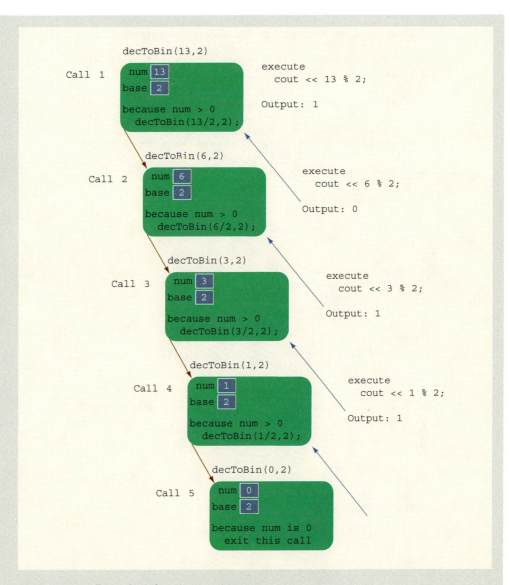

FIGURE 11-11 Execution of `decToBin(13, 2)`

Because the **if** statement in call 5 fails, this call does not print anything. The first output is produced by call 4, which prints 1; the second output is produced by call 3, which prints 1; the third output is produced by call 2, which prints 0; and the fourth output is produced by call 1, which prints 1. Thus, the output of the statement:

```
decToBin(13, 2);
```

is:

1101

The following C++ program tests the function `decToBin`:

```cpp
//*********************************************************
// Author: D.S. Malik
//
// Program: Decimal to binary
// This program uses recursion to find the binary
// representation of a nonnegative integer.
//*********************************************************

#include <iostream>

using namespace std;

void decToBin(int num, int base);

int main()
{
    int decimalNum;
    int base;

    base = 2;

    cout << "Enter number in decimal: ";
    cin >> decimalNum;
    cout << endl;

    cout << "Decimal " << decimalNum << " = ";
    decToBin(decimalNum, base);
    cout << " binary" << endl;

    return 0;
}

void decToBin(int num, int base)
{
    if (num > 0)
    {
        decToBin(num / base, base);
        cout << num % base;
    }
}
```

Sample Run: In this sample run, the user input is shaded.

```
Enter a number in decimal: 57

Decimal 57 = 111001 binary
```

QUICK REVIEW

1. The process of solving a problem by reducing it to smaller versions of itself is called recursion.

2. A recursive definition defines a problem in terms of smaller versions of itself.

3. Every recursive definition has one or more base cases.

4. A recursive algorithm solves a problem by reducing it to smaller versions of itself.

5. Every recursive algorithm has one or more base cases.

6. The solution to the problem in a base case is obtained directly.

7. A function is called recursive if it calls itself.

8. Recursive algorithms are implemented using recursive functions.

9. Every recursive function must have one or more base cases.

10. The general solution breaks the problem into smaller versions of itself.

11. The general case must eventually be reduced to a base case.

12. The base case stops the recursion.

13. While tracing a recursive function:

    - Logically, you can think of a recursive function as having an unlimited number of copies of itself.

    - Every call to a recursive function—that is, every recursive call—has its own code and its own set of parameters and local variables.

    - After completing a particular recursive call, control goes back to the calling environment, which is the previous call. The current (recursive) call must execute completely before control goes back to the previous call. The execution in the previous call begins from the point immediately following the recursive call.

14. A function is called directly recursive if it calls itself.

15. A function that calls another function and eventually results in the original function call is said to be indirectly recursive.

16. A recursive function in which the last statement executed is the recursive call is called a tail recursive function.

17. To design a recursive function, you must do the following:

    a. Understand the problem requirements.

    b. Determine the limiting conditions. For example, for a list, the limiting condition is the number of elements in the list.

    c. Identify the base cases and provide a direct solution to each base case.

    d. Identify the general cases and provide a solution to each general case in terms of smaller versions of itself.

EXERCISES

1. Mark the following statements as true or false.

   a. Every recursive definition must have one or more base cases.

   b. Every recursive function must have one or more base cases.

   c. The general case stops the recursion.

   d. In the general case, the solution to the problem is obtained directly.

   e. A recursive function always returns a value.

2. What is a base case?

3. What is a recursive case?

4. What is direct recursion?

5. What is indirect recursion?

6. What is tail recursion?

7. Consider the following recursive function:

```
int mystery(int number)                            //Line 1
{                                                   //Line 2
    if (number == 0)                                //Line 3
        return number;                              //Line 4
    else                                            //Line 5
        return(number + mystery(number - 1));       //Line 6
}                                                   //Line 7
```

   a. Identify the base case.

   b. Identify the general case.

   c. What valid values can be passed as parameters to the function `mystery`?

   d. If `mystery(0)` is a valid call, what is its value? If not, explain why.

   e. If `mystery(5)` is a valid call, what is its value? If not, explain why.

   f. If `mystery(-3)` is a valid call, what is its value? If not, explain why.

8. Consider the following recursive function:

```
void funcRec(int u, char v)                     //Line 1
{                                               //Line 2
    if (u == 0)                                 //Line 3
        cout << v;                              //Line 4
    else if (u == 1)                            //Line 5
        cout << static_cast<char>
                 (static_cast<int>(v) + 1);     //Line 6
    else                                        //Line 7
        funcRec(u - 1, v);                      //Line 8
}                                               //Line 9
```

Answer the following questions:

a. What is the base case?

b. What is the general case?

c. What is the output of the following statement?

```
funcRec(5, 'A');
```

9. Consider the following recursive function:

```cpp
void exercise(int x)
{
    if (x > 0 && x < 10)
    {
        cout << x << " ";
        exercise(x + 1);
    }
}
```

What is the output of the following statements?

a. `exercise(0);`

b. `exercise(5);`

c. `exercise(10);`

d. `exercise(-5);`

10. Consider the following function:

```cpp
int test(int x, int y)
{
    if (x == y)
        return x;
    else if (x > y)
        return (x + y);
    else
        return test(x + 1, y - 1);
}
```

What is the output of the following statements?

a. `cout << test(5, 10) << endl;`

b. `cout << test(3, 9) << endl;`

11. Consider the following function:

```cpp
int func(int x)
{
    if (x == 0)
        return 2;
    else if (x == 1)
        return 3;
    else
        return (func(x - 1) + func(x - 2));
}
```

What is the output of the following statements?

a. `cout << func(0) << endl;`

b. `cout << func(1) << endl;`

c. `cout << func(2) << endl;`

d. `cout << func(5) << endl;`

12. Suppose that `intArray` is an array of integers, and `length` specifies the number of elements in `intArray`. Also, suppose that `low` and `high` are two integers such that $0 <= low < length$, $0 <= high < length$, and $low < high$. That is, `low` and `high` are two indices in `intArray`. Write a recursive definition that reverses the elements in `intArray` between `low` and `high`.

13. Write a recursive algorithm to multiply two positive integers m and n using repeated addition. Specify the base case and the recursive case.

14. Consider the following problem: How many ways can a committee of four people be selected from a group of 10 people? There are many other similar problems, which ask you to find the number of ways to select a set of items from a given set of items. The general problem can be stated as follows: Find the number of ways r different things can be chosen from a set of n items, where r and n are nonnegative integers and $r \leq n$. Suppose $C(n, r)$ denotes the number of ways r different things can be chosen from a set of n items. Then $C(n, r)$ is given by the following formula:

$$C(n,r) = \frac{n!}{r!(n-r)!}$$

where the exclamation point denotes the factorial function. Moreover, $C(n, 0) = C(n, n) = 1$. It is also known that $C(n, r) = C(n - 1, r - 1) + C(n - 1, r)$.

a. Write a recursive algorithm to determine $C(n, r)$. Identify the base case(s) and the general case(s).

b. Using your recursive algorithm, determine $C(5, 3)$ and $C(9, 4)$.

PROGRAMMING EXERCISES

1. Write a recursive function that takes as a parameter a nonnegative integer and generates the following pattern of stars. If the nonnegative integer is 4, then the pattern generated is:

    ```
    ****
    ***
    **
    *
    *
    **
    ***
    ****
    ```

    Also, write a program that prompts the user to enter the number of lines in the pattern and uses the recursive function to generate the pattern. For example, specifying 4 as the number of lines generates the above pattern.

2. Write a recursive function to generate a pattern of stars, such as the following:

    ```
    *
    **
    ***
    ****
    ****
    ***
    **
    *
    ```

    Also, write a program that prompts the user to enter the number of lines in the pattern and uses the recursive function to generate the pattern. For example, specifying 4 as the number of lines generates the above pattern.

3. Write a recursive function to generate the following pattern of stars:

    ```
        *
       * *
      * * *
     * * * *
      * * *
       * *
        *
    ```

    Also, write a program that prompts the user to enter the number of lines in the pattern and uses the recursive function to generate the pattern. For example, specifying 4 as the number of lines generates the above pattern.

4. Write a recursive function, **vowels**, that returns the number of vowels in a string. Also, write a program to test your function.

5. Write a recursive function that finds and returns the sum of the elements of an **int** array. Also, write a program to test your function.

6. A palindrome is a string that reads the same both forward and backward. For example, the string **"madam"** is a palindrome. Write a program that uses a recursive function to check whether a string is a palindrome. Your program must contain a value-returning recursive function that returns `true` if the string is a palindrome and `false` otherwise. Do not use any global variables; use the appropriate parameters.

7. Write a program that uses a recursive function to print a string backward. Do not use any global variables; use the appropriate parameters.

8. Write a recursive function, `reverseDigits`, that takes an integer as a parameter and returns the number with the digits reversed. Also, write a program to test your function.

9. Write a recursive function, `power`, that takes as parameters two integers x and y such that x is nonzero and returns x^y. You can use the following recursive definition to calculate x^y. If $y \geq 0$,

$$power(x, y) = \begin{cases} 1 & \text{if } y = 0 \\ x & \text{if } y = 1 \\ x \times power(x, y - 1) & \text{if } y > 1. \end{cases}$$

If $y < 0$,

$$power(x, y) = \frac{1}{power(x, -y)}.$$

Also, write a program to test your function.

10. (**Greatest Common Divisor**) Given two integers x and y, the following recursive definition determines the greatest common divisor of x and y, written $gcd(x,y)$:

$$gcd(x, y) = \begin{cases} x & \text{if } y = 0 \\ gcd(y, x\%y) & \text{if } y \neq 0 \end{cases}$$

Note: In this definition, % is the mod operator.

Write a recursive function, `gcd`, that takes as parameters two integers and returns the greatest common divisor of the numbers. Also, write a program to test your function.

11. Write a recursive function to implement the recursive algorithm of Exercise 12 (reversing the elements of an array between two indices). Also, write a program to test your function.

12. Write a recursive function to implement the recursive algorithm of Exercise 13 (multiplying two positive integers using repeated addition). Also, write a program to test your function.

13. Write a recursive function to implement the recursive algorithm of Exercise 14 (determining the number of ways to select a set of things from a given set of things). Also, write a program to test your function.

14. In the Programming Example "Converting a Number from Decimal to Binary" given in this chapter, you learned how to convert a decimal number into the equivalent binary number. Two more number systems, octal (base 8) and hexadecimal (base 16), are of interest to computer scientists. In fact, in C++, you can instruct the computer to store a number in octal or hexadecimal.

The digits in the octal number system are 0, 1, 2, 3, 4, 5, 6, and 7. The digits in the hexadecimal number system are 0, 1, 2, 3, 4, 5, 6, 7, 8, 9, A, B, C, D, E, and F. So A in hexadecimal is 10 in decimal, B in hexadecimal is 11 in decimal, and so on.

The algorithm to convert a positive decimal number into an equivalent number in octal (or hexadecimal) is the same as discussed for binary numbers. Here, we divide the decimal number by 8 (for octal) and by 16 (for hexadecimal). Suppose a_b represents the number a to the base b. For example, 75_{10} means 75 to the base 10 (that is decimal), and 83_{16} means 83 to the base 16 (that is, hexadecimal). Then:

$$753_{10} = 1361_8$$
$$753_{10} = 2F1_{16}$$

The method of converting a decimal number to base 2 or 8 or 16 can be extended to any arbitrary base. Suppose you want to convert a decimal number n into an equivalent number in base b, where b is between 2 and 36. You then divide the decimal number n by b as in the algorithm for converting decimal to binary.

Note that the digits in, say, base 20, are 0, 1, 2, 3, 4, 5, 6, 7, 8, 9, A, B, C, D, E, F, G, H, I, and J.

Write a program that uses a recursive function to convert a number in decimal to a given base b, where b is between 2 and 36. Your program should prompt the user to enter the number in decimal and in the desired base.

Test your program on the following data:

9098 and base 20
692 and base 2
753 and base 16

15. **(Recursive Sequential Search)** The sequential search algorithm given in Chapter 10 is nonrecursive. Write and implement a recursive version of the sequential search algorithm.

16. The function `sqrt` from the header file `cmath` can be used to find the square root of a nonnegative real number. Using Newton's method, you can also write an algorithm to find the square root of a nonnegative real number within a given tolerance, as follows: Suppose x is a nonnegative real number, a is the approximate square root of x, and *epsilon* is the tolerance. Start with $a = x$;

a. If $|a^2 - x| \leq$ *epsilon*, then a is the square root of x within the tolerance; otherwise:

b. Replace a with $(a^2 + x) / (2a)$ and repeat Step a
where $|a^2 - x|$ denotes the absolute value of $a^2 - x$.

Write a recursive function to implement this algorithm to find the square root of a nonnegative real number. Also, write a program to test your function.

RESERVED WORDS

and	and_eq	asm	auto
bitand	bitor	bool	break
case	catch	char	class
compl	const	const_cast	continue
default	delete	do	double
dynamic_cast	else	enum	explicit
export	extern	false	float
for	friend	goto	if
include	inline	int	long
mutable	namespace	new	not
not_eq	operator	or	or_eq
private	protected	public	register
reinterpret_cast	return	short	signed
sizeof	static	static_cast	struct
switch	template	this	throw
true	try	typedef	typeid
typename	union	unsigned	using
virtual	void	volatile	wchar_t
while	xor	xor_eq	

OPERATOR PRECEDENCE

The following table shows the precedence (highest to lowest) and associativity of the operators in C++.

Operator	Associativity
:: (binary scope resolution)	Left to right
:: (unary scope resolution)	Right to left
()	Left to right
[ ] -> .	Left to right
++ -- (as postfix operators)	Right to left
typeid dynamic_cast	Right to left
static_cast const_cast	Right to left
reinterpret_cast	Right to left
++ -- (as prefix operators) ! + (unary) - (unary)	Right to left
~ & (address of) * (dereference)	Right to left
new delete sizeof	Right to left
->* -- .*	Left to right
* / %	Left to right
+ -	Left to right
<< >>	Left to right
< <= > >=	Left to right
== !=	Left to right
&	Left to right
^	Left to right
		Left to right
&&	Left to right

Operator	Associativity
||	Left to right
?:	Right to left
= += -= *= /= %=	Right to left
<<= >>= &= |= ^=	Right to left
throw	Right to left
, (the sequencing operator)	Left to right

CHARACTER SETS

ASCII (American Standard Code for Information Interchange)

The following table shows the ASCII character set.

ASCII										
	0	1	2	3	4	5	6	7	8	9
0	nul	soh	stx	etx	eot	enq	ack	bel	bs	ht
1	lf	vt	ff	cr	so	si	dle	dc1	dc2	dc3
2	dc4	nak	syn	etb	can	em	sub	esc	fs	gs
3	rs	us	<u>b</u>	!	"	#	$	%	&	'
4	(	)	*	+	,	-	.	/	0	1
5	2	3	4	5	6	7	8	9	:	;
6	<	=	>	?	@	A	B	C	D	E
7	F	G	H	I	J	K	L	M	N	O
8	P	Q	R	S	T	U	V	W	X	Y
9	Z	[	\	]	^	_	`	a	b	c
10	d	e	f	g	h	i	j	k	l	m
11	n	o	p	q	r	s	t	u	v	w
12	x	y	z	{	|	}	~	del		

The numbers 0–12 in the first column specify the left digit(s), and the numbers 0–9 in the second row specify the right digit of each character in the ASCII data set. For example, the character in the row marked 6 (the number in the first column) and the column marked 5 (the number in the second row) is A. Therefore, the character at position 65 (which is the 66th character) is A. Moreover, the character <u>b</u> at position 32 represents the space character.

The first 32 characters, that is, the characters at positions 00–31 and at position 127 are nonprintable characters. The following table shows the abbreviations and meanings of these characters.

nul	null character	ff	form feed	can	cancel
soh	start of header	cr	carriage return	em	end of medium
stx	start of text	so	shift out	sub	substitute
etx	end of text	si	shift in	esc	escape
eot	end of transmission	dle	data link escape	fs	file separator
enq	enquiry	dc1	device control 1	gs	group separator
ack	acknowledge	dc2	device control 2	rs	record separator
bel	bell	dc3	device control 3	us	unit separator
bs	back space	dc4	device control 4	b	space
ht	horizontal tab	nak	negative acknowledge	del	delete
lf	line feed	syn	synchronous idle		
vt	vertical tab	etb	end of transmitted block		

EBCDIC (Extended Binary Coded Decimal Interchange Code)

The following table shows some of the characters in the EBCDIC character set.

EBCDIC										
	0	1	2	3	4	5	6	7	8	9
6					b					
7						.	<	(	+	|
8	&									
9	!	$	*	)	;	¬	-	/		
10								,	%	_
11	>	?								
12		`	:	#	@	'	=	"		a
13	b	c	d	e	f	g	h	i		

EBCDIC

	0	1	2	3	4	5	6	7	8	9
14						j	k	l	m	n
15	o	p	q	r						
16		~	s	t	u	v	w	x	y	z
17										
18	[	]								
19				A	B	C	D	E	F	G
20	H	I								J
21	K	L	M	N	O	P	Q	R		
22							S	T	U	V
23	W	X	Y	Z						
24	0	1	2	3	4	5	6	7	8	9

The numbers 6-24 in the first column specify the left digit(s), and the numbers 0-9 in the second row specify the right digits of the characters in the EBCDIC data set. For example, the character in the row marked 19 (the number in the first column) and the column marked 3 (the number in the second row) is A. Therefore, the character at position 193 (which is the 194th character) is A. Moreover, the character b̲ at position 64 represents the space character. The preceding table does not show all the characters in the EBCDIC character set. In fact, the characters at positions 00-63 and 250-255 are nonprintable control characters.

ADDITIONAL C++ TOPICS

Binary (Base 2) Representation of a Nonnegative Integer

Converting a Base 10 Number to a Binary Number (Base 2)

Chapter 1 remarked that A is the 66th character in the ASCII character set, but its position is 65 because the position of the first character is 0. Furthermore, the binary number 1000001 is the binary representation of 65. The number system that we use daily is called the **decimal number system** or **base 10 system**. The number system that the computer uses is called the **binary number system** or **base 2 system**. In this section, we describe how to find the binary representation of a nonnegative integer, and vice versa.

Consider 65. Note that:

$$65 = 1 \times 2^6 + 0 \times 2^5 + 0 \times 2^4 + 0 \times 2^3 + 0 \times 2^2 + 0 \times 2^1 + 1 \times 2^0$$

Similarly:

$$711 = 1 \times 2^9 + 0 \times 2^8 + 1 \times 2^7 + 1 \times 2^6 + 0 \times 2^5 + 0 \times 2^4 + 0 \times 2^3 + 1 \times 2^2 + 1 \times 2^1 + 1 \times 2^0$$

In general, if m is a nonnegative integer, then m can be written as:

$$m = a_k \times 2^k + a_{k-1} \times 2^{k-1} + a_{k-2} \times 2^{k-2} + \cdots + a_1 \times 2^1 + a_0 \times 2^0$$

for some nonnegative integer k, and where $a_i = 0$ or 1, for each $i = 0, 1, 2, \ldots, k$. The binary number $a_k a_{k-1} a_{k-2} \ldots a_1 a_0$ is called the **binary** or **base 2 representation** of m. In this case, we usually write:

$$m_{10} = (a_k a_{k-1} a_{k-2} \cdots a_1 a_0)_2$$

and say that m to the base 10 is $a_k a_{k-1} a_{k-2} \ldots a_1 a_0$ to the base 2.

For example, for the integer 65, $k = 6$, $a_6 = 1$, $a_5 = 0$, $a_4 = 0$, $a_3 = 0$, $a_2 = 0$, $a_1 = 0$, $a_0 = 1$. Thus, $a_6 a_5 a_4 a_3 a_2 a_1 a_0 = 1000001$, so the binary representation of 65 is 1000001, that is:

$$65_{10} = (1000001)_2.$$

If no confusion arises, then we write $(1000001)_2$ as 1000001_2.

Similarly, for the number 711, $k = 9$, $a_9 = 1$, $a_8 = 0$, $a_7 = 1$, $a_6 = 1$, $a_5 = 0$, $a_4 = 0$, $a_3 = 0$, $a_2 = 1$, $a_1 = 1$, $a_0 = 1$. Thus:

$$711_{10} = 1011000111_2.$$

It follows that to find the binary representation of a nonnegative integer, we need to find the coefficients, which are 0 or 1, of various powers of 2. However, there is an easy algorithm, described next, that can be used to find the binary representation of a non-negative integer. First, note that:

$$0_{10} = 0_2, 1_{10} = 1_2, 2_{10} = 10_2, 3_{10} = 11_2, 4_{10} = 100_2, 5_{10} = 101_2, 6_{10} = 110_2,$$
and $7_{10} = 111_2$.

Let us consider the integer 65. Note that $65 / 2 = 32$ and $65 \% 2 = 1$, where $\%$ is the mod operator. Next, $32 / 2 = 16$, and $32 \% 2 = 0$, and so on. It can be shown that $a_0 = 65 \% 2 = 1$, $a_1 = 32 \% 2 = 0$, and so on. We can show this continuous division and obtaining the remainder with the help of Figure D-1.

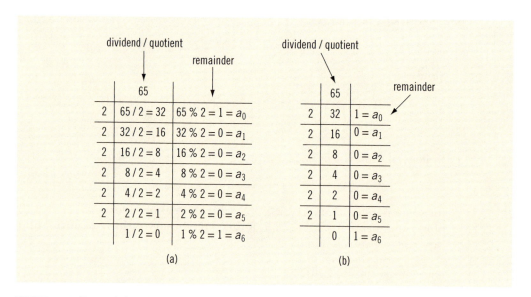

FIGURE D-1 Determining the binary representation of 65

Notice that in Figure D-1(a), starting at the second row, the second column contains the quotient when the number in the previous row is divided by 2, and the third column contains the remainder of that division. For example, in the second row, $65 / 2 = 32$, and $65 \% 2 = 1$. In the third row, $32 / 2 = 16$ and $32 \% 2 = 0$, and so on. For each row, the number in the second column is divided by 2, the quotient is written in the next row, below the current row, and the remainder is written in the third column. When using a figure, such as D-1, to find the binary representation of a nonnegative integer, typically, we show only the quotients and remainders, as in Figure D-1(b). You can write the binary representation of the number starting with the last remainder in the third column, followed by the second last remainder, and so on. Thus:

$65_{10} = 1000001_2$.

Next, consider the number 711. Figure D-2 shows the quotients and the remainders.

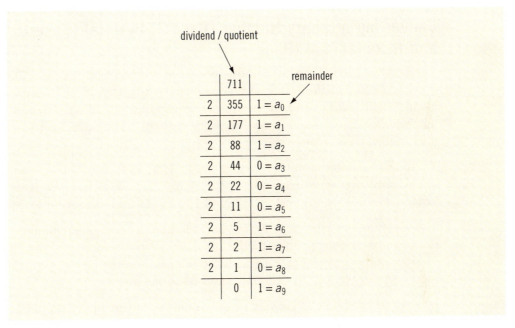

FIGURE D-2 Determining the binary representation of 711

From Figure D-2, it follows that:

$711_{10} = 1011000111_2$.

Converting a Binary Number (Base 2) to Base 10

To convert a number from base 2 to base 10, we first find the weight of each bit in the binary number. The weight of each bit in the binary number is assigned from right to left. The weight of the rightmost bit is 0. The weight of the bit immediately to the left of the rightmost bit is 1, the weight of the bit immediately to the left of it is 2, and so on. Consider the binary number 1001101. The weight of each bit is as follows:

```
weight  6  5  4  3  2  1  0
        1  0  0  1  1  0  1
```

We use the weight of each bit to find the equivalent decimal number. For each bit, we multiply the bit by 2 to the power of its weight, and then we add all of the numbers. For the above binary number, the equivalent decimal number is:

$$1 \times 2^6 + 0 \times 2^5 + 0 \times 2^4 + 1 \times 2^3 + 1 \times 2^2 + 0 \times 2^1 + 1 \times 2^0$$

$$= 64 + 0 + 0 + 8 + 4 + 0 + 1$$

$$= 77.$$

Converting a Binary Number (Base 2) to Octal (Base 8) and Hexadecimal (Base 16)

The previous sections described how to convert a binary number (base 2) to a decimal number. Even though the language of a computer is binary, if the binary number is too long, then it will be hard to manipulate it manually. To effectively deal with binary numbers, two more number systems, octal (base 8) and hexadecimal (base 16), are of interest to computer scientists.

The digits in the octal number system are 0, 1, 2, 3, 4, 5, 6, and 7. The digits in the hexadecimal number system are 0, 1, 2, 3, 4, 5, 6, 7, 8, 9, A, B, C, D, E, and F. So A in hexadecimal is 10 in decimal, B in hexadecimal is 11 in decimal, and so on.

The algorithm to convert a binary number into an equivalent number in octal (or hexadecimal) is quite simple. Before we describe the method to do so, let us review some notations. Suppose a_b represents the number a to the base b. For example, $2A0_{16}$ means 2A0 to the base 16, and 63_8 means 63 to the base 8.

First we describe how to convert a binary number into an equivalent octal number, and vice versa. Table D-1 describes the first eight octal numbers.

TABLE D-1   Binary Representation of First Eight Octal Numbers

Binary	Octal	Binary	Octal
000	0	100	4
001	1	101	5
010	2	110	6
011	3	111	7

Consider the binary number 1101100010101. To find the equivalent octal number, starting from right to left we consider three digits at a time and write their octal representation. Note that the binary number 1101100010101 has only 13 digits. So when we consider three digits at a time, at the end we will be left with only one digit. In this case, we just add two 0s to the left of the binary number; the equivalent binary number is 001101100010101. Thus,

$$1101100010101_2 = 001101100010101_2$$

$$= 001\ 101\ 100\ 010\ 101$$

$$= 15425_8 \text{ because } 001_2 = 1_8,\ 101_2 = 5_8,\ 100_2 = 4_8,\ 010_2 = 2_8,$$
$$\text{and } 101_2 = 5_8$$

Thus, $1101100010101_2 = 15425_8$.

To convert an octal number into an equivalent binary number, using Table D-1, write the binary representation of each octal digit in the number. For example,

$$3761_8 = 011\ 111\ 110\ 001_2$$

$$= 011111110001_2$$

$$= 11111110001_2$$

Thus, $3761_8 = 11111110001_2$.

Next we discuss how to convert a binary number into an equivalent hexadecimal number, and vice versa. The method to do so is similar to converting a number from binary to octal and vice versa, except that here we work with four binary digits. Table D-2 gives the binary representation of the first 16 hexadecimal numbers.

TABLE D-2 Binary Representation of First 16 Hexadecimal Numbers

Binary	Hexadecimal	Binary	Hexadecimal
0000	0	1000	8
0001	1	1001	9
0010	2	1010	A
0011	3	1011	B
0100	4	1100	C
0101	5	1101	D
0110	6	1110	E
0111	7	1111	F

Consider the binary number 1111101010001010101_2. Now,

$$1111101010001010101_2 = 111\ 1101\ 0100\ 0101\ 0101_2$$

$$= 0111\ 1101\ 0100\ 0101\ 0101_2, \text{ add one zero to the left}$$

$$= 7D455_{16}$$

Hence, $1111101010001010101_2 = 7D455_{16}$.

Next, to convert a hexadecimal number into an equivalent binary number, write the four-digit binary representation of each hexadecimal digit into that number. For example,

$$A7F32_{16} = 1010\ 0111\ 1111\ 0011\ 0010_2$$

$$= 10100111111100110010_2$$

Thus, $A7F32_{16} = 10100111111100110010_2$.

Additional Input and Output Tools

In Chapter 2, you learned how to use the functions `get`, `ignore`, and `clear` to input data, how to use the manipulators `steprecision`, `fixed`, and `showpoint` to control the output of floating-point numbers, and how to use the manipulators `setw`, `left`, and `right` to align and display the output in specific columns. Even though these functions and manipulators are adequate to input data and produce an elegant report, in some situations you might want to do more. In this section, you will learn additional input and output formatting tools.

The `putback` and `peek` Functions

Suppose you are processing data that is a mixture of numbers and characters. Moreover, the numbers must be read and processed as numbers. You have also looked at many sets of sample data and cannot determine whether the next input is a character or a number. You could read the entire data set character-by-character and check whether a certain character is a digit. If a digit is found, you could then read the remaining digits of the number and somehow convert these characters into numbers. This programming code would be somewhat complex. Fortunately, C++ provides two useful stream functions that can be used effectively in these types of situations.

The stream function `putback` lets you put the last character the `get` function extracted from the input stream back into the input stream. The stream function `peek` looks into the input stream and tells you what the next character is without removing it from the input stream. By using these functions, after determining that the next input is a number, you can read that input as a number. You do not have to read the digits of the number as characters and then convert those characters to that number.

The syntax to use the function `putback` is:

```
istreamVar.putback(ch);
```

Here, `istreamVar` is an input stream variable, such as `cin`, and `ch` is a **char** variable.

The `peek` function returns the next character from the input stream, but does not remove the character from that stream. In other words, the function `peek` looks into the input stream and checks the identity of the next input character. Moreover, after checking the next input character in the input stream, the function `peek` can store this character in a designated memory location without removing the character from the input stream. That is, when you use the `peek` function, the next input character stays the same, even though you now know what it is.

The syntax to use the function `peek` is:

```
ch = istreamVar.peek();
```

Here, `istreamVar` is an input stream variable, such as `cin`, and `ch` is a **char** variable.

The following example, Example D-1, illustrates how to use the **peek** and **putback** functions.

EXAMPLE D-1

```cpp
//*************************************************************
// Author: D.S. Malik
//
// This program shows how to use the functions peek and putback.
//*************************************************************

#include <iostream>                                     //Line 1

using namespace std;                                    //Line 2

int main()                                              //Line 3
{                                                       //Line 4
    char ch;                                            //Line 5

    cout << "Line 6: Enter a string: ";                 //Line 6
    cin.get(ch);                                        //Line 7
    cout << endl;                                       //Line 8
    cout << "Line 9: After first cin.get(ch); "
         << "ch = " << ch << endl;                      //Line 9

    cin.get(ch);                                        //Line 10
    cout << "Line 11: After second cin.get(ch); "
         << "ch = " << ch << endl;                      //Line 11

    cin.putback(ch);                                    //Line 12
    cin.get(ch);                                        //Line 13
```

```
    cout << "Line 14: After putback and then "
         << "cin.get(ch); ch = " << ch << endl;          //Line 14

    ch = cin.peek();                                       //Line 15
    cout << "Line 16: After cin.peek(); ch = "             //Line 16
         << ch << endl;

    cin.get(ch);                                           //Line 17
    cout << "Line 18: After cin.get(ch); ch = "            //Line 18
         << ch << endl;

    return 0;                                              //Line 19
}                                                          //Line 20
```

Sample Run: In this sample run, the user input is shaded.

```
Line 6: Enter a string: abcd

Line 9: After first cin.get(ch); ch = a
Line 11: After second cin.get(ch); ch = b
Line 14: After putback and then cin.get(ch); ch = b
Line 16: After cin.peek(); ch = c
Line 18: After cin.get(ch); ch = c
```

The user input, abcd, allows you to see the effect of the functions get, putback, and peek in the preceding program. The statement in Line 6 prompts the user to enter a string. In Line 7, the statement cin.get(ch); extracts the first character from the input stream and stores it in the variable ch. So after Line 7 executes, the value of ch is 'a'.

The cout statement in Line 9 outputs the value of ch. The statement cin.get(ch); in Line 10 extracts the next character from the input stream, which is 'b', and stores it in ch. At this point, the value of ch is 'b'.

The cout statement in Line 11 outputs the value of ch. The cin.putback(ch); statement in Line 12 puts the previous character extracted by the get function, which is 'b', back into the input stream. Therefore, the next character to be extracted from the input stream is 'b'.

The cin.get(ch); statement in Line 13 extracts the next character, which is still 'b', from the input stream and stores it in ch. Now the value of ch is 'b'. The cout statement in Line 14 outputs the value of ch as 'b'.

In Line 15, the statement ch = cin.peek(); checks the next character in the input stream, which is 'c', and stores it in ch. The value of ch is now 'c'. The cout statement in Line 16 outputs the value of ch. The cin.get(ch); statement in Line 17 extracts the next character from the input stream and stores it in ch. The cout statement in Line 18 outputs the value of ch, which is still 'c'.

Note that the statement ch = cin.peek(); in Line 15 did not remove the character 'c' from the input stream; it only peeked into the input stream. The output of Lines 16 and 18 demonstrates this functionality.

`setfill` **Manipulator**

Recall that in the manipulator `setw`, if the number of columns specified exceeds the number of columns required by the expression, the output of the expression is right-justified, and the unused columns to the left are filled with spaces. The output stream variables can use the manipulator `setfill` to fill the unused columns with a character other than a space.

The syntax to use the manipulator `setfill` is

```
ostreamVar << setfill(ch);
```

where `ostreamVar` is an output stream variable, and `ch` is a character. For example, the statement

```
cout << setfill('#');
```

sets the fill character to `'#'` on the standard output device.

To use the manipulator `setfill`, the program must include the header file `iomanip`.

The program in Example D-2 illustrates the effect of using `setfill` in a program.

EXAMPLE D-2

```
//************************************************************
// Author: D.S. Malik
//
// This program illustrates how to use the function setfill.
//************************************************************

#include <iostream>                                    //Line 1
#include <iomanip>                                     //Line 2

using namespace std;                                   //Line 3

int main()                                             //Line 4
{                                                      //Line 5
    int x = 15;                                        //Line 6
    int y = 7634;                                      //Line 7

    cout << "12345678901234567890" << endl;            //Line 8

    cout << setw(5) << x << setw(7) << y
         << setw(8) << "Warm" << endl;                 //Line 9

    cout << setfill('*');                              //Line 10

    cout << setw(5) << x << setw(7) << y
         << setw(8) << "Warm" << endl;                 //Line 11

    cout << setw(5) << x << setw(7) << setfill('#')
         << y << setw(8) << "Warm" << endl;            //Line 12
```

```
    cout << setw(5) << setfill('@') << x
         << setw(7) << setfill('#') << y
         << setw(8) << setfill('^') << "Warm"
         << endl;                                    //Line 13

    cout << setfill(' ');                            //Line 14

    cout << setw(5) << x << setw(7) << y
         << setw(8) << "Warm" << endl;               //Line 15

    return 0;                                        //Line 16
}                                                    //Line 17
```

Sample Run:

```
12345678901234567890
   15   7634    Warm
***15***7634****Warm
***15###7634####Warm
@@@15###7634^^^^Warm
   15   7634    Warm
```

The statements in Lines 6 and 7 declare and initialize the variables **x** and **y** to 15 and 7634, respectively. The output of the statement in Line 8—the first line of output—shows the column position when the subsequent statements output the values of the variables. The statement in Line 9 outputs the value of **x** in five columns, the value of **y** in seven columns, and the string **"Warm"** in eight columns. In this statement, the filling character is the blank character, as shown in the second line of output.

The statement in Line 10 sets the filling character to *. The statement in Line 11 outputs the value of **x** in five columns, the value of **y** in seven columns, and the string **"Warm"** in eight columns. Because **x** is a two-digit number and five columns are assigned to output its value, the first three columns are unused by **x** and are, therefore, filled by the filling character *. To print the value of **y**, seven columns are assigned. However, **y** is a four-digit number, so the filling character fills the first three columns. Similarly, to print the value of the string **"Warm"**, eight columns are assigned. The string **"Warm"** has only four characters, so the filling character fills the first four columns. See the third line of output.

The output of the statement in Line 12—the fourth line of output—is similar to the output of the statement in Line 11, except that the filling character for **y** and the string **"Warm"** is #. In the output of the statement in Line 13 (the fifth line of output), the filling character for **x** is @, the filling character for **y** is #, and the filling character for the string **"Warm"** is ^. The manipulator `setfill` sets these filling characters.

The statement in Line 14 sets the filling character to blank. The statement in Line 15 outputs the values of **x**, **y**, and the string **"Warm"** using the filling character blank, as shown in the sixth line of output.

APPENDIX E
HEADER FILES

The C++ standard library contains many predefined functions, named constants, and specialized data types. This appendix discusses some of the most widely used library routines (and several named constants). For additional explanation and information on functions, named constants, and so on, check your system documentation. The names of the Standard C++ header files are shown in parentheses.

Header File `cassert` (`assert.h`)

The following table describes the function `assert`. Its specification is contained in the header file `cassert` (`assert.h`).

`assert(expression)`	`expression` is any `int expression;` `expression` is usually a logical expression.	• If the value of `expression` is nonzero (`true`), the program continues to execute. • If the value of `expression` is 0 (`false`), execution of the program terminates immediately. The expression, the name of the file containing the source code, and the line number in the source code are displayed.

NOTE To disable all the `assert` statements, place the preprocessor directive `#define` NDEBUG before the directive `#include <cassert>`.

Header File cctype (ctype.h)

The following table shows various functions from the header file cctype (ctype.h).

Function Name and Parameters	Parameter(s) Types	Function Return Value
isalnum(ch)	ch is a char value	Function returns an int value as follows: • If ch is a letter or a digit character, that is ('A'-'Z', 'a'-'z', '0'-'9'), it returns a nonzero value (true) • 0 (false), otherwise
iscntrl(ch)	ch is a char value	Function returns an int value as follows: • If ch is a control character (in ASCII, a character value 0-31 or 127), it returns a nonzero value (true) • 0 (false), otherwise
isdigit(ch)	ch is a char value	Function returns an int value as follows: • If ch is a digit ('0'-'9'), it returns a nonzero value (true) • 0 (false), otherwise
islower(ch)	ch is a char value	Function returns an int value as follows: • If ch is lowercase ('a'-'z'), it returns a nonzero value (true) • 0 (false), otherwise
isprint(ch)	ch is a char value	Function returns an int value as follows: • If ch is a printable character, including blank (in ASCII, ' ' through '~'), it returns a nonzero value (true) • 0 (false), otherwise
ispunct(ch)	ch is a char value	Function returns an int value as follows: • If ch is a punctuation character, it returns a nonzero value (true) • 0 (false), otherwise
isspace(ch)	ch is a char value	Function returns an int value as follows: • If ch is a white space character (blank, newline, tab, carriage return, form feed), it returns a nonzero value (true) • 0 (false), otherwise

Function Name and Parameters	Parameter(s) Types	Function Return Value
isupper(ch)	ch is a char value	Function returns an int value as follows: • If ch is an uppercase letter ('A'-'Z'), it returns a nonzero value (true) • 0 (false), otherwise
tolower(ch)	ch is a char value	Function returns an int value as follows: • If ch is an uppercase letter, it returns the ASCII value of the lowercase equivalent of ch • ASCII value of ch, otherwise
toupper(ch)	ch is a char value	Function returns an int value as follows: • If ch is a lowercase letter, it returns the ASCII value of the uppercase equivalent of ch • ASCII value of ch, otherwise

Header File cfloat (float.h)

In Chapter 1, we listed the largest and smallest values belonging to the floating-point data types. We also remarked that these values are system dependent. These largest and smallest values are stored in named constants. The header file cfloat contains many such named constants. The following table lists some of these constants.

Named Constant	Description
FLT_DIG	Approximate number of significant digits in a float value
FLT_MAX	Maximum positive float value
FLT_MIN	Minimum positive float value
DBL_DIG	Approximate number of significant digits in a double value
DBL_MAX	Maximum positive double value
DBL_MIN	Minimum positive double value
LDBL_DIG	Approximate number of significant digits in a long double value
LDBL_MAX	Maximum positive long double value
LDBL_MIN	Minimum positive long double value

A program similar to the following can print the values of these named constants on your system:

```cpp
//***********************************************************
// Author: D.S. Malik
//
// This program prints the values of some of the named
// constants listed in the header file cfloat.
//***********************************************************

#include <iostream>
#include <cfloat>

using namespace std;

int main()
{
    cout << "Approximate number of significant digits "
         << "in a float value " << FLT_DIG << endl;
    cout << "Maximum positive float value " << FLT_MAX
         << endl;
    cout << "Minimum positive float value " << FLT_MIN
         << endl;
    cout << "Approximate number of significant digits "
         << "in a double value " << DBL_DIG << endl;
    cout << "Maximum positive double value " << DBL_MAX
         << endl;
    cout << "Minimum positive double value " << DBL_MIN
         << endl;
    cout << "Approximate number of significant digits "
         << "in a long double value " << LDBL_DIG << endl;
    cout << "Maximum positive long double value " << LDBL_MAX
         << endl;
    cout << "Minimum positive long double value " << LDBL_MIN
         << endl;

    return 0;
}
```

Header File `climits` (`limits.h`)

In Chapter 1, we listed the largest and smallest values belonging to the integral data types. We also remarked that these values are system dependent. These largest and smallest values are stored in named constants. The header file `climits` contains many such named constants. The following table lists some of these constants.

Named Constant	Description
CHAR_BIT	Number of bits in a byte
CHAR_MAX	Maximum `char` value
CHAR_MIN	Minimum `char` value
SHRT_MAX	Maximum `short` value

Named Constant	Description
SHRT_MIN	Minimum **short** value
INT_MAX	Maximum **int** value
INT_MIN	Minimum **int** value
LONG_MAX	Maximum **long** value
LONG_MIN	Minimum **long** value
UCHAR_MAX	Maximum **unsigned char** value
USHRT_MAX	Maximum **unsigned short** value
UINT_MAX	Maximum **unsigned int** value
ULONG_MAX	Maximum **unsigned long** value

A program similar to the following can print the values of these named constants on your system:

```cpp
//**********************************************************
// Author: D.S. Malik
//
// This program prints the values of some of the named
// constants listed in the header file climits.
//**********************************************************

#include <iostream>
#include <climits>

using namespace std;

int main()
{
    cout << "Number of bits in a byte " << CHAR_BIT << endl;
    cout << "Maximum char value " << CHAR_MAX << endl;
    cout << "Minimum char value " << CHAR_MIN << endl;
    cout << "Maximum short value " << SHRT_MAX << endl;
    cout << "Minimum short value " << SHRT_MIN << endl;
    cout << "Maximum int value " << INT_MAX << endl;
    cout << "Minimum int value " << INT_MIN << endl;
    cout << "Maximum long value " << LONG_MAX << endl;
    cout << "Minimum long value " << LONG_MIN << endl;
    cout << "Maximum unsigned char value " << UCHAR_MAX
         << endl;
    cout << "Maximum unsigned short value " << USHRT_MAX
         << endl;
    cout << "Maximum unsigned int value " << UINT_MAX << endl;
    cout << "Maximum unsigned long value " << ULONG_MAX
         << endl;

    return 0;
}
```

Header File `cmath` (`math.h`)

The following table shows various math functions.

Function Name and Parameters	Parameter(s) Type	Function Return Value
`acos(x)`	x is a floating-point expression, $-1.0 \leq x \leq 1.0$	Arc cosine of x, a value between 0.0 and π
`asin(x)`	x is a floating-point expression, $-1.0 \leq x \leq 1.0$	Arc sine of x, a value between -π/2 and π/2
`atan(x)`	x is a floating-point expression	Arc tan of x, a value between -π/2 and π/2
`ceil(x)`	x is a floating-point expression	The smallest whole number $\geq$ x, ("ceiling" of x)
`cos(x)`	x is a floating-point expression, x is measured in radians	Trigonometric cosine of the angle
`cosh(x)`	x is a floating-point expression	Hyperbolic cosine of x
`exp(x)`	x is a floating-point expression	The value e raised to the power of x; (e = 2.718...)
`fabs(x)`	x is a floating-point expression	Absolute value of x
`floor(x)`	x is a floating-point expression	The largest whole number $\leq$ x; ("floor" of x)
`log(x)`	x is a floating-point expression, where x > 0.0	Natural logarithm (base e) of x
`log10(x)`	x is a floating-point expression, where x > 0.0	Common logarithm (base 10) of x
`pow(x,y)`	x and y are floating-point expressions. If x = 0.0, y must be positive; if x $\leq$ 0.0, y must be a whole number.	x raised to the power of y
`sin(x)`	x is a floating-point expression; x is measured in radians	Trigonometric sine of the angle
`sinh(x)`	x is a floating-point expression	Hyperbolic sine of x

Function Name and Parameters	Parameter(s) Type	Function Return Value
sqrt(x)	x is a floating-point expression, where x ≥ 0.0	Square root of x
tan(x)	x is a floating-point expression; x is measured in radians	Trigonometric tangent of the angle
tanh(x)	x is a floating-point expression	Hyperbolic tangent of x

Header File cstddef (stddef.h)

Among others, this header file contains the definition of the following symbolic constant:

NULL: The system–dependent null pointer (usually 0)

Header File cstring (string.h)

The following table shows various string functions.

Function Name and Parameters	Parameter(s) Type	Function Return Value
strcat(destStr, srcStr)	destStr and srcStr are null-terminated char arrays; destStr must be large enough to hold the result	The base address of destStr is returned; srcStr, including the null character, is concatenated to the end of destStr
strcmp(str1, str2)	str1 and str2 are null terminated char arrays	The returned value is as follows: • An int value < 0, if str1 < str2 • An int value 0, if str1 = str2 • An int value > 0, if str1 > str2

Function Name and Parameters	Parameter(s) Type	Function Return Value
strcpy(destStr, srcStr)	destStr and srcStr are null-terminated **char** arrays	The base address of destStr is returned; srcStr is copied into destStr
strlen(str)	str is a null-terminated **char** array	An integer value ≥ 0 specifying the length of the str (excluding the '\0') is returned

HEADER FILE string

This header file—not to be confused with the header file cstring—supplies a programmer-defined data type named string. Associated with the string type are a data type string::size_type and a named constant string::npos. These are defined as follows:

string::size_type	An unsigned integer type
string::npos	The maximum value of type string::size_type

Several functions are associated with the string type. The following table shows some of these functions. Unless stated otherwise, str, str1, and str2 are variables (objects) of type string. The position of the first character in a string variable (such as str) is 0, the second character is 1, and so on.

Function Name and Parameters	Parameter(s) Type	Function Return Value
str.c_str()	None	The base address of a null-terminated C-string corresponding to the characters in str.
getline(istreamVar,str)	istreamVar is an input stream variable (of type istream or ifstream). str is a string object (variable).	Characters until the newline character are input from istreamVar and stored in str. (The newline character is read but not stored into str.) The value returned by this function is usually ignored.

Function Name and Parameters	Parameter(s) Type	Function Return Value
str.empty()	None	Returns true if str is empty, that is, the number of characters in str is zero, false otherwise.
str.length()	None	A value of type string::size_type giving the number of characters in the string.
str.size()	None	A value of type string::size_type giving the number of characters in the string.
str.find(strExp)	str is a string object and strExp is a string expression evaluating to a string. The string expression, strExp, can also be a character.	The find function searches str to find the first occurrence of the string or the character specified by strExp. If the search is successful, the function find returns the position in str where the match begins. If the search is unsuccessful, the function returns the special value string::npos.
str.substr(pos, len)	Two unsigned integers, pos and len. pos, represent the starting position (of the substring in str), and len represents the length (of the substring). The value of pos must be less than str.length().	A temporary string object that holds a substring of str starting at pos. The length of the substring is, at most, len characters. If len is too large, it means "to the end" of the string in str.
str1.swap(str2);	One parameter of type string. str1 and str2 are string variables.	The contents of str1 and str2 are swapped.
str.clear();	None	Removes all the characters from str.

Function Name and Parameters	Parameter(s) Type	Function Return Value
`str.erase();`	None	Removes all the characters from `str`.
`str.erase(m);`	One parameter of type `string::size_type`.	Removes all the characters from `str` starting at index m.
`str.erase(m, n);`	Two parameters of type `int`.	Starting at index m, removes the next n characters from `str`. If n > length of `str`, removes all the characters starting at the mth.
`str.insert(m, n, c);`	Parameters m and n are of type `string::size_type`; c is a character.	Inserts n occurrences of the character c at index m into `str`.
`str1.insert(m, str2);`	Parameter m is of type `string::size_type`.	Inserts all the characters of `str2` at index m into `str1`.
`str1.replace(m, n, str2);`	Parameters m and n are of type `string::size_type`.	Starting at index m, replaces the next n characters of `str1` with all the characters of `str2`. If n > length of `str1`, then all the characters until the end of `str1` are replaced.

ANSWERS TO ODD-NUMBERED EXERCISES

Chapter 0

1. a. true; b. false; c. false; d. false; e. true; f. false; g. false; h. true; i. false; j. true

3. Fetch and decode instructions, control the flow of information (instructions or data) in and out of main memory, and control the operation of the internal components of the CPU.

5. Screen and printer

7. An operating system monitors the overall activity of the computer and provides services. Some of these services include memory management, input/output activities, and storage management.

9. Because the computer cannot directly execute instructions written in a high-level language, a compiler is needed to translate a program written in high-level language into machine code.

11. Every computer directly understands its own machine language. Therefore, for the computer to execute a program written in a high-level language, the high-level language program must be translated into the computer's machine language.

13. In linking, an object program is combined with other programs in the library, that are used in the program, to create the executable code.

15. To find the weighted average of the four test scores, first, you need to know each test score and its weight. Next, you multiply each test score with its weight, and then add these numbers to get the average. Therefore,

   1. Get testScore1, weightTestScore1

   2. Get testScore2, weightTestScore2

   3. Get testScore3, weightTestScore3

   4. Get testScore4, weightTestScore4

   5. weightedAverage = testScore1 * weightTestScore1 +
                         testScore2 * weightTestScore2 +
                         testScore3 * weightTestScore3 +
                         testScore4 * weightTestScore4;

17. To find the price per square inch, first, we need to find the area of the pizza. Then we divide the price of the pizza by the area of the pizza. Let `radius` denote the radius, let `area` denote the area of the circle, and let `price` denote the price of the pizza. Also, let `pricePerSquareInch` denote the price per square inch.

    a. Get `radius`

    b. `area` = π * `radius` * `radius`

    c. Get `price`

    d. `pricePerSquareInch` = `price` / `area`

19. To calculate the area of a triangle using the given formula, we need to know the lengths of the sides—a, b, and c—of the triangle. Next, we calculate s using the formula:

    ```
    s = (1/2) (a + b + c)
    ```

    and then calculate the area using the formula:

    ```
    area = sqrt(s(s-a)(s-b)(s-c))
    ```

    where `sqrt` denotes the square root.

    The algorithm, therefore, is:

    a. Get a, b, c

    b. `s` = (1/2) (a + b + c)

    c. `area` = sqrt(s(s-a)(s-b)(s-c))

    The information needed to calculate the area of the triangle is the lengths of the sides of the triangle.

21. Suppose `callTime` denotes the number of minutes the call lasted, and `billingAmount` denotes the total charges for the call. To calculate the total charges for the call, you need to know the number of minutes the call lasted.

    If `callTime` is less than three minutes, the billing amount is connection charges plus $2.00; otherwise, the billing amount is connection charges plus $2.00 plus 45 cents per minute over three minutes. That is,

    ```
    if (callTime is less than or equal to 3)
        billingAmount = 1.99 + 2.00;
    otherwise
        billingAmount = 1.99 + 2.00 + (callTime - 3)* 0.45;
    ```

You can now write the algorithm as follows:

a. Get `callTime`.

b. Calculate billing amount using the formula:

```
if (callTime is less than or equal to 3)
    billingAmount = 1.99 + 2.00;
otherwise
    billingAmount = 1.99 + 2.00 + (callTime - 3)* 0.45;
```

Chapter 1

1. a. false; b. false; c. false; d. true; e. true; f. true; g. true; h. false; i. true; j. false

3. b, d, e

5. a. `3`

    b. Not possible. Both operands of the operator `%` must be integers. Because the second operand, `w`, is a floating-point value, the expression is invalid.

    c. Not possible. Both operands of the operator `%` must be integers. Because the first operand, which is `y + w`, is a floating-point value, the expression is invalid.

    d. `38.5`

    e. `1`

    f. `2`

    g. `2`

    h. `420.0`

7.  ```
    This is Exercise 7.
    In C++, the multiplication symbol is *."
    2 + 3 * 5 = 17
    ```

9. `7`

11. a and c are valid

13. a. `-10 * a`

    b. `'8'`

    c. `(b * b - 4 * a * c) / (2 * a)`

    d. `(-b + (b * b - 4 * a * c)) / (2 * a)`
    ```

15. x = 20
    y = 15
    z = 6
    w = 11.5
    t = 4.5

17. a. 0.50

    b. 24.50

    c. 37.6

    d. 8.3

    e. 10

    f. 38.75

19. a. cout << endl; or cout << "\n"; or cout << '\n';

    b. cout << "\t";

    c. cout << "\"";

21. a. `int` num1;
       `int` num2;

    b. cout << "Enter two numbers separated by spaces." << endl;

    c. cin >> num1 >> num2;

    d. cout << "num1 = " << num1 << "num2 = " << num2
            << "2 * num1 - num2 = " << 2 * num1 - num2 << endl;

Chapter 2

1. a. false; b. true; c. true; d. false; e. false; f. true; g. true

3. The user input is shaded.

   Enter last name: Miller

   Enter a two-digit number: 34

   Enter a positive integer less than 1000: 340

   Name: Miller
   Id: 3417
   Mystery number: 3689

5. The program requires four inputs in the following order:

   string string integer decimal_Number

7. a. x = 37, y = 86, z = 0.56

    b. x = 37, y = 32, z = 86.56

    c. Input failure: z = 37.0, x = 86, trying to read the . (period) into y.

9. Input failure: Trying to read A into y, which is an **int** variable. x = 46, y = 18, and z = 'A'. The values of y and z are unchanged.

11. a. name = "Mickey Balto", age = 35

    b. name = "Mickey Balto", age = 35

13. Invalid data might cause the input stream to enter the fail state. When an input stream enters the fail state, all further inputs associated with that input stream are ignored. The program continues to execute with whatever values the variables have.

Chapter 3

1. a. false; b. false; c. false; d. true; e. false; f. false; g. false; h. false; i. false; j. false

3. 100 200 0

5. Omit the semicolon after **else**. The correct statement is:

```
if (score >= 60)
    cout << "You pass." << endl;
else
    cout << "You fail." << endl;
```

7. 15

9. 96

11.
```
#include <iostream>

using namespace std;
const int SECRET = 5;

int main()
{
    int x, y, w, z;

    z = 9;

    if (z > 10)
    {
        x = 12;
        y = 5;
        w = x + y + SECRET;
    }
```

```
        else
        {
            x = 12;
            y = 4;
            w = x + y + SECRET;
        }

        cout << "w = " << w << endl;

        return 0;
    }
```

Chapter 4

1. a. false; b. true; c. false; d. true; e. true; f. true; g. true; h. false

3. 5

5. if ch > 'Z' or ch < 'A'

7. Sum = 158

9. Sum = 158

11. 11 18 25

13. a. 18

    b. 14

    c. false

15. 2 7 17 37 77 157 317

17. a. *

    b. infinite loop

    c. infinite loop

    d. ****

    e. ******

    f. ***

19. 11 19 30 49

21. a. both

    b. do...while

    c. while

    d. while

23. There is more than one answer to this problem. One solution is to replace the `do...while` with the following:

```
do
{
    cin >> number;
    if (number != -1)
        total = total + number;
    count++;
}
while (number != -1);
```

25. a.
```
number = 1;
while (number <= 10)
{
    cout << setw(3) << number;
    number++;
}
```

b.
```
number = 1;
do
{
    cout << setw(3) << number;
    number++;
}
while (number <= 10);
```

27. `11 18 25`

Chapter 5

1. a. false; b. true; c. true; d. true; e. false; f. true; g. false; h. true; i. false; j. true; k. false; l. false; m. false; n. true

3. a, b, c, e, f, and g are valid. In d, the function call in the output (`cout`) statement requires one more argument.

5. a. 4; `int`

   b. 2; `double`

   c. 4; `char`

   d. The function test requires four actual parameters. The order of the parameters is: `int`, `char`, `double`, `int`.

   e. `cout << test(5, 'z', 7.3, 5) << endl;`

   f. `cout << two(17.5, 18.3) << endl;`

   g. `cout << static_cast<char>(static_cast<int>`
      `                          (three(4, 3, 'A', 17.6)) + 1)`
      `    << endl;`

7. a.   i. 125   ii. 432

    b.   The function computes x^3, where x is the argument of the function.

9. 1
    2
    6
    24
    120

11. A variable declared in the heading of a function definition is called a formal parameter. A variable or expression used in a function call is called an actual parameter.

13. A value parameter receives a copy of the actual parameter's data. A reference parameter receives the address of the actual parameter.

15. A variable for which memory is allocated at block entry and deallocated at block exit is an automatic variable. A variable for which memory remains allocated as long as the program executes is a static variable.

17. 3 4 20 78
    7 3 20 4
    7 5 6 2

19.
```
#include <iostream>

using namespace std;

void func(int val1, int val2);

int main()
{
        int num1, num2;
__1__   cout << "Please enter two integers." << endl;
__2__   cin >> num1 >> num2;
__3__   func (num1, num2);
__7__   cout << " The two integers are " << num1
                << ", " << num2 << endl;
__8__   return 0;
}

void func (int val1, int val2)
{
        int val3, val4;
__4__   val3 = val1 + val2;
__5__   val4 = val1 * val2;
__6__   cout << "The sum and product are " << val3
                << " and " << val4 << endl;

}
```

21. 10 20
    5 20

23. a, b, and d are correct.

Chapter 6

1. a. true; b. true; c. false; d. false; e. true; f. false; g. false; h. false; i. true; j. false; k. false; l. false

3. a. `funcOne(list, 50);`

   b. `cout << funcSum(50, list[3]) << endl;`

   c. `cout << funcSum(list[29], list[9]) << endl;`

   d. `funcTwo(list, aList);`

5. `list elements are: 5, 6, 9, 19, 23, 37`

7. a. Invalid; the assignment operator is not defined for C-strings.

   b. Invalid; the relational operators are not defined for C-strings.

   c. Invalid; the assignment operator is not defined for C-strings.

   d. Valid

9. a. `strcpy(str1, "Sunny Day");`

   b. `length = strlen(str1);`

   c. `strcpy(str2, name);`

   d. `if (strcmp(str1, str2) <= 0)`
      `    cout << str1 << endl;`
      `else`
      `    cout << str2 << endl;`

11. `List elements: 11  16  21  26  30`

13. a. 30

    b. 5

    c. 6

    d. row

    e. column

15. a. `beta is initialized to 0.`

    b. `First row of beta: 0 1 2`
       `Second row of beta: 1 2 3`
       `Third row of beta: 2 3 4`

    c. `First row of beta: 0 0 0`
       `Second row of beta: 0 1 2`
       `Third row of beta: 0 2 4`

    d. `First row of beta: 0 2 0`
       `Second row of beta: 2 0 2`
       `Third row of beta: 0 2 0`

Chapter 7

1. a. false; b. false; c. true; d. false; e. false; f. false; g. true

3. a. 6

    b. 2

    c. 2

    d.
```cpp
void xClass::func()
{
    u = 10;
    w = 15.3;
}
```

    e.
```cpp
void xClass::print()
{
    cout << u << " " << w << endl;
}
```

    f.
```cpp
xClass::xClass()
{
    u = 0;
    w = 0;
}
```

    g. `x.print();`

    h. `xClass t(20, 35.0);`

5. a.
```cpp
int testClass::sum()
{
    return x + y;
}

void testClass::print() const
{
    cout << "x = " << x << ", y = " << y << endl;
}

testClass::testClass()
{
    x = 0;
    y = 0;
}

testClass::testClass(int a, int b)
{
    x = a;
    y = b;
}
```

b. One possible solution. (We assume that the name of the header file containing the definition of the **class** testClass is `Exercise5Ch7.h`.)

```
#include <iostream.h>
#include "Exercise5Ch7.h"

int main()
{
    testClass one;
    testClass two(4, 5);

    one.print();
    two.print();

    cout << "The sum of the instance variables of two = "
         << two.sum() << endl;

    return 0;
}
```

7. a. `personType student("Buddy", "Arora");`

   b. `student.print();`

   c. `student.setName("Susan", "Gilbert");`

9. a. `myClass::count = 0;`

   b. `myClass.incrementCount();`

   c. `myClass.printCount();`

   d. `int myClass::count = 0;`

```
void myClass::setX(int a)
{
    x = a;
}

void myClass::printX() const
{
    cout << x;
}

void myClass::printCount()
{
    cout << count;
}

void myClass::incrementCount()
{
    count++;
}
```

```
myClass::myClass(int a)
{
    x = a;
}
```

e. `myClass myObject1(5);`

f. `myClass myObject2(7);`

g. The statements in Lines 1 and 2 are valid.
    The statement in Line 3 should be: `myClass::printCount();`.

    The statement in Line 4 is invalid because the member function `printX` is not a **static** member of the class, and so cannot be called by using the name of class.

    The statement in Line 5 is invalid because `count` is a **private static** member variable of the class.

h. 5
    2
    2
    3
    14
    3
    3

Chapter 8

1. a. false; b. false; c. false; d. true; e. false; f. true; g. false; h. false; i. true; j. true; k. true;

3. The `namespace` mechanism may not be used with Standard C++ style header files, that is, header files that end with `.h`. Therefore, remove `.h` in Line 1.

5. The keyword `namespace` in Line 3 is missing.

7. Only a and c are valid.

9. a. true

    b. false

    c. true

    d. false

Chapter 9

1. a. false; b. false; c. false; d. true; e. true; f. true; g. false; h. false

3. 98 98
   98 98

5. b and c

7. 78 78

9. 4 4 5 7 10 14 19 25 32 40

11. In a shallow copy of data, two or more pointers point to the same memory space. In a deep copy of data, each pointer has its own copy of the data.

13. ```
Array p: 5 7 11 17 25
Array q: 25 17 11 7 5
```

# Chapter 10

1. a. false; b. true; c. false; d. false; e. false

3. 3

5. 10, 12, 18, 21, 25, 28, 30, 71, 32, 58, 15

7. a. 8
   b. 6
   c. 1
   d. 8

9. To use a **vector** object in a program, the program must include the header file vector.

11. 1  3  5  7  9

13. a. ```vector<int> secretList;```

    b. ```
secretList.push_back(56);
secretList.push_back(28);
secretList.push_back(32);
secretList.push_back(96);
secretList.push_back(75);
```

    c. ```
for (unsigned int i = 0; i < secretList.size(); i++)
    cout << secretList[i] << " ";

cout << endl;
```
```

15. a. `cout << myList.front() << " " << myList.back() << endl;`

    b. `length = myList.size();`

    c. ```
    for (unsigned int i = 0; i < myList.size(); i++)
          cout << myList[i] << " ";
    ```

    `cout << endl;`

# Chapter 11

1. a. true; b. true; c. false; d. false; e. false

3. The case in which the solution is defined in terms of smaller versions of itself

5. A function that calls another function and eventually results in the original function call is said to be indirectly recursive.

7. a. The statements in Lines 3 and 4

   b. The statements in Lines 5 and 6

   c. Any nonnegative integer

   d. It is a valid call. The value of `mystery(0)` is 0.

   e. It is a valid call. The value of `mystery(5)` is 15.

   f. It is an invalid call. It will result in infinite recursion.

9. a. It does not produce any output.

   b. 5  6  7  8  9

   c. It does not produce any output.

   d. It does not produce any output.

11. a. 2

    b. 3

    c. 5

    d. 21

13.

$$multiply(m,n) = \begin{cases} 0 & if\ n = 0 \\ m & if\ \ n = 1 \\ m + multiply(m, n-1) & otherwise \end{cases}$$

The base cases are when $n = 0$ or $n = 1$. The general case is specified by the option otherwise.
    ```

INDEX